Structured COBOL

Structured COBOL
A Modern Approach

HENRY MULLISH
New York University

HARPER & ROW, PUBLISHERS, New York
Cambridge, Philadelphia, San Francisco,
London, Mexico City, São Paulo, Sydney

1817

Sponsoring Editor: John Willig
Project Editor: David Nickol
Designer: Helen Iranyi
Production Supervisor: Marion Palen
Compositor: Science Typographers, Inc.
Printer and Binder: The Murray Printing Company
Art Studio: Fine Line
Cover Design: Caliber Design Planning, Inc.

Structured COBOL: A Modern Approach

Library of Congress Cataloging in Publication Data

Mullish, Henry.
  Structured COBOL.

  Includes index.
  1. COBOL (Computer program language)   2. Structured
programming.   I. Title.
QA76.73.C25M835 1983   001.64′24   82-15593
ISBN 0-06-044652-8

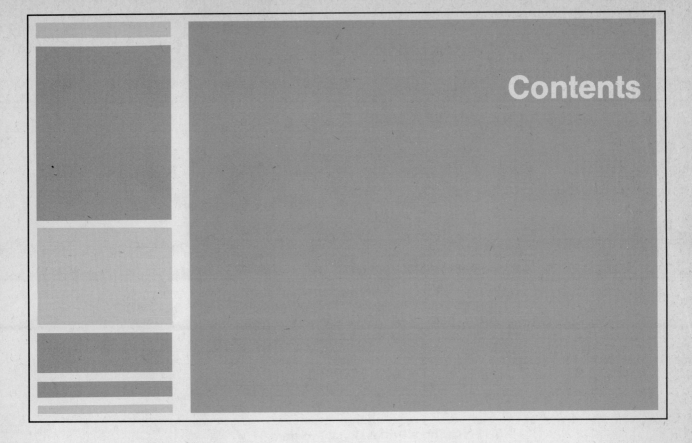

Contents

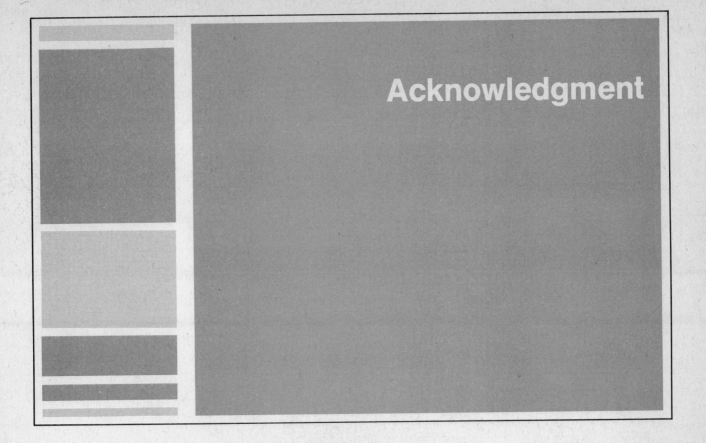

Acknowledgment

At the request of the American National Standards Institute (ANSI), the following acknowledgment is reproduced in its entirety.

Any organization interested in reproducing the COBOL standard and specifications in whole or in part, using ideas from this document as the basis for an instruction manual or for any other purpose, is free to do so. However, all such organizations are requested to reproduce the following acknowledgment paragraphs in their entirety as part of the preface to any such publication (any organization using a short passage from this document, such as in a book review, is requested to mention "COBOL" in acknowledgment of the source, but need not quote the acknowledgment):

- COBOL is an industry language and is not the property of any company or group of companies, or any organization or group of organizations.
- No warranty, expressed or implied, is made by any contributor or by the CODASYL Programming Language Committee as to the accuracy and functioning of the programming system and language. Moreover, no responsibility is assumed by any contributor, or by the committee, in connection therewith.
- The authors and copyright holders of the copyrighted material used herein have specifically authorized the use of this in whole or in part, in the COBOL specifications. Such authorization extends to the reproduction and use of COBOL specifications in programming manuals or similar publications.

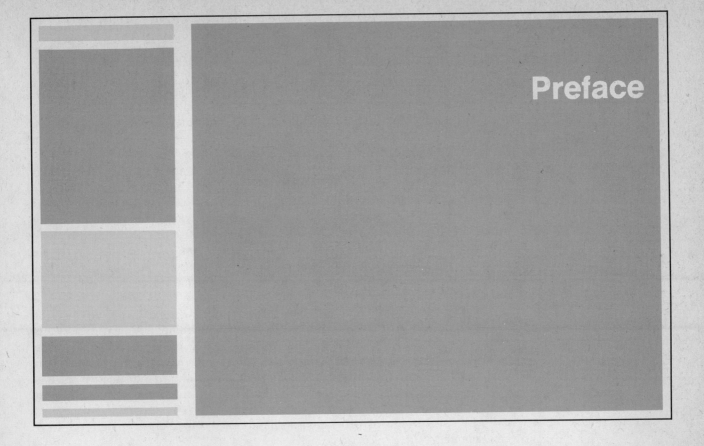

Preface

COBOL is an industry language that is not the property of any company or group of companies, or of any organization or group of organizations.

This book is based on the 1974 COBOL standard as proposed by the American National Standards Institute. This standard has been adopted for use by the U.S. government, and has also been approved unanimously by the International Organization for Standardization, a worldwide federation of national standards institutes whose member bodies include the following countries:

Australia	Italy	Romania
Belgium	Japan	Republic of South Africa
Brazil	Republic of Korea	Sweden
Canada	Mexico	Switzerland
Czechoslovakia	Netherlands	Turkey
France	New Zealand	United Kingdom
Germany	Philippines	U.S.A.
Hungary	Poland	Yugoslavia

Wide international acceptance is evident. The 1974 standard is actually a revision of a previous version known as the 1968 standard, which is still widely used throughout the world. This book attempts to clarify the major differences between the two standards as they relate to the material presented.

Since 1960 when COBOL was first designed and formulated, it has undergone regular development and improvement. Although the general format of today's COBOL is the same as that of 1960, much has been added to the language to enrich it, making it even more effective as the major computer programming language of the business and data-processing world.

The changes that have taken place are not confined only to the COBOL language. COBOL has become increasingly more available for use on other computers, particularly smaller ones (even on some home computers) and the style in which COBOL programs are now written has undergone a major advance. That style is usually referred to by the term "structured programming."

Much of the credit for structured programming is given to a Dutchman named Edsger W. Dijkstra, a professor from the University of Eindhoven, Netherlands. During the mid-1960s he and his group of computer scientists arrived at a fundamental notion of what constitutes a good program (regardless of the particular language being used), what kind of constructs should be used, what should not be used, and what style should be adopted. Until that time computer programming—whether it was done in a business or a scientific language—was primarily a "do-it-as-you-please" affair, with the major criterion on which to judge a program being: Does it work? This conventional approach often resulted in very convoluted programs whose logic was so obscure that even the author of the program had difficulty in following it, to say nothing of the person who was responsible for modifying the program to reflect new requirements that had evolved since it was written.

Under the conventional approach, programmers write programs that mirror their own personalized style. Under structured programming, however, this style is muted in favor of a more general, consistent one that enables a stranger to the program to know what to expect even before realizing the nature of the problem that the program is designed to solve. While a personal style—even a distinctive one—is often encouraged, especially in the fields of art and creative writing, one's ego must take second place to the program style when writing programs in the structured style. In fact, structured programming has often been referred to as "ego-less" programming.

Undoubtedly, learning structured COBOL initially requires a little more attention to detail than learning COBOL in the conventional, nonstructured way. This perhaps is why only 25 percent of all COBOL programs today are written in structured COBOL. Although many programmers readily acknowledge the efficiency and desirability of structured programming, they nevertheless continue to write programs in the more familiar, conventional style they were taught. Bad habits are very difficult to discard, so these programmers give only lip service to structured programming, and that's all. It becomes a question of "Do what I say, not what I do."

However, the discipline acquired by following the dictates of structured programming pays off in the end. The programs are easier to write and correct, and once working, they can be modified without difficulty by most other programmers.

Although we have already discussed the merits of programming styles, the chances are good that you have probably never before dealt with either the conventional or the structured style. Perhaps you should first get to know some general concepts and then learn a little COBOL so that you can write fine, elegant, structured COBOL programs. This will be covered in Chapter 4.

COBOL is an acronym for COmmon Business Oriented Language. The word "common" is used for several compelling reasons. COBOL is the result of a carefully planned, deliberate, collective, common effort that was undertaken by various branches of the U.S. government, business representatives, and computer manufacturers, who pooled their efforts in the late 1950s to design a language that is dedicated to the special problems of business, data processing, and finance. COBOL is a common language because with the passing of time it has become the major one in use today and eventually may be the only business language in use. Of all the programs that are written in the world today, it has been estimated that 80 percent of them are written in COBOL. Therefore, in a very real sense, COBOL has become extremely common in commercial establishments. In light of its popularity and the irreversible manner in which the business community has become dependent on COBOL to process its enormous workload, mastering the language is increasingly important. Moreover, the demand for so-called structured COBOL has recently increased so much that teaching institutions have invariably converted to this more elegant style of programming.

The unprecedented prevalence of COBOL in the world of business programming has led the more enlightened companies actively to encourage the writing of programs in the structured style, and more importantly, to vow not to hire anyone who programs in the conventional "do-it-as-you-please" style.

Most of the programs illustrated in this book have been run on the CYBER 170/720 computer, which uses the 1974 compiler. Enough material has been included on the 1968 compiler, however, to enable those readers who have access only to that equipment to run all the programs listed.

From actual classroom testing it has become clear that this book could be used to advantage at a two- or four-year college, particularly if COBOL is the student's first exposure to computer languages. The rich selection of questions and exercises should make an instructor's task easier in assigning homework problems. It is important to note that in recent years many high schools across the nation have decided to include the teaching of COBOL in their newly launched computer science curricula. Surely this trend will continue in the years to come, for COBOL is definitely a bread-and-butter language.

No one book can possibly contain everything there is to know about COBOL. This text presents enough information to give a clear picture of what COBOL programming is about, and in addition provides those fundamentals that will enable the reader to pursue topics later and in depth in other sources. The manuals published by ANSI and various manufacturers give minute details concerning a particular version of the language, although their formal presentation prevents them from being successful as vehicles from which one can learn the rudiments of the language. Unfortunately, not all manufacturers adhere to the prevailing standard, so a COBOL program that will work on one computer will not necessarily work on another without some modification, even if a minor one. Nevertheless, considerable effort has gone into making COBOL a problem-oriented rather than a computer-oriented language. Naturally the problems to which COBOL is directed are those of industry, insurance companies, government, and general business.

As you progress through this book it will soon become clear that it conforms to a strict format that incorporates the following principles:

1. No previous knowledge of computers, programming languages, or business concepts is assumed.
2. There is a conscious effort made throughout the text to avoid the use of unnecessary jargon. Topics are discussed in their proper context at which time all the appropriate terms are presented.
3. The style of writing adopted is informal, nonintimidating, and "reader-friendly."
4. The reader is introduced to the actual writing of a COBOL program at the earliest possible time—in the middle of the first chapter.
5. All the 52 programs presented are complete in all respects. Their listings are printed in full, the actual data used in running the program are shown and annotated, and the output produced is also given in full. Nothing is left to the imagination.
6. The major points covered in each chapter are provided before they are discussed in order to alert the reader to the contents ahead of time.
7. Each chapter is terminated with a list of review questions, the answers to which are supplied at the end of the book, often in detail so as to better absorb the material.
8. Each chapter contains exercises based on the material covered in that chapter. A teacher's resource manual is in preparation to supplement the textual material and to supply further pedagogical pointers.
9. The book covers the broad spectrum of material covered in a regular

introductory course in COBOL plus further material generally reserved for a more advanced course. This includes such topics as table handling, which is treated in considerable depth, as well as the much maligned topic of Report Writer which most books seem to ignore altogether. In addition a taste is given of subroutine calls. Experience has shown that a mastery of the material covered in this book will satisfy if not exceed the requirements of industry for incoming COBOL programmers.

10. All the programs are original and many are of direct use in a commercial environment—for example, the Day-of-the-week program and the Elapsed days program.

11. Finally, a strict adherence to the principles of structured programming is maintained throughout the book. It is hoped beginning students will absorb this style as their own.

Acknowledgments

It is with deep gratitude that I thank my ex-student, Irvin Poremba, of Skokie, Illinois, for the unselfish manner in which he volunteered his superb talents in the writing of this book. He was always ready to offer advice, type up programs, amend them whenever it was felt that they could be improved in one way or another. His ideas and suggestions were always sound and most of them were implemented. At the same time I would like to thank another ex-student, Susan Chan, who unselfishly gave of her hard-pressed time to review the manuscript and suggest changes that she felt would help the novice. Finally, I would like to express my appreciation to all those excellent students at New York University who, in one way or another, helped to shape the final form of this book. Thank you, all of you.

Special recognition should be given to Dr. Grace Murray Hopper, the "grandmother" of COBOL. Dr. Hopper worked on UNIVAC's first COBOL compiler and has been instrumental in helping to guide the language through its various evolutionary changes.

Welcome to the world of COBOL!

HENRY MULLISH

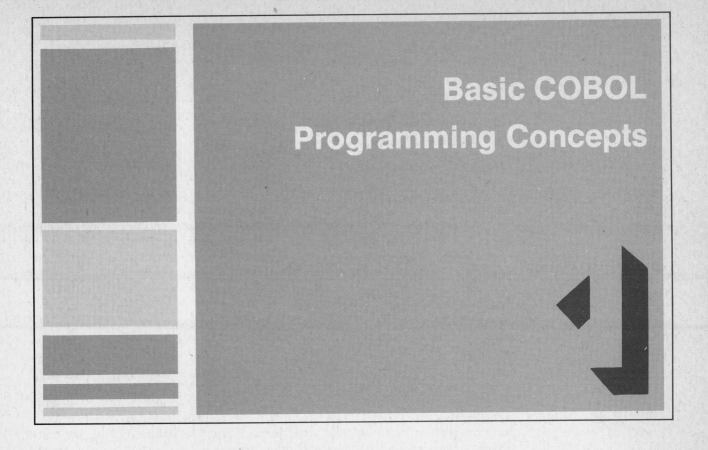

Basic COBOL Programming Concepts

In this chapter we will learn about the following important concepts.

- a computer program
- a CRT
- the speed of a computer
- the computer's blind obedience to the program instructions
- COBOL as a high level language
- why COBOL programs sometimes seem verbose
- the binary language
- the compiler
- diagnostic messages
- errors of logic
- source deck
- object deck
- the punched card and its origins
- Dr. Herman Hollerith
- the coding of characters
- the structure of a COBOL program
- the role played by column 7
- the Identification Division
- margins A and B
- the PROGRAM-ID name
- the Environment Division
- the Data Division
- the Procedure Division
- the flow of control through a program
- the DISPLAY STATEMENT
- the hierarchical nature of a COBOL program

1.1 The COBOL Compiler

> I wake up every morning
> And shout aloud in glee
> For COBOL is the language
> That's tailor made for me!

The sequence of computer instructions to solve a particular problem is called a *program*. In the case of a COBOL program, the instructions may be punched on cards by means of a keypunch machine. It is becoming increasingly popular (and cheaper) to type the instructions directly into a video terminal sometimes called a CRT (for Cathode Ray Tube), or a VDT (for Video Display Terminal). From our point of view the two methods are identical because both transmit the punched or typed information to the computer. Once in the computer the instructions are "executed," that is to say, acted upon in much the same way that you are reading this book, line by line. The major difference is, of course, that the computer operates on each successive instruction at phenomenally fast speeds. Indeed, much of the vaunted power of a computer derives precisely from this inherent characteristic. It unabashedly races through each sequential instruction without either having the slightest comprehension as to why or understanding any part of its solution. The computer is utterly ignorant of the consequences of its actions, devoid of imagination, humor, discretion, pity, and sympathy, as well as of feeling. With no soul and human sensitivity, it merely does what we command it to do via the program, performing with tantalizing speed and unerring accuracy. In fact, one of the most frustrating facts about computers is that they always do exactly what they are told to do rather than what you would like them to do. Once a computer program is executed the computer single-mindedly obeys each and every instruction in sequence.

Although the computer is a mere machine that never has an idea or matures and is bereft of any kind of motive or emotion, it is one of the most fascinating machines ever built by humans, and is destined to change the ways in which society generally interacts. Computers are built to be exploited. In this sense, however, the word "exploited" has a positive connotation, for the computer is excellent at doing those long tedious, monotonous, error-prone chores that, until the advent of the computer, was the sad lot of so many people.

Frequently when we speak to each other in ordinary conversation we can be quite imprecise in the language we select, omitting even words and parts of words without any appreciable loss of communication. This markedly contrasts with the manner in which we deal with a computer. Each command must be unambiguous, precise, and phrased exactly the way the computer demands, when instructing the computer. The omission of a period where it is supposed to be or its inclusion at a point where it is not supposed to be, can have catastrophic results. Sometimes these rules may appear to be quite arbitrary—and indeed they often are—but rigid obedience to the rules is a prime necessity.

COBOL was the first high-level business language ever written. COBOL is considered to be a high-level language because it is composed of words, phrases, and syntax not entirely dissimilar from written English. Thus anyone with a knowledge of English will find COBOL relatively easy to learn—even people without any previous programming or business experience.

A criticism sometimes leveled at COBOL is that, generally speaking, it is so verbose; and this cannot be denied. But as a matter of fact, it is intended to be precisely that so that someone who is unfamiliar with the language (it is surprising how often supervisors and managers fall into this category) can read the program and have a fairly good idea of what it is supposed to do. Because COBOL is routinely written in this English-like vocabulary, the program becomes self-documenting, which is a major asset of the language.

You might be surprised if not shocked to learn, however, that even COBOL instructions are not really "understood" by the computer. The only language a computer is capable of understanding is the so-called *binary* language. This language is composed entirely of 1's and 0's. The binary language is extremely tedious and error prone, as well as very difficult for humans like ourselves. For the computer, however, the binary language is ideal, with each 0 and 1 regarded as a tiny switch, which is either "on" or "off."

Because one COBOL instruction may produce a great number of machine level instructions, it will become apparent to the reader that programs are hardly ever written in the binary language, for it would be much too monotonous, time consuming, and difficult both to amend and understand. Amending a COBOL program, on the other hand, lightens the burden considerably. Because COBOL programs are so readily understandable and may be amended and updated so easily, U.S. government agencies are ordinarily forbidden to purchase a computer unless it comes equipped with a COBOL compiler.

Every computer that is able to accept COBOL as a programming language is equipped with a special set of highly sophisticated programs called the *compiler*. The purpose of the compiler is to scan the COBOL instructions individually and to convert them into their equivalent binary instructions. It is quite possible that one COBOL instruction is translated into 20 or even more machine language (binary) instructions. Once converted into this binary form the computer is able to follow the instructions with the speed of electricity, or at least at a rate approaching that speed.

This concept of converting from one language to another is probably not unfamiliar to you, particularly if you live in a large metropolitan area. In New York City, for example, when ordering a meal in a luncheonette, one often hears one's order converted to a jargon that seemingly has little or no relation to the original order. For example, a glass of seltzer water is encoded to number "91." A cup of hot chocolate becomes a "51" while a glass of water is converted to "81." A small glass of cola is a "shot" while a large glass is referred to as a "stretch." The number "210" means, believe it or not, that someone is leaving the restaurant without paying. The phrase "check the ice" is the jargon for "take a look at the cute looking girl who just entered the luncheonette." All this may seem rather exotic to the uninitiated. Being a native of Britain, the author takes exception to the jargon that is used for the order "one toasted English muffin." It is none other than "down with the British," or even worse, "one burnt Limey"!

The reason for converting the simple orders into a particular jargon is threefold. First, it lends a certain amount of prestige to the employees of the luncheonette; second, the converted order is generally shorter and less ambiguous; and third, it prevents the possibility of a chef hearing a duplicate order—the one voiced by the customer and that relayed by the waiter.

One might wonder what all this has to do with COBOL. In a sense, the waiter, when relaying the order from the customer to the chef, acts like a compiler in that he or she converts the customer's order that was given in common English to the jargon version, which the chef understands and processes.

Once a COBOL program is written the instructions contained in that program must be converted into a form that the computer can handle. This form, as we mentioned earlier, is the binary representation of the instructions. The compiler is composed of a bewilderingly complicated series of routines that examine each of the instructions of the COBOL program, and if after examination they are found to be valid, convert them into the binary form for subsequent execution. Only after the program is executed are the results produced. The compiler is designed to check each program instruction for correct grammatical syntax and for accurate spelling of keywords, as well as to ensure that special reserved words are used properly. What happens if a COBOL instruction is found to be invalid? In that case a *diagnostic* message is printed along with an attempt to explain the probable cause of the error. This is reminiscent of the manner in which a medical examiner performs a health checkup on a patient by administering a battery of tests. If the patient passes all the tests within certain limits, he or she is pronounced in good health. The analogy is not that farfetched because the compiler permits minor infractions to pass with just a printed warning and terminates the program immediately if the error is of a severe nature. Although a program may contain a series of syntactically correct instructions, the instructions may be put together in such a way that they do not produce the desired results. In other words, there is an error in their logical arrangement. Such an error of logic is often found in everyday life, particularly with respect to children. If a child is told, for example, to get dressed and to take a shower, the instructions themselves would be correct, but carrying out the instructions in the order stated would *not* produce the desired effects.

Unfortunately, no compiler that has yet been written is so sophisticated that it can correct an error of logic. This kind of error as well as the correcting of any other errors detected by the compiler is the responsibility of the programmer. A printed listing of the program is returned to the programmer together with any computed results. It is pointed out here that it is quite possible for a single error to create a deluge of diagnostic messages. As disappointing as this may be, one should not be too upset by this because correcting the single error will invariably clear up all the diagnostics. Programmers are sometimes discouraged when, after considerable effort, their programs are returned with more diagnostic messages than instructions. It pays not to be too thin-skinned at this juncture. Everybody makes mistakes, so why not you? With experience and dedication to the task, the number of errors decreases very quickly and correcting them becomes nothing more than a slight inconvenience.

Once the COBOL language has been converted or translated by the compiler to its equivalent binary program, it is possible to get a copy of the binary program perhaps punched on cards or written on either a magnetic tape or a magnetic disk. If the program is to be run subsequently—maybe with new data—valuable computer time can be saved by running the binary version of the program, because it does not have to undergo compilation. The binary program is readily executable.

In order to distinguish between these two versions of the program, one speaks of the original version written in COBOL as the *source* program, whereas the compiled version is referred to as the *object* program.

1.2   The Punched Card

The vast majority of computers in the world today accept the standard 80-column punched card. However, there is a strong tendency now away from punched cards in favor of the video terminal, which greatly resembles the familiar television set, except that it has a keyboard similar to the one used on both typewriters and keypunch machines—the latter being used to punch cards. It is unlikely that punched cards will ever be entirely discarded. Regardless of whether or not punched cards are here to stay, it is instructive to know something about them.

Although punched cards have been used widely since the 1930s, they originated at the end of the American Revolution, when a French weaver named Jacquard used wooden ones to control the operation of his looms.

In the preparations for the exhausting work that was necessary to compile the data for the 1880 census count in the United States, a gentleman named Dr. Herman Hollerith, a statistician, was hired by the Census Bureau as a special agent to help to alleviate the tabulating problem. It was in 1887 that Hollerith developed his concept of the machine-readable punched card. It proved to be strikingly successful. The

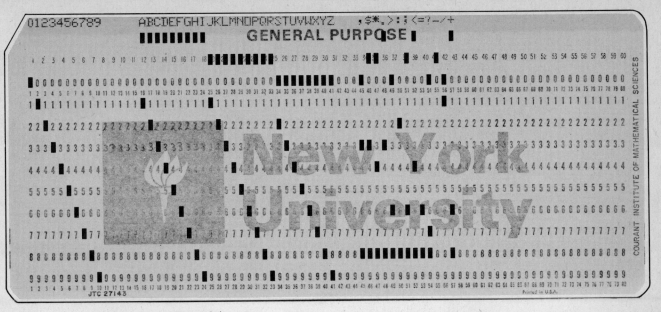

Figure 1-1

early Hollerith cards measured 3 by 5 inches. Today they measure $7\frac{3}{8}$ by $3\frac{1}{4}$ inches. Figure 1-1 shows a typical card that is punched with the numerics 0 through 9, the 26 letters of the alphabet, and some frequently used symbols.

The 80-column Hollerith card is divided from left to right into 80 consecutively numbered vertical *columns*. These columns in turn have 12 horizontal positions, or *rows*. Where each row and column intersect there is a possibility of punching a hole. Thus a complete card can have a maximum of 960 holes punched in it. Each column of the card can contain one character of information, such as a numeric, an alphabetic letter, or a special character.

Notice that to record a numeric digit only 1 hole is punched in the column. An alphabetic letter, however, requires 2 holes per column. Some of the special characters require 3 holes per column.

Naturally, there is general agreement about which holes are to represent particular characters; otherwise, information punched on a card would mean one thing on one computer and something else on another. The card is illustrated in Figure 1-2.

Figure 1-2

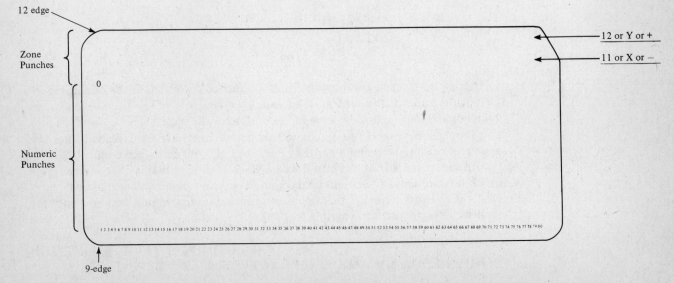

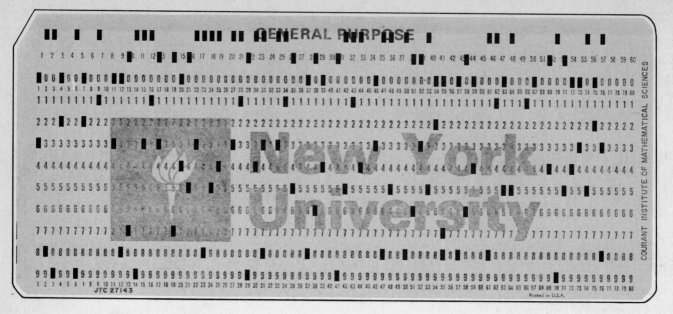

Figure 1-3

The punched card shown here contains some coded information. It would be impossible to decode the card without first being supplied with the key. The Hollerith card code key follows.

LETTER	HOLES	LETTER	HOLES	LETTER	HOLES
A	12 1	J	11 1	S	0 2
B	12 2	K	11 2	T	0 3
C	12 3	L	11 3	U	0 4
D	12 4	M	11 4	V	0 5
E	12 5	N	11 5	W	0 6
F	12 6	O	11 6	X	0 7
G	12 7	P	11 7	Y	0 8
H	12 8	Q	11 8	Z	0 9
I	12 9	R	11 9		

SYMBOL	HOLES	SYMBOL	HOLES
*	11 4 8	$	11 3 8
!	11 2 8	(	0 4 8
?	0 7 8	)	12 4 8
.	12 3 8		
>	0 6 8		
<	12 4 8		

Numerics: 1 = 1, 2 = 2, and so on

Using the key, we can now interpret a punched card such as the one in Figure 1-3. Each column of the card must be examined separately. The decoded information is printed for you upside down at the bottom of the page.

It might be of interest to know that today there are card readers that are capable of reading 80-column cards at the speed of 1200 cards per minute !

In recent years IBM has introduced a 96-column card that is only one-third the size of the traditional 80-column card. Figure 1-4 is an example of such a card.

It is sobering to realize that the more information that is punched on a card the less it weighs. Do you see why this is true ?

It reads: THIS IS A TYPICAL PUNCHED CARD. CAN YOU READ THE HOLES? YOU HAVE 10 MINUTES.

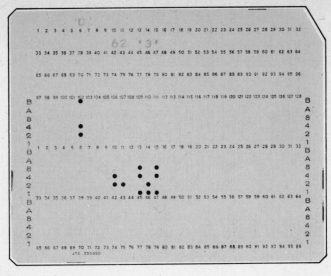

Figure 1-4

1.3 The Structure of a COBOL Program

Every COBOL program is divided into 4 main subgroupings, which are:

    a. the Identification Division
    b. the Environment Division
    c. the Data Division
    d. the Procedure Division.

The order of these divisions must be in the order shown so that it would be a good idea either to learn the order by heart or to place a bookmark in this page so that the order can be checked quickly when needed. Remember, this order must be adhered to, "In Every Darned Program." The initial letter of each word, which corresponds to the initial letter of the 4 divisions, will aid in remembering the order.

    When punching a program into the standard 80-column punch-cards, certain rules must be observed. Each of the 4 divisions previously mentioned must be punched on separate cards, but not anywhere on the card. They must be punched beginning in what is called area A or margin A, which begins in column 8 and extends to column 11 (see Figure 1-5). Area B, or margin B, about which we will say more shortly, begins in column 12 and extends to column 72. Columns 73–80 are

Figure 1-5

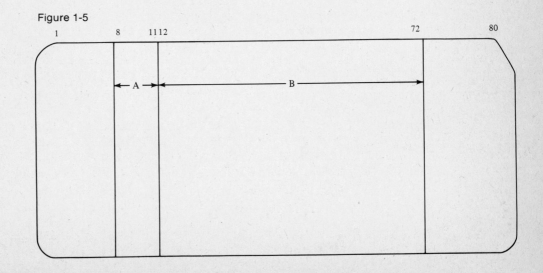

ignored so that they may be used for sequencing, identification, or anything else for that matter. These rules also apply to programs that are typed into a video terminal where the word "column" is used, read "position."

Columns 1–6 may be used, if desired, for additional sequencing. Although this is entirely optional, in long programs it would be particularly useful. Column 7, or position number 7, is used for comments as well as for so-called continuation purposes, a topic we will discuss in due course.

The Identification Division

The Identification Division is indicated by typing or punching these two words, beginning in area A, as shown in Figure 1-6. Although they may be entered in column 8, 9, 10, or 11, we will always type them beginning in column 8, and for the sake of consistency it is suggested that the reader do likewise. There must be at least one space between the two words. In COBOL, anywhere that one space is permitted, any number of spaces are also permitted.

The Identification Division header is the very first entry in any and every COBOL program to the computer system. The *header*, as are so many of the entries that are soon to be described, must be terminated by a period. The next line is always PROGRAM-ID, also an area A entry, which is followed by a period. Incidentally, the words PROGRAM and ID are always hyphenated together by a minus sign. The terminating period is followed by at least one space, after which the programmer's choice of a name for the program is entered, again ending with a period. The PROGRAM-ID paragraph is the only paragraph of the Identification Division that is actually *required*.

The rules for constructing PROGRAM-ID names are:

1. The name may consist of all alphabetics, all numerics, or a mixture of numerics and alphabetics.
2. The name may be up to 30 characters in length but different compilers might recognize only the first, possibly 8 characters, but more about this soon.
3. Hyphens (minus signs) may be used, but not at the beginning or at the end.
4. No special characters such as a period, comma, and so on are permitted.
5. No embedded blanks are allowed.

It should be pointed out that not all compilers treat the PROGRAM-ID name similarly. Many IBM machines recognize only the first 8 characters, whereas Control Data Corporation computers recognize the first 7, whereas on some Burroughs' machines only the first 6 are used. IBM compilers convert embedded hyphens to zeros.

Figure 1-6

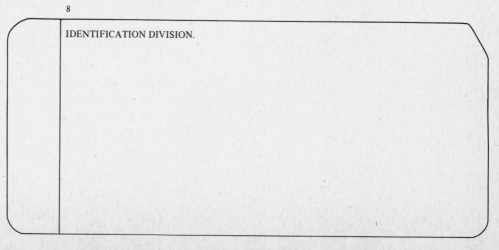

6. The name selected must not be a reserved word. In COBOL there is a list of several hundred words that are reserved for special purposes. Unless the word is being used in precisely the context for which it is intended, the word must be avoided. The words DATA, COMPUTE, INPUT, ADD, MULTIPLY, EXIT, READ, WRITE, each of which plays a special role in COBOL, are examples of reserved words. A complete list of them will be found at the back of the book. Because the list is so long it is unlikely that they will all be remembered. There are several choices that can be made.

a. Always refer to the list of reserved words when necessary.

b. Deliberately misspell a name by prefixing it with an X, or some such letter, or perhaps a numeric.

c. Commit the common ones to memory and rely on experience to avoid reserved words.

In any case here are some examples of valid Identification Division entries.

COLUMN
a. 8
```
IDENTIFICATION DIVISION.
PROGRAM-ID. ARREARS.
```
b.
```
IDENTIFICATION DIVISION.
PROGRAM-ID. FINES.
```
c.
```
IDENTIFICATION DIVISION.
PROGRAM-ID. BILLS-PAID.
```
d.
```
IDENTIFICATION DIVISION.
PROGRAM-ID. MSTR-FILE.
```

The second division is the Environment Division, which is so named because it describes the "computing environment" in which the program is to be processed. That is, it specifies the equipment on which the program is to be run. It allows for the specification of the source computer—the computer on which the COBOL program is to be compiled—and the object computer, on which it is to be executed. This section of the Environment Division is called the Configuration Section. If we assume that both the source computer and the object computer are the IBM 370/145, the Configuration Section may be omitted entirely because the IBM COBOL compiler assumes the IBM 370 by default. If it were included, the entry would look like this.

```
ENVIRONMENT DIVISION.
CONFIGURATION SECTION.
SOURCE-COMPUTER. IBM-370-145.
OBJECT-COMPUTER. IBM-370-145.
```

If the computer being used is the IBM 360 (the IBM 370's predecessor), it is suggested that if the model number is 45, for example, the specification should be:

```
IBM-360-45.
```

On the Cyber computer, on which most of the programs illustrated in this book were run, the entries are:

```
SOURCE-COMPUTER. CYBER-170-720.
OBJECT-COMPUTER. CYBER-170-720.
```

The Data Division

To solve a business problem—or any other kind of problem for that matter—one has to start out with data. Indeed, programming may be defined as the art of manipulating data. The kinds of data to be used in a COBOL program are specified and described in the Data Division. We will say more about this division later. For now we will merely include a card that is punched with the words DATA DIVISION, beginning in margin A, and expand on the concept at the appropriate time.

The Procedure Division

Finally, we arrive at the last of the 4 divisions, the Procedure Division. This is the "action" division, usually the most complicated of the four, because it is here that the precise procedure to solve a particular problem must be specified. For the time being we will concern ourselves with just a simple instruction—the DISPLAY. The DISPLAY instruction, simply prints out whatever is enclosed between single quotes. Note that some computers such as those manufactured by Control Data Corporation ordinarily require the double quote to delineate literals. However, the option to convert to single quotes (apostrophes) is provided, and thus this option has been used throughout this book. For example, to print out "HI THERE" we could use the COBOL instruction:

DISPLAY 'HI THERE'.

Such an instruction is usually punched, beginning in column 12, where the B area begins. Indeed, all instructions are punched in the B margin. Here is the formalized version of the DISPLAY statement.

$$\underline{\text{DISPLAY}} \left\{ \begin{array}{c} \text{data-name-1} \\ \text{literal-1} \end{array} \right\} \left[\begin{array}{c} \text{,data-name-2} \\ \text{,literal-2} \end{array} \right] \dots$$

COBOL Formal Notation

Just a brief word about the notation used in COBOL to specify the formal structure of statements. If a word is written in uppercase and underlined (such as the word "DISPLAY"), it is a key word in the sense that it must be present when this feature is intended. If a word is written in uppercase but is not underlined, the word is optional and may or may not be used according to the programmer's wishes. However, uppercase words, whether or not underlined, must be spelled correctly.

Lowercase words such as data-name-1 and literal-1, are generic names that are used to represent COBOL words, or literals.

If items are enclosed by braces, { }, such as data-name-1 and literal-1, a choice of one of them must be made by the programmer. It is possible in certain cases to have more than 2 choices, in which instance the choices are listed vertically. Items enclosed in brackets, [ ], are optional. They, too, are listed vertically.

An ellipsis, (...), composed of three consecutive periods, indicates the position in a general format at which repetition may occur at the user's option.

In the program that follows, execution is terminated by the instruction STOP RUN. Note that this instruction consists of two separate words—they are not hyphenated. Many novices insist on hyphenating these words, with the result that the program does not run properly. When the STOP RUN is executed, termination of the program is effected immediately. The STOP RUN is also a B margin entry.

As our first real, live program, which admittedly doesn't do anything very spectacular, we will have the computer merely print out the phrase "HI THERE." Here is the program and its output. Notice that the header cards for each of the four divisions have to appear, even in such an elementary program. Under the 1974 compiler the Procedure Division must always begin with a paragraph name. We have used the name HERE-WE-GO this time.

Program 1

```
IDENTIFICATION      DIVISION.
PROGRAM-ID.         PROG1.
*
ENVIRONMENT         DIVISION.
*
DATA                DIVISION.
*
PROCEDURE           DIVISION.
HERE-WE-GO.
    DISPLAY 'HI THERE'.
    STOP RUN.
```

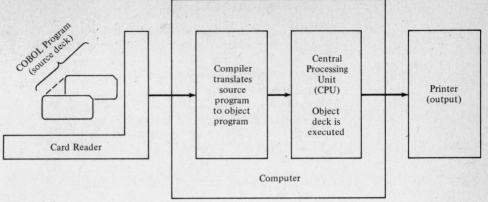

Figure 1-7

Output for Program 1

HI THERE

Figure 1-7 is a diagrammatic representation of the flow of a punched COBOL program that is being processed on a typical computer. Note the double role played by the computer. It executes the translated instructions once they are in the binary form and also compiles the source program (COBOL).

1.4   The Hierarchical Nature of a COBOL Program

Although it is not apparent from the elementary program that we have just illustrated, every COBOL program may be broken down into various subordinate parts. We have already seen that each COBOL program is broken up into four divisions. Within each of the last three divisions there may be one or more sections. Each section in turn may be written in terms of paragraphs. Each paragraph is composed of individual sentences. Finally, each sentence is constructed of verbs and clauses. This hierarchical nature is represented schematically in Figure 1-8.

Figure 1-8

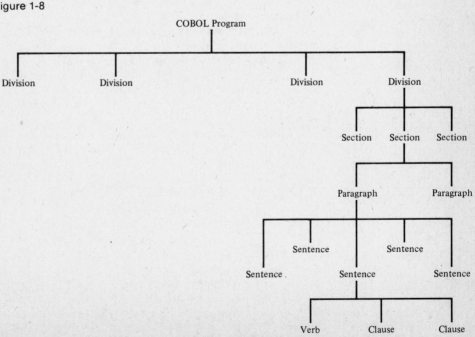

Review Questions

1. How does a COBOL *source* program differ from an *object* program?
2. What is the name given to the part of the system that converts the COBOL program to the language that the computer "understands"?
3. What does the acronym COBOL stand for?
4. The acronym ANSI stands for
   a. A New Set of Instructions
   b. All-purpose Numeric System Indicators
   c. American National Standards Institute
   d. ANother Silly Invention
5. COBOL was first written in
   a. 1984
   b. 1776
   c. 200 BC
   d. 1960
6. The process of translating a COBOL program into machine-level language is called
   a. compilation
   b. reformation
   c. restructuring
   d. proliferation
7. The term "execution" refers to
   a. elimination of errors in a program
   b. keypunching or typing of an original program
   c. carrying out the program instructions
   d. conversion from a source program to an object program
8. A "diagnostic" is
   a. an error message that is printed by the compiler after having detected an error in the program
   b. a questionable path in a program
   c. a hardware fault in the computer
   d. a medical term with no relevance to programming
9. The reason that programs are written in COBOL rather than in machine language is that
   a. it is more fun
   b. it is a commercial conspiracy to promote the language
   c. it satisfies a governmental directive
   d. it requires far fewer instructions, as well as being easier to write and understand
10. The compiler is so sophisticated that it
    a. leaves us free to be sloppy
    b. corrects errors of logic
    c. permits a mixture of COBOL, FORTRAN, BASIC, and ALGOL
    d. none of the above
11. COBOL is such an important language that
    a. according to international law, every computer must accept it
    b. no business procedure is permitted unless it can be written in COBOL
    c. no U.S. government agency may ordinarily purchase a computer that does not have a COBOL compiler
    d. every department store cashier should know it well
12. Which, if any, of the following Identification Division segments are free of error?

```
   1    8    12
a.     IDENTIFICATION DIVISION.
       PROGRAM-ID. SUSAN.

b.     IDENTIFICATION-DIVISION.
       PROGRAM-ID. CHAN.

c.     IDENTIFICATION DIVISION.
       PROGRAM-ID. LAST-TIME?.

d.     IDENTIFICATION DIVISION.
       PROGRAM-ID. COBOL

e.     IDENTIFICATION DIVISION.
       PROGRAM-ID ACCOUNTS.
```

    f.   IDENTIFICATION DIVISION.
           PROGRAM-ID. MA$$-TRANSIT

    g.   IDENTIFICATION DIVISION.
           PROGRAM-ID. DATA.

    h.   IDENTIFICATION DIVISION.
           PROGRAM-ID. AT-LAST.

13. Every COBOL program is composed of 4 divisions that are written in a specific order. They are
    a. Data, Environment, Identification, Procedure
    b. Procedure, Data, Environment, Identification
    c. Identification, Environment, Data, Procedure
    d. Identification, Data, Procedure, Environment
14. A good COBOL compiler will permit
    a. a mix-up of the 4 divisions
    b. the inclusion of an extra division
    c. the omission of any one of the 4 divisions
    d. none of the above
15. A margin A entry must appear in
    a. positions 8 through 11
    b. only position 8
    c. position 1
    d. position 11 only
16. Margin B entries must appear in
    a. positions 12 through 72
    b. positions 11 through 72
    c. positions 1 through 80
    d. positions 12 through 80
17. Who is considered the "grandmother" of COBOL?
    a. Eleanor Roosevelt
    b. Madame Curie
    c. Farrah Fawcett
    d. Grace Murray Hopper

General Research Questions

1. Write a short essay on the contributions made to computer science by
   a. Herman Hollerith
   b. Charles Babbage
   c. Von Neumann
   d. Edsger Dijkstra
2. Write a short essay differentiating between hardware and software and indicate how the two appear to be merging.
3. Where is Silicon Valley and what is its special significance to the development of computers?
4. Write a brief survey of the various computer languages through the present day, pointing out their special advantages.

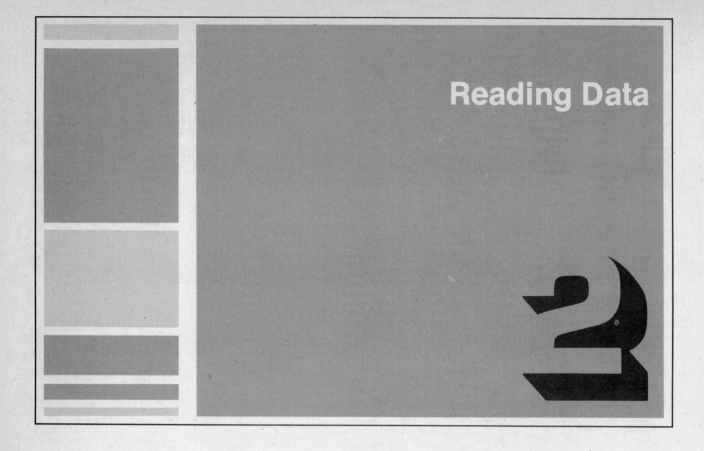

Reading Data

I don't like COBOL—I love it!

(Helen Lee)*

In this chapter you will be introduced to the following concepts:

- the ACCEPT statement
- the rules for constructing data names in COBOL
- reading data cards
- the Working-Storage Section
- the A format
- the ACCEPT and DISPLAY statements in the same program
- the X PICTURE
- optional paragraphs in the Identification Division
- the Configuration Section in the Environment Division
- the 01-level record description in the Working-Storage Section
- the reason for dropping the REMARKS paragraph when going from the 1968 to the 1974 standard
- how blank lines enhance the way a program listing looks
- the PERFORM statement

Suppose we were to punch some alphabetic information in the first 8 columns of a punch-card. When punching *data* we are not restricted in the same way as we are when punching COBOL instructions. There are no margins in data cards. We are at liberty to use any and all of the columns 1 through 80. Let the card be punched with the 8-character phrase "HI THERE." Figure 2-1 shows what the data card would look like.

*Throughout the book will appear actual quotes from students reacting to their COBOL learning experiences.

Figure 2-1

We will now write a COBOL program that *reads in* this data card and does nothing other than print out on paper the contents of the card. This differs from the previous program in that instead of merely printing out a literal message built into the program, now we want to print out the contents of the first 8 columns of an *input card*. We will do this after printing out a suitable phrase with the DISPLAY statement, exactly as was done in Program 1.

There are two implications here: (1) The data has to be appropriately described in the Data Division. (2) An appropriate command has to be given to accept the data card. Acceptance of data cards is handled in the "action" division, the Procedure Division.

2.1 Data Description

One of the subdivisions of the Data Division is called the Working-Storage Section. In the Working-Storage Section we may describe the data associated with the program by means of *level numbers* and appropriate names. The highest level number is the 01 level. The reason that it is called the 01 level rather than just the 1 level (even though 1 works just as well, to the surprise of many professional COBOL programmers!) is that lower levels can reach as high as the number 49, which is a 2-digit number; for the sake of conformity, levels 1 through 9 are preceded by a zero so that they too will be 2-digit numbers.

The question of levels is very important and has direct relevance as to how the individual items of data are related to each other, if at all, and also to the manner in which business data is normally entered. Meanwhile, however, because we are considering a somewhat atypical case, let us confine ourselves to the minimum description that is necessary to describe our data card that is punched with HI THERE. We define the data-item on the 01 level, and 01 is punched in the A margin. Now we assign an arbitrary name to the data-item, say, INFO-IN. This name is punched in margin B. It is followed by the word "PICTURE,"* which gives a physical description of the data-item in question. Then a statement is made specifying that the data-item is alphabetic in character and that there are 8-character items involved. This is done by the very brief designation A(8), where the number of characters involved is enclosed within parentheses. Alternatively, it may be written (but usually isn't) AAAAAAAA.

---

*Many COBOL systems permit the use of PIC as an abbreviation for PICTURE. If PIC is one of the reserved words that are listed for a particular system, then you may be assured that it is an acceptable substitute for PICTURE.

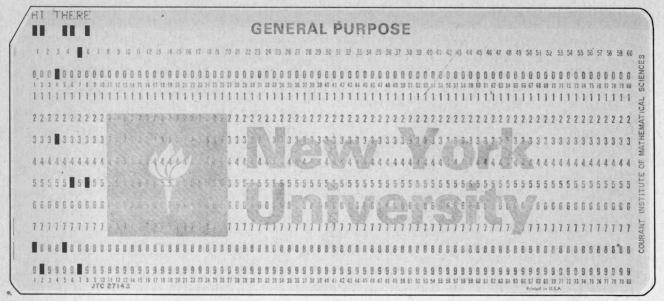

Figure 2-2

The complete data description in the Working-Storage Section of the Data Division will therefore be

01 INFO-IN PICTURE A(8).

Rules for Constructing Data Names

The rules for constructing data names are similar to those for constructing PRO-GRAM-ID names.

1. They may be up to 30 characters long.
2. No embedded spaces may be present.
3. The characters that are used may consist of alphabetics, numerics, and the hyphen but no special characters—except the hyphen.
4. The name must not begin or end with a hyphen.
5. Whereas a PROGRAM-ID name (and also a procedure name) may consist entirely of numerics, a data-name must contain at least one alphabetic character but does *not* have to be the first character.
6. The name must not be a reserved word.

The complete program to read the data card and to print out its contents will shortly be presented. Despite the fact that the program is straightforward, you will notice that the 4 divisions must nevertheless be present. The data card that was used as the sole input to the program is shown in Figure 2-2.

2.2 The ACCEPT Statement

In order to read the contents of a punched card, one may use a form of the ACCEPT statement. In its simplest form it is:

ACCEPT data-name

After deciding on a suitable data name (say, INFO-IN), one must supply an 01-level entry in the Working-Storage Section of memory. Because the data card that is punched with HI THERE occupies 8 positions (including the space between the 2 words), the PICTURE associated with the entry is specified as A(8). A data card is usually 80 columns in length. In pre-1974 compilers A(80) was the maximum that could be read in this fashion, but the 1974 compiler is much more flexible. If A(800) were specified, 10 separate cards would be "accepted." In the following program the single data card is read and its contents are printed out again. Notice that this time there is the paragraph name NOW-START at the beginning of the Procedure Division. As pointed out earlier, the 1974 compiler insists on a paragraph name at the beginning of the Procedure Division. In Program 1 we used the paragraph name HERE-WE-GO.

Program 2A

```
IDENTIFICATION          DIVISION.
PROGRAM-ID.             PROG2A.
*
ENVIRONMENT             DIVISION.
*
DATA                    DIVISION.
WORKING-STORAGE         SECTION.
01    INFO-IN           PIC A(8).
*
PROCEDURE               DIVISION.
NOW-START.
      ACCEPT            INFO-IN.
      DISPLAY 'THE INPUT CARD READS:'
      DISPLAY INFO-IN.
      STOP RUN.
```

Output for Program 2A

```
THE INPUT CARD READS:
HI THERE.
```

In Program 2A we used the instruction ACCEPT to read a data card and the instruction DISPLAY to print out both a literal text, THE INPUT CARD READS:, and the "value" of the data-item that is called in the program INFO-IN, which has the value HI THERE. Because two separate DISPLAY statements are used, the output is printed on two separate lines. If, however, the DISPLAY statement were:

```
DISPLAY 'THE INPUT CARD READS:' INFO-IN.
```

then the output would appear on a single line, as illustrated in the next version of the program.

Program 2B

Illustration of ACCEPT and DISPLAY

```
IDENTIFICATION          DIVISION.
PROGRAM-ID.             PROG 2B.
*
ENVIRONMENT             DIVISION.
*
DATA                    DIVISION.
WORKING-STORAGE         SECTION.
01    INFO-IN           PIC A(8).
*
PROCEDURE               DIVISION.
NOW-START.
      ACCEPT            INFO-IN.
      DISPLAY 'THE INPUT CARD READS:' INFO-IN.
      STOP RUN.
```

Output for Program 2B

THE INPUT CARD READS: HI THERE

    Having now illustrated the DISPLAY and the ACCEPT statements, we must state that both these instructions are used only for what is described as "low-volume" data. They are *not* normally used to read and print information because they are slow and therefore expensive to use. When dealing with mass data where there are volumes of material to read and print, we would ordinarily resort to a much faster method, to be discussed shortly. Nevertheless, each of the preceding programs work, and they help to illustrate some of the important principles involved in writing COBOL programs.

    Here are some more illustrative programs that are designed to show how the ACCEPT and DISPLAY statements operate. In Program 3 the sole input to the program is a data card that is punched (beginning in column 1) with the 12-character phrase COBOL IS FUN. The program reads in this data card and prints out its contents.

Program 3

```
IDENTIFICATION          DIVISION.
PROGRAM-ID.             PROG3.
*
ENVIRONMENT             DIVISION.
*
DATA                    DIVISION.
WORKING-STORAGE         SECTION.
01    LINE-IN           PIC A(12).
*
PROCEDURE               DIVISION.
HERE-IT-COMES.
      ACCEPT            LINE-IN.
      DISPLAY 'THE LINE BEING READ IS:'.
      DISPLAY LINE-IN.
      STOP RUN.
```

Output for Program 3

THE LINE BEING READ IS:
COBOL IS FUN

    In Program 4, three separate data cards are read into the computer's memory, using the ACCEPT instruction. They are punched, respectively,

    card 1 COBOL IS AN ACRONYM
    card 2 WHICH STANDS FOR
    card 3 COMMON BUSINESS ORIENTED LANGUAGE

Each punched card may be named separately in the program, but this would mean three separate 01 levels in the Working-Storage Section. Rather than resort to this method, another, perhaps better, method would be to assign the *same* name for each one. After each card is read, it could be displayed before the next data card is read. In this way the second card's contents would occupy the same area in memory as the first card's and subsequently so would the third card's contents. Because each of the three cards contains a varying number of characters (the first is 19; the second, 17; and the third, 33), we could either assign the maximum length of 33 characters or simply assign the complete 80 columns of the card to the single name that is selected.

Program 4

```
IDENTIFICATION          DIVISION.
PROGRAM-ID.             PROG4.
*
```

```
ENVIRONMENT              DIVISION.
*
DATA                     DIVISION.
WORKING-STORAGE          SECTION.
01      CARD-CONTENTS    PIC A(80).
*
PROCEDURE                DIVISION.
THIS-IS-IT.
        ACCEPT           CARD-CONTENTS.
        DISPLAY          CARD-CONTENTS.
        ACCEPT           CARD-CONTENTS.
        DISPLAY          CARD-CONTENTS.
        ACCEPT           CARD-CONTENTS.
        DISPLAY          CARD-CONTENTS.
        STOP RUN.
```

Output for Program 4

```
COBOL IS AN ACRONYM
WHICH STANDS FOR
COMMON BUSINESS ORIENTED LANGUAGE
```

It is worth contemplating for a moment what would have been the result if the Procedure Division were written

```
ACCEPT CARD-CONTENTS.
ACCEPT CARD-CONTENTS.
ACCEPT CARD-CONTENTS.
DISPLAY CARD-CONTENTS.
STOP RUN.
```

In this case the second data card's contents would have erased that of the first's while the third card would have erased that of the second. As a result, only the contents of the *last* data card (the third in this case) would have been displayed. Sometimes this kind of logical error is committed by a tired programmer, and the most frequent comment heard—especially if the programmer is a novice—is that "the computer made an error"! Of course, it didn't; it was the unsuspecting programmer!

As Program 4 did, Program 5 also reads in data cards by means of the ACCEPT verb and prints out their contents with the DISPLAY verb. However, some changes are worth noting.

Input for Program 5

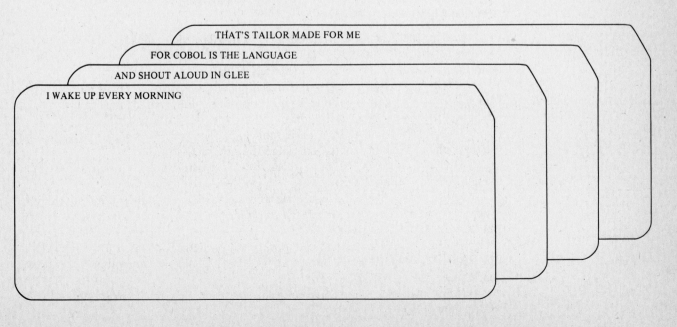

Program 5

```
1      IDENTIFICATION                      DIVISION.
2      PROGRAM-ID.                         POEM.
3      AUTHOR.                             DAVID SULLIVAN.
4      INSTALLATION.                       NYU.
5      DATE-WRITTEN.                       FEBRUARY 13, 1982.
6      DATE-COMPILED.                      NOVEMBER 16, 1982.
7      SECURITY.                           HENRY MULLISH.
8      * * * * * * * * * * * * * * * * * * * * * * * * * * * * * * * * * * * * * * * * * * * * * *
9      *   THIS PROGRAM DEMONSTRATES THE USE OF THE                    *
10     *   ACCEPT AND DISPLAY VERBS BY ACCEPTING FOUR                  *
11     *   CARDS (RECORDS) AND DISPLAYING THEM                         *
12     * * * * * * * * * * * * * * * * * * * * * * * * * * * * * * * * * * * * * * * * * * * * * *
13
14     ENVIRONMENT DIVISION.
15     CONFIGURATION SECTION.
16     SOURCE-COMPUTER.   CYBER-170-720.
17     OBJECT-COMPUTER.   CYBER-170-720.
18
19     DATA DIVISION.
20     WORKING-STORAGE SECTION.
21     01    A-LINE          PIC A(80).
22
23     PROCEDURE DIVISION.
24
25     MAKE-A-POEM.
26
27         ACCEPT A-LINE.
28         DISPLAY A-LINE.
29
30         ACCEPT A-LINE.
31         DISPLAY A-LINE.
32
33         ACCEPT A-LINE.
34         DISPLAY A-LINE.
35
36         ACCEPT A-LINE.
37         DISPLAY A-LINE.
38
39         STOP RUN.
```

Output for Program 5

```
I WAKE UP EVERY MORNING
   AND SHOUT ALOUD IN GLEE
FOR COBOL IS THE LANGUAGE
   THAT'S TAILOR MADE FOR ME
```

Detailed Description of Program 5

1. The Identification Division has been enlarged to include all the possible options on the 1974 standard. The PROGRAM-ID is mandatory in every Identification Division and in fact must immediately follow the header.

2. The AUTHOR paragraph comes after PROGRAM-ID. One generally types the name of the author of the program so that due credit (or, heaven forbid, criticism) for the program can be properly ascribed to the appropriate individual.

3. The INSTALLATION paragraph is merely documentation that states the name of the particular installation where the program is run.

4. DATE-WRITTEN is the paragraph that permits you to record the date on which the program was written.

5. DATE-COMPILED is a little unusual in that after the period, nothing is written by the programmer. When the program is run, however, the compiler inserts the current date to the right.

6. SECURITY is the last of the optional paragraphs. This could have said at the right, MANAGEMENT ONLY or TOP SECRET or any other appropriate classification.

If any of these options, 1 through 6, are used, they must be presented in the order shown.

7. In previous compilers the Identification Division had another option, namely, the REMARKS paragraph. This was intended to enable the programmer to write a short description (in the B margin) of the purpose of the program. This paragraph was dropped, beginning with the 1974 standard because in COBOL a comment card is specified simply by punching an asterisk in column 7. Anything else that appears on that line (or card) is totally ignored by the compiler, except for the fact that whatever is there will be printed in the listing of the program. As such, the comments replace the role that was previously played by the REMARKS paragraph. Although the total description of the program is enclosed in a rectangle consisting of asterisks, it is only the 5 asterisks in column 7 that make those 5 lines comments.

The reason that the REMARKS paragraph was discontinued is that by resorting to comments (placing an asterisk in column 7), one may include remarks (comments) *anywhere* in the program, not just in the Identification Division.

8. Notice how the inclusion of blank cards enhances the appearance of the listing. Lines 13, 18, 22, 24, 26, 29, 32, 35, and 38 are blank lines.

9. The Environment Division has been expanded to include the Configuration Section. In this section we state what the SOURCE-COMPUTER is (CYBER-170-720). In other words, it states on which computer the source program, written in COBOL, is compiled and on which computer the object program, produced by the compiler, is to be run. In most situations these two phases will be carried out on the same computer, as was done in our case. But it doesn't have to be.

10. The name given to the 80-column area in which to store the contents of each data card is now called A-LINE, which is given a picture (acceptably abbreviated to PIC) of X(80).

11. In the Procedure Division the cards are read. However, there is a rule under the 1974 standard to the effect that every instruction in the Procedure Division must be part of a paragraph that is introduced by a paragraph name. So an arbitrary name was selected—MAKE-A-POEM.

12. Each ACCEPT and DISPLAY has been paired off, simply for aesthetic reasons. This doesn't make the slightest bit of difference to the computer, of course, but it does make a difference to whoever has to read the listing. Notice that each instruction in the Procedure Division is terminated by a period and only one instruction appears on any single line. This is the recommended way of writing COBOL instructions.

13. On some systems, under the listing the compiler prints out a line that goes from 1 to 80. This is to permit the reader of the program to be able to know exactly in which column any character is punched or typed. This may not be printed on your system and has not been included in this book.

14. The output to the program is printed immediately following the program listing. It reflects the fact that different data was used from that used in Program 4.

2.3 A First Look at the PERFORM Statement

Using the same data and producing the same output as before, Program 5 was rewritten to illustrate the use of an instruction that has assumed considerable importance in structured programming. It is called the PERFORM instruction.

The PERFORM statement performs, or executes, a given paragraph. Immediately after performing the given paragraph it returns automatically to the instruction *following* the PERFORM. This in itself is very interesting but is not particularly useful in this case in its present form. However, we can also state how many times a paragraph is to be performed. For example, we could write:

PERFORM MAKE-A-POEM 4 TIMES.

as is done in Program 6, which follows. Immediately after the paragraph is performed 4 times it automatically "falls through" to the next instruction—the STOP RUN in this case—which terminates the program.

The general formats of some of the PERFORM statements are:

<u>PERFORM</u> procedure-name-1

OR

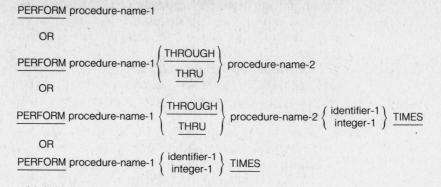

OR

which is the form that is selected in Program 6.

Program 6

```
1      IDENTIFICATION              DIVISION.
2      PROGRAM-ID.                 POEM.
3      AUTHOR.                     DAVID SULLIVAN.
4      INSTALLATION.               NYU.
5      DATE-WRITTEN.               NOVEMBER 2, 1982.
6      DATE-COMPILED.              NOVEMBER 2, 1982.
7      SECURITY.                   HENRY MULLISH.
8      * * * * * * * * * * * * * * * * * * * * * * * * * * * * * * * * * * * * * * * * *
9      *   THIS PROGRAM ALSO DEMONSTRATES THE USE OF THE              *
10     *   ACCEPT AND DISPLAY VERBS BY ACCEPTING FOUR                 *
11     *   CARDS (RECORDS) AND DISPLAYING THEM                        *
12     *   BUT IN THIS CASE STRUCTURED PROGRAMMING IS USED            *
13     *   REDUCING THE NUMBER OF ACCEPT AND DISPLAY VERBS            *
14     *   TO JUST ONE.                                               *
15     * * * * * * * * * * * * * * * * * * * * * * * * * * * * * * * * * * * * * * * * *
16
17     ENVIRONMENT DIVISION.
18     CONFIGURATION SECTION.
19     SOURCE-COMPUTER.   CYBER-170-720.
20     OBJECT-COMPUTER.   CYBER-170-720.
21
22     DATA DIVISION.
23     WORKING-STORAGE SECTION.
24     01    A-LINE          PIC A(80).
25
26     PROCEDURE DIVISION.
27
28     MAIN-LINE-ROUTINE.
29          PERFORM MAKE-A-POEM 4 TIMES.
30          STOP RUN.
31
32          MAKE-A-POEM.
33           ACCEPT A-LINE.
34           DISPLAY A-LINE.
```

(Input and output are the same as for Program 5.)

For the reading of alphabetic information the A format is perfectly in order. The fact is, however, that there are few instances in the data-processing world where any data is truly alphabetic. Even a person's name is not necessarily all alphabetic. Some people have hyphens in their name whereas others include apostrophes. Neither the hyphen nor the apostrophe is considered in COBOL to be alphabetic—only the letters of the alphabet and the space are.

For this reason A format is virtually ignored in COBOL in favor of the X format, used for alphanumeric data. A PICTURE of X will accept any character that is defined in the computer's repertoire, whether it be alphabetic, a special character, a punctuation symbol, or even a numeric. That is why there is hardly any point in using A format anymore—so we won't.

Numeric data, on the other hand, must have a PICTURE of 9's, especially if they are to be operated on arithmetically. The number 471 could be represented by a PICTURE of 999, whereas 14 may be represented by a PICTURE of 99.

Review Questions

1. What is a program?
2. How many columns are there on the standard punch card?
3. Are columns 73 – 80 of a punched card ever used?
4. Which division identifies a particular program?
5. Which division describes the computing environment in which a COBOL program is run?
6. Which division describes the format of the data to be used in a COBOL program?
7. Which division instructs the computer how to proceed to solve a COBOL problem?
8. What statement is used to print out a message enclosed by quotation marks?
9. What statement is sometimes used to read in a data card?
10. Is there anything wrong with the header DATA DIVISION?
11. What is the maximum number of positions that may be read by the ACCEPT statement?
12. What is the instruction that terminates execution of a program?
13. If a program contains a REMARKS paragraph in the Identification Division, what can you say about the program?
14. How are comments included in a program?
15. How does a simple PERFORM instruction operate?
16. Do you think the following program segment would work?

```
POEM.
    ACCEPT CARD-CONTENTS.
    DISPLAY CARD-CONTENTS.
    PERFORM POEM 4 TIMES.
    STOP RUN.
```

17. In question 16, is it true to say that because the data name CARD-CONTENTS is 13 characters long, the data to which it refers may only be 13 characters long?
18. What entry does the 1974 COBOL compiler insist be present in the Procedure Division?
19. What is the difference in the rules for designating procedure names as opposed to ordinary data-names?

Exercises

Author's note: Now that you have read 2 chapters, the time has arrived for you to attempt to write your own programs. If this is your first exposure to computer programming (which for many readers will undoubtedly be the case), it should be a most thrilling experience. Try not to let your excitement interfere with the accuracy of your keypunching or typing. For these exercises confine yourself to the ACCEPT and DISPLAY statements for input-output purposes.

1. Write a program that prints out the message I LOVE YOU.
2. Write a program that reads and prints out your name, address, and telephone number on 3 separate lines.
3. Write a program in 2 styles — structured and conventional — that prints any 4-line poem of your own choice; for example,

> I've always longed for adventure
> To do the things I've never dared
> Now here I am facing adventure
> So why am I so scared?

4. Write a program that accepts as data a card punched with the phrase

WHERE THERE IS A WILL

The program should print out this phrase, followed on the next line with the phrase THERE IS A WAY.

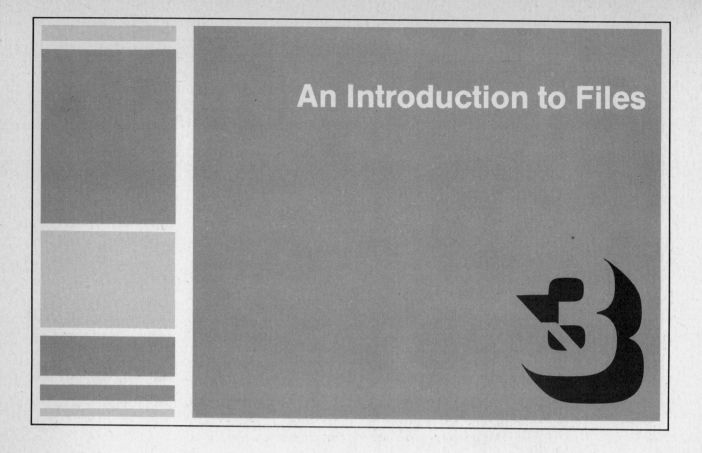

An Introduction to Files

There is no such thing as a debugged program.

(John Kesich)

In this chapter you will be introduced to the all-important notion of "files." You will examine a program that reads a file of data cards and prints them out. This process is called "listing" the data. The data is not changed in any way; the cards are printed out exactly as they are punched, or as they are typed into the CRT. Care is taken to be sure that the printer ejects to the next new page before printing so that the output will be quite separate from the program listing.

In particular you will learn:

- more about the Environment Division
- about the File Section
- a little about FILLER
- the OPEN instruction that is used to open files
- the figurative constant SPACE or SPACES
- the READ instruction that reads a record of the input file
- the WRITE instruction that is used to write (print) records of an output file onto paper
- the unconditional transfer instruction GO TO
- the CLOSE instruction that closes a file after it has been opened
- what is meant by a traditionally or conventionally written COBOL program, as opposed to one that is written in structured style.

One of the major advantages of COBOL over other programming languages is the ease with which it is able to handle *files*. A file is simply a collection of one or more *records*. We will shortly explain in detail what is meant by a record, but for now we can consider information that is punched on a single card to be a record. We can also consider the information to be printed out on a single line to be a record.

3.1 Listing Data

For our first program using files let us assume we have a list of students or clients or customers or agents and wish to record certain critical information about them on punched cards. Eventually the card information might be written out onto either magnetic tape or a disk, but it is most informative to think in terms of punched cards, even if the information isn't actually on cards.

Let us assume that we allocate different field widths of the 80-column card for the various details, as follows.

DETAILS OF PUNCHED CARD	
1. Last Name column	1–12
2. First Name	14–22
3. Address	24–57
4. Zip Code	59–63
5. Left Parenthesis	65
6. Telephone Area Code	66–68
7. Right Parenthesis	69
8. First 3 digits of Telephone No.	70–72
9. Hyphen (Minus sign)	73
10. Last 4 digits of Telephone No.	74–77
11. Department (G, B, W, E, A, or O)	79
12. Sex of Person (1 = Male, 2 = female)	80

Thus on each card we have *alphabetic* information (letters of the alphabet only including the space), *numeric* information (the digits of the number system 0 through 9), and some special characters that, because they are neither pure alphabetic nor pure numeric, are described as being *alphanumeric*.

A typical written list would look like this.

AHN	HWA-YUHN	375 RIVERSIDE DR. NEW YORK, N.Y.	10025	(212)222-7760	O2
BENLEVY	LINDA	5-11 UNIVERSITY PLACE NY NY	10003	(212)473-4322	B2
BHASIN	KULJOT	5 UNIVERSITY PLACE	10003	(212)254-0500	B1
BLITZ	CIPORA	232 E 82ND ST NY NY	10028	(212)249-4570	B2
COTTONE	JEROME	325 PACIFIC AVE	10312	(212)984-3668	W1
DAVIS	TI	5 UNIVERSITY PLACE BOX 213	10003	(212)674-6352	W2
DECATREL	RALPH	196-20 91 AVE HOLLISCOURT	11423	(212)479-7348	W1
DIBERNARDO	FRAN	65-45 79 STREET MIDDLE VILLAGE NY	11379	(212)894-1752	W2
DUGGAN	TIM	46-32 193 ST	11358	(212)357-5126	B1
DUNCAN	CHRIS	441 W 22; APT. 4-A; NEW YORK, N.Y.	10011	(212)989-3105	O1
EHLER	LINDA	55 EAST 10 ST. APT 1202 N.Y. N.Y.	10003	(212)254-2914	E2
EPIFAN	PETER	105 CLAUDY LN NEW HYDE PK NY	11040	(516)328-3337	W1
FERMANN	BARBARA	5 UNIVERSITY PL NEW YORK NY	10003	(212)475-4376	W2
FINE	LARRY	327 E. 54 ST., N.Y., N.Y., APT. C	10022	(212)752-9435	W1
GEE	KEITH	181 DAHILL ROAD	11218	(212)436-4913	B1
GOLDBERG	ALLEN	1237 E. 100 ST. BROOKLYN N.Y.	11236	(212)763-6271	W1
GOODMAN	CORINNE	90 8TH AVE. APT. 9A, BROOKLYN	11215	(212)638-5522	O2
HANLON	CHRIS	5-11 UNIVERSITY PLACE NY NY	10003	(212)475-4482	B2
HIRSCH	DORIS	75-60 188 ST	11366	(212)454-4942	B2
POREMBA	IRVIN	35 FIFTH AVENUE ROOM 1119	10003	(212)477-1708	W1

When this identical information is punched on cards the input deck would resemble the sketch on the top of page 26.

Input for Program 7

A complete COBOL program to "list" these data cards is now presented. Because the program involves both an input and an output file, obviously, much about the program will be unfamiliar. At the same time, however, a considerable portion of the program will be familiar. Study the program a while before we discuss it in detail.

| BHASIN | KULJOT | 5 UNIVERSITY PLACE | 10003 | (212) 254-0500 | B1 |

| BENLEVY | LINDA | 5-11 UNIVERSITY PLACE NY NY | 10003 | (212) 473-4322 | B2 |

| AHN | HWA-YUHN | 375 RIVERSIDE DR. NEW YORK, N.Y. | 10025 | (212) 222-7760 | D2 |

For the present we are not changing the data in any way. That we will leave for a little later.

The numbering along the left-hand side of the listing is produced by the compiler. This is convenient for it provides an accurate way of referring to each line of the program—even if it is blank.

Program 7

```
1       IDENTIFICATION DIVISION.
2       PROGRAM-ID. LISTING1.
3       AUTHOR. IRVIN POREMBA.
4       INSTALLATION. NYU.
5       DATE-WRITTEN. FEBRUARY 17, 1982.
6       DATE-COMPILED. OCTOBER 16, 1982.
7       SECURITY. HENRY MULLISH.
8       * * * * * * * * * * * * * * * * * * * * * * * * * * * * * * * * * *
9       *    THIS IS A CONVENTIONAL PROGRAM THAT              *
10      *    READS AND WRITES EIGHTY COLUMN DATA CARDS.    *
11      * * * * * * * * * * * * * * * * * * * * * * * * * * * * * * * * * *
12
13      ENVIRONMENT DIVISION.
14      CONFIGURATION SECTION.
15      SOURCE-COMPUTER. CYBER-170-720.
16      OBJECT-COMPUTER. CYBER-170-720.
17      SPECIAL-NAMES.
18      INPUT-OUTPUT SECTION.
19      FILE-CONTROL.
20          SELECT IN-FILE ASSIGN TO INPUT.
21          SELECT OUT-FILE ASSIGN TO OUTPUT.
22
23      DATA DIVISION.
24      FILE SECTION.
25
26      *    DEFINE INPUT OF THE PROGRAM.
27
28      FD   IN-FILE
29           LABEL RECORDS ARE OMITTED.
30      01   RECORD-IN              PIC X(80).
31
32      *    DEFINE OUTPUT OF THE PROGRAM.
33
34      FD   OUT-FILE
35           LABEL RECORDS ARE OMITTED.
36      01   RECORD-OUT.
37           02  FILLER            PIC X(01).
38           02  DATA-OUT          PIC X(80).
39
```

```
40          PROCEDURE DIVISION.
41
42          LETS-GO.
43              OPEN INPUT IN-FILE.
44              OPEN OUTPUT OUT-FILE.
45              MOVE SPACES TO RECORD-OUT.
46              WRITE RECORD-OUT AFTER PAGE.
47
48          READ-AND-WRITE.
49              READ IN-FILE AT END GO TO CLOSE-UP.
50              MOVE RECORD-IN TO DATA-OUT.
51              WRITE RECORD-OUT AFTER 1.
52              GO TO READ-AND-WRITE.
53
54          CLOSE-UP.
55              CLOSE IN-FILE, OUT-FILE.
56              STOP RUN.
```

Output for Program 7

AHN	HWA-YUHN	375 RIVERSIDE DR. NEW YORK, N.Y.	10025	(212)222-7760	O2
BENLEVY	LINDA	5-11 UNIVERSITY PLACE NY NY	10003	(212)473-4322	B2
BHASIN	KULJOT	5 UNIVERSITY PLACE	10003	(212)254-0500	B1
BLITZ	CIPORA	232 E 82ND ST NY NY	10028	(212)249-4570	B2
COTTONE	JEROME	325 PACIFIC AVE	10312	(212)984-3668	W1
DAVIS	TI	5 UNIVERSITY PLACE BOX 213	10003	(212)674-6352	W2
DECATREL	RALPH	196-20 91 AVE HOLLISCOURT	11423	(212)479-7348	W1
DIBERNARDO	FRAN	65-45 79 STREET MIDDLE VILLAGE NY	11379	(212)894-1752	W2
DUGGAN	TIM	46-32 193 ST	11358	(212)357-5126	B1
DUNCAN	CHRIS	441 W 22; APT. 4-A; NEW YORK, N.Y.	10011	(212)989-3105	O1
EHLER	LINDA	55 EAST 10 ST. APT 1202 N.Y. N.Y.	10003	(212)254-2914	E2
EPIFAN	PETER	105 CLAUDY LN NEW HYDE PK NY	11040	(516)328-3337	W1
FERMANN	BARBARA	5 UNIVERSITY PL NEW YORK NY	10003	(212)475-4376	W2
FINE	LARRY	327 E. 54 ST., N.Y., N.Y., APT. C	10022	(212)752-9435	W1
GEE	KEITH	181 DAHILL ROAD	11218	(212)436-4913	B1
GOLDBERG	ALLEN	1237 E. 100 ST. BROOKLYN N.Y.	11236	(212)763-6271	W1
GOODMAN	CORINNE	90 8TH AVE. APT. 9A, BROOKLYN	11215	(212)638-5522	O2
HANLON	CHRIS	5-11 UNIVERSITY PLACE NY NY	10003	(212)475-4482	B2
HIRSCH	DORIS	75-60 188 ST	11366	(212)454-4942	B2
POREMBA	IRVIN	35 FIFTH AVENUE ROOM 1119	10003	(212)477-1708	W1

3.2   Discussion of Program 7

1. In the Identification Division there is nothing new. The comments that follow the SECURITY paragraph are, of course, different so as to reflect the purpose of the current program.

2. The Environment Division has the Configuration Section that we have already come across but which now also has another section, called the INPUT-OUTPUT Section. If used, the two sections must appear in this order. Before describing the purpose of the INPUT-OUTPUT Section, notice the new paragraph name that is called SPECIAL-NAMES in the Configuration Section. Nothing is printed there, but it is used to equate what are called "user-specified" mnemonic names with function names that are used by the compiler. This probably will not be very meaningful to you at this point so don't worry about it. Just remember where it belongs if it is employed. Incidentally, among its uses, SPECIAL-NAMES provides for the ability to exchange the functions of the comma and period. This is sometimes necessary because when expressing numbers some European countries use commas where we use periods and vice versa. Furthermore, if a currency symbol other than the $ is used in a PICTURE clause, the user must specify the currency substitute symbol in this paragraph. Although optional, the paragraph will always be included so that your eye will get used to seeing it and you will know exactly where it belongs should the need to use it arise. We will discuss this SPECIAL-NAMES paragraph further when we explain the WRITE statement.

The INPUT-OUTPUT Section must always be included in any COBOL program that uses input or output files. Because all subsequent programs to be presented in this book will use files, this section, concerned with the definition of the input and output devices, will always appear. The only paragraph name in the INPUT-OUTPUT Section that we will deal with is the hyphenated paragraph name FILE-CONTROL. Subordinate to the FILE-CONTROL paragraph are the SELECT clauses that associate the names of the files to be used with the external media. On the Cyber computer the input file is associated or assigned to a special area of disk, referenced by the keyword INPUT, whereas the output file is assigned to another special area, designated by the keyword OUTPUT. We will be coming across these two special keywords again shortly, so look out for them.

The programmer has to make up a suitable name for both the input and the output file. File-names obey the same rules as data-names do. Whatever names we select follow the words SELECT. We have arbitrarily selected the name IN-FILE for the input file and OUT-FILE for the output file. Having given them such simple, obvious names, it is unlikely that we shall confuse them in the Data Division where we describe them and in the Procedure Division where we either read or write entries for them.

3. Having described everything in the Environment Division, we are now ready to tackle the Data Division. The novice might mistakenly believe that it is in the Data Division that the actual data to the program are placed. This is simply not so. It is here that the data—both the input and the output data—is *described*. Because we are dealing with an input and an output file, these must be specified and the order makes no difference. We will arbitrarily describe the input file first and then, the output file.

4. The Data Division header is always followed by the section header, FILE SECTION. A File Description now follows and the letters FD (not F.D.) are entered in the A margin. The name of the file being described is written in the B margin. Remember, it is named IN-FILE, as specified in the first of the two SELECT clauses. The phrase LABEL RECORDS ARE OMITTED follows the file-name. This LABEL RECORDS clause specifies whether or not labels are present. Usually, magnetic tape files are labeled at their beginning to identify the file. There would be another label at the other end of the file. It is possible for the label records to be STANDARD or OMITTED. Because our input is being read from data cards—for which there cannot possibly be any labels—we write the word OMITTED. The phrase LABEL RECORDS ARE OMITTED may be placed on the same line as the FD entry, which specifies the file name. Having done that we must now specify the record for that file. Records *always* have 01 written in the A margin and the name of the record written in the B margin. The arbitrarily selected name that is chosen for the record is RECORD-IN, which is a wise choice, for it clearly reflects the fact that it refers to a record and, in particular, is an input record.

Because we have alphabetic, numeric, and alphanumeric data that is punched or typed on each input record, and are reading in the whole record as a single entity without distinguishing between the various fields, we can assign a PICTURE of X(80) to the whole record.

5. As we did for the input file, we will describe the output file with its FD in the A margin and the selected name in the B margin. Because the output file, as was the input file, is a unit record device, the clause LABEL RECORDS ARE OMITTED is included. Perhaps now it will become clear why the LABEL RECORDS ARE OMITTED clause was punched on a separate line. The reason is simply that once it was punched for the input file it need only be duplicated (using the "duplicate" button on the keypunch) to produce the identical line for the output file. Of course, users of video terminals would have to type the clause again.

The output file, too, has an 01-record description and the name selected is RECORD-OUT. What would probably appear more reasonable than what appears in the program is an 01-entry reading:

01   RECORD-OUT PIC X(80).

For reasons that we have not yet explained (because we haven't yet covered the material) RECORD-OUT is "broken up" into two separate lines. The first of these two lines is given a lower level number, 02, and the special name FILLER (we will have much more to say about FILLER later on). To FILLER we attach a PICTURE of X, which is equivalent to X(01), or X(1). The second line is also given a level number of 02, which is named DATA-OUT, and is given a PICTURE of X(80).

6. The Procedure Division is, of course, the last of the four divisions. It is begun by a user-defined paragraph name, in this case LETS-GO.

The first instruction in the Procedure Division is the OPEN statement, because there is a rule in COBOL that says that whenever you are dealing with files you must first open them with an OPEN statement and close them at the end with a CLOSE statement.

The OPEN statement is strikingly different from the CLOSE statement in that when the OPEN verb is used it must be followed by the word INPUT (if it is an input file that is being opened) or the word OUTPUT (if it is an output file that is being opened). Hence the two B margin instructions are:

```
OPEN INPUT IN-FILE.
OPEN OUTPUT OUT-FILE.
```

Incidentally, it is illegal to OPEN a file that is already open or to CLOSE a file that is already closed.

7. In order to be sure that the output appears at the beginning of a fresh page (rather than on the same page as the listing of the program, which would be most unsatisfactory if not unacceptable), we must consciously make provision for this—by first "clearing out" the output line (RECORD-OUT). Moving spaces to RECORD-OUT is all that is necessary to clear out the output line. In COBOL the instruction:

```
MOVE SPACES TO RECORD-OUT
```

accomplishes the task. The reserved words SPACES and SPACE are equivalent and are also known as *figurative constants*. The figurative constants SPACE and SPACES are always available to the programmer for the purpose of moving blanks to a field. Now in order to get to the top of a new page, we must use the WRITE statement, so we merely write out that blank line after advancing the printer to a new page. This may be accomplished by the single instruction:

```
WRITE RECORD-OUT AFTER ADVANCING PAGE
```

where PAGE is again a reserved word that is designed precisely for the purpose at hand. The word ADVANCING may always be omitted from the WRITE instruction, if desired.

On the IBM computer using the 1968 compiler, the preferred method of ejecting to the top of the next new page is to insert the phrase: C01 is NEW-PAGE in the SPECIAL-NAMES paragraph of the Environment Division. The letter C stands for "channel," 01 for the channel number, and NEW-PAGE is simply a user-defined mnemonic data-name. When the WRITE instruction is used it assumes the form:

```
WRITE RECORD-NAME AFTER ADVANCING NEW-PAGE
```

which triggers channel 1 of the tape inside the printer, having the effect of ejecting to the top of the next new page.

8. Next, we arrive at the paragraph name READ-AND-WRITE. Within this paragraph the first instruction reads the first data card. When reading data cards we will not use the ACCEPT verb very much (if at all) because ACCEPT reads one record only. When reading files we generally use the READ verb. Following the word READ the name of the file to be read is written, in our case IN-FILE.

An AT END clause follows the name of the file. This is a particularly useful device that enables the programmer to specify some special instructions that are to be executed when the end of the input file is reached—when there is no more data left to be read. The AT END clause is ignored if the end of input has not yet been reached. The AT END clause terminates when the first period is encountered.

The action of the READ statement is to read a record of the file and to place the information (or, strictly speaking, a copy of the information) into the input area set aside for it by IN-FILE—80 characters of room. This information is then moved to DATA-OUT by the MOVE instruction and the record RECORD-OUT is written. The instruction to write the line may be:

WRITE RECORD-OUT

which assumes single spacing, or:

WRITE RECORD-OUT AFTER ADVANCING 1 LINE

or even the ungrammatical

WRITE RECORD-OUT AFTER ADVANCING 1 LINES

or omitting the word ADVANCING,

WRITE RECORD-OUT AFTER 1 LINE

or omitting the word LINE or LINES,

WRITE RECORD-OUT AFTER 1.

Notice that we READ a file (the FD name) but we WRITE a record (the 01-level name). Once the line has been written (remember, the first line of output will be printed at the top of a new page), a GO TO instruction is encountered, which unconditionally sends control to the paragraph READ-AND-WRITE, which starts the process of reading, moving, and writing a record all over again. Therefore we have set up a *loop*, the single, most important feature of computer programming. By means of this loop the second, third, fourth, and so on data cards will be processed. At some point (when all the data has been read) the end of file will have been reached and the AT END clause of the READ statement will have been triggered. This has the effect of unconditionally transferring control to the paragraph named CLOSE-UP.

9. Once the paragraph CLOSE-UP is reached the input and output files are closed and the program is terminated by the STOP RUN instruction. We could have written:

CLOSE IN-FILE.
CLOSE OUT-FILE.
STOP RUN.

but it is possible to close more than one file with the same CLOSE instruction. Notice we do *not* say whether it is the input or output file that we are closing when the CLOSE verb is used. We do indicate, however, whether it is the input or output file when we OPEN the files.

Backtracking to point 5, we have to justify the use of the FILLER in line 37. As you will now understand, the 80-column line of input data is moved to the output area for printing. When the WRITE instruction is executed, the *first* character of the printed line is "absorbed" for what is called "carriage-control" purposes. That will not be too meaningful at the moment but what is important to understand is that the first character of the printed line will not be printed. Worse yet, it could have the effect of printing one line to a page with the first character of each line chopped off. So before printing any line we always make sure that there is no significant information in the first print position. Placing a FILLER there with a PICTURE of X takes care of it.

As you can see, Program 7 is well documented, is neatly written, does the job well, and is quite comprehensible, even to a novice like yourself. The output begins on a fresh page, is single spaced, and terminates cleanly when all the input data has been read and printed.

It would be useful to conceptualize the way Program 7 works as follows: The 01-level item, RECORD-IN in line 30, specifies the 80-position input area of memory that is allocated automatically. The 01-level entry RECORD-OUT (in line 36) specifies 81 positions of memory to be allocated for *output* purposes. The first of these 81 positions will be used for carriage-control but the remaining 80 positions will be left intact. Whatever is in those 80 positions will be printed. Now, information read from an input card is copied into the input area. From there it is moved to the output area. It is from this output area only that any writing at all can be carried out by the WRITE statement. Once the record is written (after advancing one line, that is, on the next available line) the GO TO READ-AND-WRITE instruction is executed and the process is repeated again. However, when the READ instruction (in line 48) is executed the *second* time, it is not the same card as before that is read but the next card in line—it is the *second* card that is now read, moved, and then written. The same cycle is repeated for all the input data cards in turn.

This sequence of operations is typical of almost all COBOL programs, regardless of the style used. Understanding this simple concept will help you to follow all the subsequent programs and to assist you in writing your own programs.

It is fair to say that about 75% of all COBOL programs are written in the straightforward, traditional style that is used in Program 7. Of course, most programs are more complex than this simple listing program. This conventional style of programming, however, is increasingly coming under attack mainly because of the use of the GO TO instruction. We have used two of them in Program 7, one, in line 49 and the other, in line 52. Eventually the structured style of writing programs, in which the GO TO instruction is avoided, is bound to become conventional; it is only a matter of time.

In more complex programs that are written in the traditional style the indiscriminate use of GO TO's can lead to programs that are extremely difficult to understand. Therefore they are troublesome to maintain and awkward to transfer to another user because he or she, too, will have to suffer the frustrations of trying to comprehend it. A program that is riddled with GO TO's is spoken of as a "spaghetti-bowl"-type of program—it's difficult to tell where one strand begins and another ends.

In structured programming these GO TO's are all but eliminated. Before we are able to rewrite Program 7 in the structured style there are one or two topics that we have to cover in more detail. Stand by!

3.3 The READ Statement

The READ statement reads a card or a logical record and places the information in the input area of the computer's memory (as defined by the record description entry for the file) so that it may be accessed by the program. The format is:

READ file name [AT END imperative statement(s)]

Although the AT END clause is optional, it is recommended when the input file being accessed is sequential, as indeed it is in all the examples illustrated in this text.

Whatever data was residing in the input area prior to the execution of the READ will be overlaid (replaced) by the data transmitted by that READ, and that information will remain in that area until it is subsequently replaced by the action of another READ.

After the phrase AT END one or more statements must be written. If the READ is executed and a record is read, the AT END clause and its associated statements up to the first period are totally ignored. However, once all the records in the input file have been read—in other words, once there are no more records to be read—and an attempt to read another record is made, the end of the file is sensed and the instructions that follow the AT END clause are executed, up to the first encountered period. It is clear then that the placing of the period is of crucial significance and that none of the instructions in the AT END clause may be terminated by a period *except* the last one.

3.4 The WRITE Statement

After the reserved word WRITE the name of the record to be written is specified. (Notice the difference between the READ and the WRITE statement—you READ a *file* but WRITE a *record*.)

WRITE record-name-1 [FROM record-name-2]

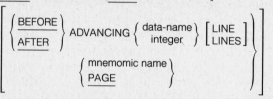

If the WRITE record-name option is used, the computer assumes you want to advance the paper a single line. However, you also have the option of controlling vertical movement of the paper by specifying either BEFORE ADVANCING or AFTER ADVANCING. If BEFORE ADVANCING is specified, the line is first written and the paper is advanced. In other words, the line is written before advancing. If the paper is to be advanced and the line is written after, the AFTER ADVANCING option is used. In practice, the AFTER ADVANCING option is much more frequently used because for many printers it is more efficient. Using both BEFORE ADVANCING and AFTER ADVANCING options in the same program can have the undesirable effect of unintentional overprinting.

On many IBM systems it is forbidden to mix WRITE record-name instructions with ADVANCING forms of the WRITE statement. If a WRITE instruction is used (and it's difficult to imagine a COBOL program without a WRITE instruction), all the WRITEs must be of the same form. I suppose you could say: "two WRITEs make a wrong."

As the format for the WRITE clearly indicates, the number of lines to be advanced may be specified by a predefined data-name or a specific integer. Also, the words LINE or LINES may be used. In pre-1974 compilers only the word LINES was permitted in this context, so that one frequently sees instructions such as:

WRITE OUT-LINE AFTER ADVANCING 1 LINES

which, despite its ungrammatical form, is entirely correct COBOL. The integer that is specified between the words ADVANCING and LINES may range between 0 and 99 on most systems.

To provide for variable line spacing with a single WRITE statement, one must use the data-name option. When the WRITE statement is executed the number of lines advanced will be equal to the current value of the data-name. Moving a 1 to it will cause single-line spacing; a 2, double spacing; and a 3, triple spacing; and so on.

Note that the words ADVANCING and LINES are optional and may be omitted entirely in much the same way as we are inclined in everyday speech to omit words or phrases without any loss of information transfer. No other computer language has this flexibility.

For advancing to a new page the PAGE option is now the standard method. (It is not available, however, on pre-1974 compilers). For example,

WRITE OUT-LINE AFTER ADVANCING PAGE.

For pre-1974 IBM compilers another method is used. The mnemonic name option of the ADVANCING phrase uses the Configuration Section of the Environment Division. In the SPECIAL-NAMES paragraph C01 (for Channel 01) is written.

One often hears the phrase "channel 01," which actually means 01. A frequently selected mnemonic name is TO-THE-TOP-OF-A-NEW-PAGE. To advance to a new page one may write, for example,

WRITE OUT-LINE AFTER ADVANCING TO-THE-TOP-OF-A-NEW-PAGE

which is so explicit that it virtually leaves nothing to the imagination.

The WRITE statement with the FROM phrase causes the record-name that follows the word FROM to be moved to the output line, where it is written directly.

3.5 The CLOSE Statement

After all the input and/or output operations for a given file have been executed and before the program is terminated, each file must be closed. This is done by the CLOSE statement, and once it is executed no further operations on the file are possible. It is not possible to close a file that is already closed or for that matter is it permissible to open an already opened file.

Unlike the OPEN statement, the reserved words INPUT and OUTPUT are not specified; the COBOL compiler retains this information from the OPEN statement. Writing CLOSE INPUT name-of-file will create an error.

3.6 Nonnumeric Literals

COBOL distinguishes between two kinds of literals: numeric and nonnumeric. The item 'YES' is an example of a nonnumeric literal.

The method by which the COBOL compiler distinguishes nonnumeric literals from data-names is that all nonnumeric literals must be enclosed by quotation marks. Now the official American National Standards COBOL calls for double quotation marks, but this is in direct opposition to the practice observed by many compilers that use the single quotation marks. Because IBM uses the single quotation marks—and to a great extent they dictate what a large segment of the data-processing world does—we have resorted to single quotation marks in this book.

The quotation marks may contain any characters, including letters of the alphabet, the 10 numeric digits, blanks, and special characters that are part of the character set of the particular computer. It is possible therefore to have a nonnumeric literal such as 'FISCAL YEAR 1984', which includes alphabetics, blank spaces, and numerics. In fact, a nonnumeric literal may even contain only numerics, such as '1984', or '12345'. Calling these examples of nonnumeric literals is a little mystifying. But they are nonnumeric in the sense that they can never be used in any arithmetic operation.

A nonnumeric literal begins with the first character after the first quotation mark and ends with the character before the last quotation mark (the maximum number of characters is 120), so that the quotation mark itself may not appear by itself as one of the characters in the literal because it would signal the end of the literal. Should it be necessary to include a single quotation mark, two contiguous marks must be used to represent the single mark. The COBOL compiler always looks at the succeeding character when it detects a quotation mark in order to "know" if it is the end of the literal or an included quotation mark. Here are some examples of literals that contain quotation marks.

LITERAL	PRINTS OUT AS
HOW"S THAT	HOW'S THAT
JOHN"S BOOK	JOHN'S BOOK
O"GRADY"S BAR	O'GRADY'S BAR

3.7   Numeric Literals

Numeric literals are values that are expressed as numbers and may include a plus or a minus sign and a decimal point. The decimal point may be placed anywhere in the literal *except as the rightmost character*, because if placed there, it would create ambiguity—is it a decimal point or is it a period?—after all, we use the same symbol for both. A numeric literal may consist of up to 18 digits.

3.8   Some Simple but Worthwhile Style Conventions

Some people are quite fanatical about style. What we present here are 7 simple-to-understand and easy-to-implement guidelines, which we suggest you follow for your own personal satisfaction—and possibly for others', too.

1. When writing program instructions by hand take special care to distinguish carefully between:
   a. the numeral 0 and the letter O
   b. the numeral 1 and the letter I
   c. the numeral 2 and the letter Z
   d. the European way of writing the numeral 7, (7), and the letter F.
2. Be sure that all user-supplied words such as PROGRAM-ID name, and data-names are both meaningful and descriptive. Using letters such as X, P, T, and R for data-names is fine in algebra but not for COBOL. If anyone has to ask what a data-name means, it is de facto a bad choice. When you consider that COBOL permits up to 30 characters for a data-name, there simply is no excuse for resorting to nonmeaningful names.
3. Whenever you want to combine more than one English word together and yet preserve separation between them, use the hyphen. You may use hyphens freely, except at the beginning and at the end.
4. Although commas and semicolons are permitted as punctuation symbols, they should not be used. It is true that they can sometimes be used to improve the readability of the program, but often a printer ribbon is worn and the code is not so perfectly printed as the print is in this text. Under such circumstances the comma and semicolon may appear to be periods and thus completely alter the logic of the program as viewed by the reader. Any advantage gained by their use is outweighed by the disadvantages.
5. The judicious use of "white space" adds immeasurably to the clarity of a program. Think for a moment how white space is used to such good effect in the printing of this text. Separate all divisions, sections, and paragraphs by inserting either blank lines or by resorting to blank comment lines.
6. Write only one COBOL sentence, or statement, clause, or phrase per coding line, terminating it with a period wherever appropriate.
7. When a sentence, statement, or clause extends over multiple coding lines, indent each line after the first by a few spaces.

Review Questions

1. What is the name of the division that comes after the Identification Division but before the Data Division?
2. When using files, what is the name of the section that describes them in the Data Division?
3. In the Data Division, which is named first — the file-name or the record-name?

4. What is the significance of an asterisk in column 7?
5. Should the FD for a file be more properly written F.D.?
6. What is the use of the reserved word FILLER?
7. Which of the following are reserved words?
   - a. DIVISION   b. DATA   c. FILE-CONTROL   d. CONFIGURATION
   - e. DATA-OUT   f. SELECT   g. INSTALLATION   h. READ-AND-WRITE
   - i. OUT-FILE   j. PROCEDURE
8. What must be done to files before they can be accessed?
9. What must be done to files before the program is terminated?
10. What is strikingly different about the OPEN and CLOSE statements?
11. What is the fundamental difference between a READ and a WRITE statement?
12. What is the method of informing the printer to eject to a new page?
13. In going to a new page, why is it necessary to clear out the output record first?
14. What is the method of ejecting to a new page on IBM pre-1974 standard compilers?
15. What is it that clearly distinguishes the READ statement from the ACCEPT?
16. What determines the end of the AT END clause?
17. What is a loop?
18. What is "carriage-control"?
19. Distinguish between a numeric literal and a nonnumeric literal.
20. A file is
    - a. a single record consisting only of numeric data
    - b. one or more records containing either numeric or nonnumeric data, or both
    - c. a rough tool used in COBOL
    - d. a list of people of questionable character
21. A record is
    - a. an unseemly past
    - b. an element of a COBOL file
    - c. a prize-winning program
    - d. a flat platter
22. The File Section is part of
    - a. the Identification Division
    - b. the Environment Division
    - c. the Data Division
    - d. the Procedure Division
23. In COBOL the letters FD stand for
    - a. Fire Department
    - b. Feel Depressed
    - c. Financial Debt
    - d. File Description
24. Which, if any, of the following is a reserved word?
    - a. FA
    - b. FB
    - c. FC
    - d. FD
    - e. FE
25. Which of the following, if any, are syntactically correct?
    - a. OPEN ABCDE INPUT
    - b. OPEN INPUT ABCDE
    - c. OPEN OUTPUT-ABCDE
    - d. OPEN OUTPUT ABCDE
26. Indicate which of the following is valid, ignoring the need to close files before program termination.
    - a. READ IN-FILE.
    - b. READ IN-FILE AT END STOP.
    - c. READ IN-FILE AT END STOP RUN.
    - d. READ IN-FILE CAREFULLY AT END STOP RUN.
27. State which of the following is correct.
    - a. MOVE X TO Y
    - b. MOVE G TO H GENTLY.
    - c. MOVE INPUT TO OUTPUT.
    - d. MOVE RECORD-IN TO RECORD-OUT.

28. Which, if any, of the following is correct?
    a. CLOSE ALL FILES
    b. CLOSE INPUT IN-FILE
    c. CLOSE INPUT
    d. CLOSE ANY FILE
29. Without looking up the list of reserved words, guess which of the following are COBOL reserved words.
    a. SECTION
    b. DIVISION
    c. PROCEDURE
    d. DATA
    e. CLOSE
    f. FILE
    g. FD
30. What type of constant is SPACE or SPACES?

Exercises

1. Prepare a deck of about a dozen different data cards as shown.
   col 1 – 20 last name
       25 – 35 first name
       40 – 80 name of school
   Write two programs to list the cards.
   a. without going to a new page
   b. taking care to go to a new page before printing the listing
2. Arrange to visit any computer center. Take your friends with you.
3. A teacher of computer science distinguishes between hardware and software as follows.

   If you can write it, it's software;
   if you can kick it, it's hardware.

   Comment on this.

Important Instructions

COBOL is fine—if you can get someone else to type the program for you.

(Maddy Cohen)

In this chapter we will become familiar with more instructions, which will enable us to rewrite Program 7 in the elegant way that is associated with structured programming. In particular, we will learn:

- more about the MOVE instruction
- the distinction between moving a numeric literal and a nonnumeric literal to a field larger than itself
- more on the PERFORM instruction
- level-77 independent items
- the use of VALUE clauses in the Working-Storage Section
- about the MOVE CORRESPONDING statement

In order to understand how to write elegant programs in the structured style, we have to extend our understanding of the MOVE and PERFORM verbs.

4.1 The MOVE Instruction

In a recent analysis of randomly selected COBOL programs it was revealed that of the instructions that are permitted in the Procedure Division, no fewer than 50% of them were MOVE instructions. As already seen, it is by means of the MOVE instruction that information is literally moved from one part of memory to another. To list data from input cards the cards are first read; this automatically moves the input data to the input areas of memory. Then the data is MOVEd from the input area to the output area. From there it is written—again, the idea of a move is involved.

Suppose we have an area named PLACE that is specified with a PICTURE of X(3). Here is a diagrammatic representation of such an area.

PLACE X(3)

```
┌──┬──┬──┐
│  │  │  │
└──┴──┴──┘
 1  2  3
```

If we now wanted to move the literal 'DOG' to PLACE we would simply write:

MOVE 'DOG' TO PLACE.

'DOG' ⟶ ☐☐☐ PLACE PIC X(3).
          1 2 3

If we could now look inside PLACE we would find it filled as shown.

PLACE X(3)

```
┌──┬──┬──┐
│ D│ O│ G│
└──┴──┴──┘
 1  2  3
```

If PLACE had a PICTURE of X(10) rather than X(3) we would need to know exactly what rules apply because the nonnumeric literal 'DOG' would be moved to a field larger than itself.

```
        1  2  3  4  5  6  7  8  9 10
'DOG' ⟶ ┌─┬─┬─┬─┬─┬─┬─┬─┬─┬─┐ PLACE PIC X(10)
        └─┴─┴─┴─┴─┴─┴─┴─┴─┴─┘
```

In such a situation the literal is "left-adjusted" into the 10-position area, which means that it begins all the way over to the left. What about the 7 remaining positions—what happens to them? The rule in COBOL is that when a nonnumeric literal is MOVEd to a field larger than itself, it is not only left-adjusted (or left-justified) but any remaining positions (that is, positions 4 through 10) are *filled with blanks*. The result of such a move would therefore be:

```
1  2  3  4  5  6  7  8  9 10
┌─┬─┬─┬─┬─┬─┬─┬─┬─┬─┐
│D│O│G│ḃ│ḃ│ḃ│ḃ│ḃ│ḃ│ḃ│
└─┴─┴─┴─┴─┴─┴─┴─┴─┴─┘
```

where the blanks are indicated by the lowercase b with a slash written over it.

Now that we have seen what happens when a nonnumeric literal is moved to a field larger than itself, let us proceed to examine what occurs when a nonnumeric literal is moved to a field smaller than itself. Suppose PLACE is now described with a PICTURE of X(2).

```
         1  2
'DOG' ⟶ ┌─┬─┐ PLACE PIC X(2)
        └─┴─┘
```

In this case the nonnumeric literal is once again left-justified, but because there is not enough room in PLACE to accommodate all of it, the rightmost character, 'G', is lost. This process is quite legitimate; it is called *truncation*.

The result of the move is:

```
'DOG' ⟶ ┌─┬─┐ PLACE PIC X(2)
        │D│O│
        └─┴─┘
         1  2
```

Numeric literals can also, of course, be moved. However, the receiving field should have a PICTURE of 9's. Moving 547 to a PICTURE of 999 (or its equivalent, 9(3)) is quite ordinary.

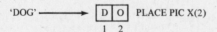

547 ⟶ ☐☐☐ PLACE PIC 9(3)

The resulting field becomes

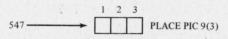

```
1  2  3
┌─┬─┬─┐
│5│4│7│
└─┴─┴─┘
```

We now ask the question: What happens when a numeric literal such as 547 is moved to a field with a PICTURE of 9(10)? In this case the number is right-justified and any unused portion is filled with zeros.

```
              1  2  3  4  5  6  7  8  9  10
547 ───────▶ | 0| 0| 0| 0| 0| 0| 0| 5| 4| 7|  PLACE PIC 9(10)
```

Moving a numeric value to a field larger than itself therefore differs in 2 important respects from that of moving a nonnumeric literal. A *nonnumeric* literal is *left-justified* and filled out with *blanks*, whereas a *numeric* literal is *right-justified* and filled out with *zeros*. Try to remember this distinction.

The formal way of showing the syntactic structure of the MOVE statement is:

MOVE { data-name-1 / literal } TO data-name-2 [data-name-3] · · ·

Because the words MOVE and TO are underlined, as well as capitalized, those key words are mandatory. The subject of the MOVE may be either a data-name, such as NET-SALES, or a literal, such as 567 or 'PROFIT = '. For any given MOVE, however, only one item may be moved to the object field, which must be a data-name. Actually, a *copy* of the subject is moved to the object field. The contents of the subject are left unchanged.

In practice, about 50% of all Procedure Division instructions are MOVEs. It is understandably so, because this instruction provides an easy way of transmitting data from one part of memory to another.

The format of the MOVE statement includes a data-name-3 (in brackets), followed by 3 successive dots (an ellipsis). This means that the subject of the MOVE may be moved to one *or more* different locations. In other words, one can write

MOVE SUPPLY TO DEPT-1 DEPT-2 DEPT-3 DEPT-4

where the number of object fields is optional.

It is considered illegal to MOVE alphanumeric data to a numeric field, numeric data with embedded decimal point to an alphanumeric field, or a group MOVE to either a numeric or a numeric-edited field. If a group item is MOVEd to an alphanumeric-edited field, no editing will take place.

The MOVE statement has another format that you might encounter on occasion. It is:

MOVE { CORRESPONDING / CORR } data-name-1 TO data-name-2.

Here the word CORRESPONDING may be abbreviated to CORR. It is an interesting instruction in that it permits the moving of more than one subject field. The only condition is that the names of the subject and the object fields must be absolutely identical. If they are, considerable programming time may be saved by using this feature. Here is an illustration of its use:

```
01    RECORD-1.       01    RECORD-2.
      02 A PIC 99.           02 A PIC 99.
      02 B PIC 999.          02 B PIC 999.
      02 C PIC 99V99.        02 C PIC 99V99.
      02 D PIC X(05).        02 D PIC X(05).

      MOVE CORRESPONDING RECORD-1 TO RECORD-2
```

The above has the effect of moving the data-names A, B, C, and D from RECORD-1 to their counternames in RECORD-2; remember, it's a *copy* that is moved.

The following record setup works exactly the same, even though the individual fields are not in the same order.

```
01    RECORD-3.       01    RECORD-4
      03 W PIC X(07).       03 Z  PIC X(03).
      03 X PIC 99V9.        03 W PIC X(07).
      03 Y PIC 999.         03 X  PIC 99V9.
      03 Z PIC X(03).       03 Y  PIC 999.

      MOVE CORR RECORD-3 TO RECORD-4.
```

So long as the sending and receiving fields have identical data-names, the MOVE CORR or MOVE CORRESPONDING statement moves each individual item. It would certainly appear therefore that this instruction is a real time-saver and one that should be used whenever feasible. As a matter of fact, however, the instruction is not only avoided by many COBOL shops, but it is often downright forbidden. Moreover, many programmers use a unique prefix or suffix name to every data item so that it reflects the record in which it is located and perhaps the sequential location within the record, as shown here.

```
01      RECORD-5.
        02 1-REC-5-ABLE      PIC X(05).
        02 2-REC-5-BAKER     PIC 99V99.
        02 3-REC-5-CHARLY    PIC 999.
        02 4-REC-5-FILLER    PIC X(10).
```

If such a device is used consistently (and a very powerful argument can be made in its favor), no individual field will have the same name in any record and thus the MOVE CORRESPONDING becomes worthless. The real opposition to the use of the MOVE CORRESPONDING derives from the possibility that during the course of the life of a program a field (or fields) may have its name changed inadvertently by a maintenance programmer. He or she may be unaware of the fact that the original name was essential for the MOVE CORRESPONDING to do its work. Even if the name is changed in the most trivial manner, for example, from ELAPSED-DAYS to ELAPSED-DAY, such a change is sufficient to negate the move of that particular field and the programmer may never know about it. Program 22 illustrates the MOVE CORRESPONDING statement.

4.2 The PERFORM... UNTIL Instruction

We have already encountered a more elementary form of the PERFORM. Now we will examine a more sophisticated version, which has some condition attached to it. For example,

PERFORM PARA-1 UNTIL J = 10

This instruction executes PARA-1 over and over until the condition, J = 10, is true, that is, until the value of J becomes exactly equal to 10. Actually, the condition is tested before the first time that the paragraph is executed. It will continue executing PARA-1 until something is done to J to make it equal to 10.

In the instruction:

PERFORM PARA-2 UNTIL X > 15

the paragraph PARA-2 will continuously be executed until the value of X becomes greater than 15. The instruction:

PERFORM PARA-3 UNTIL 1 = 0

really amounts to an infinite loop because the condition 1 = 0 will never be true. It is not so bad as you may think, however, because the paragraph being performed, PARA-3, may do something within itself to terminate the loop—such as trying to read beyond the end of the input file and thus triggering an end-of-file condition.

The condition that is associated with the PERFORM does not necessarily have to be numeric; it could just as easily be alphanumeric or alphabetic. This idea may be exploited in structured programming. It is often used in conjunction with an independent item, which we will now explain.

4.3   Independent Items and the VALUE Clause

Often there is a need for some additional memory other than the input and output areas. Occasionally it is necessary to store a temporary value, which may be done by giving the item a suitable data-name and PICTURE and assigning to it the special level number 77. According to the 1968 standard, independent items are placed in the A margin in the Working-Storage Section that *immediately* follows the section header. In the 1974 standard it is no longer necessary to place 77-level items at the beginning of the Working-Storage Section. They may be interspersed between record descriptions anywhere in the Working-Storage Section. There is a plan afoot to eliminate 77-level items altogether but this will likely not happen—if at all—until the 1980 standard is released (if it is ever released).

The 77-level items may have any of the 3 allowable PICTURE, namely, A, X, and 9. Suppose we set up a 77-level item such as:

```
77    MORE-CARDS PICTURE X(03) VALUE 'YES'.
```

This means that we have reserved a special area called MORE-CARDS to hold a 3-character word. Into this area the word 'YES' is moved automatically by virtue of the VALUE clause. The VALUE clause, (as used here) may be used only in the Working-Storage Section. However, 77-level items are also restricted to the Working-Storage Section. The VALUE clause proves to be of inestimable worth. During compilation of the program the VALUE clause MOVEs the information to the required area, thereby saving the programmer the trouble of having to MOVE it explicitly in the Procedure Division. This is such a useful device that in most professional COBOL programs the Working-Storage Section is by far the longest section of the program.

We have now covered a sufficient amount of material to present the listing program written in structured COBOL. It uses precisely the same input data as Program 7 and produces the identical output. However, the program differs significantly. Study Program 8 very carefully and try to understand how it works.

Welcome to the world of disciplined, predictable, and elegant structured programming!

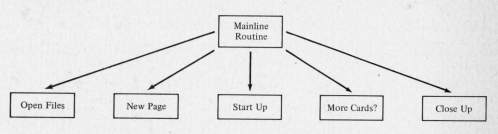

Program 8

```
1       IDENTIFICATION DIVISION.
2       PROGRAM-ID. LISTING2.
3       AUTHOR. IRVIN POREMBA.
4       INSTALLATION. NYU.
5       DATE-WRITTEN. OCTOBER 19, 1982.
6       DATE-COMPILED. OCTOBER 19, 1982.
7       SECURITY. HENRY MULLISH.
8       * * * * * * * * * * * * * * * * * * * * * * * * * * * * * * * * * * * * * * * * * * * * * * * *
9
10      *THIS PROGRAMS READS AND WRITES 80-COLUMN DATA CARDS.
11
12      ENVIRONMENT DIVISION.
13      CONFIGURATION SECTION.
14      SOURCE-COMPUTER. CYBER-170-720.
15      OBJECT-COMPUTER. CYBER-170-720.
16      SPECIAL-NAMES.
```

```
17      INPUT-OUTPUT SECTION.
18      FILE-CONTROL.
19          SELECT IN-FILE ASSIGN TO INPUT.
20          SELECT OUT-FILE ASSIGN TO OUTPUT.
21
22      DATA DIVISION.
23      FILE SECTION.
24
25    *   DEFINE INPUT OF THE PROGRAM.
26
27      FD  IN-FILE
28          LABEL RECORDS ARE OMITTED.
29      01  RECORD-IN              PIC X(80).
30
31    *   DEFINE OUTPUT OF THE PROGRAM.
32
33      FD  OUT-FILE
34          LABEL RECORDS ARE OMITTED.
35      01  OUT-RECORD.
36          02 FILLER             PIC X(01).
37          02 LINE-OUT           PIC X(80).
38
39      WORKING-STORAGE SECTION.
40      77  MORE-CARDS            PIC X(03) VALUE 'YES'.
41
42      PROCEDURE DIVISION.
43
44      MAIN-LINE-ROUTINE.
45          PERFORM OPEN-FILES.
46          PERFORM NEW-PAGE.
47          PERFORM START-UP.
48          PERFORM PROCESS-DATA UNTIL MORE-CARDS EQUAL 'NO'.
49          PERFORM CLOSE-UP.
50          STOP RUN.
51
52      OPEN-FILES.
53          OPEN INPUT IN-FILE.
54          OPEN OUTPUT OUT-FILE.
55
56      NEW-PAGE.
57          MOVE SPACES TO OUT-RECORD.
58          WRITE OUT-RECORD AFTER PAGE.
59
60      START-UP.
61          READ IN-FILE AT END
62              MOVE 'NO' TO MORE-CARDS
63              MOVE '***NO DATA IN DECK***' TO LINE-OUT
64              WRITE OUT-RECORD AFTER 30.
65
66      PROCESS-DATA.
67          MOVE RECORD-IN TO LINE-OUT.
68          WRITE OUT-RECORD AFTER ADVANCING 1 LINES.
69          READ IN-FILE AT END
70              MOVE 'NO' TO MORE-CARDS.
71
72      CLOSE-UP.
73          CLOSE IN-FILE, OUT-FILE.
```

4.4 Discussion of Program 8

The major difference between Programs 7 and 8 lies in the Procedure Division. Under the paragraph-name MAIN-LINE-ROUTINE, an A-margin entry, are a series of PERFORMs that end with STOP RUN. By looking at this main-line routine, you can get a fairly accurate idea of what the program is all about. A good analogy would be to consider the main-line routine as the boss of a large company, one in which the boss never does anything himself or herself except to bark out orders to various workteams.

The instruction PERFORM OPEN-FILES is equivalent to the boss giving instructions to the OPEN-FILES crew. Not until the OPEN-FILES crew has completed its work, namely, to open the input and output files, is the instruction to the next crew given. Again, notice that every time the OPEN verb is used it is not sufficient to name the file that is to be opened, but before the file-name is mentioned the appropriate word INPUT, if it is an input file, or OUTPUT if it is an output file, must appear.

Once the OPEN-FILES paragraph has been executed, control returns to the main-line routine, in particular, to the instruction in line 46, following the last PERFORM. This is the PERFORM NEW-PAGE instruction. The paragraph NEW-PAGE in line 56 moves spaces to OUT-RECORD and writes it out after ejecting to the next new page. Execution now returns to line 47, the line following the last PERFORM. This is the instruction PERFORM START-UP.

In paragraph START-UP the first data card is read. In the event that no data cards are present at all, the AT END condition is triggered. The literal 'NO' is moved to MORE-CARDS and the message ***NO DATA IN DECK*** is moved to LINE-OUT, which is written in the middle of the new page, that is, after advancing 30 lines. Control would then be sent to line 48, which reads:

PERFORM PROCESS-DATA UNTIL MORE-CARDS EQUAL 'NO'.

Now, if there were no data cards read at all, this instruction would not be executed because MORE-CARDS would contain the literal 'NO'. Control would be sent to the next instruction in line 49, which has the effect of closing the files, after which the STOP RUN is executed in line 50. However, this situation is unlikely; nevertheless the program has been written to allow for this possibility—and it really sometimes happens that the programmer forgets to include the data with the input deck.

Assuming now that the data cards were present—the expected situation—the AT END clause would not be triggered and the paragraph START-UP would have completed its task, returning control to line 48, which is PERFORM PROCESS-DATA UNTIL MORE-CARDS EQUAL 'NO'. This has the effect of moving the information read by the first READ instruction to LINE-OUT from where it is printed.

The next instruction (line 69) is another READ, which reads the second and subsequent data cards.

Notice that if the second READ instruction were to be located at the beginning of the paragraph PROCESS-DATA, it would have the effect of reading the next card in sequence, thus overwriting the contents of the previous data card on which no action has yet been taken.

Therefore we see that the program is clean, efficient, easy to follow and to amend, if necessary, devoid of GO TO's, and has an elegance about it that is attributable to structured programming. It could be argued that this was done at the cost of two separate READ statements. True, but this is surely a small price to pay for such elegance.

If by this time you have begun to write and run your own programs, no doubt you will have discovered that the programs seldom (if ever) work the first time they are run. Diagnostic messages are printed by the COBOL compiler each time an error is detected. This phase of the operation can be truly exasperating. As soon as you encounter diagnostic messages, perhaps you should look ahead to Chapter 12 where the whole subject of debugging a program is discussed. However, again, maybe you are such a careful programmer that you avoid making errors entirely. In that case you may want to ignore Chapter 12 altogether—but that is most unlikely.

An Approach to Solving a Problem by a Structured COBOL Program

First, examine the problem carefully and aim at a systematic approach rather than a hasty, impetuous attack. Some people have compared the writing of a good COBOL program to the writing of a symphony. Whether or not this is an exaggeration, the analogy holds in that a considerable amount of tender care is necessary so that everything fits together logically and cohesively.

The problem itself must be clearly understood. If it isn't, writing an intelligent program is virtually impossible. Understanding the problem in its entirety is equivalent to winning half the battle.

As problems emerge, try to break them down into smaller subproblems that are simpler to solve, so that they become systematically refined.

Never assume that the program will run correctly the first time. Accept the fact that you—just like everybody else in this world—are fallible. Thus print out intermediate results by using the DISPLAY statement; in other words, resort to "defensive" programming, in the spirit that "an ounce of prevention is worth a pound of cure." Check your computed values against hand-calculated ones. Use as many different types of data that you can to test out the program. If necessary, use maliciously contrived data to verify that the program works exactly as it is supposed to.

A program should be able to cope with as many logical contingencies as possible. COBOL provides numerous features for implementing such situations, more so than most programming languages in the world today. Because they exist, exploit them. Of course, it requires a fertile imagination to predict all kinds of aberrant behavior, but to be a good programmer, one needs a lively imagination. It is probably impossible to allow for *all* the possible situations that may arise, but certainly the most probable ones should be catered for. The newspapers frequently exploit those spectacular computer "accidents" such as an irate customer who is forever receiving dunning notices for $0.00 or the delighted customer who instead of receiving a refund check for $5.95 receives one for $1,000,005.95. Such errors are due to the faulty programmer who wrote the program in the first place, rather than to the computer.

The Philosophy of Structured Programming

In a letter to the editor of the prestigious journal *Communications* of the ACM, Volume 11, Number 3, dated March 1968, Edsger W. Dijkstra wrote that his observation was that the quality of programming skill in a program was a decreasing function of the density of GO TO statements in it. In other words, the more GO TO's that were present, the poorer was the programming quality. His idea of structured programming was the complete elimination of the GO TO statement.

In Dijkstra's view all programming may be reduced to 3 basic constructs.

1. simple sequence
2. selection (testing a condition)
3. repetition of a certain part of the program

Using these three constructs, one could write any meaningful program without resorting to any GO TO statements.

Rules for Structured Programming

1. Each program should be divided into separate modules or subroutines, each of which has a single function.
2. There should be a hierarchy of modules. The first is the main-line control, which directs the execution of the second level routines, and so on.
3. In COBOL there should be a restricted use of the GO TO statement.

The resulting "top-down" design leads to error-resistant programs that are faster to write, faster to execute, easier to understand, and therefore easier to maintain. A side benefit of structured programming is that it has changed the emphasis from clever to clear programming, where it properly belongs. A poorly structured program may have errors that are difficult to find, may be difficult to comprehend, and are troublesome to amend.

The programs in this book are written in a predictable, structured style. As you become familiar with the various features of the COBOL language, you will begin to write your own programs in this same structured style. Indeed, shortly it will become your natural style.

4.5 Questions and Answers Based on Program 8

Q. What is the PROGRAM-ID name?
A. *LISTING*

Q. What date was punched or typed by the programmer for DATE-COMPILED?
A. *None. The date is printed automatically during processing of the program.*

Q. What are the names of the files in the SELECT clauses and where else must these appear?
A. *The input file is named IN-FILE and the output file, OUT-FILE. These names must be part of the SELECT clause and also have individual FD's in the Data Division.*

Q. What is so special about the Working-Storage Section?
A. *It permits the use of the VALUE clause and 77-level items.*

Q. How many instructions are written in the main-line routine?
A. *6.*

Q. At what point is PERFORM NEW-PAGE executed?
A. *Immediately after paragraph OPEN-FILES has been performed.*

Q. Why is the STOP RUN instruction not the last instruction of the program?
A. *It is not the last physical instruction, being encountered only when the program has reached its natural conclusion. It is however the last logical instruction to be encountered.*

Q. How many instructions are executed as a direct result of the triggering of the AT END clause in START-UP?
A. *3; 2 MOVEs and 1 WRITE*

Q. What is the significance of the period at the end of line 64?
A. *The period plays a crucial role. It specifies that the conditional clause, AT END, terminates at that point.*

Q. How many times will 'NO' be moved to MORE-CARDS?
A. *Only once; if no data cards are present at all, 'NO' will be moved at line 62. If data cards are present, it will be moved at line 70, once all the data has been processed.*

Q. What role does the VALUE clause play?
A. *It plays the role of an implied MOVE statement. The MOVE is made during the compilation process.*

4.6 Some Frequently Made Errors — Spot and Correct Them

1. ENVIROMENT DIVISION.
2. SPECIAL NAMES.
3. 02 NUMBER PIC(999).
4. DATA-COMPILED.
5. DATA-WRITTEN.
6. INPUT-OUTPUT CONTROL.
7. FD IN-FILE.
8. OPEN IN-FILE.
9. OPEN INPUT FILE IN-FILE.
10. FILE-SECTION.

11. ASSIGN IN-FILE TO INPUT.
12. READ IN-FILE AT END PRINT 'NO DATA PRESENT'.
13. 77 MORE-CARDS PIC X(3) EQUAL 'YES'.
14. READ IN-FILE ON END STOP RUN.
15. SPECIALS-NAMES.
16. LABLE RECORDS ARE OMITTED.
17. PICX(23)
18. SELECT IN-FILE AND ASSIGN...

Review Questions

1. What is the result of moving the literal 'FINANCE' to a PICTURE of
   a. X(7)
   b. X(3)
   c. X(01)
   d. X(10)
2. What is the result of moving the literal 746 to a PICTURE of
   a. 9(3)
   b. 99
   c. 9
   d. 9(6)
3. What is an independent item?
4. What disadvantages are associated with the DISPLAY and ACCEPT verbs?
5. Write against each of the following the letters DN if it is a data-name: NL, for a numeric literal; and NNL, for a nonnumeric literal.
   a. 18
   b. '1492'
   c. 1776
   d. XTOTAL
   e. 'PRICE'
   f. 123.45
   g. −17
   h. SALE1982
   i. 246X

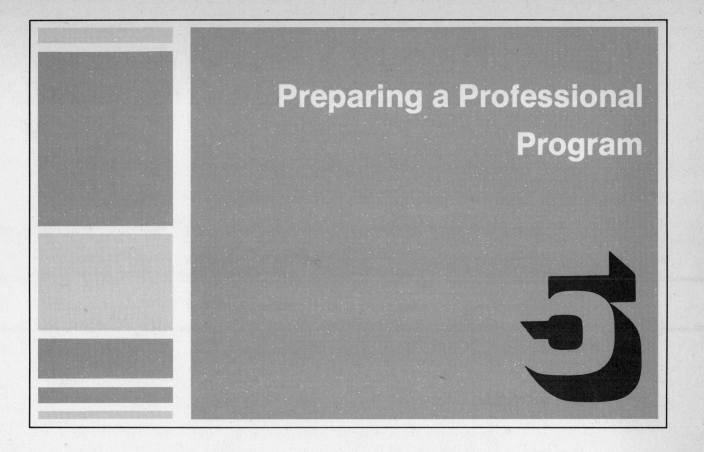

Preparing a Professional Program

In COBOL there's so much work to do you don't have time to forget anything.

(Joel Cohen)

In this chapter you will be gradually introduced to the approach used in writing quality programs. In professional COBOL circles a program must not only solve the problem at hand properly and accurately, but the output to the program must be easy to read and sensibly laid out. Because COBOL provides excellent formatting capabilities, all under the direct control of the programmer, there is no excuse for not printing the results as attractively as possible without being bogged down by cosmetic considerations.

In particular, you will learn about:

- printing a general heading
- using the full length of the printed line rather than restricting it to the length of the input card
- printing individual headings
- the use of the VALUE clause
- the figurative constant ALL
- subdividing a horizontal line into a column of vertical, partial descriptions
- making decisions in COBOL
- the IF statement and its variations
- the relational operators
- the logical operators
- compound IF statements

- the NEXT SENTENCE clause
- the test for NUMERIC
- the test for ALPHABETIC
- the test for POSITIVE, NEGATIVE, or ZERO
- the arithmetic verbs
- the COMPUTE statement
- counting
- suppressing leading zeros
- paginating the pages of a report
- restricting the output page to a given number of detail-line printouts
- printing the headings on each page
- the print chart form for planning a fancy format

There is so much information to absorb in this chapter that it might easily require repeated reading. However, this is the kind of knowledge about COBOL that you need in order to write sophisticated programs such as those you will see in real life. Look carefully now at the output for Program 9 and consider the special attention to detail that is needed in preparing such a report. You are very close to writing such programs yourself—be patient!

5.1   Printing a General Heading

In each of the listing programs shown so far the printed data appeared on a new page but without any headings. It is often advisable when printing out mass data to arrange for a suitable heading to appear at the top of the page. Let's suppose, for example, that we wanted to print the following heading.

```
******************************************
LISTING OF DETAIL CARDS
*=*=*=*=*=*=*=*=*=*=*=*=*=*=*=*=*=*=*=*=*=
```

where the first line is composed of a row of 42 asterisks; the second line, the words LISTING OF DETAIL CARDS (suitably spaced to make it look attractive); and finally, another line composed of alternate asterisk and equals sign symbols.

There is no reason to confine the output line to 80 columns because most computer printers can handle up to 132 characters per line. Adding on one for carriage control (making 133 characters altogether), we may always write the output line as:

```
01   LINE-OUT PIC X(133).
```

In COBOL each line to be printed must be set up individually. For example, an 01-record description must be written for the 42 asterisks; another, for the wording; and yet another, for the line of alternating asterisks and equal signs. It is most convenient to place these 01-record descriptions in Working-Storage because the VALUE clause may be used only in the Working-Storage Section, and for the printing of such headings the VALUE clause is extremely useful, as you will soon see.

When setting up a record one must always remember that allowance must be made for carriage control. The first character of the line is used for carriage control purposes. If there is a need to move the line away from the left-hand margin of the page, this indentation may be combined with the provision for carriage control as follows.

```
A    B
01   HEADER-1.
     02 FILLER PIC X(20) VALUE SPACES.
     02 FILLER PIC X(42) VALUE ALL ' * '.
```

When this kind of record structure is first seen it tends to seem somewhat confusing. In Chapter 7 we will study record descriptions in much greater detail and by then the concept will become crystal clear.

The name of the 01-level item is arbitrarily named HEADER-1. This is a group name that means simply that it has subordinate entries. A subordinate entry takes a level number between 02 and 49. A higher number implies a lower level. That lower level number is written in the B margin (unlike the 01, which is an A margin entry).

Rather than have to compose data-names for areas that are never referenced, COBOL supplies the reserved word FILLER, which may be used as often as required even within the same record.

Thus we may designate the first 02-level item FILLER and give it a PICTURE of X(20). This is followed by the special phrase VALUE SPACES. The word SPACES or its equivalent SPACE is one of the so-called *figurative constants*. A figurative constant has special significance to the compiler. Shortly we will learn of another figurative constant and later on, of others, too. The VALUE clause has the effect of moving the required information during compilation of the program, so that the entry:

```
02   FILLER PIC X(20) VALUE SPACES
```

has the effect of moving blanks to the 20-character area designated by the PICTURE X(20). The first of these spaces will serve for carriage control purposes while the remaining 19 blanks will merely provide sufficient spacing to center the rest of the printing.

The next entry is:

```
02   FILLER PIC X(42) VALUE ALL '*'.
```

The word ALL is another of these figurative constants that we just mentioned. It has the effect in the preceding case of filling up every one of the 42 positions set aside by PIC X(42) with asterisks. Of course, we could have written VALUE '* * * ··· * *' (42 consecutive asterisks), but look how much easier and efficient it is to use the figurative constant ALL. Another alternative is to name the 02 level with a non-FILLER name such as ASTERISKS and in the Procedure Division to use the instruction:

```
MOVE ALL '*' TO ASTERISKS
```

which would have served just as well. You can probably already get the notion that using a VALUE clause in the Data Division saves you a MOVE instruction in the Procedure Division; in other words, the VALUE clause behaves as an *implied* MOVE, even though the MOVE is made in compilation time, rather than when the program is in execution.

In order to print out this line of asterisks, we would have to move it to the output line in the Data Division before it could be written. In fact no line can be printed unless it is first moved to the output line. Therefore nothing can be printed directly from a record stored in the Working-Storage Section. It would make no sense to have an instruction in the Procedure Division that says:

```
WRITE HEADER-1.
```

If you tried it, an error would result and the program would be aborted—terminated without producing the desired results.

The record named HEADER-1 uses a total of 62 characters as may soon be checked by looking at the two PICTURES X(20) and X(42). It is not necessary to have another FILLER of X(78) VALUE SPACES because when this 62-character field is moved to the output-line of X(133) (a field larger than itself), it is left-justified and any unused positions to the right are *automatically* filled with spaces. However, to include the FILLER would not be wrong, just redundant.

To print the line

LISTING OF DETAIL CARDS

(which is spaced for its pleasing effect on the eye), another record would have to be set up in Working-Storage. One of the many attractive features of COBOL is that it permits you to set up the line in any way you wish. For example, you could write:

```
A   B
01  HEADER-2.
    02 FILLER PIC X(20) VALUE SPACES.
    02 FILLER PIC X(13) VALUE 'L I S T I N G'.
    02 FILLER PIC X(05) VALUE ' O F'.
    02 FILLER PIC X(13) VALUE ' D E T A I L'.
    02 FILLER PIC X(11) VALUE ' C A R D S'.
```

or

```
A   B
01  HEADER-2.
    02 FILLER PIC X(18) VALUE 'L I S T I N G  O F'.
    02 FILLER PIC X(24) VALUE ' D E T A I L  C A R D S'.
```

or some other variation such as we will soon illustrate in Program 9. You may subdivide any horizontal line to be printed into as many parts as you like in a vertical direction. This makes for an extremely flexible arrangement. In the event that a minor change becomes necessary, what is needed is to change possibly only one line and all the others remain exactly as they are.

To print the line of alternating asterisks and equal signs and to be sure that it lines up with the other 2 headings, we may write:

```
01  HEADER-3.
    02 FILLER PIC X(20) VALUE SPACES.
    02 FILLER PIC X(42) VALUE ALL ' * = '.
```

The use of the figurative constant ALL with the literal ' * = ' has the effect of filling the 42 positions with consecutive pairs of characters * and = . In the event that the FILLER has an odd number of characters rather than even, as many characters would be inserted as would fit.

Suppose that for some obscure reason the data was omitted. We would not, under those circumstances, want the headings to be printed. To ensure that this was so, we must examine the contents of the 77-level item MORE-CARDS immediately after the initial read. If it were now 'NO', then we would know that no data was present.

5.2   Making Elementary Decisions in COBOL

Testing for the presence or absence of a value in COBOL is done by means of the IF statement. The COBOL IF statement is particularly powerful and flexible, although its full power will not be illustrated for a while. For the moment here is how it works in its simplest form:

```
IF condition imperative-statement(s).
```

The condition is evaluated; if it is found to be true the imperative statement(s) (up to the first period) is (are) executed. If the condition is false, the imperative statement(s) is (are) ignored and execution is resumed from the statement following the period. It is clear therefore that the placing of the period is of critical importance for the correct use of the IF statement.

We could therefore write (in the B margin) immediately after the first READ.:

```
IF MORE-CARDS EQUAL 'YES' PERFORM WRITE-HEADINGS
```

or its equivalent:

```
IF MORE-CARDS = 'YES' PERFORM WRITE-HEADINGS.
```

where the paragraph WRITE-HEADINGS writes the 3 heading lines in succession.

The preceding is illustrated in Program 9, which follows. The input data is identical to previous versions; however, the output this time has a general heading. Study the program carefully and be sure you understand it. You may test your comprehension by closing the book and trying to write the whole program by yourself!

Program 9

```
1       IDENTIFICATION DIVISION.
2       PROGRAM-ID. LISTING3.
3       AUTHOR. IRVIN POREMBA.
4       INSTALLATION. NYU.
5       DATE-WRITTEN. MARCH 24, 1982.
6       DATE-COMPILED. OCTOBER 12, 1982.
7       SECURITY. HENRY MULLISH ONLY.
8    *      THIS PROGRAM READS AND WRITES 80-COLUMN DATA CARDS
9    *      AND LISTS THE DATA UNDER A GENERAL HEADING.
10
11      ENVIRONMENT DIVISION.
12      CONFIGURATION SECTION.
13      SOURCE-COMPUTER. CYBER-170-720.
14      OBJECT-COMPUTER. CYBER-170-720.
15      SPECIAL-NAMES.
16      INPUT-OUTPUT SECTION.
17      FILE-CONTROL.
18          SELECT IN-FILE ASSIGN TO INPUT.
19          SELECT OUT-FILE ASSIGN TO OUTPUT.
20
21      DATA DIVISION.
22      FILE SECTION.
23      FD   IN-FILE
24          LABEL RECORDS ARE OMITTED.
25
26      01   RECORD-IN           PIC X(80).
27
28      FD   OUT-FILE
29          LABEL RECORDS ARE OMITTED.
30
31      01   LINE-OUT            PIC X(133).
32
33      WORKING-STORAGE SECTION.
34      77   MORE-CARDS          PIC X(03) VALUE 'YES'.
35
36      01   HEADER-1.
37          02 FILLER            PIC X(20) VALUE SPACES.
38          02 FILLER            PIC X(42) VALUE ALL ' * '.
39
40      01   HEADER-2.
41          02 FILLER            PIC X(20) VALUE SPACES.
42          02 FILLER            PIC X(13) VALUE 'L I S T I N G'.
43          02 FILLER            PIC X(02) VALUE SPACES.
44          02 FILLER            PIC X(03) VALUE 'O F'.
45          02 FILLER            PIC X(02) VALUE SPACES.
46          02 FILLER            PIC X(11) VALUE 'D E T A I L'.
47          02 FILLER            PIC X(02) VALUE SPACES.
48          02 FILLER            PIC X(09) VALUE 'C A R D S'.
49
50      01   HEADER-3.
51          02 FILLER            PIC X(20) VALUE SPACES.
52          02 FILLER            PIC X(42) VALUE ALL ' * = '.
53
54      01   DETAIL-LINE.
55          02 FILLER            PIC X(01) VALUE SPACES.
56          02 OUT-RECORD        PIC X(80).
57
58      PROCEDURE DIVISION.
59
60      MAIN-LINE-ROUTINE.
61          PERFORM OPEN-FILES.
```

```
62          PERFORM NEW-PAGE.
63          PERFORM START-UP.
64          PERFORM PROCESS-DATA UNTIL MORE-CARDS EQUAL 'NO'.
65          PERFORM CLOSE-UP.
66          STOP RUN.
67
68      OPEN-FILES.
69          OPEN INPUT IN-FILE.
70          OPEN OUTPUT OUT-FILE.
71
72      NEW-PAGE.
73          MOVE SPACES TO LINE-OUT.
74          WRITE LINE-OUT AFTER PAGE.
75
76      START-UP.
77          READ IN-FILE AT END
78              MOVE 'NO' TO MORE-CARDS
79              MOVE '**NO DATA IN DECK**' TO OUT-RECORD
80              MOVE DETAIL-LINE TO LINE-OUT
81              WRITE LINE-OUT AFTER 30.
82          IF MORE-CARDS EQUAL 'YES' PERFORM WRITE-HEADINGS.
83
84      PROCESS-DATA.
85          MOVE RECORD-IN TO OUT-RECORD.
86          WRITE LINE-OUT FROM DETAIL-LINE AFTER 2.
87          READ IN-FILE AT END MOVE 'NO' TO MORE-CARDS.
88
89      CLOSE-UP.
90          CLOSE IN-FILE, OUT-FILE.
91
92      WRITE-HEADINGS.
93          WRITE LINE-OUT FROM HEADER-1 AFTER 1.
94          WRITE LINE-OUT FROM HEADER-2 AFTER 1.
95          WRITE LINE-OUT FROM HEADER-3 AFTER 1.
```

Output for Program 9

```
* * * * * * * * * * * * * * * * * * * * * * * * * * * * * * * * * * * * *
              L I S T I N G   O F   D E T A I L   C A R D S
= * = * = * = * = * = * = * = * = * = * = * = * = * = * = * = * = * = * =

AHN          HWA-YUHN    375 RIVERSIDE DR. NEW YORK, N.Y.      10025  (212)222-7760  O2
BENLEVY      LINDA       5-11 UNIVERSITY PLACE NY NY           10003  (212)473-4322  B2
BHASIN       KULJOT      5 UNIVERSITY PLACE                    10003  (212)254-0500  B1
BLITZ        CIPORA      232 E 82ND ST NY NY                   10028  (212)249-4570  B2
COTTONE      JEROME      325 PACIFIC AVE                       10312  (212)984-3668  W1
DAVIS        TI          5 UNIVERSITY PLACE BOX 213            10003  (212)674-6352  W2
DECATREL     RALPH       196-20 91 AVE HOLLISCOURT             11423  (212)479-7348  W1
DIBERNARDO   FRAN        65-45 79 STREET MIDDLE VILLAGE NY     11379  (212)894-1752  W2
DUGGAN       TIM         46-32 193 ST                          11358  (212)357-5126  B1
DUNCAN       CHRIS       441 W 22; APT. 4-A; NEW YORK, N.Y.    10011  (212)989-3105  O1
EHLER        LINDA       55 EAST 10 ST. APT 1202 N.Y. N.Y.     10003  (212)254-2914  E2
EPIFAN       PETER       105 CLAUDY LN NEW HYDE PK NY          11040  (516)328-3337  W1
FERMANN      BARBARA     5 UNIVERSITY PL NEW YORK NY           10003  (212)475-4376  W2
FINE         LARRY       327 E. 54 ST., N.Y., N.Y., APT. C     10022  (212)752-9435  W1
GEE          KEITH       181 DAHILL ROAD                       11218  (212)436-4913  B1
GOLDBERG     ALLEN       1237 E. 100 ST. BROOKLYN N.Y.         11236  (212)763-6271  W1
GOODMAN      CORINNE     90 8TH AVE. APT. 9A, BROOKLYN         11215  (212)638-5522  O2
HANLON       CHRIS       5-11 UNIVERSITY PLACE NY NY           10003  (212)475-4482  B2
HIRSCH       DORIS       75-60 188 ST                          11366  (212)454-4942  B2
POREMBA      IRVIN       35 FIFTH AVENUE ROOM 1119             10003  (212)477-1708  W1
```

5.3   The IF Statement in Detail

When processing large volumes of information, one must usually make certain critical decisions at various points in the program. As a matter of fact, we have already encountered 3 instructions in which decisions are made. The READ statement, for example, has the AT END clause associated with it. This is only a succinct way of saying: "If all the records of the input file have been read, then execute a predetermined set of instructions." Here the AT END clause behaves as though it were an implied IF statement. We used our first explicit IF statement in Program 9 where we tested the value of MORE-CARDS to determine whether or not it was equal to 'YES'. Of course, the PERFORM...UNTIL also carried the notion of a decision.

We can ask within a program whether a data value is equal to that of another, greater than, less than, and so on and whether a data item being read in is alphabetic or numeric in character. Depending on the result of such a test, we can direct the computer to follow one path if the condition being tested holds and a completely different path if the condition being tested fails. By placing these IF statements in carefully selected points within a program, the COBOL programmer can design an extremely efficient and highly sophisticated network.

The simplest form of the IF statement is, as already stated:

IF condition imperative statement(s).

For example, we could write:

IF A IS EQUAL TO B MOVE C TO D.

(although it is not part of the 1974 standard the word THEN is optional on many compilers.) This IF statement could therefore be written:

IF A IS EQUAL TO B THEN MOVE C TO D.

without any diagnostic message being printed.

The statement is interpreted to mean that if the value contained in A is exactly equal to that contained in B then move a copy of C to D. If, on the other hand, the value of A is not equal to B, the imperative statement MOVE C TO D is ignored entirely and execution continues with the statement following the period. A certain amount of flexibility is permitted in writing the IF statement. For example, it may be written as well in any of the following equivalent forms.

IF A EQUAL TO B MOVE C TO D.
IF A EQUAL B MOVE C TO D.
IF A = B MOVE C TO D.

The relational condition need not, of course, be restricted to equality or for that matter must the operands such as A and B be data-names; they can just as easily be numeric or nonnumeric literals, or even arithmetic expressions that are automatically evaluated before the comparisons are made. The general format for comparisons is:

$$\begin{Bmatrix} \text{data-name-1} \\ \text{literal-1} \\ \text{expression-1} \end{Bmatrix} \begin{Bmatrix} \text{IS [NOT] } \underline{\text{GREATER}} \text{ THAN} \\ \text{IS [NOT] } \underline{\text{LESS}} \text{ THAN} \\ \text{IS [NOT] } \underline{\text{EQUAL}} \text{ TO} \end{Bmatrix} \begin{Bmatrix} \text{data-name-2} \\ \text{literal-2} \\ \text{expression-2} \end{Bmatrix}$$

The symbols < and > may be used for "less than" and "greater than", respectively, but some COBOL shops insist that these symbols, including the equal sign, be avoided because not all printers print alike. Some printers may print out these mathematical symbols in a strange manner, which might be quite incomprehensible to a human reader of the program. The philosophy seems to be that although it takes longer, writing the program in its English form is preferable because no matter what printer is used, it will always print out correctly in its English form. Note, however, that if the symbols are used, they must be preceded and followed by at least one space.

The reader is cautioned that there is always a strong temptation to use the word EQUALS instead of EQUAL. Although EQUALS is accepted by some compilers, it is not in the 1974 standard. Some compilers will accept UNEQUAL and even EXCEEDS, but these are commercial extensions to the standard.

More than one imperative statement may be written after the condition that is being tested. For example,

```
IF A EQUAL B MOVE C TO D
            DISPLAY 'I TOLD YOU'
            CLOSE IN-FILE, OUT-FILE
            STOP RUN.
```

In this example if A is, in fact, equal to B not only is C moved to D, but "I TOLD YOU" is displayed, the 2 files IN-FILE and OUT-FILE are closed, and the program is terminated by the STOP RUN statement. The first period that is encountered determines the end of the scope of the IF. There is no limit to the number of statements that may appear before the terminating period.

It should therefore be clear that in the Procedure Division a terminating period is ordinarily not necessary and must not be there if it is in a conditioned sequence of instructions. Nevertheless it is highly recommended that in an ordinary sequence of statements each one is given a line to itself (and additional lines, if necessary) and that each is terminated by a period. Wherever a period appears in COBOL it must be followed by at least one space. A statement may optionally be separated from another by a comma or a semicolon. If either of these is used, however, it too must be followed by at least one space. Commas and semicolons are sometimes used for added clarity. In fact, though, they are entirely ignored by the compiler.

We may always ask if A is *not* equal to B by use of the NOT operator. For example,

```
IF A NOT EQUAL TO B MOVE C TO D.
```

In certain situations it is very useful to be able to make 2 or more tests in a single IF statement. This may be done by means of the logical operators AND and OR, which serve distinctly different functions. For example, to determine whether the value A is less than or equal to that of B, we would write:

```
IF A LESS B OR A EQUAL B ...
```

The logical operator OR means that if either one or both of the related conditions hold, then the statement as a whole is true. If neither one is true, the whole statement is regarded as false.

Actually, COBOL permits a flexibility that few other languages permit. In the preceding example the subject of both comparisons is A. Therefore it is possible to write the instruction more concisely, very close indeed to the manner in which it is used in everyday English:

```
IF A LESS B OR EQUAL B ....
```

where the subject, A, may be implied in subsequent comparisons. So that the compound statement:

```
IF A LESS B OR EQUAL B OR GREATER C ...
```

will be true if any of the conditions $A < B$, $A = B$, or $A > C$ is true. Moreover, if the subject and the comparison are both common to each comparison test, both the subject and the comparison operator may be implied after the first one is explicitly stated, as shown in the next example:

```
IF A < B OR C OR D ...
```

where if $A < B$ or $A < C$ or $A < D$, the whole statement is considered to be true.

We can in a single IF statement test whether one or more conditions hold simultaneously. For example, a certain action might be required only in the event that A is equal to B *at the same time* that C is greater than D. These 2 conditions may be associated together by the means of the logical operator AND as follows.

```
IF A EQUAL B AND C GREATER D ....
```

5.4 The IF... ELSE Statement

We have already seen examples of the simplest IF statement. If the condition is true the statement(s) following the condition is (are) executed. If the condition is false, the statement(s) following the condition is (are) ignored and control is sent to the statement following the period.

It often transpires that if a condition that is being tested is false, some other action should be taken before you go to the next statement. For such situations COBOL provides an ELSE clause. For example,

```
IF A EQUAL B MOVE C TO D
ELSE MOVE E TO F.
```

When this statement is executed the condition is evaluated. If A is equal to B a copy of C is moved to D and control goes to the next sentence, the one following the period of the IF statement. If, however, A is not equal to B, the clause MOVE C TO D is ignored and instead the ELSE clause is executed, resulting in a copy of E being moved to F.

Both parts of the IF statement may contain one or more imperative statements. Thus the following example is valid.

```
IF X = Y MOVE Z TO BINGO
        WRITE RECORD-OUT
ELSE MOVE ALL '*' TO MESSAGE
        WRITE RECORD-OUT AFTER PAGE.
```

Notice the single period at the end of the IF statement. This is both a powerful feature and a reason for criticizing COBOL. On the one hand, all that is necessary to define the scope of the IF statement is the placing of a single period at the end of the sentence. On the other hand, if the period is placed in some other position, all manner of difficult problems may arise. It is wise then to pay extra attention when writing IF statements. Doing it correctly is just as easy as being sloppy and doing it incorrectly. Incidentally, IBM compilers permit the use of the word OTHERWISE in place of ELSE.

The clause NEXT SENTENCE is permitted in either clause of the IF statement. Here is the general format of the IF statement.

$$\underline{\text{IF}} \text{ condition} \begin{Bmatrix} \text{imperative statement(s)} \\ \underline{\text{NEXT}} \ \underline{\text{SENTENCE}} \end{Bmatrix} \begin{Bmatrix} \underline{\text{ELSE}} \text{ imperative statement(s)} \\ \underline{\text{ELSE}} \ \underline{\text{NEXT}} \ \underline{\text{SENTENCE}} \end{Bmatrix}$$

If the NEXT SENTENCE option is used, its action is simply to transfer control out of the IF statement to the next sentence. Notice, we do not write GO TO NEXT SENTENCE even though it may be considered as such.

With the IF statement we can also test whether a data item is numeric or alphabetic.

```
IF X IS NUMERIC ...
```

tests whether the data-name X consists entirely of the digits 0 through 9. The presence of *any* other character will cause the test to fail.

```
IF X IS ALPHABETIC ...
```

determines whether X consists entirely of the characters A through Z, including the space character. The numeric and alphabetic tests are known as the Class Condition tests. Both of them may be preceded by the logical operator NOT.

The Sign test determines whether or not the algebraic value of an arithmetic expression is less than, greater than, or equal to zero. Its general format is:

$$\text{arithmetic-expression IS [\underline{NOT}]} \begin{Bmatrix} \underline{\text{POSITIVE}} \\ \underline{\text{NEGATIVE}} \\ \underline{\text{ZERO}} \end{Bmatrix}$$

5.5 Erroneous IF Statements

Each of the following IF statements is in error. Try to spot the errors. The solutions immediately follow.

   a. IF X = Y S = T
   b. IF A = B GO TO EOJ, ADD 1 TO X.
   c. IF X = '345' ADD X TO Y.
   d. IF A EQUALS B MOVE C TO D.
   e. GO TO PARA-2 IF X > Y.
   f. IF HOURS AND RATE NUMERIC ...
   g. IF A AND B ARE EQUAL TO C ...
   h. IF X ISN'T NUMERIC ...
   i. IF X > Y GO TO NEXT SENTENCE.
   j. IF A > = B ADD 1 TO X.
   k. IF X > Y MOVE A TO B.
      ELSE MOVE C TO D.
   l. IF C = D COMPUTE* X + Y = Z.
   m. IF A > B C < D

a. The word COMPUTE after Y is omitted; the instruction

IF X = Y MOVE S TO T

would be just as effective.

b. If A is equal to B, control would be sent to paragraph EOJ but the ADD part of the instruction would never be reached.

c. If X is in fact equal to the nonnumeric literal '345' (even though within the quotes is a number, the quotes designate it a nonnumeric literal), it is impossible to add anything to a nonnumeric literal.

d. Some compilers might complain about the use of the word EQUALS rather than the standard EQUAL.

e. The compiler (if not a structured programming purist) would accept

IF X > Y GO TO PARA-2

but neither could accept it the way it is written here.

f. This instruction must be written:

IF HOURS NUMERIC AND RATE NUMERIC ...

because only the subject of the clause may be omitted.

g. This must be written:

IF A IS EQUAL TO C AND B IS EQUAL TO C ...

where the words IS and TO may be omitted.

h. This must be written:

IF X IS NOT NUMERIC ...

where IS may be omitted.

i. The words GO TO must be omitted, not because they offend the sensitivity of a structured COBOL programmer but because the clause NEXT SENTENCE implies a preceding GO TO. In other words, you think GO TO but do not write it.

j. There is no arithmetic operator > = in COBOL.

k. The period after B must be omitted because an instruction cannot begin with the word ELSE. It must always be part of an IF statement, if used at all.

*The COMPUTE statement is discussed in detail in the next section.

l. The COMPUTE part must be written:

COMPUTE Z = X + Y

with the left and right sides interchanged and spaces placed before and after the operators.

m. This is quite meaningless; C < D is not an imperative statement.

5.6   Doing Arithmetic in COBOL with the Arithmetic Verbs

The time has arrived to learn how to compute in COBOL. So far we have managed to avoid all calculations but when we work with computers a certain amount of arithmetic computation is always necessary. There are 4 arithmetic verbs.

1. ADD
2. SUBTRACT
3. MULTIPLY
4. DIVIDE

Without knowing much more, examine the following B margin entry.

ADD A TO B

This instruction, which is understandable to just about everybody who understands English, is actually the way in which an addition is written in COBOL. Look at how simple it is—how self-documenting and how little one has to know in order to understand what it means. COBOL was intentionally written in this manner so that even people without expertise in the field could learn it quickly or, at least, could follow a program fairly well.

Having said that, we should caution you that the preceding ADD instruction is also quite profound. It carries certain implications that must be clearly understood.

1. The instruction is a B-margin entry.
2. Both A and B must be numeric quantities; that is, they must have PICTUREs of 9's.
3. Both A and B must be predefined. It would be impossible to add A to B unless both A and B had actual values.
4. The result of the addition is stored in the second operand B, replacing whatever was there previously.
5. The value of A is left intact.

Other examples of valid ADD instructions follow.

ADD 1 TO A.
ADD 1.5 TO B.
ADD −2.7 TO C.

It is *not* legal to write:

ADD B TO 1

because when we use the arithmetic verbs the second operand must *always* be a data-name, never a constant.

Let us now examine the instruction:

SUBTRACT C FROM D

Once again, both C and D must be predefined with PICTUREs of 9's and the instruction must be written in the B margin. The result of subtracting C from D is placed in the second operand, D, replacing its previous contents while the value C remains as it was.

Other valid SUBTRACT instructions are:

```
SUBTRACT 1 FROM A.
SUBTRACT 1.5 FROM B.
SUBTRACT −25 FROM C.
```

The instruction:

```
MULTIPLY E BY F
```

behaves in exactly the same way, namely, the predefined numeric values E and F are multiplied together and the result is stored in the *second* operand, F, while E is left unchanged. You must avoid the temptation to write MULTIPLY E TIMES F. This is *not* a valid statement and will create errors if attempted.

```
DIVIDE G INTO H
```

is, like the other arithmetic instructions, a B-margin entry. G and H must be predefined and have PICTUREs of 9's, and the result of dividing G into H is stored in the second operand, H, replacing the previous contents of H and leaving G unchanged.

So you see there is a striking consistency in how these arithmetic verbs behave. Occasionally it is necessary to carry out an arithmetic operation and not to change either operand as a result of the calculation. For precisely this purpose each of the 4 arithmetic verbs is capable of taking an optional GIVING clause into which the result is sent, leaving *both* operands unchanged.

To add together the values A and B without destroying either one, we may write the instruction:

```
ADD A B GIVING C
```

where the result is placed in C, replacing whatever number was previously stored there. Note that the word TO is not used with the GIVING clause. It is one of the most frequent mistakes made by novices, even after repeated warnings. If desired, a comma may be placed after A and B. The object of the GIVING clause, C, must be a data-name with a PICTURE of 9's, but it need not be predefined with a given value because it will be replaced by the new value of C. To add A, B, C, and D together, we could write:

```
ADD A, B, C, D GIVING E
```

which places the sum in E. If we wrote:

```
ADD A, B, C, D GIVING E, F, G
```

the sum of A, B, C, and D would be placed in E, F, and G.

Here are some valid examples of other ADD instructions that use the GIVING clause.

```
ADD   2 A GIVING B.
ADD   C 3 GIVING D.
ADD   E −4 GIVING F.
ADD   −5 6 GIVING H.
ADD   I, J, 6, K, −7 GIVING L.
```

To subtract H from I such that the result goes into J, leaving H and I as they were, we could write:

```
SUBTRACT H FROM I GIVING J.
```

To subtract a series of items from another item, we may write:

```
SUBTRACT A, B, C FROM D
```

which adds A, B, and C and subtracts their sum from D, replacing D with this result. If we did not want to change D, we could simply use the GIVING clause:

```
SUBTRACT A, B, C FROM D GIVING E.
```

To multiply A by B, we could write:

MULTIPLY A BY B GIVING C

which places the product into C.

The divide instruction is the most interesting of the arithmetic verbs. First of all, we can write:

DIVIDE A INTO B GIVING C

which is the COBOL equivalent of the algebraic

$$c = \frac{b}{a}$$

however, we may also write:

DIVIDE A BY B GIVING C

which is equivalent to the algebraic

$$c = \frac{a}{b}$$

This is decidedly different from the INTO counterpart. Be sure that you understand the difference. Note, however, that we can *not* say:

DIVIDE A BY B

without the GIVING clause. This would imply that it is the first operand that changes, contrary to the general pattern.

The DIVIDE has an extension that is seldom found in other programming languages. It is:

DIVIDE A INTO B GIVING C REMAINDER D

and the corresponding

DIVIDE A BY B GIVING C REMAINDER D

These instructions assume, of course, that data-names A, B, C, and D each have a PICTURE of 9's. A and B must be predefined, but not C and D. Suppose A has a PICTURE of 99 and has the value 17 while B has a PICTURE of 9 and the value 6. Let both C and D have a PICTURE of 9.

Dividing 17 by 6 yields 2 with a remainder of 5. The value of 2 will be stored in C while D will have the value 5.

It would be instructive to examine the following instructions, each of which is in error. Try to spot the nature of the error.

a. ADD X TO Y GIVING Z.
b. ADD LIGHT TO DARK GIVING MILD.
c. SUBTRACT WEAK FROM STRONG GIVING 1500.
d. SUBTRACT COLD FROM 212.
e. MULTIPLY A TIMES B.
f. DIVIDE TOTAL BY DAYS.

a and b have TO and GIVING in the same clause.
c and d have constants to store a result instead of data-names.
e uses TIMES instead of BY.
f uses BY without the GIVING clause.

5.7 The COMPUTE Statement

Suppose we wanted to find the square root of a number. In COBOL there are no functions such as those found in other more scientifically oriented languages. After all, COBOL is geared to business-type problems. In mathematics we could calculate the square root of a number by raising that number to the exponent one half ($\frac{1}{2}$). But there is no verb EXPONENTIATE in COBOL. To provide for the calculation of algebraic expressions, COBOL supplies the COMPUTE verb in which the arithmetic verbs are substituted by symbols.

In general, the COMPUTE statement (a B-margin entry) is of the following form.

COMPUTE data-name = arithmetic-expression.

For example,

a. COMPUTE A = B + C
b. COMPUTE D = E − F
c. COMPUTE G = H ∗ I
d. COMPUTE J = K / L
e. COMPUTE M = N ∗∗ M

where the symbol for addition is the plus sign; subtraction, the minus sign; multiplication, the asterisk; division, the slash; and exponentiation, the double asterisk. There must be at least one space after the word COMPUTE, before and after the equal sign, and before and after each arithmetic operator. However, it would be an error to place a space in the middle of the exponentiation symbol.

The arithmetic symbols have a mathematical hierarchy as shown.

highest (strongest)	∗∗		exponentiation
	∗	/	multiplication and division
lowest (weakest)	+	−	addition and subtraction

This means that in any expression that is evaluated, exponentiation will be done first, followed by multiplication and division, followed in turn by addition and subtraction. In each of the last 2 cases, where 2 operators have the same hierarchy, that which comes first in a left-to-right scan is done first. In other words, if we had a COMPUTE instruction such as:

COMPUTE A = B / C + D ∗ E ∗∗ F

the computation would proceed as:

1. E ∗∗ F; this is reduced to a single number.
2. B/C; reduced to a single number
3. D ∗ (E ∗∗ F); reduced to a single number
4. (B/C) + (D ∗ (E ∗∗ F))

which, after it is reduced to a single number, is stored in A.

Parentheses may be used freely to group terms but within the parentheses the preceding hierarchy applies.

In order to find the square root of X, for example, we would be wrong to write:

COMPUTE Y = X ∗∗ 1/2

because, according to the previous hierarchy, X would be raised to the power 1 and the result would be divided by 2. This is *not* the square root. Either parentheses are placed around the fraction $\frac{1}{2}$ or it is replaced by the constant 0.5.

Using this method, one can calculate the third root, the fourth root, and so on. The number in question is merely raised to the reciprocal of the desired root.

Although it is perfectly legal in algebra to write:

$a + b = c$

it is not legal to write in COBOL:

COMPUTE A + B = C

because the data-name specified on the left-hand side of the equal sign represents the location in memory where the result of the expression on the right is stored. It is not possible to store C in location A + B. Therefore the expression must be translated into COBOL by simply reversing the expression:

COMPUTE C = A + B

where the sense of the expression is in no way impaired.

The algebraic expression:

$$a = b + c$$

may therefore be written in 2 different ways in COBOL:

COMPUTE A = B + C

or

ADD B, C GIVING A

but not

ADD B TO C GIVING A

because COBOL forbids the use of TO and GIVING in the same clause.

The expression:

$$d = e^2fg$$

may be written by using the COMPUTE statement:

COMPUTE D = E ** 2 * F * G

but not as:

COMPUTE D = E ** 2FG

because implied multiplication is not accepted in COBOL as it is in algebra. If multiplication is intended the asterisks must be included. However, the following is still incorrect:

COMPUTE D = E ** 2 * F * G

because before and after every operator (including the equal sign) there must be at least one space. It should be written as:

COMPUTE D = E ** 2 * F * G

The expression may be evaluated by using the arithmetic verbs—"lingo-longo"—as follows.

MULTIPLY E BY E (places e^2 into E)
MULTIPLY F BY G (places fg into G)
MULTIPLY E BY G GIVING D (places e^2fg in D)

The reader is cautioned against trying to solve the problem in one step by writing:

MULTIPLY E BY E BY F BY G GIVING D

because this defies the acceptable format of the MULTIPLY verb.

The algebraic expression:

$$h = \frac{ij}{km}$$

may be evaluated by the COMPUTE verb as:

COMPUTE H = (I * J) / (K * M)

or

COMPUTE H = I * J / (K * M)

where in both cases the numerator ij is divided by the denominator km, but the instruction:

COMPUTE H = I * J / K * M

which would be perfectly acceptable by the compiler, would nevertheless produce an incorrect result. That is because according to the hierarchical rules previously described, each of the operations, multiplication and division, are of equal strength, being on the same level. In such cases the compiler executes them in a left-to-right scan. Therefore I will first be multiplied by J and the result will be divided by K. So far so good, but then the expression:

$$\frac{ij}{k}$$

is multiplied by M, producing a result for:

$$\frac{ijm}{k} \quad \text{and not} \quad \frac{ij}{km}$$

The algebraic expression:

$$d = \sqrt{b^2 - 4ac}$$

may be computed by using the COMPUTE statement in the following manner:

COMPUTE D = (B ** 2 − 4 * A * C) ** .5

but not by using the arithmetic verbs.

As a final example, let us evaluate the algebraic expression:

$$x = \frac{b^3 c^5}{d + g} - ef^4$$

by using both methods. There are many different and correct ways by employing both methods.

a. COMPUTE X = (B ** 3 * C ** 5) / (D + G) − E * F ** 4

b. MULTIPLY B BY B GIVING B2. (places b^2 in B2)
MULTIPLY B2 BY B. (places b^3 in B)
MULTIPLY C BY C GIVING C2. (places c^2 in C2)
MULTIPLY C2 BY C2. (places c^4 in C2)
MULTIPLY C2 BY C. (places c^5 in C)
MULTIPLY B BY C. (places $b^3 c^5$ in C)
ADD D TO G. (places $d + g$ in G)
DIVIDE G INTO C. (places $\dfrac{b^3 c^5}{d + g}$ into C)
MULTIPLY F BY F. (places f^2 in F)
MULTIPLY F BY F. (places f^4 in F)
MULTIPLY F BY E. (places ef^4 in E)
SUBTRACT E FROM C GIVING X.

5.8   The Final Version of the Listing Program

The information (or, at least, parts of it) presented in this chapter is necessary for a complete understanding of our next illustrative program. Using the same input data, what we want to do is to list the data in an elegant fashion, where the individual items of information are printed across the page, each under its separate heading, and the whole report under a general heading. Moreover, we want to paginate the output printing PAGE 1 in the top left-hand corner of the first page, PAGE 2 on the second page, and so on. We want to count the cards and print out the count on each line of the report, suppressing leading zeros if necessary. We do not want to print more than 15 lines of data per page, and finally, we want to translate or interpret each of the coded items in columns 79 and 80.

The program to satisfy all these conditions contains many of the characteristics of a professional program. You will be able to follow its features once they are

Print Chart for Program 10

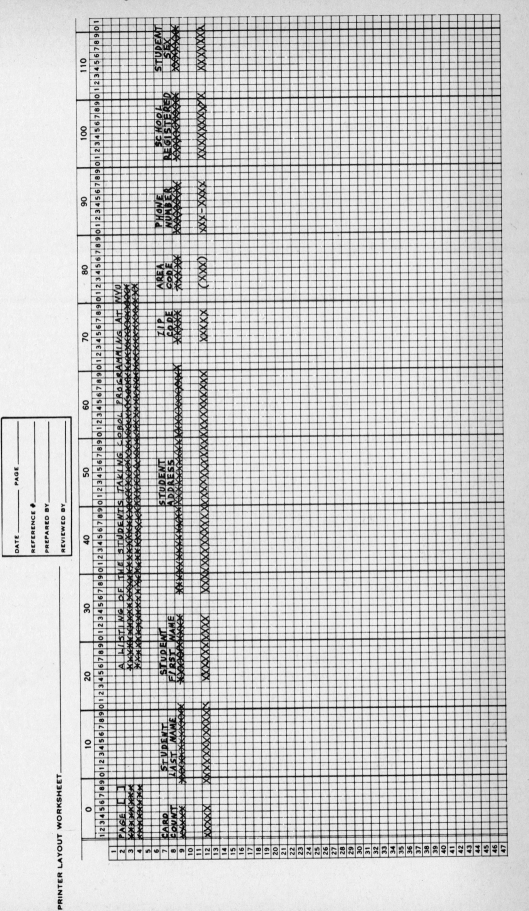

explained. A print chart or layout sheet is generally used to assist a programmer to plan out the format of the output. Several such print charts are included at the back of the book to help you in planning your own sophisticated layouts. The print chart used for Program 10 is presented on page 63. Look at it. You may want to refer to it in the discussion of Program 10.

Program 10

```
1       IDENTIFICATION DIVISION.
2       PROGRAM-ID. LISTING4.
3       AUTHOR. IRVIN POREMBA.
4       INSTALLATION. NYU.
5       DATE-WRITTEN. MARCH 24, 1982.
6       DATE-COMPILED. OCTOBER 12, 1982.
7       SECURITY. HENRY MULLISH ONLY.
8       * * * * * * * * * * * * * * * * * * * * * * * * * * * * * * * * * * * * * * * * * * * * * * * * * * *
9       *     THIS PROGRAM IS A LISTING OF DATA CARDS PUNCHED:                          *
10      *       COLUMNS 1-12:   LAST NAME                                               *
11      *       COLUMNS 14-22:  FIRST NAME                                             *
12      *       COLUMNS 24-57:  ADDRESS (NUMBER AND STREET)                            *
13      *       COLUMNS 59-63:  ZIP CODE                                              *
14      *       COLUMN    65:   (                                                     *
15      *       COLUMNS 66-68:  TELEPHONE AREA CODE                                   *
16      *       COLUMN    69:   )                                                     *
17      *       COLUMNS 70-72:  FIRST 3 DIGITS OF TELEPHONE #                         *
18      *       COLUMN    73:   -                                                     *
19      *       COLUMNS 74-77:  LAST 4 DIGITS OF TELEPHONE #                          *
20      *       COLUMN    79:   SCHOOL REGISTERED (G = GRADUATE,                       *
21      *                       B = BPA, W = WSUC, E = EDUCATION,                      *
22      *                       A = SCHOOL OF THE ARTS, O = OTHER)                     *
23      *       COLUMN    80:   SEX (1 FOR MALE, 2 FOR FEMALE)                         *
24      *     THIS PROGRAM THEN PRINTS OUT THE DATA CARDS                              *
25      *     UNDER A SUITABLE HEADING WITH A PAGE COUNT,                              *
26      *     A CARD COUNT AND ANY CODED INFORMATION DECODED.                          *
27      * * * * * * * * * * * * * * * * * * * * * * * * * * * * * * * * * * * * * * * * * * * * * * * * * * *
28
29      ENVIRONMENT DIVISION.
30      CONFIGURATION SECTION.
31      SOURCE-COMPUTER. CYBER-170-720.
32      OBJECT-COMPUTER. CYBER-170-720.
33      SPECIAL-NAMES.
34      INPUT-OUTPUT SECTION.
35      FILE-CONTROL.
36          SELECT IN-FILE ASSIGN TO INPUT.
37          SELECT OUT-FILE ASSIGN TO OUTPUT.
38
39      DATA DIVISION.
40      FILE SECTION.
41      FD   IN-FILE
42          LABEL RECORDS ARE OMITTED.
43
44      *    DEFINE DATA.
45
46      01   RECORD-IN.
47           02 LAST-NAME            PIC X(12).
48           02 FILLER               PIC X(01).
49           02 FIRST-NAME           PIC X(09).
50           02 FILLER               PIC X(01).
51           02 ADDRESS-IN           PIC X(34).
52           02 FILLER               PIC X(01).
53           02 ZIP-CODE             PIC 99999.
54           02 FILLER               PIC X(01).
55           02 AREA-CODE            PIC X(05).
56           02 PHONE-NO             PIC X(08).
57           02 FILLER               PIC X(01).
58           02 SCHOOL               PIC X(01).
59           02 SEX                  PIC 9.
60
61      FD   OUT-FILE
62          LABEL RECORDS ARE OMITTED.
```

```
63
64      *       DEFINE OUTPUT OF PROGRAM
65
66      01      LINE-OUT                    PIC X(133).
67
68      WORKING-STORAGE SECTION.
69
70      77      PAGE-COUNT                  PIC 999   VALUE ZERO.
71      77      CARD-COUNT                  PIC 9999  VALUE ZERO.
72      77      CARD-COUNT-2                PIC 99    VALUE ZERO.
73      77      MORE-CARDS                  PIC X(03) VALUE 'YES'.
74
75      01      HEADER-1
76              02 FILLER                   PIC X(01) VALUE SPACES.
77              02 FILLER                   PIC X(05) VALUE 'PAGE'.
78              02 PAGE-COUNT-OUT           PIC ZZ9.
79              02 FILLER                   PIC X(17) VALUE SPACES.
80              02 FILLER                   PIC X(13) VALUE 'A LISTING OF'.
81              02 FILLER                   PIC X(13) VALUE 'THE STUDENTS'.
82              02 FILLER                   PIC X(13) VALUE 'TAKING COBOL'.
83              02 FILLER                   PIC X(18) VALUE 'PROGRAMMING AT NYU'.
84
85      01      HEADER-2.
86              02 FILLER                   PIC X(01) VALUE SPACES.
87              02 FILLER                   PIC X(08) VALUE ALL '*'.
88              02 FILLER                   PIC X(17) VALUE SPACES.
89              02 FILLER                   PIC X(57) VALUE ALL '*'.
90
91      01      HEADER-3.
92              02 FILLER                   PIC X(01) VALUE SPACES.
93              02 FILLER                   PIC X(10) VALUE 'CARD'.
94              02 FILLER                   PIC X(07) VALUE 'STUDENT'.
95              02 FILLER                   PIC X(07) VALUE SPACES.
96              02 FILLER                   PIC X(07) VALUE 'STUDENT'.
97              02 FILLER                   PIC X(18) VALUE SPACES.
98              02 FILLER                   PIC X(07) VALUE 'STUDENT'.
99              02 FILLER                   PIC X(18) VALUE SPACES.
100             02 FILLER                   PIC X(16) VALUE 'ZIP AREA'.
101             02 FILLER                   PIC X(12) VALUE 'PHONE'.
102             02 FILLER                   PIC X(11) VALUE 'SCHOOL'.
103             02 FILLER                   PIC X(07) VALUE 'STUDENT'.
104
105     01      HEADER-4.
106             02 FILLER                   PIC X(01) VALUE SPACES.
107             02 FILLER                   PIC X(09) VALUE 'COUNT'.
108             02 FILLER                   PIC X(14) VALUE 'LAST NAME'.
109             02 FILLER                   PIC X(10) VALUE 'FIRST NAME'.
110             02 FILLER                   PIC X(16) VALUE SPACES.
111             02 FILLER                   PIC X(07) VALUE 'ADDRESS'.
112             02 FILLER                   PIC X(18) VALUE SPACES.
113             02 FILLER                   PIC X(11) VALUE 'CODE CODE'.
114             02 FILLER                   PIC X(05) VALUE SPACES.
115             02 FILLER                   PIC X(10) VALUE 'NUMBER'.
116             02 FILLER                   PIC X(10) VALUE 'REGISTERED'.
117             02 FILLER                   PIC X(08) VALUE 'SEX'.
118
119     01      HEADER-5.
120             02 FILLER                   PIC X(01) VALUE SPACES.
121             02 FILLER                   PIC X(05) VALUE ALL '*'.
122             02 FILLER                   PIC X(03) VALUE SPACES.
123             02 FILLER                   PIC X(12) VALUE ALL '*'.
124             02 FILLER                   PIC X(03) VALUE SPACES.
125             02 FILLER                   PIC X(10) VALUE ALL '*'.
126             02 FILLER                   PIC X(03) VALUE SPACES.
127             02 FILLER                   PIC X(34) VALUE ALL '*'.
128             02 FILLER                   PIC X(03) VALUE SPACES.
129             02 FILLER                   PIC X(05) VALUE ALL '*'.
130             02 FILLER                   PIC X(03) VALUE SPACES.
131             02 FILLER                   PIC X(05) VALUE ALL '*'.
132             02 FILLER                   PIC X(03) VALUE SPACES.
133             02 FILLER                   PIC X(08) VALUE ALL '*'.
134             02 FILLER                   PIC X(03) VALUE SPACES.
135             02 FILLER                   PIC X(10) VALUE ALL '*'.
136             02 FILLER                   PIC X(03) VALUE SPACES.
137             02 FILLER                   PIC X(07) VALUE ALL '*'.
```

```
138
139    01    DETAIL-LINE.
140          02 FILLER                PIC X(02) VALUE SPACES.
141          02 CARD-COUNT-OUT        PIC ZZZ9.
142          02 FILLER                PIC X(03) VALUE SPACES.
143          02 LAST-NAME-OUT         PIC X(12).
144          02 FILLER                PIC X(04) VALUE SPACES.
145          02 FIRST-NAME-OUT        PIC X(09).
146          02 FILLER                PIC X(03) VALUE SPACES.
147          02 ADDRESS-OUT           PIC X(34).
148          02 FILLER                PIC X(03) VALUE SPACES.
149          02 ZIP-CODE-OUT          PIC 99999.
150          02 FILLER                PIC X(03) VALUE SPACES.
151          02 AREA-CODE-OUT         PIC X(05).
152          02 FILLER                PIC X(03) VALUE SPACES.
153          02 PHONE-NO-OUT          PIC X(08).
154          02 FILLER                PIC X(03) VALUE SPACES.
155          02 SCHOOL-OUT            PIC X(09).
156          02 FILLER                PIC X(04) VALUE SPACES.
157          02 SEX-OUT               PIC X(06).
158
159    PROCEDURE DIVISION.
160
161    *     THIS IS THE MAIN PARAGRAPH WHICH USES
162    *     THE PERFORM STATEMENT TO ACCESS OTHER PARAGRAPHS.
163
164    MAIN-LINE-ROUTINE.
165          PERFORM OPEN-FILES.
166          PERFORM NEW-PAGE.
167          PERFORM START-UP.
168          PERFORM PROCESS-DATA UNTIL MORE-CARDS EQUAL 'NO'.
169          PERFORM CLOSE-UP.
170          STOP RUN.
171
172    *     THIS PARAGRAPH OPENS UP THE FILES.
173
174    OPEN-FILES.
175          OPEN INPUT IN-FILE.
176          OPEN OUTPUT OUT-FILE.
177
178    NEW-PAGE.
179          MOVE SPACES TO LINE-OUT.
180          WRITE LINE-OUT AFTER PAGE.
181
182    *     START-UP PRINTS THE HEADINGS AND
183    *     CHECKS TO SEE IF THERE IS ANY DATA.
184    *     IF THERE IS NO DATA AN ERROR MESSAGE IS PRINTED
185    *     AND THE PROGRAM IS THEN TERMINATED BY MOVING 'NO'
186    *     TO MORE-CARDS.
187
188    START-UP.
189          READ IN-FILE AT END
190              MOVE 'NO' TO MORE-CARDS
191              MOVE '**NO DATA IN DECK**' TO LINE-OUT
192              WRITE LINE-OUT AFTER 30.
193          IF MORE-CARDS EQUAL 'YES' PERFORM WRITE-HEADINGS-PARA.
194
195    *     IF THERE IS DATA PROCESS-DATA SENDS THE DATA
196    *     TO SCHOOL-SEX-PARA WHERE IT IS DECODED, MOVES
197    *     THE DATA TO DETAIL-LINE, WRITES DETAIL-LINE,
193    *     AND THEN READS ANOTHER DATA CARD.
199
200    PROCESS-DATA.
201          ADD 1 TO CARD-COUNT.
202          ADD 1 TO CARD-COUNT-2.
203          PERFORM SCHOOL-SEX-PARA.
204          MOVE CARD-COUNT TO CARD-COUNT-OUT.
205          MOVE LAST-NAME TO LAST-NAME-OUT.
206          MOVE FIRST-NAME TO FIRST-NAME-OUT.
207          MOVE ADDRESS-IN TO ADDRESS-OUT.
208          MOVE ZIP-CODE TO ZIP-CODE-OUT.
209          MOVE AREA-CODE TO AREA-CODE-OUT.
210          MOVE PHONE-NO TO PHONE-NO-OUT.
211          WRITE LINE-OUT FROM DETAIL-LINE AFTER 2.
212          READ IN-FILE AT END MOVE ZEROS TO CARD-COUNT-2
```

```
213              MOVE 'NO' TO MORE-CARDS.
214          IF CARD-COUNT-2 EQUAL 15 MOVE ZEROS TO CARD-COUNT-2
215              PERFORM NEW-PAGE
216              PERFORM WRITE-HEADINGS-PARA.
217
218      *   CLOSE-UP CLOSES THE FILES.
219
220      CLOSE-UP.
221          CLOSE IN-FILE, OUT-FILE.
222
223      *   SCHOOL-SEX-PARA TRANSFORMS THE CODES FOR THE
224      *   STUDENT'S SEX AND SCHOOL INTO MEANINGFUL
225      *   WORDS WITH THE USE OF THE IF-ELSE CONDITION
226      *   STATEMENTS.
227
228      SCHOOL-SEX-PARA.
229          IF SCHOOL EQUAL 'G' MOVE 'GRADUATE' TO SCHOOL-OUT
230          ELSE IF SCHOOL EQUAL 'B' MOVE 'BPA' TO SCHOOL-OUT
231           ELSE IF SCHOOL EQUAL 'W' MOVE 'WSUC' TO SCHOOL-OUT
232            ELSE IF SCHOOL EQUAL 'E' MOVE 'EDUCATION' TO SCHOOL-OUT
233             ELSE IF SCHOOL EQUAL 'A' MOVE 'ARTS' TO SCHOOL-OUT
234              ELSE IF SCHOOL EQUAL 'O' MOVE 'OTHER' TO SCHOOL-OUT.
235          IF SEX EQUAL 1 MOVE 'MALE' TO SEX-OUT
236          ELSE MOVE 'FEMALE' TO SEX-OUT.
237
238      *   WRITE-HEADINGS-PARA WRITES OUT THE HEADERS
239      *   AFTER ADVANCING TO A NEW PAGE.
240
241      WRITE-HEADINGS-PARA.
242          ADD 1 TO PAGE-COUNT.
243          MOVE PAGE-COUNT TO PAGE-COUNT-OUT.
244          WRITE LINE-OUT FROM HEADER-1 AFTER 1.
245          WRITE LINE-OUT FROM HEADER-2 AFTER 1.
246          WRITE LINE-OUT FROM HEADER-2 AFTER 1.
247          WRITE LINE-OUT FROM HEADER-3 AFTER 2.
248          WRITE LINE-OUT FROM HEADER-4 AFTER 1.
249          WRITE LINE-OUT FROM HEADER-5 AFTER 1.
```

Output for Program 10

PAGE 1 A LISTING OF THE STUDENTS TAKING COBOL PROGRAMMING AT NYU

CARD COUNT	STUDENT LAST NAME	STUDENT FIRST NAME	STUDENT ADDRESS	ZIP CODE	AREA CODE	PHONE NUMBER	SCHOOL REGISTERED	STUDENT SEX
1	AHN	HWA-YUHN	375 RIVERSIDE DR. NEW YORK, N.Y.	10025	(212)	222-7760	OTHER	FEMALE
2	BENLEVY	LINDA	5-11 UNIVERSITY PLACE NY NY	10003	(212)	473-4322	BPA	FEMALE
3	BHASIN	KULJOT	5 UNIVERSITY PLACE	10003	(212)	254-0500	BPA	MALE
4	BLITZ	CIPORA	232 E 82ND ST NY NY	10028	(212)	249-4570	BPA	FEMALE
5	COTTONE	JEROME	325 PACIFIC AVE	10312	(212)	984-3668	WSUC	MALE
6	DAVIS	TI	5 UNIVERSUTY PLACE BOX 213	10003	(212)	674-6352	WSUC	FEMALE
7	DECATREL	RALPH	196-20 91 AVE HOLLISCOURT	11423	(212)	479-7348	WSUC	MALE
8	DIBERNARDO	FRAN	65-45 79 STREET MIDDLE VILLAGE NY	11379	(212)	894-1752	WSUC	FEMALE
9	DUGGAN	TIM	46-32 193 ST	11358	(212)	357-5126	BPA	MALE
10	DUNCAN	CHRIS	441 W 22; APT. 4-A; NEW YORK, N.Y.	10011	(212)	989-3105	OTHER	MALE
11	EHLER	LINDA	55 EAST 10 ST. APT 1202 N.Y. N.Y.	10003	(212)	254-2914	EDUCATION	FEMALE
12	EPIFAN	PETER	105 CLAUDY LN NEW HYDE PK NY	11040	(516)	328-3337	WSUC	MALE
13	FERMANN	BARBARA	5 UNIVERSITY PL NEW YORK NY	10003	(212)	475-4376	WSUC	FEMALE
14	FINE	LARRY	327 E. 54 ST., N.Y., N.Y., APT. C	10022	(212)	752-9435	WSUC	MALE
15	GEE	KEITH	181 DAHILL ROAD	11218	(212)	436-4913	BPA	MALE

PAGE 2 A LISTING OF THE STUDENTS TAKING COBOL PROGRAMMING AT NYU

CARD COUNT	STUDENT LAST NAME	STUDENT FIRST NAME	STUDENT ADDRESS	ZIP CODE	AREA CODE	PHONE NUMBER	SCHOOL REGISTERED	STUDENT SEX
16	GOLDBERG	ALLEN	1237 E. 100 ST. BROOKLYN N.Y.	11236	(212)	763-6271	WSUC	MALE
17	GOODMAN	CORINNE	80 8TH AVE. APT. 9A, BROOKLYN	11215	(212)	638-5522	OTHER	FEMALE
18	HANLON	CHRIS	5-11 UNIVERSITY PLACE NY NY	10003	(212)	475-4482	BPA	FEMALE
19	HIRSCH	DORIS	75-60 188 ST	11366	(212)	454-4942	BPA	FEMALE
20	POREMBA	IRVIN	35 FIFTH AVENUE ROOM 119	10003	(212)	477-1708	WSUC	MALE

5.9 Explanation of Program 10

1. The Identification Division is identical to previous ones, except that a full description of the program is provided in a rectangle of asterisks, which are really a series of comments by virtue of the fact that each line has an asterisk in column 7. This is an extremely important part of the internal documentation of the program. As a portion of the program itself, the comments are unlikely to become detached from it.

2. The Environment Division, too, has no changes whatsoever in it.

3. In order to handle each of the fields individually in the Procedure Division, one has to read in each field individually. This is done by means of RECORD-IN in the Data Division. Each separate field of the input record is carefully described in the record description.

The first 02-level item is LAST-NAME and has a PICTURE of X(12). Because nothing is punched in column 13, a FILLER of X(01) is provided. If this FILLER were omitted, it would imply that the next field begins in column 13, which it doesn't. Only the numeric fields, ZIP-CODE and SEX are given a PICTURE of 9's; all the rest are alphanumeric and receive a PICTURE of X. If the characters in each of these 02-level items is totaled, the number of columns used on the card will be found to be exactly 80. Making this simple check often saves hours of aggravation later.

4. Under the FD for the output file, OUT-FILE, there is nothing new. The 01 for LINE-OUT is assigned a PICTURE of X(133), exactly as was done in the last program and will in fact be done in all subsequent programs.

5. Under the Working-Storage Section there are four 77-level items. One is a page counter; another, a card counter; and another, a second card counter. The second card counter CARD-COUNT-2 is needed because we want to keep 15 detail-lines printouts per page. One way to do this easily is to keep 2 separate counts. Every time a card is read each count is incremented by 1. As soon as CARD-COUNT-2 reaches 15, it is a signal to eject to the next page and reset this counter back to zero. Meanwhile, the printout of the detail-line is based on the first card counter so that we have a sequential count printed.

The fourth 77-level item is our usual device for determining if we have read all the data cards. MORE-CARDS is initialized to 'YES', whereas the other 3 numeric items are initialized to zero.

6. The various headers and the detail-line are set up in Working-Storage as before. An explanation is required only for the field ZZ9 for PAGE-COUNT-OUT in HEADER-1 and the field ZZZ9, for CARD-COUNT-OUT in the detail-line. If these fields were 999 and 9999, respectively, the counts would be printed with leading zeros. Because we do not wish to print out leading zeros, we may take advantage of what in COBOL is called an editing technique. If a Z is substituted for each leading 9 of the output PICTURE, any leading zero will be suppressed and substituted by a blank space. We will discuss the various editing techniques at great length later, but this short explanation of leading zero suppression should suffice for now.

7. The main-line routine is exactly the same as that used in earlier versions and all future programs that are illustrated in this text will be quite similar, if not identical.

8. In the paragraph START-UP, after the first data card has been read, the question is asked whether MORE-CARDS is equal to 'YES'. If it is, then we must write the headings; so the paragraph WRITE-HEADINGS-PARA is performed. Notice that this is the first instance that we have encountered where a PERFORMed paragraph itself contains another PERFORM. This is a perfectly legal strategy.

9. Under WRITE-HEADINGS-PARA, 1 is added to PAGE-COUNT. The value of PAGE-COUNT is then moved to PAGE-COUNT-OUT in the detail-line where the PICTURE is ZZ9. Any leading zeros will therefore be suppressed.

What we would want to do now is to print HEADER-1. Ordinarily we would write:

```
MOVE HEADER-1 TO LINE-OUT.
WRITE LINE-OUT AFTER 1.
```

In order to print HEADER-2, we would similarly write:

```
MOVE HEADER-2 TO LINE-OUT.
WRITE LINE-OUT AFTER 1.
```

Now there is nothing wrong with these pairs of instructions. However, COBOL permits a contraction of this pattern of actions to a single instruction. These pairs of instructions may be contracted to:

```
WRITE LINE-OUT FROM HEADER-1 AFTER 1.
WRITE LINE-OUT FROM HEADER-2 AFTER 1.
```

HEADER-2 prints out the first line of asterisks. Under this line, however, we again want an identical line of asterisks printed. So the instruction:

```
WRITE LINE-OUT FROM HEADER-2
```

is repeated. It is not necessary to write a duplicate record in the program.

In printing out HEADER-3 we want to double space. Thus the appropriate instruction to move HEADER-3 to the output line and to print it is:

```
WRITE LINE-OUT FROM HEADER-3 AFTER 2.
```

The headings HEADER-4 and HEADER-5 are printed on consecutive lines in what is by now the ordinary way.

10. The paragraph PROCESS-DATA is then performed until MORE-CARDS is equal to 'NO'. It is within this paragraph that 1 is added to both CARD-COUNT and CARD-COUNT-2. Again, we encounter a PERFORM within a PERFORMed paragraph.

11. The instruction PERFORM SCHOOL-SEX-PARA examines the code punched in column 79 of the data card. If 'G' is punched there it means that that individual is a graduate student and the literal 'GRADUATE' is moved to SCHOOL-OUT. If it is not 'G', 'B' is tested for, then 'W', 'E', 'A', and finally, 'O'. These tests could have been made with individual IF statements without having to resort to ELSE clauses at all. But if it were programmed in that way and the first test were true, all the remaining tests would have had to be made although it would have been an absolute waste of time. By stringing together all the IF and ELSE clauses, control is sent immediately to the sentence following the period, as soon as a "hit is made" (so to speak). This strategy makes for a much more efficient program.

12. Once the appropriate literal is moved to SCHOOL-OUT, the test is made for the sex of the individual. By means of a simple IF... ELSE the word 'MALE' or 'FEMALE' is sent to SEX-OUT.

13. Returning back to PROCESS-DATA, CARD-COUNT is moved to CARD-COUNT-OUT, LAST-NAME to LAST-NAME-OUT, FIRST-NAME to FIRST-NAME-OUT, ADDRESS-IN to ADDRESS-OUT, ZIP-CODE to ZIP-CODE-OUT, and PHONE-NO to PHONE-NO-OUT. Now that the complete detail-line is taken care of, the line is printed after advancing 2 lines and the next input card is read.

14. If the end-of-file has been reached, zeros are sent to CARD-COUNT-2 (to avoid printing the headings after the report if it is equal to 15) and 'NO' is moved to MORE-CARDS. Otherwise, if CARD-COUNT-2 is equal to 15, meaning that we have already printed 15 detail-lines on the current page, zeros are moved to CARD-COUNT-2 (it is reinitialized), paragraph NEW-PAGE is again executed, and the paragraph WRITE-HEADINGS-PARA performed once more.

5.10 Some Frequently Made Errors — Spot and Correct Them

1. $y = \dfrac{w}{t}$

DIVIDE W INTO T GIVING Y.

2. $p = q^3$

MULTIPLY Q BY Q
MULTIPLY Q BY Q
MULTIPLY Q BY Q

3. $r = t^5$

COMPUTE R = T******5.

4. $m = \dfrac{pq}{r + t}$

COMPUTE M = P * Q / R + T

5. 77 BINGO PICX(23).

6. OPEN INPUT IN-FILE.
  MOVE A TO B.
  OPEN INPUT IN-FILE.

7. $p = e^2$

COMPUT P = E**E

8. $V = abcd$

COMPUTE V = ABCD

9. $v = abcd$

MULTIPLY A BY B BY C BY D GIVING V.

10. $\dfrac{g}{h}$

DIVIDE G BY H.

11. 02 FILLER PIC X(06) VALUE ZERO.
12. READ IN-FILE AT END PRINT 'NO DATA'.

Review Questions

1. What is the effect of the following.

   02 FILLER PICTURE X(05) VALUE ALL ' =

2. What role does the VALUE clause play?
3. Why is the placing of the period in an IF statement so critical?
4. Check each of the following independent COBOL statements and, if an error is found, mark it with an X and rewrite it correctly.
   a. FD OUT-FILE.
   b. OPEN IN-FILE OUT-FILE.
   c. MOVE BLANKS TO OUT-FIELD.
   d. MOVE YES TO MORE-CARDS.
5. If the input record to a program is RECORD-IN, would writing

   WRITE RECORD-IN

   be acceptable?

6. Check with a √ all those IF statements that are valid.
    a. IF A IS EQUAL TO B MOVE X TO Y.
    b. IF A = B MOVE X TO Y.
    c. ELSE MOVE T TO W.
    d. IF X < Y GO TO NEXT SENTENCE.
    e. IF X = '345' ADD X TO Y.
    f. GO TO PARA-1 IF X > Y.
    g. IF A OR B = C MOVE D TO E.
    h. IF A AND B = C MOVE D TO E.
    i. IF X = SPACE ADD 1 TO X.
    j. IF Y = NUMERIC ADD A TO B.
    k. IF X > Y GO TO PARA-1
              ADD 1 TO Z
        ELSE ADD P TO Q.
    l. IF X IS LESS THEN Y PERFORM PARA.
7. Which of the following are valid?
    a. ADD A TO B.
    b. ADD B TO A.
    c. ADD A TO B GIVING C.
    d. ADD X TO Y GIVING Z.
    e. SUBTRACT X FROM Z.
    f. MULTIPLY A TIMES B.
    g. MULTIPLY A BY B YIELDING C.
    h. MULTIPLY A BY B GIVING C.
    i. DIVIDE A INTO B.
    j. DIVIDE A BY B.
    k. DIVIDE AB BY BA.
    l. DIVIDE C INTO D GIVING E.
    m. DIVIDE A BY A GIVING A.
8. Each of the following algebraic expressions has been converted into COBOL by 2 different methods.
   Examine each conversion carefully and indicate whether each has been done correctly.
    a. $y = ab$ MULTIPLY A BY B GIVING Y.   COMPUTE Y = A * B
    b. $f = p - t$ SUBTRACT T FROM P GIVING F.   COMPUTE F = P − T.
    c. $q = rst$ MULTIPLY R, S, T, GIVING Q.   COMPUTE Q = R * S * T.
    d. $r = s/t$ DIVIDE T INTO S GIVING R.   COMPUTE R = S/T.
    e. $w = \sqrt{Y}$ ROOT-OF Y GIVING W.   COMPUTE W = Y ** 1/2
9. Examine each of the following COBOL instructions and determine which are valid and which are invalid. If you think an instruction is invalid, state your reasons in full. (It is suggested that you have a list of the reserved words readily available.)
    a. ADD ACTUAL TO REAL.
    b. SUBTRACT EVERY FROM END.
    c. MULTIPLY DAY BY NIGHT.
    d. DIVIDE WEEK BY DATE.
    e. ADD DATA, SUM, GIVING COLUMN.
    f. SUBTRACT DAY-OF-WEEK FROM MONTH GIVING NEXT.
    g. MULTIPLY PAGE BY PAGE-COUNTER.
    h. ADD FINAL TO LENGTH.
    i. SUBTRACT TOP FROM BOTTOM.
    j. MULTIPLY UP BY DOWN.
    k. DIVIDE DIVIDE BY CHARACTER.
    l. ADD COMPUTE TO CONSTANT.
    m. SUBTRACT ADDRESS FROM AREA.
10. Verify that each of the following algebraic expressions has been correctly converted to its COBOL equivalent.
    a. $b = c^2 d$ COMPUTE B = C↑2 * D.
    b. $c = \dfrac{a + b}{d}$ COMPUTE C = A + B / D.
    c. $d = b^2 - 4ac$ COMPUTE D = B ** 2 − 4A C.
    d. $e = \dfrac{ab}{cd}$ COMPUTE E = A * B / C * D.
    e. $f = (w^2 + v)^3$ COMPUTE F = (W ** 2 + V) *** 3.

11. Assume an input file called INPUTPHILE, consisting of a number of record cards. The program that is shown initializes a count called KOUNT to zero and counts the cards, printing the result. However, the program contains a bug. Find it!

```
PROCEDURE DIVISION.
GET-READY.
      OPEN INPUT INPUTPHILE.
      COMPUTE KOUNT = 0.
ON-YOUR-MARK.
      READ INPUTPHILE ON END GO AWAY.
      COMPUTE KOUNT = KOUNT + 1.
      GO TO ON-YOUR-MARK.
AWAY.
      DISPLAY 'THE NUMBER OF CARDS = 'KOUNT.
      CLOSE INPUTPHILE.
      STOP RUN.
```

12. Using the arithmetic verbs (not the COMPUTE), calculate the following expression without using any location in memory other than C and D.

$$c = (c - 1)d - c$$

13. A program segment reads:

```
READ IN-FILE AT END CLOSE IN-FILE, OUT-FILE, STOP RUN
ADD 1 TO DAYS.
MOVE A TO B.
```

and so on
Will it work?

14. Study the following English instructions and translate them into COBOL.
    a. If X is equal to 5, go to the end-of-job paragraph.
    b. If A is greater than B and C is less than D, perform the totals paragraph.
    c. If E is greater than or equal to F, move 'CAT' to flag.
    d. If G is less than H, then set I to 15.
    e. If A or B or C is less than 10, stop execution of the program.
    f. If X is greater than Y, then double the value of P and triple the value of R.

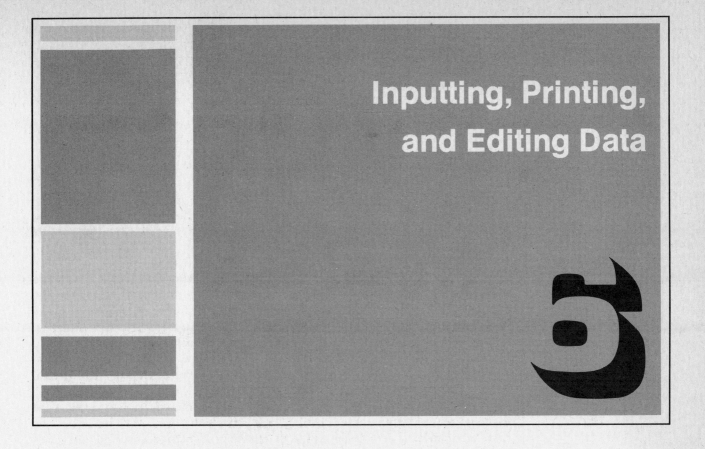

Inputting, Printing, and Editing Data

Programming COBOL involves both frustration and *eventual* satisfaction. You can't have one without the other.

(Collette Briody)

In this chapter you will be introduced to those aspects of programming that will enable you to write elegant-looking programs for a variety of different situations. In particular, you will learn:

- how to punch fractional numbers
- how to handle decimal points
- what is meant by an *implied* decimal point
- how to punch negative numbers
- the PICTURE prefix S
- how to suppress leading zeros (in detail)
- that the object of a COMPUTE and the GIVING clause may be edited items
- how to print out a number with a decimal point
- how to insert a fixed position dollar sign in a report
- how to insert commas
- how to insert asterisks
- how to insert a minus sign
- how to insert a plus sign
- how to insert DB or CR for negative values
- how to insert blanks
- how to insert zeros

- what is meant by a floating dollar sign
- about a floating minus sign
- about a floating plus sign
- the BLANK WHEN ZERO clause

6.1 Inputting Fractional Numbers

COBOL, being the language of business, is geared to handle values representing dollars and cents. Until now, although we have dealt with numeric data representing dollars, on each occasion those numbers were integers. Suppose, however, we wanted to read in the value 123.45 (representing $123.45) from data cards?

It might be shocking for you to learn that in COBOL there is no way to read in a number containing a decimal point. The number has to be read in without the decimal point and it is up to the programmer to allow for the decimal point in the input record description.

Actually, there are rather good reasons that the decimal point is not punched on data cards. If there were 40 items to be punched on a single card and each item needed a decimal point, half of the input card would be consumed with decimal points. This would represent a waste of vital space. In addition, punching the decimal points would entail extra work on the part of the operator who enters the data and thus extra time would be required. Finally, the more work that has to be done in submitting data (even typing or punching a single decimal point is extra work—it is after all an extra keystroke), the more chance there is of introducing faulty data.

In COBOL the PICTURE associated with a number containing a fractional portion is the key to the solution. If we had a 5-digit number, say, 12345, that was to be read in columns 1–5 of the data card, we would simply use a PICTURE of 9(05) as the first item in the input record description. If, however, the number to be read is 123.45, the special PICTURE symbol V is used to represent the location of the *implied* decimal point. The PICTURE would be 999V99 or its equivalent 9(03)V9(02) or 9(3)V9(2), whichever is preferred. The V signifies only the location of the implied decimal point and therefore occupies no room in storage. The width of the field 999V99 is still only 5 columns even though the related PICTURE has a V in it, giving it the *appearance* of a 6-digit field.

In the same way that any number may not contain more than one decimal point, so no PICTURE may contain more than one V symbol. If no V is present in a PICTURE, it is regarded as if it were present after the rightmost digit of the field. Hence placing a V at the extreme right of a PICTURE will not cause an error but would be redundant.

6.2 Inputting Negative Numbers

If a *negative number* is to be read in from data cards, it is punched *as if it were* not negative; a negative sign is then *overpunched* over the rightmost digit of the field. This might make the printed character difficult for humans to read but not for the computer. However, for the reading of negative numbers the associated PICTURE clause must be prefixed by the sign symbol S. Thus the number -12345 would have to have a PICTURE of S99999 and would appear on a punched card as 12345, with the minus sign punched over the 5. In the same way that the V does not take up memory, neither does the S. Therefore a PICTURE of S999 represents a signed

3-digit number. Sometimes a negative number is described in a text with the minus sign printed above the rightmost digit, such as 12345, thereby making it easier for the reader to read it correctly. Later we will learn another way to enter negative numbers.

6.3   Editing Output

In order to make output look both attractive and more meaningful, COBOL provides some unique and intriguing features. We have already come across cases where we wanted to suppress leading zeros on the output. This process of changing output items either for enhancing their appearance or for other possible reasons is called *editing*. Both numeric and alphanumeric items may be edited. We will see that final output can be made to look more attractive to the human reader by the judicious use of selective editing. In the industrial environment, computerized reports are often read by high-level management so that due consideration should be given to this aspect of the program when it is written.

Suppressing Leading Zeros

When a number such as 00427 is moved to a field of 99999, the result will be the same, namely, 00427. However, if we wanted to suppress the leading zeros, which have no significant value, we could move the number 00427 to an output area that contains the PICTURE ZZZZ9. This would then print out as ♭♭427, where ♭ is a space. Generally, all leading zeros should be suppressed for printed reports. It is of critical importance to understand that the edited item is not capable of being acted on arithmetically. The inclusion of a single editing item such as a Z is sufficient to prevent that edited item from computational use. Editing is an end process, something like making a cake with all manner of ingredients. Once the cake has been baked and taken out of the oven, it is too late to include any further ingredients.

The number 010203 has only one leading zero, not 3. When this number is moved to an editing field of ZZZZZ9 the result would print as ♭10203, with only the leading zero being replaced by a blank. Similarly, moving 100000 to ZZZZZ9 would cause it to be printed out as 100000 because it has no leading zeros. All the zeros in this number are significant and we would not want to lose any of them. The following examples illustrate the action of editing leading zeros.

Here are some other examples of the suppression of leading zeros.

Suppression of Leading Zeros

Sending Item	Editing Field	Printed Result
0058	ZZZZ	⬚⬚5 8
0980	ZZZ9	9 8 0
1000	ZZ99	1 0 0 0
0001	ZZZZ	⬚⬚⬚1
0000	ZZZZ	⬚⬚⬚⬚
0980	ZZZZ	9 8 0

Note that in the case of the suppression of leading zeros, if there are no leading zeros the number is printed exactly the way it is. Also, the field in which the sending item is stored must have a PICTURE of 9. The receiving field containing the editing symbols should have the same number of digits as the sending item. The editing PICTURE ZZZZ may also be written as Z(4). It is customary to make the rightmost position of a field of Z's a 9 in order that in the event zero is moved into it, at least a zero will print out rather than a blank field. Blank fields are distrusted by many people.

Combining Z's and 9's in editing fields is always possible, provided that *all* the Z's precede the 9's. That is to say, editing fields such as Z99Z9 or Z99Z are not permitted.

The typical way of using edited fields is by means of the statement MOVE A TO B, where A is the item to be moved (actually, it is a *copy* of it—the value of A remains unchanged) and B is the editing item. Usually, item B is part of a detail line that is eventually moved to the output area for subsequent printing. However, the GIVING clause as used in the ADD, SUBTRACT, MULTIPLY, and DIVIDE verbs also acts as a MOVE, and therefore the object of a GIVING clause may be an editing item, thus saving the programmer the need to write an extra MOVE in the Procedure Division. However, if the object of the GIVING or the COMPUTE instruction is going to be used in subsequent calculations, it can*not* be an editing item.

Printing the Decimal Point

You will recall that when fractional values are *read* into the computer the implied decimal point is specified by the position of the V in the corresponding PICTURE, for example, 999V99. If this value is now *printed* with a V in its PICTURE, the decimal point would not be visible. The number would simply look like it is 100 times larger than it is supposed to be. In order to print a decimal point in the place of the V, the editing PICTURE must actually contain a decimal point. The symbol V is automatically aligned with the implied decimal point.

For example, let's say that the number 12345 is read in with a PICTURE of 999V99. The implied decimal point would therefore be located between the 3 and the 4. We may represent its position conceptually as 123‸45, where the caret specifies the implied decimal point. Now if the value is moved to an editing PICTURE of 999.99, the decimal point is aligned with the implied decimal point and is printed out as 123.45.

PIC   999V99

value   123‸45
                 ↓↓↓↓↓
editing PIC   9 9 9 . 9 9
                 ↓↓↓↓↓↓
printed result   1 2 3 . 4 5

Some more examples of editing using the decimal point follow.

Sending Item	Editing Field	Printed Result
12∧34	99.99	12.34
9876∧54	9999.99	9876.54
40∧5	99.9	40.5
123	999.99	123.00
0002	9.99	2.00
024∧68	ZZZ.99	24.68
0000	ZZ.ZZ	

(Note that the decimal point, as opposed to the implied decimal point, actually takes up a position of memory.)

Normally digits to the right of the decimal point are not zero-suppressed, but if zero is moved to a PICTURE of ZZ.ZZ, as was done in the preceding example, the digits to the right are zero-suppressed and a blank field is printed. This is a somewhat exceptional case in that the decimal point is not printed.

Notice what happens when, say, the number 1234.567 is moved to a field of 99.99. As before, the implied decimal point is aligned with the actual decimal point in the editing PICTURE, but because this is not wide enough to accommodate the number fully, what is actually printed is 34.56, where the two most significant and the rightmost digit are lost.

Inserting a Fixed Dollar Sign

It is to be expected that COBOL would permit the printing of the dollar sign. All that is necessary is for the $ to appear (on the extreme left) in the PICTURE of the editing field. For example, if 123.45 is moved to an editing field of $999.99, it will print out as $123.45. Here are some examples. In each case the dollar sign takes up a position of memory.

PIC	999V99
value	123∧45
	↓↓↓↓↓↓
editing PIC	$999.99
	↓↓↓↓↓↓
printed result	$123.45

Often an item to be edited is moved to a field that is wider than itself, in order to allow for the printing of additional symbols. In the preceding example a 5-digit number is moved to a field containing 7 positions. The additional 2 places are to accommodate the dollar sign and the decimal point.

Some additional examples are:

Sending Item	Editing Field	Printed Result
12∧34	$99.99	$12.34
4096∧12	$9999.99	$4096.12
033∧33	$ZZZ.99	$ 33.33
000	$999.99	$000.00
00058∧91	$ZZZZZ.99	$ 58.91

Suppose we moved the number 456 with a PICTURE of 999 to an editing field of $99, where the number of 9's present is insufficient to accommodate the number of significant digits. The manner in which COBOL handles this situation is probably not to your liking. It assumes that you really want the dollar sign printed so it prints the dollar sign at the *expense of the leading digit*! As a result, the value $56 is printed. In this case "all" we lost was $400. Think how much more serious this would be if the amount were 100005 and it was moved to an editing field of $ZZZZ9. Because the leading 1 would be replaced by the dollar sign, the zeros present in the number would be treated as leading zeros and so the printed result would be $ƀƀƀƀ5. To appreciate the gravity of the situation, pretend for a moment that the check being printed was *your* personal paycheck!

Notice that in each of the cases shown the position of the printed dollar sign is fixed according to the location it occupies in the editing field, even if it is followed by blank spaces that are caused by zero suppression. We will shortly discuss ways to avoid printing those blank spaces that follow the dollar sign.

Inserting Commas

For even greater clarity in reading large numbers, commas may be inserted at the appropriate places. For example, if the number 234567.89 is moved to a field of $ZZZ,ZZZ.99, the printed result would be $234,567.89. Here are a few more examples. In each case the dollar sign, the comma, and the decimal point each take up a position.

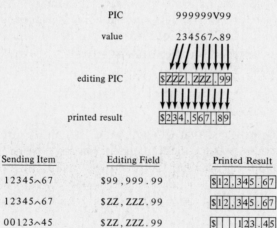

Sending Item	Editing Field	Printed Result
12345∧67	$99,999.99	$12,345.67
12345∧67	$ZZ,ZZZ.99	$12,345.67
00123∧45	$ZZ,ZZZ.99	$ 123.45

In the last case a comma is not printed because there is no significant digit to its left. In such situations COBOL replaces the comma by a space.

Inserting Asterisks as Check Protection

Many business documents are enhanced when leading zeros are suppressed by the use of the Z. However, for those documents (such as checks) it is not advisable to print a dollar sign that is followed by blanks. For example, suppose we moved the value 000123.45 to a PICTURE of $ZZZ,ZZZ.99. The result would be a printing of $ƀƀƀƀ123.45, with 4 spaces following the dollar sign. Someone might yield to the temptation of typing in some high-order digits in these locations, especially if the check were made out to him or her, or to an accomplice.

To eliminate such a possibility, the check protection symbol, (*), is used. Thus moving 000123.45 to $ * * * , * * * .99 will print out $ * * * * 123.45. Notice that if the comma is not needed it is not printed, and instead, an asterisk is printed in its place. Isn't the COBOL compiler smart?

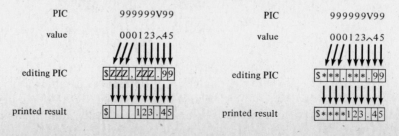

Here are some more examples of check protection.

Sending Item	Editing Field	Printed Result
123∧45	$* * *.99	$|1|2|3|.|4|5|
24∧68	$* * *.99	$|*|2|4|.|6|8|
3∧57	$* * *.99	$|*|*|3|.|5|7|
∧69	$* * *.99	$|*|*|*|.|6|9|
0000	$* * *	$* * *
0000	* * * *	* * * *.

Inserting Minus Sign to Indicate the Sign of a Value

Normally, numbers printed without a sign are regarded as positive and most numbers in everyday life are treated this way. If a value turns out to be negative, the negative sign can be retained within the computer only if its PICTURE is prefixed by the letter S. However, even if the PICTURE does have an S in front of it, this will not cause that number to be printed out as a negative number. It would print out as an unsigned number and be regarded as positive, not negative. In order to print out a negative number, one may place the edit symbol, " − ", either to the left or right of the editing field. Whichever side is used, the negative sign will appear on that side of the printed result.

Suppose, for example, that the negative number 123.45, with a PICTURE of S999V99 is moved to an editing PICTURE of − 999.99. It would be printed out as − 123.45. If the editing PICTURE were 999.99 − instead, the result printed would be 123.45 − . Whether the negative sign is placed before or after the editing PICTURE is up to the programmer. The minus sign will appear on whichever side of the PICTURE was selected.

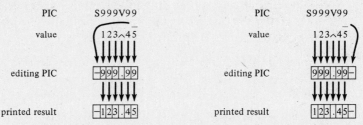

Additional examples of the insertion of the minus sign for editing purposes follow. Notice that only if the item number being sent is negative—its PICTURE is prefixed with S—and the editing PICTURE contains a minus sign, is the result printed as a negative value.

Sending Item	Sending PICTURE	Editing Field	Printed Result
456̄	S999	999−	4|5|6|−
456̄	999	999−	4|5|6|
456̄	S999	−999	−|4|5|6
456̄	999	−999	4|5|6
456̄	S999	999	4|5|6

Inserting Plus Sign to Indicate Sign of Value

It is not common to see numbers that are prefixed with plus signs, but if this is required the associated PICTURE must have an S prefix. The plus sign is punched over the rightmost digit of the number, as was the case with the minus sign. In order that the printed item carry a plus sign, the edit symbol, " + ", is placed either to the left or right of the editing PICTURE, whichever side is desired by the programmer. The plus sign will print out for all positive numbers, as well as for unsigned numbers. What is interesting about the plus sign as an edit symbol is that if a negative value is moved into its field, the negative sign will print out instead of the plus sign. In other words, the correct sign will always print out if a plus sign is part of the editing field. Looked at from another angle, you can always be "positive" about the sign if a plus sign is used in the editing field.

Sending Item	Sending PICTURE	Editing Field	Printed Result
+123	S999	+999	+123
+123	S999	999+	123+
+123	S999	+999	+123
+123	S999	999+	123+
−123	S999	999+	123−
−123	S999	+999	−123
+01234.56	S99999V99	+ZZ,ZZZ.99	+ 1,234.56

Printing CR or DB for Negative Values

We have already learned how to deal with negative numbers. Accountants, however, sometimes want negative values to be specified by the letters CR (for credit) or DB (for debit) rather than by a minus sign, depending on the kind of account. Actually, accountants prefer the letters DR instead of DB but COBOL provides DB. The seeming contradiction of using CR and DB for negative values can be explained by the fact that in some accounts negative values have to be credited, whereas in others they have to be debited. In any event, whichever pair of symbols is used, DB or CR, their printing is triggered *only* by negative values. Moreover, unlike the printing of the negative sign that may appear on either side of the edited result, when CR or DB is specified it may appear only to the immediate right. Each uses 2 storage positions of memory in contrast to the minus sign that uses only one. If CR or DB are not triggered, 2 blanks are printed in their place.

Sending Item	Sending PICTURE	Editing Field	Printed Result
−123	S999	999CR	123CR
−123	S999	999DB	123DB
123	999	999CR	123
123	999	999DB	123
+123	S999	999CR	123
−0987.65	S9999V99	$Z,ZZZ.99DB	$ 987.65DB

We therefore have a choice of printing a minus sign, CR, or DB for a negative value. Only one of these options is possible for a given number.

Inserting Blank Spaces in Fields

If a Social Security number is read in as a data item, the 2 embedded hyphens (minus signs) would probably be omitted for reasons of economy of space. On a printed report, however, it would probably be a good idea to insert a blank space where the hyphens appear. COBOL permits the insertion of blank spaces but not of

Sending Item	Sending PICTURE	Editing Field	Printed Result
1234	9999	99B99	12 34
13579	99999	9B9B9B9B9	1 3 5 7 9
109282011	999999999	999B99B9999	109 28 2011
'ABCD'	XXXX	XXBXX	AB CD

hyphens, except as previously described. The symbol that is used for inserting a blank space is the letter B, which may be inserted in a numeric, alphabetic, or alphanumeric field. As many as are desired may be used.

Inserting Zeros in Fields

Zeros may be inserted in any kind of field in the same way as blank spaces are. The symbol that is used is the numeric zero, 0, and as before, as many as are required may appear.

Sending Item	Sending PICTURE	Editing Field	Printed Result
894	999	99900	89400
'CAT'	XXX	XX0X0	CA0T0
01234	99999	9909909	0102304

The Floating Dollar Sign

We have already seen how to print out a fixed dollar sign. The dollar sign is simply placed at the beginning of the editing field. The instruction:

MOVE AMOUNT TO AMOUNT-OUT

where AMOUNT is 00059.36 and AMOUNT-OUT has a PICTURE of $ZZ,ZZZ.99 will cause the printing of $ƀƀƀƀ59.36, with 4 spaces following the dollar sign. Frequently, however, it is desirable to print the dollar sign immediately to the left of the first significant digit. To accomplish this, we use the floating dollar sign. The word "floating" implies that the printed symbol will appear to the immediate left of the most significant digit, all unused symbols preceding the printed one being replaced by blanks.

In order to float the dollar sign, we repeat the dollar symbol, $, everywhere a Z would otherwise appear in the editing PICTURE. In other words, instead of moving 00059.36 to a PICTURE of $ZZ,ZZZ.99, move it to a PICTURE of $$$,$$$.99. Here are some examples of floating dollar sign edits.

Sending Item	Sending PICTURE	Editing Field	Printed Result
1234	9999	$$$$9	$1234
123∧45	999V99	$$$$.99	$123.45
0001∧23	9999V99	$$$$$.99	⬚⬚⬚$1.23
45∧67 +	S99V99	$$$.99DB	$45.67DB
019∧64 +	S999V99	$$,$$$.99CR	⬚⬚⬚$19.64⬚⬚
45∧76	S99V99	+$$$.99	+$45.76

The Floating Minus Sign

A floating minus sign may also be printed but just as a string of floating dollar signs must appear to the left of the editing PICTURE, so too must the string of successive minus signs. This contrasts with the fixed minus sign that could appear either at the beginning or the end of the editing PICTURE. Like the floating dollar sign, the floating minus sign suppresses leading zeros and prints one minus sign to the left of the most significant digit. Some examples are:

Sending Item	Sending PICTURE	Editing Field	Printed Result
1̄2̄3̄	S999	———9	−123
123	999	———9	⬚⬚123
1234∧56	S9999V99	————.99	−1234.56
00145∧98	S99999V99	——————.99	⬚⬚−145.98⬚
2̄3̄4̄	S999	————	−234

The Floating Plus Sign

The plus sign is another of the editing symbols that may be floated. It must also be a string of plus signs to the left of the editing PICTURE. It has the effect of suppressing leading zeros and printing the plus sign or the minus sign (whichever is appropriate) to the left of the most significant digit. All unused plus signs are replaced by blanks.

Sending Item	Sending PICTURE	Editing Field	Printed Result
+123	S999	+++9	+123
+123	999	+++9	123
+246∧80	S999V99	++++.99	+246.80
+487	S999	++++	+487
−487	S999	++++	−487

The BLANK WHEN ZERO Clause

For those situations in which the sending of zeros to an editing field would cause the printing of items such as $.00 or −0 or +0, it is possible to replace such questionable output with blanks by using the BLANK WHEN ZERO clause immediately following its PICTURE in the DATA Division; for example,

```
01  DETAIL-LINE.
    02 AMOUNT-OUT PICTURE $$,$$$.99 BLANK WHEN ZERO.
```

Sending Item	Sending PIC	Editing Field	Printed Result
0000	99V99	$$,$$$.99 BLANK WHEN ZERO	
1234	99V99	$$,$$$.99 BLANK WHEN ZERO	$12.34

Here is a table showing all the permitted symbols that may be used for editing purposes.

SYMBOL	EXPLANATION
A	alphabetic character or space
B	insert blank space
P	decimal position mover for scaling purposes, not included in field count
S	allows for signed numbers and is not included in field count
V	implied decimal point and is not included in field count
X	alphanumeric character
Z	zero suppression character (floating)
9	numeric character
0	zero insertion character
,	comma insertion character
.	decimal point or period insertion character
+	plus sign insertion character (floating)
−	minus sign insertion character (floating)
CR	credit editing symbols
DB	debit editing symbols
*	check protection insertion character (floating)
$	dollar sign insertion character (floating)
/	slash

Review Questions

1. How are fractional numbers read in as data?
2. Are actual decimal points ever punched on data cards?
3. How are negative numbers read in from data cards?

4. What is the result of moving the following items.

ITEM	EDITING FIELD	RESULT
a. 3904	Z999	
b. 472	Z99	
c. 00056	ZZZ99	
d. 00074	ZZ999	
e. 00048	Z9999	
f. 5000	ZZZZ	
g. 00001	Z(5)	
h. 010203	Z(6)	
i. 00000	Z(5)	

5. What is the result of moving the following items.

ITEM	EDITING FIELD	RESULT
a. 123ˬ4	999.999	
b. 1ˬ234	999.99	
c. 123ˬ45	9999.99	
d. 1ˬ68	9.99	
e. 16ˬ8	9.99	
f. ˬ214	.99	
g. ˬ287	.99	
h. 12ˬ34	999.999	
i. 1234	999	

6. What is the result of moving the following items.

ITEM	EDITING FIELD	RESULT
a. 123	$999	
b. 123	$$99	
c. 1234	$$99	
d. 0123	$$$9	
e. 9123	$$$9	
f. 123456	$$,$$$.99	
g. 1234	$$,$$$.99	
h. 12	$$,$$$.99	
i. 12345	$$,$$$,$$$.99	

7. What is the result of moving the following items.

ITEM	EDITING FIELD	RESULT
a. 123	$*999	
b. 123	*****	
c. 123	**9	
d. 000	***	
e. 12345	$**,***.99	
f. 123ˬ456	$***.99	
g. 123ˬ45	$**,**9.99	

8. What is the result of moving the following items.

ITEM	EDITING FIELD	RESULT
a. 12345	99,999	
b. 123456	999,999	
c. 3	999,999	
d. 1234567	9,999,999	
e. 0123	$ZZ,ZZ9.99	
f. 1234	$ZZ,ZZ9.99	
g. 123	$ZZ,ZZ9.99	
h. 1000ˬ01	$ZZZ.99	

9. What is the result of the following moves.

ITEM	EDITING FIELD	RESULT
a. 12345	99B999	
b. 1234	9B9B9B9	
c. 1489	9BB99BB9	
d. 1234	99BBB99	
e. 109282011	999B99B9999	
f. 123	999000	
g. 1234	9B999000	
h. 1234	XBXXX000	

10. What is the effect of the following moves.

ITEM	PICTURE	EDITING FIELD	RESULT
a. 123	S999	+999	
b. 123	S999	999+	
c. 123	S999	++99	
d. 123	S999	++++	
e. 456	S999	+99	
f. 123	S999	+++	
g. −123	S999	+999	
h. +123	S999	+999	
i. 123+	S999	999+	

11. What result is produced by the following moves.

ITEM	PICTURE	EDITING FIELD	RESULT
a. 123	999	−999	
b. −123	S999	−999	
c. −123	S999	999−	
d. −1234	S9999	−−−99	
e. −123	S999	−−−−	
f. −123	S999	+999	
g. −123	S999	++++	
h. −123	S999	−−−	
i. 123	S999	999DB	
j. 123	S999	999CR	
k. −123	S999	999DB	
l. −123	S999	999CR	

12. Spot the error.
    a. 02 SALES-OUT PIX $$$,$$$.99.
    b. 02 PURCHASE PIC $99,999V99.99.
    c. 02 TOTAL-OUT PIC $$,ZZZ.99.
    d. 02 COST-OUT PIC $$,$$$V99.
    e. 02 ID-OUT PIC 99Z9Z9
    f. IF SALARY > $1000.00 . . .

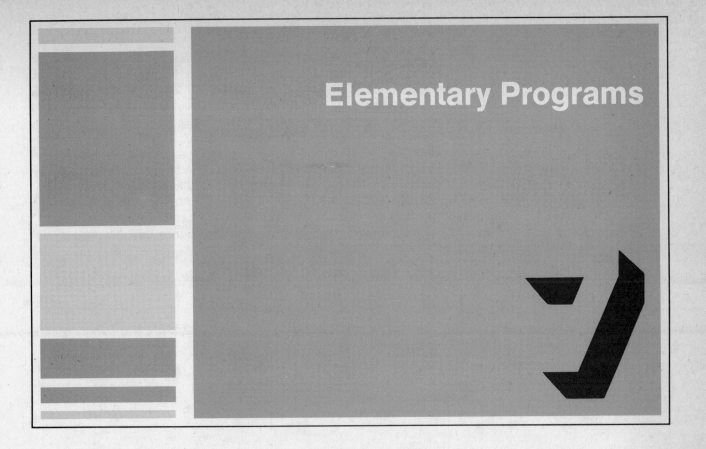

Elementary Programs

In the two weeks I've been learning COBOL I've lost 10 pounds in weight—I've been so busy I just haven't had time to eat.

(Sidney Schwecky)

We have now covered considerable important material. The time has now arrived to put that knowledge to work. In this chapter you will be introduced to 3 programs that will help you to learn about:

- record description entries in more detail
- qualification of fields with identical names
- elementary calculations
- making specific decisions with the aid of the logical operator AND
- testing whether or not a year is a leap year
- validating data
- calculating the day of the week on which any arbitrary date falls
- the case statement (GO TO... DEPENDING ON)
- how to obtain the integer portion of a number
- how to derive the fractional portion of a number
- the PERFORM... THRU option

7.1 More on Record Descriptions

We have already seen in the most recently presented programs that after a file has been described by its FD, a record description entry follows. In each of the illustrated programs the FD for the input file preceded that for the output file, but it does not necessarily have to be in that order. We could just have easily reversed the two. Whichever is described first, an appropriate record description, describing the format of the record, must follow the FD. Later we will see that it is possible for a single file to contain more than one different kind of record. In such cases a record description for each different record must be present.

What is the role played by a record description? It describes in detail the structure of the record, in particular, the various items that appear on a record and the order in which they are related to each other. However, the items may not be related to each other. The file-name is specified on the FD level while the record-name is coded on the 01 level. Both FD and 01 must be written in the A margin; the data-names that they describe are always B margin entries.

Let's examine some records and write appropriate record descriptions for them.

(a)

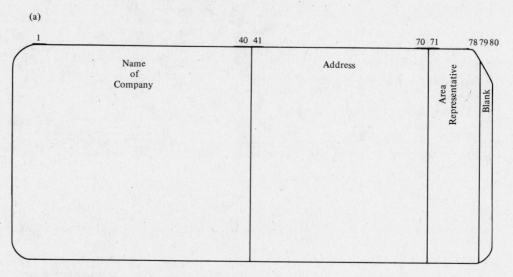

```
01   COMPANY-CARD.
     02   NAME-OF-COMPANY    PIC X(40).
     02   COMPANY-ADDRESS    PIC X(30).
     02   AREA-REP           PIC X(08).
     02   FILLER             PIC X(02).
```

The record-name, COMPANY-CARD, is a general name for the whole record. It is broken into a series of separate fields. A lower level is given a higher number; the number 01 is considered to be a higher level number than 02. The next entry, also on the 02 level, implies that the first 02-level entry with a PICTURE of X(40) is the field, NAME-OF-COMPANY, which begins in column 1 of the data card and extends to column 40. The next entry is also on the 02 level. It implies that the field associated with COMPANY-ADDRESS follows immediately after the previous field, in columns 41–70. The field for AREA-REP is defined as the next 8 columns of the input record, that is, columns 71–78, and the unreferenced portion of the card is in columns 79 and 80. Each level entry is therefore contiguous to the previous entry.

It is always wise to use a FILLER to represent any unreferenced area to the end of the card so that the record may quickly be verified that all 80 columns have been accounted for. Be careful of the word ADDRESS, which would ordinarily have been an ideal choice of a name for the middle field. Although ADDRESS is not a reserved word in the ANSI 1974 standard, both IBM and CDC computers regard it as a reserved word. The question of reserved words is always vexing. The best approach is to keep a copy of your particular computer's list of reserved words close by for easy reference.

When defining fields on a card all of the columns 1 through 80 are available. There are no restrictions such as those that apply when punching or coding a COBOL *instruction* on a card.

(b)

1	30 31	39 40	47 48	55 56	80
Salesman	Social Security Number	Annual Quota in Dollars	Current Date	Blank	

```
01   QUOTA-CARD.
     02   SALESMANS-NAME   PIC X(30).
     02   SOC-SEC-NO       PIC 9(09).
     02   ANNUAL-QUOTA     PIC 9(08).
     02   CURRENT--DATE    PIC 9(08).
     02   FILLER           PIC X(25).
```

Once again, each of the four data-fields is contiguous. The data begins in column 1 and extends through column 55. The only point that is worth mentioning is that the fourth field (columns 48–55) could have been named CURRENT-DATE, with a single hyphen. However, this name is a reserved word on the IBM version of COBOL. There are many hyphenated words that are reserved words even in the 1974 standard. We are very familiar with PROGRAM-ID, DATE-WRITTEN, DATE-COMPILED, INPUT-OUTPUT, and so on. However, there are no reserved words that have two *adjacent* hyphens in any COBOL compiler. That is why the data-name that is selected is CURRENT--DATE, spelled with two adjacent hyphens.

(c)

1	30	33	37	40	44	50	54	80
Product Name		Color Code		Stock Available		Price	Blank	

```
01   PRODUCT-CARD.
     02   PRODUCT-NAME   PIC X(30).
     02   FILLER         PIC X(02).
     02   COLOR-CODE     PIC X(05).
     02   FILLER         PIC X(02).
     02   STOCK          PIC 9(05).
     02   FILLER         PIC X(05).
     02   PRICE          PIC 9(05).
     02   FILLER         PIC X(26).
```

If the FILLER lines were omitted from the preceding record description, the computer would assume that the fields were contiguous, which they clearly are not.

Therefore if the data was read without the FILLER lines, incorrect data would be accessed. This usually leads to considerable trouble.

(d)

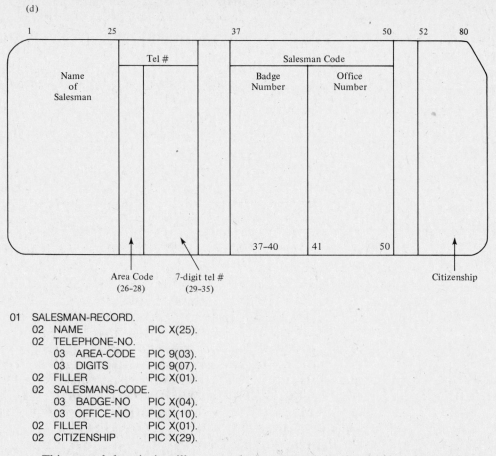

```
01   SALESMAN-RECORD.
     02   NAME              PIC X(25).
     02   TELEPHONE-NO.
          03   AREA-CODE    PIC 9(03).
          03   DIGITS       PIC 9(07).
     02   FILLER            PIC X(01).
     02   SALESMANS-CODE.
          03   BADGE-NO     PIC X(04).
          03   OFFICE-NO    PIC X(10).
     02   FILLER            PIC X(01).
     02   CITIZENSHIP       PIC X(29).
```

This record description illustrates the concept of one level being dependent on a higher level. For example, the group item TELEPHONE-NO, which is on the 02 level, does not itself have a PICTURE. Instead, it is "broken up" or subdivided into 2 dependent items, each of which carries its own PICTURE clause. In other words, AREA-CODE and DIGITS, both of which are coded on the 03 level, are subordinate to TELEPHONE-NO (a group item) in the same way that both NAME and TELEPHONE-NO are subordinate to SALESMAN-RECORD.

SALESMANS-CODE is also coded on the 02 level and therefore is an independent item. However, it does not have a PICTURE. The 2 subordinate 03-level items BADGE-NO and OFFICE-NO have PICTURES of X(04) and X(10), respectively. Although they are both dependent on SALESMANS-CODE, they are independent of each other.

The indentation of subordinate items is for purposes of enhanced visual clarity rather than to meet any compiler requirements. Except for the 01 level, which is always coded in the A margin, all subordinate entries are coded in the B margin.

When assigning names to individual items (data-names) only letters of the alphabet, the numeric digits, and the hyphen may be used. The rules are simply that the data-name may not be greater than 30 characters; it must contain at least one alphabetic, no embedded blanks are permitted (after all, a blank is not alphabetic, numeric, or a hyphen), no special characters other than the hyphen may be used, and finally, no reserved words are permitted. Should you inadvertently use a reserved word, all manner of perplexing diagnostic messages may ensue.

When assigning level numbers below the 01 level any level between 02 and 49 (inclusive) may be used. Although our examples show level numbers that are consecutive, this does not necessarily have to be the case. One can write, for example,

```
01   RECORD-1.
        04   ITEM-1 PIC X(05).
        04   ITEM-2.
                09   SUB-ITEM-2-1 PIC 9.
                09   SUB-ITEM-2-2 PIC 99.
        04   ITEM-3 PIC X(10).
```

where the two 09-level items SUB-ITEM-2-1 and SUB-ITEM-2-2 are subordinate to the group item ITEM-2.

As already mentioned, the COBOL reserved word FILLER may be used to designate any unreferenced field of data and as many FILLER entries as needed may be written in any record or records. This saves you the trouble of concocting names yourself. It would not necessarily be true to say that the FILLERs associated with areas on an input card are blank; rather, you could say that the areas are unreferenced. It would ordinarily be an error to name more than one item *in the same record* with the same data-name, other than FILLER. It is possible, however, to name different items in *different* records with the same name. If this occurs the item would have to be *qualified*; otherwise, the computer would not know which data item was being referred to. Qualification is done in the Procedure Division by means of the words IN or OF.

For example, suppose we have two records, RECORD-1 and RECORD-2.

```
01   RECORD-1.                          01   RECORD-2.
        02   SALES PIC 9(06).                   02   SALES PIC 9(06).
        02   CANCELLATIONS PIC 9(04).           02   CANCELLATIONS PIC 9(04).
        02   QUOTA PIC 9(06).                    02   QUOTA PIC 9(06).
```

If, in the Procedure Division, we wanted to move the elementary item, SALES, in RECORD-1 to DETAIL-LINE, we would write:

```
MOVE SALES OF RECORD-1 TO DETAIL-LINE
```

or its equivalent

```
MOVE SALES IN RECORD-1 TO DETAIL-LINE.
```

The words OF and IN may be used interchangeably. Similarly, we could write:

```
ADD QUOTA IN RECORD-1 TO QUOTA OF RECORD-2.
MULTIPLY CANCELLATIONS OF RECORD-1 BY CANCELLATIONS IN RECORD-2
GIVING CROSS-CANCELLATIONS.
```

and so on.

7.2   The Arithmetic Operation Code Problem

The purpose of the following program is to reinforce some of the concepts we learned in the previous chapter and to introduce some new ideas, rather than to present an industrial-type problem of striking importance. The program reads in a series of cards, each of which is punched with a numeric code and two associated numbers. The code specifies the arithmetic operation that is to be performed on the two numbers.

The input to the program is punched on cards. In the first 2 columns of each card a 2-digit code number is punched. The codes are as follows.

> 10 = addition
> 20 = subtraction
> 30 = multiplication
> 40 = division
> 50 = no more data follows

The last data card is punched with the number 50 to signal the fact that no data follows. Such a card is sometimes spoken of as a *trailer* card because it *trails* all the way at the end of the data card.

In addition to the code number, 2 numbers that are to be operated on are punched according to the particular operation code. Of course, for the trailer card there are no other numbers punched.

What is important to understand in this program is that the data are not punched just anywhere on the cards but are punched in specific columns, in specific "fields." Let's examine a typical data card.

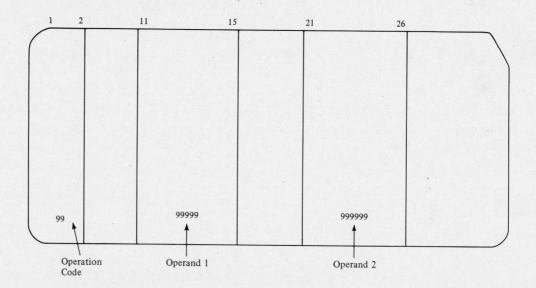

Operand 1 is punched in the field between columns 11 and 15 inclusive and operand 2, in columns 21 through 26. It is imperative to punch the data in the correct field and that the number be right-justified in the field, with any unused columns being filled with leading zeros. If operand 1, for example, were 13 it would have to be punched, beginning in column 11 with the number 00013. Similarly, if operand 2 were 169 it would have to be punched as 000169, beginning in column 21. Leaving leading blanks instead of zeros might be acceptable on some compilers but doing so is an invitation to trouble because in COBOL (unlike some other computer languages), blanks are not considered to be numeric characters.

The 80-column input record will therefore be of the form:

```
01   RECORD-IN.
     02   OPERATION-CODE   PIC 9(02).
     02   FILLER           PIC X(08).
     02   OPERAND-1        PIC 9(05).
     02   FILLER           PIC X(05).
     02   OPERAND-2        PIC 9(06).
     02   FILLER           PIC X(54).
```

where each FILLER gets a PICTURE of X and the numeric items, a PICTURE of 9's. Adding up the numbers in parentheses alongside the PICTURE, we confirm that RECORD-IN totals 80; this is always a good idea. For this reason it is better to write X(08) rather than XXXXXXXX even though they work equally well. It is an equally good idea to use a FILLER for the remaining unused columns of the card.

Once again, we will paginate each page of output, print headings at the top of each page, count the data cards and print out the count, suppressing leading zeros, restrict the printout to 15 lines per page, and decode each operation code into its English meaning.

Input for Program 11

There are 20 cards, followed by the trailer card.

OPERATION CODE	OPERAND 1	OPERAND 2
10	12453	265345
30	20000	003000
40	00013	000169
30	00142	000110
30	00004	000025
10	00500	000600
10	00001	000002
20	00100	000300
20	00008	000009
40	00002	000012
30	00004	000005
20	00122	000240
40	00100	400000
30	23561	189234
20	02354	015000
10	45132	452786
30	00012	000012
20	45623	234567
40	00023	000023
10	00015	000012
50		

TRAILER CODE	OPERAND 1	OPERAND 2

Program 11

```
1       IDENTIFICATION DIVISION.
2       PROGRAM-ID. MATH.
3       AUTHOR. IRVIN POREMBA.
4       INSTALLATION. NYU.
5       DATE-WRITTEN. JULY 1, 1982.
6       DATE-COMPILED. JULY 1, 1982.
7       SECURITY. HENRY MULLISH ONLY.
8       ************************************************************
9       *     THIS PROGRAM READS IN A DECK OF CARDS PUNCHED:       *
10      *                                                          *
11      *     COLUMNS    1-2: ARITHMETIC OPERATION CODE            *
12      *     COLUMNS 11-15: FIRST OPERAND                         *
13      *     COLUMNS 21-26: SECOND OPERAND                        *
14      *                                                          *
15      *     THE OUTPUT OF THE PROGRAM SPELLS OUT                 *
16      *     THE OPERATION BEING PERFORMED AND THE RESULT         *
17      *     OF THE OPERATION.                                    *
18      ************************************************************
19
20      ENVIRONMENT DIVISION.
21      CONFIGURATION SECTION.
22      SOURCE-COMPUTER. CYBER-170-720.
23      OBJECT-COMPUTER. CYBER-170-720.
24      SPECIAL-NAMES.
25      INPUT-OUTPUT SECTION.
26          SELECT IN-FILE ASSIGN TO INPUT.
27          SELECT OUT-FILE ASSIGN TO OUTPUT.
28
29      DATA DIVISION.
30      FILE SECTION.
31
32      FD   IN-FILE
33          LABEL RECORDS ARE OMITTED.
34
35      *    DEFINE DATA.
36
37      01   RECORD-IN.
38          02 OPERATION-CODE      PIC 9(02).
```

```
39              02 FILLER              PIC X(08).
40              02 OPERAND-1           PIC 9(05).
41              02 FILLER              PIC X(05).
42              02 OPERAND-2           PIC 9(06).
43              02 FILLER              PIC X(54).
44
45      *       DEFINE OUTPUT OF PROGRAM
46
47      FD   OUT-FILE
48              LABEL RECORDS ARE OMITTED.
49
50      01   LINE-OUT                  PIC X(133).
51
52      WORKING-STORAGE SECTION.
53      77   CARD-COUNT                PIC 9999 VALUE ZERO.
54      77   CARD-COUNT-2              PIC 99 VALUE ZERO.
55      77   PAGE-COUNT                PIC 999 VALUE ZERO.
56      77   MORE-CARDS                PIC X(03) VALUE 'YES'.
57
58      01   HEADER-1.
59              02 FILLER              PIC X(01) VALUE SPACES.
60              02 FILLER              PIC X(05) VALUE 'PAGE'.
61              02 PAGE-COUNT-OUT      PIC ZZ9.
62              02 FILLER              PIC X(15) VALUE SPACES.
63              02 FILLER              PIC X(10) VALUE 'ARITHMETIC'.
64              02 FILLER              PIC X(06) VALUE 'CODES'.
65
66      01   HEADER-2.
67              02 FILLER              PIC X(01) VALUE SPACES.
68              02 FILLER              PIC X(08) VALUE ALL ' * '.
69              02 FILLER              PIC X(15) VALUE SPACES.
70              02 FILLER              PIC X(16) VALUE ALL ' * '.
71
72
73      01   HEADER-3.
74              02 FILLER              PIC X(01) VALUE SPACES.
75              02 FILLER              PIC X(08) VALUE 'CARD NO.'.
76              02 FILLER              PIC X(05) VALUE SPACES.
77              02 FILLER              PIC X(09) VALUE 'OPERATION'.
78              02 FILLER              PIC X(06) VALUE SPACES.
79              02 FILLER              PIC X(09) VALUE 'OPERAND 1'.
80              02 FILLER              PIC X(03) VALUE SPACES.
81              02 FILLER              PIC X(09) VALUE 'OPERAND 2'.
82              02 FILLER              PIC X(06) VALUE SPACES.
83              02 FILLER              PIC X(06) VALUE 'RESULT'.
84
85      01   HEADER 4.
86              02 FILLER              PIC X(01) VALUE SPACES.
87              02 FILLER              PIC X(08) VALUE ALL ' * '.
88              02 FILLER              PIC X(03) VALUE SPACES.
89              02 FILLER              PIC X(14) VALUE ALL ' * '.
90              02 FILLER              PIC X(03) VALUE SPACES.
91              02 FILLER              PIC X(09) VALUE ALL ' * '.
92              02 FILLER              PIC X(03) VALUE SPACES.
93              02 FILLER              PIC X(09) VALUE ALL ' * '.
94              02 FILLER              PIC X(03) VALUE SPACES.
95              02 FILLER              PIC X(11) VALUE ALL ' * '.
96
97      01   DETAIL-LINE.
98              02 FILLER              PIC X(01) VALUE SPACES.
99              02 CARD-COUNT-OUT      PIC ZZZ9.
100             02 FILLER              PIC X(07) VALUE SPACES.
101             02 CODE-OUT            PIC X(14).
102             02 FILLER              PIC X(03) VALUE SPACES.
103             02 OPERAND-1-OUT       PIC ZZZZ9.
104             02 FILLER              PIC X(07) VALUE SPACES.
105             02 OPERAND-2-OUT       PIC ZZZZZ9.
106             02 FILLER              PIC X(06) VALUE SPACES.
107             02 RESULT              PIC ZZZZZZZZZ9.
108
109     PROCEDURE DIVISION.
110
111     *       THIS IS THE MAIN PARAGRAPH WHICH USES
112     *       THE PERFORM STATEMENT TO ACCESS OTHER PARAGRAPHS.
113
```

```
114    MAIN-LINE-ROUTINE.
115        PERFORM OPEN-FILES.
116        PERFORM NEW-PAGE.
117        PERFORM START-UP.
118        PERFORM PROCESS-DATA UNTIL MORE-CARDS EQUAL 'NO'.
119        PERFORM CLOSE-UP.
120        STOP RUN.
121
122    OPEN-FILES.
123        OPEN INPUT IN-FILE.
124        OPEN OUTPUT OUT-FILE.
125
126    NEW-PAGE.
127        MOVE SPACES TO LINE-OUT.
128        WRITE LINE-OUT AFTER PAGE.
129
130  *    START-UP PRINTS THE HEADERS AND CHECKS IF
131  *    THERE IS ANY DATA IN THE PROGRAM, OTHERWISE PRINTS AN
132  *    ERROR MESSAGE.
133
134    START-UP.
135        READ IN-FILE AT END MOVE 'NO' TO MORE-CARDS
136            MOVE ' **NO DATA IN DECK**' TO LINE-OUT
137            WRITE LINE-OUT AFTER 30.
138        IF MORE-CARDS EQUAL 'YES' AND OPERATION-CODE EQUAL 50
139            MOVE 'NO' TO MORE-CARDS
140        ELSE IF MORE-CARDS EQUAL 'YES' PERFORM WRITE-HEADINGS.
141
142  *    IF THERE IS DATA AND OPERATION CODE 50 IS NOT
143  *    FOUND, PROCESS-DATA PROCESSES THE DATA CARD THEN
144  *    READS IN ANOTHER DATA CARD.
145
146    PROCESS-DATA.
147        PERFORM WORK-PARA.
148        READ IN-FILE AT END MOVE 'NO' TO MORE-CARDS
149            PERFORM NEW-PAGE
150            MOVE ZEROS TO CARD-COUNT-2
151            MOVE ' **NO TRAILER CARD 50 IS IN DECK**' TO LINE-OUT
152            WRITE LINE-OUT AFTER 30.
153        IF OPERATION-CODE EQUAL 50 MOVE 'NO' TO MORE-CARDS
154            MOVE ZEROS TO CARD-COUNT-2.
155        IF CARD-COUNT-2 EQUAL 15 MOVE ZEROS TO CARD-COUNT-2
156            PERFORM NEW-PAGE
157            PERFORM WRITE-HEADINGS.
158
159    CLOSE-UP.
160        CLOSE IN-FILE, OUT-FILE.
161
162    WORK-PARA.
163        ADD 1 TO CARD-COUNT.
164        ADD 1 TO CARD-COUNT-2.
165        IF OPERATION-CODE EQUAL 10 MOVE 'ADDITION' TO CODE-OUT
166            ADD OPERAND-1, OPERAND-2 GIVING RESULT
167        ELSE IF OPERATION-CODE EQUAL 20
168            MOVE 'SUBTRACTION' TO CODE-OUT
169            SUBTRACT OPERAND-1 FROM OPERAND-2 GIVING RESULT
170        ELSE IF OPERATION-CODE EQUAL 30
171            MOVE 'MULTIPLICATION' TO CODE-OUT
172            MULTIPLY OPERAND-1 BY OPERAND-2 GIVING RESULT
173        ELSE IF OPERATION-CODE EQUAL 40
174            MOVE 'DIVISION' TO CODE-OUT
175            DIVIDE OPERAND-1 INTO OPERAND-2 GIVING RESULT.
176        MOVE CARD-COUNT TO CARD-COUNT-OUT.
177        MOVE OPERAND-1 TO OPERAND-1-OUT.
178        MOVE OPERAND-2 TO OPERAND-2-OUT.
179        WRITE LINE-OUT FROM DETAIL-LINE AFTER 2.
180
181    WRITE-HEADINGS.
182        ADD 1 TO PAGE-COUNT.
183        MOVE PAGE-COUNT TO PAGE-COUNT-OUT.
184        WRITE LINE-OUT FROM HEADER-1 AFTER 1.
185        WRITE LINE-OUT FROM HEADER-2 AFTER 1.
186        WRITE LINE-OUT FROM HEADER-2 AFTER 1.
187        WRITE LINE-OUT FROM HEADER-3 AFTER 2.
188        WRITE LINE-OUT FROM HEADER-4 AFTER 1.
```

Output for Program 11

PAGE 1		ARITHMETIC CODES		
* * * * * * * *		* * * * * * * * * * * * * * * * *		
* * * * * * * *		* * * * * * * * * * * * * * * * *		
CARD NO.	OPERATION	OPERAND 1	OPERAND 2	RESULT
* * * * * * * *	* * * * * * * * * * * * *	* * * * * * * * *	* * * * * * * * *	* * * * * * * * * *
1	ADDITION	12453	265345	277798
2	MULTIPLICATION	20000	3000	60000000
3	DIVISION	13	169	13
4	MULTIPLICATION	142	110	15620
5	MULTIPLICATION	4	25	100
6	ADDITION	500	600	1100
7	ADDITION	1	2	3
8	SUBTRACTION	100	300	200
9	SUBTRACTION	8	9	1
10	DIVISION	2	12	6
11	MULTIPLICATION	4	5	20
12	SUBTRACTION	122	240	118
13	DIVISION	100	400000	4000
14	MULTIPLICATION	23561	189234	4458542274
15	SUBTRACTION	2354	15000	12646

PAGE 2		ARITHMETIC CODES		
* * * * * * * *		* * * * * * * * * * * * * * * * *		
* * * * * * * *		* * * * * * * * * * * * * * * * *		
CARD NO.	OPERATION	OPERAND 1	OPERAND 2	RESULT
* * * * * * * *	* * * * * * * * * * * * *	* * * * * * * * *	* * * * * * * * *	* * * * * * * * * *
16	ADDITION	45132	452786	497918
17	MULTIPLICATION	12	12	144
18	SUBTRACTION	45623	234567	188944
19	DIVISION	23	23	1
20	ADDITION	15	12	27

7.3 Discussion of Program 11

1. The data as shown contains a trailer with 50 in columns 1–2. Suppose this item were inadvertently omitted, what kind of result would this have had on the program?

The program would have produced the identical output, except that the phrase " * *NO TRAILER CARD IS IN DECK * *" would have been printed 30 lines after the last line of output.

2. If no data at all was supplied to the program, how would this have affected its execution? The phrase " * *NO DATA IN DECK * *" would have been printed out in the middle of a new page.

3. What would happen if the second READ instruction—the one in the paragraph PROCESS-DATA—were omitted? This would result in an infinite loop because the paragraph would repeatedly operate on the same data items, printing out line after line of similar output.

7.4 The Senior Student Problem

Let us suppose that the administration of a college has been given a gift of $1 million with the express instructions that the money be divided among those senior students who are enrolled in the most useful of the various disciplines. Naturally, the selected discipline would have to be computer science.

On record in the administration offices there is a file of punched cards of every student in the school. In addition to the name, the number of credits accumulated and the name of the student's major field are punched as shown here.

1	30	35	37	42	66 67	80
Student Name		Number of Credits		Name of Major Field		

A college senior is regarded as a student who has accumulated more than 95 college credits, or points. The idea behind the program is to examine each student's record and to determine whether or not the student is a senior, and if so, whether his or her major field is computer science.

These 2 tests may be accomplished by a single IF statement.

IF NUMBER-CREDITS > 95 AND MAJOR EQUAL 'COMPUTER SCIENCE' PERFORM PRINT-ROUTINE.

For the IF statement to be true, both parts must be true simultaneously because they are connected by the logical operator AND.

All computer science seniors are counted and the relevant information is printed under suitable headings, 15 students per page.

Input for Program 12

IRVIN POREMBA	110	ECONOMICS
JEFFERY KARP	112	COMPUTER SCIENCE
JERRY GEISLER	111	COMPUTER SCIENCE
DAVID FIRE	053	COMPUTER SCIENCE
WENDY WONG	096	COMPUTER SCIENCE
CHESTER JAFFEE	122	DRAMA
ARTHUR FIELDS	035	HISTORY
SUSAN PERLES	114	ENGLISH
STEVEN LEVY	123	JAPANESE
JANE MURROW	120	COMPUTER SCIENCE
ELI OPAS	096	COMPUTER SCIENCE
MARY HARTMAN	115	MATHEMATICS
MARY JANE	103	COMPUTER SCIENCE
ANN ASTER	123	COMPUTER SCIENCE
HARVEY RENMAN	113	COMPUTER SCIENCE
SAMUEL SMITH	125	COMPUTER SCIENCE
MARGIE BRAND	114	COMPUTER SCIENCE
EDWARD JONES	099	COMPUTER SCIENCE
HARRY JONES	115	COMPUTER SCIENCE
ANDREA ROSS	116	COMPUTER SCIENCE
ALINA CHU	105	COMPUTER SCIENCE
GEORGE THOMAS	122	FRENCH
JOHN WELLER	102	COMPUTER SCIENCE
EARL DENTOM	025	COMPUTER SCIENCE
LINDA FIORELLO	109	COMPUTER SCIENCE
SUPER SAM	107	COMPUTER SCIENCE
BEATRICE TIER	120	GEOLOGY
SAMUEL JONES	045	COMPUTER SCIENCE
WILLIAM TELLE	020	COMPUTER SCIENCE

Program 12

```
1        IDENTIFICATION DIVISION.
2        PROGRAM-ID. SENIOR.
3        AUTHOR. IRVIN POREMBA.
4        INSTALLATION. NYU.
5        DATE-WRITTEN. MARCH 30, 1982.
6        DATE-COMPILED. OCTOBER 19, 1982.
7        SECURITY. HENRY MULLISH.
8        * * * * * * * * * * * * * * * * * * * * * * * * * * * * * * * * * * * * * * * * * * * * * * *
9        *       THIS PROGRAM READS IN A DECK OF CARDS PUNCHED:                   *
10       *                                                                        *
11       *       COLUMNS  1-30: STUDENT'S NAME                                    *
12       *       COLUMNS 35-37: NUMBER OF CREDITS COMPLETED                       *
13       *       COLUMNS 42-66: STUDENTS'S MAJOR                                  *
14       *                                                                        *
15       *       THIS PROGRAM THEN PRINTS OUT THE DATA CARDS                      *
16       *       REPRESENTING THOSE STUDENTS WHO HAVE OVER 95                     *
17       *       CREDITS AND ARE COMPUTER SCIENCE MAJORS                          *
18       * * * * * * * * * * * * * * * * * * * * * * * * * * * * * * * * * * * * * * * * * * * * * * *
19
20       ENVIRONMENT DIVISION.
21       CONFIGURATION SECTION
22       SOURCE-COMPUTER. CYBER-170-720.
23       OBJECT-COMPUTER. CYBER-170-720.
24       SPECIAL-NAMES.
25       INPUT-OUTPUT SECTION.
26       FILE-CONTROL.
27            SELECT IN-FILE ASSIGN TO INPUT.
28            SELECT OUT-FILE ASSIGN TO OUTPUT.
29
30       DATA DIVISION.
31       FILE SECTION.
32
33       FD   IN-FILE
34            LABEL RECORDS ARE OMITTED.
35
36       01   RECORD-IN.
37            02 STUDENT-NAME      PIC X(30).
38            02 FILLER            PIC X(04).
39            02 NUMBER-CREDITS    PIC 9(03).
40            02 FILLER            PIC X(04).
41            02 MAJOR             PIC X(25).
42            02 FILLER            PIC X(14).
43
44       FD OUT-FILE
45            LABEL RECORDS ARE OMITTED.
46
47       01   LINE-OUT             PIC X(133).
48
49       WORKING-STORAGE SECTION.
50       77   STUDENT-COUNT        PIC 99999 VALUE ZERO.
51       77   STUDENT-COUNT-2      PIC 99 VALUE ZERO.
52       77   MORE-CARDS           PIC X(03) VALUE 'YES'.
53
54       01   HEADER-1.
55            02 FILLER            PIC X(01) VALUE SPACES.
56            02 FILLER            PIC X(05) VALUE 'COUNT'.
57            02 FILLER            PIC X(13) VALUE SPACES.
58            02 FILLER            PIC X(12) VALUE 'STUDENT NAME'.
59            02 FILLER            PIC X(13) VALUE SPACES.
60            02 FILLER            PIC X(07) VALUE 'CREDITS'.
61            02 FILLER            PIC X(14) VALUE SPACES.
62            02 FILLER            PIC X(05) VALUE 'MAJOR'.
63
64       01   HEADER-2.
65            02 FILLER            PIC X(01) VALUE SPACES.
66            02 FILLER            PIC X(05) VALUE ALL '*'.
67            02 FILLER            PIC X(04) VALUE SPACES.
68            02 FILLER            PIC X(30) VALUE ALL '*'.
69            02 FILLER            PIC X(04) VALUE SPACES.
70            02 FILLER            PIC X(07) VALUE ALL '*'.
71            02 FILLER            PIC X(04) VALUE SPACES.
72            02 FILLER            PIC X(25) VALUE ALL '*'.
```

```
73
74      01    DETAIL-LINE.
75            02 FILLER                    PIC X(01) VALUE SPACES.
76            02 STUDENT-COUNT-OUT         PIC ZZZZ9.
77            02 FILLER                    PIC X(04) VALUE SPACES.
78            02 STUDENT-NAME-OUT          PIC X(30).
79            02 FILLER                    PIC X(06) VALUE SPACES.
80            02 NUMBER-CREDITS-OUT        PIC ZZ9.
81            02 FILLER                    PIC X(06) VALUE SPACES.
82            02 MAJOR-OUT                 PIC X(25).
83
84      PROCEDURE DIVISION.
85
86      MAIN-LINE-ROUTINE.
87            PERFORM OPEN-FILES.
88            PERFORM NEW-PAGE.
89            PERFORM START-UP.
90            PERFORM PROCESS-DATA UNTIL MORE-CARDS EQUAL 'NO'.
91            PERFORM CLOSE-UP.
92            STOP RUN.
93
94      OPEN-FILES.
95            OPEN INPUT IN-FILE.
96            OPEN OUTPUT OUT-FILE.
97
98      NEW-PAGE.
99            MOVE SPACES TO LINE-OUT.
100           WRITE LINE-OUT AFTER PAGE.
101
102     START-UP.
103           READ IN-FILE AT END MOVE 'NO' TO MORE-CARDS
104               MOVE ' **NO DATA IN DECK**' TO LINE-OUT
105               WRITE LINE-OUT AFTER 30.
106           IF MORE-CARDS EQUAL 'YES' PERFORM WRITE-HEADINGS.
107
108     PROCESS-DATA.
109           IF NUMBER-CREDITS > 95 AND MAJOR EQUAL
110               'COMPUTER SCIENCE' PERFORM PRINT-ROUTINE.
111           READ IN-FILE AT END MOVE 'NO' TO MORE-CARDS.
112
113     CLOSE-UP.
114           CLOSE IN-FILE, OUT-FILE.
115
116     PRINT-ROUTINE.
117           IF STUDENT-COUNT-2 EQUAL 15 MOVE ZEROS TO STUDENT-COUNT-2
118               PERFORM NEW-PAGE
119               PERFORM WRITE-HEADINGS.
120           ADD 1 TO STUDENT-COUNT.
121           ADD 1 TO STUDENT-COUNT-2.
122           MOVE STUDENT-COUNT TO STUDENT-COUNT-OUT.
123           MOVE STUDENT-NAME TO STUDENT-NAME-OUT.
124           MOVE NUMBER-CREDITS TO NUMBER-CREDITS-OUT.
125           MOVE MAJOR TO MAJOR-OUT.
126           WRITE LINE-OUT FROM DETAIL-LINE AFTER 2.
127
128     WRITE-HEADINGS.
129           WRITE LINE-OUT FROM HEADER-1 AFTER 1.
130           WRITE LINE-OUT FROM HEADER-2 AFTER 1.
```

Output for Program 12

COUNT	STUDENT NAME	CREDITS	MAJOR
* * * * *	* * * * * * * * * * * * *	* * * * * * *	* * * * * * * * * * * * * * * * * *
1	JEFFERY KARP	112	COMPUTER SCIENCE
2	JERRY GEISLER	111	COMPUTER SCIENCE
3	WENDY WONG	96	COMPUTER SCIENCE
4	JANE MURROW	120	COMPUTER SCIENCE
5	ELI OPAS	96	COMPUTER SCIENCE
6	MARY JANE	103	COMPUTER SCIENCE
7	ANN ASTER	123	COMPUTER SCIENCE
8	HARVEY RENMAN	113	COMPUTER SCIENCE
9	SAMUEL SMITH	125	COMPUTER SCIENCE
10	MARGIE BRAND	114	COMPUTER SCIENCE

COUNT	STUDENT NAME	CREDITS	MAJOR
* * * * *	* * * * * * * * * * * * *	* * * * * * *	* * * * * * * * * * * * * * * * *
11	EDWARD JONES	99	COMPUTER SCIENCE
12	HARRY JONES	115	COMPUTER SCIENCE
13	ANDREA ROSS	116	COMPUTER SCIENCE
14	ALINA CHU	105	COMPUTER SCIENCE
15	JOHN WELLER	102	COMPUTER SCIENCE
16	LINDA FIORELLO	109	COMPUTER SCIENCE
17	SUPER SAM	107	COMPUTER SCIENCE

7.5 The Leap Year Problem

A leap year is defined as one that, when divided by 4, leaves a remainder of zero. This is true except if the year in question is a century year such as 1700, 1800, 1900, and so on. The year 1600 is a leap year but 1700, 1800, and 1900, are not even though each of the last 3 years are evenly divisible by 4. In the case of a century year it has to be evenly divisible by 400 to be a leap year.

In the next program a series of input cards are read, each punched with a 4-digit year in columns 1 through 4. The purpose of the program is to read each card and to determine whether or not the year punched on it is a leap year.

Of course, it is also possible that the data is not punched correctly. After all, we humans are the ones who punch the data onto cards or type it into a terminal; and even if the computer is close to being infallible, we certainly aren't. Take a quick look down the list of input years and see if you can spot any invalid data. Would you believe that there are no fewer than 3 items that are incorrectly punched? One is punched K532; another, HHHJ, and yet another, I335. Trying to do arithmetic on these data items is bound to lead to severe problems. How can we handle such a contingency?

First, we can always test immediately after reading each data item whether or not the year is numeric. If not, then a special detail-line set up for that purpose in the Working-Storage Section can be utilized. We can move the card count to this detail-line, move the invalid punched data to a field of X(04), rather than to one of 9(04), and print out an appropriate message to the effect that an error in data has been encountered. In this way we will avoid any unpleasant shocks we might otherwise receive when using such data in an arithmetic operation.

If the data passes the numeric test, then we are in a position to determine whether or not the year is a leap year. We would first have to know if the year in question is a century year. One way to find out is to move the year to a PICTURE of 99. The year will be right-adjusted and the leading 2 digits will be truncated. In order to test if it is a century year, we are just interested in the 2 rightmost digits and not in the 2 leading digits. This can be tested against zero. If it is equal to zero, the year is a century year, otherwise it is not. Once it has been established that the year is a century year, the year would have to be divided by 400. Because we are concerned about the remainder of such a division, we may exploit the version of the DIVIDE statement that contains the REMAINDER clause. If the remainder is equal to zero, then there is no question that the year is, in fact, a leap year. If the remainder is greater than zero, then clearly the year is not a leap year.

If it turns out that the year is not a century year, then the year must be divided by 4 and again the remainder must be tested against zero. If it is equal to zero, then the year is a leap year; if not, it is not a leap year.

Two additional detail-lines are included in Working-Storage to print out whether or not the year is a leap year.

The reader's attention is drawn to HEADER-3. It differs from all the other headers in the program, in that other than the leading blank (for carriage control), it has no other FILLERs and yet the literals are printed with the correct spacing between them. In case this baffles you, think about what happens when the 8-character literal 'CARD NO.' is moved to a PICTURE of X(11). Because it is a nonnumeric literal, the VALUE clause has the effect of a MOVE by which the nonnumeric literal is left-justified and filled out to the right with spaces. The same applies to the entry:

02 FILLER PIC X(13) VALUE 'YEAR'.

where the 4-character literal 'YEAR' is implicitly MOVEd to the 13-character field, left-justified, and filled out to the right with spaces.

Once again, 15 detail-lines are printed per page, the pages are counted, and the card-count is printed in ascending sequence throughout.

Input for Program 13

There are 36 items of data.

```
1981
1976
1776
1979
1980
1900
1800
1600
1066
2053
1990
1914
1492
1972
1562
1200
1876
K532
1300
HHHJ
0200
2344
1945
1818
1335
1865
1932
1964
1864
1515
2002
1780
1856
1924
2037
1904
```

Program 13

```
1       IDENTIFICATION DIVISION.
2       PROGRAM-ID. LEAP.
3       AUTHOR. IRVIN POREMBA.
4       INSTALLATION. NYU.
5       DATE-WRITTEN. MARCH 25, 1982.
6       DATE-COMPILED. MARCH 31, 1982.
7       SECURITY. HENRY MULLISH ONLY.
8       ***********************************************************
9       *    THIS PROGRAM DECIDES WHETHER A YEAR PUNCHED IN       *
10      *    THE FIRST FOUR COLUMNS OF A DATA CARD                *
11      *    IS A LEAP YEAR OR NOT. A LEAP YEAR IS DEFINED        *
12      *    AS A YEAR THAT IS DIVISIBLE BY 4 EXCEPT IN THE       *
13      *    CASE OF A CENTURY YEAR. FOR A CENTURY YEAR IT        *
14      *    MUST BE DIVISIBLE BY 400 TO BE A LEAP YEAR.          *
15      ***********************************************************
```

```
16
17        ENVIRONMENT DIVISION.
18        CONFIGURATION SECTION.
19        SOURCE-COMPUTER. CYBER-170-720.
20        OBJECT-COMPUTER. CYBER-170-720.
21        SPECIAL-NAMES.
22        INPUT-OUTPUT SECTION.
23        FILE-CONTROL.
24            SELECT IN-FILE ASSIGN TO INPUT.
25            SELECT OUT-FILE ASSIGN TO OUTPUT.
26
27        DATA DIVISION.
28        FILE SECTION.
29
30        FD   IN-FILE
31            LABEL RECORDS ARE OMITTED.
32
33        *    DEFINE DATA.
34
35        01   RECORD-IN.
36             02 YEAR-IN            PIC 9(04).
37             02 FILLER             PIC X(76).
38
39        *    DEFINE OUTPUT OF PROGRAM
40
41        FD   OUT-FILE
42            LABEL RECORDS ARE OMITTED.
43
44        01   LINE-OUT              PIC X(133).
45
46        WORKING-STORAGE SECTION.
47        77   CARD-COUNT            PIC 9999 VALUE ZERO.
48        77   CARD-COUNT-2          PIC 99 VALUE ZERO.
49        77   PAGE-COUNT            PIC 999 VALUE ZERO.
50        77   MORE-CARDS            PIC X(03) VALUE 'YES'.
51        77   CENTURY-YEAR          PIC 99.
52        77   YEAR-DIVIDED          PIC 9999.
53        77   LEAP-YEAR             PIC 999.
54
55        01   HEADER-1.
56             02 FILLER             PIC X(01) VALUE SPACES.
57             02 FILLER             PIC X(05) VALUE 'PAGE'.
58             02 PAGE-COUNT-OUT     PIC ZZ9.
59             02 FILLER             PIC X(02) VALUE SPACES.
60             02 FILLER             PIC X(09) VALUE 'LEAP YEAR'.
61             02 FILLER             PIC X(08) VALUE 'PROGRAM'.
62
63        01   HEADER-2.
64             02 FILLER             PIC X(01) VALUE SPACES.
65             02 FILLER             PIC X(08) VALUE ALL ' * '.
66             02 FILLER             PIC X(02) VALUE SPACES.
67             02 FILLER             PIC X(17) VALUE ALL ' * '.
68
69        01   HEADER-3.
70             02 FILLER             PIX X(01) VALUE SPACES.
71             02 FILLER             PIC X(11) VALUE 'CARD NO.'.
72             02 FILLER             PIC X(13) VALUE 'YEAR'.
73             02 FILLER             PIC X(07) VALUE 'REMARKS'.
74
75        01   HEADER-4.
76             02 FILLER             PIC X(01) VALUE SPACES.
77             02 FILLER             PIC X(08) VALUE ALL ' * '.
78             02 FILLER             PIC X(03) VALUE SPACES.
79             02 FILLER             PIC X(04) VALUE ALL ' * '.
80             02 FILLER             PIC X(03) VALUE SPACES.
81             02 FILLER             PIC X(18) VALUE ALL ' * '.
82
83        01   DETAIL-LINE.
84             02 FILLER             PIC X(03) VALUE SPACES.
85             02 CARD-COUNT-OUT     PIC Z,ZZ9.
86             02 FILLER             PIC X(04) VALUE SPACES.
87             02 YEAR-OUT           PIC 9999.
88             02 FILLER             PIC X(03) VALUE SPACES.
89             02 FILLER             PIC X(14) VALUE 'IS A LEAP YEAR'.
```

```
90
91      01    DETAIL-LINE-2.
92            02 FILLER                    PIC X(03) VALUE SPACES.
93            02 CARD-COUNT-OUT-2          PIC Z,ZZ9.
94            02 FILLER                    PIC X(04) VALUE SPACES.
95            02 YEAR-OUT-2                PIC 9999.
96            02 FILLER                    PIC X(03) VALUE SPACES.
97            02 FILLER                    PIC X(18) VALUE 'IS NOT A LEAP YEAR'.
98
99      01    DETAIL-LINE-3.
100           02 FILLER                    PIC X(03) VALUE SPACES.
101           02 CARD-COUNT-OUT-3          PIC Z,ZZ9.
102           02 FILLER                    PIC X(04) VALUE SPACES.
103           02 YEAR-OUT-3                PIC X(04).
104           02 FILLER                    PIC X(03) VALUE SPACES.
105           02 FILLER                    PIC X(13) VALUE 'ERROR IN DATA'.
106
107     PROCEDURE DIVISION.
108
109     *     THIS IS THE MAIN PARAGRAPH WHICH USES
110     *     THE PERFORM STATEMENT TO GO TO OTHER PARAGRAPHS.
111
112     MAIN-LINE-ROUTINE.
113           PERFORM OPEN-FILES.
114           PERFORM NEW-PAGE.
115           PERFORM START-UP.
116           PERFORM PROCESS-DATA UNTIL MORE-CARDS EQUAL 'NO'.
117           PERFORM CLOSE-UP.
118           STOP RUN.
119
120     OPEN-FILES.
121           OPEN INPUT IN-FILE.
122           OPEN OUTPUT OUT-FILE.
123
124     NEW-PAGE.
125           MOVE SPACES TO LINE-OUT.
126           WRITE LINE-OUT AFTER PAGE.
127
128     *     START-UP PRINTS THE HEADERS AND CHECKS IF
129     *     THERE IS ANY DATA IN THE PROGRAM, OTHERWISE PRINTS AN
130     *     ERROR MESSAGE.
131
132     START-UP.
133           READ IN-FILE AT END MOVE 'NO' TO MORE-CARDS
134               MOVE ' **NO DATA IN DECK**' TO LINE-OUT
135               WRITE LINE-OUT AFTER 30.
136           IF MORE-CARDS EQUAL 'YES' PERFORM WRITE-HEADINGS.
137
138     *     IF THERE IS DATA PROCEED TO PROCESS-DATA. IF DATA
139     *     IS NOT NUMERIC PRINTS OUT ERROR MESSAGE ELSE
140     *     SENDS THE DATA TO BE TESTED AND LATER
141     *     READS ANOTHER DATA CARD.
142
143     PROCESS-DATA.
144           ADD 1 TO CARD-COUNT.
145           ADD 1 TO CARD-COUNT-2.
146           IF YEAR-IN NOT NUMERIC PERFORM ERROR-PARA
147           ELSE PERFORM TEST-PARA.
148           READ IN-FILE AT END MOVE ZEROS TO CARD-COUNT-2
149               MOVE 'NO' TO MORE-CARDS.
150           IF CARD-COUNT-2 EQUAL 15 MOVE ZEROS TO CARD-COUNT-2
151               PERFORM NEW-PAGE
152               PERFORM WRITE-HEADINGS.
153
154     CLOSE-UP.
155           CLOSE IN-FILE, OUT-FILE.
156
157     *     TEST-PARA TEST TO SEE WHETHER YEAR IS A CENTURY YEAR.
158
159     TEST-PARA.
160           MOVE YEAR-IN TO CENTURY-YEAR.
161           IF CENTURY-YEAR EQUAL ZERO PERFORM CENTURY-PARA
162           ELSE PERFORM YEAR-PARA.
163
```

```
164     *       CENTURY-PARA DETERMINES IF CENTURY YEAR IS A LEAP YEAR.
165
166     CENTURY-PARA.
167         DIVIDE 400 INTO YEAR-IN GIVING YEAR-DIVIDED
168             REMAINDER LEAP-YEAR.
169         IF LEAP-YEAR EQUAL ZERO PERFORM LEAP-YEAR-PARA
170         ELSE PERFORM NOT-LEAP-YEAR-PARA.
171
172     *       YEAR-PARA DETERMINES IF REGULAR YEAR IS A LEAP YEAR.
173
174     YEAR-PARA.
175         DIVIDE 4 INTO YEAR-IN GIVING YEAR-DIVIDED
176             REMAINDER LEAP-YEAR.
177         IF LEAP-YEAR EQUAL ZERO PERFORM LEAP-YEAR-PARA
178         ELSE PERFORM NOT-LEAP-YEAR-PARA.
179
180     LEAP-YEAR-PARA.
181         MOVE CARD-COUNT TO CARD-COUNT-OUT.
182         MOVE YEAR-IN TO YEAR-OUT.
183         WRITE LINE-OUT FROM DETAIL-LINE AFTER 2.
184
185     NOT-LEAP-YEAR-PARA.
186         MOVE CARD-COUNT TO CARD-COUNT-OUT-2.
187         MOVE YEAR-IN TO YEAR-OUT-2.
188         WRITE LINE-OUT FROM DETAIL-LINE-2 AFTER 2.
189
190     ERROR-PARA.
191         MOVE CARD-COUNT TO CARD-COUNT-OUT-3.
192         MOVE YEAR-IN TO YEAR-OUT-3.
193         WRITE LINE-OUT FROM DETAIL-LINE-3 AFTER 2.
194
195     WRITE-HEADINGS.
196         ADD 1 TO PAGE-COUNT.
197         MOVE PAGE-COUNT TO PAGE-COUNT-OUT.
198         WRITE LINE-OUT FROM HEADER-1 AFTER 1.
199         WRITE LINE-OUT FROM HEADER-2 AFTER 1.
200         WRITE LINE-OUT FROM HEADER-2 AFTER 1.
201         WRITE LINE-OUT FROM HEADER-3 AFTER 2.
202         WRITE LINE-OUT FROM HEADER-4 AFTER 1.
```

Output for Program 13

```
      PAGE 1                         LEAP YEAR PROGRAM
      * * * * * * *                  * * * * * * * * * * * * * * *
      * * * * * * *                  * * * * * * * * * * * * * * *
      CARD NO.          YEAR              REMARKS
      * * * * * *        * * * *    * * * * * * * * * * * * * * * * * *
              1          1981         IS NOT A LEAP YEAR
              2          1976         IS A LEAP YEAR
              3          1776         IS A LEAP YEAR
              4          1979         IS NOT A LEAP YEAR
              5          1980         IS A LEAP YEAR
              6          1900         IS NOT A LEAP YEAR
              7          1800         IS NOT A LEAP YEAR
              8          1600         IS A LEAP YEAR
              9          1066         IS NOT A LEAP YEAR
             10          2053         IS NOT A LEAP YEAR
             11          1990         IS NOT A LEAP YEAR
             12          1914         IS NOT A LEAP YEAR
             13          1492         IS A LEAP YEAR
             14          1972         IS A LEAP YEAR
             15          1562         IS NOT A LEAP YEAR
```

```
      PAGE 2                         LEAP YEAR PROGRAM
      * * * * * * *                  * * * * * * * * * * * * * * *
      * * * * * * *                  * * * * * * * * * * * * * * *
      CARD NO.          YEAR              REMARKS
      * * * * * * *      * * * *    * * * * * * * * * * * * * * * * * *
             16          1200         IS A LEAP YEAR
             17          1876         IS A LEAP YEAR
             18          K532         ERROR IN DATA
```

19	1300	IS NOT A LEAP YEAR
20	HHHJ	ERROR IN DATA
21	0200	IS NOT A LEAP YEAR
22	2344	IS A LEAP YEAR
23	1945	IS NOT A LEAP YEAR
24	1818	IS NOT A LEAP YEAR
25	I335	ERROR IN DATA
26	1865	IS NOT A LEAP YEAR
27	1932	IS A LEAP YEAR
28	1964	IS A LEAP YEAR
29	1864	IS A LEAP YEAR
30	1515	IS NOT A LEAP YEAR

```
PAGE 3                         LEAP YEAR PROGRAM
* * * * * * * *                * * * * * * * * * * * * * * *
* * * * * * * *                * * * * * * * * * * * * * * *
CARD NO.        YEAR                      REMARKS
* * * * * * * *  * * * *        * * * * * * * * * * * * * * * * * *
```

31	2002	IS NOT A LEAP YEAR
32	1780	IS A LEAP YEAR
33	1856	IS A LEAP YEAR
34	1924	IS A LEAP YEAR
35	2037	IS NOT A LEAP YEAR
36	1904	IS A LEAP YEAR

7.6 The Day of the Week Problem

The problem we will now discuss is a natural successor to the leap year program that was just presented. The purpose of the next program is to read in a set of data cards, each of which is punched with the standard date in MM/DD/YYYY format, such as 01/01/2000 for January 1st, 2000. The program examines the date and prints out the day of the week on which that date falls. Once the date is read in it is tested to be sure that it is NUMERIC. If the date is found to be NUMERIC the data is then validated—the input is tested to determine whether it is reasonable. For instance, if the month, MM, is less than 1 or greater than 12, obviously something is wrong because in the generally used calendar system there are only 12 months to the year—the first, denoted by 1 and the last, by 12. Similarly, if the day, DD, is less than 1 or greater than 31, again an error is indicated because in no month can the day be less than 1 or greater than 31. Finally, the method we use to calculate the day of the week on which a particular date falls does not apply to any date before the year 1582, the year that Pope Gregory changed the calendar system from the Julian format to Gregorian.

The Julian date is sometimes more convenient. For example, April 15, 1981, is the 105th day of the year 1981. The date may therefore be expressed as a Julian date in the form

1051981

By the same token, December 31, 1984 would have as its Julian date:

3661984

because 1984 is a leap year, making December 31st day 366 of that year.

The formula used to calculate the day of the week is:

Day of the week (rounded)

$$= 7 \times \frac{\text{fractional}}{\text{portion}} \left[\frac{D + Y + \text{integer portion}\left(\frac{Y-1}{4}\right) - \text{integer portion}\left(\frac{Y-1}{100}\right) + \text{integer portion}\left(\frac{Y-1}{400}\right)}{7} \right]$$

where the day of the week (rounded) is found according to the code:

NUMBER CODE	DAY	NUMBER CODE	DAY
1	Sunday	5	Thursday
2	Monday	6	Friday
3	Tuesday	0	Saturday
4	Wednesday		

and

D = number of days since the beginning of the year
Y = year

Here is the distribution of days in the 12 months of the year.

January 31	April 30	July 31	October 31
February 28	May 31	August 31	November 30
March 31	June 30	September 30	December 31

If the year is a leap year the month of February has one additional day.

In order to calculate D, the Julian day, the number of days that has elapsed in all previous months has to be calculated. To this total is added the number of days in the current month. If the year in question is a leap year and the month in question is after February, 1 has to be added to the total days to account for February 29th.

The GO TO... DEPENDING ON Statement

Advantage may be taken of a statement called the GO TO... DEPENDING ON, a construct that is particularly suited to this situation. It behaves in the following manner. Assume there are 5 different paragraphs (procedures) we want to branch to depending on the value of a data-name, which we will call Q. The instruction:

```
GO TO PARA-A, PARA-B, PARA-C, PARA-D, PARA-E DEPENDING ON Q
```

has the effect of first evaluating Q. If Q is equal to 1, control is sent to the *first* named paragraph, in this case PARA-A. If Q is equal to 2, branching is effected to the *second* paragraph, PARA-B, and so on. If Q is less than 1 or greater than, in this case, 5, the statement is ignored. This statement is often regarded as the case structure, which uses a GO TO but in a highly controlled way, thereby not violating the rules of structured programming.

In Program 14 the value of D (in the formula) is represented by the more descriptive data-name TOTAL-DAYS, a 77-level item with a PICTURE of 999 initialized to zero in the Working-Storage Section. In order to calculate D, we first find the total number of days in all the previous months by using the following method:

```
GO TO JAN, FEB, MAR, APR, MAY, JUNE, JULY, AUG, SEPT,
OCT, NOV, DEC DEPENDING ON MONTH-IN.

DEC.    ADD 30 TO TOTAL-DAYS.
NOV.    ADD 31 TO TOTAL-DAYS.
OCT.    ADD 30 TO TOTAL-DAYS.
SEPT.   ADD 31 TO TOTAL-DAYS.
AUG.    ADD 31 TO TOTAL-DAYS.
JULY.   ADD 30 TO TOTAL-DAYS.
JUNE.   ADD 31 TO TOTAL-DAYS.
MAY.    ADD 30 TO TOTAL-DAYS.
APRIL.  ADD 31 TO TOTAL-DAYS.
MAR.    ADD 28 TO TOTAL-DAYS.
FEB.    ADD 31 TO TOTAL-DAYS.
JAN.    ADD DAY-IN TO TOTAL-DAYS.
```

where a branch to one of the paragraphs DEC, NOV,... JAN is effected depending on the value of MONTH-IN. If MONTH-IN is equal to 12, a branch is made to the paragraph named DEC, the first of the list of 12 paragraph names. Once there, 30 is added to TOTAL-DAYS to account for December's *previous* month, November. After this is done, 31 is immediately added for October, and so on until the paragraph named FEB is reached. Here 31 days is added for the previous month of January. At this point the value of DAY-IN is added to account for the number of days to be added for the month being read in. For example, if the date being read in is December 25, D is computed by totaling 30 for November; 31, for October; plus 30, plus 31, plus 31, plus 30, plus 31, plus 30, plus 31, plus 28, plus 31, plus 25 for the number of days to be added in December.

By means of this technique the computer dutifully sums all the days together, automatically regardless of the month being read in. If the date being inputted is, say, January 27 (January has no previous months) the value of MONTH-IN is 01 and control is sent directly to JAN where 27 is added to TOTAL-DAYS, bypassing all the other paragraph names.

However, if MONTH-IN is greater than 02 and YEAR-IN is a leap year, an additional 1 has to be added to TOTAL-DAYS. This final figure represents the value D in the formula. Returning once again to the formula, we notice that the third term in the bracket is:

$$\text{integer portion}\left(\frac{Y-1}{4}\right)$$

This value has to be computed separately in order to be sure that only the integer portion is used. The data-name MATH-1 is really $Y - 1$, MATH-2 is $(Y - 1)/4$, MATH-3 is $(Y - 1)/100$, and MATH-4 is $(Y - 1)/400$. MATH-1, MATH-2, and MATH-4 each has a PICTURE of 9999 while MATH-3 has a PICTURE of 99.

In line 212 of the program the numerator is evaluated and is given the name MATH-5. This is divided by 7 and the quotient is stored in MATH-6, which has a PICTURE of 9999V9999. This allows for a fractional portion. When MATH-6 is moved to MATH-7 (which has a PICTURE of 9999) only the integral portion of MATH-6 is retained in MATH-7. To get the fractional portion, we subtract MATH-7 from MATH-6, which places the fractional portion *only* in MATH-6. This fractional portion is then multiplied by 7 and the result is rounded, yielding a number that may be an integer from 0 to 6. This integer specifies the day of the week, the object of the program.

Notice that the program uses a form of the PERFORM we have not yet encountered. It is worth careful inspection.

The PERFORM PARA-A THRU PARA-Z Statement

The PERFORM, as we have seen, is used to transfer control explicitly to a procedure and to return control implicitly whenever execution of the specified procedure is complete. So far we have PERFORMed only a single paragraph (or procedure). COBOL also provides for the situation where 2 or more procedures may be PERFORMed. Suppose we have 5 sequential paragraphs named PARA-1, PARA-2, PARA-3, PARA-4, and PARA-5, respectively. We may then write instructions such as:

    a. PERFORM PARA-1 THRU PARA-2
    b. PERFORM PARA-1 THRU PARA-2 3 TIMES
    c. PERFORM PARA-1 THRU PARA-3
    d. PERFORM PARA-1 THROUGH PARA-5
    e. PERFORM PARA-2 THRU PARA-5 4 TIMES.

where the words THRU and THROUGH are equivalent. However, because THRU is shorter to write than THROUGH, the former is preferred. In each of these examples where the THRU option is specified, control is transferred to the first paragraph that is specified and is returned after the last statement of the second paragraph name mentioned is executed.

There are COBOL experts who maintain that the simpler version of the PERFORM should never be used. Instead, they insist that the PERFORM with the THRU option should always be used because someone someday might come along and in the middle of the PERFORMed paragraph would insert another paragraph. If this were to happen the original paragraph would no longer be performed in its entirety but would terminate where the newly inserted paragraph appears. To allow for the THRU option (even with a single paragraph) we specify a "dummy" last paragraph. This "dummy" paragraph has as its sole entry the word EXIT in the B margin.

If you take a close look at the input to Program 14 you will notice that 5 dates are invalid for reasons that were specifically tested for within the program. In order to allow for the possibility of a suitable printout if the date was invalid, 2 detail-lines are set up. In the detail-line for correct, valid data the literal 'LEAP YEAR' is printed out in the event that the year in question is in fact a leap year. If it is not a leap year, spaces are moved into this field. (Note carefully lines 274–276 of the program in which either 'LEAP YEAR' or blank spaces are MOVEd to BLANK-OR-LEAP-YEAR.)

Input for Program 14

```
MONTH DAY YEAR
  01/01/2000
  12/31/1978
  12/31/1980
  07/04/1976
  07/04/1978
  10/30/1927
  05/15/1948
  11/05/1700
  04/KH/1980
  03/00/1865
  12/12/1623
  13/25/1705
  05/13/1677
  06/28/1959
  07/04/1776
  09/29/1800
  02/06/1400
  02/25/1853
  08/16/2155
```

Program 14

```
1     IDENTIFICATION      DIVISION.
2     PROGRAM-ID.         JULIAN.
3     AUTHOR.             IRVIN POREMBA.
4     INSTALLATION.       NYU.
5     DATE-WRITTEN.       APRIL 3, 1982.
6     DATE-COMPILED.      APRIL 16, 1982.
7     SECURITY.           HENRY MULLISH.
8     * * * * * * * * * * * * * * * * * * * * * * * * * * * * * * * * * * * * * * * * * * * * * *
9     *    THIS PROGRAM READS IN DATA CARDS PUNCHED:                              *
10    *                                                                          *
11    *    COLUMNS  1-2: MONTH                                                    *
12    *    COLUMN      3: SLASH                                                   *
13    *    COLUMNS  4-5: DAY                                                      *
14    *    COLUMN      6: SLASH                                                   *
15    *    COLUMNS 7-13: YEAR                                                     *
16    *                                                                          *
17    *    THIS PROGRAM THEN USES THE DATA TO FIND THE                           *
18    *    JULIAN DATE FOR EACH GREGORIAN DATE GIVEN,                            *
19    *    ALONG WITH THE DAY OF THE WEEK AND WHETHER                            *
20    *    THE YEAR WAS A LEAP YEAR OR NOT.                                      *
21    * * * * * * * * * * * * * * * * * * * * * * * * * * * * * * * * * * * * * * * * * * * * * *
22
23    ENVIRONMENT DIVISION.
```

```
24        CONFIGURATION SECTION.
25        SOURCE-COMPUTER.  CYBER-170-720.
26        OBJECT-COMPUTER.  CYBER-170-720.
27        SPECIAL-NAMES.
28        INPUT-OUTPUT SECTION.
29        FILE-CONTROL.
30              SELECT IN-FILE ASSIGN TO INPUT.
31              SELECT OUT-FILE ASSIGN TO OUTPUT.
32
33        DATA DIVISION.
34        FILE SECTION.
35
36        FD    IN-FILE
37              LABEL RECORDS ARE OMITTED.
38
39        01    RECORD-IN.
40              02 MONTH-IN            PIC 9(02).
41              02 SLASH-1             PIC X(01).
42              02 DAY-IN              PIC 9(02).
43              02 SLASH-2             PIC X(01).
44              02 YEAR-IN             PIC 9(04).
45              02 FILLER              PIC X(70).
46
47        FD    OUT-FILE
48              LABEL RECORDS ARE OMITTED.
49
50        01    LINE-OUT               PIC X(133).
51
52        WORKING-STORAGE SECTION.
53        77    PAGE-COUNT             PIC 9999 VALUE ZERO.
54        77    CARD-COUNT             PIC 99999 VALUE ZERO.
55        77    CARD-COUNT-2           PIC 99 VALUE ZERO.
56        77    TOTAL-DAYS             PIC 999 VALUE ZERO.
57        77    CENTURY                PIC 99.
58        77    YEAR-X                 PIC 9999.
59        77    LEAP-YEAR              PIC 999.
60        77    WEEKDAY-ROUNDED        PIC 9.
61        77    MATH-1                 PIC 9999.
62        77    MATH-2                 PIC 9999.
63        77    MATH-3                 PIC 99.
64        77    MATH-4                 PIC 9999.
65        77    MATH-5                 PIC 9999.
66        77    MATH-6                 PIC 9(04)V9(04).
67        77    MATH-7                 PIC 9999.
68        77    MORE-CARDS             PIC X(03) VALUE 'YES'.
69
70        01    HEADER-1.
71              02 FILLER              PIC X(01) VALUE SPACES.
72              02 FILLER              PIC X(05) VALUE 'PAGE'.
73              02 PAGE-COUNT-OUT      PIC Z,ZZ9.
74              02 FILLER              PIC X(04) VALUE SPACES.
75              02 FILLER              PIC X(16) VALUE 'JULIAN CALENDAR'.
76              02 FILLER              PIC X(10) VALUE 'CONVERSION'.
77
78        01    HEADER-2.
79              02 FILLER              PIC X(01) VALUE SPACES.
80              02 FILLER              PIC X(10) VALUE ALL '*'.
81              02 FILLER              PIC X(04) VALUE SPACES.
82              02 FILLER              PIC X(26) VALUE ALL '*'.
83
84        01    HEADER-3.
85              02 FILLER              PIC X(01) VALUE SPACES.
86              02 FILLER              PIC X(04) VALUE 'CARD'.
87              02 FILLER              PIC X(06) VALUE SPACES.
88              02 FILLER              PIC X(09) VALUE 'GREGORIAN'.
89              02 FILLER              PIC X(05) VALUE SPACES.
90              02 FILLER              PIC X(06) VALUE 'JULIAN'.
91              02 FILLER              PIC X(08) VALUE SPACES.
92              02 FILLER              PIC X(03) VALUE 'DAY'.
93
94        01    HEADER-4.
95              02 FILLER              PIC X(01) VALUE SPACES.
96              02 FILLER              PIC X(05) VALUE 'COUNT'.
97              02 FILLER              PIC X(08) VALUE SPACES.
98              02 FILLER              PIC X(04) VALUE 'DATE'.
99              02 FILLER              PIC X(08) VALUE SPACES.
```

```
100        02 FILLER              PIC X(04) VALUE 'DATE'.
101        02 FILLER              PIC X(07) VALUE SPACES.
102        02 FILLER              PIC X(07) VALUE 'OF WEEK'.
103
104    01  HEADER-5.
105        02 FILLER              PIC X(01) VALUE SPACES.
106        02 FILLER              PIC X(06) VALUE ALL '*'.
107        02 FILLER              PIC X(04) VALUE SPACES.
108        02 FILLER              PIC X(10) VALUE ALL '*'.
109        02 FILLER              PIC X(04) VALUE SPACES.
110        02 FILLER              PIC X(07) VALUE ALL '*'.
111        02 FILLER              PIC X(04) VALUE SPACES.
112        02 FILLER              PIC X(09) VALUE ALL '*'.
113
114    01  DETAIL-LINE.
115        02 FILLER              PIC X(01) VALUE SPACES.
116        02 CARD-COUNT-OUT      PIC ZZ,ZZ9.
117        02 FILLER              PIC X(04) VALUE SPACES.
118        02 MONTH-OUT           PIC 99.
119        02 SLASH-1-OUT         PIC X(01).
120        02 DAY-OUT             PIC 99.
121        02 SLASH-2-OUT         PIC X(01).
122        02 YEAR-OUT            PIC 9999.
123        02 FILLER              PIC X(04) VALUE SPACES.
124        02 JULIAN-DAY-OUT      PIC 999.
125        02 YEAR-2-OUT          PIC 9999.
126        02 FILLER              PIC X(04) VALUE SPACES.
127        02 DAY-OF-WEEK-OUT     PIC X(09).
128        02 FILLER              PIC X(04) VALUE SPACES.
129        02 BLANK-OR-LEAP-YEAR  PIC X(09).
130
131    01  DETAIL-LINE-2.
132        02 FILLER              PIC X(01) VALUE SPACES.
133        02 CARD-COUNT-OUT-2    PIC ZZ,ZZ9.
134        02 FILLER              PIC X(04) VALUE SPACES.
135        02 MONTH-OUT-2         PIC X(02).
136        02 SLASH-1-OUT-2       PIC X(01).
137        02 DAY-OUT-2           PIC X(02).
138        02 SLASH-2-OUT-2       PIC X(01).
139        02 YEAR-OUT-2          PIC X(04).
140        02 FILLER              PIC X(04) VALUE SPACES.
141        02 FILLER              PIC X(15) VALUE 'GREGORIAN DATE'.
142        02 FILLER              PIC X(07) VALUE 'INVALID'.
143
144    PROCEDURE DIVISION.
145
146    MAIN-LINE-ROUTINE.
147        PERFORM OPEN-FILES.
148        PERFORM NEW-PAGE.
149        PERFORM START-UP.
150        PERFORM PROCESS-DATA UNTIL MORE-CARDS EQUAL 'NO'.
151        PERFORM CLOSE-UP.
152        STOP RUN.
153
154    OPEN-FILES.
155        OPEN INPUT IN-FILE.
156        OPEN OUTPUT OUT-FILE.
157
158    NEW-PAGE.
159        MOVE SPACES TO LINE-OUT.
160        WRITE LINE-OUT AFTER PAGE.
161
162    START-UP.
163        READ IN-FILE AT END MOVE 'NO' TO MORE-CARDS
164            MOVE ' **NO DATA IN DECK**' TO LINE-OUT
165            WRITE LINE-OUT AFTER 30.
166        IF MORE-CARDS EQUAL 'YES' PERFORM WRITE-HEADINGS.
167
168    PROCESS-DATA.
169        ADD 1 TO CARD-COUNT.
170        ADD 1 TO CARD-COUNT-2.
171        IF MONTH-IN NOT NUMERIC
172            OR DAY-IN NOT NUMERIC
173            OR YEAR-IN NOT NUMERIC
174            OR MONTH-IN > 12
175            OR MONTH-IN < 1
```

```
176                 OR DAY-IN > 31
177                 OR DAY-IN < 1
178                 OR YEAR-IN < 1582
179                 PERFORM ERROR-PARA
180                 PERFORM CHECK-READ
181             ELSE
182                 PERFORM GO-PARA THRU CHECK-READ.
183
184     CLOSE-UP.
185             CLOSE IN-FILE, OUT-FILE.
186
187     GO-PARA.
188             GO TO JAN, FEB, MAR, APR, MAY, JUNE, JULY, AUG, SEPT,
189                 OCT, NOV, DEC DEPENDING ON MONTH-IN.
190
191     DEC.    ADD 30 TO TOTAL-DAYS.
192     NOV.    ADD 31 TO TOTAL-DAYS.
193     OCT.    ADD 30 TO TOTAL-DAYS.
194     SEPT.   ADD 31 TO TOTAL-DAYS.
195     AUG.    ADD 31 TO TOTAL-DAYS.
196     JULY.   ADD 30 TO TOTAL-DAYS.
197     JUNE.   ADD 31 TO TOTAL-DAYS.
198     MAY.    ADD 30 TO TOTAL-DAYS.
199     APR.    ADD 31 TO TOTAL-DAYS.
200     MAR.    ADD 28 TO TOTAL-DAYS.
201     FEB.    ADD 31 TO TOTAL-DAYS.
202     JAN.    ADD DAY-IN TO TOTAL-DAYS.
203             MOVE YEAR-IN TO CENTURY.
204             IF CENTURY EQUAL ZERO PERFORM LEAP-1
205             ELSE PERFORM LEAP-2.
206
207     WEEKDAY.
208             SUBTRACT 1 FROM YEAR-IN GIVING MATH-1.
209             DIVIDE 4 INTO MATH-1 GIVING MATH-2.
210             DIVIDE 100 INTO MATH-1 GIVING MATH-3.
211             DIVIDE 400 INTO MATH-1 GIVING MATH-4.
212             ADD TOTAL-DAYS, YEAR-IN, MATH-2, MATH-4 GIVING MATH-5.
213             SUBTRACT MATH-3 FROM MATH-5.
214             DIVIDE 7 INTO MATH-5 GIVING MATH-6.
215             MOVE MATH-6 TO MATH-7.
216             SUBTRACT MATH-7 FROM MATH-6.
217             MULTIPLY 7 BY MATH-6 GIVING WEEKDAY-ROUNDED ROUNDED.
218
219     GET-WEEKDAY.
220             IF WEEKDAY-ROUNDED = 0 MOVE 'SATURDAY' TO DAY-OF-WEEK-OUT
221             ELSE IF WEEKDAY-ROUNDED = 1 MOVE 'SUNDAY' TO DAY-OF-WEEK-OUT
222                 ELSE IF WEEKDAY-ROUNDED = 2 MOVE 'MONDAY' TO
223                     DAY-OF-WEEK-OUT
224                     ELSE IF WEEKDAY-ROUNDED = 3 MOVE 'TUESDAY' TO
225                         DAY-OF-WEEK-OUT
226                         ELSE IF WEEKDAY-ROUNDED = 4 MOVE 'WEDNESDAY'
227                             TO DAY-OF-WEEK-OUT
228                             ELSE IF WEEKDAY-ROUNDED = 5 MOVE
229                                 'THURSDAY' TO DAY-OF-WEEK-OUT
230                                 ELSE IF WEEKDAY-ROUNDED = 6 MOVE
231                                     'FRIDAY' TO DAY-OF-WEEK-OUT
232                                     ELSE PERFORM ERROR-PARA-2.
233
234     WRITE-PARA.
235             MOVE CARD-COUNT TO CARD-COUNT-OUT.
236             MOVE MONTH-IN TO MONTH-OUT.
237             MOVE SLASH-1 TO SLASH-1-OUT.
238             MOVE DAY-IN TO DAY-OUT.
239             MOVE SLASH-2 TO SLASH-2-OUT.
240             MOVE YEAR-IN TO YEAR-OUT.
241             MOVE TOTAL-DAYS TO JULIAN-DAY-OUT.
242             MOVE YEAR-IN TO YEAR-2-OUT.
243             WRITE LINE-OUT FROM DETAIL-LINE AFTER 2.
244
245     CHECK-READ.
246             READ IN-FILE AT END MOVE ZEROS TO CARD-COUNT-2
247                 MOVE 'NO' TO MORE-CARDS.
248             IF CARD-COUNT-2 = 10 MOVE ZEROS TO CARD-COUNT-2
249                 PERFORM NEW-PAGE
250                 PERFORM WRITE-HEADINGS.
251             MOVE ZEROS TO TOTAL-DAYS.
```

```
252
253     WRITE-HEADINGS.
254         ADD 1 TO PAGE-COUNT.
255         MOVE PAGE-COUNT TO PAGE-COUNT-OUT.
256         WRITE LINE-OUT FROM HEADER-1 AFTER 1.
257         WRITE LINE-OUT FROM HEADER-2 AFTER 1.
258         WRITE LINE-OUT FROM HEADER-3 AFTER 2.
259         WRITE LINE-OUT FROM HEADER-4 AFTER 1.
260         WRITE LINE-OUT FROM HEADER-5 AFTER 1.
261
262     LEAP-1.
263         DIVIDE 400 INTO YEAR-IN GIVING YEAR-X
264             REMAINDER LEAP-YEAR.
265         IF LEAP-YEAR EQUAL ZERO
266             MOVE 'LEAP YEAR' TO BLANK-OR-LEAP-YEAR
267         ELSE MOVE SPACES TO BLANK-OR-LEAP-YEAR
268         IF LEAP-YEAR EQUAL ZERO AND MONTH-IN > 2
269             ADD 1 TO TOTAL-DAYS.
270
271     LEAP-2.
272         DIVIDE 4 INTO YEAR-IN GIVING YEAR-X
273             REMAINDER LEAP-YEAR.
274         IF LEAP-YEAR EQUAL ZERO
275             MOVE 'LEAP YEAR' TO BLANK-OR-LEAP-YEAR
276         ELSE MOVE SPACES TO BLANK-OR-LEAP-YEAR.
277         IF LEAP-YEAR EQUAL ZERO AND MONTH-IN > 2
278             ADD 1 TO TOTAL-DAYS.
279
280     ERROR-PARA.
281         MOVE CARD-COUNT TO CARD-COUNT-OUT-2.
282         MOVE MONTH-IN TO MONTH-OUT-2.
283         MOVE SLASH-1 TO SLASH-1-OUT-2.
284         MOVE DAY-IN TO DAY-OUT-2.
285         MOVE SLASH-2-OUT-2.
286         MOVE YEAR-IN TO YEAR-OUT-2.
287         WRITE LINE-OUT FROM DETAIL-LINE-2 AFTER 2.
288
289     ERROR-PARA-2.
290         MOVE ' **ERROR IN PROGRAMMING**' TO LINE-OUT.
291         WRITE LINE-OUT AFTER 2.
292         PERFORM CLOSE-UP.
293         STOP RUN.
```

Output for Program 14

PAGE 1		JULIAN CALENDAR CONVERSION		
**********		***************************		
CARD	GREGORIAN	JULIAN	DAY	
COUNT	DATE	DATE	OF WEEK	
******	**********	*******	*********	
1	01/01/2000	0012000	SATURDAY	LEAP YEAR
2	12/31/1978	3651978	SUNDAY	
3	12/31/1980	3661980	WEDNESDAY	LEAP YEAR
4	07/04/1976	1861976	SUNDAY	LEAP YEAR
5	07/04/1978	1851978	TUESDAY	
6	10/30/1927	3031927	SUNDAY	
7	05/15/1948	1361948	SATURDAY	LEAP YEAR
8	11/05/1700	3091700	FRIDAY	
9	04/KH/1980	GREGORIAN DATE INVALID		
10	03/00/1865	GREGORIAN DATE INVALID		

PAGE 2		JULIAN CALENDAR CONVERSION		
**********		***************************		
CARD	GREGORIAN	JULIAN	DAY	
COUNT	DATE	DATE	OF WEEK	
*******	**********	*******	*********	
11	12/12/1623	GREGORIAN DATE INVALID		
12	13/25/1705	GREGORIAN DATE INVALID		
13	05/13/1677	1331677	THURSDAY	
14	06/28/1959	1791959	SUNDAY	
15	07/04/1776	1861776	THURSDAY	LEAP YEAR
16	09/29/1800	2721800	MONDAY	
17	02/06/1400	GREGORIAN DATE INVALID		
18	02/25/1853	0561853	FRIDAY	
19	08/16/2155	2282155	SATURDAY	

Review Questions

1. Write a record description entry for the 4 following records. In each case assign an appropriate name to the record.

(a)

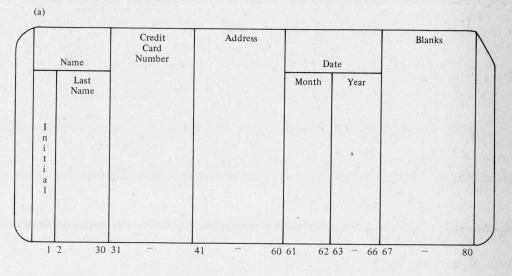

(b)

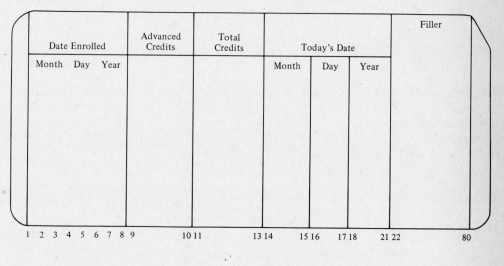

(c)

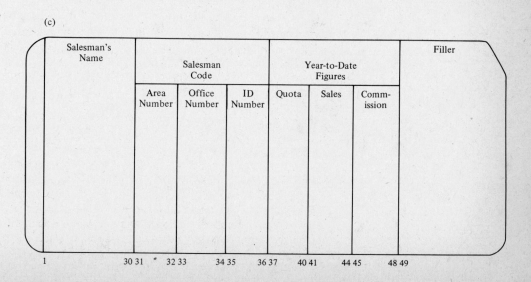

(d)

	Low Priced Calculators			Medium Priced Calculators			High Priced Calculators			Filler
	Units Sold 1982	Units Sold 1983	Units Sold 1984	1982	1983	1984	1982	1983	1984	

```
1      4 5      8 9    12 13    16 17    20 21    24 25    28 29    32 33    36 37                    80
```

2. Write a record description entry appropriate to the following data. The record name is MILITARY. Each input card is punched with a numeric ID number in the first 8 columns, followed by 6 spaces. In the next 5 columns there is punched the monthly wage with an implied decimal point that separates dollars from cents. A further 15 columns are left blank and the following 2 columns are punched with the years of service. The remaining columns of the card are blank. Use FILLER to account for any unused portions of the card.

3. Study the following record description.

```
01   STUDENT-HISTORY.
     05 YEAR-OF-BIRTH                    PICTURE 9(4).
     05 YEAR-GRADUATED-HIGH-SCHOOL       PICTURE 9(4).
     05 COLLEGE-CREDITS-EARNED           PICTURE 999.
     05 FILLER                           PICTURE X(69).
```

   a. The record name is _____ .
   b. The elementary item names are _____ _____ .
   c. The last elementary item is called _____ .
   d. The total length of the record is _____ .
   e. The number of numeric fields in this record is _____ ; alphanumeric fields _____ .
   f. The largest number of credits that can be recorded is _____ .
   g. The year of birth that allowed for can be no greater than _____ .
   h. The only item that cannot be referenced is _____ .
   i. No record can have more than _____ 01-level entries.

4. If the same data-name is used in different records, they must be _____ when referred to individually in the _____ Division, unless they are referenced by the MOVE _____ . Ordinarily, such data-names must be qualified by use of the key words _____ or _____ .

5. When the MOVE CORRESPONDING instruction is used
   a. the 01 names must be identical
   b. the spelling of the data-names in both records must be identical
   c. the order in which the names appear is of no consequence
   d. qualification is unnecessary

Exercises

1. THE MURDER PROBLEM
   As you are probably aware, the use of computers is not confined solely to business establishments. Computers have been particularly useful to the police department in the fight against crime in a great number of varied ways. Perhaps the reader knows to his or her regret that automobile license plate numbers, together with any offenses registered against them, are stored in computers by many cities in the United States. This affords police departments instantaneous access to this kind of information when required.

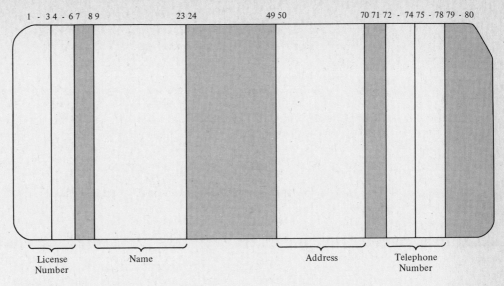

1 - 34 - 67 8 9   23 24   49 50   70 71 72 - 74 75 - 78 79 - 80

License   Name   Address   Telephone
Number   Number

Figure 7-1

For the purposes of the next program, assume that the license plates in a particular state are all of a uniform type, namely, they are composed of two 3-digit numbers that are separated by a star. A typical license plate would therefore be

587 * 633

For each license plate issued a punched card is filed at police headquarters, which contains the license plate number, name, address, and telephone number of the person who is assigned that particular license plate. Figure 7-1 shows a typical input data card.

Subsequent to a murder being committed, a police investigation is undertaken. As a result of the investigation, a witness to the crime is asked to identify the license plate of the automobile in which the perpetrator of the crime was seen to make his escape.

Unfortunately, the best information that the witness can produce is that the first 3-digit number on the left of the license plate was *identical* to the 3-digit number on the right. Exactly what they were could not be recalled, despite strenuous efforts to do so. The exact details of the license plate were lost in the excitement of the moment. In the absence of any further evidence the detectives working in the computer section have little alternative but to write a program that examines each individual license plate issued and that for each license plate tests whether the first 3-digit number is equal to the second 3-digit number. It is apparent that there would be no point in writing the program in such a way that as soon as the first occurrence of such a plate is detected the relevant information is printed out and the program is terminated. This might seem to make the job of the detectives easier, because they would have a single suspect to apprehend. However, such a course of action would be self-defeating for there are probably many, perhaps dozens — even hundreds — of license plates on which the first 3-digit number is equal to the second 3-digit number. It is therefore imperative that *every* such license plate be examined by the computer and a list of suspects be printed.

In order to counter a possible question that might be raised in court, the police programmer decides to compute also the percentage of license plates that conform to this pattern. To compute a percentage, we must keep 2 separate counts. The first is the total card count, whereas the second is the count for the number of suspects. As each card of the input file is read, CARD-COUNT is updated by 1. Each time LEFT-3, (the left 3 digits of the license plate number) is equal to RIGHT-3 (the right 3 digits of the license plate number) 1 is added to NUMBER-OF-SUSPECTS. Write the program.

2. Referring to the murder problem (exercise 1) assume that the first 2 letters of the car manufacturer's name are punched in columns 7 and 8 of the data cards. For example, CH could stand for Chevrolet, FO for Ford, PO for Pontiac, and so on. Assume also that another witness has been found who remembers the make of the escape vehicle. Rewrite the program to take advantage of this additional information, again printing out all the relevant information, including the percentage of suspects.

3. Assume a deck of 80-column student registration cards is punched with the student name, ID number, address, and the number of credits to be taken in the forthcoming semester. Select any columns you desire for the individual fields. Write a program that will print, for the benefit of the college bursar, the tuition costs for each student and the total tuition for all students.

    If the student registers for less than 12 credits, he or she is charged $100 per credit. If the student takes between 12 and 18 credits, the charge is a flat fee of $1500. For more than 18 credits the student is charged the flat fee of $1500 plus $100 for every credit over 18.

4. A salesman employed by the McKay T-Shirt Company sells only 3 types of T-shirts.
   a. plain white at $2.95 a shirt
   b. imprinted with the name in black at $3.95 a shirt.
   c. imprinted with the name in color at $5.95 a shirt.
       Assume that a card for each sale is punched as follows.
   columns 1 – 20: salesman's name
   column 25: type of shirt sold (1, 2, or 3 as detailed here)
   columns 30 – 33: number of shirts sold
       The salesman earns 5% commission on every shirt of type 1; 9%, on every shirt of type 2; and 15%, on every shirt of type 3. Write a program that prints and calculates
   a. a report of all the transactions
   b. the commission for each sale
   c. the gross amount for each sale
   d. the total commission for each salesman
   e. the grand total of sales
   f. the grand total commission.
       It may be assumed that all the data cards are sorted by salesman's name.

5. Write a COBOL program to process a monthly payroll. There is an input file and an output file. The cards in the input file are punched as follows.
   col 1 – 25   employee name
       26 – 29   blank
       30 – 33   hours worked 999V9
       34 – 35   blank
       36 – 39   rate of pay per hour 99V99
       40 – 80   blank
   The program should print out
   a. a count of the cards
   b. employee name
   c. gross pay (hours worked times rate)
   d. Social Security tax (0.0613 times gross pay)
   e. net pay (gross pay less tax).
       If a net pay exceeds $1000.00, print out 10 asterisks alongside the line so that it can be checked for accuracy. Each output field must be edited as necessary. Use all the options you know, but do not concern yourself with elaborate cosmetics.

7.8   To Hire or Not to Hire...

The manager of Universal Computer Services advertised for a COBOL programmer in the local newspaper. Among the people who responded to the ad was a Mr. Jimmy Smiley who presented credentials that weren't particularly convincing. The manager decided to ask Mr. Smiley if he would agree to write a short structured program in COBOL. Mr. Smiley hesitated at first and then agreed. Here is the program he wrote.

    Would you hire him?

```
1       IDENTIFICATION DIVISION
2       PROGRAMME-ID MONEY$
3       OTHER. GRACE MURRAY HOPPER
4       DATA-COMPILED.
5       DATE-WRITTEN. FEB 30, 1981
```

```
6      SEKURITY. BOTTOM MANAGMENT ONLY
7      REMARK. NONE WHATEVER.
8
9      ENVIRONMENT-DIVISION.
10     COFIGERATION SECTION.
11     SAUCE COMPUTER. IBM-370-145.
12     OBJECTCOMPUTER. IBM-370-145.
13     SPECIAL NAME CO1 IS SUN-YIP.
14     INPUT-OUTPUT AREA.
15         FILE SECTION.
16         SELECT IN-FILE ASSIGN TO SYSIN.
17         SELECT OUT-FILE ASSIGN TO SYSIN.
18
19     DATER DIVISION.
20     FILE-CONTROL.
21     FD OUT-FILE
22         RECORDS LABELS ARE OMITTED.
23       01   OUT-LINE PIC X(500).
24     FD   IN-FILE
25         RECORD LABELS ARE OMMITED.
26     01    RECORD-IN.
27         02 CUSTOMER-NAME PIC X(30).
28         03 FILLER            PIC X(03) VALUE BLANKS.
29         02 ADDRESS           PIC X(30).
30         02 HEAD OFFICE       PIC X(30).
31     WORKING STORAGE DIVISION.
32     01    DETAIL LINE.
33         02 CUST-NAME-OUT  PIC X(30).
34         02 FILLER            PIC X(30) VALUE BLANKS.
35         02 ADDRESS-OU-       PIC X(30).
36         02 FILLER            PIC X(30).
37         02 HEAD-OFFICE-OUT   PIC X(20).
38     PROCEEDURE DIVISION.
39     MAIN-LINE-ROUTINE
40         PERFORM OPEN-FILES.
41         PERFORM START-UP.
42         PERFORM PROCESS-DATA UNTIL ANY-MORE-CARDS EQUAL 'NO'.
43         PERFORM CLOSE-FILES.
44         STOP-RUN.
45
46         START-DOWN.
47         READ CUSTOMER-NAME, FILLER, ADDRESS, HEAD OFFICE
48     PROCESS-DATA.
49         MOVE CUST-NAME TO CUST-NAME-OUT.
50         MOVE ADDRESS TO ADDRESS-OUT.
51         MOVD FILLER TO FILLER.
52         WRITE OUT-LINE TO DETAIL-LINE.
53         READ IN-FILE ON END CLOSE-UP.
54         CLOSE-UP.
55         CLOSE BOTH FILES.
```

For your information this "program" was run on the computer. It created no fewer than 112 diagnostic messages.

I wonder what Mr. Smiley is doing now....

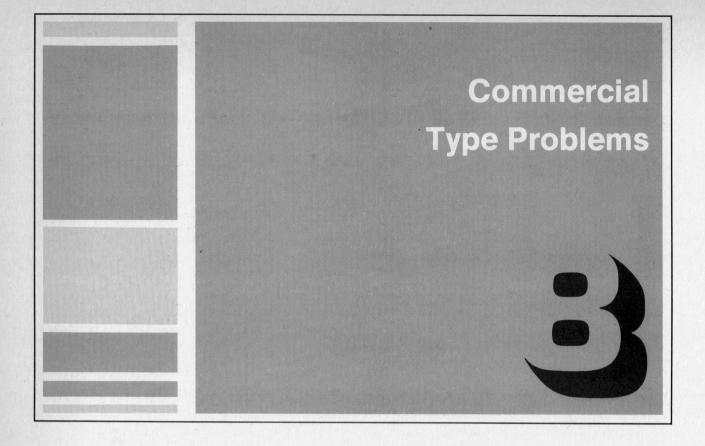

Commercial Type Problems

3

Man does not live by COBOL alone.

(Don Lee)

The time has arrived to examine the ways that COBOL can handle financial problems. After all, COBOL is the major commercial data processing language. In particular, you will learn:

- when more than a single detail line is necessary
- how to edit fully dollars and cents values
- how to write a payroll problem
- how to test for invalid data
- how to use the REDEFINES clause and to restrict the output to a single detail-line
- how to flag large payments so that they may be verified by the payroll personnel
- how to calculate compound interest by using 2 different methods
- how to include the current date in a report
- how CURRENT-DATE works on IBM computers
- the PERFORM... VARYING statement.
- that paragraph names may be composed of numeric digits only
- how to eliminate 77-level items
- about control breaks
- the ON SIZE ERROR option

8.1   The Sales Report Problem

A typical commercial application is the printing of a sales report. If a product sells for a given price and the number of units sold is known, the cost is found simply by multiplying the unit price by the quantity purchased.

In this program the input data is punched as shown here.

1	25	30	34	40	44	50	53
Salesman's Name		Product Code		Unit Price		Quantity Purchased	
X(25)		9(05)		999V99		9999	

In our sample data deck there are 20 cards punched in this format. The program reads in each card, counts the card, and prints out the count, the salesman's name, the product code, the unit price (edited), the quantity purchased (edited), and the net sales cost for each particular transaction (edited). Once all the data has been read and the net sales figure for each transaction computed and printed, the total net sales is printed directly underneath the last net sales figure, with a suitable printout.

Separate 77-level items are kept in the Working-Storage Section in order to accumulate a total net sales figure. One is called NET-SALES with a PICTURE of 9(07)V99. It is not initialized to zero because this value is computed by multiplying UNIT-PRICE by NO-PURCHASED. The unedited PICTURE for NET-SALES provides the means to add NET-SALES to TOTAL-NET-SALES, the instruction in line 188. In order to add anything to TOTAL-NET-SALES it has to be initialized to some value. Because it is an accumulator, it is initialized to zero.

Once all the data has been read the AT END clause of the READ instruction in line 196 is triggered. This has a dual effect; first, it PERFORMs TOTAL-PARA and then moves 'NO' to MORE-CARDS to terminate the program.

Input for Program 15

IRVIN POREMBA	01234	23199	1010
AARON GEENFELD	98950	69100	2156
DAVID SAKS	24231	14314	3752
ROGER POOL	73445	22930	1743
THOMAS MCGREEHAM	59017	10519	0125
JULIEN GUILFORD	02000	07029	0636
ANDREW DORSEY	19271	31055	3848
CARLOS BILBAO	30071	10702	4260
LEONARD AUBREY	42519	76771	3052
HENRY FREEDMAN	12034	33061	0546
ROBERT MORRISON	01200	03600	6167
FERNANDO TORRES	00099	13913	1485
GEORGE YOUNG	30230	37954	3957
ARNOLD KRONENBERG	43557	23055	3337
JOSEPH WADE	25930	20173	1140
BERNARD ZIMMERMAN	00458	61535	0570
SOLOMON SAPERMAN	13912	00201	3079

MICHAEL DAVIDSON	51585	16024	2138
FRANK JASPER	00939	10059	2292
RICHARD LESTER	30779	02138	1567
NAME	PRODUCT CODE	UNIT PRICE 999V99	QUANTITY PURCHASED

Program 15

```
1       IDENTIFICATION DIVISION.
2       PROGRAM-ID. SALES.
3       AUTHOR. IRVIN POREMBA.
4       INSTALLATION. NYU.
5       DATE-WRITTEN. MARCH 24, 1982.
6       DATE-COMPILED. APRIL 16, 1982.
7       SECURITY. HENRY MULLISH ONLY.
8       ***********************************************************
9       *       THIS PROGRAM IS A SALES REPORT. THE DATA CARDS        *
10      *       ARE PUNCHED AS FOLLOWS:                               *
11      *                                                            *
12      *       COLUMNS   1-25: SALESMAN'S NAME                       *
13      *       COLUMNS 30-34: PRODUCT CODE                           *
14      *       COLUMNS 40-44: UNIT PRICE                             *
15      *       COLUMNS 50-53: QUANTITY PURCHASED                     *
16      *                                                            *
17      *       THE OUTPUT OF THE PROGRAM NOT ONLY CONTAINS           *
18      *       THE DATA CARDS LISTED UNDER A SUITABLE HEADING,       *
19      *       BUT ALSO THE NET SALES BY EACH SALESMAN AND           *
20      *       AT THE END OF THE OUTPUT THE TOTAL NET SALES          *
21      *       FOR ALL THE SALESMEN.                                 *
22      ***********************************************************
23
24      ENVIRONMENT DIVISION.
25      CONFIGURATION SECTION.
26      SOURCE-COMPUTER. CYBER-170-720.
27      OBJECT-COMPUTER. CYBER-170-720.
28      SPECIAL-NAMES.
29      INPUT-OUTPUT SECTION.
30      FILE-CONTROL.
31          SELECT IN-FILE ASSIGN TO INPUT.
32          SELECT OUT-FILE ASSIGN TO OUTPUT.
33
34      DATA DIVISION.
35      FILE SECTION.
36
37      FD  IN-FILE
38          LABEL RECORDS ARE OMITTED.
39
40      *   DEFINE DATA.
41
42      01  RECORD-IN.
43          02  SALESMANS-NAME        PIC X(25).
44          02  FILLER                PIC X(04).
45          02  PRODUCT-CODE          PIC 9(05).
46          02  FILLER                PIC X(05).
47          02  UNIT-PRICE            PIC 9(03)V9(02).
48          02  FILLER                PIC X(05).
49          02  NO-PURCHASED          PIC 9(04).
50          02  FILLER                PIC X(27).
51
52      FD  OUT-FILE
53          LABEL RECORDS ARE OMITTED.
54
55      *   DEFINE OUTPUT OF PROGRAM
56
57      01  LINE-OUT               PIC X(133).
58
59      WORKING-STORAGE SECTION.
60      77  PAGE-COUNT             PIC 9999  VALUE ZERO.
61      77  CARD-COUNT             PIC 99999 VALUE ZERO.
62      77  CARD-COUNT-2           PIC 99    VALUE ZERO.
63      77  MORE-CARDS             PIC X(03) VALUE 'YES'.
64      77  NET-SALES              PIC 9(07)V99.
```

65	77	TOTAL-NET-SALES		PIC 9(11)V99 VALUE ZERO.
66				
67	01	HEADER-1.		
68		02	FILLER	PIC X(01) VALUE SPACES.
69		02	FILLER	PIC X(05) VALUE 'PAGE'.
70		02	PAGE-COUNT-OUT	PIC Z,ZZ9.
71		02	FILLER	PIC X(32) VALUE SPACES.
72		02	FILLER	PIC X(12) VALUE 'SALES REPORT'.
73				
74	01	HEADER-2.		
75		02	FILLER	PIC X(01) VALUE SPACES.
76		02	FILLER	PIC X(10) VALUE ALL '*'.
77		02	FILLER	PIC X(32) VALUE SPACES.
78		02	FILLER	PIC X(12) VALUE ALL '*'.
79				
80	01	HEADER-3.		
81		02	FILLER	PIC X(01) VALUE SPACES.
82		02	FILLER	PIC X(04) VALUE 'ITEM'.
83		02	FILLER	PIC X(15) VALUE SPACES.
84		02	FILLER	PIC X(10) VALUE 'SALESMANS'.
85		02	FILLER	PIC X(12) VALUE SPACES.
86		02	FILLER	PIC X(07) VALUE 'PRODUCT'.
87		02	FILLER	PIC X(06) VALUE SPACES.
88		02	FILLER	PIC X(04) VALUE 'UNIT'.
89		02	FILLER	PIC X(07) VALUE SPACES.
90		02	FILLER	PIC X(08) VALUE 'QUANTITY'.
91		02	FILLER	PIC X(11) VALUE SPACES.
92		02	FILLER	PIC X(03) VALUE 'NET'.
93				
94	01	HEADER-4.		
95		02	FILLER	PIC X(02) VALUE SPACES.
96		02	FILLER	PIC X(03) VALUE 'NO.'.
97		02	FILLER	PIC X(18) VALUE SPACES.
98		02	FILLER	PIC X(04) VALUE 'NAME'.
99		02	FILLER	PIC X(16) VALUE SPACES.
100		02	FILLER	PIC X(04) VALUE 'CODE'.
101		02	FILLER	PIC X(08) VALUE SPACES.
102		02	FILLER	PIC X(05) VALUE 'PRICE'.
103		02	FILLER	PIC X(06) VALUE SPACES.
104		02	FILLER	PIC X(09) VALUE 'PURCHASED'.
105		02	FILLER	PIC X(10) VALUE SPACES.
106		02	FILLER	PIC X(05) VALUE 'SALES'.
107				
108	01	HEADER-5.		
109		02	FILLER	PIC X(01) VALUE SPACES.
110		02	FILLER	PIC X(06) VALUE ALL '*'.
111		02	FILLER	PIC X(05) VALUE SPACES.
112		02	FILLER	PIC X(25) VALUE ALL '*'.
113		02	FILLER	PIC X(05) VALUE SPACES.
114		02	FILLER	PIC X(07) VALUE ALL '*'.
115		02	FILLER	PIC X(05) VALUE SPACES.
116		02	FILLER	PIC X(07) VALUE ALL '*'.
117		02	FILLER	PIC X(05) VALUE SPACES.
118		02	FILLER	PIC X(09) VALUE ALL '*'.
119		02	FILLER	PIC X(05) VALUE SPACES.
120		02	FILLER	PIC X(18) VALUE ALL '*'.
121				
122	01	HEADER-6.		
123		02	FILLER	PIC X(80) VALUE SPACES.
124		02	FILLER	PIC X(18) VALUE ALL '*'.
125				
126	01	DETAIL-LINE.		
127		02	FILLER	PIC X(01) VALUE SPACES.
128		02	CARD-COUNT-OUT	PIC ZZ,ZZ9.
129		02	FILLER	PIC X(05) VALUE SPACES.
130		02	SALESMANS-NAME-OUT	PIC X(25).
131		02	FILLER	PIC X(07) VALUE SPACES.
132		02	PRODUCT-CODE-OUT	PIC ZZZZ9.
133		02	FILLER	PIC X(05) VALUE SPACES.
134		02	UNIT-PRICE-OUT	PIC $$$9.99.
135		02	FILLER	PIC X(09) VALUE SPACES.
136		02	NO-PURCHASED-OUT	PIC Z,ZZ9.
137		02	FILLER	PIC X(10) VALUE SPACES.
138		02	NET-SALES-OUT	PIC $$,$$$,$$9.99.
139				

```
140    01    DETAIL-LINE-2.
141          02    FILLER               PIC X(62) VALUE SPACES.
142          02    FILLER               PIC X(18) VALUE 'TOTAL NET SALES:'.
143          02    TOTAL-SALES-OUT      PIC $$$,$$$,$$$,$$9.99.
144
145    PROCEDURE DIVISION.
146
147    *     THIS IS THE MAIN PARAGRAPH WHICH USES
148    *     THE PERFORM STATEMENT TO ACCESS TO THE OTHER PARAGRAPHS.
149
150    MAIN-LINE-ROUTINE.
151          PERFORM OPEN-FILES.
152          PERFORM NEW-PAGE.
153          PERFORM START-UP.
154          PERFORM PROCESS-DATA UNTIL MORE-CARDS EQUAL 'NO'.
155          PERFORM CLOSE-UP.
156          STOP RUN.
157
158    OPEN-FILES.
159          OPEN INPUT IN-FILE.
160          OPEN OUTPUT OUT-FILE.
161
162    NEW-PAGE.
163          MOVE SPACES TO LINE-OUT.
164          WRITE LINE-OUT AFTER PAGE.
165
166    *     START-UP WRITES THE HEADINGS AND CHECKS TO SEE
167    *     IF THERE IS ANY DATA. IF THERE IS NO DATA, AN ERROR
168    *     MESSAGE IS WRITTEN.
169
170    START-UP.
171          READ IN-FILE AT END MOVE 'NO' TO MORE-CARDS
172                MOVE ' **NO DATA IN DECK**' TO LINE-OUT
173                WRITE LINE-OUT AFTER 30.
174          IF MORE-CARDS EQUAL 'YES' PERFORM WRITE-HEADINGS.
175
176    *     IF THERE IS DATA, PROCESS-DATA DOES THE ARITHMETIC
177    *     NEEDED TO GET NET-SALES, ADDS THAT NUMBER TO
178    *     TOTAL-NET-SALES, WRITES DETAIL-LINE AND READS ANOTHER
179    *     DATA CARD.
180
181    PROCESS-DATA.
182          IF CARD-COUNT-2 EQUAL 15 MOVE ZEROS TO CARD-COUNT-2,
183                PERFORM NEW-PAGE
184                PERFORM WRITE-HEADINGS.
185          ADD 1 TO CARD-COUNT.
186          ADD 1 TO CARD-COUNT-2.
187          MULTIPLY UNIT-PRICE BY NO-PURCHASED GIVING NET-SALES.
188          ADD NET-SALES TO TOTAL-NET-SALES.
189          MOVE CARD-COUNT TO CARD-COUNT-OUT.
190          MOVE SALESMANS-NAME TO SALESMANS-NAME-OUT.
191          MOVE PRODUCT-CODE TO PRODUCT-CODE-OUT.
192          MOVE UNIT-PRICE TO UNIT-PRICE-OUT.
193          MOVE NO-PURCHASED TO NO-PURCHASED-OUT.
194          MOVE NET-SALES TO NET-SALES-OUT.
195          WRITE LINE-OUT FROM DETAIL-LINE AFTER 2.
196          READ IN-FILE AT END PERFORM TOTAL-PARA
197                MOVE 'NO' TO MORE-CARDS.
198
199    CLOSE-UP.
200          CLOSE IN-FILE, OUT-FILE.
201
202    TOTAL-PARA.
203          MOVE TOTAL-NET-SALES TO TOTAL-SALES-OUT.
204          WRITE LINE-OUT FROM HEADER-6 AFTER 1.
205          WRITE LINE-OUT FROM DETAIL-LINE-2 AFTER 2.
206
207    WRITE-HEADINGS.
208          ADD 1 TO PAGE-COUNT.
209          MOVE PAGE-COUNT TO PAGE-COUNT-OUT.
210          WRITE LINE-OUT FROM HEADER-1 AFTER 1.
211          WRITE LINE-OUT FROM HEADER-2 AFTER 1.
212          WRITE LINE-OUT FROM HEADER-2 AFTER 1.
213          WRITE LINE-OUT FROM HEADER-3 AFTER 2.
214          WRITE LINE-OUT FROM HEADER-4 AFTER 1.
215          WRITE LINE-OUT FROM HEADER-5 AFTER 1.
```

Output for Program 15

PAGE 1					
ITEM NO.	SALESMANS NAME	PRODUCT CODE	UNIT PRICE	QUANTITY PURCHASED	NET SALES
1	IRVIN POREMBA	1234	$231.99	1,010	$234,309.90
2	AARON GEENFELD	98950	$691.00	2,156	$1,489,796.00
3	DAVID SAKS	24231	$143.14	3,752	$537,061.28
4	ROGER POOL	73445	$229.30	1,743	$399,669.90
5	THOMAS MCGREEHAM	59017	$105.19	125	$13,148.75
6	JULIEN GUILFORD	2000	$70.29	636	$44,704.44
7	ANDREW DORSEY	19271	$310.55	3,848	$1,194,996.40
8	CARLOS BILBAO	30071	$107.02	4,260	$455,905.20
9	LEONARD AUBREY	42519	$767.71	3,052	$2,343,050.92
10	HENRY FREEDMAN	12034	$330.61	546	$180,513.06
11	ROBERT MORRISON	1200	$36.00	6,167	$222,012.00
12	FERNANDO TORRES	99	$139.13	1,485	$206,608.05
13	GEORGE YOUNG	30230	$379.54	3,957	$1,501,839.78
14	ARNOLD KRONENBERG	43557	$230.55	3,337	$769,345.35
15	JOSEPH WADE	25930	$201.73	1,140	$229,972.20

PAGE 2					
ITEM NO.	SALESMAN NAME	PRODUCT CODE	UNIT PRICE	QUANTITY PURCHASED	NET SALES
16	BERNARD ZIMMERMAN	458	$615.35	570	$350,749.50
17	SOLOMON SAPERMAN	13912	$2.01	3,079	$6,188.79
18	MICHAEL DAVIDSON	51585	$160.24	2,138	$342,593.12
19	FRANK JASPER	939	$100.59	2,292	$230,552.28
20	RICHARD LESTER	30779	$21.38	1,567	$33,502.46

TOTAL NET SALES: $10,786,519.38

8.2 The Weekly Payroll Problem

The program that is given top priority in most businesses is the payroll. If the weekly check is not forthcoming at the end of the week, employees will not be very happy.

A fairly straightforward payroll follows. The input data consists of a deck of cards that are punched in this format.

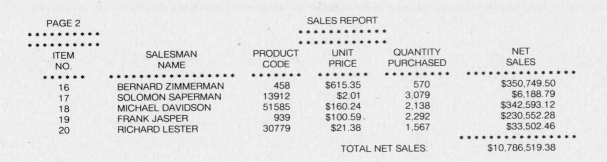

The program contains a single detail-line that shows the count, the employee's name, the rate of pay (edited), hours worked (edited), number of regular hours worked (edited and up to 40), regular pay (edited), overtime hours worked (edited—over 40), overtime pay (edited), gross pay (edited—regular pay plus overtime pay), Social Security tax (edited—6.13% of gross pay), net pay (edited), and finally, if the net pay is greater than $1000, a string of 5 asterisks so that it receives special attention from the payroll manager.

Because the critical information in a payroll problem is the number of hours worked and the rate of pay per hour, this information would have to be entered manually through a CRT or keypunched on cards. Whichever method is used, it is a fact of life that there is a good chance that some of the data will be entered incorrectly. To minimize the risk of running the program with bad data, clearly one should give both these fields—the number of hours worked and the rate of pay—the NUMERIC test. If it is not numeric and a computation is attempted, the program will "blow up"—will be aborted prematurely in the middle of the run.

Thus in the PROCESS-DATA paragraph, immediately after 1 has been added to the two card counts, both HOURS-WORKED and RATE-OF-PAY are tested to be sure they are numeric. (You should realize, of course, that even if these two fields pass the numeric test, it is no guarantee that they are correct—it merely confirms that they are numeric.) If either one or the other (or both) are not numeric, control is sent to ERROR-PARA.

What are the possibilities? Hopefully, both fields are numeric. This is the ideal case. Possibly HOURS-WORKED is not numeric but RATE-OF-PAY is. This is case number 2. Perhaps the reverse is true—RATE-OF-PAY is not numeric but HOURS-WORKED is. This is case number 3. Of course, it is also possible that both fields are not numeric. Case number 4 would indeed be a sorry state of affairs but it is not improbable. In fact, the philosophy that most professional COBOL programmers adopt is that "if it is inputted by a human being, assume it is wrong!" Despite this fatalistic tone, it is nevertheless a sound concept.

Ordinarily, we would be forced to set up in Working-Storage four separate detail-lines to cater to the 4 previous possibilities. However, COBOL provides a very neat feature to take care of such eventualities so that only one detail-line is necessary. It is the REDEFINES clause.

The REDEFINES Clause

It is possible in the Data Division to define a field with one PICTURE and, immediately afterward, on the same level, redefine that same area with a different PICTURE. For example, suppose we have in the detail-line an entry that reads:

02   RATE-OF-PAY-OUT PIC $$9.99.

If the RATE-OF-PAY were numeric, it could then be moved to RATE-OF-PAY-OUT and everything would be fine. However, should RATE-OF-PAY prove not to be numeric, we could hardly move it to RATE-OF-PAY-OUT because its PICTURE accommodates only numeric data. The PICTURE $$9.99 takes up 6 places—count them yourself, for this is a critical feature of the REDEFINES clause. This area of memory can be redefined by following it with another 02-level entry of the form:

02   ERROR-RATE-OF-PAY REDEFINES RATE-OF-PAY-OUT PIC X(06).

where the 6-character numeric edited field is redefined by the 6-character X field. The same could be done for any numeric to alphanumeric and alphanumeric to numeric field. In Program 16, which follows, a numeric edited field is redefined as an alphanumeric field. If the item is, in fact, numeric, the numeric edited field is used; otherwise, the X field is used and the word 'VOID' may be moved there. In this way only one detail-line is needed. The REDEFINES entry must have the level number of the entry it is redefining and the redefining field may not be wider than the field being redefined, although it may be equal in width to it or shorter.

If the net pay, after subtracting Social Security tax, exceeds $1000, '* * * * *' is moved to the field called BLANK-OR-AST; otherwise, blanks are moved there.

Notice that there are 7 separate 02-level items that carry the BLANK WHEN ZERO clause. If zero is moved to any of these fields, a blank field will be printed.

Input for Program 16

IRVIN POREMBA	5300	3575
HENRY MULLISH	2000	0100
AARON GREENFELD	1234	3150
DAVID SAKS	4230	4315
ROGER POOL	3455	2930
THOMAS MCGEEHAM	J010	0515
JUIEN GUILFORD	2000	7030
ANDREW DORSEY	9270	1055
CARLOS BILBAO	1000	0720
LEONARD AUBREY	2500	6770
HENRY FREEDMAN	2035	3060
ROBERT MORRISON	1200	3600
FERNANDO TORRES	0190	F930
GEORGE YOUNG	0230	7950
ARNOLD KRONENBERG	3550	3000
JOSEPH WADE	5930	0750
BERNALD ZIMMERMAN	0450	1535
SOLOMAN SAPERSTEIN	3915	0200
MICHAEL DAVIDSON	1585	6025
FRANK JASPER	0940	0050
RICHARD LESTER	JKIU	GT4U
BRIAN MILLER	1515	0810
CHARLES O'CONNER	2450	2270
ROGER BEGELMAN	1950	2635
HENRI ERICKSON	JK63	2535
LEO MARX	4415	3345
FRED NUSSBAUM	3930	1290
MARTIN SMITH	3254	5110
HOWARD WASHINGTON	0120	5140
JACOB HELLER	9280	3080
HAMILTON POSNER	4750	0250
RONALD KRAMER	6010	0500
JOHN DODGE	2050	1375
EDGAR GREGERSON	1455	1065
STEVEN ROBERTS	2025	1095

Program 16

```
1       IDENTIFICATION DIVISION.
2       PROGRAM-ID. PAYROLL.
3       AUTHOR. IRVIN POREMBA.
4       INSTALLATION. NYU.
5       DATE-WRITTEN. MARCH 24, 1982.
6       DATE-COMPILED. APRIL 17, 1982.
7       SECURITY. HENRY MULLISH ONLY.
8       *************************************************************
9       *      THIS PROGRAM IS A PAYROLL. THE DATA CARDS            *
10      *      ARE PUNCHED AS FOLLOWS:                              *
11      *                                                          *
12      *      COLUMNS  1-25: EMPLOYEE NAME                         *
13      *      COLUMNS 30-33: HOURS WORKED                          *
14      *      COLUMNS 36-39: RATE OF PAY                           *
15      *                                                          *
16      *      THIS PROGRAM PRINTS OUT A CARD COUNT,                *
17      *      THE EMPLOYEE NAME, THE TOTAL HOURS WORKED,           *
18      *      THE RATE OF PAY, THE REGULAR HOURS WORKED,           *
19      *      THE REGULAR PAY, THE OVERTIME HOURS WORKED,          *
20      *      THE OVERTIME PAY, THE GROSS PAY, THE SOCIAL          *
21      *      SECURITY TAX, AND THE NET PAY FOR EACH CARD.         *
22      *      ALL NUMERIC DATA IS TESTED FOR VALIDITY; THE WORD    *
23      *      VOID IS PRINTED IN ANY AREA NOT NUMERIC. ALL         *
24      *      NUMERIC OUTPUT IS FULLY EDITED. IF AN EMPLOYEE'S     *
25      *      NET PAY IS GREATER THAN $1,000.00, ASTERISKS         *
26      *      ARE PRINTED FOLLOWING THE NET PAY.                   *
27      *************************************************************
28
29      ENVIRONMENT DIVISION.
30      CONFIGURATION SECTION.
```

```
31      SOURCE-COMPUTER. CYBER-170-720.
32      OBJECT-COMPUTER. CYBER-170-720.
33      SPECIAL-NAMES.
34      INPUT-OUTPUT SECTION.
35      FILE-CONTROL.
36          SELECT IN-FILE ASSIGN TO INPUT.
37          SELECT OUT-FILE ASSIGN TO OUTPUT.
38
39      DATA DIVISION.
40      FILE SECTION.
41
42      FD  IN-FILE
43          LABEL RECORDS ARE OMITTED.
44
45      *   DEFINE DATA.
46
47      01  RECORD-IN.
48          02    EMPLOYEE-NAME       PIC X(25).
49          02    FILLER             PIC X(04).
50          02    HOURS-WORKED       PIC 9(02)V9(02).
51          02    FILLER             PIC X(02).
52          02    RATE-OF-PAY        PIC 9(02)V9(02).
53          02    FILLER             PIC X(41).
54
55      FD  OUT-FILE
56          LABEL RECORDS ARE OMITTED.
57
58      *   DEFINE OUTPUT OF THE PROGRAM.
59
60      01  LINE-OUT                 PIC X(133).
61
62      WORKING-STORAGE SECTION.
63      77  CARD-COUNT               PIC 99999 VALUE ZERO.
64      77  CARD-COUNT-2             PIC 99 VALUE ZERO.
65      77  PAGE-COUNT               PIC 9999 VALUE ZERO.
66      77  REGULAR-HOURS            PIC 99V99.
67      77  OVERTIME-HOURS           PIC 99V99.
68      77  OVERTIME-PAY             PIC 9999V99.
69      77  REGULAR-PAY              PIC 9999V99.
70      77  GROSS-PAY                PIC 99999V99.
71      77  SOC-SEC-TAX              PIC 999V99.
72      77  NET-PAY                  PIC 99999V99.
73      77  MORE-CARDS               PIC X(03) VALUE 'YES'.
74
75      01  HEADER-1.
76          02    FILLER             PIC X(06) VALUE 'PAGE'.
77          02    PAGE-COUNT-OUT     PIC Z,ZZ9.
78          02    FILLER             PIC X(48) VALUE SPACES.
79          02    FILLER             PIC X(14) VALUE 'WEEKLY PAYROLL'.
80
81      01  HEADER-2.
82          02    FILLER             PIC X(01) VALUE SPACES.
83          02    FILLER             PIC X(10) VALUE ALL '*'.
84          02    FILLER             PIC X(48) VALUE SPACES.
85          02    FILLER             PIC X(14) VALUE ALL '*'.
86
87      01  HEADER-3.
88          02    FILLER             PIC X(05) VALUE 'CARD'.
89          02    FILLER             PIC X(13) VALUE SPACES.
90          02    FILLER             PIC X(08) VALUE 'EMPLOYEE'.
91          02    FILLER             PIC X(11) VALUE SPACES.
92          02    FILLER             PIC X(13) VALUE 'RATE HOURS'.
93          02    FILLER             PIC X(12) VALUE 'REGULAR'.
94          02    FILLER             PIC X(10) VALUE 'REGULAR'.
95          02    FILLER             PIC X(10) VALUE 'OVERTIME'.
96          02    FILLER             PIC X(13) VALUE 'OVERTIME'.
97          02    FILLER             PIC X(10) VALUE 'GROSS'.
98          02    FILLER             PIC X(14) VALUE 'SOC. SEC.'.
99          02    FILLER             PIC X(11) VALUE 'NET BLANK'.
100
101     01  HEADER-4.
102         02    FILLER             PIC X(01) VALUE SPACES.
103         02    FILLER             PIC X(19) VALUE 'COUNT'.
```

```
104        02   FILLER                    PIC X(16) VALUE 'NAME'.
105        02   FILLER                    PIC X(17) VALUE 'OF PAY WORKED'.
106        02   FILLER                    PIC X(11) VALUE 'HOURS'.
107        02   FILLER                    PIC X(09) VALUE 'PAY'.
108        02   FILLER                    PIC X(12) VALUE 'HOURS'.
109        02   FILLER                    PIC X(11) VALUE 'PAY'.
110        02   FILLER                    PIC X(11) VALUE 'PAY'.
111        02   FILLER                    PIC X(12) VALUE 'TAX'.
112        02   FILLER                    PIC X(11) VALUE 'PAY OR CK'.
113
114   01   HEADER-5.
115        02   FILLER                    PIC X(01) VALUE SPACES.
116        02   FILLER                    PIC X(06) VALUE ALL '*'.
117        02   FILLER                    PIC X(02) VALUE SPACES.
118        02   FILLER                    PIC X(25) VALUE ALL '*'.
119        02   FILLER                    PIC X(02) VALUE SPACES.
120        02   FILLER                    PIC X(06) VALUE ALL '*'.
121        02   FILLER                    PIC X(02) VALUE SPACES.
122        02   FILLER                    PIC X(06) VALUE ALL '*'.
123        02   FILLER                    PIC X(02) VALUE SPACES.
124        02   FILLER                    PIC X(07) VALUE ALL '*'.
125        02   FILLER                    PIC X(02) VALUE SPACES.
126        02   FILLER                    PIC X(09) VALUE ALL '*'.
127        02   FILLER                    PIC X(02) VALUE SPACES.
128        02   FILLER                    PIC X(08) VALUE ALL '*'.
129        02   FILLER                    PIC X(02) VALUE SPACES.
130        02   FILLER                    PIC X(09) VALUE ALL '*'.
131        02   FILLER                    PIC X(02) VALUE SPACES.
132        02   FILLER                    PIC X(10) VALUE ALL '*'.
133        02   FILLER                    PIC X(02) VALUE SPACES.
134        02   FILLER                    PIC X(08) VALUE ALL '*'.
135        02   FILLER                    PIC X(02) VALUE SPACES.
136        02   FILLER                    PIC X(15) VALUE ALL '*'.
137
138   01   DETAIL-LINE.
139        02   FILLER                    PIC X(01) VALUE SPACES.
140        02   CARD-COUNT-OUT            PIC ZZ,ZZ9.
141        02   FILLER                    PIC X(02) VALUE SPACES.
142        02   EMPLOYEE-NAME-OUT         PIC X(25).
143        02   FILLER                    PIC X(02) VALUE SPACES.
144        02   RATE-OF-PAY-OUT           PIC $$9.99.
145        02   ERROR-RATE-OF-PAY           REDEFINES RATE-OF-PAY-OUT PIC X(06).
146        02   FILLER                    PIC X(03) VALUE SPACES.
147        02   HOURS-WORKED-OUT          PIC Z9.99.
148        02   ERROR-HOURS REDEFINES HOURS-WORKED-OUT PIC X(05).
149        02   FILLER                    PIC X(03) VALUE SPACES.
150        02   REGULAR-HOURS-OUT         PIC Z9.99 BLANK WHEN ZERO.
151        02   FILLER                    PIC X(03) VALUE SPACES.
152        02   REGULAR-PAY-OUT           PIC $$,$$9.99 BLANK WHEN ZERO.
153        02   FILLER                    PIC X(04) VALUE SPACES.
154        02   OVERTIME-HOURS-OUT        PIC Z9.99 BLANK WHEN ZERO.
155        02   FILLER                    PIC X(03) VALUE SPACES.
156        02   OVERTIME-PAY-OUT          PIC $$,$$9.99 BLANK WHEN ZERO.
157        02   FILLER                    PIC X(02) VALUE SPACES.
158        02   GROSS-PAY-OUT             PIC $$$,$$9.99 BLANK WHEN ZERO.
159        02   FILLER                    PIC X(03) VALUE SPACES.
160        02   SOC-SEC-TAX-OUT           PIC $$$9.99 BLANK WHEN ZERO.
161        02   FILLER                    PIC X(02) VALUE SPACES.
162        02   NET-PAY-OUT               PIC $$$,$$9.99 BLANK WHEN ZERO.
163        02   BLANK-OR-AST              PIC X(05).
164
165   PROCEDURE DIVISION.
166
167   *    THIS IS THE MAIN PARAGRAPH OF THE PROGRAM WHICH
168   *    USES THE PERFORM STATEMENT TO ACCESS THE
169   *    OTHER PARAGRAPHS.
170
171   MAIN-LINE-ROUTINE.
172        PERFORM OPEN-FILES.
173        PERFORM NEW-PAGE.
174        PERFORM START-UP.
175        PERFORM PROCESS-DATA UNTIL MORE-CARDS EQUAL 'NO'.
176        PERFORM CLOSE-UP.
```

```
177          STOP RUN.
178
179      OPEN-FILES.
180          OPEN INPUT IN-FILE.
181          OPEN OUTPUT OUT-FILE.
182
183      NEW-PAGE.
184          MOVE SPACES TO LINE-OUT.
185          WRITE LINE-OUT AFTER PAGE.
186
187   *      START-UP CHECKS TO SEE IF THERE IS ANY DATA
188   *      TO BE READ IN. IF THERE IS NOT, AN ERROR MESSAGE
189   *      IS PRINTED. IF THERE IS DATA THE HEADERS ARE PRINTED.
190
191      START-UP.
192          READ IN-FILE AT END MOVE 'NO' TO MORE-CARDS
193              MOVE ' **NO DATA IN DECK**' TO LINE-OUT
194              WRITE LINE-OUT AFTER 30.
195          IF MORE-CARDS EQUAL 'YES' PERFORM WRITE-HEADINGS.
196
197   *      IF THERE IS DATA PROCESS-DATA TESTS THE
198   *      NUMERIC DATA FOR VALIDITY. IF THE TESTS ARE PASSED
199   *      THE PERFORM STATEMENT SENDS CONTROL TO ANOTHER
200   *      PARAGRAPH DEPENDING ON WHETHER THE NUMBER OF
201   *      HOURS WORKED IS LESS THAN OR EQUAL TO 40 HOURS OR
202   *      THAT THE NUMBER OF HOURS WORKED IS GREATER THAN 40 HOURS.
203
204      PROCESS-DATA.
205          ADD 1 TO CARD-COUNT.
206          ADD 1 TO CARD-COUNT-2.
207          IF HOURS-WORKED NOT NUMERIC OR RATE-OF-PAY
208              NOT NUMERIC PERFORM ERROR-PARA
209          ELSE IF HOURS-WORKED < 40 OR = 40 PERFORM REGULAR-ONLY-PARA
210              ELSE PERFORM OVERTIME-TOO-PARA.
211          READ IN-FILE AT END MOVE ZEROS TO CARD-COUNT-2
212              MOVE 'NO' TO MORE-CARDS.
213          IF CARD-COUNT-2 = 15 MOVE ZEROS TO CARD-COUNT-2
214              PERFORM NEW-PAGE
215              PERFORM WRITE-HEADINGS.
216
217      CLOSE-UP.
218          CLOSE IN-FILE, OUT-FILE.
219
220   *      REGULAR-ONLY-PARA DOES THE CALCULATIONS NECESSARY
221   *      TO GET THE OUTPUT DESIRED WHEN THE TOTAL NUMBER
222   *      OF HOURS WORKED BY A WORKER IS LESS THAN OR EQUAL TO 40.
223
224      REGULAR-ONLY-PARA.
225          MULTIPLY HOURS-WORKED BY RATE-OF-PAY
226              GIVING GROSS-PAY ROUNDED.
227          MULTIPLY 0.0613 BY GROSS-PAY GIVING SOC-SEC-TAX ROUNDED.
228          SUBTRACT SOC-SEC-TAX FROM GROSS-PAY GIVING NET-PAY.
229          MOVE GROSS-PAY TO REGULAR-PAY-OUT, GROSS-PAY-OUT.
230          MOVE HOURS-WORKED TO REGULAR-HOURS-OUT, HOURS-WORKED-OUT.
231          MOVE SOC-SEC-TAX TO SOC-SEC-TAX-OUT.
232          MOVE ZEROS TO OVERTIME-HOURS-OUT, OVERTIME-PAY-OUT.
233          MOVE NET-PAY TO NET-PAY-OUT.
234          MOVE CARD-COUNT TO CARD-COUNT-OUT.
235          MOVE EMPLOYEE-NAME TO EMPLOYEE-NAME-OUT.
236          MOVE RATE-OF-PAY TO RATE-OF-PAY-OUT.
237          IF NET-PAY > 1000 MOVE '*****' TO BLANK-OR-AST
238          ELSE MOVE SPACES TO BLANK-OR-AST.
239          WRITE LINE-OUT FROM DETAIL-LINE AFTER 2.
240
241   *      OVERTIME-TOO-PARA DOES THE CALCULATIONS NECESSARY
242   *      TO GET THE OUTPUT DESIRED WHEN THE NUMBER OF HOURS WORKED
243   *      BY A WORKER IS GREATER THAN 40.
244
245      OVERTIME-TOO-PARA.
246          SUBTRACT 40 FROM HOURS-WORKED GIVING OVERTIME-HOURS.
247          MOVE 40.00 TO REGULAR-HOURS.
248          MULTIPLY REGULAR-HOURS BY RATE-OF-PAY
249              GIVING REGULAR-PAY ROUNDED.
```

```
250          COMPUTE OVERTIME-PAY ROUNDED = 1.5*RATE-OF-PAY*
251              OVERTIME-HOURS.
252          ADD OVERTIME-PAY, REGULAR-PAY GIVING GROSS-PAY.
253          MULTIPLY 0.0613 BY GROSS-PAY GIVING SOC-SEC-TAX ROUNDED.
254          SUBTRACT SOC-SEC-TAX FROM GROSS-PAY GIVING NET-PAY.
255          MOVE CARD-COUNT TO CARD-COUNT-OUT.
256          MOVE EMPLOYEE-NAME TO EMPLOYEE-NAME-OUT.
257          MOVE HOURS-WORKED TO HOURS-WORKED-OUT.
258          MOVE RATE-OF-PAY TO RATE-OF-PAY-OUT.
259          MOVE REGULAR-HOURS TO REGULAR-HOURS-OUT.
260          MOVE REGULAR-PAY TO REGULAR-PAY-OUT.
261          MOVE OVERTIME-HOURS TO OVERTIME-HOURS-OUT.
262          MOVE OVERTIME-PAY TO OVERTIME-PAY-OUT.
263          MOVE GROSS-PAY TO GROSS-PAY-OUT.
264          MOVE SOC-SEC-TAX TO SOC-SEC-TAX-OUT.
265          MOVE NET-PAY TO NET-PAY-OUT.
266          IF NET-PAY > 1000 MOVE '*****' TO BLANK-OR-AST
267          ELSE MOVE SPACES TO BLANK-OR-AST.
268          WRITE LINE-OUT FROM DETAIL-LINE AFTER 2.
269
270     *    ERROR-PARA IS USED TO MAKE MENTION OF NUMERIC FIELDS
271     *    WHICH HAVE BEEN FOUND TO BE NOT NUMERIC. THIS IS
272     *    DONE BY MOVING THE WORD "VOID" TO THE REDEFINED FIELD
273     *    OF THE AREAS NOT FOUND TO BE NUMERIC, THEN WRITING
274     *    THE DETAIL-LINE OUT.
275
276     ERROR-PARA.
277          IF HOURS-WORKED NOT NUMERIC MOVE 'VOID' TO
278              ERROR-HOURS
279          ELSE MOVE HOURS-WORKED TO HOURS-WORKED-OUT.
280          IF RATE-OF-PAY NOT NUMERIC MOVE 'VOID' TO
281              ERROR-RATE-OF-PAY
282          ELSE MOVE RATE-OF-PAY TO RATE-OF-PAY-OUT.
283          MOVE ZEROS TO REGULAR-HOURS-OUT, REGULAR-PAY-OUT,
284              OVERTIME-HOURS-OUT, OVERTIME-PAY-OUT, SOC-SEC-TAX-OUT,
285              GROSS-PAY-OUT, NET-PAY-OUT.
286          MOVE SPACES TO BLANK-OR-AST.
287          MOVE CARD-COUNT TO CARD-COUNT-OUT.
288          MOVE EMPLOYEE-NAME TO EMPLOYEE-NAME-OUT.
289          WRITE LINE-OUT FROM DETAIL-LINE AFTER 2.
290
291     WRITE-HEADINGS.
292          ADD 1 TO PAGE-COUNT.
293          MOVE PAGE-COUNT TO PAGE-COUNT-OUT.
294          WRITE LINE-OUT FROM HEADER-1 AFTER 1.
295          WRITE LINE-OUT FROM HEADER-2 AFTER 1.
296          WRITE LINE-OUT FROM HEADER-2 AFTER 1.
297          WRITE LINE-OUT FROM HEADER-3 AFTER 2.
298          WRITE LINE-OUT FROM HEADER-4 AFTER 1.
299          WRITE LINE-OUT FROM HEADER-5 AFTER 1.
```

Output for Program 16

PAGE 1

WEEKLY PAYROLL

CARD COUNT	EMPLOYEE NAME	RATE OF PAY	HOURS WORKED	REGULAR HOURS	REGULAR PAY	OVERTIME HOURS	OVERTIME PAY	GROSS PAY	SOC. SEC. TAX	NET PAY	BLANK OR CK
1	IRVIN POREMBA	$35.75	53.00	40.00	$1,430.00	13.00	$697.13	$2,127.13	$130.39	$1,996.74	*****
2	HENRY MULLISH	$1.00	20.00	20.00	$20.00			$20.00	$1.23	$18.77	
3	AARON GREENFELD	$31.50	12.34	12.34	$388.71			$388.71	$23.83	$364.88	
4	DAVID SAKS	$43.15	42.30	40.00	$1,726.00	2.30	$148.87	$1,874.87	$114.93	$1,759.94	*****
5	ROGER POOL	$29.30	34.55	34.55	$1,012.32			$1,012.32	$62.06	$950.26	
6	THOMAS MCGEEHAM	$5.15	VOID								
7	JUIEN GUILFORD	$70.30	20.00	20.00	$1,406.00			$1,406.00	$86.19	$1,319.81	*****
8	ANDREW DORSEY	$10.55	92.70	40.00	$422.00	52.70	$833.98	$1,255.98	$76.99	$1,178.99	*****
9	CARLOS BIBAO	$7.20	10.00	10.00	$72.00			$72.00	$4.41	$67.59	
10	LEONARD AUBREY	$67.70	25.00	25.00	$1,692.50			$1,692.50	$103.75	$1,588.75	*****
11	HENRY FREEDMAN	$30.60	20.35	20.35	$622.71			$622.71	$38.17	$584.54	
12	ROBERT MORRISON	$36.00	12.00	12.00	$432.00			$432.00	$26.48	$405.52	
13	FERNANDO TORRES	VOID	1.90								
14	GEORGE YOUNG	$79.50	2.30	2.30	$182.85			$182.85	$11.21	$171.64	
15	ARNOLD KRONENBERG	$30.00	35.50	35.50	$1,065.00			$1,065.00	$65.28	$999.72	

PAGE 2
* * * * * * * *
* * * * * * * *

WEEKLY PAYROLL
* * * * * * * * * * * * * * *
* * * * * * * * * * * * * * *

CARD COUNT	EMPLOYEE NAME	RATE OF PAY	HOURS WORKED	REGULAR HOURS	REGULAR PAY	OVERTIME HOURS	OVERTIME PAY	GROSS PAY	SOC. SEC. TAX	NET PAY	BLANK OR CK
* * * * * *	* * * * * * * * * * * * * *	* * * * * *	* * * * * *	* * * * * * *	* * * * * * *	* * * * * * *	* * * * * *	* * * * * *	* * * * * * *	* * * * * * *	* * * * *
16	JOSEPH WADE	$7.50	59.30	40.00	$300.00	19.30	$217.13	$517.13	$31.70	$485.43	
17	BERNALD ZIMMERMAN	$15.35	4.50	4.50	$69.08			$69.08	$4.23	$64.85	
18	SOLOMAN SAPERSTEIN	$2.00	39.15	39.15	$78.30			$78.30	$4.80	$73.50	
19	MICHAEL DAVIDSON	$60.25	15.85	15.85	$954.96			$954.96	$58.54	$896.42	
20	FRANK JASPER	$0.50	9.40	9.40	$4.70			$4.70	$0.29	$4.41	
21	RICHARD LÉSTER	VOID	VOID								
22	BRIAN MILLER	$8.10	15.15	15.15	$122.72			$122.72	$7.52	$115.20	
23	CHARLES O'CONNER	$22.70	24.50	24.50	$556.15			$556.15	$34.09	$522.06	
24	ROGER BEGELMAN	$26.35	19.50	19.50	$513.83			$513.83	$31.50	$482.33	
25	HENRI ERICKSON	$25.35	VOID								
26	LEO MARX	$33.45	44.15	40.00	$1,338.00	4.15	$208.23	$1,546.23	$94.78	$1,451.45	* * * * *
27	FRED NUSSBAUM	$12.90	39.30	39.30	$506.97			$506.97	$31.08	$475.89	
28	MARTIN SMITH	$51.10	32.54	32.54	$1,662.79			$1,662.79	$101.93	$1,560.86	* * * * *
29	HOWARD WASHINGTON	$51.40	1.20	1.20	$61.68			$61.68	$3.78	$57.90	
30	JACOB HELLER	$30.80	92.80	40.00	$1,232.00	52.80	$2,439.36	$3,671.36	$235.05	$3,446.31	* * * * *

PAGE 3
* * * * * * * *
* * * * * * * *

WEEKLY PAYROLL
* * * * * * * * * * * * * * *
* * * * * * * * * * * * * * *

CARD COUNT	EMPLOYEE NAME	RATE OF PAY	HOURS WORKED	REGULAR HOURS	REGULAR PAY	OVERTIME HOURS	OVERTIME PAY	GROSS PAY	SOC. SEC. TAX	NET PAY	BLANK OR CK
* * * * * *	* * * * * * * * * * * * * *	* * * * * *	* * * * * *	* * * * * * *	* * * * * * *	* * * * * * *	* * * * * *	* * * * * *	* * * * * * *	* * * * * * *	* * * * *
31	HAMILTON POSNER	$2.50	47.50	40.00	$100.00	7.50	$28.13	$128.13	$7.85	$120.28	
32	RONALD KRAMER	$5.00	60.10	40.00	$200.00	20.10	$150.75	$350.75	$21.50	$329.25	
33	JOHN DODGE	$13.75	20.50	20.50	$281.88			$281.88	$17.28	$264.60	
34	EDGAR GREGERSON	$10.65	14.55	14.55	$154.96			$154.96	$9.50	$145.46	
35	STEVEN ROBERTS	$10.95	20.25	20.25	$221.74			$221.74	$13.59	$208.15	

8.3   The Manhattan Island Problem

Legend has it that back in 1627 the island of Manhattan was bought from the Indians for the equivalent of $24 in trinkets. As you probably know, it is worth considerably more than that today.

In the program that follows each input card is punched in the first 4 columns with a year subsequent to 1627. A rate of interest is punched in columns 10–15 in 9V99999 format. The idea of the program is to calculate the final amount that the original $24, invested in 1627, would have become if the $24 had been invested at the specified rate and compounded annually through whatever year is punched. There are 2 basic methods for calculating this. In the first, the interest accrued each year can be added to the original $24. When calculating the interest for the following year, the new principal becomes the previous principal plus the accrued interest. This procedure is then repeated (PERFORMed) for each successive year until the final year, as punched on the data card, is reached. This approach may be regarded as the brute-force method. A more elegant and direct way to compute the final principal is to resort to the customary compound interest formula, which is:

$$S = P(1 + r)^n$$

where

P is the original $24
r is the rate of interest (for example, 03650 = 3.65%)
n is the number of years the investment is compounded annually.

In theory, the final values calculated by the brute-force and formula methods should be the same, but in practice, these can differ considerably. One of the purposes of presenting this particular problem is to alert the reader to the inconsistencies that can result when working with financial problems. These inconsistencies can be minimized by taking advantage of the ROUNDED option. The formula method is far quicker as well as more reliable.

This program also introduces us to several features that have not yet been illustrated in preceding programs. One is that, unlike data-names and PROGRAM-ID names, paragraph names in the Procedure Division (procedure names) may be completely numeric. For example, the main-line procedure is labeled 100, followed by 200, which opens the files, and so on. There is a certain utility to such an idea because by presenting the numeric procedure names in sequence, it is much easier to locate them when they are referenced. However, a number is just a number; it has no descriptive meaning to someone who is reading the main-line routine, which really acts as a table of contents for the program as a whole. After all, COBOL is deliberately designed to be self-documenting. A better idea therefore, especially for programs considerably longer than those illustrated in this text, is to combine a number with some meaningful name such as:

100-MAIN-LINE-ROUTINE, 200-OPEN-FILES, ETC.

In procedure 300 a test of ANY-MORE-CARDS is made to determine whether to proceed. If it contains the literal 'YES', procedure 800 is performed, which has the effect of adding 1 to the page count (it was initialized to zero in the Working-Storage Section). We now come across a new version of the ACCEPT.

The ACCEPT FROM Statement

We encountered the ACCEPT verb very early on in the text. It was used to "read" a record. Now we are using it for a totally different purpose, one that is provided only by the 1974 compiler. Its format is:

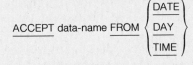

ACCEPT data-name FROM { DATE / DAY / TIME }

Line 200 of the program reads:

ACCEPT DATE--WRITTEN FROM DATE

where the first of the three options is specified. DATE--WRITTEN is written with two adjacent hyphens to avoid conflict with the familiar DATE-WRITTEN that, as you know, is a reserved word. DATE--WRITTEN is an 01-level entry in Working-Storage and has three subordinate 02-level entries. Accessing DATE with the ACCEPT/FROM statement has the effect of moving a copy of the current date (stored within the computer) to a 6-digit numeric field as specified by the data-name used. The date is in the form YYMMDD, where YY represents the last two digits of the year; MM, the month; and DD, the day. The value of YY will therefore be moved to the 02-level entry YEAR, MM to MONTH, and DD to DAAY, which is deliberately misspelled to avoid conflict with the second option, DAY, which we will illustrate later. The current date is moved to the second line of the printed report.

On IBM systems the current date is stored in a special 8-character register. It may be accessed only by a MOVE. The format of CURRENT-DATE (a reserved word on IBM systems with this option) is MM/DD/YY, with the two slashes forming part of the field. Using CURRENT-DATE (if it is available) is therefore more convenient, but if a particular compiler has both CURRENT-DATE and ACCEPT/FROM available, it would be wise to use only the latter because this is the official 1974 standard option.

The PERFORM... VARYING Statement

Doubtless, in COBOL the PERFORM statement with all its various forms is a veritable workhorse. Now we will use yet another version of it. Procedure 600 multiplies the original principal of $24 by the interest (rounded) and adds the interest to the principal. The same is done to another copy of the original $24, this time without rounding the result of the multiplication. The unrounded result is then added to the original principal. This process is repeated for each year of the investment, starting from 1627.

This may be done by a form of the PERFORM that reads:

PERFORM procedure-name VARYING data-name-1 FROM data-name-2 BY data-name-3 UNTIL condition

So that we could write:

PERFORM 600 VARYING KOUNT FROM 1627 BY 1 UNTIL KOUNT > YEAR-IN

When the condition is satisfied the loop will have been performed the correct number of times, placing the compounded (rounded) amount in ARITHMETIC-1 and the unrounded result in ARITHMETIC-2.

In procedure 700 the formula method is used, again using the ROUNDED option the first time and without it, the second. (Note there is no UNROUNDED option—the ROUNDED option is merely omitted.)

Also of interest is the fact that there are no 77-level items in Program 17. All independent items that ordinarily would have been written as 77-level items are part of a separate record description with the 01-level entry INDEPENDENT-ITEMS-USED, whose series of 02-level items act as a "catch-all" for all the independent items. If there were more of them, these could be placed in alphabetical order as an added refinement. Today many COBOL shops prefer collecting independent items in this way—or even assigning to each one a separate 01-level entry, together with its PICTURE and VALUE clause, if needed.

Once procedure 400 has been performed the full number of times, as specified by the PERFORM VARYING, all the moves to the detail-line will have been made, including the interest rate, multiplied by 100, so that it can be expressed as a percentage. The output is a little more decorative than previous ones and it is headed by a printout of the current date. No more than 15 cases are printed per page. Notice the discrepancies between the results that are produced. In case number 12 there is a difference of about $15 million.

Input for Program 17

YEAR	RATE OF INTEREST 9V99999
1933	003650
1628	010000
1776	005100
1812	004500
1865	005250
1876	003575
1900	006000
1927	002500
1945	003750
1960	005000
1972	004500
1980	004750
1981	003250
1975	002550
1700	005220
1800	004200
1914	002000
1850	001500

Program 17

```
1       IDENTIFICATION DIVISION.
2       PROGRAM-ID. MANHATTAN.
3       AUTHOR. IRVIN POREMBA.
```

```
4       INSTALLATION. NYU.
5       DATE-WRITTEN. JULY 1, 1982.
6       DATE-COMPILED. JULY 1, 1982.
7       SECURITY. HENRY MULLISH.
8       * * * * * * * * * * * * * * * * * * * * * * * * * * * * * * * * * * * * * * * * *
9       *      THIS PROGRAM PRINTS OUT THE VALUE OF                              *
10      *      MANHATTAN ISLAND AT THE END OF A GIVEN YEAR                       *
11      *      USING FOUR VALUES: COMPUTE AND THE ARITHMETIC                     *
12      *      VERBS BOTH WITH AND WITHOUT THE ROUNDED OPTION.                   *
13      *      THE DATA CARDS ARE PUNCHED:                                       *
14      *                                                                        *
15      *      COLUMNS  1-4: A YEAR AFTER 1627 PICTURE 9(04)                     *
16      *      COLUMNS 10-15: RATE OF INTEREST PICTURE 9V9(05)                   *
17      *                                                                        *
18      *      ORIGINAL VALUE OF MANHATTAN IN 1627 WAS $24                       *
19      * * * * * * * * * * * * * * * * * * * * * * * * * * * * * * * * * * * * * * * * *
20
21      ENVIRONMENT DIVISION.
22      CONFIGURATION SECTION.
23      SOURCE-COMPUTER. CYBER-170-720.
24      OBJECT-COMPUTER. CYBER-170-720.
25      SPECIAL-NAMES.
26      INPUT-OUTPUT SECTION.
27      FILE-CONTROL.
28          SELECT IN-FILE ASSIGN TO INPUT.
29          SLECT OUT-FILE ASSIGN TO OUTPUT.
30
31      DATA  DIVISION.
32      FILE SECTION.
33
34      FD   IN-FILE
35          LABEL RECORDS ARE OMITTED.
36
37      01   RECORD-IN.
38          02   YEAR-IN           PIC 9(04).
39          02   FILLER            PIC X(05).
40          02   INTEREST-IN       PIC 9V9(05).
41          02   FILLER            PIC X(65).
42
43      FD   OUT-FILE
44          LABEL RECORDS ARE OMITTED.
45
46      01   LINE-OUT              PIC X(133).
47
48      WORKING-STORAGE SECTION.
49
50      01   INDEPENDENT-ITEMS-USED.
51          02   PAGE-COUNT        PIC 9999 VALUE ZERO.
52          02   ANY-MORE-CARDS    PIC X(03) VALUE 'YES'.
53          02   INTEREST-ACC-1    PIC 9(11)V99.
54          02   INTEREST-ACC-2    PIC 9(11)V9(06).
55          02   ARITHMETIC-1      PIC 9(12)V9(06).
56          02   ARITHMETIC-2      PIC 9(12)V9(06).
57          02   COMPUTE-1         PIC 9(12)V99.
58          02   COMPUTE-2         PIC 9(12)V9(06).
59          02   CARD-COUNT        PIC 9999 VALUE ZERO.
60          02   CARD-COUNT-2      PIC 99 VALUE ZERO.
61          02   KOUNT             PIC 9999.
62
63      01   DATE--WRITTEN.
64          02   YEAR              PIC 99.
65          02   MONTH             PIC 99.
66          02   DAAY              PIC 99.
67
68      01   HEADER-1.
69          02   FILLER            PIC X(45) VALUE SPACES.
70          02   FILLER            PIC X(10) VALUE 'MANHATTAN'.
71          02   FILLER            PIC X(06) VALUE 'ISLAND'.
72          02   FILLER            PIC X(01) VALUE QUOTE.
73          02   FILLER            PIC X(08) VALUE 'S VALUES'.
74
75      01   HEADER-2.
76          02   FILLER            PIC X(09) VALUE 'PAGE'.
77          02   PAGE-COUNT-OUT    PIC ZZZ9.
78          02   FILLER            PIC X(34) VALUE SPACES.
79          02   FILLER            PIC X(13) VALUE 'REPORT DATED'.
```

```
80          02    MONTH-OUT         PIC 99.
81          02    FILLER            PIC X(01) VALUE '/'.
82          02    DAY-OUT           PIC 99.
83          02    FILLER            PIC X(01) VALUE '/'.
84          02    YEAR-OUT-2        PIC 99.
85
86    01    HEADER-3.
87          02    FILLER            PIC X(04) VALUES SPACES.
88          02    FILLER            PIC X(09) VALUE ALL '*'.
89          02    FILLER            PIC X(32) VALUE SPACES.
90          02    FILLER            PIC X(25) VALUE ALL '*'.
91
92    01    HEADER-4.
93          02    FILLER            PIC X(04) VALUE SPACES.
94          02    FILLER            PIC X(107) VALUE ALL '*'.
95
96    01    HEADER-5.
97          02    FILLER            PIC X(04) VALUE SPACES.
98          02    FILLER            PIC X(11) VALUE '*CARD*'.
99          02    FILLER            PIC X(15) VALUE 'YEAR *INTEREST'.
100         02    FILLER            PIC X(14) VALUE '*ARITHMETIC'.
101         02    FILLER            PIC X(09) VALUE 'VERB *'.
102         02    FILLER            PIC X(17) VALUE 'ARITHMETIC VERB'.
103         02    FILLER            PIC X(10) VALUE '* USING'.
104         02    FILLER            PIC X(14) VALUE 'COMPUTE*'.
105         02    FILLER            PIC X(17) VALUE 'USING COMPUTE*'.
106
107   01    HEADER-6.
108         02    FILLER            PIC X(04) VALUE SPACES.
109         02    FILLER            PIC X(11) VALUE '*COUNT*'.
110         02    FILLER            PIC X(08) VALUE 'END*'.
111         02    FILLER            PIC X(14) VALUE 'RATE*'.
112         02    FILLER            PIC X(13) VALUE 'ROUNDED'.
113         02    FILLER            PIC X(20) VALUE '*UNROUNDED'.
114         02    FILLER            PIC X(20) VALUE '*ROUNDED'.
115         02    FILLER            PIC X(20) VALUE '*UNROUNDED'.
116         02    FILLER            PIC X(01) VALUE '*'.
117
118   01    DETAIL-LINE.
119         02    FILLER            PIC X(06) VALUE '*'.
120         02    CARD-COUNT-OUT    PIC Z,ZZ9.
121         02    FILLER            PIC X(04) VALUE '*'.
122         02    YEAR-OUT          PIC 9999.
123         02    FILLER            PIC X(03) VALUE '*'.
124         02    INTEREST-OUT      PIC Z9.999.
125         02    FILLER            PIC X(04) VALUE '%*'.
126         02    ARITHMETIC-1-OUT  PIC $$$$,$$$,$$$,$$9.
127         02    FILLER            PIC X(04) VALUE '*'.
128         02    ARITHMETIC-2-OUT  PIC $$$$,$$$,$$$,$$9.
129         02    FILLER            PIC X(04) VALUE '*'.
130         02    COMPUTE-1-OUT     PIC $$$$,$$$,$$$,$$9.
131         02    FILLER            PIC X(04) VALUE '*'.
132         02    COMPUTE-2-OUT     PIC $$$$,$$$,$$$,$$9.
133         02    FILLER            PIC X(03) VALUE '*'.
134
135   PROCEDURE DIVISION.
136
137   100.
138         PERFORM 200.
139         PERFORM 250.
140         PERFORM 300.
141         PERFORM 400 UNTIL ANY-MORE-CARDS EQUAL 'NO'.
142         PERFORM 500.
143         STOP RUN.
144
145   200.
146         OPEN INPUT IN-FILE.
147         OPEN OUTPUT OUT-FILE.
148
149   250.
150         MOVE SPACES TO LINE-OUT.
151         WRITE LINE-OUT AFTER PAGE.
152
153   300.
154         READ IN-FILE AT END MOVE 'NO' TO ANY-MORE-CARDS
155             MOVE ' **NO DATA IN DECK**' TO LINE-OUT
```

```
156              WRITE LINE-OUT AFTER 30.
157              IF ANY-MORE-CARDS EQUAL 'YES' PERFORM 800.
158
159     400.
160              ADD 1 TO CARD-COUNT.
161              ADD 1 TO CARD-COUNT-2.
162              MOVE 24 TO ARITHMETIC-1, ARITHMETIC-2.
163              PERFORM 600 VARYING KOUNT FROM 1627 BY 1
164                  UNTIL KOUNT > YEAR-IN.
165              PERFORM 700.
166              MOVE CARD-COUNT TO CARD-COUNT-OUT.
167              MOVE YEAR-IN TO YEAR-OUT.
168              MULTIPLY 100 BY INTEREST-IN GIVING INTEREST-OUT.
169              MOVE ARITHMETIC-1 TO ARITHMETIC-1-OUT.
170              MOVE ARITHMETIC-2 TO ARITHMETIC-2-OUT.
171              MOVE COMPUTE-1 TO COMPUTE-1-OUT.
172              MOVE COMPUTE-2 TO COMPUTE-2-OUT.
173              WRITE LINE-OUT FROM DETAIL-LINE AFTER 1.
174              WRITE LINE-OUT FROM HEADER-4 AFTER 1.
175              READ IN-FILE AT END MOVE 'NO' TO ANY-MORE CARDS
176                  MOVE ZEROS TO CARD-COUNT-2.
177              IF CARD-COUNT-2 EQUAL 15 MOVE ZEROS TO CARD-COUNT-2
178                  PERFORM 250
179                  PERFORM 800.
180
181     500.
182              CLOSE IN-FILE, OUT-FILE.
183
184     600.
185              MULTIPLY ARITHMETIC-1 BY INTEREST-IN GIVING
186                  INTEREST-ACC-1 ROUNDED.
187              ADD INTEREST-ACC-1 TO ARITHMETIC-1.
188              MULTIPLY ARITHMETIC-2 BY INTEREST-IN GIVING
189                  INTEREST-ACC-2 ON SIZE ERROR DISPLAY 'FIELD TOO SMALL'.
190              ADD INTEREST-ACC-2 TO ARITHMETIC-2.
191
192     700.
193              SUBTRACT 1627 FROM YEAR-IN GIVING KOUNT.
194              COMPUTE COMPUTE-1 ROUNDED = 24*(1 + INTEREST-IN)**KOUNT.
195              COMPUTE COMPUTE-2 = 24*(1 + INTEREST-IN)**KOUNT.
196
197     800.
198              ADD 1 TO PAGE-COUNT.
199              MOVE PAGE-COUNT TO PAGE-COUNT-OUT.
200              ACCEPT DATE -- WRITTEN FROM DATE.
201              MOVE YEAR TO YEAR-OUT-2.
202              MOVE DAAY TO DAY-OUT.
203              MOVE MONTH TO MONTH-OUT.
204              WRITE LINE-OUT FROM HEADER-1 AFTER 1.
205              WRITE LINE-OUT FROM HEADER-2 AFTER 1.
206              WRITE LINE-OUT FROM HEADER-3 AFTER 1.
207              WRITE LINE-OUT FROM HEADER-3 AFTER 1.
208              WRITE LINE-OUT FROM HEADER-4 AFTER 2.
209              WRITE LINE-OUT FROM HEADER-5 AFTER 1.
210              WRITE LINE-OUT FROM HEADER-6 AFTER 1.
211              WRITE LINE-OUT FROM HEADER-4 AFTER 1.
```

Output for Program 17

```
                                   MANHATTAN ISLAND'S VALUES
      PAGE 1                        REPORT DATED 03/31/82
* * * * * * * *
* * * * * * * * *              * * * * * * * * * * * * * * * * * * * * * * *
                               * * * * * * * * * * * * * * * * * * * * * * *
* * * * * * * * * * * * * * * * * * * * * * * * * * * * * * * * * * * * * * * * * * * * *
*  CARD    *  YEAR  * INTEREST * ARITHMETIC VERB * ARITHMETIC VERB * USING COMPUTE * USING COMPUTE *
*  COUNT   *  END   *  RATE    *    ROUNDED      *    UNROUNDED    *    ROUNDED    *   UNROUNDED   *
* * * * * * * * * * * * * * * * * * * * * * * * * * * * * * * * * * * * * * * * * * * *
*    1     *  1933  *  3.650%  *   $1,446,522    *   $1,445,400    *  $1,394,501   *  $1,394,501   *
* * * * * * * * * * * * * * * * * * * * * * * * * * * * * * * * * * * * * * * * * * * *
*    2     *  1628  * 10.000%  *       $29       *       $29       *      $26      *      $26      *
* * * * * * * * * * * * * * * * * * * * * * * * * * * * * * * * * * * * * * * * * * * *
*    3     *  1776  *  5.100%  *     $41,726     *     $41,746     *    $39,720    *    $39,720    *
* * * * * * * * * * * * * * * * * * * * * * * * * * * * * * * * * * * * * * * * * * * *
*    4     *  1812  *  4.500%  *     $86,285     *     $86,266     *    $82,551    *    $82,551    *
```

	CARD COUNT		YEAR END		INTEREST RATE		ARITHMETIC VERB ROUNDED		ARITHMETIC VERB UNROUNDED		USING COMPUTE ROUNDED		USING COMPUTE UNROUNDED	
*	5	*	1865	*	5.250%	*	$4,914,692	*	$4,912,403	*	$4,667,368	*	$4,667,368	*
*	6	*	1876	*	3.575%	*	$156,256	*	$156,295	*	$150,900	*	$150,900	*
*	7	*	1900	*	6.000%	*	$206,134,085	*	$206,071,628	*	$194,407,250	*	$194,407,250	*
*	8	*	1927	*	2.500%	*	$40,570	*	$40,559	*	$39,570	*	$39,570	*
*	9	*	1945	*	3.750%	*	$3,022,230	*	$3,022,850	*	$2,913,592	*	$2,913,592	*
*	10	*	1960	*	5.000%	*	$286,639,278	*	$286,706,135	*	$273,053,553	*	$273,053,553	*
*	11	*	1972	*	4.500%	*	$98,752,090	*	$98,729,640	*	$94,478,164	*	$94,478,164	*
*	12	*	1980	*	4.750%	*	$327,008,350	*	$327,143,483	*	$312,308,935	*	$312,308,935	*
*	13	*	1981	*	3.250%	*	$2,048,342	*	$2,047,304	*	$1,982,862	*	$1,982,862	*
*	14	*	1975	*	2.550%	*	$157,406	*	$157,310	*	$153,399	*	$153,399	*
*	15	*	1700	*	5.220%	*	$1,036	*	$1,036	*	$984	*	$984	*

PAGE 2

MANHATTAN ISLAND'S VALUES
REPORT DATED 03/31/82

	CARD COUNT		YEAR END		INTEREST RATE		ARITHMETIC VERB ROUNDED		ARITHMETIC VERB UNROUNDED		USING COMPUTE ROUNDED		USING COMPUTE UNROUNDED	
*	16	*	1800	*	4.200%	*	$30,830	*	$30,845	*	$29,602	*	$29,602	*
*	17	*	1914	*	2.000%	*	$7,195	*	$7,195	*	$7,054	*	$7,054	*
*	18	*	1850	*	1.500%	*	$673	*	$673	*	$663	*	$663	*

8.4 Control Breaks

Each of the programs illustrated so far was only concerned with individual records of a file; no consideration was given to any relationship between records. This could easily be, however, a critical factor. Suppose, for example, that a sales report for a given set of salespeople were required and each salesperson had several entries. As soon as all the relevant information for a particular salesperson is printed, a total is required before processing the next one's data. In other words, what we want to do is to print a total-line after a group of data cards have been processed. In this example

Employee Name	Item Number	Price	Number Sold	
X(25)	9999	99V99	9999	

the total would be printed as soon as a change of the salesperson's name was detected. If this is the only criterion for printing a group total, it is called a single-level control break. More complex programs might use multilevel control breaks.

For the purpose of illustration, assume we have a deck of input cards that are punched as shown.

Input for Program 18

	ITEM #	PRICE 99V99	$ SOLD
AMY COBOL	2388	3366	0532
AMY COBOL	5322	1350	0890
AMY COBOL	1234	5730	1200
AMY COBOL	5342	1475	0055
AMY COBOL	3599	5520	2424
AMY COBOL	1230	5533	2366
AMY COBOL	1355	2000	0250
AMY COBOL	3333	1111	0055
JACK DANIELS	6425	2433	1002
JACK DANIELS	1133	1125	0357
JACK DANIELS	2369	1732	0683
JACK DANIELS	4486	1065	0056
JACK DANIELS	5321	1420	2200
JACK DANIELS	7771	4200	0300
JACK DANIELS	2536	3050	1352
JACK DANIELS	3526	1455	0035
IRVIN POREMBA	2300	0530	0053
IRVIN POREMBA	1542	1050	0123
IRVIN POREMBA	3689	2500	0230
IRVIN POREMBA	9953	1230	0356
IRVIN POREMBA	1257	2655	0258
IRVIN POREMBA	5533	3575	1200

where Amy Cobol has 8 sales recorded, Jack Daniels also has 8, and Irvin Poremba, 6.

We would like the printed report to be suitably headed, one salesperson per page, with a total sales figure for that person printed with a suitable message. At the end of the report, again on a separate page, we want to print a total sales figure for all the employees. We will therefore need 3 separate detail-lines.

In order to prepare for a control break on EMPLOYEE-NAME, we must save a copy of the employee name of the first data card read. This is done by moving EMPLOYEE-NAME to a Working-Storage area—EMPLOYEE-NAME-SAVE. A comparison is made between EMPLOYEE-NAME and EMPLOYEE-NAME-SAVE on reading the next card in sequence. If they are the same, it is not necessary to print out the name again because they are identical. Thus spaces are moved to EMPLOYEE-NAME-OUT. If, on the other hand, there is a change of name, a control break is detected. In this way each group is printed on a new page with an individual total for each salesperson.

When the AT END clause in line 156 is reached, the total sales figure is printed on a new page and the program is terminated.

Program 18

```
1    IDENTIFICATION    DIVISION.
2    PROGRAM-ID.       ABREAK.
3    AUTHOR.           IRVIN POREMBA.
4    INSTALLATION.     NYU.
5    DATE-WRITTEN.     JULY 1, 1982.
6    DATE-COMPILED.    JULY 1, 1982.
7    SECURITY.         HENRY MULLISH.
```

```
8    * * * * * * * * * * * * * * * * * * * * * * * * * * * * * * * * * * * * * * * * * * * * * * * * * *
9    *        THIS PROGRAM SHOWS THE USE OF A CONTROL BREAK                    *
10   *        TO WRITE A SALES REPORT. THE DATA CARDS ARE                      *
11   *        PUNCHED:                                                         *
12   *                                                                         *
13   *        COLUMNS  1-25: EMPLOYEE NAME                                     *
14   *        COLUMNS 30-33: ITEM NUMBER                                       *
15   *        COLUMNS 38-41: PRICE OF ITEM                                     *
16   *        COLUMNS 46-49: NUMBER OF ITEMS SOLD                              *
17   *                                                                         *
18   *        THE PROGRAM READS IN THE DATA CARDS AND PRINTS                   *
19   *        THE INFORMATION OUT UNDER A HEADING FOR EACH                     *
20   *        EMPLOYEE UNTIL THE DATA CARD HAS A NEW EMPLOYEE                   *
21   *        NAME PUNCHED ON IT. THEN A BREAK IN THE                          *
22   *        PROGRAM IS TRIGGERED PRINTING THE NEW EMPLOYEE                    *
23   *        AND THE INFORMATION ASSOCIATED WITH THE                          *
24   *        EMPLOYEE ON A NEW PAGE WITH A HEADING.                           *
25   * * * * * * * * * * * * * * * * * * * * * * * * * * * * * * * * * * * * * * * * * * * * * * * * * *
26
27   ENVIRONMENT         DIVISION.
28   CONFIGURATION       SECTION.
29   SOURCE-COMPUTER. CYBER-170-720.
30   OBJECT-COMPUTER. CYBER-170-720.
31   SPECIAL-NAMES.
32   INPUT-OUTPUT        SECTION.
33   FILE-CONTROL.
34        SELECT IN-FILE ASSIGN TO INPUT.
35        SELECT OUT-FILE ASSIGN TO OUTPUT.
36
37   DATA DIVISION.
38   FILE SECTION.
39
40   FD IN-FILE
41        LABEL RECORDS ARE OMITTED.
42
43   01   RECORD-IN.
44        02 EMPLOYEE-NAME        PIC X(25).
45        02 FILLER               PIC X(04).
46        02 ITEM-NO              PIC 9(04).
47        02 FILLER               PIC X(04).
48        02 PRICE                PIC 9(02)V9(02).
49        02 FILLER               PIC X(04).
50        02 NUMBER-SOLD          PIC 9(04).
51        02 FILLER               PIC X(31).
52
53   FD   OUT-FILE
54        LABEL RECORDS ARE OMITTED.
55
56   01   LINE-OUT                PIC X(133).
57
58   WORKING-STORAGE SECTION.
59   77   EMPLOYEE-NAME-SAVE      PIC X(25).
60   77   MORE-CARDS              PIC X(03) VALUE 'YES'.
61   77   SALES-TOTAL             PIC 9(07)V99.
62   77   EMPLOYEE-TOTAL          PIC 9(09)V99.
63   77   GRAND-TOTAL             PIC 9(11)V99 VALUE ZERO.
64
65   01   HEADER-1.
66        02 FILLER               PIC X(27) VALUE SPACES.
67        02 FILLER               PIC X(11) VALUE 'SALES'.
68        02 FILLER               PIC X(11) VALUE 'REPORT'.
69
70   01   HEADER-2.
71        02 FILLER               PIC X(27) VALUE SPACES.
72        02 FILLER               PIC X(22) VALUE ALL ' * = '.
73
74   01   HEADER-3.
75        02 FILLER               PIC X(12) VALUE SPACES.
76        02 FILLER               PIC X(08) VALUE 'EMPLOYEE'.
77        02 FILLER               PIC X(13) VALUE SPACES.
78        02 FILLER               PIC X(09) VALUE 'ITEM'.
79        02 FILLER               PIC X(10) VALUE 'PRICE'.
80        02 FILLER               PIC X(11) VALUE 'AMOUNT'.
81        02 FILLER               PIC X(12) VALUE 'TOTAL PRICE'.
```

```
82
83    01    HEADER-4.
84          02 FILLER                  PIC X(14) VALUE SPACES.
85          02 FILLER                  PIC X(04) VALUE 'NAME'.
86          02 FILLER                  PIC X(16) VALUE SPACES.
87          02 FILLER                  PIC X(14) VALUE 'NO OF ITEM'.
88          02 FILLER                  PIC X(11) VALUE 'OF ITEM'.
89          02 FILLER                  PIC X(07) VALUE SPACES.
90          02 FILLER                  PIC X(07) VALUE 'OF SALE'.
91
92    01    HEADER-5.
93          02 FILLER                  PIC X(04) VALUE SPACES.
94          02 FILLER                  PIC X(25) VALUE ALL '*'.
95          02 FILLER                  PIC X(04) VALUE SPACES.
96          02 FILLER                  PIC X(04) VALUE ALL '*'.
97          02 FILLER                  PIC X(04) VALUE SPACES.
98          02 FILLER                  PIC X(07) VALUE ALL '*'.
99          02 FILLER                  PIC X(04) VALUE SPACES.
100         02 FILLER                  PIC X(07) VALUE ALL '*'.
101         02 FILLER                  PIC X(04) VALUE SPACES.
102         02 FILLER                  PIC X(13) VALUE ALL '*'.
103
104   01    DETAIL-LINE.
105         02 FILLER                  PIC X(04) VALUE SPACES.
106         02 EMPLOYEE-NAME-OUT       PIC X(25).
107         02 FILLER                  PIC X(04) VALUE SPACES.
108         02 ITEM-NO-OUT             PIC 9(04).
109         02 FILLER                  PIC X(05) VALUE SPACES.
110         02 PRICE-OUT               PIC $$$.99.
111         02 FILLER                  PIC X(05) VALUE SPACES.
112         02 NUMBER-SOLD-OUT         PIC Z,ZZZ.
113         02 FILLER                  PIC X(05) VALUE SPACES.
114         02 SALES-TOTAL-OUT         PIC $$,$$$,$$$.99.
115
116   01    DETAIL-LINE-2.
117         02 FILLER                  PIC X(04) VALUE SPACES.
118         02 FILLER                  PIC X(09) VALUE 'EMPLOYEE'.
119         02 FILLER                  PIC X(11) VALUE 'SALES TOTAL'.
120         02 FILLER                  PIC X(05) VALUE 'IS'.
121         02 EMPLOYEE-TOTAL-OUT      PIC $$$$,$$$,$$$.99.
122
123   01    DETAIL-LINE-3.
124         02 FILLER                  PIC X(05) VALUE SPACES.
125         02 FILLER                  PIC X(12) VALUE 'TOTAL SALES'.
126         02 FILLER                  PIC X(07) VALUE 'OF ALL'.
127         02 FILLER                  PIC X(14) VALUE 'EMPLOYEES IS'.
128         02 GRAND-TOTAL-OUT         PIC $$$,$$$,$$$,$$$.99.
129
130   PROCEDURE DIVISION.
131
132   MAIN-LINE-ROUTINE.
133         PERFORM OPEN-FILES.
134         PERFORM NEW-PAGE.
135         PERFORM START-UP.
136         PERFORM PROCESS-DATA UNTIL MORE-CARDS EQUAL 'NO'.
137         PERFORM CLOSE-UP.
138         STOP RUN.
139
140   OPEN-FILES.
141         OPEN INPUT IN-FILE.
142         OPEN OUTPUT OUT-FILE.
143
144
145   NEW-PAGE.
146         MOVE SPACES TO LINE-OUT.
147         WRITE LINE-OUT AFTER PAGE.
148
149   START-UP.
150         READ IN-FILE AT END MOVE 'NO' TO MORE-CARDS
151             MOVE ' ***NO DATA IN DECK***' TO LINE-OUT
152             WRITE LINE-OUT AFTER 30.
153         IF MORE-CARDS EQUAL 'YES' PERFORM WORK-PARA.
154
155   PROCESS-DATA.
```

```
156          READ IN-FILE AT END MOVE 'NO' TO MORE-CARDS.
157          IF MORE-CARDS EQUAL 'NO' PERFORM TOTAL-PARA
158          ELSE IF EMPLOYEE-NAME EQUAL EMPLOYEE-NAME-SAVE
159                    PERFORM WORK-PARA-2
160              ELSE PERFORM EMPLOYEE-TOTAL-PARA
161                 PEFORM NEW-PAGE
162                    PERFORM WORK-PARA.
163
164      TOTAL-PARA.
165          PERFORM EMPLOYEE-TOTAL-PARA.
166            MOVE GRAND-TOTAL TO GRAND-TOTAL-OUT.
167              PERFORM NEW-PAGE.
168                WRITE LINE-OUT FROM DETAIL-LINE-3 AFTER 30.
169
170      CLOSE-UP.
171          CLOSE IN-FILE, OUT-FILE.
172
173      WORK-PARA.
174            PERFORM WRITE-HEADINGS.
175              MOVE ZEROS TO EMPLOYEE-TOTAL.
176                MOVE EMPLOYEE-NAME TO EMPLOYEE-NAME-SAVE.
177                MOVE EMPLOYEE-NAME TO EMPLOYEE-NAME-OUT.
178              MOVE ITEM-NO TO ITEM-NO-OUT.
179              MOVE PRICE TO PRICE-OUT.
180                MOVE NUMBER-SOLD TO NUMBER-SOLD-OUT.
181                  MULTIPLY NUMBER-SOLD BY PRICE GIVING SALES-TOTAL.
182              ADD SALES-TOTAL TO EMPLOYEE-TOTAL.
183                MOVE SALES-TOTAL TO SALES-TOTAL-OUT.
184                  WRITE LINE-OUT FROM DETAIL-LINE AFTER 2.
185
186      WORK-PARA-2.
187            MOVE SPACES TO EMPLOYEE-NAME-OUT.
188            MOVE ITEM-NO TO ITEM-NO-OUT.
189            MOVE PRICE TO PRICE-OUT.
190              MOVE NUMBER-SOLD TO NUMBER-SOLD-OUT.
191              MOVE PRICE TO PRICE-OUT.
192                MULTIPLY NUMBER-SOLD BY PRICE GIVING SALES-TOTAL.
193              ADD SALES-TOTAL TO EMPLOYEE-TOTAL.
194                MOVE SALES-TOTAL TO SALES-TOTAL-OUT.
195                  WRITE LINE-OUT FROM DETAIL-LINE AFTER 2.
196
197      EMPLOYEE-TOTAL-PARA.
198            ADD EMPLOYEE-TOTAL TO GRAND-TOTAL.
199            MOVE EMPLOYEE-TOTAL TO EMPLOYEE-TOTAL-OUT.
200            WRITE LINE-OUT FROM DETAIL-LINE-2 AFTER 2.
201
202      WRITE-HEADINGS,
203          WRITE LINE-OUT FROM HEADER-1 AFTER 1.
204          WRITE LINE-OUT FROM HEADER-2 AFTER 1.
205          WRITE LINE-OUT FROM HEADER-2 AFTER 1.
206            WRITE LINE-OUT FROM HEADER-3 AFTER 2.
207              WRITE LINE-OUT FROM HEADER-4 AFTER 1.
208                WRITE LINE-OUT FROM HEADER-5 AFTER 1.
```

Output for Program 18

```
                      SALES REPORT
        * = * = * = * = * = * = * = * = * = * = * = * =
        * = * = * = * = * = * = * = * = * = * = * = * =
        EMPLOYEE         ITEM      PRICE      AMOUNT      TOTAL PRICE
          NAME            NO      OF ITEM     OF ITEM       OF SALE
    * * * * * * * * * * * *   * * * *   * * * * * * *   * * * * * * *   * * * * * * * * * * * *
    AMY COBOL             2388     $33.66        532        $17,907.12
                         5322     $13.50        890        $12,015.00
                         1234     $57.30      1,200        $68,760.00
                         5342     $14.75         55           $811.25
                         3599     $55.20      2,424       $133,804.80
                         1230     $55.33      2,366       $130,910.78
                         1355     $20.00        250         $5,000.00
                         3333     $11.11         55           $611.05
    EMPLOYEE SALES TOTAL IS                  $369,820.00
```

```
                      SALES REPORT
          * = * = * = * = * = * = * = * = * = * =
          * = * = * = * = * = * = * = * = * = * =
     EMPLOYEE         ITEM      PRICE      AMOUNT      TOTAL PRICE
      NAME             NO      OF ITEM    OF ITEM       OF SALE
  * * * * * * * * * * * *    * * * *    * * * * * * *    * * * * * * *    * * * * * * * * * * * *
  JACK DANIELS        6425     $24.33      1,002       $24,378.66
                      1133     $11.25       357         $4,016.25
                      2369     $17.32       683        $11,829.56
                      4486     $10.65        56           $596.40
                      5321     $14.20      2,200       $31,240.00
                      7771     $42.00       300        $12,600.00
                      2536     $30.50      1,352       $41,236.00
                      3526     $14.55        35           $509.25
  EMPLOYEE SALES TOTAL IS                 $126,406.12
```

```
                      SALES REPORT
          * = * = * = * = * = * = * = * = * = * =
          * = * = * = * = * = * = * = * = * = * =
     EMPLOYEE         ITEM      PRICE      AMOUNT      TOTAL PRICE
      NAME             NO      OF ITEM    OF ITEM       OF SALE
  * * * * * * * * * * * *    * * * *    * * * * * * *    * * * * * * *    * * * * * * * * * * * *
  IRVIN POREMBA       2300     $5.30         53          $280.90
                      1542     $10.50       123        $1,291.50
                      3689     $25.00       230        $5,750.00
                      9953     $12.30       356        $4,378.80
                      1257     $26.55       258        $6,849.90
                      5533     $33.75      1,200       $42,900.00
  EMPLOYEE SALES TOTAL IS                 $61,451.10
```

```
  TOTAL SALES OF ALL EMPLOYEES IS            $557,677.22
```

8.5 Multilevel Control Breaks

The simplest type of control break is the kind that we have just encountered—the single-level control break. We often have to allow, however, for those situations where control breaks may occur on more than one level. For example, we might want to have control breaks for divisions of a company and within the divisions, different departments, and within the departments, different accounts.

For our next program, a sales report, the company is divided up into 4 different regions—north, south, east, and west. Within each region there is a subdivision into salespeople, according to their last name and then within that, their first name. Once again, the data is presorted as shown.

Input for Program 19

```
NORTHPOREMBA    IRVIN     035000
NORTHPOREMBA    IRVIN     007550
NORTHPOREMBA    IRVIN     012500
NORTHPOREMBA    MICHAEL   005500
NORTHPOREMBA    MICHAEL   045075
NORTHMULLISH    HENRY     025000
NORTHMULLISH    HENRY     036500
NORTHMULLISH    HENRY     012345
NORTHMULLISH    HENRY     024535
SOUTHFREEDMAN   MARC      025700
SOUTHFREEDMAN   MARC      002500
SOUTHFREEDMAN   MARC      014550
SOUTHDOYLE      PETER     023100
SOUTHDOYLE      PETER     028500
```

SOUTHDOYLE	PETER	063320
SOUTHBERGEN	CINDY	037500
SOUTHBERGEN	CINDY	120000
SOUTHBERGEN	CINDY	014575
SOUTHBERGEN	CINDY	055900
SOUTHBERGEN	CINDY	012545
WEST GREENBERG	HAROLD	032500
WEST GREENBERG	HAROLD	042500
WEST GREENBERG	HAROLD	042755
WEST GREENBERG	HAROLD	100000
EAST COHEN	BARBARA	003575
EAST COHEN	BARBARA	024500
EAST COHEN	ALAN	078500
EAST COHEN	ALAN	014250
EAST FLINT	MATT	032100
EAST FLINT	MATT	035625
EAST FLINT	JAMES	042530
EAST FLINT	JAMES	002500

As you will see, the data is grouped, beginning with those employees in the northern, southern, western, and eastern regions. Within those regions the salespeople are grouped according to the last name and for those cases where the last name is the same, according to first name.

The purpose of the program is to print out a sales report in which changes in regions causes an eject to a new page. Within a region, salespeople's names are listed. Each time there is a change in the last or first name the previous salesperson's total sales is printed out, and after skipping 4 or 5 lines (depending on whether it's a last or first name change) the succeeding salesperson's sales are listed. At the conclusion of a region the total for the region is printed out. At the termination of the report the grand total for all regions is printed out.

The only time that a region or a last or first name is printed out is at its first occurrence, thus avoiding repetition of data. The extra "white space" that is created provides for greater clarity and ease of reading.

In the previous program the technique used to prevent repetitions in printing was to place a copy of the last name in Working-Storage and to check each successive last name against that saved in Working-Storage. If no change in the last name was detected, spaces were moved to EMPLOYEE-NAME-OUT. As soon as a change was detected, the new name replaced that in Working-Storage and the name rather than spaces was moved to the detail-line. In the next program exactly the same technique is followed for a change in region, last name, and first name, in order stated.

Program 19

```
1       IDENTIFICATION      DIVISION.
2       PROGRAM-ID.         MULTICONTROL.
3       AUTHOR.             IRVIN POREMBA.
4       INSTALLATION.       NYU.
5       DATE-WRITTEN.       APRIL 19, 1982.
6       DATE-COMPILED.      APRIL 30, 1982.
7       SECURITY.           HENRY MULLISH.
8       * * * * * * * * * * * * * * * * * * * * * * * * * * * * * * * * * * * * * * * * *
9       *     THIS PROGRAM READS IN DATA CARDS PUNCHED:                              *
10      *                                                                           *
11      *     COLUMNS    1-5: REGION OF COUNTRY                                      *
12      *     COLUMNS 11-25: LAST NAME                                              *
13      *     COLUMNS 31-40: FIRST NAME                                             *
14      *     COLUMNS 45-50: AMOUNT OF SALES                                        *
15      *                                                                           *
16      *     THIS PROGRAM PRINTS OUT A SALES REPORT BY USING                       *
17      *     CONTROL BREAKS FOR REGIONS, LAST NAMES, AND                           *
18      *     FIRST NAMES. A TOTAL IS PRINTED OUT FOR EACH                          *
19      *     EMPLOYEE AND REGION. A GRAND TOTAL IS PRINTED                         *
20      *     OUT ON A NEW PAGE.                                                     *
21      * * * * * * * * * * * * * * * * * * * * * * * * * * * * * * * * * * * * * * * * *
22
```

```
23     ENVIRONMENT        DIVISION.
24     CONFIGURATION      SECTION.
25     SOURCE-COMPUTER.CYBER-170-720.
26     OBJECT-COMPUTER.CYBER-170-720.
27     SPECIAL-NAMES.
28     INPUT-OUTPUT       SECTION.
29     FILE-CONTROL.
30          SELECT IN-FILE ASSIGN TO INPUT.
31          SELECT OUT-FILE ASSIGN TO OUTPUT.
32
33     DATA DIVISION.
34     FILE SECTION.
35
36     FD    IN-FILE
37          LABEL RECORDS ARE OMITTED.
38
39     01    RECORD-IN.
40           02 REGION-IN            PIC X(05).
41           02 FILLER               PIC X(05).
42           02 LAST-NAME-IN         PIC X(15).
43           02 FILLER               PIC X(05).
44           02 FIRST-NAME-IN        PIC X(10).
45           02 FILLER               PIC X(04).
46           02 AMOUNT-IN            PIC 9(04)V9(02).
47           02 FILLER               PIC X(30).
48
49     FD    OUT-FILE
50          LABEL RECORDS ARE OMITTED.
51
52     01    LINE-OUT                PIC X(133).
53
54     WORKING-STORAGE SECTION.
55
56     01    INDEPENDENT-ITEMS-USED.
57           02 EMPLOYEE-TOTAL       PIC 9(06)V99 VALUE ZERO.
58           02 REGION-TOTAL         PIC 9(08)V99 VALUE ZERO.
59           02 GRAND-TOTAL          PIC 9(09)V99 VALUE ZERO.
60           02 ANY-MORE-CARDS       PIC X(03) VALUE 'YES'.
61           02 CARD-COUNT           PIC 9(04) VALUE ZERO.
62           02 PAGE-COUNT           PIC 9(03) VALUE ZERO.
63           02 REGION-SAVE          PIC X(05) VALUE SPACES.
64           02 LAST-NAME-SAVE       PIC X(15) VALUE SPACES.
65           02 FIRST-NAME-SAVE      PIC X(10).
66
67     01    HEADER-1.
68           02 FILLER               PIC X(01) VALUE SPACES.
69           02 FILLER               PIC X(05) VALUE 'PAGE'.
70           02 PAGE-COUNT-OUT       PIC ZZ9.
71           02 FILLER               PIC X(13) VALUE SPACES.
72           02 FILLER               PIC X(12) VALUE 'SALES REPORT'.
73
74     01    HEADER-2.
75           02 FILLER               PIC X(01) VALUE SPACES.
76           02 FILLER               PIC X(08) VALUE ALL '*'.
77           02 FILLER               PIC X(13) VALUE SPACES.
78           02 FILLER               PIC X(12) VALUE ALL '*'.
79
80     01    HEADER-3.
81           02 FILLER               PIC X(01) VALUE SPACES.
82           02 FILLER               PIC X(08) VALUE 'COUNT'.
83           02 FILLER               PIC X(12) VALUE 'REGION'.
84           02 FILLER               PIC X(15) VALUE 'LAST NAME'.
85           02 FILLER               PIC X(15) VALUE 'FIRST NAME'.
86           02 FILLER               PIC X(06) VALUE 'AMOUNT'.
87
88     01    HEADER-4.
89           02 FILLER               PIC X(01) VALUE SPACES.
90           02 FILLER               PIC X(05) VALUE ALL '*'.
91           02 FILLER               PIC X(03) VALUE SPACES.
92           02 FILLER               PIC X(06) VALUE ALL '*'.
93           02 FILLER               PIC X(03) VALUE SPACES.
94           02 FILLER               PIC X(15) VALUE ALL '*'.
95           02 FILLER               PIC X(03) VALUE SPACES.
96           02 FILLER               PIC X(10) VALUE ALL '*'.
97           02 FILLER               PIC X(03) VALUE SPACES.
```

```
98            02 FILLER                    PIC X(09) VALUE ALL ' * '.
99
100    01    HEADER-5.
101           02 FILLER                    PIC X(10) VALUE SPACES.
102           02 FILLER                    PIC X(27) VALUE ALL '-'.
103
104    01    DETAIL-LINE.
105           02 FILLER                    PIC X(01) VALUE SPACES.
106           02 CARD-COUNT-OUT            PIC Z,ZZ9.
107           02 FILLER                    PIC X(03) VALUE SPACES.
108           02 REGION-OUT                PIC X(05).
109           02 FILLER                    PIC X(04).
110           02 LAST-NAME-OUT             PIC X(15).
111           02 FILLER                    PIC X(03) VALUE SPACES.
112           02 FIRST-NAME-OUT            PIC X(10).
113           02 FILLER                    PIC X(03) VALUE SPACES.
114           02 AMOUNT-OUT                PIC $$,$$9.99.
115
116    01    DETAIL-LINE-2.
117           02 FILLER                    PIC X(20) VALUE SPACES.
118           02 FILLER                    PIC X(08) VALUE 'EMPLOYEE'.
119           02 FILLER                    PIC X(07) VALUE 'TOTAL'.
120           02 EMPLOY-TOTAL-OUT          PIC $$$$,$$9.99.
121
122    01    DETAIL-LINE-3.
123           02 FILLER                    PIC X(20) VALUE SPACES.
124           02 REGION-OUT-2              PIC X(05).
125           02 FILLER                    PIC X(06) VALUE 'TOTAL'.
126           02 FILLER                    PIC X(01) VALUE SPACES.
127           02 REGION-TOTAL-OUT          PIC $$$,$$$,$$9.99.
128
129    01    DETAIL-LINE-4.
130           02 FILLER                    PIC X(10) VALUE SPACES.
131           02 FILLER                    PIC X(11) VALUE 'GRAND TOTAL'.
132           02 FILLER                    PIC X(01) VALUE SPACES.
133           02 GRAND-TOTAL-OUT           PIC $$$$,$$$,$$9.99.
134
135    PROCEDURE DIVISION.
136
137    MAIN-LINE-ROUTINE.
138          PERFORM OPEN-FILES.
139          PERFORM NEW-PAGE.
140          PERFORM START-UP.
141          PERFORM PROCESS-DATA UNTIL ANY-MORE-CARDS EQUAL 'NO'.
142          PERFORM CLOSE-UP.
143          STOP RUN.
144
145    OPEN-FILES.
146          OPEN INPUT IN-FILE.
147          OPEN OUTPUT OUT-FILE.
148
149    NEW-PAGE.
150          MOVE SPACES TO LINE-OUT.
151          WRITE LINE-OUT AFTER PAGE.
152
153    START-UP.
154          READ IN-FILE AT END MOVE 'NO' TO ANY-MORE-CARDS
155              MOVE ' * *NO DATA IN DECK * *' TO LINE-OUT
156              WRITE LINE-OUT AFTER 30.
157          IF ANY-MORE-CARDS EQUAL 'YES' ADD 1 TO CARD-COUNT
158              PERFORM REGION-CHANGE.
159
160    PROCESS-DATA.
161          READ IN-FILE AT END PERFORM THE-GRAND-TOTAL
162              MOVE 'NO' TO ANY-MORE-CARDS.
163          IF ANY-MORE-CARDS EQUAL 'YES' PERFORM TEST-PARA.
164
165    CLOSE-UP.
166          CLOSE IN-FILE, OUT-FILE.
167
168    TEST-PARA.
169          ADD 1 TO CARD-COUNT.
170          IF REGION-IN NOT EQUAL REGION-SAVE PERFORM EMPLOY-TOTAL
171              PERFORM REGIONX-TOTAL PERFORM NEW-PAGE
172              PERFORM REGION-CHANGE
```

```
173        ELSE IF LAST-NAME-IN NOT EQUAL LAST-NAME-SAVE PERFORM
174            LAST-NAME-CHANGE
175          ELSE IF FIRST-NAME-IN NOT EQUAL FIRST-NAME-SAVE
176            PERFORM FIRST-NAME-CHANGE
177            ELSE PERFORM NO-CHANGE-NEEDED.
178
179    REGION-CHANGE.
180        PERFORM WRITE-HEADINGS.
181        MOVE REGION-IN TO REGION-SAVE.
182        MOVE LAST-NAME-IN TO LAST-NAME-SAVE.
183        MOVE FIRST-NAME-IN TO FIRST-NAME-SAVE.
184        MOVE CARD-COUNT TO CARD-COUNT-OUT.
185        MOVE REGION-IN TO REGION-OUT.
186        MOVE LAST-NAME-IN TO LAST-NAME-OUT.
187        MOVE FIRST-NAME-IN TO FIRST-NAME-OUT.
188        MOVE AMOUNT-IN TO AMOUNT-OUT.
189        ADD AMOUNT-IN TO REGION-TOTAL, EMPLOYEE-TOTAL, GRAND-TOTAL.
190        WRITE LINE-OUT FROM DETAIL-LINE AFTER 2.
191
192    LAST-NAME-CHANGE.
193        PERFORM EMPLOY-TOTAL.
194        MOVE LAST-NAME-IN TO LAST-NAME-SAVE.
195        MOVE FIRST-NAME-IN TO FIRST-NAME-SAVE.
196        MOVE CARD-COUNT TO CARD-COUNT-OUT.
197        MOVE SPACES TO REGION-OUT.
198        MOVE LAST-NAME-IN TO LAST-NAME-OUT.
199        MOVE FIRST-NAME-IN TO FIRST-NAME-OUT.
200        MOVE AMOUNT-IN TO AMOUNT-OUT.
201        ADD AMOUNT-IN TO EMPLOYEE-TOTAL, REGION-TOTAL, GRAND-TOTAL.
202        WRITE LINE-OUT FROM DETAIL-LINE AFTER 5.
203
204    FIRST-NAME-CHANGE.
205        PERFORM EMPLOY-TOTAL.
206        MOVE FIRST-NAME-IN TO FIRST-NAME-SAVE.
207        MOVE CARD-COUNT TO CARD-COUNT-OUT.
208        MOVE SPACES TO REGION-OUT, LAST-NAME-OUT.
209        MOVE FIRST-NAME-IN TO FIRST-NAME-OUT.
210        MOVE AMOUNT-IN TO AMOUNT-OUT.
211        ADD AMOUNT-IN TO REGION-TOTAL, EMPLOYEE-TOTAL, GRAND-TOTAL.
212        WRITE LINE-OUT FROM DETAIL-LINE AFTER 4.
213
214    NO-CHANGE-NEEDED.
215        MOVE CARD-COUNT TO CARD-COUNT-OUT.
216        MOVE SPACES TO REGION-OUT, LAST-NAME-OUT, FIRST NAME-OUT.
217        MOVE AMOUNT-IN TO AMOUNT-OUT.
218        ADD AMOUNT-IN TO REGION-TOTAL, EMPLOYEE-TOTAL, GRAND-TOTAL.
219        WRITE LINE-OUT FROM DETAIL-LINE AFTER 2.
220
221    EMPLOY-TOTAL.
222        MOVE EMPLOYEE-TOTAL TO EMPLOY-TOTAL-OUT.
223        WRITE LINE-OUT FROM DETAIL-LINE-2 AFTER 2.
224        MOVE ZEROS TO EMPLOYEE-TOTAL.
225
226    REGIONX-TOTAL.
227        MOVE REGION-SAVE TO REGION-OUT-2.
228        MOVE REGION-TOTAL TO REGION-TOTAL-OUT.
229        WRITE LINE-OUT FROM DETAIL-LINE-3 AFTER 3.
230        MOVE ZEROS TO REGION-TOTAL.
231
232    THE-GRAND-TOTAL.
233        PERFORM EMPLOY-TOTAL.
234        PERFORM REGIONX-TOTAL.
235        PERFORM NEW-PAGE.
236        MOVE GRAND-TOTAL TO GRAND-TOTAL-OUT.
237        WRITE LINE-OUT FROM DETAIL-LINE-4 AFTER 30.
238        WRITE LINE-OUT FROM HEADER-5 AFTER 0.
239
240    WRITE-HEADINGS.
241        ADD 1 TO PAGE-COUNT.
242        MOVE PAGE-COUNT TO PAGE-COUNT-OUT.
243        WRITE LINE-OUT FROM HEADER-1 AFTER 1.
244        WRITE LINE-OUT FROM HEADER-2 AFTER 1.
245        WRITE LINE-OUT FROM HEADER-2 AFTER 1.
246        WRITE LINE-OUT FROM HEADER-3 AFTER 2.
247        WRITE LINE-OUT FROM HEADER-4 AFTER 1.
```

Output for Program 19

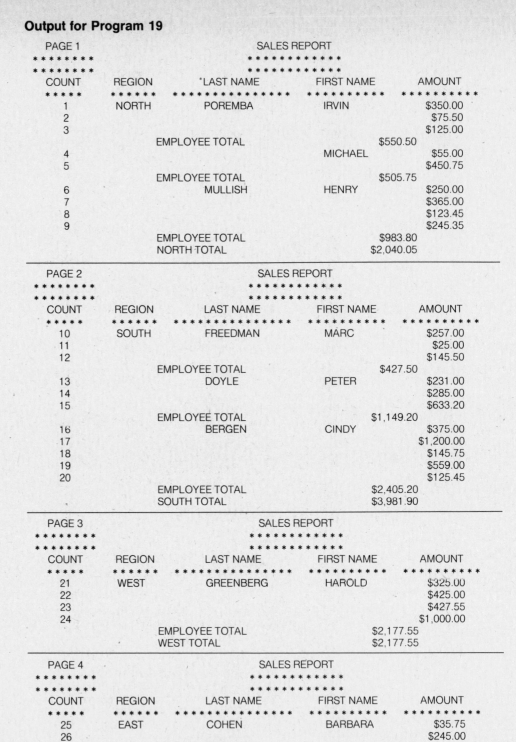

PAGE 1   SALES REPORT
* * * * * * *   * * * * * * * * * * *
* * * * * * *   * * * * * * * * * * *
COUNT   REGION   LAST NAME   FIRST NAME   AMOUNT
* * * * *   * * * * * *   * * * * * * * * * * * * *   * * * * * * * * *   * * * * * * * * * *
1   NORTH   POREMBA   IRVIN $350.00
2 $75.50
3 $125.00
            EMPLOYEE TOTAL $550.50
4   MICHAEL $55.00
5 $450.75
            EMPLOYEE TOTAL $505.75
6   MULLISH   HENRY $250.00
7 $365.00
8 $123.45
9 $245.35
            EMPLOYEE TOTAL $983.80
            NORTH TOTAL $2,040.05

PAGE 2   SALES REPORT
* * * * * * *   * * * * * * * * * * *
* * * * * * *   * * * * * * * * * * *
COUNT   REGION   LAST NAME   FIRST NAME   AMOUNT
* * * * *   * * * * * *   * * * * * * * * * * * * *   * * * * * * * * *   * * * * * * * * * *
10   SOUTH   FREEDMAN   MARC $257.00
11 $25.00
12 $145.50
            EMPLOYEE TOTAL $427.50
13   DOYLE   PETER $231.00
14 $285.00
15 $633.20
            EMPLOYEE TOTAL $1,149.20
16   BERGEN   CINDY $375.00
17 $1,200.00
18 $145.75
19 $559.00
20 $125.45
            EMPLOYEE TOTAL $2,405.20
            SOUTH TOTAL $3,981.90

PAGE 3   SALES REPORT
* * * * * * *   * * * * * * * * * * *
* * * * * * *   * * * * * * * * * * *
COUNT   REGION   LAST NAME   FIRST NAME   AMOUNT
* * * * *   * * * * * *   * * * * * * * * * * * * *   * * * * * * * * *   * * * * * * * * * *
21   WEST   GREENBERG   HAROLD $325.00
22 $425.00
23 $427.55
24 $1,000.00
            EMPLOYEE TOTAL $2,177.55
            WEST TOTAL $2,177.55

PAGE 4   SALES REPORT
* * * * * * *   * * * * * * * * * * *
* * * * * * *   * * * * * * * * * * *
COUNT   REGION   LAST NAME   FIRST NAME   AMOUNT
* * * * *   * * * * * *   * * * * * * * * * * * * *   * * * * * * * * *   * * * * * * * * * *
25   EAST   COHEN   BARBARA $35.75
26 $245.00
            EMPLOYEE TOTAL $280.75
27   ALAN $785.00
28 $142.50
            EMPLOYEE TOTAL $927.50
29   FLINT   MATT $321.00
30 $356.25
            EMPLOYEE TOTAL $677.25
31   JAMES $425.30
32 $25.00
            EMPLOYEE TOTAL $450.30
            EAST TOTAL $2,335.80

            GRAND TOTAL $10,535.30

8.6 More on the ACCEPT FROM Statement

The purpose of the next program is to exploit fully the use of the ACCEPT FROM statement. As you may recall, the ACCEPT FROM statement allows you to access the time, day, and date from the computer. In Program 17 we illustrated how the date only could be accessed, but in the next program we will utilize all 3 options. Here again is the format of the statement.

$$\underline{\text{ACCEPT}} \text{ data-name } \underline{\text{FROM}} \left\{ \begin{array}{l} \underline{\text{DATE}} \\ \underline{\text{DAY}} \\ \underline{\text{TIME}} \end{array} \right\}$$

You can see at a glance that the words ACCEPT, FROM, DATE, DAY, and TIME are all reserved words; they can be used only in the special contexts for which they are intended. This version of the ACCEPT is not present in pre-1974 compilers so you should not try to use it unless the compiler that you are using conforms to the 1974 standard.

As already shown, the ACCEPT data-name FROM DATE (by far the most frequently accessed of the 3 options) moves the date in the form of YYMMDD to a 6-digit numeric field. If the format YYMMDD is not acceptable to you (and will probably not be for printing reports), you will have to move the individual items to appropriate fields, as we have done. The date is in this possibly strange format because when presented in this way a direct arithmetic comparison may be made between one date and another. For example, the date 811215 clearly precedes the date 820101, simply because the "number" 811215 is less than 820101. Therefore it is easy within a program to determine if, say, a payment is overdue.

In the paragraph PROCESS-DATA the first instruction is:

ACCEPT DAAY FROM DAY.

The reason for the peculiar spelling DAAY is that whatever data-name is selected it must not be a reserved word. Because DAAY resembles DAY but is not the same and is not itself a reserved word, it is quite acceptable.

DAAY is an 02-level item with an unsigned numeric PICTURE of 9(05). When DAY is accessed by the ACCEPT FROM statement it returns a 5-digit number in the format YYDDD, where YY represents the last 2 digits of the year and DDD is the sequential day number of the year. For example, the date October 30, 1982 would be accessed as 82303 because October 30th is the 303rd day of 1982.

The second instruction is:

ACCEPT TI-ME FROM TIME.

Accessing TIME with the ACCEPT FROM statement moves the current time to a field that must have a PICTURE 9(08). It is in the form HHMMSSCC, where HH is the hour (based on the 24-hour clock); that is, HH may vary from 0 to 23. MM is the minutes, ranging from 0 to 59, SS is the seconds, again ranging from 0 to 59, and CC is the number of hundredths of seconds, going from 0 to 99.

Notice that when DAAY is moved to DAY-OUT in the detail-line, the receiving field is not 99999 but rather, 99/999, where the slash has been inserted. The ability to use the slash as an insertion symbol in edited fields is new. It has been implemented in the 1974 standard only. The slash may be inserted in both a numeric and an alphanumeric field.

In DETAIL-LINE-2, recourse to the slash as an editing symbol has been made in the printing of TIME-OUT, where the editing field has 3 slashes inserted.

Because there is no input to this program, no input data is illustrated or is there a need for an input file in the program.

Program 20

```
1        IDENTIFICATION      DIVISION.
2        PROGRAM-ID.         THEACCEPT.
3        AUTHOR.             IRVIN POREMBA.
4        INSTALLATION.       NYU.
5        DATE-WRITTEN.       APRIL 19, 1981.
6        DATE-COMPILED.      APRIL 24, 1981.
7        SECURITY.           HENRY MULLISH.
8     * * * * * * * * * * * * * * * * * * * * * * * * * * * * * * * * * * * * * * * * *
9     *      THIS PROGRAM SHOWS THE USES OF THE ACCEPT VERB              *
10    *      TO RETRIEVE THE DATE, JULIAN DAY AND THE TIME               *
11    *      FROM THE COMPUTER. NOTE THAT THERE IS ONLY AN               *
12    *      OUTPUT FILE.                                                *
13    * * * * * * * * * * * * * * * * * * * * * * * * * * * * * * * * * * * * * * * * *
14
15       ENVIRONMENT         DIVISION.
16       CONFIGURATION       SECTION.
17       SOURCE-COMPUTER.    CYBER-170-720.
18       OBJECT-COMPUTER.    CYBER-170-720.
19       SPECIAL-NAMES.
20       INPUT-OUTPUT        SECTION.
21       FILE-CONTROL.
22           SELECT OUT-FILE ASSIGN TO OUTPUT.
23
24       DATA DIVISION.
25       FILE SECTION.
26
27       FD   OUT-FILE
28            LABEL RECORDS ARE OMITTED.
29
30       01   LINE-OUT                 PIC X(133).
31
32       WORKING-STORAGE SECTION.
33
34       01   ITEMS-USED.
35            02 DAAY                  PIC 9(05).
36            02 TI-ME                 PIC 9(08).
37            02 DATE--WRITTEN.
38               03 YEAR               PIC 9(02).
39               03 MONTH              PIC 9(02).
40               03 DA-Y               PIC 9(02).
41
42       01   HEADER-1.
43            02 FILLER                PIC X(10) VALUE SPACES.
44            02 FILLER                PIC X(14) VALUE 'USES OF ACCEPT'.
45
46       01   HEADER-2.
47            02 FILLER                PIC X(10) VALUE SPACES.
48            02 FILLER                PIC X(14) VALUE ALL ' * '.
49
50       01   DETAIL-LINE.
51            02 FILLER                PIC X(10) VALUE SPACES.
52            02 FILLER                PIC X(05) VALUE 'TODAY'.
53            02 FILLER                PIC X(01) VALUE QUOTE.
54            02 FILLER                PIC X(14) VALUE 'S DATE IN THE'.
55            02 FILLER                PIC X(16) VALUE 'JULIAN CALENDAR'.
56            02 FILLER                PIC X(03) VALUE 'IS'.
57            02 DAAY-OUT              PIC 99/999.
58
59       01   DETAIL-LINE-2.
60            02 FILLER                PIC X(10) VALUE SPACES.
61            02 FILLER                PIC X(13) VALUE 'THE TIME NOW'.
62            02 FILLER                PIC X(06) VALUE 'IS:'.
63            02 TIME-OUT              PIC 99/99/99/99.
64
65       01   DETAIL-LINE-3.
66            02 FILLER                PIC X(10) VALUE SPACES.
67            02 FILLER                PIC X(05) VALUE 'TODAY'.
68            02 FILLER                PIC X(01) VALUE QUOTE.
69            02 FILLER                PIC X(12) VALUE 'S DATE IS:'.
70            02 DATE-OUT.
71               03  MONTH-OUT         PIC 99.
72               03  FILLER            PIC X(01) VALUE '/'.
```

```
73              03  DAY-OUT          PIC 99.
74              03  FILLER           PIC X(01) VALUE '/'.
75              03  YEAR-OUT         PIC 99.
76
77      PROCEDURE DIVISION.
78      MAIN-LINE-ROUTINE.
79          PERFORM OPEN-FILE.
80          PERFORM NEW-PAGE.
81          PERFORM START-UP.
82          PERFORM PROCESS-DATA.
83          PERFORM CLOSE-UP.
84          STOP RUN.
85
86      OPEN-FILE.
87          OPEN OUTPUT OUT-FILE.
88
89      NEW-PAGE.
90          MOVE SPACES TO LINE-OUT.
91          WRITE LINE-OUT AFTER PAGE.
92
93      START-UP.
94          WRITE LINE-OUT FROM HEADER-1 AFTER 1.
95          WRITE LINE-OUT FROM HEADER-2 AFTER 1.
96          WRITE LINE-OUT FROM HEADER-2 AFTER 1.
97
98      PROCESS-DATA.
99          ACCEPT DAAY FROM DAY.
100         ACCEPT TI-ME FROM TIME.
101         ACCEPT DATE--WRITTEN FROM DATE.
102         MOVE DAAY TO DAAY-OUT.
103         MOVE TI-ME TO TIME-OUT.
104         MOVE MONTH TO MONTH-OUT.
105         MOVE DA-Y TO DAY-OUT.
106         MOVE YEAR TO YEAR-OUT.
107         WRITE LINE-OUT FROM DETAIL-LINE AFTER 2.
108         WRITE LINE-OUT FROM DETAIL-LINE-2 AFTER 2.
109         WRITE LINE-OUT FROM DETAIL-LINE-3 AFTER 2.
110
111     CLOSE-UP.
112         CLOSE OUT-FILE.
```

Output for Program 20

```
USES OF ACCEPT
* * * * * * * * * * * * *
* * * * * * * * * * * * *
TODAY'S DATE IN THE JULIAN CALENDAR IS 81/114
THE TIME NOW IS:15/14/50/00
TODAY'S DATE IS: 04/24/81
```

Review Questions

1. What is the purpose of the REDEFINES clause?
2. May the area of a REDEFINES and the redefined area be of unequal length?
3. Must the REDEFINES clause have the same level number as that item being redefined?
4. Is it permissible for paragraph names in the Procedure Division to be composed only of digits?
5. If the date is December 25, 1983, what would be the result of executing the instruction:

   ACCEPT QQQQQQ FROM DATE

   if QQQQQQ is a 6-digit numeric field?
6. In order to separate the year, month, and day from the result in question 5, what could be done?
7. When CURRENT-DATE is moved to an 8-character field on IBM computers, how would the date December 25, 1983 appear?
8. How does one stipulate that the result of a computation is to be rounded?
9. How does one specify that the result of a calculation is *not* to be rounded?

10. What is the effect of executing the following statement in the Working-Storage Section?

    02 FILLER PICTURE X(09) VALUE ALL ' * = '.

11. What is a control break?
12. How may the current Julian day and the current time be accessed within a program?

Exercises

1. Assume an input file is composed of cards that are punched in the following format.
    1 – 12 last name
    14 – 22 first name
    24 – 58 address
    59 – 63 zip code
    65 – 69 area code (in parentheses)
    70 – 77 numeric telephone number
    79 – 80 alphabetic school code

    Write a program to read each card of the input deck and to print out a listing of the cards. In particular, check that each numeric field is in fact punched with numeric data. If it is not, print a string of 10 asterisks to the right of the listed card. If the percentage of cards with invalid data is greater than 10%, print out the correct percentage.

2. Devise a method of determining in COBOL whether a number is odd or even.

3. For a series of special courses given by a leading university, attendance is recorded by punching a card for each student for every meeting of the class. The card is punched by columns as follows.
    1 – 20 name
    25 attendance code (A – Absent
              P = Present
              E = excused)

    28 – 31 course number
    80 section number

    List all the cards, printing the course number and section number once only each time there is a change either in the course number or the class number. Be sure that only attendance codes A, P, and E are used. At the end of the job, beginning on a new page, print the grand total absent, grand total present, the grand total excused, followed by the grand total listed and the grand total of errors that are punched in column 25.

4. The input deck for a factory's payroll is punched as follows.
    1 – 5 department number
    10 – 18 Social Security number
    20 – 24 rate per hour 99V999
    31 – 34 hours worked (straight time) 99V99
    41 – 44 hours worked (at time and a half) 99V99

    Write a program that prints the department number, Social Security number, rate per hour, straight hours worked, straight pay, overtime hours worked, overtime pay, and gross pay. Appropriate headings, including the current date, should be provided.

    There should be a totals line showing the totals for straight time, straight pay, overtime, overtime pay, and gross pay.

    To impress your teacher with your proficiency, you may wish to print subtotals for each department.

5. Sloppy Sam wanted to amuse himself by writing a short COBOL program that appears here to sum all the integers from 1 to 10. He made sure that all his data-names were correctly defined. From his knowledge of mathematics he was convinced that the sum of the integers from 1 to 10 was 55. For some unexplained reason, however, he could not get the computer to confirm this result. Like most novices, he suspected at first that the computer had made an error. What, in fact, is the reason for the incorrect result?

```
MOVE ZERO TO TOTAL.
PERFORM PARA-1 VARYING DATA-POINTER
    FROM 1 BY 1 UNTIL DATA-POINTER > 10.
PARA-1. ADD DATA-POINTER TO TOTAL.
```

6. Write a COBOL program by using the PERFORM... VARYING... UNTIL version of PERFORM to print the following output.

```
6 BOTTLES OF BEER ON THE WALL,
6 BOTTLES OF BEER.
  IF ONE OF THE BOTTLES SHOULD HAPPEN TO FALL,
5 BOTTLES OF BEER ON THE WALL.

5 BOTTLES OF BEER ON THE WALL,
5 BOTTLES OF BEER,
  IF ONE OF THE BOTTLES SHOULD HAPPEN TO FALL,
4 BOTTLES OF BEER ON THE WALL.

4 BOTTLES OF BEER ON THE WALL,
4 BOTTLES OF BEER,
  IF ONE OF THE BOTTLES SHOULD HAPPEN TO FALL,
3 BOTTLES OF BEER ON THE WALL.

3 BOTTLES OF BEER ON THE WALL,
3 BOTTLES OF BEER,
  IF ONE OF THE BOTTLES SHOULD HAPPEN TO FALL,
2 BOTTLES OF BEER ON THE WALL.

2 BOTTLES OF BEER ON THE WALL,
2 BOTTLES OF BEER,
  IF ONE OF THE BOTTLES SHOULD HAPPEN TO FALL,
1 BOTTLES OF BEER ON THE WALL.

1 BOTTLES OF BEER ON THE WALL,
1 BOTTLES OF BEER,
  IF ONE OF THE BOTTLES SHOULD HAPPEN TO FALL,
0 BOTTLES OF BEER ON THE WALL.
```

7. A local newspaper vendor offers its customers 3 types of services for its delivered newspapers. Type 1 is for weekly delivery of the daily newspapers, Monday through Saturday; type 2, Sunday edition only; and type 3, both weekdays, Saturdays, and Sundays.

   For each customer a record is kept as shown here.

   col 1 – 20 : customer name
       25 – 50 : address
       52   : code 1, 2 or 3
       54 – 55 : number of weeks requested

   Write a program that produces a report containing

   a. card count
   b. name of computer
   c. address
   d. the coded type
   e. the number of weeks requested
   f. rate per week
   g. the amount owed by each customer
   h. the grand total owed by all customers

   Validate all incoming data with the NUMERIC test and check that the code number is within range.

8. A foreign exchange company keeps a record of each day's transactions in the following way.

   col 1 – 10 : name of foreign currency
       15 – 21 : rate of exchange 9V9(6)
       25 – 30 : amount of foreign currency exchanged 9(4)V99

   Write a program that writes a comprehensive report on the day's trading, showing the current date. The output should contain

   a. card count
   b. name of the currency traded
   c. the amount of currency traded
   d. the current exchange rate
   e. the dollar value of the exchange

9. Write a program that reads such data as
   col: 1 – 25 customer name
       30 – 34 code name of item

36 – 40 no. of items bought
42 – 46 price per item 999V99
48 – 50 % discount 9V99
54 – 55 no. of days elapsed since purchase

The discount is given only if the number of days that have elapsed since the purchase is 10 days or less. The program should first determine whether the discount is due and then if it is, calculate the discount and print an invoice. At the end a total of the net due should be printed.

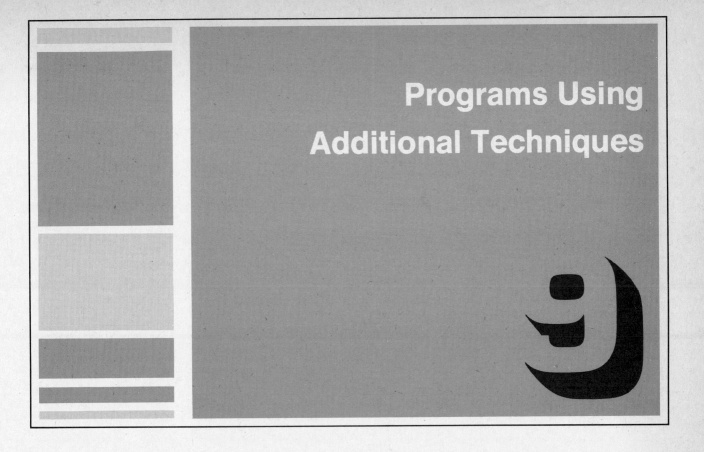

Programs Using Additional Techniques

The only part of a COBOL program I can't figure out is the Procedure Division.

(Natalie Cooper)

At this point in the text you will probably welcome some additional techniques to enhance your programs. In this chapter you will be introduced to the concepts of:

- condition-names—88-level items
- a new kind of VALUE clause
- computing percentages
- solving a crime with a computer
- the figurative constant QUOTE
- an alternative to the figurative constant QUOTE
- computing the windchill factor
- inputting data with either a leading or a trailing sign as a separate character
- the use of the PERFORM... VARYING statement
- multiformat records in the input file

9.1 88-Level Items — Condition Names

Suppose we are reading some input cards containing a person's name, address, and a code number designating the person's marital status, such as 1 for single; 2 for married, and 3 for divorced, according to the following format.

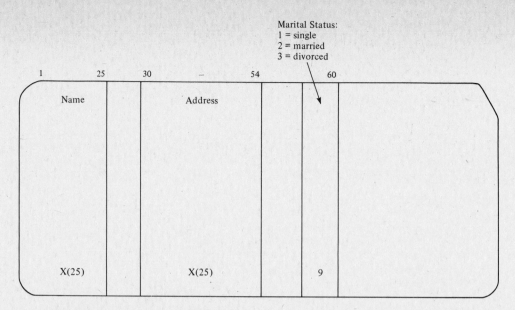

In order to determine the marital status, we could (in the Procedure Division, of course) write:

```
IF MARITAL-STATUS = 1 ADD 1 TO PARA-1.
IF MARITAL-STATUS = 2 ADD 1 TO PARA-2.
IF MARITAL-STATUS = 3 ADD 1 TO PARA-3.
```

To the casual reader the significance of the codes 1, 2, and 3 would be hidden because there is no way to find out what they mean short of looking at PARA-1, PARA-2, and PARA-3 and somehow deducing their significance. In order that such IF statements convey the maximum information to the reader in the Procedure Division, COBOL provides a novel method of coding the item in question as an 88-level entry in the Data Division. All 88-level entries are called condition-names and are always coded in the B margin immediately following the independent item associated with it. The data card shown here would be described in the Data Division as:

```
FD   IN-FILE LABEL RECORDS ARE OMITTED.
01   RECORD-IN.
     02   NAME-IN      PIC X(25).
     02   FILLER       PIC X(04).
     02   ADDRESS-IN PIC X(25).
     02   FILLER       PIC X(05).
     02   MARITAL-STATUS PIC 9.
          88   SINGLE VALUE 1.
          88   MARRIED VALUE 2.
          88   DIVORCED VALUE 3.
     02 FILLER         PIC X(20).
```

After the number 88 a *condition*-name (not a data-name) is written. Then comes the word VALUE, which is followed by a constant value. Notice that each of the three 88-level items (SINGLE, MARRIED, and DIVORCED) are subordinate to the same 02-level entry, which alone has a PICTURE. An 88-level item *never* takes a PICTURE but *always* takes a VALUE. This is interesting because we have repeatedly maintained that the VALUE clause may be used only in the Working-Storage Section and here it is clearly not in Working-Storage. That is perfectly true; but the VALUE clause of an 88-level item is not the same as the VALUE clauses we have used until now. The VALUE clauses used in the Working-Storage Section are implied MOVEs of a literal, numeric, or nonnumeric. The VALUE clause of an 88-level item is merely a way of expressing a condition. It doesn't really do any extra work for you; it merely provides a more descriptive test in the Procedure Division, as you will soon see.

In the Procedure Division we may still use the sequence of IF's as previously shown, but now we can write:

```
IF SINGLE ADD 1 TO SINGLE-PARA.
IF MARRIED ADD 1 TO MARRIED-PARA.
IF DIVORCED ADD 1 TO DIVORCED-PARA.
```

where the statement is much more meaningful. If MARITAL-STATUS is equal to 1 in the input record, then SINGLE takes on the value "true" and 1 is added to SINGLE-PARA. You may *not* write:

```
IF SINGLE = 1
```

because SINGLE is not a data-name with a PICTURE clause.

Condition-names are very flexible. Here are some examples of how they may be used.

a. 02 FLAG PIC X.
    88 ONN VALUE 'Y'.
    88 OFFF VALUE 'N'.

b. 02 GPA PIC 9V99.
    88 HONORS VALUE 3.8 THRU 4.00.
    88 DEANS-LIST VALUE 3.4 THRU 3.79.
    88 AVERAGE VALUE 2.0 THRU 2.39.
    88 PROBATION VALUE 0.0 THRU 1.99.

c. 02 SCORE PIC 99.
    88 INVALID VALUE 1, 5, 9, 33.

d. 02 SUBSCRIPTION-BASIS PIC X.
    88 REGULAR VALUE '1'.
    88 SPECIAL VALUE '2'.
    88 CHARTER VALUE '3'.

Remember:

a. The condition-name is the name of the *value* of an item, not the item itself.

b. An associated entry with a PICTURE clause is needed in order to describe an 88-level item.

c. A level 88 must be used in every condition-name entry.

d. The condition-name relates to an elementary item in a group of items.

e. The condition-name is used in the Procedure Division relational test statement.

f. The only clause required in a condition-name entry is the VALUE clause.

g. An 88-level item must immediately follow its associated item.

h. The type of literal used with the condition-name must be consistent with the data type of the condition data-name.

In the program that follows the cards are listed; the marital status decoded and printed; and on a new page the percentage of single, married, and divorced people is calculated.

Input for Program 21

ELSIA BAZARNIK	580 PARK AVE. NEW YORK, NY	3
STEVEN BEISPEL	290 WEST END AVE N.Y., NY	2
LARISA BELFOR	600 WEST 186 STREET	1
JAMES BIANCO	255 FIELDSTON TER. BX, NY	1
MARY CURATOLO	1825 80 ST. BROOKLYN, NY	2
THOMAS DELUCA	1320 ODELL ST. NY, NY	1
ALEXANDER EHRLICH	35 FIFTH AV NEW YORK, NY	3
ANGLEA FAZIO	1764 66 ST BROOKLYN, NY	2
BARBARA GERMAIN	1 MARK LANE BLOOMFIELD CON	1
CHARLES HOFFMAN	44 NEW STREET	2
JOSEPH INTERLIGI	2501 85 ST. BROOKLYN, NY	3
BRIAN KEENAN	908 EAST 46 ST. BKLYN, NY	2
ROBERT LA PLANT	6132 64 ST. MIDDLE VILLAGE	1
JOANNE LABARBERA	54 BAY 14 ST BKLYN, NY	1
STEVEN LACORAZZA	77 SULLIVAN ST. NEW YORK	2
NANCY LUCADAMO	1919 BAY AVENUE BK, NY	2

KEITH MCCAFFREY	35 FIFTH AVENUE NY, NY	2
PETER MENDELSOHN	1133 E. 82 ST. BKLYN, NY	1
NANCY MILLER	130-06 97 AVE RICHMONDHILL	3
VANESSA ROSA	2453 BELLMORE AVE. NY, NY	3
JOHN ROSS	2177 E. 69 ST. BROOKLYN, NY	2
JOHN SAKETOS	78-04 21 AVE NY, NY	1
WILLIAM TAYLOR	90 MORRIC AVENUE	1
GRACE TORRES	170-62 CEDARCROFT RD.	2
ALEXANDER VIRVO	38 ELYSIAN AVE. NYACK, NY	1
DORIS WOO	5921 4 AVE. BROOKLYN, NY	1
ELEANOR YU	23-22 82 ST. JACKSON HGTS	1
ELIZABETH ZOLCHAK	83 GREENWD DR BEACON, NY	1

Program 21

```
1       IDENTIFICATION DIVISION.
2       PROGRAM-ID. MARITALSTATUS.
3       AUTHOR. IRVIN POREMBA.
4       INSTALLATION. NYU.
5       DATE-WRITTEN. MARCH 27, 1982.
6       DATE-COMPILED. MARCH 31, 1982.
7       SECURITY. HENRY MULLISH ONLY.
8       * * * * * * * * * * * * * * * * * * * * * * * * * * * * * * * * * * * * * * * * * * * * * * * * *
9       *       THIS PROGRAM READS IN DATA CARDS PUNCHED:                    *
10      *                                                                    *
11      *       COLUMNS  1-25:   NAME                                        *
12      *       COLUMNS 30-55:   ADDRESS                                     *
13      *       COLUMN     60:   MARITAL STATUS (1-SINGLE,                   *
14      *                         2-MARRIED, 3-DIVORCED)                     *
15      *                                                                    *
16      *       THE PROGRAM THEN PRINTS OUT THE INFORMATION WITH             *
17      *       THE MARITAL STATUS DECODED AND THEN PRINTS OUT               *
18      *       THE PERCENTAGE OF EACH MARITAL STATUS                        *
19      *       REPRESENTED IN THE DATA. THIS PROGRAM MAKES                  *
20      *       USE OF THE 88 LEVEL METHOD OF TESTING                        *
21      * * * * * * * * * * * * * * * * * * * * * * * * * * * * * * * * * * * * * * * * * * * * * * * * *
22
23      ENVIRONMENT DIVISION.
24      CONFIGURATION SECTION.
25      SOURCE-COMPUTER. CYBER-170-720.
26      OBJECT-COMPUTER. CYBER-170-720.
27      SPECIAL-NAMES.
28      INPUT-OUTPUT SECTION.
29      FILE-CONTROL.
30          SELECT IN-FILE ASSIGN TO INPUT.
31          SELECT OUT-FILE ASSIGN TO OUTPUT.
32
33      DATA DIVISION.
34      FILE SECTION.
35
36      FD   IN-FILE
37           LABEL RECORDS ARE OMITTED
38
39      01   RECORD-IN.
40           02   NAME-IN           PIC X(25).
41           02   FILLER            PIC X(04).
42           02   ADDRESS-IN        PIC X(25).
43           02   FILLER            PIC X(05).
44           02   MARITAL-STATUS    PIC 9.
45               88   SINGLE        VALUE 1.
46               88   MARRIED       VALUE 2.
47               88   DIVORCED      VALUE 3.
48           02   FILLER            PIC X(20).
49
50      FD   OUT-FILE
51           LABEL RECORDS ARE OMITTED.
52
53      01   LINE-OUT               PIC X(133).
54
55      WORKING-STORAGE SECTION.
56      77   PAGE-COUNT             PIC 9999 VALUE ZERO.
57      77   CARD-COUNT             PIC 9999 VALUE ZERO.
```

```
58      77   CARD-COUNT-2              PIC 99 VALUE ZERO.
59      77   TOTAL-COUNT               PIC 9999 VALUE ZERO.
60      77   SINGLE-COUNT              PIC 9999 VALUE ZERO.
61      77   MARRIED-COUNT             PIC 9999 VALUE ZERO.
62      77   DIVORCE-COUNT             PIC 9999 VALUE ZERO.
63      77   ANY-MORE-CARDS            PIC X(03) VALUE 'YES'.
64
65      01   HEADER-1.
66           02   FILLER               PIC X(06) VALUE 'PAGE'.
67           02   PAGE-COUNT-OUT       PIC ZZZ9.
68           02   FILLER               PIC X(16) VALUE SPACES.
69           02   FILLER               PIC X(08) VALUE 'LISTING'.
70           02   FILLER               PIC X(09) VALUE 'OF PEOPLE'.
71
72      01   HEADER-2.
73           02   FILLER               PIC X(01) VALUE SPACES.
74           02   FILLER               PIC X(09) VALUE ALL '*'.
75           02   FILLER               PIC X(16) VALUE SPACES.
76           02   FILLER               PIC X(17) VALUE ALL '*'.
77
78      01   HEADER-3.
79           02   FILLER               PIC X(20) VALUE 'COUNT'.
80           02   FILLER               PIC X(28) VALUE 'NAME'.
81           02   FILLER               PIC X(21) VALUE 'ADDRESS'.
82           02   FILLER               PIC X(06) VALUE 'STATUS'.
83
84      01   HEADER-4.
85           02   FILLER               PIC X(01) VALUE SPACES.
86           02   FILLER               PIC X(05) VALUE ALL '*'.
87           02   FILLER               PIC X(04) VALUE SPACES.
88           02   FILLER               PIC X(25) VALUE ALL '*'.
89           02   FILLER               PIC X(04) VALUE SPACES.
90           02   FILLER               PIC X(25) VALUE ALL '*'.
91           02   FILLER               PIC X(04) VALUE SPACES.
92           02   FILLER               PIC X(08) VALUE ALL '*'.
93
94      01   DETAIL-LINE.
95           02   FILLER               PIC X(01) VALUE SPACES.
96           02   CARD-COUNT-OUT       PIC Z,ZZ9.
97           02   FILLER               PIC X(04) VALUE SPACES.
98           02   NAME-OUT             PIC X(25).
99           02   FILLER               PIC X(04) VALUE SPACES.
100          02   ADDRESS-OUT          PIC X(25).
101          02   FILLER               PIC X(04) VALUE SPACES.
102          02   MARITAL-STATUS-OUT   PIC X(09).
103
104     01   DETAIL-LINE-2.
105          02   FILLER               PIC X(12) VALUE 'PERCENTAGE'.
106          02   FILLER               PIC X(10) VALUE 'OF SINGLE'.
107          02   FILLER               PIC X(19) VALUE 'PEOPLE IN DATA = '.
108          02   PERCENT-SINGLE       PIC ZZ9.99.
109          02   FILLER               PIC X(02) VALUE '%.'.
110
111     01   DETAIL-LINE-3.
112          02   FILLER               PIC X(12) VALUE 'PERCENTAGE'.
113          02   FILLER               PIC X(11) VALUE 'OF MARRIED'.
114          02   FILLER               PIC X(18) VALUE 'PEOPLE IN DATA = '.
115          02   PERCENT-MARRIED      PIC ZZ9.99.
116          02   FILLER               PIC X(02) VALUE '%.'.
117
118     01   DETAIL-LINE-4.
119          02   FILLER               PIC X(12) VALUE 'PERCENTAGE'.
120          02   FILLER               PIC X(12) VALUE 'OF DIVORCED'.
121          02   FILLER               PIC X(17) VALUE 'PEOPLE IN DATA = '.
122          02   PERCENT-DIVORCED     PIC ZZ9.99.
123          02   FILLER               PIC X(02) VALUE '%.'.
124
125     PROCEDURE DIVISION.
126
127     MAIN-LINE-ROUTINE.
128          PERFORM OPEN-FILES.
129          PERFORM NEW-PAGE.
130          PERFORM START-UP.
131          PERFORM PROCESS-DATA UNTIL ANY-MORE-CARDS EQUAL 'NO'.
132          PERFORM CLOSE-UP.
```

```
133          STOP RUN.
134
135      OPEN-FILES.
136          OPEN INPUT IN-FILE.
137          OPEN OUTPUT OUT-FILE.
138
139      NEW-PAGE.
140          MOVE SPACES TO LINE-OUT.
141          WRITE LINE-OUT AFTER PAGE.
142
143      START-UP.
144          READ IN-FILE AT END MOVE 'NO' TO ANY-MORE-CARDS
145              MOVE ' **NO DATA IN DECK**' TO LINE-OUT
146              WRITE LINE-OUT AFTER 30.
147          IF ANY-MORE-CARDS EQUAL 'YES' PERFORM WRITE-HEADINGS.
148
149      PROCESS-DATA.
150          ADD 1 TO CARD-COUNT.
151          ADD 1 TO CARD-COUNT-2.
152          ADD 1 TO TOTAL-COUNT.
153          MOVE CARD-COUNT TO CARD-COUNT-OUT.
154          MOVE NAME-IN TO NAME-OUT.
155          MOVE ADDRESS-IN TO ADDRESS-OUT.
156          PERFORM STATUS-DECODE.
157          WRITE LINE-OUT FROM DETAIL-LINE AFTER 2.
158          READ IN-FILE AT END MOVE 'NO' TO ANY-MORE-CARDS
159              MOVE ZEROS TO CARD-COUNT-2
160              PERFORM PERCENT-WRITE.
161          IF CARD-COUNT-2 = 20 MOVE ZEROS TO CARD-COUNT-2
162              PERFORM NEW-PAGE
163              PERFORM WRITE-HEADINGS.
164
165      CLOSE-UP.
166          CLOSE IN-FILE, OUT-FILE.
167
168      STATUS-DECODE.
169          IF SINGLE MOVE 'SINGLE' TO MARITAL-STATUS-OUT
170              ADD 1 TO SINGLE-COUNT
171          ELSE IF MARRIED MOVE 'MARRIED' TO MARITAL-STATUS-OUT
172                  ADD 1 TO MARRIED-COUNT
173              ELSE IF DIVORCED MOVE 'DIVORCED' TO MARITAL-STATUS-OUT
174                  ADD 1 TO DIVORCE-COUNT
175              ELSE MOVE 'INCORRECT' TO MARITAL-STATUS-OUT
176                  SUBTRACT 1 FROM TOTAL-COUNT.
177
178      PERCENT-WRITE.
179          COMPUTE PERCENT-SINGLE ROUNDED = 100*
180              SINGLE-COUNT / TOTAL-COUNT.
181          COMPUTE PERCENT-MARRIED ROUNDED = 100*
182              MARRIED-COUNT / TOTAL-COUNT.
183          COMPUTE PERCENT-DIVORCED ROUNDED = 100*
184              DIVORCE-COUNT / TOTAL-COUNT.
185          PERFORM NEW-PAGE.
186          WRITE LINE-OUT FROM DETAIL-LINE-2 AFTER 20.
187          WRITE LINE-OUT FROM DETAIL-LINE-3 AFTER 3.
188          WRITE LINE-OUT FROM DETAIL-LINE-4 AFTER 3.
189
190      WRITE-HEADINGS.
191          ADD 1 TO PAGE-COUNT.
192          MOVE PAGE-COUNT TO PAGE-COUNT-OUT.
193          WRITE LINE-OUT FROM HEADER-1 AFTER 1.
194          WRITE LINE-OUT FROM HEADER-2 AFTER 1.
195          WRITE LINE-OUT FROM HEADER-2 AFTER 1.
196          WRITE LINE-OUT FROM HEADER-3 AFTER 2.
197          WRITE LINE-OUT FROM HEADER-4 AFTER 1.
```

Output for Program 21

```
   PAGE 1                                        LISTING OF PEOPLE
* * * * * * * * *                         * * * * * * * * * * * * * * * *
* * * * * * * * *                         * * * * * * * * * * * * * * * *
   COUNT              NAME                      ADDRESS                STATUS
* * * * *     * * * * * * * * * * * * * *  * * * * * * * * * * * * * * * *  * * * * * * *
     1         ELSIA BAZARNIK          580 PARK AVE. NEW YORK, NY      DIVORCED
     2         STEVEN BEISPEL          290 WEST END AVE N.Y., NY       MARRIED
```

3	LARISA BELFOR	600 WEST 186 STREET	SINGLE
4	JAMES BIANCO	255 FIELDSTON TER. BX, NY	SINGLE
5	MARY CURATOLO	1825 80 ST. BROOKLYN, NY	MARRIED
6	THOMAS DELUCA	1320 ODELL ST. NY, NY	SINGLE
7	ALEXANDER EHRLICH	35 FIFTH AV NEW YORK, NY	DIVORCED
8	ANGLEA FAZIO	1764 66 ST BROOKLYN, NY	MARRIED
9	BARBARA GERMAIN	1 MARK LANE BLOOMFIELD CO	SINGLE
10	CHARLES HOFFMAN	44 NEW STREET	MARRIED
11	JOSEPH INTERLIGI	2501 85 ST. BROOKLYN, NY	DIVORCED
12	BRIAN KEENAN	908 EAST 46 ST. BKLYN, NY	MARRIED
13	ROBERT LA PLANT	6132 64 ST. MIDDLE VILLAGE	SINGLE
14	JOANNE LABARBERA	54 BAY 14 ST BKLYN, NY	SINGLE
15	STEVEN LACORAZZA	77 SULLIVAN ST. NEW YORK	MARRIED
16	NANCY LUCADAMO	1919 BAY AVENUE BK, NY	MARRIED
17	KEITH MCCAFFREY	35 FIFTH AVENUE NY, NY	MARRIED
18	PETER MENDELSOHN	1133 E. 82 ST. BKLYN, NY	SINGLE
19	NANCY MILLER	130-06 97 AVE RICHMONDHIL	DIVORCED
20	VANESSA ROSA	2453 BELLMORE AVE. NY, NY	DIVORCED

PAGE 2		LISTING OF PEOPLE	
*********		*****************	
*********		*****************	
COUNT	NAME	ADDRESS	STATUS
*****	******************	*********************	*********
21	JOHN ROSS	2177 E. 69 ST. BROOKLYN, NY	MARRIED
22	JOHN SAKETOS	78-04 21 AVE NY, NY	SINGLE
23	WILLIAM TAYLOR	90 MORRIC AVENUE	SINGLE
24	GRACE TORRES	170-62 CEDARCROFT RD.	MARRIED
25	ALEXANDER VIRVO	38 ELYSIAN AVE. NYACK, NY	SINGLE
26	DORIS WOO	5921 4 AVE. BROOKLYN, NY	SINGLE
27	ELEANOR YU	23-22 82 ST. JACKSON HGTS	SINGLE
28	ELIZABETH ZOLCHAK	83 GREENWD DR BEACON, NY	SINGLE

PERCENTAGE OF SINGLE PEOPLE IN DATA = 46.43%.
PERCENTAGE OF MARRIED PEOPLE IN DATA = 35.71%.
PERCENTAGE OF DIVORCED PEOPLE IN DATA = 17.86%.

9.2 The Case of the Murdered Mathematician

The COBOL language may be used to advantage for many situations, other than for normal business applications. It may be employed in any instance where there is a need to examine and manipulate data to produce a suitable report at computer speed. Even in the investigation of crime, computers play a unique role.

An Historical Anecdote

The central figure in our scenario is an American mathematician whose contribution to the world was so great that he was awarded the Nobel prize in mathematics. (In fact, there is no Nobel prize for mathematics.) Students seem to relish the purported reason for this, so for their benefit and enjoyment we will repeat the story here. When Mr. Nobel was deciding upon the categories of human endeavor that were to receive prizes, the question of awarding a prize for mathematics naturally arose. The leading mathematician of the time was a fellow Swede named Dr. Mittag-Leffler. If a Nobel prize for mathematics were to be awarded, there was little question in the minds of those in authority that Dr. Mittag-Leffler would be the recipient. Now, according to the story, Nobel's wife was having a romantic affair with the good doctor, and what's more, Nobel was well aware of the situation. In order to avoid having to award a prize to Dr. Mittag-Leffler, Nobel declined to name mathematics among the selected disciplines.

In his earlier days our fictional Nobel-prize-winning mathematician was a high school teacher of mathematics. When teaching his students the Pythagorean Theorem ($A^2 = B^2 + C^2$ for a right triangle) he learned by rote to recognize Pythagorean triplets instantly. It just became second nature to him. In case you do not know, a Pythagorean triplet is a set of 3 integer numbers such that the square of one of them is equal to the sum of the squares of the other two. Here are some examples of Pythagorean triplets.

3	4	5	(since $5^2 = 4^2 + 3^2$)
5	12	13	(since $13^2 = 5^2 + 12^2$)
10	8	6	(since $10^2 = 8^2 + 6^2$)
4	5	3	(since $5^2 = 4^2 + 3^2$)

and so on.

Now our fictitious mathematician lived in a state where automobile license plates were all of the form:

> nn–nn–nn

where each plate is composed of three 2-digit numbers, separated by dashes.

One night he was awakened by the stealthy steps of uninvited guests prowling through his living room. Investigating the matter, he was shocked to discover that the thieves were about to depart with his new color TV set and recently acquired video cassette recorder. Although momentarily stunned, his natural instincts soon compelled him to make chase. On seeing the furious mathematician rushing at them, the robbers dropped their ill-gotten gains and dashed to a getaway vehicle, their accomplice at the wheel, the engine running. As the automobile pulled away, they fired a parting shot at the mathematician who fell down in a pool of blood. The sound of the shot was heard by the neighbors who immediately called the police. The detective who appeared on the scene did his best to comfort the stricken man and radioed for an ambulance. While waiting for the ambulance, the detective, in an effort to get as many clues as possible, asked the mathematician if, by chance, he noticed the license plate number of the escape vehicle. "Officer," he replied, "I made a determined attempt to catch a glimpse of the license plate, but unfortunately, in the excitement of the moment I forgot the exact number, although I do remember that it was a Pythagorean triplet!" Sad to relate, these were his last words.

The Pythagorean Triplet Search

Based on this evidence alone, namely, the license plate number of the vehicle used in the getaway was a Pythagorean triplet, it behooves us to examine each license plate issued by the state. Fortunately, for every license plate issued, a record was kept at the Motor Vehicle Bureau in the form of a punched card in the following format.

1 Driver's Name	25	30 Address	54	59 License Plate Number	60 –	62 License Plate Number	63 –	65 License Plate Number	66
X(25)		X(25)		99		99		99	

When examining the whole deck of data we must remember that of the three 2-digit numbers, we do not know in advance which of the 3 numbers represents the hypotenuse. The hypotenuse, the longest of the 3 sides of a right triangle, is the line opposite the right angle. We certainly could not assume that the first or the last number was the hypotenuse. It is encumbent upon us therefore to test for each of the 3 possibilities on each input card. These possibilities are:

$$A^2 = B^2 + C^2$$
$$B^2 = A^2 + C^2$$
$$C^2 = A^2 + B^2$$

Moreover, it would be foolish to terminate the search once the first Pythagorean triplet had been discovered because, after all, each triplet found constitutes only a suspect, not necessarily the culprit. However, the field will have been narrowed considerably by printing out all the suspect license numbers. For the purposes of additional information it is probably a good idea to calculate the percentage of suspects over all the cards read.

In the heading of the printout to Program 22 there is the word DRIVER'S; as a matter of fact, it appears 3 times on a single line. We *cannot* write an apostrophe as shown here because it would terminate the literal and create an error message.

```
02 FILLER PIC X(08) VALUE 'DRIVER'S'.
```

COBOL provides yet another figurative constant, which is called (as you may already have guessed) QUOTE or QUOTES. An entry such as:

```
02 FILLER PIC X VALUE QUOTE.
```

will place an apostrophe in that FILLER position. This feature is also part of previous compilers. The 1974 standard, however, provides an additional method of printing a single apostrophe. Whenever you want a single apostrophe to appear, write 2 adjacent single quotes (not a double quotation symbol). For example,

```
02 FILLER PIC X(08) VALUE 'DRIVER''S'.
```

where the 2 consecutive apostrophes are stored as a *single* symbol and therefore the PICTURE allows for only 8 characters, not 9.

Input for Program 22

LINDA BENLEVY	5-11 UNIVERSITY PLACE	05-08-11
CORINNE GOODMAN	90 8TH AVE APT. A	16-12-20
CHRIS HANLON	5-11 UNIVERSITY PLACE	25-36-44
KULJOT BHASIN	5 UNIVERSITY PLACE	06-22-23
JEROME COTTONE	325 PACIFIC AVENUE	25-13-35
CIPORA BLITZ	232 E 82ND STREET	04-03-05
TI DAVIS	5 UNIVERSITY PLACE	08-06-10
RALPH DECATREL	196-20 91 AVE HOLLISCOURT	23-58-75
TERI CHIN	1196 NECK RD	13-75-26
FRAN DIBERNARDO	65-45 79 STREET	35-26-78
JAMES LAFLEUR	69 WILLOWBROOK RD.	25-33-24
IRVIN POREMBA	35 FIFTH AVENUE ROOM 1119	05-12-13
LUDO COPPENS	148 WEST 11 STREET	10-11-12
TIM DUGGAN	46-32 193 STREET	03-05-04
CHRIS DUNCAN	441 W 22 ST. APT 4-A	12-25-45
LINDA EHLER	55 EAST 10 ST APT 1202	75-36-33
SABRINA ELLIS	1470 AMSTERDAM AVE	05-12-13
PETER EPIFAN	105 CLAUDY LINE	43-25-11
BARBARA FERMANN	5 UNIVERSITY PLACE	23-88-56
LARRY FINE	327 E. 54 STREET APT C	26-13-05
KEITH GEE	181 DAHILL ROAD	43-55-17
HWA-YUHN AHN	375 RIVERSIDE DR.	02-03-12
ALLEN GOLDBERG	1237 E. 100 STREET	23-24-66

Program 22

```
1      IDENTIFICATION DIVISION.
2      PROGRAM-ID. CRIME.
3      AUTHOR. IRVIN POREMBA.
```

```
 4         INSTALLATION. NYU.
 5         DATE-WRITTEN. MARCH 20, 1982.
 6         DATE-COMPILED. APRIL 21, 1982.
 7         SECURITY. HENRY MULLISH.
 8         * * * * * * * * * * * * * * * * * * * * * * * * * * * * * * * * * * * * * * * * * * * * * *
 9         *       THIS PROGRAM IS USED TO SOLVE A CRIME WHERE                      *
10         *       THE ONLY CLUE TO THE CRIMINAL IS THE FACT THAT                   *
11         *       THE CRIMINAL'S LICENSE PLATE NUMBER IS A PERFECT                 *
12         *       PYTHAGOREAN TRIPLET IN WHICH THE SUM OF THE                      *
13         *       SQUARES OF THE TWO NUMBERS EQUALS THE SQUARE                     *
14         *       OF THE THIRD                                                     *
15         *                                                                        *
16         *       THE DATA CARDS ARE PUNCHED:                                      *
17         *                                                                        *
18         *       COLUMNS  1-25: DRIVER'S NAME                                     *
19         *       COLUMNS 30-54: DRIVER'S ADDRESS                                  *
20         *       COLUMNS 59-60: LEFT LICENSE PLATE NUMBER                         *
21         *       COLUMN     61: –                                                 *
22         *       COLUMNS 62-63: MIDDLE LICENSE NUMBER                             *
23         *       COLUMN     64: –                                                 *
24         *       COLUMNS 65-66: RIGHT LICENSE NUMBER                              *
25         * * * * * * * * * * * * * * * * * * * * * * * * * * * * * * * * * * * * * * * * * * * * * *
26
27         ENVIRONMENT DIVISION.
28         CONFIGURATION SECTION.
29         SOURCE-COMPUTER. CYBER-170-720.
30         OBJECT-COMPUTER. CYBER-170-720.
31         SPECIAL-NAMES.
32         INPUT-OUTPUT SECTION.
33         FILE-CONTROL.
34             SELCT IN-FILE ASSIGN TO INPUT.
35             SELECT OUT-FILE ASSIGN TO OUTPUT.
36
37         DATA DIVISION.
38         FILE SECTION.
39
40         FD   IN-FILE
41             LABEL RECORDS ARE OMITTED.
42
43         01   RECORD-IN.
44             02   DRIVER              PIC X(25).
45             02   FILLER              PIC X(04).
46             02   DRIVER-ADDRESS      PIC X(25).
47             02   FILLER              PIC X(04).
48             02   LEFT-IN             PIC 9(02).
49             02   DASH-1              PIC X(01).
50             02   MIDDLE-IN           PIC 9(02).
51             02   DASH-2              PIC X(01).
52             02   RIGHT-IN            PIC 9(02).
53             02   FILLER              PIC X(14).
54
55         FD OUT-FILE
56             LABEL RECORDS ARE OMITTED.
57
58         01   LINE-OUT                PIC X(133).
59
60         WORKING-STORAGE SECTION.
61
62         01   INDEPENDENT-ITEMS-USED.
63             02   LEFT-2              PIC 9999.
64             02   MIDDLE-2            PIC 9999.
65             02   RIGHT-2             PIC 9999.
66             02   SUM-TWO-2           PIC 99999.
67             02   CARD-COUNT          PIC 9999 VALUE ZERO.
68             02   CARD-COUNT-2        PIC 9999 VALUE ZERO.
69             02   CARD-COUNT-3        PIC 99 VALUE ZERO.
70             02   MORE-CARDS          PIC X(03) VALUE 'YES'.
71             02   W-S-LEFT            PIC 99.
72             02   W-S-MIDDLE          PIC 99.
73             02   W-S-RIGHT           PIC 99.
74
75         01   HEADER-1.
76             02   FILLER              PIC X(30) VALUE SPACES.
77             02   FILLER              PIC X(13) VALUE 'SUSPECTS LIST'.
78
```

```
79    01   HEADER-2.
80         02   FILLER            PIC X(30) VALUE SPACES.
81         02   FILLER            PIC X(13) VALUE ALL '*'.
82
83    01   HEADER-3.
84         02   FILLER            PIC X(20) VALUE 'CARD'.
85         02   FILLER            PIC X(06) VALUE 'DRIVER'.
86         02   FILLER            PIC X(01) VALUE QUOTE.
87         02   FILLER            PIC X(22) VALUE 'S'.
88         02   FILLER            PIC X(06) VALUE 'DRIVER'.
89         02   FILLER            PIC X(01) VALUE QUOTE.
90         02   FILLER            PIC X(12) VALUE 'S'.
91         02   FILLER            PIC X(06) VALUE 'DRIVER'.
92         02   FILLER            PIC X(01) VALUE QUOTE.
93         02   FILLER            PIC X(01) VALUE 'S'.
94
95    01   HEADER-4.
96         02   FILLER            PIC X(22) VALUE 'COUNT'.
97         02   FILLER            PIC X(27) VALUE 'NAME'.
98         02   FILLER            PIC X(19) VALUE 'ADDRESS'.
99         02   FILLER            PIC X(08) VALUE 'LICENSE#'.
100
101   01   HEADER-5.
102        02   FILLER            PIC X(01) VALUE SPACES.
103        02   FILLER            PIC X(05) VALUE ALL '*'.
104        02   FILLER            PIC X(04) VALUE SPACES.
105        02   FILLER            PIC X(25) VALUE ALL '*'.
106        02   FILLER            PIC X(04) VALUE SPACES.
107        02   FILLER            PIC X(25) VALUE ALL '*'.
108        02   FILLER            PIC X(04) VALUE SPACES.
109        02   FILLER            PIC X(08) VALUE ALL '*'.
110
111   01   DETAIL-LINE.
112        02   FILLER            PIC X(01) VALUE SPACES.
113        02   CARD-COUNT-OUT    PIC Z,ZZ9.
114        02   FILLER            PIC X(04) VALUE SPACES.
115        02   DRIVER            PIC X(25).
116        02   FILLER            PIC X(04) VALUE SPACES.
117        02   DRIVER-ADDRESS    PIC X(25).
118        02   FILLER            PIC X(04) VALUE SPACES.
119        02   LEFT-IN           PIC 99.
120        02   DASH-1            PIC X(01).
121        02   MIDDLE-IN         PIC 99.
122        02   DASH-2            PIC X(01).
123        02   RIGHT-IN          PIC 99.
124
125   01   PERCENT-LINE.
126        02   FILLER            PIC X(20) VALUE SPACES.
127        02   FILLER            PIC X(11) VALUE 'PERCENTAGE'.
128        02   FILLER            PIC X(09) VALUE 'SUSPECTS'.
129        02   FILLER            PIC X(15) VALUE 'OUT OF TOTAL = '.
130        02   PERCENT-OUT       PIC ZZ9.
131
132   PROCEDURE DIVISION.
133
134   MAIN-LINE-ROUTINE.
135        PERFORM OPEN-FILES.
136        PERFORM NEW-PAGE.
137        PERFORM START-UP.
138        PERFORM PROCESS-DATA UNTIL MORE-CARDS EQUAL 'NO'.
139        PERFORM CLOSE-UP.
140        STOP RUN.
141
142   OPEN-FILES.
143        OPEN INPUT IN-FILE.
144        OPEN OUTPUT OUT-FILE.
145
146   NEW-PAGE.
147        MOVE SPACES TO LINE-OUT.
148        WRITE LINE-OUT AFTER PAGE.
149
150   START-UP.
151        READ IN-FILE AT END MOVE 'NO' TO MORE-CARDS
152             MOVE ' **NO DATA IN DECK**' TO LINE-OUT
153             WRITE LINE-OUT AFTER 2.
```

```
154          IF MORE-CARDS EQUAL 'YES' PERFORM WRITE-HEADINGS.
155
156     PROCESS-DATA.
157          ADD 1 TO CARD-COUNT.
158          MOVE LEFT-IN OF RECORD-IN TO W-S-LEFT.
159          MOVE MIDDLE-IN OF RECORD-IN TO W-S-MIDDLE.
160          MOVE RIGHT-IN OF RECORD-IN TO W-S-RIGHT.
161          MULTIPLY W-S-LEFT BY W-S-LEFT GIVING LEFT-2.
162          MULTIPLY W-S-MIDDLE BY W-S-MIDDLE GIVING MIDDLE-2.
163          MULTIPLY W-S-RIGHT BY W-S-RIGHT GIVING RIGHT-2.
164          ADD LEFT-2, MIDDLE-2 GIVING SUM-TWO-2.
165          IF SUM-TWO-2 EQUAL RIGHT-2 PERFORM WORK-PARA
166          ELSE ADD MIDDLE-2, RIGHT-2 GIVING SUM-TWO-2.
167               IF SUM-TWO-2 EQUAL LEFT-2 PERFORM WORK-PARA
168               ELSE ADD RIGHT-2, LEFT-2 GIVING SUM-TWO-2.
169               IF SUM-TWO-2 EQUAL MIDDLE-2 PERFORM WORK-PARA.
170          READ IN-FILE AT END PERFORM PERCENT-PARA
171               MOVE 'NO' TO MORE-CARDS.
172
173     WORK-PARA.
174          IF CARD-COUNT-3 EQUAL 15 MOVE ZEROS TO CARD-COUNT-3
175               PERFORM NEW-PAGE
176               PERFORM WRITE-HEADINGS.
177          ADD 1 TO CARD-COUNT-2.
178          ADD 1 TO CARD-COUNT-3.
179          MOVE CARD-COUNT TO CARD-COUNT-OUT.
180          MOVE CORR RECORD-IN TO DETAIL-LINE.
181          WRITE LINE-OUT FROM DETAIL-LINE AFTER 2.
182
183     PERCENT-PARA.
184          COMPUTE PERCENT-OUT ROUNDED = 100 * CARD-COUNT-2
185               / CARD-COUNT.
186          PERFORM NEW-PAGE.
187          WRITE LINE-OUT FROM PERCENT-LINE AFTER 20.
188
189     CLOSE-UP.
190          CLOSE IN-FILE, OUT-FILE.
191
192     WRITE-HEADINGS.
193          WRITE LINE-OUT FROM HEADER-1 AFTER 1.
194          WRITE LINE-OUT FROM HEADER-2 AFTER 1.
195          WRITE LINE-OUT FROM HEADER-2 AFTER 1.
196          WRITE LINE-OUT FROM HEADER-3 AFTER 2.
197          WRITE LINE-OUT FROM HEADER-4 AFTER 1.
198          WRITE LINE-OUT FROM HEADER-5 AFTER 1.
```

Output for Program 22

```
                              SUSPECTS LIST
                        * * * * * * * * * * * *
                        * * * * * * * * * * * *
     CARD          DRIVER'S              DRIVER'S              DRIVER'S
     COUNT           NAME                 ADDRESS              LICENSE #
     * * * * *   * * * * * * * * * * * * * *  * * * * * * * * * * * * * * * * *  * * * * * * * * *
        2       CORINNE GOODMAN      90 8TH AVE APT. A            16-12-20
        6       CIPORA BLITZ         232 E 82ND STREET           04-03-05
        7       TI DAVIS             5 UNIVERSITY PLACE          08-06-10
       12       IRVIN POREMBA        35 FIFTH AVENUE ROOM 1119   05-12-13
       14       TIM DUGGAN           46-32 193 STREET            03-05-04
```

PERCENTAGE SUSPECTS OUT OF TOTAL = 23

9.3 The Windchill Problem

During the cold season the weather forecasters who broadcast the expected temperatures also include what is known as the "windchill factor." This additional information is given, because if the weather is cold and the wind is blowing, humans feel as though the temperature is lower than it is due to the action of the wind on the body's surface. Weather bureaus have charts from which they quote the appropriate outside temperatures and wind velocities and simply quote the appropriate windchill temperatures corresponding to a given wind velocity and temperature.

The purpose of the next program is to produce several such charts. Each chart's data card contains 4 items.

a. an initial Fahrenheit temperature
b. a final Fahrenheit temperature
c. a wind velocity in miles per hour
d. an incremental value to be added to the initial value

For each data card read in, a table is to be printed of the windchill temperatures in both the Fahrenheit and Celsius scales so that it will have universal utility. Each table is to be headed by a caption that specifies the sequence number, the particular wind velocity, the increment used, and the temperature range with leading plus or minus signs, whichever is appropriate. No more than 15 lines of table results are to be printed per page. If a particular table exceeds this number, the remainder of the table is to be printed on a fresh page, suitably annotated to show that it is a continuation of the previous table. All data is to be validated, that is, checked to be sure that it is all numeric.

It is not surprising that this program is the first in this text that uses a considerable amount of computation, for the problem at hand is much more mathematical in content than a typical commercial data-processing application. Because we will be dealing with both positive and negative temperatures, all PICTUREs *must* be prefixed with the letter S so that the correct sign is retained.

The windchill temperatures are derived as shown.

$$T_{cent-1} = (T_{fahr-1} - 32)/1.8$$
$$V_{mps} = 0.44704 * V_{mph}$$
$$X = \left(10 * \sqrt{V_{mps}} - V_{mps} + 10.5\right) * (33 - T_{cent-1})$$
$$T_{cent-2} = 33 - X/23.1324$$
$$T_{fahr-2} = T_{cent-2} * 1.8 + 32$$

where

T_{fahr-1} = outside temperature in degrees Fahrenheit
T_{cent-1} = outside temperature converted to Celsius
V_{mph} = wind velocity in miles per hour
V_{mps} = wind velocity converted to meters per second
T_{cent-2} = windchill temperature in degrees Celsius
T_{fahr-2} = windchill temperature in degrees Fahrenheit

The windchill calculation is very sensitive to the number of digits of accuracy that are retained in the intermediate steps. For this reason the PICTUREs have rather large fractional portions.

The reader's attention is directed to the input record RECORD-IN. The signed PICTURE on 3 occasions is followed by the phrase SIGN IS LEADING SEPARATE CHARACTER. This is a new clause, born with the 1974 standard, which permits the programmer to read in signed data without having to overpunch it in the rightmost digit of the field. If the sign precedes the number (as we customarily write a number), the phrase LEADING is used. However, we also have the option of following the number with the sign. Then we would write TRAILING instead of LEADING, in accordance with the following general format.

$$[\underline{SIGN\ IS}] \left\{ \begin{array}{c} \underline{LEADING} \\ \underline{TRAILING} \end{array} \right\} [\underline{SEPARATE}\ CHARACTER]$$

When this option is used the sign actually takes up a space of its own, unlike the situation where it is overpunched. Notice that in the detail-line each of the temperatures is assigned a PICTURE with floating plus signs. As you may recall from Chapter 6, this ensures that the appropriate sign, plus or minus, is printed immediately to the left of the most significant digit.

Input for Program 23

```
+030000   +050000   01500   +01000
+010000   +020000   01000   +00500
+000000   +010000   00750   +00400
-010000   -005000   02000   +00250
+J00000   +020000   02500   +00100
```

Program 23

```
1       IDENTIFICATION DIVISION.
2       PROGRAM-ID. WIND.
3       AUTHOR. IRVIN POREMBA.
4       INSTALLATION. NYU.
5       DATE-WRITTEN. JANUARY 30, 1982.
6       DATE-COMPILED. APRIL 21, 1982.
7       SECURITY. HENRY MULLISH.
8       * * * * * * * * * * * * * * * * * * * * * * * * * * * * * * * * * * * * * * * * * * * * * * * * * *
9       *       THIS PROGRAM IS A WIND CHILL FACTOR TABLE.                  *
10      *       THE DATA CARDS ARE PUNCHED:                                 *
11      *                                                                   *
12      *       COLUMNS  1-7  : BEGINNING TEMPERATURE (F).                  *
13      *       COLUMNS 10-16: ENDING TEMPERATURE (F)                       *
14      *       COLUMNS 19-23: WIND VELOCITY (MPH)                          *
15      *       COLUMNS 26-31: INCREMENT BETWEEN TEMPERATURES (F)           *
16      *                                                                   *
17      *       THE PROGRAM USES THE INFORMATION GIVEN                      *
18      *       TO PRINT OUT A TABLE UNDER A SUITABLE HEADING.              *
19      *       AFTER EVERY 15 INCREMENT STEPS THE TABLE IS                 *
20      *       CONTINUED ON A NEW PAGE. THE TABLE GIVES OUT                *
21      *       THE TEMPERATURES BOTH IN FAHRENHEIT AND                     *
22      *       CELSIUS DEGREES ALONG WITH THE CORRESPONDING                *
23      *       WIND CHILL TEMPERATURES.                                    *
24      * * * * * * * * * * * * * * * * * * * * * * * * * * * * * * * * * * * * * * * * * * * * * * * * * *
25
26      ENVIRONMENT DIVISION.
27      CONFIGURATION SECTION.
28      SOURCE-COMPUTER. CYBER-170-720.
29      OBJECT-COMPUTER. CYBER-170-720.
30      SPECIAL-NAMES.
31      INPUT-OUTPUT SECTION.
32      FILE-CONTROL.
33          SELECT IN-FILE ASSIGN TO INPUT.
34          SELECT OUT-FILE ASSIGN TO OUTPUT.
35
36      DATA DIVISION.
37      FILE SECTION.
38
39      FD    IN-FILE
40            LABEL RECORDS ARE OMITTED.
41
42      *     DEFINE DATA.
43
44      01    RECORD-IN.
45            02    BEGIN-TEMP       PIC S9(03)V9(03) SIGN IS LEADING
46                                                    SEPARATE CHARACTER.
47            02    FILLER           PIC X(02).
48            02    END-TEMP         PIC S9(03)V9(03) SIGN IS LEADING
49                                                    SEPARATE CHARACTER.
50            02    FILLER           PIC X(02).
51            02    WIND-VELOCITY    PIC 9(03)V9(02).
52            02    FILLER           PIC X(02).
```

```
53           02    INCREMENT           PIC S9(02)V9(03) SIGN IS LEADING
54                                         'SEPARATE CHARACTER.
55           02    FILLER              PIC X(49).
56
57     FD    OUT-FILE
58           LABEL RECORDS ARE OMITTED.
59
60     *     DEFINE OUTPUT OF PROGRAM
61
62     01    LINE-OUT                  PIC X(133).
63
64     WORKING-STORAGE SECTION.
65     77    MORE-CARDS                PIC X(03) VALUE 'YES'.
66     77    INCREMENT-NO              PIC 99999 VALUE ZERO.
67     77    INCREMENT-NO-2            PIC 99 VALUE ZERO.
68     77    F-TEMP                    PIC S999V999.
69     77    C-TEMP                    PIC S999V999.
70     77    C-TEMP-WIND               PIC S999V9(10).
71     77    C-TEMP-CAL                PIC S999V9(10).
72     77    VMPS                      PIC 999V9(10).
73     77    X-CAL                     PIC S9999V9(10).
74     77    F-TEMP-WIND               PIC S999V999.
75     77    TABLE-COUNT               PIC 99999 VALUE ZERO.
76     77    MATH-1                    PIC S999V9(10).
77     77    MATH-2                    PIC S999V9(10).
78     77    MATH-3                    PIC S999V9(10).
79
80     01    HEADER-1.
81           02    FILLER              PIC X(38) VALUE SPACES.
82           02    FILLER              PIC X(11) VALUE 'WIND CHILL'.
83           02    FILLER              PIC X(14) VALUE 'FACTOR TABLE #'.
84           02    TABLE-COUNT-OUT     PIC ZZ,ZZ9.
85           02    FILLER              PIC X(02) VALUE SPACES.
86           02    BLANK-OR-MESSAGE    PIC X(11).
87
88     01    HEADER-2.
89           02    FILLER              PIC X(38) VALUE SPACES.
90           02    FILLER              PIC X(31) VALUE ALL '*'.
91           02    BLANK-OR-AST        PIC X(13).
92
93     01    HEADER-3.
94           02    FILLER              PIC X(29) VALUE SPACES.
95           02    FILLER              PIC X(67) VALUE ALL '*'.
96
97     01    HEADER-4.
98           02    FILLER              PIC X(29) VALUE SPACES.
99           02    FILLER              PIC X(14) VALUE '*INCREMENT*'.
100          02    FILLER              PIC X(14) VALUE 'TEMPERATURE*'.
101          02    FILLER              PIC X(13) VALUE 'WIND CHILL*'.
102          02    FILLER              PIC X(14) VALUE 'TEMPERATURE*'.
103          02    FILLER              PIC X(12) VALUE 'WIND CHILL*'.
104
105    01    HEADER-5.
106          02    FILLER              PIC X(29) VALUE SPACES.
107          02    FILLER              PIC X(14) VALUE '*NUMBER*'.
108          02    FILLER              PIC X(14) VALUE 'FAHRENHEIT*'.
109          02    FILLER              PIC X(15) VALUE 'FACTOR (F)*'.
110          02    FILLER              PIC X(12) VALUE 'CELSIUS*'.
111          02    FILLER              PIC X(12) VALUE 'FACTOR (C)*'.
112
113    01    HEADER-6.
114          02    FILLER              PIC X(29) VALUE SPACES.
115          02    FILLER              PIC X(67) VALUE ALL '*'.
116
117    01    DETAIL-LINE.
118          02    FILLER              PIC X(29) VALUE SPACES.
119          02    FILLER              PIC X(03) VALUE '*'.
120          02    INCREMENT-NO-OUT    PIC ZZZZ9.
121          02    FILLER              PIC X(07) VALUE '*'.
122          02    F-TEMP-OUT          PIC ++++.999.
123          02    FILLER              PIC X(06) VALUE '*'.
124          02    F-TEMP-WIND-OUT     PIC ++++.999.
125          02    FILLER              PIC X(05) VALUE '*'.
126          02    C-TEMP-OUT          PIC ++++.999.
127          02    FILLER              PIC X(06) VALUE '*'.*
```

```
128         02    C-TEMP-WIND-OUT      PIC + + + + .999.
129         02    FILLER               PIC X(03) VALUE ' * '.
130
131   01    DETAIL-LINE-2.
132         02    FILLER               PIC X(29) VALUE SPACES.
133         02    FILLER               PIC X(05) VALUE 'WIND'.
134         02    FILLER               PIC X(14) VALUE 'VELOCITY (MPH):'.
135         02    FILLER               PIC X(02) VALUE SPACES.
136         02    WIND-VELOCITY-OUT    PIC ZZ9.99.
137
138   01    DETAIL-LINE-3.
139         02    FILLER               PIC X(29) VALUE SPACES.
140         02    FILLER               PIC X(15) VALUE 'INCREMENT USED'.
141         02    FILLER               PIC X(14) VALUE 'IN TABLE (F):'.
142         02    INCREMENT-OUT        PIC + + + + .999.
143
144   01    DETAIL-LINE-4.
145         02    FILLER               PIC X(29) VALUE SPACES.
146         02    FILLER               PIC X(12) VALUE 'TEMPERATURE'.
147         02    FILLER               PIC X(11) VALUE 'RANGE (F):'.
148         02    BEGIN-TEMP-OUT       PIC + + + + .999.
149         02    FILLER               PIC X(04) VALUE 'TO'.
150         02    END-TEMP-OUT         PIC + + + + .999.
151
152   01    DETAIL-LINE-5.
153         02    FILLER               PIC X(29) VALUE SPACES.
154         02    FILLER               PIC X(15) VALUE 'AN ERROR FOUND'.
155         02    FILLER               PIC X(12) VALUE 'IN THE DATA'.
156         02    FILLER               PIC X(14) VALUE 'PREVENTED THE'.
157         02    FILLER               PIC X(17) VALUE 'TABLE FROM BEING'.
158
159   01    DETAIL-LINE-6.
160         02    FILLER               PIC X(29) VALUE SPACES.
161         02    FILLER               PIC X(12) VALUE 'PRINTED OUT.'.
162         02    FILLER               PIC X(16) VALUE 'CARD NUMBER = '.
163         02    TABLE-COUNT-OUT-2    PIC ZZ,ZZ9.
164
165   01    DETAIL-LINE-7.
166         02    FILLER               PIC X(29) VALUE SPACES.
167         02    FILLER               PIC X(13) VALUE 'BEGIN TEMP = '.
168         02    BEGIN-TEMP-OUT-2     PIC 999V999.
169         02    FILLER               PIC X(14) VALUE 'END TEMP = '.
170         02    END-TEMP-OUT-2       PIC 999V999.
171
172   01    DETAIL-LINE-8.
173         02    FILLER               PIC X(29) VALUE SPACES.
174         02    FILLER               PIC X(05) VALUE 'WIND'.
175         02    FILLER               PIC X(11) VALUE 'VELOCITY = '.
176         02    WIND-OUT-2           PIC 999V99.
177         02    FILLER               PIC X(15) VALUE 'INCREMENT = '.
178         02    INCREMENT-OUT-2      PIC 99V999.
179
180   01    DETAIL-LINE-9.
181         02    FILLER               PIC X(29) VALUE SPACES.
182         02    FILLER               PIC X(57) VALUE ALL ' * '.
183
184   PROCEDURE DIVISION.
185
186   *     THIS IS THE MAIN PARAGRAPH WHICH USES
187   *     THE PERFORM STATEMENT TO ACCESS TO OTHER PARAGRAPHS
188
189   MAIN-LINE-ROUTINE.
190         PERFORM OPEN-FILES.
191         PERFORM START-UP.
192         PERFORM PROCESS-DATA UNTIL MORE-CARDS EQUAL 'NO'.
193         PERFORM CLOSE-UP.
194         STOP RUN.
195
196   OPEN-FILES.
197         OPEN INPUT IN-FILE.
198         OPEN OUTPUT OUT-FILE.
199
200   NEW-PAGE.
201         MOVE SPACES TO LINE-OUT.
202         WRITE LINE-OUT AFTER PAGE.
```

```
203
204   *        START-UP CHECKS TO SEE IF THERE IS ANY DATA.
205   *        IF THE IS NO DATA AN ERROR MESSAGE IS PRINTED.
206
207        START-UP.
208            READ IN-FILE AT END MOVE 'NO' TO MORE-CARDS
209                MOVE SPACES TO LINE-OUT
210                WRITE LINE-OUT AFTER PAGE
211                MOVE ' **NO DATA IN DECK**' TO LINE-OUT
212                WRITE LINE-OUT AFTER 30.
213
214   *        PROCESS-DATA CHECKS TO SEE IF THE DATA READ IN
215   *        IS NUMERIC. IF IT NOT NUMERIC AN ERROR MESSAGE
216   *        IS PRINTED, OTHERWISE THE HEADINGS ARE WRITTEN AND
217   *        THRU THE USE OF THE PERFORM-VARYING-UNTIL STATEMENT,
218   *        CONTROL IS DIRECTED TO WORK-PARA. AFTERWARDS ANOTHER
219   *        DATA CARD IS READ IN.
220
221        PROCESS-DATA.
222            ADD 1 TO TABLE-COUNT.
223            IF WIND-VELOCITY NOT NUMERIC
224                OR BEGIN-TEMP NOT NUMERIC
225                OR END-TEMP NOT NUMERIC
226                OR INCREMENT NOT NUMERIC
227                PERFORM ERROR-PARA
228            ELSE MOVE TABLE-COUNT TO TABLE-COUNT-OUT
229                MOVE BEGIN-TEMP TO BEGIN-TEMP-OUT
230                MOVE END-TEMP TO END-TEMP-OUT
231                MOVE WIND-VELOCITY TO WIND-VELOCITY-OUT
232                MOVE INCREMENT TO INCREMENT-OUT
233                PERFORM NEW-PAGE
234                PERFORM WRITE-HEADINGS-PARA
235                PERFORM WORK-PARA VARYING F-TEMP FROM BEGIN-TEMP
236                    BY INCREMENT UNTIL F-TEMP > END-TEMP
237            WRITE LINE-OUT FROM HEADER-6 AFTER 1.
238            READ IN-FILE AT END MOVE 'NO' TO MORE-CARDS.
239            MOVE ZEROS TO INCREMENT-NO, INCREMENT-NO-2.
240            MOVE SPACES TO BLANK-OR-MESSAGE, BLANK-OR-AST.
241
242        CLOSE-UP.
243            CLOSE IN-FILE, OUT-FILE.
244
245   *        WORK-PARA PERFORMS THE CALCULATIONS FOR EACH VALUE
246   *        OF THE FAHRENHEIT TEMPERATURE BETWEEN THE INITIAL
247   *        VALUE AND THE FINAL VALUE IN STEPS OF INCREMENT.
248
249        WORK-PARA.
250            ADD 1 TO INCREMENT-NO.
251            ADD 1 TO INCREMENT-NO-2.
252            MOVE INCREMENT-NO TO INCREMENT-NO-OUT.
253            MOVE F-TEMP TO F-TEMP-OUT.
254            SUBTRACT 32 FROM F-TEMP GIVING MATH-1.
255            DIVIDE 1.8 INTO MATH-1 GIVING C-TEMP-CAL.
256            ADD 0.0005, C-TEMP-CAL GIVING C-TEMP-OUT.
257            MULTIPLY 0.44704 BY WIND-VELOCITY GIVING VMPS.
258            COMPUTE X-CAL = (10 * VMPS ** 0.5 − VMPS + 10.5)
259                * (33 - C-TEMP-CAL).
260            DIVIDE 23.1324 INTO X-CAL GIVING MATH-2.
261            SUBTRACT MATH-2 FROM 33 GIVING C-TEMP-WIND.
262            ADD 0.0005, C-TEMP-WIND GIVING C-TEMP-WIND-OUT.
263            MULTIPLY C-TEMP-WIND BY 1.8 GIVING MATH-3.
264            ADD 32, MATH-3 GIVING F-TEMP-WIND-OUT ROUNDED.
265            WRITE LINE-OUT FROM HEADER-6 AFTER 1.
266            WRITE LINE-OUT FROM DETAIL-LINE AFTER 1.
267            IF F-TEMP EQUAL END-TEMP MOVE ZEROS TO INCREMENT-NO-2.
268            IF INCREMENT-NO-2 = 15 MOVE ZEROS TO INCREMENT-NO-2
269                MOVE '(CONTINUED)' TO BLANK-OR-MESSAGE
270                WRITE LINE-OUT FROM HEADER-6 AFTER 1
271                MOVE '**************' TO BLANK-OR-AST
272                PERFORM NEW-PAGE
273                PERFORM WRITE-HEADINGS-PARA.
274
275   *        WRITE-HEADINGS-PARA WRITES THE HEADINGS.
276
277        WRITE-HEADINGS-PARA.
```

```
278        WRITE LINE-OUT FROM HEADER-1 AFTER 1.
279        WRITE LINE-OUT FROM HEADER-2 AFTER 1.
280        WRITE LINE-OUT FROM HEADER-2 AFTER 1.
281        WRITE LINE-OUT FROM DETAIL-LINE-2 AFTER 2.
282        WRITE LINE-OUT FROM DETAIL-LINE-3 AFTER 1.
283        WRITE LINE-OUT FROM DETAIL-LINE-4 AFTER 1.
284        WRITE LINE-OUT FROM HEADER-3 AFTER 1.
285        WRITE LINE-OUT FROM HEADER-4 AFTER 1.
286        WRITE LINE-OUT FROM HEADER-5 AFTER 1.
287        WRITE LINE-OUT FROM HEADER-6 AFTER 1.
288
289    *   ERROR-PARA MOVES THE DATA TO THEIR CORRESPONDING FIELDS
290    *.  AND THEN PRINTS OUT THE DATA ON A NEW PAGE SO THAT
291    *   THE USER WILL KNOW WHICH DATA IS NOT NUMERIC.
292
293    ERROR-PARA.
294        MOVE TABLE-COUNT TO TABLE-COUNT-OUT-2.
295        MOVE WIND-VELOCITY TO WIND-OUT-2.
296        MOVE BEGIN-TEMP TO BEGIN-TEMP-OUT-2.
297        MOVE END-TEMP TO END-TEMP-OUT-2.
298        MOVE INCREMENT TO INCREMENT-OUT-2.
299        PERFORM NEW-PAGE.
300        WRITE LINE-OUT FROM DETAIL-LINE-5 AFTER 1.
301        WRITE LINE-OUT FROM DETAIL-LINE-6, AFTER 1.
302        WRITE LINE-OUT FROM DETAIL-LINE-7.
303        WRITE LINE-OUT FROM DETAIL-LINE-8.
304        WRITE LINE-OUT FROM DETAIL-LINE-9 AFTER 1.
```

Output for Program 23

```
                           WIND CHILL FACTOR TABLE # 1
           * * * * * * * * * * * * * * * * * * * * * * * * * * * * *
           * * * * * * * * * * * * * * * * * * * * * * * * * * * * *
WIND VELOCITY(MPH): 15.00
INCREMENT USED IN TABLE(F): +1.005
TEMPERATURE RANGE(F): +30.000 TO +50.000
```

INCREMENT NUMBER	TEMPERATURE FAHRENHEIT	WIND CHILL FACTOR(F)	TEMPERATURE CELSIUS	WIND CHILL FACTOR(C)
1	+30.000	+12.595	−1.110	−10.779
2	+31.000	+13.879	−.555	−10.066
3	+32.000	+15.162	+.000	−9.353
4	+33.000	+16.446	+.556	−8.640
5	+34.000	+17.729	+1.111	−7.927
6	+35.000	+19.013	+1.667	−7.214
7	+36.000	+20.296	+2.222	−6.501
8	+37.000	+21.580	+2.778	−5.788
9	+38.000	+22.863	+3.333	−5.075
10	+39.000	+24.147	+3.889	−4.362
11	+40.000	+25.430	+4.444	−3.649
12	+41.000	+26.713	+5.000	−2.936
13	+42.000	+27.997	+5.556	−2.223
14	+43.000	+29.280	+6.111	−1.510
15	+44.000	+30.564	+6.667	−.797

WIND CHILL FACTOR TABLE # 1 (CONTINUED)

* *

* *

WIND VELOCITY(MPH): 15.00
INCREMENT USED IN TABLE(F): +1.005
TEMPERATURE RANGE(F): +30.000 TO +50.000

INCREMENT NUMBER	TEMPERATURE FAHRENHEIT	WIND CHILL FACTOR(F)	TEMPERATURE CELSIUS	WIND CHILL FACTOR(C)
16	+45.000	+31.847	+7.222	−.084
17	+46.000	+33.131	+7.778	+.628
18	+47.000	+34.414	+8.333	+1.341
19	+48.000	+35.698	+8.889	+2.054
20	+49.000	+36.981	+9.444	+2.767
21	+50.000	+38.265	+10.000	+3.480

WIND CHILL FACTOR TABLE # 2

* *

* *

WIND VELOCITY(MPH): 10.00
INCREMENT USED IN TABLE(F): +.500
TEMPERATURE RANGE(F): +10.000 TO +20.000

INCREMENT NUMBER	TEMPERATURE FAHRENHEIT	WIND CHILL FACTOR(F)	TEMPERATURE CELSIUS	WIND CHILL FACTOR(C)
1	+10.000	−4.218	−12.221	−20.120
2	+10.500	−3.631	−11.943	−19.794
3	+11.000	−3.043	−11.666	−19.468
4	+11.500	−2.456	−11.388	−19.141
5	+12.000	−1.869	−11.110	−18.815
6	+12.500	−1.281	−10.832	−18.489
7	+13.000	−.694	−10.555	−18.162
8	+13.500	−.107	−10.277	−17.836
9	+14.000	+.481	−9.999	−17.510
10	+14.500	+1.068	−9.721	−17.183
11	+15.000	+1.655	−9.443	−16.857
12	+15.500	+2.243	−9.166	−16.531
13	+16.000	+2.830	−8.888	−16.205
14	+16.500	+3.417	−8.610	−15.878
15	+17.000	+4.005	−8.332	−15.552

WIND CHILL FACTOR TABLE # 2 (CONTINUED)

* *
* *

WIND VELOCITY(MPH): 10.00
INCREMENT USED IN TABLE(F): +.500
TEMPERATURE RANGE(F): +10.000 TO +20.000

INCREMENT NUMBER	TEMPERATURE FAHRENHEIT	WIND CHILL FACTOR(F)	TEMPERATURE CELSIUS	WIND CHILL FACTOR(C)
16	+17.500	+4.592	−8.055	−15.226
17	+18.000	+5.179	−7.777	−14.899
18	+18.500	+5.767	−7.499	−14.573
19	+19.000	+6.354	−7.221	−14.247
20	+19.500	+6.941	−6.943	−13.921
21	+20.000	+7.529	−6.666	−13.594

WIND CHILL FACTOR TABLE # 3

* *
* *

WIND VELOCITY(MPH): 7.50
INCREMENT USED IN TABLE(F): +.407
TEMPERATURE RANGE(F): +.000 TO +10.000

INCREMENT NUMBER	TEMPERATURE FAHRENHEIT	WIND CHILL FACTOR(F)	TEMPERATURE CELSIUS	WIND CHILL FACTOR(C)
1	+.000	−9.188	−17.777	22.881
2	+.400	−8.748	−17.555	−22.637
3	+.800	−8.308	−17.332	−22.392
4	+1.200	−7.868	−17.110	−22.148
5	+1.600	−7.427	−16.888	−21.903
6	+2.000	−6.987	−16.666	−21.659
7	+2.400	−6.547	−16.443	−21.414
8	+2.800	−6.107	−16.221	−21.169
9	+3.200	−5.667	−15.999	−20.925
10	+3.600	−5.226	−15.777	−20.680
11	+4.000	−4.786	−15.555	−20.436
12	+4.400	−4.346	−15.332	−20.191
13	+4.800	−3.906	−15.110	−19.947
14	+5.200	−3.466	−14.888	−19.702
15	+5.600	−3.025	−14.666	−19.457

WIND CHILL FACTOR TABLE # 3 (CONTINUED)

* *
* *

WIND VELOCITY(MPH): 7.50
INCREMENT USED IN TABLE(F): +.407
TEMPERATURE RANGE(F): +.000 TO +10.000

INCREMENT NUMBER	TEMPERATURE FAHRENHEIT	WIND CHILL FACTOR(F)	TEMPERATURE CELSIUS	WIND CHILL FACTOR(C)
16	+6.000	−2.585	−14.443	−19.213
17	+6.400	−2.145	−14.221	−18.968
18	+6.800	−1.705	−13.999	−18.724
19	+7.200	−1.264	−13.777	−18.479
20	+7.600	−.824	−13.555	−18.235
21	+8.000	−.384	−13.332	−17.990
22	+8.400	+.056	−13.110	−17.746
23	+8.800	+.496	−12.888	−17.501
24	+9.200	+.937	−12.666	−17.256
25	+9.600	+1.377	−12.443	−17.012
26	+10.000	+1.817	−12.221	−16.767

WIND CHILL FACTOR TABLE # 4

* *
* *

WIND VELOCITY(MPH): 20.00
INCREMENT USED IN TABLE(F): +.250
TEMPERATURE RANGE(F): −10.000 TO −5.000

INCREMENT NUMBER	TEMPERATURE FAHRENHEIT	WIND CHILL FACTOR(F)	TEMPERATURE CELSIUS	WIND CHILL FACTOR(C)
1	−10.000	−46.505	−23.332	−43.613
2	−9.750	−46.165	−23.193	−43.424
3	−9.500	−45.825	−23.055	−43.235
4	−9.250	−45.485	−22.916	−43.046
5	−9.000	−45.145	−22.777	−42.858
6	−8.750	−44.805	−22.638	−42.669
7	−8.500	−44.465	−22.499	−42.480
8	−8.250	−44.125	−22.360	−42.291
9	−8.000	−43.785	−22.221	−42.102
10	−7.750	−43.445	−22.082	−41.913
11	−7.500	−43.105	−21.943	−41.724
12	−7.250	−42.765	−21.805	−41.535
13	−7.000	−42.425	−21.666	−41.346
14	−6.750	−42.085	−21.527	−41.158
15	−6.500	−41.745	−21.388	−40.969

```
                    WIND CHILL FACTOR TABLE # 4 (CONTINUED)
      * * * * * * * * * * * * * * * * * * * * * * * * * * * * * * * * * * * * * * * *
      * * * * * * * * * * * * * * * * * * * * * * * * * * * * * * * * * * * * *
WIND VELOCITY(MPH): 20.00
INCREMENT USED IN TABLE(F): +.250
TEMPERATURE RANGE(F): −10.000 TO −5.000
* * * * * * * * * * * * * * * * * * * * * * * * * * * * * * * * * * * * * * * * * * * *
*   INCREMENT   *   TEMPERATURE   *   WIND CHILL   *   TEMPERATURE   *   WIND CHILL   *
*    NUMBER     *   FAHRENHEIT     *   FACTOR(F)    *    CELSIUS      *   FACTOR(C)    *
* * * * * * * * * * * * * * * * * * * * * * * * * * * * * * * * * * * * * * * * * * * *
* * * * * * * * * * * * * * * * * * * * * * * * * * * * * * * * * * * * * * * * * * * *
*      16       *      −6.250      *    −41.405     *     −21.249     *    −40.780     *
* * * * * * * * * * * * * * * * * * * * * * * * * * * * * * * * * * * * * * * * * * * *
*      17       *      −6.000      *    −41.065     *     −21.110     *    −40.591     *
* * * * * * * * * * * * * * * * * * * * * * * * * * * * * * * * * * * * * * * * * * * *
*      18       *      −5.750      *    −40.725     *     −20.971     *    −40.402     *
* * * * * * * * * * * * * * * * * * * * * * * * * * * * * * * * * * * * * * * * * * * *
*      19       *      −5.500      *    −40.385     *     −20.832     *    −40.213     *
* * * * * * * * * * * * * * * * * * * * * * * * * * * * * * * * * * * * * * * * * * * *
*      20       *      −5.250      *    −40.045     *     −20.693     *    −40.024     *
* * * * * * * * * * * * * * * * * * * * * * * * * * * * * * * * * * * * * * * * * * * *
*      21       *      −5.000      *    −39.705     *     −20.555     *    −39.835     *
* * * * * * * * * * * * * * * * * * * * * * * * * * * * * * * * * * * * * * * * * * * *
```

AN ERROR FOUND IN THE DATA PREVENTED THE TABLE FROM BEING
PRINTED OUT. CARD NUMBER = 5
BEGIN TEMP = J00000 END TEMP = + J0000
WIND VELOCITY = 02500 INCREMENT = 00100
```
* * * * * * * * * * * * * * * * * * * * * * * * * * * * * * * * * * * * * * * * * * * *
```

9.4   The Branch Banks Problem

This problem is introduced now for a special reason. It is the first time that we will deal with a program in which the input file consists of records of different formats, not a particularly uncommon occurrence in commercial data processing.

The input file consists of "sets" of data. Each "set" is composed of a bank head office card, followed by one card for each of its various branches.

Each *head office* card is punched with the name of the bank, the headquarters location, the number of employees in the head office, and the number of branches.

Each *branch* card is punched with the name of the branch, the total dollar assets of the branch, and the number of employees in the branch.

The purpose of the program is to prepare a report in which, for each bank, a separate page is printed with the name of the bank, its address, the number of branches, and the number of employees. The name of each branch, its dollar assets, and the number of its employees are then printed under the name of the head office. The total assets are then computed and printed, and the average branch assets, together with the total number of employees, are calculated and printed. In addition, each page of output is numbered sequentially.

The main bank record is formatted as shown.

1	30	35	57	60	62	77 78 — 80
Bank Name		Address		Number of Branches		Number of Employees

whereas the format for each branch bank record is:

1	25	30	38	55	57
Branch Name		Branch Assets		Number of Employees	

If there are too many data cards following the main bank card—or if there are too few—an error will result and eventually the end-of-file condition will be raised and an appropriate error message is printed.

Input for Program 24

IRVIN POREMBA BANKING CORP.		NEW YORK, NEW YORK	004	100
IRVIN NORTH BRANCH	550000000	050		
IRVIN SOUTH BRANCH	350000000	125		
IRVIN EAST BRANCH	750000000	175		
IRVIN WEST BRANCH	125000000	075		
AMERICAN SAVING CORP.		CHICAGO, ILLINOIS	003	088
NORTH SIDE BRANCH	007500000	035		
SKOKIE BRANCH	035000000	050		
WILMETTE BRANCH	005000000 *	025		
PACIFIC COMMERCIAL BANK CORP.		SAN DIEGO, CALIFORNIA	002	035
L.A. BRANCH	025000000	055		
SAN FRANCISCO BRANCH	035000000	090		

The situation we are confronting—a single input file with more than one record description—can be very confusing to the novice. How is such a file described? It is, of course, described in the Data Division where a single FD for the file-name is specified. However, under that FD, *2 separate* record descriptions are entered, one for each of the 2 input records. The order in which they appear is of no consequence, as we will see shortly.

Despite the fact that there are 2 record descriptions for the same input file, only 80 characters of memory space are provided by the computer. Because the 2 records have little, if anything, in common with each other, how does the programmer know to which of the 2 records to refer? The answer is that the 2 separate record descriptions describe precisely the same area of memory. So long as the programmer knows with which kind of data card he or she is dealing at any given time, the appropriate record description is referred to when working with individual fields. In other words, one record description is only a *redefinition* of the other.

Once the main bank record has been read, provision must be made either to process the appropriate data on that card immediately or to save it for subsequent use. That is, once the first of the following branch bank records is read, the information from the main bank record will be lost, being overwritten by whatever is read into the input area next. Therefore whatever information is needed from the main bank record must be utilized while it is available. As soon as the next record is read in, that information will otherwise be lost.

Program 24

```
1        IDENTIFICATION   DIVISION.
2        PROGRAM-ID.      BANKING.
3        AUTHOR.          IRVIN POREMBA.
4        INSTALLATION.    NYU.
5        DATE-WRITTEN.    JUNE 10, 1982.
6        DATE-COMPILED.   JUNE 13, 1982.
7        SECURITY.        HENRY MULLISH.
8
9        ENVIRONMENT   DIVISION.
10       CONFIGURATION  SECTION.
11       SOURCE-COMPUTER. CYBER-170-720.
12       OBJECT-COMPUTER. CYBER-170-720.
13       SPECIAL-NAMES.
14       INPUT-OUTPUT    SECTION.
15       FILE-CONTROL.
16           SELECT IN-FILE ASSIGN TO INPUT.
17           SELECT OUT-FILE ASSIGN TO OUTPUT.
18
19       DATA DIVISION.
20       FILE SECTION.
21
22       FD  IN-FILE
23           LABEL RECORDS ARE OMITTED.
24
25       01  MAIN-BANK-RECORD.
26           02   BANK-NAME-IN          PIC X(30).
27           02   FILLER                PIC X(04).
28           02   HEAD-ADDRESS          PIC X(23).
29           02   FILLER                PIC X(02).
30           02   BRANCH-NUMBERS        PIC 9(03).
31           02   FILLER                PIC X(15).
32           02   EMPLOYEE-NUMBER-1     PIC 9(03).
33
34       01  BRANCH-BANK-RECORD.
35           02   BRANCH-NAME           PIC X(25).
36           02   FILLER                PIC X(04).
37           02   BRANCH-ASSET          PIC 9(09).
38           02   FILLER                PIC X(16).
39           02   BRANCH-EMPLOYEES      PIC 9(03).
40           02   FILLER                PIC X(23).
41
42       FD  OUT-FILE
43           LABEL RECORDS ARE OMITTED.
44
45       01  LINE-OUT                   PIC X(133).
46
47       WORKING-STORAGE SECTION.
48
49       01  INDEPENDENT-ITEMS-USED.
50           02   ANY-MORE-CARDS        PIC X(03) VALUE 'YES'.
51           02   CARD-COUNT            PIC 9(03).
52           02   PAGE-COUNT            PIC 9(02) VALUE ZERO.
53           02   TOTAL-ASSETS          PIC 9(11).
54           02   TOTAL-EMPLOYEES       PIC 9(05).
55           02   WS-BRANCH-NUMBERS     PIC 9(03).
56
57       01  HEADER-1.
58           02   FILLER                PIC X(10) VALUE SPACES.
59           02   FILLER                PIC X(09) VALUE 'AMERICAN'.
60           02   FILLER                PIC X(08) VALUE 'BANKING'.
61           02   FILLER                PIC X(14) VALUE 'ASSOCIATION:'.
62           02   FILLER                PIC X(13) VALUE 'BANK FILE'.
63           02   FILLER                PIC X(05) VALUE 'PAGE'.
64           02   PAGE-COUNT-OUT        PIC Z9.
65
66       01  HEADER-2.
67           02   FILLER                PIC X(10) VALUE SPACES.
68           02   FILLER                PIC X(51) VALUE ALL ' * '.
69
70       01  HEADER-3.
71           02   FILLER                PIC X(01) VALUE SPACES.
72           02   FILLER                PIC X(14) VALUE 'COUNT'.
73           02   FILLER                PIC X(23) VALUE 'BRANCH NAME'.
```

```
74        02    FILLER                    PIC X(14) VALUE 'ASSETS'.
75        02    FILLER                    PIC X(09) VALUE 'EMPLOYEES'.
76
77   01   HEADER-4.
78        02    FILLER                    PIC X(01) VALUE SPACES.
79        02    FILLER                    PIC X(05) VALUE ALL '-'.
80        02    FILLER                    PIC X(02) VALUE SPACES.
81        02    FILLER                    PIC X(25) VALUE ALL '-'.
82        02    FILLER                    PIC X(02) VALUE SPACES.
83        02    FILLER                    PIC X(15) VALUE ALL '-'.
84        02    FILLER                    PIC X(02) VALUE SPACES.
85        02    FILLER                    PIC X(09) VALUE ALL '-'.
86
87   01   DETAIL-LINE.
88        02    FILLER                    PIC X(01) VALUE SPACES.
89        02    FILLER                    PIC X(12) VALUE 'BANK NAME:'.
90        02    BANK-NAME-OUT             PIC X(30).
91        02    FILLER                    PIC X(02) VALUE SPACES.
92        02    FILLER                    PIC X(10) VALUE 'ADDRESS:'.
93        02    ADDRESS-OUT               PIC X(23).
94        02    FILLER                    PIC X(02) VALUE SPACES.
95
96   01   DETAIL-LINE-2.
97        02    FILLER                    PIC X(01) VALUE SPACES.
98        02    FILLER                    PIC X(11) VALUE 'BRANCHES:'.
99        02    BRANCH-NO-OUT             PIC ZZ9.
100       02    FILLER                    PIC X(02) VALUE SPACES.
101       02    FILLER                    PIC X(12) VALUE 'HEAD OFFICE'.
102       02    FILLER                    PIC X(12) VALUE 'EMPLOYEES:'.
103       02    EMPLOYEES-OUT-1           PIC ZZ9.
104
105  01   DETAIL-LINE-3.
106       02    FILLER                    PIC X(03) VALUE SPACES.
107       02    CARD-COUNT-OUT            PIC ZZ9.
108       02    FILLER                    PIC X(02) VALUE SPACES.
109       02    BRANCH-NAME-OUT           PIC X(25).
110       02    FILLER                    PIC X(02) VALUE SPACES.
111       02    ASSETS-OUT                PIC $$$$,$$$,$$9.00.
112       02    FILLER                    PIC X(05) VALUE SPACES.
113       02    EMPLOYEE-OUT-2            PIC ZZ9.
114
115  01   DETAIL-LINE-4.
116       02    FILLER                    PIC X(02) VALUE SPACES.
117       02    FILLER                    PIC X(15) VALUE 'TOTAL ASSETS = '.
118       02    TOTAL-ASSETS-OUT          PIC $$$,$$$,$$$,$$9.00.
119
120  01   DETAIL-LINE-5.
121       02    FILLER                    PIC X(02) VALUE SPACES.
122       02    FILLER                    PIC X(15) VALUE 'AVERAGE BRANCH'.
123       02    FILLER                    PIC X(09) VALUE 'ASSETS = '.
124       02    AVERAGE-OUT               PIC $$$,$$$,$$$,$$9.99.
125
126  01   DETAIL-LINE-6.
127       02    FILLER                    PIC X(02) VALUE SPACES.
128       02    FILLER                    PIC X(18) VALUE 'TOTAL EMPLOYEES = '.
129       02    TOTAL-EMPLOYEE-OUT        PIC ZZ,ZZ9.
130
131  PROCEDURE DIVISION.
132
133  MAIN-LINE-ROUTINE.
134       PERFORM OPEN-FILES.
135       PERFORM NEW-PAGE.
136       PERFORM START-UP.
137       PERFORM PROCESS-DATA UNTIL ANY-MORE-CARDS EQUAL 'NO'.
138       PERFORM CLOSE-UP.
139       STOP RUN.
140
141  OPEN-FILES.
142       OPEN INPUT IN-FILE.
143       OPEN OUTPUT OUT-FILE.
144
145  NEW-PAGE.
146       MOVE SPACES TO LINE-OUT.
147       WRITE LINE-OUT AFTER PAGE.
148
149  START-UP.
```

```
150         READ IN-FILE AT END MOVE 'NO' TO ANY-MORE-CARDS
151             MOVE ' **NO DATA IN DECK**' TO LINE-OUT
152             WRITE LINE-OUT AFTER 30.
153
154     PROCESS-DATA.
155         PERFORM WRITE-HEADINGS-1.
156         MOVE ZEROS TO CARD-COUNT, TOTAL-EMPLOYEES, TOTAL-ASSETS.
157         MOVE BANK-NAME-IN TO BANK-NAME-OUT.
158         MOVE HEAD-ADDRESS TO ADDRESS-OUT.
159         MOVE BRANCH-NUMBERS TO BRANCH-NO-OUT.
160         MOVE EMPLOYEE-NUMBER-1 TO EMPLOYEES-OUT-1.
161         ADD EMPLOYEE-NUMBER-1 TO TOTAL-EMPLOYEES.
162         WRITE LINE-OUT FROM DETAIL-LINE AFTER 2.
163         WRITE LINE-OUT FROM DETAIL-LINE-2 AFTER 1.
164         MOVE BRANCH-NUMBERS TO WS-BRANCH-NUMBERS.
165         PERFORM WRITE-HEADINGS-2.
166         PERFORM READ-BRANCH-CARDS WS-BRANCH-NUMBERS TIMES.
167         PERFORM AVERAGE-AND-TOTAL.
168         READ IN-FILE AT END MOVE 'NO' TO ANY-MORE-CARDS.
169         IF ANY-MORE-CARDS EQUAL 'YES' PERFORM NEW-PAGE.
170
171     CLOSE-UP.
172         CLOSE IN-FILE, OUT-FILE.
173
174     READ-BRANCH-CARDS.
175         READ IN-FILE AT END PERFORM ERROR-PARA.
176         ADD 1 TO CARD-COUNT.
177         MOVE CARD-COUNT TO CARD-COUNT-OUT.
178         MOVE BRANCH-NAME TO BRANCH-NAME-OUT.
179         MOVE BRANCH-ASSET TO ASSETS-OUT.
180         ADD BRANCH-ASSET TO TOTAL-ASSETS.
181         MOVE BRANCH-EMPLOYEES TO EMPLOYEE-OUT-2.
182         ADD BRANCH-EMPLOYEES TO TOTAL-EMPLOYEES.
183         WRITE LINE-OUT FROM DETAIL-LINE-3 AFTER 2.
184
185     AVERAGE-AND-TOTAL.
186         MOVE TOTAL-ASSETS TO TOTAL-ASSETS-OUT.
187         DIVIDE WS-BRANCH-NUMBERS INTO TOTAL-ASSETS GIVING
188             AVERAGE-OUT ROUNDED.
189         MOVE TOTAL-EMPLOYEES TO TOTAL-EMPLOYEE-OUT.
190         WRITE LINE-OUT FROM DETAIL-LINE-4 AFTER 2.
191         WRITE LINE-OUT FROM DETAIL-LINE-5 AFTER 1.
192         WRITE LINE-OUT FROM DETAIL-LINE-6 AFTER 1.
193
194     WRITE-HEADINGS-1.
195         ADD 1 TO PAGE-COUNT.
196         MOVE PAGE-COUNT TO PAGE-COUNT-OUT
197         WRITE LINE-OUT FROM HEADER-1 AFTER 1.
198         WRITE LINE-OUT FROM HEADER-2 AFTER 1.
199
200     WRITE-HEADINGS-2.
201         WRITE LINE-OUT FROM HEADER-3 AFTER 2.
202         WRITE LINE-OUT FROM HEADER-4 AFTER 0.
203
204     ERROR-PARA.
205         PERFORM NEW-PAGE.
206         MOVE ' **ERROR IN SEQUENCE TO DATA CARDS**' TO LINE-OUT.
207         WRITE LINE-OUT AFER 30.
208         PERFORM CLOSE-UP.
209         STOP RUN.
```

Output for Program 24

```
            AMERICAN BANKING ASSOCIATION: BANK FILE   PAGE 1
* * * * * * * * * * * * * * * * * * * * * * * * * * * * * * * * * * * * * * * * *
BANK NAME: IRVIN POREMBA BANKING CORP.     ADDRESS: NEW YORK, NEW YORK
BRANCHES: 4     HEAD OFFICE EMPLOYEES: 100
    COUNT           BRANCH NAME           ASSETS            EMPLOYEES
    _ _ _ _ _   _ _ _ _ _ _ _ _ _ _   _ _ _ _ _ _ _ _   _ _ _ _ _ _ _
        1       IRVIN NORTH BRANCH    $550,000,000.00         50
        2       IRVIN SOUTH BRANCH    $350,000,000.00        125
        3       IRVIN EAST BRANCH     $750,000,000.00        175
        4       IRVIN WEST BRANCH     $125,000,000.00         75
TOTAL ASSETS = $1,775,000,000.00
AVERAGE BRANCH ASSETS = $443,750,000.00
TOTAL EMPLOYEES = 525
```

AMERICAN BANKING ASSOCIATION: BANK FILE   PAGE 2

* *

BANK NAME: AMERICAN SAVING CORP.   ADDRESS: CHICAGO, ILLINOIS
BRANCHES: 3   HEAD OFFICE EMPLOYEES: 88

COUNT	BRANCH NAME	ASSETS	EMPLOYEES
1	NORTH SIDE BRANCH	$7,500,000.00	35
2	SKOKIE BRANCH	$35,000,000.00	50
3	WILMETTE BRANCH	$5,000,000.00	25

TOTAL ASSETS = $47,500,000.00
AVERAGE BRANCH ASSETS = $15,833,333.33
TOTAL EMPLOYEES = 198

AMERICAN BANKING ASSOCIATION: BANK FILE   PAGE 3

* *

BANK NAME: PACIFIC COMMERCIAL BANK CORP.   ADDRESS: SAN DIEGO, CALIFORNIA
BRANCHES: 2   HEAD OFFICE EMPLOYEES: 35

COUNT	BRANCH NAME	ASSETS	EMPLOYEES
1	L.A. BRANCH	$25,000,000.00	55
2	SAN FRANCISCO BRANCH	$35,000,000.00	90

TOTAL ASSETS = $60,000,000.00
AVERAGE BRANCH ASSETS = $30,000,000.00
TOTAL EMPLOYEES = 180

9.5   The Traffic Problem

This is another program in which the input file consists of records of different formats.

For the purposes of this program the data is organized in the following way. The first card of a "set" of cards contains the last name of a traffic violator, his or her first name, the driver's license number, and the number of violations recorded against the violator, in this format.

1 20	25 40	45 50	60 61
Last Name	First Name	License Plate Number	Number of Violations
X(20)	X(16)	X(06)	99

If the number of violations recorded in columns 60–61 were, say, 03, then behind the card 3 violations cards would be placed, each one giving details of the violations recorded against the individual named in the first card. These violator cards are punched in the format, shown at the top of the next page, where the license plate number, date of violation, nature of the violation, and the amount of the fine are recorded.

The goal of the program is to print a detailed report in which for each violator all the pertinent information appears neatly on a single page. At the foot of the printout a statement giving the total sum due and the average amount per violation should be given. Finally, at the end of the run the total amount due the Motor Vehicles Bureau in fines should be printed on a separate page—the last page of the output.

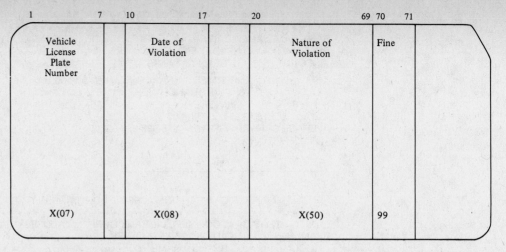

It is clear from the input for the program that the single input file consists of 2 totally different records.

Input for Program 25

```
COLE                      JERRY           C12398      06
MX13456    11/15/80   SPEEDING 25 IN 10 MPH ZONE          40
MX13456    09/07/80   DRIVING IN EMERGENCY ONLY ZONE      40
124ABCD    05/08/80   SPEEDING 80 IN 55 MPH ZONE          53
124ABDF    03/24/80   SPEEDING 45 IN 30 MPH ZONE          40
ABD8910    02/10/80   PARKING ON WRONG SIDE OF STREET     10
Z100001    04/05/79   FAILURE TO SIGNAL ON TURN           15
CORNER                    MICHELLE        G95134      04
MX13456    04/14/79   FAILURE TO SIGNAL WHILE CHANGING LANES   35
ABCB765    01/01/79   SPEEDING 25 IN 15 MPH ZONE          05
ABCB765    12/31/79   DRINKING WHILE DRIVING              80
ABCB765    12/30/79   SPEEDING 45 IN 30 MPH ZONE          25
FREEDMAN                  ROBERT          F00274      05
NGIEDRF    01/15/81   DRIVING ON WRONG SIDE OF STREET     20
SDF1234    01/02/81   SPEEDING 56 IN 55 MPH ZONE          01
HJK1245    12/21/81   RECKLESS DRIVING                    95
FREED-2    08/13/80   HITTING MAILBOX                     35
ABCDEFG    06/22/80   PARKING TOO FAR FROM CURB           15
POREMBA                   IRVIN           P32152      05
PIRVIN1    01/01/81   DRINKING WHILE DRIVING              75
PIRVIN1    01/01/81   SPEEDING 100 IN 55 MPH ZONE         45
IRVIN-1    07/28/80   SPEEDING 75 IN 30 MPH ZONE          72
IRVIN-1    01/01/80   HITTING LAMPOST                     50
IRVIN-1    10/20/79   RUNNING A RED LIGHT                 25
ZIMMERMAN                 THOMAS          Z07029      06
ZIMMER4    10/25/80   HONKING HORN FOR NO REASON          25
ZIMMER4    09/05/80   SPEEDING IN SCHOOL ZONE             55
ZIMMER4    07/04/80   DRIVING AT NIGHT WITHOUT HEADLIGHTS ON   15
ZIMMER4    04/03/80   FAILURE TO YIELD RIGHT OF WAY       15
ZIMMER5    03/23/80   SPEEDING 45 IN 30 MPH ZONE          30
ZIMMER5    02/14/80   DRIVING WITHOUT A VALID DRIVER'S LICENSE  50
```

Because there is only one input file, only one FD appears in the File Section of the Data Division for the input file. Of course, an FD has to be written for the output file, too. In fact an FD has to appear for every file that is used in a program. It should again be emphasized here that although 2 separate kinds of records are shown in the input file, (1) only one FD for the output file is required and (2) a separate record description is required for each type of record. For the latter reason the program has one 01-level entry, named DRIVERS-CARD, and another, called VIOLATIONS-CARD. Both these records are 80 characters long.

As already stated, it is important to understand that one record is an *implied redefinition* of the other. The FD allows for only 80 characters of room for the input record and "doesn't care" which record description you, the programmer, are looking at. They could just as easily be in the reverse order, so far as the computer is concerned. What must concern you, however, is the fact that after the first card of a set is read, any information in that record that is to be used after the next card is read should be saved by moving it to Working-Storage. Otherwise, it will be overwritten when the subsequent card is read.

Because the value of NO-VIOLATIONS is required for later use to compute the average, it is moved to W-S-NO-VIOLATIONS in line 239, before the second card of a set is read. So that we are completely sure that the PERFORM "knows" this value, paragraph READ-PARA is performed W-S-NO-VIOLATIONS times rather than NO-VIOLATIONS, which trusts the compiler a little too much for some people.

Program 25

```
1      IDENTIFICATION DIVISION.
2      PROGRAM-ID. TRAFFIC.
3      AUTHOR. IRVIN POREMBA.
4      INSTALLATION. NYU.
5      DATE-WRITTEN. MARCH 24, 1982.
6      DATE-COMPILED. APRIL 16, 1982.
7      SECURITY. FOR THE READERS OF THIS BOOK ONLY.
8      * * * * * * * * * * * * * * * * * * * * * * * * * * * * * * * * * * * * * * * * * * * * * *
9      *      THIS PROGRAM IS A MOTOR VEHICLE VIOLATIONS                     *
10     *      REPORT. THERE ARE TWO DIFFERENT DATA CARD                      *
11     *      FORMATS THAT ARE READ IN. THE FIRST DATA CARD                  *
12     *      IS PUNCHED:                                                    *
13     *                                                                     *
14     *      COLUMNS  1-20:  DRIVER'S LAST NAME                             *
15     *      COLUMNS 25-40:  DRIVER'S FIRST NAME                            *
16     *      COLUMNS 45-50:  DRIVER'S LICENSE NUMBER                        *
17     *      COLUMNS 60-61:  NUMBER OF VIOLATIONS                           *
18     *                                                                     *
19     *      THE ABOVE DATA CARD IS FOLLOWED BY A GROUP                     *
20     *      OF DATA CARDS, THE NUMBER OF WHICH IS DEPENDENT                *
21     *      ON THE NUMBER OF VIOLATIONS IN THE FIRST DATA                  *
22     *      CARD. THEY ARE PUNCHED:                                        *
23     *                                                                     *
24     *      COLUMNS  1-7:   VEHICLE PLATE NUMBER                           *
25     *      COLUMNS 10-17:  DATE OF VIOLATION                              *
26     *      COLUMNS 20-69:  REASON FOR VIOLATION                           *
27     *      COLUMNS 70-71:  FINE GIVEN FOR VIOLATION                       *
28     *                                                                     *
29     *      EACH GROUP OF DATA CARDS IS THEN PRINTED OUT ON                *
30     *      A NEW PAGE WITH A HEADING AND THE TOTAL AMOUNT                 *
31     *      OF TICKETS, THE TOTAL AMOUNT OWED AND THE                      *
32     *      AVERAGE FINE FOR EACH DRIVER. AT THE END OF THE                *
33     *      PROGRAM, THE GRAND TOTAL OF ALL FINES DUE TO                   *
34     *      THE MOTOR VEHICLE DEPARTMENT IS PRINTED ON A                   *
35     *      NEW PAGE.                                                      *
36     * * * * * * * * * * * * * * * * * * * * * * * * * * * * * * * * * * * * * * * * * * * * * *
37
38     ENVIRONMENT DIVISION.
39     CONFIGURATION SECTION.
40     SOURCE-COMPUTER.    CYBER-170-720.
41     OBJECT-COMPUTER.    CYBER-170-720.
42     SPECIAL-NAMES.
43     INPUT-OUTPUT SECTION.
44     FILE-CONTROL.
45         SELECT IN-FILE ASSIGN TO INPUT.
46         SELECT OUT-FILE ASSIGN TO OUTPUT.
47
48     DATA DIVISION.
49     FILE SECTION.
50
51     FD  IN-FILE
52         LABEL RECORDS ARE OMITTED.
53
54     *      DEFINE INPUT OF THE FIRST DATA CARD.
55
```

```
56      01    DRIVERS-CARD.
57            02   LAST-NAME          PIC X(20).
58            02   FILLER             PIC X(04).
59            02   FIRST-NAME         PIC X(16).
60            02   FILLER             PIC X(04).
61            02   LICENSE-NO         PIC X(06).
62            02   FILLER             PIC X(09).
63            02   NO-VIOLATIONS      PIC 9(02).
64            02   FILLER             PIC X(19).
65
66      *     DEFINE INPUT OF THE OTHER DATA CARDS ASSOCIATED
67      *     WITH THE DATA CARD.
68
69      01    VIOLATIONS-CARD.
70            02   VEHICLE-PLATE      PIC X(07).
71            02   FILLER             PIC X(02).
72            02   DATE-VIOLATION     PIC X(08).
73            02   FILLER             PIC X(02).
74            02   REASON             PIC X(50).
75            02   FINE               PIC 9(02).
76            02   FILLER             PIC X(09).
77
78      FD    OUT-FILE
79            LABEL RECORDS ARE OMITTED.
80
81      *     DEFINE OUTPUT OF PROGRAM
82
83      01    LINE-OUT               PIC X(133).
84
85      WORKING-STORAGE SECTION.
86
87      77    CASE-COUNTER          PIC 99 VALUE ZERO.
88      77    TICKET-AMOUNT         PIC 9999 VALUE ZERO.
89      77    PAGE-COUNT            PIC 9999 VALUE ZERO.
90      77    AVERAGE               PIC 999V99.
91      77    TOTAL-AMOUNT          PIC 99999 VALUE ZERO.
92      77    W-S-NO-VIOLATIONS     PIC 99.
93      77    MORE-CARDS            PIC X(03) VALUE 'YES'.
94      77    CARD-COUNT            PIC 9999 VALUE ZERO.
95
96      01    HEADER-1.
97            02   FILLER             PIC X(01) VALUE SPACES.
98            02   FILLER             PIC X(05) VALUE 'PAGE'.
99            02   PAGE-COUNT-OUT     PIC Z,ZZ9.
100           02   FILLER             PIC X(30) VALUE SPACES.
101           02   FILLER             PIC X(13) VALUE 'MOTOR VEHICLE'.
102           02   FILLER             PIC X(10) VALUE 'BUREAU:'.
103           02   FILLER             PIC X(17) VALUE 'VIOLATIONS REPORT'.
104
105     01    HEADER-2.
106           02   FILLER             PIC X(01) VALUE SPACES.
107           02   FILLER             PIC X(10) VALUE ALL '*'.
108           02   FILLER             PIC X(30) VALUE SPACES.
109           02   FILLER             PIC X(40) VALUE ALL '*'.
110
111     01    HEADER-3.
112           02   FILLER             PIC X(01) VALUE SPACES.
113           02   FILLER             PIC X(123) VALUE ALL '*'.
114
115     01    HEADER-4.
116           02   FILLER             PIC X(01) VALUE SPACES.
117           02   FILLER             PIC X(14) VALUE 'VIOLATION'.
118           02   FILLER             PIC X(12) VALUE 'VEHICLE'.
119           02   FILLER             PIC X(09) VALUE 'VIOLATION'.
120           02   FILLER             PIC X(24) VALUE SPACES.
121           02   FILLER             PIC X(10) VALUE 'REASON FOR'.
122           02   FILLER             PIC X(26) VALUE SPACES.
123           02   FILLER             PIC X(08) VALUE 'CITATION'.
124
125     01    HEADER-5.
126           02   FILLER             PIC X(15) VALUE 'NUMBER'.
127           02   FILLER             PIC X(14) VALUE 'PLATE #'.
128           02   FILLER             PIC X(04) VALUE 'DATE'.
129           02   FILLER             PIC X(29) VALUE SPACES.
130           02   FILLER             PIC X(08) VALUE 'CITATION'.
131           02   FILLER             PIC X(28) VALUE SPACES.
```

```
132          02   FILLER                PIC X(04) VALUE 'FINE'.
133
134     01   HEADER-6.
135          02   FILLER                PIC X(01) VALUE SPACES.
136          02   FILLER                PIC X(09) VALUE ALL '*'.
137          02   FILLER                PIC X(05) VALUE SPACES.
138          02   FILLER                PIC X(07) VALUE ALL '*'.
139          02   FILLER                PIC X(05) VALUE SPACES.
140          02   FILLER                PIC X(09) VALUE ALL '*'.
141          02   FILLER                PIC X(04) VALUE SPACES.
142          02   FILLER                PIC X(50) VALUE ALL '*'.
143          02   FILLER                PIC X(06) VALUE SPACES.
144          02   FILLER                PIC X(08) VALUE ALL '*'.
145
146     01   DETAIL-LINE.
147          02   FILLER                PIC X(11) VALUE 'VIOLATOR #'.
148          02   CARD-COUNT-OUT        PIC Z,ZZ9.
149          02   FILLER                PIC X(13) VALUE 'LAST NAME:'.
150          02   LAST-NAME-OUT         PIC X(20).
151          02   FILLER                PIC X(15) VALUE 'FIRST NAME:'.
152          02   FIRST-NAME-OUT        PIC X(16).
153          02   FILLER                PIC X(08) VALUE 'DRIVER'.
154          02   FILLER                PIC X(01) VALUE QUOTE.
155          02   FILLER                PIC X(02) VALUE 'S'.
156          02   FILLER                PIC X(10) VALUE 'LICENSE:'.
157          02   LICENSE-NO-OUT        PIC X(06).
158          02   FILLER                PIC X(15) VALUE 'VIOLATIONS:'.
159          02   NO-VIOLATIONS-OUT     PIC Z9.
160
161     01   DETAIL-LINE-2.
162          02   FILLER                PIC X(04) VALUE SPACES.
163          02   CASE-COUNTER-OUT      PIC Z9.
164          02   FILLER                PIC X(09) VALUE SPACES.
165          02   VEHICLE-PLATE-OUT     PIC X(07).
166          02   FILLER                PIC X(05) VALUE SPACES.
167          02   DATE-VIOLATION-OUT    PIC X(08).
168          02   FILLER                PIC X(05) VALUE SPACES.
169          02   REASON-OUT            PIC X(50).
170          02   FILLER                PIC X(10) VALUE SPACES.
171          02   FINE-OUT              PIC $$9.
172
173     01   DETAIL-LINE-3.
174          02   FILLER                PIC X(01) VALUE SPACES.
175          02   FILLER                PIC X(14) VALUE 'VIOLATOR HAS'.
176          02   VIOLATIONS-OUT        PIC Z9.
177          02   FILLER                PIC X(18) VALUE 'TICKETS AND OWES'.
178          02   TICKET-AMOUNT-OUT     PIC $$,$$9.
179          02   FILLER                PIC X(19) VALUE 'FOR AN AVERAGE OF'.
180          02   AVERAGE-OUT           PIC $$,$$9.99.
181          02   FILLER                PIC X(01) VALUE '.'.
182
183     01   DETAIL-LINE-4.
184          02   FILLER                PIC X(18) VALUE 'TOTAL AMOUNT DUE'.
185          02   FILLER                PIC X(17) VALUE 'TO MOTOR VEHICLE'.
186          02   FILLER                PIC X(14) VALUE 'DEPARTMENT IS'.
187          02   TOTAL-AMOUNT-OUT      PIC $$$,$$9.
188          02   FILLER                PIC X(01) VALUE '.'.
189
190     PROCEDURE DIVISION.
191
192   * THIS IS THE MAIN PARAGRAPH WHICH USES THE PERFORM
193   * STATEMENT TO ACCESS OTHER PARAGRAPHS.
194
195     MAIN-LINE-ROUTINE.
196          PERFORM OPEN-FILES.
197          PERFORM NEW-PAGE.
198          PERFORM START-UP.
199          PERFORM PROCESS-DATA UNTIL MORE-CARDS EQUAL 'NO'.
200          PERFORM CLOSE-UP.
201          STOP RUN.
202
203     OPEN-FILES.
204          OPEN INPUT IN-FILE.
205          OPEN OUTPUT OUT-FILE.
206
207     NEW-PAGE.
```

```
208              MOVE SPACES TO LINE-OUT.
209              WRITE LINE-OUT AFTER PAGE.
210
211    *     START-UP WRITES THE HEADINGS THEN CHECKS
212    *     TO SEE IF THERE IS ANY DATA. IF THERE IS NO
213    *     DATA, AN ERROR MESSAGE IS PRINTED.
214
215    START-UP.
216              READ IN-FILE AT END MOVE 'NO' TO MORE-CARDS
217                   MOVE ' **NO DATA IN DECK**' TO LINE-OUT
218                   WRITE LINE-OUT AFTER 30.
219              IF MORE-CARDS EQUAL 'YES' PERFORM WRITE-HEADINGS-PARA.
220
221    *     IF THERE IS DATA PROCESS-DATA PRINTS OUT THE
222    *     OUTPUT OF THE FIRST DATA CARD THEN USING THE
223    *     PERFORM STATEMENT SEND CONTROL FIRST TO READ-PARA
224    *     AND THEN AVERAGE-PARA. FINALLY ANOTHER DATA
225    *     CARD IS READ.
226
227    PROCESS-DATA.
228              ADD 1 TO CARD-COUNT.
229              MOVE CARD-COUNT TO CARD-COUNT-OUT.
230              MOVE LAST-NAME TO LAST-NAME-OUT.
231              MOVE FIRST-NAME TO FIRST-NAME-OUT.
232              MOVE LICENSE-NO TO LICENSE-NO-OUT.
233              MOVE NO-VIOLATIONS TO NO-VIOLATIONS-OUT.
234              WRITE LINE-OUT FROM DETAIL-LINE AFTER 2.
235              WRITE LINE-OUT FROM HEADER-3 AFTER 1.
236              WRITE LINE-OUT FROM HEADER-4 AFTER 2.
237              WRITE LINE-OUT FROM HEADER-5 AFTER 1.
238              WRITE LINE-OUT FROM HEADER-6 AFTER 1.
239              MOVE NO-VIOLATIONS TO W-S-NO-VIOLATIONS.
240              PERFORM READ-PARA W-S-NO-VIOLATIONS TIMES.
241              PERFORM AVERAGE-PARA.
242              READ IN-FILE AT END MOVE 'NO' TO MORE-CARDS
243                   PERFORM TOTAL-PARA.
244              IF MORE-CARDS EQUAL 'YES' PERFORM NEW-PAGE
245                   PERFORM WRITE-HEADINGS-PARA.
246
247    *     TOTAL-PARA PRINTS OUT THE TOTAL AMOUNT OF THE FINES
248    *     DUE TO THE MOTOR VEHICLE DEPARTMENT ON A NEW PAGE.
249
250    TOTAL-PARA.
251              MOVE TOTAL-AMOUNT TO TOTAL-AMOUNT-OUT.
252              PERFORM NEW-PAGE.
253              WRITE LINE-OUT FROM DETAIL-LINE-4 AFTER 2.
254
255    CLOSE-UP.
256              CLOSE IN-FILE, OUT-FILE.
257
258    *     READ-PARA IS PERFORMED NO-VIOLATIONS TIMES,
259    *     EACH TIME READING AND PRINTING THE INFORMATION
260    *     ASSOCIATED WITH EACH VIOLATION.
261
262    READ-PARA.
263              READ IN-FILE AT END MOVE ' **NO DATA IN DECK**' TO LINE-OUT
264                   WRITE LINE-OUT AFTER 2
265                   PERFORM CLOSE-UP STOP RUN.
266              ADD 1 TO CASE-COUNTER.
267              MOVE CASE-COUNTER TO CASE-COUNTER-OUT.
268              ADD FINE TO TICKET-AMOUNT.
269              MOVE VEHICLE-PLATE TO VEHICLE-PLATE-OUT.
270              MOVE DATE-VIOLATION TO DATE-VIOLATION-OUT.
271              MOVE REASON TO REASON-OUT.
272              MOVE FINE TO FINE-OUT.
273              WRITE LINE-OUT FROM DETAIL-LINE-2 AFTER 2.
274
275    *     AVERAGE-PARA PRINTS OUT THE AVERAGE OF THE FINES
276    *     OWED BY EACH VIOLATOR.
277
278    AVERAGE-PARA.
279              DIVIDE TICKET-AMOUNT BY W-S-NO-VIOLATIONS GIVING
280                   AVERAGE ROUNDED.
281              ADD TICKET-AMOUNT TO TOTAL-AMOUNT.
282              MOVE W-S-NO-VIOLATIONS TO VIOLATIONS-OUT.
283              MOVE TICKET-AMOUNT TO TICKET-AMOUNT-OUT.
```

```
284            MOVE AVERAGE TO AVERAGE-OUT.
285            WRITE LINE-OUT FROM DETAIL-LINE-3 AFTER 2.
286            MOVE ZEROS TO CASE-COUNTER, TICKET-AMOUNT.
287
288    WRITE-HEADINGS-PARA.
289            ADD 1 TO PAGE-COUNT.
290            MOVE PAGE-COUNT TO PAGE-COUNT-OUT.
291            WRITE LINE-OUT FROM HEADER-1 AFTER 1.
292            WRITE LINE-OUT FROM HEADER-2 AFTER 1.
293            WRITE LINE-OUT FROM HEADER-2 AFTER 1.
```

Output for Program 25

```
        PAGE 1                                  MOTOR VEHICLE BUREAU: VIOLATIONS REPORT
        * * * * * * * * *              * * * * * * * * * * * * * * * * * * * * * * * * * * * *
        * * * * * * * * *              * * * * * * * * * * * * * * * * * * * * * * * * * * * *
VIOLATOR # 1     LAST NAME: COLE      FIRST NAME: JERRY     DRIVER'S LICENSE: C12398    VIOLATIONS: 6
* * * * * * * * * * * * * * * * * * * * * * * * * * * * * * * * * * * * * * * * * * * * * * * * * * * * * * *
        VIOLATION               VEHICLE          VIOLATION                 REASON FOR                 CITATION
        NUMBER                  PLATE #          DATE                      CITATION                   FINE
        * * * * * * * * *       * * * * * * * *  * * * * * * * *  * * * * * * * * * * * * * * * * * *  * * * * * * * *
            1                   MX13456          11/15/80        SPEEDING 25 IN 10 MPH ZONE          $40
            2                   MX13456          09/07/80        DRIVING IN EMERGENCY ONLY ZONE      $40
            3                   124ABCD          05/08/80        SPEEDING 80 IN 55 MPH ZONE          $53
            4                   124ABDF          03/24/80        SPEEDING 45 IN 30 MPH ZONE          $40
            5                   ABD8910          02/10/80        PARKING ON WRONG SIDE OF STREET     $10
            6                   Z100001          04/05/79        FAILURE TO SIGNAL ON TURN           $15
VIOLATOR HAS 6 TICKETS AND OWES $198 FOR AN AVERAGE OF $33.00.
```

```
        PAGE 2                                  MOTOR VEHICLE BUREAU: VIOLATIONS REPORT
        * * * * * * * * *              * * * * * * * * * * * * * * * * * * * * * * * * * * * *
        * * * * * * * * *              * * * * * * * * * * * * * * * * * * * * * * * * * * * *
VIOLATOR # 2    LAST NAME: CORNER    FIRST NAME: MICHELLE     DRIVER'S LICENSE: G95134    VIOLATIONS: 4
* * * * * * * * * * * * * * * * * * * * * * * * * * * * * * * * * * * * * * * * * * * * * * * * * * * * * * *
        VIOLATION               VEHICLE          VIOLATION                 REASON FOR                 CITATION
        NUMBER                  PLATE #          DATE                      CITATION                   FINE
        * * * * * * * * *       * * * * * * * *  * * * * * * * *  * * * * * * * * * * * * * * * * * *  * * * * * * * *
            1                   MX13456          04/14/79        FAILURE TO SIGNAL WHILE CHANGING LANES   $35
            2                   ABCB765          01/01/79        SPEEDING 25 IN 15 MPH ZONE          $5
            3                   ABCB765          12/31/79        DRINKING WHILE DRIVING              $80
            4                   ABCB765          12/30/79        SPEEDING 45 IN 30 MPH ZONE          $25
VIOLATOR HAS 4 TICKETS AND OWES $145 FOR AN AVERAGE OF $36.25.
```

```
        PAGE 3                                  MOTOR VEHICLE BUREAU: VIOLATIONS REPORT
        * * * * * * * * *              * * * * * * * * * * * * * * * * * * * * * * * * * * * *
        * * * * * * * * *              * * * * * * * * * * * * * * * * * * * * * * * * * * * *
VIOLATOR # 3     LAST NAME: FREEDMAN    FIRST NAME: ROBERT     DRIVER'S LICENSE: F00274    VIOLATIONS: 5
* * * * * * * * * * * * * * * * * * * * * * * * * * * * * * * * * * * * * * * * * * * * * * * * * * * * * * *
        VIOLATION               VEHICLE          VIOLATION                 REASON FOR                 CITATION
        NUMBER                  PLATE #          DATE                      CITATION                   FINE
        * * * * * * * * *       * * * * * * * *  * * * * * * * *  * * * * * * * * * * * * * * * * * *  * * * * * * * *
            1                   NGIEDRF          01/15/81        DRIVING ON WRONG SIDE OF STREET     $20
            2                   SDF1234          01/02/81        SPEEDING 56 IN 55 MPH ZONE          $1
            3                   HJK1245          12/21/81        RECKLESS DRIVING                    $95
            4                   FREED-2          08/13/80        HITTING MAILBOX                     $35
            5                   ABCDEFG          06/22/80        PARKING TOO FAR FROM CURB           $15
VIOLATOR HAS 5 TICKETS AND OWES $166 FOR AN AVERAGE OF $33.20.
```

```
        PAGE 4                                  MOTOR VEHICLE BUREAU: VIOLATIONS REPORT
        * * * * * * * * *              * * * * * * * * * * * * * * * * * * * * * * * * * * * *
        * * * * * * * * *              * * * * * * * * * * * * * * * * * * * * * * * * * * * *
VIOLATOR # 4    LAST NAME: POREMBA    FIRST NAME: IRVIN     DRIVER'S LICENSE: P32152    VIOLATIONS: 5
* * * * * * * * * * * * * * * * * * * * * * * * * * * * * * * * * * * * * * * * * * * * * * * * * * * * * * *
        VIOLATION               VEHICLE          VIOLATION                 REASON FOR                 CITATION
        NUMBER                  PLATE #          DATE                      CITATION                   FINE
        * * * * * * * * *       * * * * * * * *  * * * * * * * *  * * * * * * * * * * * * * * * * * *  * * * * * * * *
            1                   PIRVIN1          01/01/81        DRINKING WHILE DRIVING              $75
            2                   PIRVIN1          01/01/81        SPEEDING 100 IN 55 MPH ZONE         $45
            3                   IRVIN-1          07/28/80        SPEEDING 75 IN 30 MPH ZONE          $72
            4                   IRVIN-1          01/01/80        HITTING LAMPOST                     $50
            5                   IRVIN-1          10/20/79        RUNNING A RED LIGHT                 $25
VIOLATOR HAS 5 TICKETS AND OWES $267 FOR AN AVERAGE OF $53.40.
```

```
        PAGE 5                                        MOTOR VEHICLE BUREAU: VIOLATIONS REPORT
    * * * * * * * * * *                    * * * * * * * * * * * * * * * * * * * * * * * * * * * * * * * * * * * * * *
    * * * * * * * * * *                    * * * * * * * * * * * * * * * * * * * * * * * * * * * * * * * * * * * * * *
  VIOLATOR # 5    LAST NAME: ZIMMERMAN    FIRST NAME: THOMAS    DRIVER'S LICENSE: Z07029    VIOLATIONS: 6

  * * * * * * * * * * * * * * * * * * * * * * * * * * * * * * * * * * * * * * * * * * * * * * * * * * * * * * * * * * *
         VIOLATION              VEHICLE         VIOLATION                    REASON FOR                  CITATION
          NUMBER                PLATE #           DATE                       CITATION                      FINE
      * * * * * * * *        * * * * * * * *    * * * * * * * *    * * * * * * * * * * * * * * * * * * * * * * * *    * * * * * * * *
             1                ZIMMER4          10/25/80         HONKING HORN FOR NO REASON                   $25
             2                ZIMMER4          09/05/80         SPEEDING IN SCHOOL ZONE                      $55
             3                ZIMMER4          07/04/80         DRIVING AT NIGHT WITHOUT HEADLIGHTS ON       $15
             4                ZIMMER4          04/03/80         FAILURE TO YIELD TO THE RIGHT OF WAY         $40
             5                ZIMMER5          03/23/80         SPEEDING 45 IN 30 MPH ZONE                   $20
             6                ZIMMER5          02/14/80         DRIVING WITHOUT A VALID DRIVER'S LICENSE     $50
  VIOLATOR HAS 6 TICKETS AND OWES $205 FOR AN AVERAGE OF $34.17.
```

TOTAL AMOUNT DUE TO MOTOR VEHICLE DEPARTMENT IS $966.

Review Questions

1. Does an 88-level item take a PICTURE?
2. Does an 88-level item take a VALUE?
3. Must an 88-level item always be placed in Working-Storage?
4. Is it possible to MOVE an 88-level item?
5. What is a figurative constant? Give some examples.
6. If a negative number such as −1234 is read in from data and the minus sign is not overpunched but precedes the number, what clause must be used after the signed PICTURE?
7. If the sign follows the number?
8. If an input file contains records with 3 different formats, how many FD's must be present?

Tables

COBOL is a health-spa for the mind.
(Mark Altshul)

In this chapter you will be introduced to the concept of tables. Tables are so useful that surely much of COBOL's popularity is due to them. They are called arrays in other programming languages. There are special ways to handle tables and because of their importance a whole chapter will be devoted to the subject. Some of the significant aspects you will be learning include:

- setting up a table in memory
- the OCCURS clause
- the use of subscripting
- single-level tables
- multi-entry tables
- HIGH-VALUE and HIGH-VALUES
- LOW-VALUE and LOW-VALUES
- searching a table
- indexing
- the SEARCH verb
- SEARCH ALL
- the binary search
- double-dimensioned tables
- triple-dimensioned tables
- reading in a table from data cards
- the OCCURS... DEPENDING ON clause
- the SET verb

Tables in COBOL are very popular because they are powerful data-processing tools that are capable of extreme flexibility and utility. We are familiar with the concept of tables from everyday life. The common calendar divided up into 12 months is an example. If we want to find out on which day a certain date falls we merely "look it up" in the calendar. Similarly, we often consult bus and railroad tables when necessary. The Internal Revenue Service consults very long tables when processing annual income tax returns. What is so special about tables is that they permit a great deal of information to be accessed quickly and effectively.

In COBOL, advantage is taken of the concept of tables in various ways. We will be learning many different techniques of handling tables and using them in a variety of contexts—some already familiar from previous problems and others totally new. By the time you have absorbed the ideas embodied in this chapter you will be conversant with one of the most sophisticated methods employed in the commercial data-processing world.

10.1 Setting up a One-Dimensioned Table

The fundamental notion behind tables is that, given a sequence of table entries, any particular entry can be located and accessed quickly and efficiently. Taking again our example of a calendar, its 12 entries would be the names of the months, JANUARY through DECEMBER. Such a table is called a *single-dimensioned* table. In COBOL a maximum of 3 dimensions is possible, but single-dimensioned tables are very common indeed, if not the most frequently used.

In order to refer to a particular element in a table of elements, we use the concept of either *subscripting* or *indexing*. Although these terms are different, they have remarkably similar functions, as you will see.

First, a "skeleton" of the table is set up in Working-Storage because it is advantageous to use a series of VALUE clauses. Here is what it might look like:

```
01   MONTH-SKELETON.
     02    FILLER   PIC X(09) VALUE 'JANUARY'.
     02    FILLER   PIC X(09) VALUE 'FEBRUARY'.
     02    FILLER   PIC X(09) VALUE 'MARCH'.
     02    FILLER   PIC X(09) VALUE 'APRIL'.
     02    FILLER   PIC X(09) VALUE 'MAY'.
     02    FILLER   PIC X(09) VALUE 'JUNE'.
     02    FILLER   PIC X(09) VALUE 'JULY'.
     02    FILLER   PIC X(09) VALUE 'AUGUST'.
     02    FILLER   PIC X(09) VALUE 'SEPTEMBER'.
     02    FILLER   PIC X(09) VALUE 'OCTOBER'.
     02    FILLER   PIC X(09) VALUE 'NOVEMBER'.
     02    FILLER   PIC X(09) VALUE 'DECEMBER'.
```

By itself the preceding skeleton is quite useless. After all, each element is a FILLER and, as you already know, no FILLER can ever be referred to. Nevertheless the elements do reflect the correct order of the 12 months of the year.

Now we have to convert the skeleton into a table. This is done by redefining the skeleton and using the OCCURS clause as shown. The reason for this is that in COBOL an OCCURS clause may not appear on an 01 level statement.

```
01   MONTH-TABLE REDEFINES MONTH-SKELETON.
     02    NAME-OF-MONTH PIC X(09) OCCURS 12 TIMES.
```

This redefinition of the skeleton permits us to access any element in terms of a subscript. Suppose we had input cards punched as shown at the top of the next page, where a 2-digit number 01 through 12, corresponding to the 12 months of the year, is punched in the first 2 columns of each input card. After the first card is read (MONTH-IN is 03), we could write in the Procedure Division:

```
MOVE NAME-OF-MONTH (MONTH-IN) TO MONTH-OUT
```

where NAME-OF-MONTH is *subscripted* by MONTH-IN. In order to indicate that a value is a *subscript*, we must enclose it in parentheses.

Because MONTH-IN is 03 in the first data card, NAME-OF-MONTH (MONTH-IN) refers to the third element of the table, which is 'MARCH'. It is therefore the literal 'MARCH' that is moved to MONTH-OUT, an output area in the detail-line. If MONTH-IN is 12, it is the 12th element, 'DECEMBER', that is referenced.

Look once again at the first FILLER in the table skeleton. The PICTURE assigned to it is X(09). Clearly, 'JANUARY' is not X(09), but rather, X(07). True, but the largest month (in terms of the number of letters required to spell it) is SEPTEMBER, which has 9 letters. Because the OCCURS clause states that NAME-OF-MONTH with a PICTURE of X(09) OCCURS 12 TIMES, consistency must be maintained. This is accomplished by virtue of the fact that it is always a 9-character X field that is involved, for when, for example, the table element is 'MAY', the nature of the VALUE clause is to move 'MAY' into the 9-character X field, justified to the left, with the rightmost 6 positions filled with spaces.

In other words, the table may be conceptualized as a continuous string of 12 by 9 characters such as:

'JANUARYbbFEBRUARYbMARCHbbbbAPRILbbbb ... NOVEMBERbDECEMBERb'

1st occurrence   2nd   3rd   4th   11th   12th occurrence

where b specifies a blank space. Because there is inadequate room to show 108 characters on one line, the string of characters has been foreshortened. However, enough is shown to clarify the concept that each unit of 9 characters is contiguous to its succeeding unit of 9 characters.

To set up a table for the 7 days of the week, we could write in Working-Storage:

```
01   DAY-OF-THE-WEEK-SKELETON.
     02   FILLER   PIC   X(09) VALUE 'SUNDAY'.
     02   FILLER   PIC   X(09) VALUE 'MONDAY'.
     02   FILLER   PIC   X(09) VALUE 'TUESDAY'.
     02   FILLER   PIC   X(09) VALUE 'WEDNESDAY'.
     02   FILLER   PIC   X(09) VALUE 'THURSDAY'.
     02   FILLER   PIC   X(09) VALUE 'FRIDAY'.
     02   FILLER   PIC   X(09) VALUE 'SATURDAY'.
01   DAY-OF-THE-WEEK-TABLE REDEFINES DAY-OF-THE-WEEK-SKELETON.
     02   WEEKDAY PIC X(09) OCCURS 7 TIMES.
```

The resulting string of characters will be 7 by 9 = 63 characters long and could be viewed conceptually as:

'SUNDAYbbbMONDAYbbbTUESDAYbbWEDNESDAYTHURSDAYbFRIDAYbbbSATURDAYb

occurrence 1   2   3   4   5   6   7

Assuming we have data cards punched as shown:

where DAY-NUM is punched with an integer number in the range 1 through 7, this number acts as a subscript when used as follows.

MOVE WEEKDAY (DAY-NUM) TO WEEKDAY-OUT.

Let us now put this information to work. Suppose we have data punched as shown:

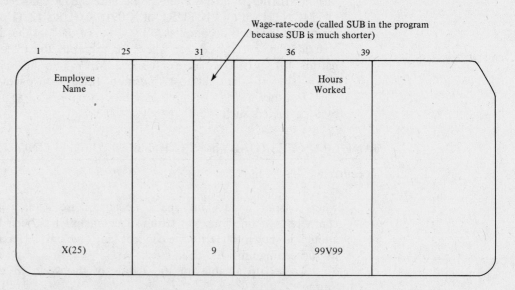

where a code number 1 through 9, representing the wage-rate code for an employee, is punched in column 31. The name and the number of hours worked is also punched on the same data card.

The purpose of the program is to determine what wage-rate code is punched and to compute the net pay by multiplying the number of hours worked by the appropriate wage rate. The wage rate is defined in accordance with the following table.

CODE	RATE PER HOUR($)
1	25.50
2	6.50
3	12.50
4	3.25
5	5.00
6	4.50
7	2.50
8	4.75
9	6.75

Of course, this could be done by a series of IF tests, but it would be an arduous task. By resorting to tables we minimize our effort and keep the program simple to code and comprehend.

The kind of table that could be set up is one in which each of the rates of pay is set up in sequence, such as:

```
01   WAGE-RATE-SKELETON.
     02    FILLER   PIC   99V99   VALUE   25.50
     02    FILLER   PIC   99V99   VALUE   06.50.
     02    FILLER   PIC   99V99   VALUE   12.50.
     02    FILLER   PIC   99V99   VALUE   03.25.
     02    FILLER   PIC   99V99   VALUE   05.00.
     02    FILLER   PIC   99V99   VALUE   04.50.
     02    FILLER   PIC   99V99   VALUE   02.50.
     02    FILLER   PIC   99V99   VALUE   04.75.
     02    FILLER   PIC   99V99   VALUE   06.75.
01   WAGE-RATE REDEFINES WAGE-RATE-SKELETON.
     02    RATE PIC 99V99 OCCURS 9 TIMES.
```

The wage-rate code on the first input card is 1. Therefore in paragraph **PROCESS-DATA** of the program the following actions take place.

a. 1 is added to CARD-COUNT.

b. CARD-COUNT is moved to the detail-line.

c. The employee-name is moved to the detail-line.

d. HOURS-WORKED is moved to the detail-line.

e. RATE (1) is moved to the detail-line. This is the first element in the table. Therefore the value 25.50 is printed as the rate of pay per hour.

f. To calculate the net pay RATE (SUB), or since SUB is equal to 1, RATE (1) is multiplied by HOURS-WORKED, giving NET-PAY.

g. NET-PAY is moved to the detail-line.

h. NET-PAY is added to TOTAL-PAY, which is to be printed on a separate page at the end of the report.

A word of caution—it is very tempting to write in the skeleton an entry such as:

```
02 FILLER PIC 99V99 VALUE 2550.
```

Unfortunately, when 2550 is moved to a PICTURE of 99V99, 50.00 is stored in the receiving area, due to the implied decimal point aligning itself with the rightmost digit of the number 2550. Nevertheless, a PICTURE of 9999 with a VALUE of 2550 would work because it is redefined later on (in the REDEFINES and OCCURS clauses) as 99V99. However, this is not so straightforward as the method we have illustrated.

In the program that follows the wage-rate code is used as a subscript to access the appropriate rate of pay per hour in the table.

Input for Program 26

IRVIN POREMBA	1	5000
JULIAN COLE	5	0450
MICHELLE CORNER	9	3525
FERN FREIDMAN	3	1450
BARBARA HODGES	4	1245
SALLY DEMBERG	8	0585
JACKIE MURDOCK	6	2500
MARY LAGOUMIS	2	5235
FRANS LISTZ	7	0500
BERT STURZA	5	1250
HAIN TOPOL	4	2000
ANTUA BORG	6	4000
GEORGE WASHINGTON	7	2536
AARON GREENFELD	7	2156
ROGER POOL	8	1740

Program 26

```
1       IDENTIFICATION  DIVISION.
2       PROGRAM-ID.     TABLE-1.
3       AUTHOR.         IRVIN POREMBA.
4       INSTALLATION.   NYU.
5       DATE-WRITTEN.   APRIL 24, 1982.
6       DATE-COMPILED.  APRIL 27, 1982.
7       SECURITY.       HENRY MULLISH.
8       * * * * * * * * * * * * * * * * * * * * * * * * * * * * * * * * * * * * * * * * * * * * * * *
9       *     THIS PROGRAM READS DATA CARDS PUNCHED:                                              *
10      *                                                                                         *
11      *     COLUMNS  1-25: EMPLOYEE NAME                                                        *
12      *     COLUMN     31: A SUBSCRIPT                                                          *
13      *     COLUMNS 36-39: HOURS-WORKED                                                        *
14      *                                                                                         *
15      *     THIS PROGRAM USES A TABLE AND THE SUBSCRIPT                                         *
16      *     TO FIND THE WAGE RATE. IT THEN USES THE                                            *
17      *     WAGE RATE TO FIND THE NET PAY FOR EACH EMPLOYEE.                                    *
18      * * * * * * * * * * * * * * * * * * * * * * * * * * * * * * * * * * * * * * * * * * * * * * *
19
20      ENVIRONMENT    DIVISION.
21      CONFIGURATION  SECTION.
22      SOURCE-COMPUTER. CYBER-170-720.
23      OBJECT-COMPUTER. CYBER-170-720.
24      SPECIAL-NAMES.
25      INPUT-OUTPUT SECTION.
26      FILE-CONTROL.
27            SELECT IN-FILE ASSIGN TO INPUT.
28            SELECT OUT-FILE ASSIGN TO OUTPUT.
29
30      DATA DIVISION.
31      FILE SECTION.
32
33      FD   IN-FILE
34           LABEL RECORDS ARE OMITTED.
35
36      01   RECORD-IN.
37           02   EMPLOYEE-NAME      PIC X(25).
38           02   FILLER            PIC X(05).
39           02   SUB               PIC 9(01).
40           02   FILLER            PIC X(04).
41           02   HOURS-WORKED      PIC 9(01)V9(02).
42           02   FILLER            PIC X(41).
43
44      FD   OUT-FILE
45           LABEL RECORDS ARE OMITTED.
46
47      01   LINE-OUT               PIC X(133).
48
49      WORKING-STORAGE SECTION.
50      77   ANY-MORE-CARDS         PIC X(03) VALUE 'YES'.
51      77   NET-PAY                PIC 9(04)V9(02).
```

```
52    77    TOTAL-PAY                    PIC 9(06)V9(02) VALUE ZERO.
53    77    CARD-COUNT                   PIC 9(04) VALUE ZERO.
54
55    01    WAGE-RATE-SKELETON.
56          02    FILLER                 PIC 9(02)V9(02) VALUE 25.50.
57          02    FILLER                 PIC 9(02)V9(02) VALUE 06.50.
58          02    FILLER                 PIC 9(02)V9(02) VALUE 12.50.
59          02    FILLER                 PIC 9(02)V9(02) VALUE 03.25.
60          02    FILLER                 PIC 9(02)V9(02) VALUE 05.00.
61          02    FILLER                 PIC 9(02)V9(02) VALUE 04.50.
62          02    FILLER                 PIC 9(02)V9(02) VALUE 02.50.
63          02    FILLER                 PIC 9(02)V9(02) VALUE 04.75.
64          02    FILLER                 PIC 9(02)V9(02) VALUE 06.75.
65
66    01    WAGE-RATE REDEFINES WAGE-RATE-SKELETON.
67          02    RATE                   PIC 99V99 OCCURS 9 TIMES.
68
69    01    HEADER-1.
70          02    FILLER                 PIC X(25) VALUE SPACES.
71          02    FILLER                 PIC X(14) VALUE 'PAYROLL REPORT'.
72
73    01    HEADER-2.
74          02    FILLER                 PIC X(25) VALUE SPACES.
75          02    FILLER                 PIC X(14) VALUE ALL ' * '.
76
77    01    HEADER-3.
78          02    FILLER                 PIC X(01) VALUE SPACES.
79          02    FILLER                 PIC X(14) VALUE 'COUNT'.
80          02    FILLER                 PIC X(22) VALUE 'EMPLOYEE NAME'.
81          02    FILLER                 PIC X(09) VALUE 'HOURS'.
82          02    FILLER                 PIC X(09) VALUE 'RATE'.
83          02    FILLER                 PIC X(07) VALUE 'NET PAY'.
84
85    01    HEADER-4.
86          02    FILLER                 PIC X(01) VALUE SPACES.
87          02    FILLER                 PIC X(05) VALUE ALL ' * '.
88          02    FILLER                 PIC X(03) VALUE SPACES.
89          02    FILLER                 PIC X(25) VALUE ALL ' * '.
90          02    FILLER                 PIC X(03) VALUE SPACES.
91          02    FILLER                 PIC X(05) VALUE ALL ' * '.
92          02    FILLER                 PIC X(03) VALUE SPACES.
93          02    FILLER                 PIC X(06) VALUE ALL ' * '.
94          02    FILLER                 PIC X(03) VALUE SPACES.
95          02    FILLER                 PIC X(09) VALUE ALL ' * '.
96
97    01    DETAIL-LINE.
98          02    FILLER                 PIC X(01) VALUE SPACES.
99          02    CARD-COUNT-OUT         PIC Z,ZZ9.
100         02    FILLER                 PIC X(03) VALUE SPACES.
101         02    EMPLOY-NAME-OUT        PIC X(25).
102         02    FILLER                 PIC X(03) VALUE SPACES.
103         02    HOURS-OUT              PIC Z9.99.
104         02    FILLER                 PIC X(03) VALUE SPACES.
105         02    RATE-OUT               PIC $$9.99.
106         02    FILLER                 PIC X(03) VALUE SPACES.
107         02    NET-PAY-OUT            PIC $$,$$9.99.
108
109   01    DETAIL-LINE-2.
110         02    FILLER                 PIC X(10) VALUE SPACES.
111         02    FILLER                 PIC X(14) VALUE 'TOTAL PAY FOR'.
112         02    FILLER                 PIC X(16) VALUE 'ALL EMPLOYEES = '.
113         02    TOTAL-PAY-OUT          PIC $$$$,$$9.99.
114
115   PROCEDURE DIVISION.
116
117   MAIN-LINE-ROUTINE.
118         PERFORM OPEN-FILES.
119         PERFORM NEW-PAGE.
120         PERFORM START-UP.
121         PERFORM PROCESS-DATA UNTIL ANY-MORE-CARDS EQUAL 'NO'.
122         PERFORM CLOSE-UP.
123         STOP RUN.
124
125   OPEN-FILES.
126         OPEN INPUT IN-FILE.
```

```
127          OPEN OUTPUT OUT-FILE.
128
129     NEW-PAGE.
130          MOVE SPACES TO LINE-OUT.
131          WRITE LINE-OUT AFTER PAGE.
132
133     START-UP.
134          READ IN-FILE AT END MOVE 'NO' TO ANY-MORE-CARDS
135               MOVE ' **NO DATA IN DECK**' TO LINE-OUT
136               WRITE LINE-OUT AFTER 30.
137          IF ANY-MORE-CARDS EQUAL 'YES' PERFORM WRITE-HEADINGS.
138
139     PROCESS-DATA.
140          ADD 1 TO CARD-COUNT.
141          MOVE CARD-COUNT TO CARD-COUNT-OUT.
142          MOVE EMPLOYEE-NAME TO EMPLOY-NAME-OUT.
143          MOVE HOURS-WORKED TO HOURS-OUT.
144          MOVE RATE (SUB) TO RATE-OUT.
145          MULTIPLY RATE (SUB) BY HOURS-WORKED GIVING NET-PAY ROUNDED.
146          MOVE NET-PAY TO NET-PAY-OUT.
147          ADD NET-PAY TO TOTAL-PAY.
148          WRITE LINE-OUT FROM DETAIL-LINE AFTER 2.
149          READ IN-FILE AT END MOVE 'NO' TO ANY-MORE-CARDS
150               PERFORM GRAND-TOTAL.
151
152     CLOSE-UP.
153          CLOSE IN-FILE, OUT-FILE.
154
155     GRAND-TOTAL.
156          PERFORM NEW-PAGE.
157          MOVE TOTAL-PAY TO TOTAL-PAY-OUT.
158          WRITE LINE-OUT FROM DETAIL-LINE-2 AFTER 30.
159
160     WRITE-HEADINGS.
161          WRITE LINE-OUT FROM HEADER-1 AFTER 1.
162          WRITE LINE-OUT FROM HEADER-2 AFTER 1.
163          WRITE LINE-OUT FROM HEADER-2 AFTER 1.
164          WRITE LINE-OUT FROM HEADER-3 AFTER 2.
165          WRITE LINE-OUT FROM HEADER-4 AFTER 1.
```

Output for Program 26

```
                            PAYROLL REPORT
                         * * * * * * * * * * * * *
                         * * * * * * * * * * * * *
     COUNT          EMPLOYEE NAME          HOURS       RATE         NET PAY
     * * * * *      * * * * * * * * * * * * * *      * * * * *      * * * * * * * *
         1          IRVIN POREMBA          50.00      $25.50       $1,275.00
         2          JULIAN COLE             4.50       $5.00          $22.50
         3          MICHELLE CORNER        35.25       $6.75         $237.94
         4          FERN FREIDMAN          14.50      $12.50         $181.25
         5          BARBARA HODGES         12.45       $3.25          $40.46
         6          SALLY DEMBERG           5.85       $4.75          $27.79
         7          JACKIE MURDOCK         25.00       $4.50         $112.50
         8          MARY LAGOUMIS          52.35       $6.50         $340.28
         9          FRANS LISTZ             5.00       $2.50          $12.50
        10          BERT STURZA            12.50       $5.00          $62.50
        11          HAIN TOPOL             20.00       $3.25          $65.00
        12          ANTUA BORG             40.00       $4.50         $180.00
        13          GEORGE WASHINGTON      25.36       $2.50          $63.40
        14          AARON GREENFELD        21.56       $2.50          $53.90
        15          ROGER POOL             17.40       $4.75          $82.65
```

TOTAL PAY FOR ALL EMPLOYEES = $2,757.67

10.2 Another Example of an Elementary Table

In industry the more years employees are associated with a company, the larger their annual bonus may be. Let us assume that the system for allocating annual bonuses is dependent on the years of service that employees have been employed by the firm, in accordance with the following table.

SENIORITY IN YEARS	PERCENTAGE BONUS
1	1.5
2	2.0
3	4.5
4	7.0
5	9.5
6	10.1
7	12.5
8	15.0
9	20.0
10 or more	25.0

The percentages are read in as decimal numbers. For example, 1.5% is read into a PICTURE of 9V999 as 0.015, as shown in this table entry.

```
01     BONUS-TABLE-SKELETON.
       02     FILLER   PIC    9V999 VALUE 0.015.
       02     FILLER   PIC    9V999 VALUE 0.020.
       02     FILLER   PIC    9V999 VALUE 0.045.
       02     FILLER   PIC    9V999 VALUE 0.070.
       02     FILLER   PIC    9V999 VALUE 0.095.
       02     FILLER   PIC    9V999 VALUE 0.110.
       02     FILLER   PIC    9V999 VALUE 0.125.
       02     FILLER   PIC    9V999 VALUE 0.150.
       02     FILLER   PIC    9V999 VALUE 0.200.
       02     FILLER   PIC    9V999 VALUE 0.250.
01     BONUS-TABLE REDEFINES BONUS-TABLE-SKELETON.
       02     BONUS-RATE PIC 9V999 OCCURS 10 TIMES.
```

The input to the program is formatted:

1	25	31	37	41	42
Employee Name		Annual Salary		Years of Service	
X(25)		99999V99		99	

where the years of service is treated as a subscript to access the appropriate bonus in the table.

Input for Program 27

IRVIN POREMBA	7500000	10
HENRY MULLISH	8000000	08
FRANK BERNS	2000000	05
ROBIN MORK	1250000	02
DAVID JOHNSON	2500000	06
WILLIAM FORD	0750000	01
JACK RIPPER	1675000	09
SUSAN WELLS	3050000	04
KATHY BERNSTEIN	4300000	07
JEFF GREEN	1725000	03
HARVEY JACKSON	2900000	04
THOMAS GREENSPAN	5500000	07
LINDA WASHINGTON	4565000	05

Program 27

```
1        IDENTIFICATION   DIVISION.
2        PROGRAM-ID.      TABLE-2.
3        AUTHOR.          IRVIN POREMBA.
4        INSTALLATION.    NYU.
5        DATE-WRITTEN.    APRIL 23, 1982.
6        DATE-COMPILED.   APRIL 27, 1982.
7        SECURITY.        HENRY MULLISH.
8        ************************************************************
9        *      THIS PROGRAM READS DATA CARDS PUNCHED:             *
10       *                                                         *
11       *      COLUMNS  1-25: EMPLOYEE NAME                       *
12       *      COLUMNS 31-37: ANNUAL SALARY                       *
13       *      COLUMNS 41-42: YEARS IN SERVICE UP TO 10 YEARS     *
14       *                                                         *
15       *      THIS PROGRAM USES A TABLE WITH THE NUMBER OF       *
16       *      YEARS OF SERVICE TO FIND THE BONUS RATE. THE       *
17       *      RATE ALONG WITH THE YEARLY BONUS FOR EACH          *
18       *      EMPLOYEE IS PRINTED OUT. A GRAND TOTAL OF          *
19       *      ALL EMPLOYEES IS PRINTED OUT ON A NEW PAGE.        *
20       ************************************************************
21
22       ENVIRONMENT    DIVISION.
23       CONFIGURATION SECTION.
24       SOURCE-COMPUTER. CYBER-170-720.
25       OBJECT-COMPUTER. CYBER-170-720.
26       SPECIAL-NAMES.
27       INPUT-OUTPUT    SECTION.
28       FILE-CONTROL.
29            SELECT IN-FILE ASSIGN TO INPUT.
30            SELECT OUT-FILE ASSIGN TO OUTPUT.
31
32       DATA DIVISION.
33       FILE SECTION.
34
35       FD    IN-FILE
36            LABEL RECORDS ARE OMITTED.
37
38       01    RECORD-IN.
39            02    EMPLOYEE-NAME      PIC X(25).
40            02    FILLER            PIC X(05).
41            02    ANNUAL-SALARY     PIC 9(05)V9(02).
42            02    FILLER            PIC X(03).
43            02    YEARS             PIC 9(02).
44            02    FILLER            PIC X(38).
45
46       FD    OUT-FILE
47            LABEL RECORDS ARE OMITTED.
48
49       01    LINE-OUT              PIC X(133).
50
51       WORKING-STORAGE SECTION.
52
53       01    BONUS-TABLE-SKELETON.
54            02    FILLER            PIC 9V9(03) VALUE 0.015.
55            02    FILLER            PIC 9V9(03) VALUE 0.020.
56            02    FILLER            PIC 9V9(03) VALUE 0.045.
57            02    FILLER            PIC 9V9(03) VALUE 0.070.
58            02    FILLER            PIC 9V9(03) VALUE 0.095.
59            02    FILLER            PIC 9V9(03) VALUE 0.110.
60            02    FILLER            PIC 9V9(03) VALUE 0.125.
61            02    FILLER            PIC 9V9(03) VALUE 0.150.
62            02    FILLER            PIC 9V9(03) VALUE 0.200.
63            02    FILLER            PIC 9V9(03) VALUE 0.250.
64
65       01    BONUS-TABLE REDEFINES BONUS-TABLE-SKELETON.
66            02    BONUS-RATE        PIC 9V9(03) OCCURS 10 TIMES.
67
68       01    INDEPENDENT-ITEMS-USED.
69            02    ANY-MORE-CARDS    PIC X(03) VALUE 'YES'.
70            02    BONUS             PIC 9(05)V9(02).
71            02    CARD-COUNT        PIC 9(04) VALUE ZERO.
72            02    TOTAL-BONUSES     PIC 9(07)V9(02) VALUE ZERO.
```

```
73
74      01    HEADER-1.
75            02    FILLER              PIC X(28) VALUE SPACES.
76            02    FILLER              PIC X(16) VALUE 'EMPLOYEE BONUSES'.
77
78      01    HEADER-2.
79            02    FILLER              PIC X(28) VALUE SPACES.
80            02    FILLER              PIC X(16) VALUE ALL '*'.
81
82      01    HEADER-3.
83            02    FILLER              PIC X(01) VALUE SPACES.
84            02    FILLER              PIC X(14) VALUE 'COUNT'.
85            02    FILLER              PIC X(22) VALUE 'EMPLOYEE NAME'.
86            02    FILLER              PIC X(10) VALUE 'YEARS'.
87            02    FILLER              PIC X(11) VALUE 'SALARY'.
88            02    FILLER              PIC X(10) VALUE 'RATE'.
89            02    FILLER              PIC X(05) VALUE 'BONUS'.
90
91      01    HEADER-4.
92            02    FILLER              PIC X(01) VALUE SPACES.
93            02    FILLER              PIC X(05) VALUE ALL '-'.
94            02    FILLER              PIC X(03) VALUE SPACES.
95            02    FILLER              PIC X(25) VALUE ALL '-'.
96            02    FILLER              PIC X(03) VALUE SPACES.
97            02    FILLER              PIC X(05) VALUE ALL '-'.
98            02    FILLER              PIC X(03) VALUE SPACES.
99            02    FILLER              PIC X(10) VALUE ALL '-'.
100           02    FILLER              PIC X(03) VALUE SPACES.
101           02    FILLER              PIC X(05) VALUE ALL '-'.
102           02    FILLER              PIC X(03) VALUE SPACES.
103           02    FILLER              PIC X(10) VALUE ALL '-'.
104
105     01    DETAIL-LINE.
106           02    FILLER              PIC X(01) VALUE SPACES.
107           02    CARD-COUNT-OUT      PIC Z,ZZ9.
108           02    FILLER              PIC X(03) VALUE SPACES.
109           02    EMPLOY-NAME-OUT     PIC X(25).
110           02    FILLER              PIC X(05) VALUE SPACES.
111           02    YEARS-OUT           PIC Z9.
112           02    FILLER              PIC X(04) VALUE SPACES.
113           02    SALARY-OUT          PIC $$$,$$9.99.
114           02    FILLER              PIC X(03) VALUE SPACES.
115           02    RATE-OUT            PIC Z9.9.
116           02    FILLER              PIC X(01) VALUE '%'.
117           02    FILLER              PIC X(03) VALUE SPACES.
118           02    BONUS-OUT           PIC $$$,$$9.99.
119
120     01    DETAIL-LINE-2.
121           02    FILLER              PIC X(05) VALUE SPACES.
122           02    FILLER              PIC X(17) VALUE 'TOTAL BONUSES = '.
123           02    TOTAL-BONUSES-OUT PIC $$,$$$,$$9.99.
124
125     PROCEDURE DIVISION.
126
127     MAIN-LINE-ROUTINE.
128           PERFORM OPEN-FILES.
129           PERFORM NEW-PAGE.
130           PERFORM START-UP.
131           PERFORM PROCESS-DATA UNTIL ANY-MORE-CARDS EQUAL 'NO'.
132           PERFORM CLOSE-UP.
133           STOP RUN.
134
135     OPEN-FILES.
136           OPEN INPUT IN-FILE.
137           OPEN OUTPUT OUT-FILE.
138
139     NEW-PAGE.
140           MOVE SPACES TO LINE-OUT.
141           WRITE LINE-OUT AFTER PAGE.
142
143     START-UP.
144           READ IN-FILE AT END MOVE 'NO' TO ANY-MORE-CARDS
145                 MOVE ' **NO DATA IN DECK**' TO LINE-OUT
146                 WRITE LINE-OUT AFTER 30.
147           IF ANY-MORE-CARDS EQUAL 'YES' PERFORM WRITE-HEADINGS.
```

```
148
149    PROCESS-DATA.
150        ADD 1 TO CARD-COUNT.
151        MOVE CARD-COUNT TO CARD-COUNT-OUT.
152        MOVE EMPLOYEE-NAME TO EMPLOY-NAME-OUT.
153        MOVE ANNUAL-SALARY TO SALARY-OUT.
154        MOVE YEARS TO YEARS-OUT.
155        MULTIPLY 100 BY BONUS-RATE (YEARS) GIVING RATE-OUT.
156        MULTIPLY ANNUAL-SALARY BY BONUS-RATE (YEARS)
157            GIVING BONUS ROUNDED.
158        ADD BONUS TO TOTAL-BONUSES.
159        MOVE BONUS TO BONUS-OUT.
160        WRITE LINE-OUT FROM DETAIL-LINE AFTER 2.
161        READ IN-FILE AT END MOVE 'NO' TO ANY-MORE-CARDS
162            PERFORM GRAND-TOTAL.
163
164    CLOSE-UP.
165        CLOSE IN-FILE, OUT-FILE.
166
167    GRAND-TOTAL.
168        PERFORM NEW-PAGE.
169        MOVE TOTAL-BONUSES TO TOTAL-BONUSES-OUT.
170        WRITE LINE-OUT FROM DETAIL-LINE-2 AFTER 30.
171
172    WRITE-HEADINGS.
173        WRITE LINE-OUT FROM HEADER-1 AFTER 1.
174        WRITE LINE-OUT FROM HEADER-2 AFTER 1.
175        WRITE LINE-OUT FROM HEADER-2 AFTER 1.
176        WRITE LINE-OUT FROM HEADER-3 AFTER 2.
177        WRITE LINE-OUT FROM HEADER-4 AFTER 0.
```

Output for Program 27

EMPLOYEE BONUSES

* * * * * * * * * * * * * * *

* * * * * * * * * * * * * * *

COUNT	EMPLOYEE NAME	YEARS	SALARY	RATE	BONUS
1	IRVIN POREMBA	10	$75,000.00	25.0%	$18,750.00
2	HENRY MULLISH	8	$80,000.00	15.0%	$12,000.00
3	FRANK BERNS	5	$20,000.00	9.5%	$1,900.00
4	ROBIN MORK	2	$12,500.00	2.0%	$250.00
5	DAVID JOHNSON	6	$25,000.00	11.0%	$2,750.00
6	WILLIAM FORD	1	$7,500.00	1.5%	$112.50
7	JACK RIPPER	9	$16,750.00	20.0%	$3,350.00
8	SUSAN WELLS	4	$30,500.00	7.0%	$2,135.00
9	KATHY BERNSTEIN	7	$43,000.00	12.5%	$5,375.00
10	JEFF GREEN	3	$17,250.00	4.5%	$776.25
11	HARVEY JACKSON	4	$29,000.00	7.0%	$2,030.00
12	THOMAS GREENSPAN	7	$55,000.00	12.5%	$6,875.00
13	LINDA WASHINGTON	5	$45,650.00	9.5%	$4,336.75

TOTAL BONUSES = $60,640.50

10.3 A Modified Single-Dimensioned Table

The two previous programs could be criticized for a variety of reasons, one of which is that no steps are taken to ensure that when reading the data cards the subscript is equal to or greater than 1. After all, the critical field could be punched 0 by accident. This would have catastrophic effects on our program because we are unable to handle a subscript of zero.

For the purposes of the next program we will assume that the U.S. government, in recognition of the crucial role its computer programmers play in the nation's destiny, lays down minimum pay scales that are carefully tailored to compensate fairly for the programmer's level of expertise. The 9 pay scales decided on are:

RATE PER HOUR ($)	NAME OF LANGUAGE	CODE NUMBER
4.50	BASIC	1
6.50	PI/I	2
3.25	SNOBOL	3
2.50	ALGOL	4
6.75	FORTRAN	5
25.50	COBOL	6
12.50	ASSEMBLER	7
5.00	RPG	8
4.75	APL	9

(Any bias toward any particular computer language is purely coincidental!)

Let us further assume that these languages are assigned code numbers of 1 through 9 so that these code numbers may be used as subscripts. The input to the next version of the tables program is formatted as:

Name of Employee		Code Number	Hours Worked	
X(25)		9	99V99	

The output this time is to show the sequential count of each card, the employee-name, the number of hours worked, the rate of pay, the name of the language, and the net pay. At the end of the report, on a fresh page, the total net pay is to be printed.

This time the skeleton to the table will contain 2 items, not one. We want the rate of pay to appear alongside its associated language-name so that for a given subscript *each* item of a table element may be accessed. However, it is clear that because the rate of pay is numeric while the language-name is alphanumeric, we cannot use a PICTURE of 9's. It turns out that this does not present very much of a problem; we may use a PICTURE of X, omit the decimal point from the rate of pay, and take care of the details in the redefinition, as follows.

```
01   WAGE-RATE-SKELETON.
     02   FILLER   PIC   X(13) VALUE '0450BASIC'.
     02   FILLER   PIC   X(13) VALUE '0650PL/I'.
     02   FILLER   PIC   X(13) VALUE '0325SNOBOL'.
     02   FILLER   PIC   X(13) VALUE '0250ALGOL'.
     02   FILLER   PIC   X(13) VALUE '0675FORTRAN'.
     02   FILLER   PIC   X(13) VALUE '2550COBOL'.
     02   FILLER   PIC   X(13) VALUE '1250ASSEMBLER'.
     02   FILLER   PIC   X(13) VALUE '0500RPG'.
     02   FILLER   PIC   X(13) VALUE '0475APL'.
```

The PICTURE is specified to be X(13) because the longest language-name is ASSEMBLER, which consists of 9 letters, plus the 4 digits (without the decimal point) for the rate of pay. The skeleton is now redefined as:

```
01   WAGE-RATE REDEFINES WAGE-RATE-SKELETON.
     02   TABLE-ELEMENT OCCURS 9 TIMES.
          03   RATE PIC 99V99.
          03   LANGUAGE PIC X(09).
```

where the name TABLE-ELEMENT has been given to each element of the table. Remember, however, that each element is composed of 2 distinct parts. These are clearly seen in the redefinition where RATE is given a PICTURE of 99V99 (assigning to it the first 4 characters of the table element) and LANGUAGE is given a PICTURE of X(09), thereby assigning to it the last 9 characters of the element.

Conceptually, the table may now be viewed as a contiguous string of 9 by 13 characters.

'0450BASICbbbb0650PL/Ibbbbb ... 1250ASSEMBLER0500RPGbbbbbb'

| 1st element | 2nd element | 8th element | 9th element |

It is quite reasonable to define the table elements with the language-name preceding the rate of pay. However, if this were done, spaces would have to be placed after the language-name so that each name occupied exactly 9 positions. It is simply easier to write it the way shown. When the VALUE clause moves the language-name, together with its associated rate, it is justified left automatically and whatever room is left is padded with blanks.

In the Procedure Division TABLE-ELEMENT is not mentioned at all. However, because it is the subject of the OCCURS clause, TABLE-ELEMENT would have to be subscripted if it were cited. Now any item that is subordinate to TABLE-ELEMENT such as RATE and LANGUAGE, which are referenced, must always take a subscript. For this reason in the paragraph WRITE-LINE we have instructions such as:

```
MOVE RATE (SUB) TO RATE-OUT.
MOVE LANGUAGE (SUB) TO LANGUAGE-OUT.
MULTIPLY RATE (SUB) BY HOURS-WORKED GIVING NET-PAY.
```

Notice that in the paragraph PROCESS-DATA the value of SUB is tested to determine if it is less than 1. It is just as well, for examining the input closely will reveal 2 items with a value of 0 punched for the language code number. When this is detected by the program an appropriate message is printed.

Input for Program 28

EMPLOYEE - NAME	LANGUAGE CODE	HOURS WORKED (99V99)
IRVIN POREMBA	1	5000
JULIAN COLE	5	0450
MICHELLE CORNER	9	3525
FERN FREIDMAN	0	3526
BARBARA HODGES	4	1245
SALLY DEMBERG	8	0585
JACKIE MURDOCK	6	2500
MARY LAGOUMIS	0	2352
FRANS LISTZ	7	0500
BERT STURZA	5	1250
HAIN TOPOL	4	2000
ANTUA BORG	6	4000
GEORGE WASHINGTON	7	2536
AARON GREENFELD	7	2156
ROGER POOL	8	1740

Program 28

```
1    IDENTIFICATION   DIVISION.
2    PROGRAM-ID.      TABLE-3.
3    AUTHOR.          IRVIN POREMBA.
4    INSTALLATION.    NYU.
5    DATE-WRITTEN.    APRIL 24, 1982.
6    DATE-COMPILED.   APRIL 27, 1982.
7    SECURITY.        HENRY MULLISH.
```

```
8      * * * * * * * * * * * * * * * * * * * * * * * * * * * * * * * * * * * * * * * * * * *
9      *       THIS PROGRAM READS DATA CARDS PUNCHED:                               *
10     *                                                                            *
11     *       COLUMNS   1-25:  EMPLOYEE NAME                                        *
12     *       COLUMN      31:  A SUBSCRIPT                                          *
13     *       COLUMNS 36-39:  HOURS-WORKED                                          *
14     *                                                                            *
15     *       THIS PROGRAM USES A TABLE AND THE SUBSCRIPT                           *.
16     *       TO FIND THE WAGE RATE AND THE NAME OF THE                            *
17     *       COMPUTER LANGUAGE ASSOCIATED WITH THE WAGE RATE.                     *
18     *       IT THEN USES THE WAGE RATE TO FIND THE NET PAY                       *
19     *       FOR EACH EMPLOYEE.                                                   *
20     * * * * * * * * * * * * * * * * * * * * * * * * * * * * * * * * * * * * * * * * * * *
21
22     ENVIRONMENT  DIVISON.
23     CONFIGURATION  SECTION.
24     SOURCE-COMPUTER. CYBER-170-720.
25     OBJECT-COMPUTER. CYBER-170-720.
26     SPECIAL-NAMES.
27     INPUT-OUTPUT SECTION.
28     FILE-CONTROL.
29          SELECT IN-FILE ASSIGN TO INPUT.
30          SELECT OUT-FILE ASSIGN TO OUTPUT.
31
32     DATA DIVISION.
33     FILE SECTION.
34
35     FD   IN-FILE
36          LABEL RECORDS ARE OMITTED.
37
38     01   RECORD-IN.
39          02   EMPLOYEE-NAME      PIC X(25).
40          02   FILLER            PIC X(05).
41          02   SUB               PIC 9(01).
42          02   FILLER            PIC X(04).
43          02   HOURS-WORKED      PIC 9(02)V9(02).
44          02   FILLER            PIC X(41).
45
46     FD   OUT-FILE
47          LABEL RECORDS ARE OMITTED.
48
49     01   LINE-OUT               PIC X(133).
50
51     WORKING-STORAGE SECTION.
52     77   ANY-MORE-CARDS         PIC X(03) VALUE 'YES'.
53     77   NET-PAY                PIC 9(04)V9(02).
54     77   TOTAL-PAY              PIC 9(06)V9(02) VALUE ZERO.
55     77   CARD-COUNT             PIC 9(04) VALUE ZERO.
56
57     01   WAGE-RATE-SKELETON.
58          02   FILLER            PIC X(13) VALUE '0450BASIC'.
59          02   FILLER            PIC X(13) VALUE '0650PL1'.
60          02   FILLER            PIC X(13) VALUE '0325SNOBOL'.
61          02   FILLER            PIC X(13) VALUE '0250ALGOL'.
62          02   FILLER            PIC X(13) VALUE '0675FORTRAN'.
63          02   FILLER            PIC X(13) VALUE '2550COBOL'.
64          02   FILLER            PIC X(13) VALUE '1250ASSEMBLER'.
65          02   FILLER            PIC X(13) VALUE '0500RPG'.
66          02   FILLER            PIC X(13) VALUE '0475APL'.
67
68     01   WAGE-RATE REDEFINES WAGE-RATE-SKELETON.
69          02   TABLE-ELEMENT OCCURS 9 TIMES.
70               03   RATE         PIC 9(02)V9(02).
71               03   LANGUAGE     PIC X(09).
72
73     01   HEADER-1.
74          02   FILLER            PIC X(29) VALUE SPACES.
75          02   FILLER            PIC X(14) VALUE 'PAYROLL REPORT'.
76
77     01   HEADER-2.
78          02   FILLER            PIC X(29) VALUE SPACES.
79          02   FILLER            PIC X(14) VALUE ALL '*'.
80
81     01   HEADER-3.
82          02   FILLER            PIC X(01) VALUE SPACES.
```

```
83          02    FILLER              PIC X(14) VALUE 'COUNT'.
84          02    FILLER              PIC X(22) VALUE 'EMPLOYEE NAME'.
85          02    FILLER              PIC X(09) VALUE 'HOURS'.
86          02    FILLER              PIC X(09) VALUE 'RATE'.
87          02    FILLER              PIC X(12) VALUE 'LANGUAGE'.
88          02    FILLER              PIC X(07) VALUE 'NET PAY'.
89
90    01    HEADER-4.
91          02    FILLER              PIC X(01) VALUE SPACES.
92          02    FILLER              PIC X(05) VALUE ALL '*'.
93          02    FILLER              PIC X(03) VALUE SPACES.
94          02    FILLER              PIC X(25) VALUE ALL '*'.
95          02    FILLER              PIC X(03) VALUE SPACES.
96          02    FILLER              PIC X(05) VALUE ALL '*'.
97          02    FILLER              PIC X(03) VALUE SPACES.
98          02    FILLER              PIC X(06) VALUE ALL '*'.
99          02    FILLER              PIC X(03) VALUE SPACES.
100         02    FILLER              PIC X(09) VALUE ALL '*'.
101         02    FILLER              PIC X(03) VALUE SPACES.
102         02    FILLER              PIC X(09) VALUE ALL '*'.
103
104   01    DETAIL-LINE.
105         02    FILLER              PIC X(01) VALUE SPACES.
106         02    CARD-COUNT-OUT      PIC Z,ZZ9.
107         02    FILLER              PIC X(03) VALUE SPACES.
108         02    EMPLOY-NAME-OUT     PIC X(25).
109         02    FILLER              PIC X(03) VALUE SPACES.
110         02    HOURS-OUT           PIC Z9.99.
111         02    FILLER              PIC X(03) VALUE SPACES.
112         02    RATE-OUT            PIC $$9.99.
113         02    FILLER              PIC X(03) VALUE SPACES.
114         02    LANGUAGE-OUT        PIC X(09).
115         02    FILLER              PIC X(03) VALUE SPACES.
116         02    NET-PAY-OUT         PIC $$,$$9.99.
117
118   01    DETAIL-LINE-2.
119         02    FILLER              PIC X(01) VALUE SPACES.
120         02    CARD-COUNT-OUT-2    PIC Z,ZZ9.
121         02    FILLER              PIC X(03) VALUE SPACES.
122         02    FILLER              PIC X(19) VALUE 'ERROR IN SUBSCRIPT'.
123         02    FILLER              PIC X(08) VALUE 'FOUND:'.
124         02    SUBSCRIPT-OUT       PIC 9.
125
126   01    DETAIL-LINE-3.
127         02    FILLER              PIC X(10) VALUE SPACES.
128         02    FILLER              PIC X(14) VALUE 'TOTAL PAY FOR'.
129         02    FILLER              PIC X(16) VALUE 'ALL EMPLOYEES = '.
130         02    TOTAL-PAY-OUT       PIC $$$$,$$9.99.
131
132   PROCEDURE DIVISION.
133
134   MAIN-LINE-ROUTINE.
135         PERFORM OPEN-FILES.
136         PERFORM NEW-PAGE.
137         PERFORM START-UP.
138         PERFORM PROCESS-DATA UNTIL ANY-MORE-CARDS EQUAL 'NO'.
139         PERFORM CLOSE-UP.
140         STOP RUN.
141
142   OPEN-FILES.
143         OPEN INPUT IN-FILE.
144         OPEN OUTPUT OUT-FILE.
145
146   NEW-PAGE.
147         MOVE SPACES TO LINE-OUT.
148         WRITE LINE-OUT AFTER PAGE.
149
150   START-UP.
151         READ IN-FILE AT END MOVE 'NO' TO ANY-MORE-CARDS
152              MOVE ' **NO DATA IN DECK**' TO LINE-OUT
153              WRITE LINE-OUT AFTER 30.
154         IF ANY-MORE-CARDS EQUAL 'YES' PERFORM WRITE-HEADINGS.
155
156   PROCESS-DATA.
157         ADD 1 TO CARD-COUNT.
```

```
158          IF SUB < 1 PERFORM ERROR-ROUTINE
159          ELSE PERFORM WRITE-LINE.
160          READ IN-FILE AT END MOVE 'NO' TO ANY-MORE-CARDS
161               PERFORM GRAND-TOTAL.
162
163      CLOSE-UP.
164          CLOSE IN-FILE, OUT-FILE.
165
166      GRAND-TOTAL.
167          PERFORM NEW-PAGE.
168          MOVE TOTAL-PAY TO TOTAL-PAY-OUT.
169          WRITE LINE-OUT FROM DETAIL-LINE-3 AFTER 30.
170
171      WRITE-LINE.
172          MOVE CARD-COUNT TO CARD-COUNT-OUT.
173          MOVE EMPLOYEE-NAME TO EMPLOY-NAME-OUT.
174          MOVE HOURS-WORKED TO HOURS-OUT.
175          MOVE RATE (SUB) TO RATE-OUT.
176          MOVE LANGUAGE (SUB) TO LANGUAGE-OUT.
177          MULTIPLY RATE (SUB) BY HOURS-WORKED GIVING NET-PAY ROUNDED.
178          MOVE NET-PAY TO NET-PAY-OUT.
179          ADD NET-PAY TO TOTAL-PAY.
180          WRITE LINE-OUT FROM DETAIL-LINE AFTER 2.
181
182      ERROR-ROUTINE.
183          MOVE CARD-COUNT TO CARD-COUNT-OUT-2.
184          MOVE SUB TO SUBSCRIPT-OUT.
185          WRITE LINE-OUT FROM DETAIL-LINE-2 AFTER 2.
186
187      WRITE-HEADINGS.
188          WRITE LINE-OUT FROM HEADER-1 AFTER 1.
189          WRITE LINE-OUT FROM HEADER-2 AFTER 1.
190          WRITE LINE-OUT FROM HEADER-2 AFTER 1.
191          WRITE LINE-OUT FROM HEADER-3 AFTER 2.
192          WRITE LINE-OUT FROM HEADER-4 AFTER 1.
```

Output for Program 28

```
                              PAYROLL REPORT
                          * * * * * * * * * * * * *
                          * * * * * * * * * * * * *
COUNT       EMPLOYEE NAME      HOURS     RATE      LANGUAGE      NET PAY
* * * * *   * * * * * * * * * * * * * *  * * * * *  * * * * * *  * * * * * * * * *  * * * * * * * * *
    1       IRVIN POREMBA      50.00     $4.50     BASIC          $225.00
    2       JULIAN COLE         4.50     $6.75     FORTRAN         $30.38
    3       MICHELLE CORNER    35.25     $4.75     APL            $167.44
    4       FERN FREIDMAN      14.50     $3.25     SNOBOL          $47.13
    5       BARBARA HODGES     12.45     $2.50     ALGOL           $31.13
    6       SALLY DEMBERG       5.85     $5.00     RPG             $29.25
    7       JACKIE MURDOCK     25.00    $25.50     COBOL          $637.50
    8       MARY LAGOUMIS      52.35     $6.50     PL1            $340.28
    9       FRANS LISTZ         5.00    $12.50     ASSEMBLER       $62.50
   10       BERT STURZA        12.50     $6.75     FORTRAN         $84.38
   11       HAIN TOPOL         20.00     $2.50     ALGOL           $50.00
   12       ANTUA BORG         40.00    $25.50     COBOL        $1,020.00
   13       GEORGE WASHINGTON  25.36    $12.50     ASSEMBLER      $317.00
   14       AARON GREENFELD    21.56    $12.50     ASSEMBLER      $269.50
   15       ROGER POOL         17.40     $5.00     RPG             $87.00
```

TOTAL PAY FOR ALL EMPLOYEES = $3,398.49

10.4   An Example of a Triple-Entry Table Using Subscripting

We have seen tables where each entry contained either a single element or an element composed of 2 items. There is no reason, however, that a single table entry cannot have 3 or even more items. The next program illustrates the use of a table in which each element consists of 3 items.

The problem concerns a retail bookstore. To keep the problem manageable within the limits imposed by a textbook such as this, we confine ourselves to a stock of only 10 different book titles. Naturally this is most unrealistic but the techniques used in the program are the same nevertheless.

The 10 books our fictitious bookstore carries are:

TITLE NUMBER	BOOK CODE	BOOK PRICE ($)	TITLE
1	T253	12.50	COBOL IS FUN
2	FX35	8.95	INSTANT COBOL
3	TI14	15.65	BUSINESS COBOL
4	PL33	14.75	A POET'S VIEW OF COBOL
5	EX11	10.55	STRUCTURED COBOL
6	JX00	25.35	HAVING A GOOD TIME WITH COBOL
7	QA87	11.99	LIFE WITH COBOL
8	AB44	5.75	COBOL POWER
9	TX56	13.55	COBOL NOW
10	GG34	15.65	COBOL AND I

where the book code is a 4-character alphanumeric number.

All this information may be included in a single table, which could then be accessed by the title number, which is used as a subscript.

Here is how the table may be set up.

```
01   BOOK-VALUE-SKELETON.
     02   FILLER    PIC   X(37) VALUE 'T2531250COBOL IS FUN'.
     02   FILLER    PIC   X(37) VALUE 'FX350895INSTANT COBOL'.
     02   FILLER    PIC   X(37) VALUE 'TI411565BUSINESS COBOL'.
     02   FILLER    PIC   X(37) VALUE 'PL331475A POET''S VIEW OF COBOL'.
     02   FILLER    PIC   X(37) VALUE 'EX111055STRUCTURED COBOL'.
     02   FILLER    PIC   X(37) VALUE 'JX002535HAVING A GOOD TIME WITH COBOL'.
     02   FILLER    PIC   X(37) VALUE 'QA871199LIFE WITH COBOL'.
     02   FILLER    PIC   X(37) VALUE 'AB440575COBOL POWER'.
     02   FILLER    PIC   X(37) VALUE 'TX561355COBOL NOW'.
     02   FILLER    PIC   X(37) VALUE 'GG31565 COBOL AND I'.
01   BOOK-VALUE REDEFINES BOOK-VALUE-SKELETON.
     02   TABLE-ELEMENT OCCURS 10 TIMES.
          03   BOOK-CODE  PIC X(04).
          03   BOOK-PRICE PIC 99V99.
          03   BOOK-NAME  PIC X(29).
```

Once again, whenever any of the 3 items subordinate to TABLE-ELEMENT (which is the subject of the OCCURS clause) is referenced, they must be subscripted.

The input is formatted as:

where the first 2 columns contain the subscript for accessing the appropriate table entry and columns 6 through 9 contain the number of books in question that are ordered.

The program is not very different from the previous one, except that it is a little more elaborate. It does serve to introduce the figurative constant HIGH-VALUES, which is the highest possible value a given computer system can store internally. It is often used for comparison purposes. Here we are using it to signal the end of file. HIGH-VALUES is equivalent to HIGH-VALUE, and their counterparts are LOW-VALUES and LOW-VALUE.

Input for Program 29

```
03   0100
06   0125
01   1500
08   0750
03   0050
04   0365
09   1100
02   0075
05   0450
10   1250
05   0120
07   0357
```

Program 29

```
1         IDENTIFICATION   DIVISION.
2         PROGRAM-ID.      TABLE-4.
3         AUTHOR.          IRVIN POREMBA.
4         INSTALLATION.    NYU.
5         DATE-WRITTEN.    NOVEMBER 9, 1982.
6         DATE-COMPILED.   NOVEMBER 11, 1982.
7         SECURITY.        HENRY MULLISH.
8         * * * * * * * * * * * * * * * * * * * * * * * * * * * * * * * * * * * * * * * * * * * * * * *
9         *      THIS PROGRAM READS IN DATA CARDS PUNCHED:                  *
10        *                                                                 *
11        *         COLUMNS 1-2: BOOK-SUBSCRIPT                             *
12        *         COLUMNS 6-9: QUANTITY ORDERED                          *
13        *                                                                 *
14        *         THIS PROGRAM USES A SUBSCRIPT TO ACCESS                 *
15        *         A TABLE WHICH CONTAINS A BOOK'S CODE, ITS               *
16        *         NAME AND ITS PRICE. ALL OF THIS IS PRINTED              *
17        *         OUT ALONG WITH THE NET SALE FOR EACH ORDER.             *
18        * * * * * * * * * * * * * * * * * * * * * * * * * * * * * * * * * * * * * * * * * * * * * * *
19
20        ENVIRONMENT    DIVISION.
21        CONFIGURATION  SECTION.
22        SOURCE-COMPUTER. CYBER-170-720.
23        OBJECT-COMPUTER. CYBER-170-720.
24        SPECIAL-NAMES.
25        INPUT-OUTPUT SECTION.
26        FILE-CONTROL.
27             SELECT IN-FILE ASSIGN TO INPUT.
28             SELECT OUT-FILE ASSIGN TO OUTPUT.
29
30        DATA DIVISION.
31        FILE SECTION.
32
33        FD   IN-FILE
34             LABEL RECORDS ARE OMITTED.
35
36        01   RECORD-IN.
37             02   BOOK-SUB            PIC 9(02).
38             02   FILLER             PIC X(03).
39             02   QUANTITY-ORDERED   PIC 9(04).
40             02   FILLER             PIC X(71).
41
42        FD   OUT-FILE
43             LABEL RECORDS ARE OMITTED.
```

```
44
45      01    LINE-OUT                      PIC X(133).
46
47    WORKING-STORAGE SECTION.
48
49      01    BOOK-VALUE-SKELETON.
50            02    FILLER                  PIC X(37) VALUE
51                                    'T2531250COBOL IS FUN'.
52            02    FILLER                  PIC X(37) VALUE
53                                    'FX350895INSTANT COBOL'.
54            02    FILLER                  PIC X(37) VALUE
55                                    'TI141565BUSINESS COBOL'.
56            02    FILLER                  PIC X(37) VALUE
57                                    'PL331475A POET''S VIEW OF COBOL'.
58            02    FILLER                  PIC X(37) VALUE
59                                    'EX111055STRUCTURED COBOL'.
60            02    FILLER                  PIC X(37) VALUE
61                                    'JX002535HAVING A GOOD TIME WITH COBOL'.
62            02    FILLER                  PIC X(37) VALUE
63                                    'QA871199LIFE WITH COBOL'.
64            02    FILLER                  PIC X(37) VALUE
65                                    'AB440575COBOL POWER'.
66            02    FILLER                  PIC X(37) VALUE
67                                    'TX561355COBOL NOW'.
68            02    FILLER                  PIC X(37) VALUE
69                                    'GG341565COBOL AND I'.
70
71      01    BOOK-VALUE REDEFINES BOOK-VALUE-SKELETON.
72            02    TABLE-ELEMENT OCCURS 10 TIMES.
73                  03    BOOK-CODE         PIC X(04).
74                  03    BOOK-PRICE        PIC 99V99.
75                  03    BOOK-NAME         PIC X(29).
76
77      01    INDEPENDENT-ITEMS-USED.
78            02    ANY-MORE-CARDS          PIC X(03) VALUE 'YES'.
79            02    CARD-COUNT              PIC 9(04) VALUE ZERO.
80
81      01    HEADER-1.
82            02    FILLER                  PIC X(28) VALUE SPACES.
83            02    FILLER                  PIC X(11) VALUE 'BOOK SALES'.
84            02    FILLER                  PIC X(06) VALUE 'REPORT'.
85
86      01    HEADER-2.
87            02    FILLER                  PIC X(28) VALUE SPACES.
88            02    FILLER                  PIC X(17) VALUE ALL '∗'.
89
90      01    HEADER-3.
91            02    FILLER                  PIC X(09) VALUE 'COUNT'.
92            02    FILLER                  PIC X(16) VALUE 'CODE'.
93            02    FILLER                  PIC X(23) VALUE 'NAME OF BOOK'.
94            02    FILLER                  PIC X(09) VALUE 'ORDER'.
95            02    FILLER                  PIC X(08) VALUE 'PRICE'.
96            02    FILLER                  PIC X(11) VALUE 'TOTAL PRICE'.
97
98      01    HEADER-4.
99            02    FILLER                  PIC X(01) VALUE SPACES.
100           02    FILLER                  PIC X(05) VALUE ALL '-'.
101           02    FILLER                  PIC X(03) VALUE SPACES.
102           02    FILLER                  PIC X(04) VALUE ALL '-'.
103           02    FILLER                  PIC X(03) VALUE SPACES.
104           02    FILLER                  PIC X(29) VALUE ALL '-'.
105           02    FILLER                  PIC X(03) VALUE SPACES.
106           02    FILLER                  PIC X(05) VALUE ALL '-'.
107           02    FILLER                  PIC X(03) VALUE SPACES.
108           02    FILLER                  PIC X(06) VALUE ALL '-'.
109           02    FILLER                  PIC X(03) VALUE SPACES.
110           02    FILLER                  PIC X(11) VALUE ALL '-'.
111
112     01    DETAIL-LINE.
113           02    FILLER                  PIC X(01) VALUE SPACES.
114           02    CARD-COUNT-OUT          PIC Z,ZZ9.
115           02    FILLER                  PIC X(03) VALUE SPACES.
116           02    BOOK-CODE-OUT           PIC X(04).
117           02    FILLER                  PIC X(03) VALUE SPACES.
```

```
118        02   BOOK-NAME-OUT        PIC X(29).
119        02   FILLER               PIC X(03) VALUE SPACES.
120        02   QUANTITY-ORDER-OUT   PIC Z,ZZ9.
121        02   FILLER               PIC X(03) VALUE SPACES.
122        02   BOOK-PRICE-OUT       PIC $$9.99.
123        02   FILLER               PIC X(03) VALUE SPACES.
124        02   TOTAL-PRICE-OUT      PIC $$$$,$$$.99.
125
126   PROCEDURE DIVISION.
127
128   MAIN-LINE-ROUTINE.
129        PERFORM OPEN-FILES.
130        PERFORM NEW-PAGE.
131        PERFORM START-UP.
132        PERFORM PROCESS-DATA UNTIL ANY-MORE-CARDS EQUAL HIGH-VALUES.
133        PERFORM CLOSE-UP.
134        STOP RUN.
135
136   OPEN-FILES.
137        OPEN INPUT IN-FILE.
138        OPEN OUTPUT OUT-FILE.
139
140   NEW-PAGE.
141        MOVE SPACES TO LINE-OUT.
142        WRITE LINE-OUT AFTER PAGE.
143
144   START-UP.
145        READ IN-FILE AT END
146                        MOVE 'NO' TO ANY-MORE-CARDS
147                        MOVE '**NO DATA IN DECK**' TO LINE-OUT
148                        WRITE LINE-OUT AFTER 30 LINES.
149        IF ANY-MORE-CARDS EQUAL 'YES' PERFORM WRITE-HEADINGS.
150
151   PROCESS-DATA.
152        ADD 1 TO CARD-COUNT.
153        MOVE CARD-COUNT TO CARD-COUNT-OUT.
154        MOVE QUANTITY-ORDERED TO QUANTITY-ORDER-OUT.
155        MOVE BOOK-CODE (BOOK-SUB) TO BOOK-CODE-OUT.
156        MOVE BOOK-NAME (BOOK-SUB) TO BOOK-NAME-OUT.
157        MOVE BOOK-PRICE (BOOK-SUB) TO BOOK-PRICE-OUT.
158        MULTIPLY QUANTITY-ORDERED BY BOOK-PRICE (BOOK-SUB)
159             GIVING TOTAL-PRICE-OUT.
160        WRITE LINE-OUT FROM DETAIL-LINE AFTER 2.
161        READ IN-FILE AT END MOVE HIGH-VALUES TO ANY-MORE-CARDS.
162
163   CLOSE-UP.
164        CLOSE IN-FILE, OUT-FILE.
165
166   WRITE-HEADINGS.
167        WRITE LINE-OUT FROM HEADER-1 AFTER 1.
168        WRITE LINE-OUT FROM HEADER-2 AFTER 1.
169        WRITE LINE-OUT FROM HEADER-2 AFTER 1.
170        WRITE LINE-OUT FROM HEADER-3 AFTER 2.
171        WRITE LINE-OUT FROM HEADER-4 AFTER 0.
```

Output for Program 29

```
                         BOOK SALES REPORT
                      * * * * * * * * * * * * * * *
                      * * * * * * * * * * * * * * *
    COUNT   CODE           NAME OF BOOK            ORDER   PRICE   TOTAL PRICE
       1    TI14    BUSINESS COBOL                   100   $15.65    $1,565.00
       2    JX00    HAVING A GOOD TIME WITH COBOL    125   $25.35    $3,168.75
       3    T253    COBOL IS FUN                   1,500   $12.50   $18,750.00
       4    AB44    COBOL POWER                      750    $5.75    $4,312.50
       5    TI14    BUSINESS COBOL                    50   $15.65      $782.50
       6    PL33    A POET'S VIEW OF COBOL           365   $14.75    $5,383.75
       7    TX56    COBOL NOW                      1,100   $13.55   $14,905.00
       8    FX35    INSTANT COBOL                     75    $8.95      $671.25
       9    EX11    STRUCTURED COBOL                 450   $10.55    $4,747.50
      10    GG34    COBOL AND I                    1,250   $15.65   $19,562.50
      11    EX11    STRUCTURED COBOL                 120   $10.55    $1,266.00
      12    QA87    LIFE WITH COBOL                  357   $11.99    $4,280.43
```

10.5 Two Versions of a Triple-Entry Table Program Using an Artificial Subscript

Searching a Table Using a Devised Subscript Written in the Conventional Style

In program 28 (the programmer's pay problem) we were very fortunate in that the subscript read in from data cards pointed directly to the location of the desired element of the table. The subscripts ranged from 1 to 9 and the corresponding elements of the table were located in positions 1 through 9. In practice, in commercial data processing this ideal set of circumstances is seldom realized. The government might decide to allow for many other languages as well as to delete certain languages as they become obsolete. The result would be that we are left with language code numbers that are no longer in sequence, as depicted in the following table.

LANGUAGE CODE NUMBER	RATE OF PAY ($)	LANGUAGE - NAME
204	4.50	BASIC
052	6.50	PL/I
128	3.25	SNOBOL
428	2.50	ALGOL
943	6.75	FORTRAN
005	22.50	COBOL
110	12.50	ASSEMBLER
148	5.00	RPG
456	4.75	APL

A single-dimensioned table can now be set up.

```
01  RATE-TABLE-SKELETON.
    02  FILLER   PIC X(16) VALUE '2040450BASIC'.
    02  FILLER   PIC X(16) VALUE '1480500RPG'.
    02  FILLER   PIC X(16) VALUE '1280325SNOBOL'.
    02  FILLER   PIC X(16) VALUE '4280250ALGOL'.
    02  FILLER   PIC X(16) VALUE '9430675FORTRAN'.
    02  FILLER   PIC X(16) VALUE '0052550COBOL'.
    02  FILLER   PIC X(16) VALUE '1101250ASSEMBLER'.
    02  FILLER   PIC X(16) VALUE '1480500RPG'.
    02  FILLER   PIC X(16) VALUE '4560475APL'.

01  RATE-TABLE REDEFINES RATE-TABLE-SKELETON.
    02 TABLE-ELEMENT OCCURS 9 TIMES.
        03   ASSIGNED-LANG-NO PIC 999.
        03   RATE-OF-PAY       PIC 99V99.
        03   LANG-NAME         PIC X(09).
```

This time when we read in a language code number we can not use it as a subscript because the first element now has a code number of 204, not 1, the second has a code number of 052, not 2, and so on.

Note carefully that the language code numbers jump about in random fashion, as well as being out of sequence.

However we cope with this situation, the fact remains that in order to access the first element of the table, we must have a subscript of 1; to access the second element, we need a subscript of 2, and so on. Thus we make up an artificial subscript (called SUB in the program), which is a 77-level item with a PICTURE of 99. We want initially to set the value of SUB to 1 and test to see whether the code number being read in matches the code number of the first element of the table. If it is not, 1 is added to SUB and a test is made against the second item, and so on. As soon as a match is successful, the appropriate information is retrieved by using the subscript SUB.

If the whole table has been searched in this way without a successful match, it could mean either one of 2 things.

1. The data card was in error for some reason.

2. The matching code was omitted from the table.

Whatever the reason, the value of SUB would have exceeded the value specified in the OCCURS clause. Therefore a test is made in line 226 of the program to determine whether SUB has exceeded its bounds. If SUB has, then the indication is that an error has occurred. When it is detected, an appropriate error message is printed.

As soon as a match succeeds between an incoming data card and an item in the table, the appropriate moves and calculations are performed, the line is printed, and the process is repeated, with SUB being reinitialized to 1.

You may wonder why we have resorted to conventional style rather than to structured programming to illustrate the point of the program. It is simply a case of presenting the solution as clearly as possible, in particular, for those people who are exposed to these concepts for the first time.

Input for Program 30

IRVIN POREMBA	342425393	005	12550
JULIAN COLE	253415583	204	04575
MICHELLE CORNER	453267789	943	10025
FERN FREIDMAN	123254789	450	45832
BARBARA HODGES	645236632	110	01245
SALLY DEMBERG	554613214	KIJ	00236
JACKIE MURDOCK	225321122	428	20000
MARY LAGOUMIS	521239816	001	45200
FRANS LISTZ	234257832	943	00500
BERT STURZA	451021411	148	32000
AARON GREENFELD	989506910	204	02156
ROGER POOL	73J552293	005	01740
ANDREW DORSEY	192713105	110	24260
RICHARD LESTER	259302305	456	02290
FRANK JASPER	319501263	148	00622
RICHARD MILLER	615140081	943	23550
MICHAEL DIAVIDSON	515851602	052	42100
RONALD KRAMER	160130059	128	11325
MARTIN SMITH	232544511	456	00720
MARC FRIEDMAN	625431982	128	05160
MARC NEFF	253147654	943	07520
ROBERT TROTENBERG	456237531	110	10000

Program 30

```
1       IDENTIFICATION   DIVISION.
2       PROGRAM-ID.      TABLE-5.
3       AUTHOR.          IRVIN POREMBA.
4       DATE-WRITTEN.    OCTOBER 21, 1982.
5       DATE-COMPILED.   OCTOBER 21, 1982.
6       SECURITY.        HENRY MULLISH.
7       * * * * * * * * * * * * * * * * * * * * * * * * * * * * * * * * * * * * * * * * * * * * * * *
8       *       THIS PROGRAM IS A U.S. GOVERNMENT PAYROLL.                    *
9       *       CARDS ARE PUNCHED AS FOLLOWED:                                *
10      *                                                                     *
11      *       COLUMNS  1-25: EMPLOYEE NAME                                  *
12      *       COLUMNS 30-38: SOCIAL SECURITY NUMBER                         *
13      *       COLUMNS 40-42: PROGRAM LANGUAGE NUMBER                        *
14      *       COLUMNS 45-49: HOURS-WORKED                                   *
15      *                                                                     *
16      *       THIS PROGRAM THEN USES A TABLE AND THE                        *
17      *       SUBSCRIPTING METHOD TO LOOK UP THE NAME OF THE                *
18      *       LANGUAGE USED BY EACH PROGRAMMER WITH THE                     *
19      *       CORRESPONDING RATE OF PAY, PRINTING OUT ALL THE               *
20      *       INFORMATION UNDER A SUITABLE HEADING WITH THE                 *
21      *       NET PAY DUE TO EACH PROGRAMMER AND, AT THE END,               *
22      *       THE TOTAL PAY DUE TO ALL PROGRAMMERS.                         *
23      *       NOTE THAT THIS PROGRAM USES A BRUTE FORCE METHOD              *
24      * * * * * * * * * * * * * * * * * * * * * * * * * * * * * * * * * * * * * * * * * * * * * * *
25
26      ENVIRONMENT DIVISION.
27      CONFIGURATION SECTION.
```

```
28      SOURCE-COMPUTER. CYBER-170-720.
29      OBJECT-COMPUTER. CYBER-170-720.
30      SPECIAL-NAMES.
31      INPUT-OUTPUT SECTION.
32      FILE-CONTROL.
33          SELECT IN-FILE ASSIGN TO INPUT.
34          SELECT OUT-FILE ASSIGN TO OUTPUT.
35
36      DATA DIVISION.
37      FILE SECTION.
38
39      FD  IN-FILE
40          LABEL RECORDS ARE OMITTED.
41
42      *   DEFINE INPUT.
43
44      01  RECORD-IN.
45          02   EMPLOYEE-NAME         PIC X(25).
46          02   FILLER               PIC X(04).
47          02   SOC-SEC-NO           PIC 9(09).
48          02   FILLER               PIC X(01).
49          02   LANGUAGE-NO          PIC 9(03).
50          02   FILLER               PIC X(02).
51          02   HOURS-WORKED         PIC 9(03)V9(02).
52          02   FILLER               PIC X(21).
53
54      FD  OUT-FILE
55          LABEL RECORDS ARE OMITTED.
56
57      *   DEFINE OUT OF PROGRAM.
58
59      01  LINE-OUT                   PIC X(133).
60
61      WORKING-STORAGE SECTION.
62      77  SUB                        PIC 99.
63      77  CARD-COUNT                 PIC 99999 VALUE ZERO.
64      77  AMOUNT-PAID                PIC 9(05)V99.
65      77  TOTAL-AMOUNT-PAID          PIC 9(09)V99 VALUE ZERO.
66      77  W-S-RATE-OF-PAY            PIC 99V99.
67
68      *   BELOW IS THE SKELETON OF THE TABLE USED IN THIS
69      *   PROGRAM. AFTERWARDS, THE TABLE (RATE-TABLE-SKELETON,
70      *   AS IT IS CALLED) IS REDEFINED AND BROKEN UP INTO
71      *   ITS DIFFERENT PARTS, NAMELY: ASSIGNED-LANG-NO,
72      *   RATE-OF-PAY, AND LANG-NAME.
73
74      01  RATE-TABLE-SKELETON.
75          02   FILLER               PIC X(16) VALUE '2040450BASIC'.
76          02   FILLER               PIC X(16) VALUE '0520650PL/I'.
77          02   FILLER               PIC X(16) VALUE '1280325SNOBOL'.
78          02   FILLER               PIC X(16) VALUE '4280250ALGOL'.
79          02   FILLER               PIC X(16) VALUE '9430675FORTRAN'.
80          02   FILLER               PIC X(16) VALUE '0052550COBOL'.
81          02   FILLER               PIC X(16) VALUE '1101250ASSEMBLER'.
82          02   FILLER               PIC X(16) VALUE '1480500RPG'.
83          02   FILLER               PIC X(16) VALUE '4560475APL'.
84
85      01  RATE-TABLE REDEFINES RATE-TABLE-SKELETON.
86          02   TABLE-ELEMENT OCCURS 9 TIMES.
87              03 ASSIGNED-LANG-NO    PIC 999.
88              03 RATE-OF-PAY         PIC 99V99.
89              03 LANG-NAME           PIC X(09).
90
91      01  HEADER-1.
92          02   FILLER               PIC X(41) VALUE SPACES.
93          02   FILLER               PIC X(14) VALUE 'UNITED STATES'.
94          02   FILLER               PIC X(11) VALUE 'GOVERNMENT'.
95          02   FILLER               PIC X(18) VALUE 'PAYROLL: COMPUTER'.
96          02   FILLER               PIC X(09) VALUE 'DIVISION'.
97
98      01  HEADER-2.
99          02   FILLER               PIC X(41) VALUE SPACES.
100         02   FILLER               PIC X(52) VALUE ALL ' * '.
101
102     01  HEADER-3.
103         02   FILLER               PIC X(01) VALUE SPACES.
```

```
104          02   FILLER              PIC X(17) VALUE 'CARD'.
105          02   FILLER              PIC X(22) VALUE 'EMPLOYEE'.
106          02   FILLER              PIC X(14) VALUE 'SOC. SEC.'.
107          02   FILLER              PIC X(19) VALUE 'ASSIGNED LANG.'.
108          02   FILLER              PIC X(10) VALUE 'HOURS'.
109          02   FILLER              PIC X(12) VALUE 'RATE PER'.
110          02   FILLER              PIC X(15) VALUE 'LANGUAGE'.
111          02   FILLER              PIC X(06) VALUE 'AMOUNT'.
112
113    01    HEADER-4.
114          02   FILLER              PIC X(01) VALUE SPACES.
115          02   FILLER              PIX X(19) VALUE 'COUNT'.
116          02   FILLER              PIC X(21) VALUE 'NAME'.
117          02   FILLER              PIC X(17) VALUE 'NUMBER'.
118          02   FILLER              PIC X(15) VALUE 'NUMBER'.
119          02   FILLER              PIC X(12) VALUE 'WORKED'.
120          02   FILLER              PIC X(12) VALUE 'HOUR'.
121          02   FILLER              PIC X(14) VALUE 'NAME'.
122          02   FILLER              PIC X(04) VALUE 'PAID'.
123
124    01    HEADER-5.
125          02   FILLER              PIC X(01) VALUE SPACES.
126          02   FILLER              PIC X(06) VALUE ALL '*'.
127          02   FILLER              PIC X(03) VALUE SPACES.
128          02   FILLER              PIC X(25) VALUE ALL '*'.
129          02   FILLER              PIC X(04) VALUE SPACES.
130          02   FILLER              PIC X(11) VALUE ALL '*'.
131          02   FILLER              PIC X(04) VALUE SPACES.
132          02   FILLER              PIC X(14) VALUE ALL '*'.
133          02   FILLER              PIC X(05) VALUE SPACES.
134          02   FILLER              PIC X(06) VALUE ALL '*'.
135          02   FILLER              PIC X(04) VALUE SPACES.
136          02   FILLER              PIC X(08) VALUE ALL '*'.
137          02   FILLER              PIC X(04) VALUE SPACES.
138          02   FILLER              PIC X(09) VALUE ALL '*'.
139          02   FILLER              PIC X(04) VALUE SPACES.
140          02   FILLER              PIC X(10) VALUE ALL '*'.
141
142    01    DETAIL-LINE.
143          02   FILLER              PIC X(01) VALUE SPACES.
144          02   CARD-COUNT-OUT      PIC ZZ,ZZ9.
145          02   FILLER              PIC X(03) VALUE SPACES.
146          02   EMPLOYEE-NAME-OUT   PIC X(25).
147          02   FILLER              PIC X(04) VALUE SPACES.
148          02   SOC-SEC-NO-OUT      PIC 999B99B9999.
149          02   FILLER              PIC X(09) VALUE SPACES.
150          02   LANGUAGE-NO-OUT     PIC 999.
151          02   FILLER              PIC X(11) VALUE SPACES.
152          02   HOURS-WORKED-OUT    PIC ZZ9.99.
153          02   FILLER              PIC X(05) VALUE SPACES.
154          02   RATE-OF-PAY-OUT     PIC $$9.99.
155          02   FILLER              PIC X(05) VALUE SPACES.
156          02   LANG-NAME-OUT       PIC X(09).
157          02   FILLER              PIC X(04) VALUE SPACES.
158          02   AMOUNT-PAID-OUT     PIC $$$,$$9.99.
159
160    01    DETAIL-LINE-2.
161          02   FILLER              PIC X(01) VALUE SPACES.
162          02   FILLER              PIC X(13) VALUE 'TOTAL AMOUNT'.
163          02   FILLER              PIC X(17) VALUE 'PAID TO COMPUTER'.
164          02   FILLER              PIC X(15) VALUE 'PROGRAMMERS IS'.
165          02   TOTAL-AMOUNT-OUT    PIC $,$$$,$$$,$$9.99.
166          02   FILLER              PIC X(01) VALUE '.'.
167
168    01    DETAIL-LINE-3.
169          02   FILLER              PIC X(01) VALUE SPACES.
170          02   CARD-COUNT-OUT-2    PIC ZZ,ZZ9.
171          02   FILLER              PIC X(03) VALUE SPACES.
172          02   EMPLOY-NAME-OUT-2   PIC X(25).
173          02   FILLER              PIC X(04) VALUE SPACES.
174          02   SOC-SEC-NO-OUT-2    PIC X(09).
175          02   FILLER              PIC X(11) VALUE SPACES.
176          02   LANGUAGE-NO-OUT-2   PIC X(03).
177          02   FILLER              PIC X(11) VALUE SPACES.
178          02   HOURS-WORKED-OUT-2  PIC 999.99
179          02   FILLER              PIC X(06) VALUE SPACES.
```

```
180          02   FILLER                    PIC X(13) VALUE 'ERROR IN DATA'.
181
182
183     01   DETAIL-LINE-4.
184          02   FILLER                    PIC X(01) VALUE SPACES.
185          02   CARD-COUNT-OUT-3          PIC ZZ,ZZ9.
186          02   FILLER                    PIC X(03) VALUE SPACES.
187          02   EMPLOY-NAME-OUT-3         PIC X(25).
188          02   FILLER                    PIC X(04) VALUE SPACES.
189          02   SOC-SEC-NO-OUT-3          PIC 999B99B9999.
190          02   FILLER                    PIC X(09) VALUE SPACES.
191          02   LANGUAGE-NO-OUT-3         PIC 999.
192          02   FILLER                    PIC X(11) VALUE SPACES.
193          02   HOURS-WORKED-OUT-3        PIC ZZ9.99.
194          02   FILLER                    PIC X(04) VALUE SPACES.
195          02   FILLER                    PIC X(09) VALUE 'LANGUAGE'.
196          02   FILLER                    PIC X(10) VALUE 'NUMBER NOT'.
197          02   FILLER                    PIC X(15) VALUE 'FOUND IN TABLE'.
198
199     PROCEDURE DIVISION.
200
201     OPEN-FILES.
202          OPEN INPUT IN-FILE.
203          OPEN OUTPUT OUT-FILE.
204
205     NEW-PAGE.
206          MOVE SPACES TO LINE-OUT.
207          WRITE LINE-OUT AFTER PAGE.
208
209     THE-WRITE-HEADINGS.
210          PERFORM WRITE-HEADINGS.
211
212     PROCESS-DATA.
213          READ IN FILE AT END GO TO TOTAL-PARA.
214          MOVE 1 TO SUB.
215          ADD 1 TO CARD-COUNT.
216          IF HOURS-WORKED NOT NUMERIC
217               OR SOC-SEC-NO NOT NUMERIC
218               OR LANGUAGE-NO NOT NUMERIC
219               PERFORM ERROR-PARA-1
220               GO TO PROCESS-DATA.
221
222     TEST-PARA.
223          IF LANGUAGE-NO EQUAL ASSIGNED-LANG-NO (SUB)
224               GO TO WORK-PARA
225          ELSE ADD 1 TO SUB
226               IF SUB > 9 GO TO ERROR-PARA-2
227               ELSE GO TO TEST-PARA.
228
229     WORK-PARA.
230          MOVE RATE-OF-PAY (SUB) TO W-S-RATE-OF-PAY.
231          MULTIPLY HOURS-WORKED BY W-S-RATE-OF-PAY
232               GIVING AMOUNT-PAID ROUNDED.
233          ADD AMOUNT-PAID TO TOTAL-AMOUNT-PAID.
234          MOVE CARD-COUNT TO CARD-COUNT-OUT.
235          MOVE EMPLOYEE-NAME TO EMPLOYEE-NAME-OUT.
236          MOVE SOC-SEC-NO TO SOC-SEC-NO-OUT.
237          MOVE LANGUAGE-NO TO LANGUAGE-NO-OUT.
238          MOVE HOURS-WORKED TO HOURS-WORKED-OUT.
239          MOVE LANG-NAME (SUB) TO LANG-NAME-OUT.
240          MOVE RATE-OF-PAY (SUB) TO RATE-OF-PAY-OUT.
241          MOVE AMOUNT-PAID TO AMOUNT-PAID-OUT.
242          WRITE LINE-OUT FROM DETAIL-LINE AFTER 2.
243          GO TO PROCESS-DATA.
244
245     TOTAL-PARA.
246          PERFORM NEW-PAGE.
247          MOVE TOTAL-AMOUNT-PAID TO TOTAL-AMOUNT-OUT.
248          WRITE LINE-OUT FROM DETAIL-LINE-2 AFTER 2.
249          GO TO CLOSE-UP.
250
251     ERROR-PARA-1.
252          MOVE CARD-COUNT TO CARD-COUNT-OUT-2.
253          MOVE EMPLOYEE-NAME TO EMPLOY-NAME-OUT-2.
254          MOVE SOC-SEC-NO TO SOC-SEC-NO-OUT-2.
```

```
255          MOVE LANGUAGE-NO TO LANGUAGE-NO-OUT-2.
256          MOVE HOURS-WORKED TO HOURS-WORKED-OUT-2.
257          WRITE LINE-OUT FROM DETAIL-LINE-3 AFTER 2.
258
259     ERROR-PARA-2.
260          MOVE CARD-COUNT TO CARD-COUNT-OUT-3.
261          MOVE EMPLOYEE-NAME TO EMPLOY-NAME-OUT-3.
262          MOVE SOC-SEC-NO TO SOC-SEC-NO-OUT-3.
263          MOVE LANGUAGE-NO TO LANGUAGE-NO-OUT-3.
264          MOVE HOURS-WORKED TO HOURS-WORKED-OUT-3.
265          WRITE LINE-OUT FROM DETAIL-LINE-4 AFTER 2.
266          GO TO PROCESS-DATA.
267
268     WRITE-HEADINGS.
269          WRITE LINE-OUT FROM HEADER-1 AFTER 1.
270          WRITE LINE-OUT FROM HEADER-2 AFTER 1.
271          WRITE LINE-OUT FROM HEADER-2 AFTER 1.
272          WRITE LINE-OUT FROM HEADER-3 AFTER 2.
273          WRITE LINE-OUT FROM HEADER-4 AFTER 1.
274          WRITE LINE-OUT FROM HEADER-5 AFTER 1.
275
276     CLOSE-UP.
277          CLOSE IN-FILE, OUT-FILE.
278          STOP RUN.
```

Output for Program 30

UNITED STATES GOVERNMENT PAYROLL: COMPUTER DIVISION

CARD COUNT	EMPLOYEE NAME	SOC. SEC NUMBER	ASSIGNED LANG. NUMBER	HOURS WORKED	RATE PER HOUR	LANGUAGE NAME	AMOUNT PAID
1	IRVIN POREMBA	342 42 5393	005	125.50	$25.50	COBOL	$3,200.25
2	JULIAN COLE	253 41 5583	204	45.75	$4.50	BASIC	$205.88
3	MICHELLE CORNER	453 26 7789	943	100.25	$6.75	FORTRAN	$676.69
4	FERN FREIDMAN	123 25 4789	450	458.32	LANGUAGE NUMBER NOT FOUND IN TABLE		
5	BARBARA HODGES	645 23 6632	110	12.45	$12.50	ASSEMBLER	$155.63
6	SALLY DEMBERG	554613214	KIJ	002.36	ERROR IN DATA		
7	JACKIE MURDOCK	225 32 1122	428	200.00	$2.50	ALGOL	$500.00
8	MARY LAGOUMIS	521 23 9816	001	452.00	LANGUAGE NUMBER NOT FOUND IN TABLE		
9	FRANS LISTZ	234 25 7832	943	5.00	$6.75	FORTRAN	$33.75
10	BERT STURZA	451 02 1411	148	320.00	$5.00	RPG	$1,600.00
11	AARON GREENFELD	989 50 6910	204	21.56	$4.50	BASIC	$97.02
12	ROGER POOL	73J552293	005	017.40	ERROR IN DATA		
13	ANDREW DORSEY	192 71 3105	110	242.60	$12.50	ASSEMBLER	$3,032.50
14	RICHARD LESTER	259 30 2305	456	22.90	$4.75	APL	$108.78
15	FRANK JASPER	319 50 1263	148	6.22	$5.00	RPG	$31.10
16	RICHARD MILLER	615 14 0081	943	235.50	$6.75	FORTRAN	$1,589.63
17	MICHAEL DIAVIDSON	515 85 1602	052	421.00	$6.50	PL/I	$2,736.50
18	RONALD KRAMER	160 13 0059	128	113.25	$3.25	SNOBOL	$368.06
19	MARTIN SMITH	232 54 4511	456	7.20	$4.75	APL	$34.20
20	MARC FRIEDMAN	625 43 1982	128	51.60	$3.25	SNOBOL	$167.70
21	MARC NEFF	253 14 7654	943	75.20	$6.75	FORTRAN	$507.60
22	ROBERT TROTENBERG	456 23 7531	110	100.00	$12.50	ASSEMBLER	$1,250.00

TOTAL AMOUNT PAID TO COMPUTER PROGRAMMERS IS $16,295.29.

Searching and Subscripting in Structured Style

In the previous program we relaxed our adherence to structured programming in order to enhance both our explanation and comprehension. The next version uses the identical input, produces almost the identical output (it prints 15 lines to the page), however, it is written in structured style.

Instead of increasing the value of SUB by 1 and testing for a match until SUB is greater than 9, we now accomplish the same thing in one statement:

```
PERFORM TEST-PARA THRU TEST-PARA-EXIT VARYING
     SUB FROM 1 BY 1 UNTIL SUB > 9
```

in lines 245 and 246.

This automatically sets SUB to 1 initially and increments SUB by 1 until SUB becomes greater than 9. If SUB actually becomes greater than 9, the performed paragraph is exhausted and control is returned to the instruction following the PERFORM.

As in the previous version, when a match is made we wish to print out the relevant information. Having done this, we want to "short-circuit" the performed paragraph so that the table will not again be searched for that particular input card. Otherwise, it would eventually trigger a nonapplicable error message, as well as be a waste of valuable computer time. All this may be avoided by simply raising the value of SUB beyond its legitimate range. We have arbitrarily selected 11 for this "short-circuiting" technique. Thus when we return to the PERFORM statement in lines 245 and 246, a test is made to see whether SUB is greater than 9. Because SUB now contains 11, control falls through to the next instruction in sequence.

Suppose each element of the table has been scanned and a match has not been made. The value of SUB would now be 10. In this instance we would definitely want to print out some error message to alert the programmer to this fact, which is accomplished by the instruction:

IF SUB = 10 PERFORM ERROR-PARA-2.

Program 31

```
1       IDENTIFICATION   DIVISION.
2       PROGRAM-ID.      TABLE-6.
3       AUTHOR.          IRVIN POREMBA.
4       INSTALLATION.    NYU.
5       DATE-WRITTEN.    APRIL 27, 1982.
6       DATE-COMPILED.   JUNE 20, 1982.
7       SECURITY.        HENRY MULLISH.
8       * * * * * * * * * * * * * * * * * * * * * * * * * * * * * * * * * * * * * * * * * * * * * * * * *
9       *       THIS PROGRAM IS A U.S. GOVERNMENT PAYROLL.                    *
10      *       CARDS ARE PUNCHED AS FOLLOWED:                                *
11      *                                                                     *
12      *       COLUMNS  1-25: EMPLOYEE NAME                                  *
13      *       COLUMNS 30-38: SOCIAL SECURITY NUMBER                         *
14      *       COLUMNS 40-42: PROGRAM LANGUAGE NUMBER                        *
15      *       COLUMNS 45-49: HOURS-WORKED                                   *
16      *                                                                     *
17      *       THIS PROGRAM USES A TABLE AND THE                             *
18      *       SUBSCRIPTING METHOD TO LOOK UP THE NAME OF THE                *
19      *       LANGUAGE USED BY EACH PROGRAMMER WITH THE                     *
20      *       CORRESPONDING RATE OF PAY, PRINTING OUT ALL THE               *
21      *       INFORMATION UNDER A SUITABLE HEADING WITH THE                 *
22      *       NET PAY DUE TO EACH PROGRAMMER AND, AT THE END,               *
23      *       THE TOTAL PAY DUE TO ALL PROGRAMMERS.                         *
24      *       NOTE THAT THIS PROGRAM USES THE PERFORM VARYING               *
25      *       STATEMENT TO INCREMENT THE SUBSCRIPT.                         *
26      * * * * * * * * * * * * * * * * * * * * * * * * * * * * * * * * * * * * * * * * * * * * * * * * *
27
28      ENVIRONMENT  DIVISION.
29      CONFIGURATION  SECTION.
30      SOURCE-COMPUTER. CYBER-170-720.
31      OBJECT-COMPUTER. CYBER-170-720.
32      SPECIAL-NAMES.
33      INPUT-OUTPUT SECTION.
34      FILE-CONTROL.
35          SELECT IN-FILE ASSIGN TO INPUT.
36          SELECT OUT-FILE ASSIGN TO OUTPUT.
37
38      DATA DIVISION.
39      FILE SECTION.
40
41      FD   IN-FILE
42           LABEL RECORDS ARE OMITTED.
43
44      *       DEFINE INPUT.
```

```
45
46    01    RECORD-IN.
47          02    EMPLOYEE-NAME         PIC X(25).
48          02    FILLER                PIC X(04).
49          02    SOC-SEC-NO            PIC 9(09).
50          02    FILLER                PIC X(01).
51          02    LANGUAGE-NO           PIC 9(03).
52          02    FILLER                PIC X(02).
53          02    HOURS-WORKED          PIC 9(03)V9(02).
54          02    FILLER                PIC X(21).
55
56    FD    OUT-FILE
57          LABEL RECORDS ARE OMITTED.
58
59    *     DEFINE OUTPUT OF PROGRAM.
60
61    01          LINE-OUT              PIC X(133).
62
63    WORKING-STORAGE SECTION.
64    77    SUB                         PIC 99.
65    77    PAGE-COUNT                  PIC 9999 VALUE ZERO.
66    77    CARD-COUNT                  PIC 99999 VALUE ZERO.
67    77    CARD-COUNT-2                PIC 99 VALUE ZERO.
68    77    AMOUNT-PAID                 PIC 9(05)V99.
69    77    TOTAL-AMOUNT-PAID           PIC 9(09)V99 VALUE ZERO.
70    77    W-S-RATE-OF-PAY             PIC 99V99.
71    77    MORE-CARDS                  PIC X(03) VALUE 'YES'.
72
73
74    *     BELOW IS THE SKELETON OF THE TABLE USED IN THIS
75    *     PROGRAM. AFTERWARDS, THE TABLE(RATE-TABLE-SKELETON,
76    *     AS IT IS CALLED) IS REDEFINED AND BROKEN UP INTO
77    *     ITS DIFFERENT PARTS, NAMELY: ASSIGNED-LANG-NO,
78    *     RATE-OF-PAY, AND LANG-NAME.
79
80    01    RATE-TABLE-SKELETON.
81          02    FILLER                PIC X(16) VALUE '2040450BASIC'.
82          02    FILLER                PIC X(16) VALUE '0520650PL/I'.
83          02    FILLER                PIC X(16) VALUE '1280325SNOBOL'.
84          02    FILLER                PIC X(16) VALUE '4280250ALGOL'.
85          02    FILLER                PIC X(16) VALUE '9430675FORTRAN'.
86          02    FILLER                PIC X(16) VALUE '0052550COBOL'.
87          02    FILLER                PIC X(16) VALUE '1101250ASSEMBLER'.
88          02    FILLER                PIC X(16) VALUE '1480500RPG'.
89          02    FILLER                PIC X(16) VALUE '4560475APL'.
90
91    01    RATE-TABLE REDEFINES RATE-TABLE-SKELETON.
92          02    TABLE-ELEMENT OCCURS 9 TIMES.
93                03 ASSIGNED-LANG-NO   PIC 999.
94                03 RATE-OF-PAY        PIC 99V99.
95                03 LANG-NAME          PIC X(09).
96
97    01    HEADER-1.
98          02    FILLER                PIC X(01) VALUE SPACES.
99          02    FILLER                PIC X(05) VALUE 'PAGE'.
100         02    PAGE-COUNT-OUT        PIC Z,ZZ9.
101         02    FILLER                PIC X(30) VALUE SPACES.
102         02    FILLER                PIC X(14) VALUE 'UNITED STATES'.
103         02    FILLER                PIC X(11) VALUE 'GOVERNMENT'.
104         02    FILLER                PIC X(18) VALUE 'PAYROLL: COMPUTER'.
105         02    FILLER                PIC X(09) VALUE 'DIVISION'.
106
107   01    HEADER-2.
108         02    FILLER                PIC X(01) VALUE SPACES.
109         02    FILLER                PIC X(10) VALUE ALL '*'.
110         02    FILLER                PIC X(30) VALUE SPACES.
111         02    FILLER                PIC X(52) VALUE ALL '*'.
112
113   01    HEADER-3.
114         02    FILLER                PIC X(01) VALUE SPACES.
115         02.   FILLER                PIC X(17) VALUE 'CARD'.
116         02    FILLER                PIC X(22) VALUE 'EMPLOYEE'.
117         02    FILLER                PIC X(14) VALUE 'SOC. SEC.'.
118         02    FILLER                PIC X(19) VALUE 'ASSIGNED LANG.'.
119         02    FILLER                PIC X(10) VALUE 'HOURS'.
```

```
120        02    FILLER                    PIC X(12) VALUE 'RATE PER'.
121        02    FILLER                    PIC X(15) VALUE 'LANGUAGE'.
122        02    FILLER                    PIC X(06) VALUE 'AMOUNT'.
123
124   01   HEADER-4.
125        02    FILLER                    PIC X(01) VALUE SPACES.
126        02    FILLER                    PIC X(19) VALUE 'COUNT'.
127        02    FILLER                    PIC X(21) VALUE 'NAME'.
128        02    FILLER                    PIC X(17) VALUE 'NUMBER'.
129        02    FILLER                    PIC X(15) VALUE 'NUMBER'.
130        02    FILLER                    PIC X(12) VALUE 'WORKED'.
131        02    FILLER                    PIC X(12) VALUE 'HOUR'.
132        02    FILLER                    PIC X(14) VALUE 'NAME'.
133        02    FILLER                    PIC X(04) VALUE 'PAID'.
134
135   01   HEADER-5.
136        02    FILLER                    PIC X(01) VALUE SPACES.
137        02    FILLER                    PIC X(06) VALUE ALL ' * '.
138        02    FILLER                    PIC X(03) VALUE SPACES.
139        02    FILLER                    PIC X(25) VALUE ALL ' * '.
140        02    FILLER                    PIC X(04) VALUE SPACES.
141        02    FILLER                    PIC X(11) VALUE ALL ' * '.
142        02    FILLER                    PIC X(04) VALUE SPACES.
143        02    FILLER                    PIC X(14) VALUE ALL ' * '.
144        02    FILLER                    PIC X(05) VALUE SPACES.
145        02    FILLER                    PIC X(06) VALUE ALL ' * '.
146        02    FILLER                    PIC X(04) VALUE SPACES.
147        02    FILLER                    PIC X(08) VALUE ALL ' * '.
148        02    FILLER                    PIC X(04) VALUE SPACES.
149        02    FILLER                    PIC X(09) VALUE ALL ' * '.
150        02    FILLER                    PIC X(04) VALUE SPACES.
151        02    FILLER                    PIC X(10) VALUE ALL ' * '.
152
153   01   DETAIL-LINE.
154        02    FILLER                    PIC X(01) VALUE SPACES.
155        02    CARD-COUNT-OUT            PIC ZZ,ZZ9.
156        02    FILLER                    PIC X(03) VALUE SPACES.
157        02    EMPLOYEE-NAME-OUT         PIC X(25).
158        02    FILLER                    PIC X(04) VALUE SPACES.
159        02    SOC-SEC-NO-OUT            PIC 999B99B9999.
160        02    FILLER                    PIC X(09) VALUE SPACES.
161        02    LANGUAGE-NO-OUT           PIC 999.
162        02    FILLER                    PIC X(11) VALUE SPACES.
163        02    HOURS-WORKED-OUT          PIC ZZ9.99.
164        02    FILLER                    PIC X(05) VALUE SPACES.
165        02    RATE-OF-PAY-OUT           PIC $$9.99.
166        02    FILLER                    PIC X(05) VALUE SPACES.
167        02    LANG-NAME-OUT             PIC X(09).
168        02    FILLER                    PIC X(04) VALUE SPACES.
169        02    AMOUNT-PAID-OUT           PIC $$$,$$9.99.
170
171   01   DETAIL-LINE-2.
172        02    FILLER                    PIC X(01) VALUE SPACES.
173        02    FILLER                    PIC X(13) VALUE 'TOTAL AMOUNT'.
174        02    FILLER                    PIC X(17) VALUE 'PAID TO COMPUTER'.
175        02    FILLER                    PIC X(15) VALUE 'PROGRAMMERS IS'.
176        02    TOTAL-AMOUNT-OUT          PIC $,$$$,$$$,$$9.99.
177        02    FILLER                    PIC X(01) VALUE '.'.
178
179   01   DETAIL-LINE-3.
180        02    FILLER                    PIC X(01) VALUE SPACES.
181        02    CARD-COUNT-OUT-2          PIC ZZ,ZZ9.
182        02    FILLER                    PIC X(03) VALUE SPACES.
183        02    EMPLOY-NAME-OUT-2         PIC X(25).
184        02    FILLER                    PIC X(04) VALUE SPACES.
185        02    SOC-SEC-NO-OUT-2          PIC X(09).
186        02    FILLER                    PIC X(11) VALUE SPACES.
187        02    LANGUAGE-NO-OUT-2         PIC X(03).
188        02    FILLER                    PIC X(11) VALUE SPACES.
189        02    HOURS-WORKED-OUT-2        PIC 999.99.
190        02    FILLER                    PIC X(06) VALUE SPACES.
191        02    FILLER                    PIC X(13) VALUE 'ERROR IN DATA'.
192
193   01   DETAIL-LINE-4.
194        02    FILLER                    PIC X(01) VALUE SPACES.
195        02    CARD-COUNT-OUT-3          PIC ZZ,ZZ9.
```

```
196          02    FILLER                    PIC X(03) VALUE SPACES.
197          02    EMPLOY-NAME-OUT-3         PIC X(25).
198          02    FILLER                    PIC X(04) VALUE SPACES.
199          02    SOC-SEC-NO-OUT-3          PIC 999B99B9999.
200          02    FILLER                    PIC X(09) VALUE SPACES.
201          02    LANGUAGE-NO-OUT-3         PIC 999.
202          02    FILLER                    PIC X(11) VALUE SPACES.
203          02    HOURS-WORKED-OUT-3        PIC ZZ9.99.
204          02    FILLER                    PIC X(04) VALUE SPACES.
205          02    FILLER                    PIC X(09) VALUE 'LANGUAGE'.
206          02    FILLER                    PIC X(10) VALUE 'NUMBER NOT'.
207          02    FILLER                    PIC X(15) VALUE 'FOUND IN TABLE'.
208
209    PROCEDURE DIVISION.
210
211    MAIN-LINE-ROUTINE.
212          PERFORM OPEN-FILES.
213          PERFORM NEW-PAGE.
214          PERFORM START-UP.
215          PERFORM PROCESS-DATA UNTIL MORE-CARDS EQUAL 'NO'.
216          PERFORM CLOSE-UP.
217          STOP RUN.
218
219    OPEN-FILES.
220          OPEN INPUT IN-FILE.
221          OPEN OUTPUT OUT-FILE.
222
223    NEW-PAGE.
224          MOVE SPACES TO LINE-OUT.
225          WRITE LINE-OUT AFTER PAGE.
226
227    START-UP.
228          READ IN-FILE AT END MOVE 'NO' TO MORE-CARDS
229                MOVE '  **NO DATA IN DECK**' TO LINE-OUT
230                WRITE LINE-OUT AFTER 30.
231          IF MORE-CARDS EQUAL 'YES' PERFORM WRITE-HEADINGS.
232
233    *     PROCESS-DATA CHECKS TO SEE IF THE DATA IS PUNCHED
234    *     CORRECTLY. IF THE DATA IS CORRECT, THE PERFORM-VARYING
235    *     STATEMENT NEXT TO THE ELSE CLAUSE IS TRIGGERED.
236    *     THIS INITIATES THE TABLE LOOK UP.
237
238    PROCESS-DATA.
239          ADD 1 TO CARD-COUNT.
240          ADD 1 TO CARD-COUNT-2.
241          IF HOURS-WORKED NOT NUMERIC
242                OR SOC-SEC-NO NOT NUMERIC
243                OR LANGUAGE-NO NOT NUMERIC
244                PERFORM ERROR-PARA-1
245          ELSE PERFORM TEST-PARA THRU TEST-PARA-EXIT
246                VARYING SUB FROM 1 BY 1 UNTIL SUB > 9.
247          IF SUB = 10 PERFORM ERROR-PARA-2.
248          READ IN-FILE AT END MOVE 'NO' TO MORE-CARDS
249                MOVE ZEROS TO CARD-COUNT-2 PERFORM TOTAL-PARA.
250          IF CARD-COUNT-2 = 15 MOVE ZEROS TO CARD-COUNT-2
251                PERFORM NEW-PAGE
252          PERFORM WRITE-HEADINGS.
253
254    *     TOTAL-PARA PRINTS THE TOTAL PAY DUE TO PROGRAMMERS.
255
256    TOTAL-PARA.
257          MOVE TOTAL-AMOUNT-PAID TO TOTAL-AMOUNT-OUT.
258          PERFORM NEW-PAGE.
259          WRITE LINE-OUT FROM DETAIL-LINE-2 AFTER 2.
260
261    CLOSE-UP.
262          CLOSE IN-FILE, OUT-FILE.
263
264    *     TEST-PARA SCANS THE TABLE AND TRIES TO MATCH
265    *     THE LANGUAGE-NO GIVEN IN THE DATA WITH THE ASSIGNED-LANG-NO
266    *     IN THE ORDER THAT IS GIVEN BY THE SUBSCRIPT, SUB.
267    *     IF A MATCH IS MADE, WORK-PARA IS PERFORMED; OTHERWISE THE
268    *     VALUE OF SUB IS RAISED BY 1 AND TEST-PARA IS EXECUTED AGAIN
269    *     UNTIL SUB IS GREATER THAN 9. IF SUB EVER BECOMES GREATER
270    *     THAN 9(IN THIS CASE 10), AN ERROR MESSAGE WOULD BE
271    *     PRINTED OUT.
```

```
272
273        TEST-PARA.
274            IF LANGUAGE-NO EQUAL ASSIGNED-LANG-NO (SUB)
275                PERFORM WORK-PARA.
276
277        TEST-PARA-EXIT.
278            EXIT.
279
280    *      WORK-PARA DOES THE WORK NECESSARY TO CREATE THE
281    *      OUTPUT DESIRED BY THE PROGRAM.
282
283        WORK-PARA.
284            MOVE RATE-OF-PAY (SUB) TO W-S-RATE-OF-PAY.
285            MULTIPLY HOURS-WORKED BY W-S-RATE-OF-PAY.
286
287            ADD AMOUNT-PAID TO TOTAL-AMOUNT-PAID.
288            MOVE CARD-COUNT TO CARD-COUNT-OUT.
289            MOVE EMPLOYEE-NAME TO EMPLOYEE-NAME-OUT.
290            MOVE SOC-SEC-NO TO SOC-SEC-NO-OUT.
291            MOVE LANGUAGE-NO TO LANGUAGE-NO-OUT.
292            MOVE HOURS-WORKED TO HOURS-WORKED-OUT.
293            MOVE LANG-NAME (SUB) TO LANG-NAME-OUT.
294            MOVE RATE-TO-PAY (SUB) TO RATE-OF-PAY-OUT.
295            MOVE AMOUNT-PAID TO AMOUNT-PAID-OUT.
296            WRITE LINE-OUT FROM DETAIL-LINE AFTER 2.
297            MOVE 11 TO SUB.
298
299        ERROR-PARA-1.
300            MOVE CARD-COUNT TO CARD-COUNT-OUT-2.
301            MOVE EMPLOYEE-NAME TO EMPLOY-NAME-OUT-2.
302            MOVE SOC-SEC-NO TO SOC-SEC-NO-OUT-2.
303            MOVE LANGUAGE-NO TO LANGUAGE-NO-OUT-2.
304            MOVE HOURS-WORKED TO HOURS-WORKED-OUT-2.
305            WRITE LINE OUT FROM DETAIL-LINE-3 AFTER 2.
306
307        ERROR-PARA-2.
308            MOVE CARD-COUNT TO CARD-COUNT-OUT-3.
309            MOVE EMPLOYEE-NAME TO EMPLOY-NAME-OUT-3.
310            MOVE SOC-SEC-NO TO SOC-SEC-NO-OUT-3.
311            MOVE LANGUAGE-NO TO LANGUAGE-NO-OUT-3.
312            MOVE HOURS-WORKED TO HOURS-WORKED-OUT-3.
313            WRITE LINE-OUT FROM DETAIL-LINE-4 AFTER 2.
314
315        WRITE-HEADINGS.
316            ADD 1 TO PAGE-COUNT.
317            MOVE PAGE-COUNT TO PAGE-COUNT-OUT.
318            WRITE LINE-OUT FROM HEADER-1 AFTER 1.
319            WRITE LINE-OUT FROM HEADER-2 AFTER 1.
320            WRITE LINE-OUT FROM HEADER-2 AFTER 1.
321            WRITE LINE-OUT FROM HEADER-3 AFTER 2.
322            WRITE LINE-OUT FROM HEADER-4 AFTER 1.
323            WRITE LINE-OUT FROM HEADER-5 AFTER 1.
```

Output for Program 31

PAGE 1   UNITED STATES GOVERNMENT PAYROLL: COMPUTER DIVISION

* * * * * * * * * *

* * * * * * * * * *   *

                 *

CARD COUNT	EMPLOYEE NAME	SOC. SEC. NUMBER	ASSIGNED LANG. NUMBER	HOURS WORKED	RATE PER HOUR	LANGUAGE NAME	AMOUNT PAID
* * * * *	* * * * * * * * * * * * * *	* * * * * * * * *	* * * * * * * * * *	* * * * * *	* * * * * * * * *	* * * * * * * *	* * * * * * * * * *
1	IRVIN POREMBA	342 42 5393	005	125.50	$25.50	COBOL	$3,200.25
2	JULIAN COLE	253 41 5583	204	45.75	$4.50	BASIC	$205.88
3	MICHELLE CORNER	453 26 7789	943	100.25	$6.75	FORTRAN	$676.69
4	FERN FREIDMAN	123 25 4789	450	458.32		LANGUAGE NUMBER NOT FOUND IN TABLE	
5	BARBARA HODGES	645 23 6632	110	12.45	$12.50	ASSEMBLER	$155.63
6	SALLY DEMBERG	554613214	KIJ	002.36		ERROR IN DATA	
7	JACKIE MURDOCK	225 32 1122	428	200.00	$2.50	ALGOL	$500.00
8	MARY LAGOUMIS	521 23 9816	001	452.00		LANGUAGE NUMBER NOT FOUND IN TABLE	
9	FRANS LISTZ	234 25 7832	943	5.00	$6.75	FORTRAN	$33.75
10	BERT STURZA	451 02 1411	148	320.00	$5.00	RPG	$1,600.00
11	AARON GREENFELD	989 50 6910	204	21.56	$4.50	BASIC	$97.02
12	ROGER POOL	73J552293	005	017.40		ERROR IN DATA	
13	ANDREW DORSEY	192 71 3105	110	242.60	$12.50	ASSEMBLER	$3,032.50
14	RICHARD LESTER	259 30 2305	456	22.90	$4.75	APL	$108.78
15	FRANK JASPER	319 50 1263	148	6.22	$5.00	RPG	$31.10

PAGE 2		UNITED STATES GOVERNMENT PAYROLL: COMPUTER DIVISION					
CARD COUNT	EMPLOYEE NAME	SOC. SEC. NUMBER	ASSIGNED LANG. NUMBER	HOURS WORKED	RATE PER HOUR	LANGUAGE NAME	AMOUNT PAID
16	RICHARD MILLER	615 14 0081	943	235.50	$6.75	FORTRAN	$1,589.63
17	MICHAEL DIAVIDSON	515 85 1602	052	421.00	$6.50	PL/I	$2,736.50
18	RONALD KRAMER	160 13 0059	128	113.25	$3.25	SNOBOL	$368.06
19	MARTIN SMITH	232 54 4511	456	7.20	$4.75	APL	$34.20
20	MARC FRIEDMAN	625 43 1982	128	51.60	$3.25	SNOBOL	$167.70
21	MARC NEFF	253 14 7654	943	75.20	$6.75	FORTRAN	$507.60
22	ROBERT TROTENBERG	456 23 7531	110	100.00	$12.50	ASSEMBLER	$1,250.00

TOTAL AMOUNT PAID TO COMPUTER PROGRAMMERS IS $16,295.29.

In every table discussed so far we have accessed the table—looked it up—by virtue of the fixed positions of its elements. Each time the table is searched the element in question is accessed by a process of counting down to the element located at the address specified by the subscript. It is a question of "count down and pull out," if you will. In order to expedite the process it would be advantageous, if at all possible, for the elements of the table to be arranged in a sequence that reflects the frequency of their normal use. The more often an element is used, the closer it should be to the top of the table. We will now study other methods of searching tables by using the technique known as indexing.

10.6   Indexing

Another way of referencing a table is by *indexing*, a method that is closely related to subscripting—at least from the programmer's logical point of view, if not from considerations of the internal workings of the computer. The transition from subscripting to indexing is (you will be pleased to know) rather easy.

Instead of using a subscript, we may address the table by means of an index. The use of the index is closely tied in to a verb called (appropriately enough) SEARCH, which has the format:

SEARCH (table) [AT END imperative-statement(s)]

WHEN condition-1 $\left\{ \begin{array}{l} \text{imperative-statement(s)} \\ \text{NEXT SENTENCE} \end{array} \right\}$

$\left[\text{WHEN condition-2} \left\{ \begin{array}{l} \text{imperative-statement(s)} \\ \text{NEXT SENTENCE} \end{array} \right\} \right] \dots$

Notice that, like the READ statement, the SEARCH has an optional AT END clause. The WHEN clause is merely a disguised IF statement. Whenever the SEARCH verb is used, at least one WHEN clause must be specified. Before explaining how to use the SEARCH verb let us state clearly that it can only be used in conjunction with indexing and not with subscripting. The difference between indexing and subscripting is quite distinct. In subscripting the table elements are counted down until the required one is reached, whereas in indexing the appropriate entry is accessed directly.

The AT END clause behaves as a safety net for the situation when LANGUAGE-NO, which is read in from the input card, either is mispunched (so that a match with ASSIGNED-LANG-NO is never successful) or is correctly punched but the appropriate ASSIGNED-LANG-NO is not in the table. In either case a match is not made and an error message is printed.

What is so interesting about the SEARCH verb is that once the index has been initialized to 1 (so that the search of the table proceeds from the first element), it is *automatically* incremented by 1 each time a pass through the entire table is made. It doesn't increment its value by 1 indefinitely, however. It does so only until either the value of the index reaches the number that is the subject of the OCCURS clause or the WHEN condition is satisfied. Therefore if the REDEFINES part of the table says that TABLE-ELEMENT OCCURS 9 TIMES, the index will reach a maximum of 9.

The searching of the table may be conceptualized as shown.

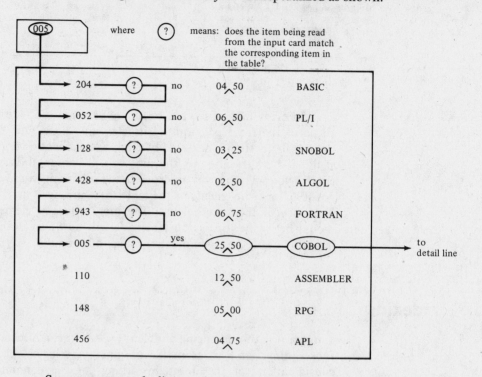

Suppose we are dealing again with our familiar computer language pay scale problem. Once the skeleton of the table has been set up (exactly as is done in subscripting), it is redefined as follows:

```
01   RATE-TABLE REDEFINES RATE-TABLE-SKELETON.
  02   TABLE-ELEMENT OCCURS 9 TIMES INDEXED BY TABLE-INDEX.
    03   ASSIGNED-LANG-NO PIC 999.
    03   RATE-OF-PAY       PIC 99V99.
    03   LANG-NAME         PIC X(09).
```

where the INDEXED BY clause specifies the name of the index—in this case, TABLE-INDEX. This index is not a decimal value that has to be converted to binary as in subscripting. The value of the index has to be initialized to 1 by the SET verb. We write before the table is searched:

```
SET TABLE-INDEX TO 1.
```

What is important to remember is that you cannot do ordinary arithmetic on an index. Attempting to write

```
ADD 1 TO TABLE-INDEX
```

will cause an error. This helps to protect the value of the index from unintended alteration in its value. By contrast a subscript is quite vulnerable.

When searching the table we make the object of the SEARCH verb the item that appears as the subject of the OCCURS clause in the table, rather than the name of the table (which is the natural although incorrect choice). Thus, after setting TABLE-INDEX to 1, we would write:

```
SEARCH TABLE-ELEMENT AT END PERFORM ERROR-PARA-2
WHEN LANGUAGE-NO EQUAL ASSIGNED-LANG-NO (TABLE-INDEX)
    PERFORM WORK-PARA.
```

Keep in mind that the table elements happen to be in random order and therefore the whole table has to be searched from the beginning to the end until a match is made. This could be rather costly in terms of computer time, especially if the table is lengthy and a match is not made until the latter part of the table is searched. We will indicate how this process may be expedited in the next section. Meanwhile, study Program 32 carefully until you are sure that you understand how it works.

Input for Program 32

IRVIN POREMBA	342425393	005	12550
JULIAN COLE	253415583	204	04575
MICHELLE CORNER	453267789	943	10025
FERN FREIDMAN	123254789	450	45832
BARBARA HODGES	645236632	110	01245
SALLY DEMBERG	554613214	KIJ	00236
JACKIE MURDOCK	225321122	428	20000
MARY LAGOUMIS	521239816	001	45200
FRANS LISTZ	234257832	943	00500
BERT STURZA	451021411	148	32000
AARON GREENFELD	989506910	204	02156
ROGER POOL	73J552293	005	01740
ANDREW DORSEY	192713105	110	24260
RICHARD LESTER	259302305	456	02290
FRANK JASPER	319501263	148	00622
RICHARD MILLER	615140081	943	23550
MICHAEL DIAVIDSON	515851602	052	42100
RONALD KRAMER	160130059	128	11325
MARTIN SMITH	232544511	456	00720
MARC FRIEDMAN	625431982	128	05160
MARC NEFF	253147654	943	07520
ROBERT TROTENBERG	456237531	110	10000

Program 32

```
1       IDENTIFICATION   DIVISION.
2       PROGRAM-ID.      TABLE-7.
3       AUTHOR.          IRVIN POREMBA.
4       INSTALLATION.    NYU.
5       DATE-WRITTEN.    APRIL 28, 1982.
6       DATE-COMPILED.   APRIL 28, 1982.
7       SECURITY.        HENRY MULLISH.
8       * * * * * * * * * * * * * * * * * * * * * * * * * * * * * * * * * * * * * * * * * * *
9       *       THIS PROGRAM IS A U.S. GOVERNMENT PAYROLL.            *
10      *       CARDS ARE PUNCHED AS FOLLOWED:                        *
11      *                                                            *
12      *       COLUMNS  1-25: EMPLOYEE NAME                          *
13      *       COLUMNS 30-38: SOCIAL SECURITY NUMBER                 *
14      *       COLUMNS 40-42: PROGRAM LANGUAGE NUMBER                *
15      *       COLUMNS 45-49: HOURS-WORKED                           *
16      *                                                            *
17      *       THIS PROGRAM THEN USES A TABLE AND THE INDEXING       *
18      *       METHOD TO FIND THE RATE OF PAY AND THE                *
19      *       PROGRAMMING LANGUAGE NAME, PRINTING ALL THE           *
20      *       INFORMATION OUT UNDER A SUITABLE HEADING WITH         *
21      *       THE NET PAY DUE TO EACH PROGRAMMER AND ON A NEW       *
22      *       PAGE, THE TOTAL PAY DUE TO ALL PROGRAMMERS BY         *
23      *       THE U.S. GOVERNMENT.                                  *
24      * * * * * * * * * * * * * * * * * * * * * * * * * * * * * * * * * * * * * * * * * * *
25
26      ENVIRONMENT DIVISION.
27      CONFIGURATION SECTION.
28      SOURCE-COMPUTER. CYBER-170-720.
29      OBJECT-COMPUTER. CYBER-170-720.
30      SPECIAL-NAMES.
31      INPUT-OUTPUT SECTION.
32      FILE-CONTROL.
33          SELECT IN-FILE ASSIGN TO INPUT.
```

```
34              SELECT OUT-FILE ASSIGN TO OUTPUT.
35
36      DATA DIVISION.
37      FILE SECTION.
38
39      FD   IN-FILE
40              LABEL RECORDS ARE OMITTED.
41
42      *       DEFINE INPUT.
43
44      01   RECORD-IN.
45              02   EMPLOYEE-NAME        PIC X(25).
46              02   FILLER              PIC X(04).
47              02   SOC-SEC-NO          PIC 9(09).
48              02   FILLER              PIC X(01).
49              02   LANGUAGE-NO         PIC 9(03).
50              02   FILLER              PIC X(02).
51              02   HOURS-WORKED        PIC 9(03)V9(02).
52              02   FILLER              PIC X(21).
53
54      FD   OUT-FILE
55              LABEL RECORDS ARE OMITTED.
56
57      *       DEFINE OUTPUT OF PROGRAM.
58
59      01   LINE-OUT                    PIC X(133).
60
61      WORKING-STORAGE SECTION.
62      77   PAGE-COUNT                  PIC 9999 VALUE ZERO.
63      77   CARD-COUNT                  PIC 99999 VALUE ZERO.
64      77   CARD-COUNT-2                PIC 99 VALUE ZERO.
65      77   AMOUNT-PAID                 PIC 9(05)V99.
66      77   TOTAL-AMOUNT-PAID           PIC 9(09)V99 VALUE ZERO.
67      77   W-S-RATE-OF-PAY             PIC 99V99.
68      77   MORE-CARDS                  PIC X(03) VALUE 'YES'.
69
70      *       BELOW IS THE SKELETON OF THE TABLE USED IN THIS
71      *       PROGRAM. AFTERWARDS, THE TABLE(RATE-TABLE-SKELETON
72      *       AS IT IS CALLED) IS REDEFINED AND BROKEN UP INTO
73      *       ITS DIFFERENT PARTS NAMELY: ASSIGNED-LANG-NO,
74      *       RATE-OF-PAY, AND LANG-NAME.
75
76      01   RATE-TABLE-SKELETON.
77              02   FILLER        PIC X(16) VALUE '2040450BASIC'.
78              02   FILLER        PIC X(16) VALUE '0520650PL/I'.
79              02   FILLER        PIC X(16) VALUE '1280325SNOBOL'.
80              02   FILLER        PIC X(16) VALUE '4280250ALGOL'.
81              02   FILLER        PIC X(16) VALUE '9430675FORTRAN'.
82              02   FILLER        PIC X(16) VALUE '0052550COBOL'.
83              02   FILLER        PIC X(16) VALUE '1101250ASSEMBLER'.
84              02   FILLER        PIC X(16) VALUE '1480500RPG'.
85              02   FILLER        PIC X(16) VALUE '4560475APL'.
86
87      *       UNDER THE INDEXING METHOD, TABLE-ELEMENT IN THE
88      *       REDEFINES STATEMENT IS INDEXED BY A VARIABLE NAME CALLED
89      *       TABLE-INDEX.
90
91      01   RATE-TABLE REDEFINES RATE-TABLE- SKELETON.
92              02   TABLE-ELEMENT OCCURS 9 TIMES INDEXED BY TABLE-INDEX.
93                   03 ASSIGNED-LANG-NO  PIC 999.
94                   03 RATE-OF-PAY       PIC 99V99.
95                   03 LANG-NAME         PIC X(09).
96
97      01   HEADER-1.
98              02   FILLER              PIC X(01) VALUE SPACES.
99              02   FILLER              PIC X(05) VALUE 'PAGE'.
100             02   PAGE-COUNT-OUT      PIC Z,ZZ9.
101             02   FILLER              PIC X(30) VALUE SPACES.
102             02   FILLER              PIC X(14) VALUE 'UNITED STATES'.
103             02   FILLER              PIC X(11) VALUE 'GOVERNMENT'.
104             02   FILLER              PIC X(18) VALUE 'PAYROLL: COMPUTER'.
105             02   FILLER              PIC X(09) VALUE 'DIVISION'.
106
107     01   HEADER-2.
108             02   FILLER              PIC X(01) VALUE SPACES.
109             02   FILLER              PIC X(10) VALUE ALL ' * '.
```

```
110          02   FILLER              PIC X(30) VALUE SPACES.
111          02   FILLER              PIC X(52) VALUE ALL '*'.
112
113     01   HEADER-3.
114          02   FILLER              PIC X(01) VALUE SPACES.
115          02   FILLER              PIC X(17) VALUE 'CARD'.
116          02   FILLER              PIC X(22) VALUE 'EMPLOYEE'.
117          02   FILLER              PIC X(14) VALUE 'SOC.SEC.'.
118          02   FILLER              PIC X(19) VALUE 'ASSIGNED LANG.'.
119          02   FILLER              PIC X(10) VALUE 'HOURS'.
120          02   FILLER              PIC X(12) VALUE 'RATE PER'.
121          02   FILLER              PIC X(15) VALUE 'LANGUAGE'.
122          02   FILLER              PIC X(06) VALUE 'AMOUNT'.
123
124     01   HEADER-4.
125          02   FILLER              PIC X(01) VALUE SPACES.
126          02   FILLER              PIC X(19) VALUE 'COUNT'.
127          02   FILLER              PIC X(21) VALUE 'NAME'.
128          02   FILLER              PIC X(17) VALUE 'NUMBER'.
129          02   FILLER              PIC X(15) VALUE 'NUMBER'.
130          02   FILLER              PIC X(12) VALUE 'WORKED'.
131          02   FILLER              PIC X(12) VALUE 'HOUR'.
132          02   FILLER              PIC X(14) VALUE 'NAME'.
133          02   FILLER              PIC X(04) VALUE 'PAID'.
134
135     01   HEADER-5.
136          02   FILLER              PIC X(01) VALUE SPACES.
137          02   FILLER              PIC X(06) VALUE ALL '*'.
138          02   FILLER              PIC X(03) VALUE SPACES.
139          02   FILLER              PIC X(25) VALUE ALL '*'.
140          02   FILLER              PIC X(04) VALUE SPACES.
141          02   FILLER              PIC X(11) VALUE ALL '*'.
142          02   FILLER              PIC X(04) VALUE SPACES.
143          02   FILLER              PIC X(14) VALUE ALL '*'.
144          02   FILLER              PIC X(05) VALUE SPACES.
145          02   FILLER              PIC X(06) VALUE ALL '*'.
146          02   FILLER              PIC X(04) VALUE SPACES.
147          02   FILLER              PIC X(08) VALUE ALL '*'.
148          02   FILLER              PIC X(04) VALUE SPACES.
149          02   FILLER              PIC X(09) VALUE ALL '*'.
150          02   FILLER              PIC X(04) VALUE SPACES.
151          02   FILLER              PIC X(10) VALUE ALL '*'.
152
153     01   DETAIL-LINE.
154          02   FILLER              PIC X(01) VALUE SPACES.
155          02   CARD-COUNT-OUT      PIC ZZ,ZZ9.
156          02   FILLER              PIC X(03) VALUE SPACES.
157          02   EMPLOYEE-NAME-OUT   PIC X(25).
158          02   FILLER              PIC X(04) VALUE SPACES.
159          02   SOC-SEC-NO-OUT      PIC 999B99B9999.
160          02   FILLER              PIC X(09) VALUE SPACES.
161          02   LANGUAGE-NO-OUT     PIC 999.
162          02   FILLER              PIC X(11) VALUE SPACES.
163          02   HOURS-WORKED-OUT    PIC ZZ9.99.
164          02   FILLER              PIC X(05) VALUE SPACES.
165          02   RATE-OF-PAY-OUT     PIC $$9.99.
166          02   FILLER              PIC X(05) VALUE SPACES.
167          02   LANG-NAME-OUT       PIC X(09).
168          02   FILLER              PIC X(04) VALUE SPACES.
169          02   AMOUNT-PAID-OUT     PIC $$$,$$9.99.
170
171     01   DETAIL-LINE-2.
172          02   FILLER              PIC X(01) VALUE SPACES.
173          02   FILLER              PIC X(13) VALUE 'TOTAL AMOUNT'.
174          02   FILLER              PIC X(17) VALUE 'PAID TO COMPUTER'.
175          02   FILLER              PIC X(15) VALUE 'PROGRAMMERS IS'.
176          02   TOTAL-AMOUNT-OUT    PIC $,$$$,$$$,$$9.99.
177          02   FILLER              PIC X(01) VALUE '.'.
178
179     01   DETAIL-LINE-3.
180          02   FILLER              PIC X(01) VALUE SPACES.
181          02   CARD-COUNT-OUT-2    PIC ZZ,ZZ9.
182          02   FILLER              PIC X(03) VALUE SPACES.
183          02   EMPLOY-NAME-OUT-2   PIC X(25).
184          02   FILLER              PIC X(04) VALUE SPACES.
185          02   SOC-SEC-NO-OUT-2    PIC X(09).
```

```
186         02   FILLER                    PIC X(11) VALUE SPACES.
187         02   LANGUAGE-NO-OUT-2         PIC X(03).
188         02   FILLER                    PIC X(11) VALUE SPACES.
189         02   HOURS-WORKED-OUT-2        PIC 999.99.
190         02   FILLER                    PIC X(06) VALUE SPACES.
191         02   FILLER                    PIC X(13) VALUE 'ERROR IN DATA'.
192
193     01  DETAIL-LINE-4.
194         02   FILLER                    PIC X(01) VALUE SPACES.
195         02   CARD-COUNT-OUT-3          PIC ZZ,ZZ9.
196         02   FILLER                    PIC X(03) VALUE SPACES.
197         02   EMPLOY-NAME-OUT-3         PIC X(25).
198         02   FILLER                    PIC X(04) VALUE SPACES.
199         02   SOC-SEC-NO-OUT-3          PIC 999B99B9999.
200         02   FILLER                    PIC X(09) VALUE SPACES.
201         02   LANGUAGE-NO-OUT-3         PIC 999.
202         02   FILLER                    PIC X(11) VALUE SPACES.
203         02   HOURS-WORKED-OUT-3        PIC ZZ9.99.
204         02   FILLER                    PIC X(04) VALUE SPACES.
205         02   FILLER                    PIC X(09) VALUE 'LANGUAGE'.
206         02   FILLER                    PIC X(10) VALUE 'NUMBER NOT'.
207         02   FILLER                    PIC X(15) VALUE 'FOUND IN TABLE'.
208
209     PROCEDURE DIVISION.
210
211     MAIN-LINE-ROUTINE.
212         PERFORM OPEN-FILES.
213         PERFORM NEW-PAGE.
214         PERFORM START-UP.
215         PERFORM PROCESS-DATA UNTIL MORE-CARDS EQUAL 'NO'.
216         PERFORM CLOSE-UP.
217         STOP RUN.
218
219     OPEN-FILES.
220         OPEN INPUT IN-FILE.
221         OPEN OUTPUT OUT-FILE.
222
223     NEW-PAGE.
224         MOVE SPACES TO LINE-OUT.
225         WRITE LINE-OUT AFTER PAGE.
226
227     START-UP.
228         READ IN-FILE AT END MOVE 'NO' TO MORE-CARDS
229             MOVE ' **NO DATA IN DECK**' TO LINE-OUT
230             WRITE LINE-OUT AFTER 30.
231         IF MORE-CARDS EQUAL 'YES' PERFORM WRITE-HEADINGS.
232
233  *      PROCESS-DATA CHECKS TO SEE IF THE DATA IS PUNCHED
234  *      CORRECTLY. IF THE DATA IS CORRECT, THE PERFORM TEST-PARA
235  *      STATEMENT SENDS THE CONTROL OF THE PROGRAM DOWN TO
236  *      TEST-PARA WHERE A TABLE SEARCH IS DONE.
237
238     PROCESS-DATA.
239         ADD 1 TO CARD-COUNT.
240         ADD 1 TO CARD-COUNT-2.
241         IF HOURS-WORKED NOT NUMERIC
242             OR SOC-SEC-NO NOT NUMERIC
243             OR LANGUAGE-NO NOT NUMERIC
244             PERFORM ERROR-PARA-1
245         ELSE PERFORM TEST-PARA.
246         READ IN-FILE AT END MOVE 'NO' TO MORE-CARDS
247             MOVE ZEROS TO CARD-COUNT-2 PERFORM TOTAL-PARA.
248         IF CARD-COUNT-2 = 15 MOVE ZEROS TO CARD-COUNT-2
249             PERFORM NEW-PAGE
250             PERFORM WRITE-HEADINGS.
251
252  *      TOTAL-PARA PRINTS THE TOTAL PAY DUE TO PROGRAMMERS.
253
254     TOTAL-PARA.
255         MOVE TOTAL-AMOUNT-PAID TO TOTAL-AMOUNT-OUT.
256         PERFORM NEW-PAGE.
257         WRITE LINE-OUT FROM DETAIL-LINE-2 AFTER 2.
258
259     CLOSE-UP.
260         CLOSE IN-FILE, OUT-FILE.
261
```

```
262   *     TEST-PARA SETS THE INDEX EQUAL TO 1. THEN A SEARCH IS
263   *     DONE INCREASING THE INDEX BY 1 UNTIL THE CONDITION
264   *     FOLLOWING THE WHEN STATEMENT IS MET. OTHERWISE
265   *     THE AT END CLAUSE IS TRIGGERED, PRINTING AN ERROR MESSAGE.
266
267       TEST-PARA.
268           SET TABLE-INDEX TO 1.
269           SEARCH TABLE-ELEMENT AT END PERFORM ERROR-PARA-2
270           WHEN LANGUAGE-NO EQUAL ASSIGNED-LANG-NO (TABLE-INDEX)
271               PERFORM WORK-PARA.
272
273   *     WORK-PARA DOES THE WORK NECESSARY TO CREATE THE
274   *     THE OUTPUT DESIRED BY THE PROGRAM
275
276       WORK-PARA.
277           MOVE RATE-OF-PAY (TABLE-INDEX) TO W-S-RATE-OF-PAY.
278           MULTIPLY HOURS-WORKED BY W-S-RATE-OF-PAY
279               GIVING AMOUNT-PAID ROUNDED.
280           ADD AMOUNT-PAID TO TOTAL-AMOUNT-PAID.
281           MOVE CARD-COUNT TO CARD-COUNT-OUT.
282           MOVE EMPLOYEE-NAME TO EMPLOYEE-NAME-OUT.
283           MOVE SOC-SEC-NO TO SOC-SEC-NO-OUT.
284           MOVE LANGUAGE-NO TO LANGUAGE-NO-OUT.
285           MOVF HOURS-WORKED TO HOURS-WORKED-OUT.
286           MOVE LANG-NAME (TABLE-INDEX) TO LANG-NAME-OUT.
287           MOVE RATE-OF-PAY (TABLE-INDEX) TO RATE-OF-PAY-OUT.
288           MOVE AMOUNT-PAID TO AMOUNT-PAID-OUT.
289           WRITE LINE-OUT FROM DETAIL-LINE AFTER 2.
290
291       ERROR-PARA-1.
292           MOVE CARD-COUNT TO CARD-COUNT-OUT-2.
293           MOVE EMPLOYEE-NAME TO EMPLOY-NAME-OUT-2.
294           MOVE SOC-SEC-NO TO SOC-SEC-NO-OUT-2.
295           MOVE LANGUAGE-NO TO LANGUAGE-NO-OUT-2.
296           MOVE HOURS-WORKED TO HOURS-WORKED-OUT-2.
297           WRITE LINE-OUT FROM DETAIL-LINE-3 AFTER 2.
298
299       ERROR-PARA-2.
300           MOVE CARD-COUNT TO CARD-COUNT-OUT-3.
301           MOVE EMPLOYEE-NAME TO EMPLOY-NAME-OUT-3.
302           MOVE SOC-SEC-NO TO SOC-SEC-NO-OUT-3.
303           MOVE LANGUAGE-NO TO LANGUAGE-NO-OUT-3.
304           MOVE HOURS-WORKED TO HOURS-WORKED-OUT-3.
305           WRITE LINE-OUT FROM DETAIL-LINE-4 AFTER 2.
306
307       WRITE-HEADINGS.
308           ADD 1 TO PAGE-COUNT.
309           MOVE PAGE-COUNT TO PAGE-COUNT-OUT.
310           WRITE LINE-OUT FROM HEADER-1 AFTER 1.
311           WRITE LINE-OUT FROM HEADER-2 AFTER 1.
312           WRITE LINE-OUT FROM HEADER-2 AFTER 1.
313           WRITE LINE-OUT FROM HEADER-3 AFTER 2.
314           WRITE LINE-OUT FROM HEADER-4 AFTER 1.
315           WRITE LINE-OUT FROM HEADER-5 AFTER 1.
```

Output for Program 32

PAGE 1

UNITED STATES GOVERNMENT PAYROLL: COMPUTER DIVISION

CARD COUNT	EMPLOYEE NAME	SOC. SEC. NUMBER	ASSIGNED LANG. NUMBER	HOURS WORKED	RATE PER HOUR	LANGUAGE NAME	AMOUNT PAID
1	IRVIN POREMBA	342 42 5393	005	125.50	$25.50	COBOL	$3,200.25
2	JULIAN COLE	253 41 5583	204	45.75	$4.50	BASIC	$205.88
3	MICHELLE CORNER	453 76 7789	943	100.25	$6.75	FORTRAN	$676.69
4	FERN FRIEDMAN	123 25 4789	450	458.32		LANGUAGE NUMBER NOT FOUND IN TABLE	
5	BARBARA HODGES	645 23 6632	110	12.45	$12.50	ASSEMBLER	$155.68
6	SALLY DEMBERG	554613214	KIJ	002.36		ERROR IN DATA	
7	JACKIE MURDOCK	225 32 1122	428	200.00	$2.50	ALGOL	$500.00
8	MARY LAGOUMIS	521 23 9816	001	452.00		LANGUAGE NUMBER NOT FOUND IN TABLE	
9	FRANS LISTZ	234 25 7832	943	5.00	$6.75	FORTRAN	$33.75
10	BERT STURZA	451 02 1411	148	320.00	$5.00	RPG	$1,600.00
11	AARON GREENFELD	989 50 6910	204	21.56	$4.50	BASIC	$97.02
12	ROGER POOL	73J552293	005	017.40		ERROR IN DATA	
13	ANDREW DORSEY	192 71 3105	110	242.60	$12.50	ASSEMBLER	$3,032.50
14	RICHARD LESTER	259 30 2305	456	22.90	$4.75	APL	$108.78
15	FRANK JASPER	319 50 1263	148	6.22	$5.00	RPG	$31.10

UNITED STATES GOVERNMENT PAYROLL: COMPUTER DIVISION

CARD COUNT	EMPLOYEE NAME	SOC.SEC. NUMBER	ASSIGNED LANG. NUMBER	HOURS WORKED	RATE PER HOUR	LANGUAGE NAME	AMOUNT PAID
16	RICHARD MILLER	615 14 0081	943	235.50	$6.75	FORTRAN	$1,589.63
17	MICHAEL DIAVIDSON	515 85 1602	052	421.00	$6.50	PL/I	$2,736.50
18	RONALD KRAMER	160 13 0059	128	113.25	$3.25	SNOBOL	$368.06
19	MARTIN SMITH	232 54 4511	456	7.20	$4.75	APL	$34.20
20	MARC NEFF	253 14 7654	943	75.20	$6.75	FORTRAN	$507.60
21	MARC FRIEDMAN	625 43 1982	128	51.60	$3.25	SNOBOL	$167.70
22	ROBERT TROTENBERG	456 23 7531	110	100.00	$12.50	ASSEMBLER	$1,250.00

TOTAL AMOUNT PAID TO COMPUTER PROGRAMMERS IS $16,295.29.

10.7   The Binary Search

In order to appreciate the utilitarian value of the binary search, just imagine how laborious it would be to look up someone's telephone number in a large telephone directory if the names of the subscribers had not been printed in alphabetical order. Of course, we take it for granted that the names are arranged in an orderly way. When looking for a particular number we simply open up the directory to any page and then go in a backward or forward direction until we hit on the required name. Suppose the name we are seeking is POREMBA Irvin. A good first move would be to open the directory at about the middle, say, at the J's. Now POREMBA comes after J in the alphabet so we make another stab at opening it halfway between J and Z. Suppose we reach T this time. Because T is beyond POREMBA and we know that the directory is sorted alphabetically, we have to go backward. Now we try for somewhere between J and T. POREMBA comes after N so again we go forward and aim at a point midway between N and T. This process continues until we finally narrow it down to the required name and make note of the associated telephone number.

This is precisely the method used in the binary search of a table. It is called a binary search because we continuously *halve* (split into 2—hence binary) the scope of the search and not because of the 2 binary digits 0 and 1.

To specify that a binary search is required "all" we need to write instead of SEARCH are the words SEARCH ALL. However, it would make no sense to specify a binary search unless, like our analogy with the telephone directory, all the items that are to be searched are arranged in some order—either ascending or descending order, it makes no difference which one. Whether the order is ascending or descending, this information must be communicated to the computer. This is done in the OCCURS clause, immediately following the INDEXED BY clause.

The definition of the table now becomes:

```
01   RATE-TABLE-SKELETON.
     02   FILLER PIC X(16) VALUE '005 2550COBOL'.
     02   FILLER PIC X(16) VALUE '052 0650PL/I'.
     02   FILLER PIC X(16) VALUE '110 1250ASSEMBLER'.
     02   FILLER PIC X(16) VALUE '128 0325SNOBOL'.
     02   FILLER PIC X(16) VALUE '148 0500RPG'.
     02   FILLER PIC X(16) VALUE '204 0450BASIC'.
     02   FILLER PIC X(16) VALUE '428 0250ALGOL'.
     02   FILLER PIC X(16) VALUE '456 0475APL'.
     02   FILLER PIC X(16) VALUE '943 0675FORTRAN'.
```

where a space has deliberately been left (for purposes of illustration only) between the ascending language number key and the rest of the table entry. In practice, no space is left there. Note, however, that the key is ascending—going from small to large.

The redefinition of the table skeleton now becomes:

```
01  RATE-TABLE REDEFINES RATE-TABLE-SKELETON.
    02  TABLE-ELEMENT OCCURS 9 TIMES
        INDEXED BY TABLE-INDEX
        ASCENDING KEY IS ASSIGNED-LANG-NO.
        03  ASSIGNED-LANG-NO PIC 999.
        03  RATE-OF-PAY        PIC 99V99.
        03  LANG-NAME          PIC X(09).
```

where, because the key is ascending, the clause ASCENDING KEY IS is used. If it were a descending key (going from 943 to 005), we would have to substitute the word DESCENDING for ASCENDING. Whether it is an ascending or descending key, that key must be one of the items mentioned in the list of subordinate items of the table entries and in the order specified by the programmer.

If a SET instruction is used, it is ignored because the action of the binary search is always to make for the middle of the unscanned range of elements.

The binary search is a particularly powerful table-handling tool. If we had, say, 1000 ordered elements through which to search, the maximum number of actual comparisons that would have to be made to assure a match is given by x, where x is:

$$2^x \leqslant 1000$$

Since 2^9 is 512 and 2^{10} is 1024, the maximum number of comparisons that would have to be made is 10—and this is a "worst-case" figure; it could easily be fewer than 10.

The format for the binary search instruction is:

SEARCH ALL (table) [AT END imperative statement(s)]

WHEN condition $\left\{ \begin{array}{l} \text{imperative statement(s)} \\ \text{NEXT SENTENCE} \end{array} \right\}$

There are 2 restrictions associated with the SEARCH ALL: (1) The only condition permitted is equality. You cannot say LESS or GREATER. (2) The indexed item must appear to the left of the condition, according to the 1974 standard.

Input for Program 33

Same as for Programs 30, 31, and 32.

Program 33

```
1    IDENTIFICATION  DIVISION.
2    PROGRAM-ID.     TABLE-8.
3    AUTHOR.         IRVIN POREMBA.
4    INSTALLATION.   NYU.
5    DATE-WRITTEN.   APRIL 28, 1982.
6    DATE-COMPILED.  APRIL 28, 1982.
7    SECURITY.       HENRY MULLISH.
8    *************************************************************
9    *       THIS PROGRAM IS A U.S. GOVERNMENT PAYROLL.          *
10   *       CARDS ARE PUNCHED AS FOLLOWED:                      *
11   *                                                           *
12   *       COLUMNS  1-25: EMPLOYEE NAME                        *
13   *       COLUMNS 30-38: SOCIAL SECURITY NUMBER               *
14   *       COLUMNS 40-42: PROGRAM LANGUAGE NUMBER              *
15   *       COLUMNS 45-49: HOURS-WORKED                         *
16   *                                                           *
17   *       THIS PROGRAM USES A BINARY SEARCH OF THE TABLE      *
18   *       TO FIND THE RATE OF PAY AND THE PROGRAMMING         *
19   *       LANGUAGE NAME, PRINTING ALL THIS OUT UNDER          *
20   *       A SUITABLE HEADING WITH THE NET PAY DUE TO          *
21   *       EACH PROGRAMMER. ON A NEW PAGE, THE TOTAL           *
22   *       PAY DUE TO ALL PROGRAMMERS BY THE U.S.              *
23   *       GOVERNMENT IS PRINTED.                              *
24   *************************************************************
```

```
25
26      ENVIRONMENT DIVISION.
27      CONFIGURATION SECTION.
28      SOURCE-COMPUTER. CYBER-170-720.
29      OBJECT-COMPUTER. CYBER-170-720.
30      SPECIAL-NAMES.
31      INPUT-OUTPUT SECTION.
32      FILE-CONTROL.
33          SELECT IN-FILE ASSIGN TO INPUT.
34          SELECT OUT-FILE ASSIGN TO OUTPUT.
35
36      DATA DIVISION.
37      FILE SECTION.
38
39      FD   IN-FILE
40           LABEL RECORDS ARE OMITTED.
41
42      *    DEFINE INPUT.
43
44      01   RECORD-IN.
45           02   EMPLOYEE-NAME        PIC X(25).
46           02   FILLER              PIC X(04).
47           02   SOC-SEC-NO          PIC 9(09).
48           02   FILLER              PIC X(01).
49           02   LANGUAGE-NO         PIC 9(03).
50           02   FILLER              PIC X(02).
51           02   HOURS-WORKED        PIC 9(03)V9(02).
52           02   FILLER              PIC X(21).
53
54      FD   OUT-FILE
55           LABEL RECORDS ARE OMITTED.
56
57      *    DEFINE OUTPUT OF PROGRAM.
58
59      01   LINE-OUT                 PIC X(133).
60
61      WORKING-STORAGE SECTION.
62      77   PAGE-COUNT               PIC 9999 VALUE ZERO.
63      77   CARD-COUNT               PIC 99999 VALUE ZERO.
64      77   CARD-COUNT-2             PIC 99 VALUE ZERO.
65      77   AMOUNT-PAID              PIC 9(05)V99.
66      77   TOTAL-AMOUNT-PAID        PIC 9(09)V99 VALUE ZERO.
67      77   W-S-RATE-OF-PAY          PIC 99V99.
68      77   MORE-CARDS               PIC X(03) VALUE 'YES'.
69
70      *    BELOW IS THE SKELETON OF THE TABLE USED IN THIS
71      *    PROGRAM. AFTERWARDS, THE TABLE (RATE-TABLE-SKELETON
72      *    AS IT IS CALLED) IS REDEFINED AND BROKEN UP INTO
73      *    ITS DIFFERENT PARTS NAMELY: ASSIGNED-LANG-NO,
74      *    RATE-OF-PAY, AND LANG-NAME.
75
76      01   RATE-TABLE-SKELETON.
77           02   FILLER              PIC X(16) VALUE '0052550COBOL'.
78           02   FILLER              PIC X(16) VALUE '0520650PL/I'.
79           02   FILLER              PIC X(16) VALUE '1101250ASSEMBLER'.
80           02   FILLER              PIC X(16) VALUE '1280325SNOBOL'.
81           02   FILLER              PIC X(16) VALUE '1480500RPG'.
82           02   FILLER              PIC X(16) VALUE '2040450BASIC'.
83           02   FILLER              PIC X(16) VALUE '4280250ALGOL'.
84           02   FILLER              PIC X(16) VALUE '4560475APL'.
85           02   FILLER              PIC X(16) VALUE '9430675FORTRAN'.
86
87      *    UNDER A BINARY SEARCH, THE TABLE IS LINED UP
88      *    IN THIS CASE IN THE ASCENDING ORDER OF THE
89      *    ASSIGNED-LANG-NO WHICH IS KEYED WHEN RATE-TABLE-SKELETON
90      *    IS REDEFINED. ALSO TABLE-ELEMENT IS INDEXED BY TABLE-INDEX
91      *    AS IN THE INDEXING METHOD USED FOR TABLES.
92
93      01   RATE-TABLE REDEFINES RATE-TABLE-SKELETON.
94           02   TABLE-ELEMENT OCCURS 9 TIMES INDEXED BY TABLE-INDEX
95                ASCENDING KEY IS ASSIGNED-LANG-NO.
96                03 ASSIGNED-LANG-NO  PIC 999.
97                03 RATE-OF-PAY       PIC 99V99.
```

```
98              03 LANG-NAME          PIC X(09).
99
100   01   HEADER-1.
101        02   FILLER               PIC X(01) VALUE SPACES.
102        02   FILLER               PIC X(05) VALUE 'PAGE'.
103        02   PAGE-COUNT-OUT       PIC Z,ZZ9.
104        02   FILLER               PIC X(30) VALUE SPACES.
105        02   FILLER               PIC X(14) VALUE 'UNITED STATES'.
106        02   FILLER               PIC X(11) VALUE 'GOVERNMENT'.
107        02   FILLER               PIC X(18) VALUE 'PAYROLL: COMPUTER'.
108        02   FILLER               PIC X(09) VALUE 'DIVISION'.
109
110   01   HEADER-2.
111        02   FILLER               PIC X(01) VALUE SPACES.
112        02   FILLER               PIC X(10) VALUE ALL '*'.
113        02   FILLER               PIC X(30) VALUE SPACES.
114        02   FILLER               PIC X(52) VALUE ALL '*'.
115
116   01   HEADER-3.
117        02   FILLER               PIC X(01) VALUE SPACES.
118        02   FILLER               PIC X(17) VALUE 'CARD'.
119        02   FILLER               PIC X(22) VALUE 'EMPLOYEE'.
120        02   FILLER               PIC X(14) VALUE 'SOC.SEC.'.
121        02   FILLER               PIC X(19) VALUE 'ASSIGNED LANG.'.
122        02   FILLER               PIC X(10) VALUE 'HOURS'.
123        02   FILLER               PIC X(12) VALUE 'RATE PER'.
124        02   FILLER               PIC X(15) VALUE 'LANGUAGE'.
125        02   FILLER               PIC X(06) VALUE 'AMOUNT'.
126
127   01   HEADER-4.
128        02   FILLER               PIC X(01) VALUE SPACES.
129        02   FILLER               PIC X(19) VALUE 'COUNT'.
130        02   FILLER               PIC X(21) VALUE 'NAME'.
131        02   FILLER               PIC X(17) VALUE 'NUMBER'.
132        02   FILLER               PIC X(15) VALUE 'NUMBER'.
133        02   FILLER               PIC X(12) VALUE 'WORKED'.
134        02   FILLER               PIC X(12) VALUE 'HOUR'.
135        02   FILLER               PIC X(14) VALUE 'NAME'.
136        02   FILLER               PIC X(04) VALUE 'PAID'.
137
138   01   HEADER-5.
139        02   FILLER               PIC X(01) VALUE SPACES.
140        02   FILLER               PIC X(06) VALUE ALL '*'.
141        02   FILLER               PIC X(03) VALUE SPACES.
142        02   FILLER               PIC X(25) VALUE ALL '*'.
143        02   FILLER               PIC X(04) VALUE SPACES.
144        02   FILLER               PIC X(11) VALUE ALL '*'.
145        02   FILLER               PIC X(04) VALUE SPACES.
146        02   FILLER               PIC X(14) VALUE ALL '*'.
147        02   FILLER               PIC X(05) VALUE SPACES.
148        02   FILLER               PIC X(06) VALUE ALL '*'.
149        02   FILLER               PIC X(04) VALUE SPACES.
150        02   FILLER               PIC X(08) VALUE ALL '*'.
151        02   FILLER               PIC X(04) VALUE SPACES.
152        02   FILLER               PIC X(09) VALUE ALL '*'.
153        02   FILLER               PIC X(04) VALUE SPACES.
154        02   FILLER               PIC X(10) VALUE ALL '*'.
155
156        01   DETAIL-LINE.
157        02   FILLER               PIC X(01) VALUE SPACES.
158        02   CARD-COUNT-OUT       PIC ZZ,ZZ9.
159        02   FILLER               PIC X(03) VALUE SPACES.
160        02   EMPLOYEE-NAME-OUT    PIC X(25).
161        02   FILLER               PIC X(04) VALUE SPACES.
162        02   SOC-SEC-NO-OUT       PIC 999B99B9999.
163        02   FILLER               PIC X(09) VALUE SPACES.
164        02   LANGUAGE-NO-OUT      PIC 999.
165        02   FILLER               PIC X(11) VALUE SPACES.
166        02   HOURS-WORKED-OUT     PIC ZZ9.99.
167        02   FILLER               PIC X(05) VALUE SPACES.
168        02   RATE-OF-PAY-OUT      PIC $$9.99.
169        02   FILLER               PIC X(05) VALUE SPACES.
170        02   LANG-NAME-OUT        PIC X(09).
```

```
171        02   FILLER              PIC X(04) VALUE SPACES.
172        02   AMOUNT-PAID-OUT     PIC $$$,$$9.99.
173
174   01   DETAIL-LINE-2.
175        02   FILLER              PIC X(01) VALUE SPACES.
176        02   FILLER              PIC X(13) VALUE 'TOTAL AMOUNT'.
177        02   FILLER              PIC X(17) VALUE 'PAID TO COMPUTER'.
178        02   FILLER              PIC X(15) VALUE 'PROGRAMMERS IS'.
179        02   TOTAL-AMOUNT-OUT    PIC $,$$$,$$$,$$9.99.
180        02   FILLER              PIC X(01) VALUE '.'.
181
182   01   DETAIL-LINE-3.
183        02   FILLER              PIC X(01) VALUE SPACES.
184        02   CARD-COUNT-OUT-2    PIC ZZ,ZZ9.
185        02   FILLER              PIC X(03) VALUE SPACES.
186        02   EMPLOY-NAME-OUT-2   PIC X(25).
187        02   FILLER              PIC X(04) VALUE SPACES.
188        02   SOC-SEC-NO-OUT-2    PIC X(09).
189        02   FILLER              PIC X(11) VALUE SPACES.
190        02   LANGUAGE-NO-OUT-2   PIC X(03).
191        02   FILLER              PIC X(11) VALUE SPACES.
192        02   HOURS-WORKED-OUT-2  PIC 999.99.
193        02   FILLER              PIC X(06) VALUE SPACES.
194        02   FILLER              PIC X(13) VALUE 'ERROR IN DATA'.
195
196   01   DETAIL-LINE-4.
197        02   FILLER              PIC X(01) VALUE SPACES.
198        02   CARD-COUNT-OUT-3    PIC ZZ,ZZ9.
199        02   FILLER              PIC X(03) VALUE SPACES.
200        02   EMPLOY-NAME-OUT-3   PIC X(25).
201        02   FILLER              PIC X(04) VALUE SPACES.
202        02   SOC-SEC-NO-OUT-3    PIC 999B99B9999.
203        02   FILLER              PIC X(09) VALUE SPACES.
204        02   LANGUAGE-NO-OUT-3   PIC 999.
205        02   FILLER              PIC X(11) VALUE SPACES.
206        02   HOURS-WORKED-OUT-3  PIC ZZ9.99.
207        02   FILLER              PIC X(04) VALUE SPACES.
208        02   FILLER              PIC X(09) VALUE 'LANGUAGE'.
209        02   FILLER              PIC X(10) VALUE 'NUMBER NOT'.
210        02   FILLER              PIC X(15) VALUE 'FOUND IN TABLE'.
211
212   PROCEDURE DIVISION.
213
214   MAIN-LINE-ROUTINE.
215        PERFORM OPEN-FILES.
216        PERFORM NEW-PAGE.
217        PERFORM START-UP.
218        PERFORM PROCESS-DATA UNTIL MORE-CARDS EQUAL 'NO'.
219        PERFORM CLOSE-UP.
220        STOP RUN.
221
222   OPEN-FILES.
223        OPEN INPUT IN-FILE.
224        OPEN OUTPUT OUT-FILE.
225
226   NEW-PAGE.
227        MOVE SPACES TO LINE-OUT.
228        WRITE LINE-OUT AFTER PAGE.
229
230   START-UP.
231        READ IN-FILE AT END MOVE 'NO' TO MORE-CARDS
232             MOVE ' **NO DATA IN DECK**' TO LINE-OUT
233             WRITE LINE-OUT AFTER 30.
234        IF MORE-CARDS EQUAL 'YES' PERFORM WRITE-HEADINGS.
235
236   *    PROCESS-DATA CHECKS TO SEE IF THE DATA IS PUNCHED
237   *    CORRECTLY. IF THE DATA IS CORRECT, THE PERFORM TEST-PARA
238   *    STATEMENT SENDS THE CONTROL OF THE PROGRAM DOWN TO
239   *    TEST-PARA WHERE A BINARY SEARCH IS DONE.
240
241   PROCESS-DATA.
242        ADD 1 TO CARD-COUNT.
243        ADD 1 TO CARD-COUNT-2.
```

```
244            IF HOURS-WORKED NOT NUMERIC
245                 OR SOC-SEC-NO NOT NUMERIC
246                 OR LANGUAGE-NO NOT NUMERIC
247                 PERFORM ERROR-PARA-1
248            ELSE PERFORM TEST-PARA.
249            READ IN-FILE AT END MOVE 'NO' TO MORE-CARDS
250                 MOVE ZEROS TO CARD-COUNT-2 PERFORM TOTAL-PARA.
251            IF CARD-COUNT-2 = 15 MOVE ZEROS TO CARD-COUNT-2
252                 PERFORM NEW-PAGE
253                 PERFORM WRITE-HEADINGS.
254
255      *     TOTAL-PARA PRINTS THE TOTAL PAY DUE TO PROGRAMMERS.
256
257      TOTAL-PARA.
258            MOVE TOTAL-AMOUNT-PAID TO TOTAL-AMOUNT-OUT.
259            PERFORM NEW-PAGE.
260            WRITE LINE-OUT FROM DETAIL-LINE-2 AFTER 2.
261
262      CLOSE-UP.
263            CLOSE IN-FILE, OUT-FILE.
264
265      *     TEST-PARA DOES THE BINARY SEARCH UNTIL THE CONDITION
266      *     FOLLOWING THE WHEN STATEMENT IS MET. OTHERWISE
267      *     THE AT END CLAUSE IS TRIGGERED, PRINTING AN ERROR MESSAGE
268
269      TEST-PARA.
270            SEARCH ALL TABLE-ELEMENT AT END PERFORM ERROR-PARA-2
271            WHEN ASSIGNED-LANG-NO (TABLE-INDEX) EQUAL LANGUAGE-NO
272                 PERFORM WORK-PARA.
273
274      *     WORK-PARA DOES THE WORK NECESSARY TO CREATE THE
275      *     THE OUTPUT DESIRED BY THE PROGRAM
276
277      WORK-PARA.
278            MOVE RATE-TO-PAY (TABLE-INDEX) TO W-S-RATE-OF-PAY.
279            MULTIPLY HOURS-WORKED BY W-S-RATE-OF-PAY
280                 GIVING AMOUNT-PAID ROUNDED.
281            ADD AMOUNT-PAID TO TOTAL-AMOUNT-PAID.
282            MOVE CARD-COUNT TO CARD-COUNT-OUT.
283            MOVE EMPLOYEE-NAME TO EMPLOYEE-NAME-OUT.
284            MOVE SOC-SEC-NO TO SOC-SEC-NO-OUT.
285            MOVE LANGUAGE-NO TO LANGUAGE-NO-OUT.
286            MOVE HOURS-WORKED TO HOURS-WORKED-OUT.
287            MOVE LANG-NAME (TABLE-INDEX) TO LANG-NAME-OUT.
288            MOVE RATE-OF-PAY (TABLE-INDEX) TO RATE-OF-PAY-OUT.
289            MOVE AMOUNT-PAID TO AMOUNT-PAID-OUT.
290            WRITE LINE-OUT FROM DETAIL-LINE AFTER 2.
291
292      ERROR-PARA-1.
293            MOVE CARD-COUNT TO CARD-COUNT-OUT-2.
294            MOVE EMPLOYEE-NAME TO EMPLOY-NAME-OUT-2.
295            MOVE SOC-SEC-NO TO SOC-SEC-NO-OUT-2.
296            MOVE LANGUAGE-NO TO LANGUAGE-NO-OUT-2.
297            MOVE HOURS-WORKED TO HOURS-WORKED-OUT-2.
298            WRITE LINE-OUT FROM DETAIL-LINE-3 AFTER 2.
299
300      ERROR-PARA-2.
301            MOVE CARD-COUNT TO CARD-COUNT-OUT-3.
302            MOVE EMPLOYEE-NAME TO EMPLOY-NAME-OUT-3.
303            MOVE SOC-SEC-NO TO SOC-SEC-NO-OUT-3.
304            MOVE LANGUAGE-NO TO LANGUAGE-NO-OUT-3.
305            MOVE HOURS-WORKED TO HOURS-WORKED-OUT-3.
306            WRITE LINE-OUT FROM DETAIL-LINE-4 AFTER 2.
307
308      WRITE-HEADINGS.
309            ADD 1 TO PAGE-COUNT.
310            MOVE PAGE-COUNT TO PAGE-COUNT-OUT.
311            WRITE LINE-OUT FROM HEADER-1 AFTER 1.
312            WRITE LINE-OUT FROM HEADER-2 AFTER 1.
313            WRITE LINE-OUT FROM HEADER-2 AFTER 1.
314            WRITE LINE-OUT FROM HEADER-3 AFTER 2.
315            WRITE LINE-OUT FROM HEADER-4 AFTER 1.
316            WRITE LINE-OUT FROM HEADER-5 AFTER 1.
```

Output for Program 33

PAGE 1
* * * * * * * * *
* * * * * * * * *

UNITED STATES GOVERNMENT PAYROLL: COMPUTER DIVISION

CARD COUNT	EMPLOYEE NAME	SOC.SEC. NUMBER	ASSIGNED LANG. NUMBER	HOURS WORKED	RATE PER HOUR	LANGUAGE NAME	AMOUNT PAID
1	IRVIN POREMBA	342 42 5393	005	125.50	$25.50	COBOL	$3,200.25
2	JULIAN COLE	253 41 5583	204	45.75	$4.50	BASIC	$205.88
3	MICHELLE CORNER	453 26 7789	943	100.25	$6.75	FORTRAN	$676.69
4	FERN FREIDMAN	123 25 4789	450	458.32	LANGUAGE NUMBER NOT FOUND IN TABLE		
5	BARBARA HODGES	645 23 6632	110	12.45	$12.50	ASSEMBLER	$155.63
6	SALLY DEMBERG	554613214	KIJ	002.36	ERROR IN DATA		
7	JACKIE MURDOCK	225 32 1122	428	200.00	$2.50	ALGOL	$500.00
8	MARY LAGOUMIS	521 23 9816	001	452.00	LANGUAGE NUMBER NOT FOUND IN TABLE		
9	FRANS LISTZ	234 25 7832	943	5.00	$6.75	FORTRAN	$33.75
10	BERT STURZA	451 02 1411	148	320.00	$5.00	RPG	$1,600.00
11	AARON GREENFELD	989 50 6910	204	21.56	$4.50	BASIC	$97.02
12	ROGER POOL	73J552293	005	017.40	ERROR IN DATA		
13	ANDREW DORSEY	192 71 3105	110	242.60	$12.50	ASSEMBLER	$3,032.50
14	RICHARD LESTER	259 30 2305	456	22.90	$4.75	APL	$108.78
15	FRANK JASPER	319 50 1263	148	6.22	$5.00	RPG	$31.10

PAGE 2
* * * * * * * * *
* * * * * * * * *

UNITED STATES GOVERNMENT PAYROLL: COMPUTER DIVISION

CARD COUNT	EMPLOYEE NAME	SOC.SEC. NUMBER	ASSIGNED LANG. NUMBER	HOURS WORKED	RATE PER HOUR	LANGUAGE NAME	AMOUNT PAID
16	RICHARD MILLER	615 14 0081	943	235.50	$6.75	FORTRAN	$1,589.63
17	MICHAEL DIAVIDSON	515 85 1602	052	421.00	$6.50	PL/I	$2,736.50
18	RONALD KRAMER	160 13 0059	128	113.25	$3.25	SNOBOL	$368.06
19	MARTIN SMITH	232 54 4511	456	7.20	$4.75	APL	$34.20
20	MARC FRIEDMAN	625 43 1982	128	51.60	$3.25	SNOBOL	$167.70
21	MARC NEFF	253 14 7654	943	75.20	$6.75	FORTRAN	$507.60
22	ROBERT TROTENBERG	456 23 7531	110	100.00	$12.50	ASSEMBLER	$1,250.00

TOTAL AMOUNT PAID TO COMPUTER PROGRAMMERS IS $16,295.29.

10.8   Using a Binary Search for Finding the Day of the Week

We are familiar with the program that reads in a date and by means of a remarkably simple formula computes the day of the week on which that date falls (see Program 14). The computation involves a division by 7. The fractional portion of the result was then multiplied by 7 and rounded in order to produce the single digit 0 through 6, which specifies the day of the week corresponding to that date.

Suppose the division were:

$$\frac{12345}{7} = 1763.5714$$

Multiplying the fractional portion by 7, we get:

$0.5714 \times 7 = 3.9998$

which when rounded yields the number 4, specifying that the date falls on a Wednesday.

However, we can arrive at this same figure 4 by a much simpler method, one that exploits the DIVIDE with REMAINDER option. Let us again divide 12345 by 7, but this time we will stop the division as soon as we know what the remainder is.

$$
\begin{array}{r}
1763 \\
7\overline{)12345} \\
\underline{7} \\
53 \\
\underline{49} \\
44 \\
\underline{42} \\
25 \\
\underline{21} \\
4 \quad \text{Remainder} = 4
\end{array}
$$

The remainder of 4 is precisely the number we were seeking by the previous method. The next version of the program uses this second approach.

If an integer is divided by 7, the only remainder possible is one between 0 and 6, inclusive. This integer could then be used to search a table in which each integer is associated with its corresponding day of the week. However, as already indicated, zero is a possible remainder, but a subscript of zero or an index of zero creates severe difficulties. After all, what does it mean to access element zero?

This problem may be resolved simply by adding 1 to whatever the remainder is and using the numbers 1 through 7 in the table rather than 0 through 6. The table can now be set up as shown where, because it has been decided to use a binary search, the ASCENDING KEY clause is used. Actually a binary search should be used with tables of at least 30 or so elements but it works for this case even if in terms of compiler time it is a little expensive.

```
01   WEEKDAY-TABLE-SKELETON.
     02   FILLER PIC X(10) VALUE '1SATURDAY'.
     02   FILLER PIC X(10) VALUE '2SUNDAY'.
     02   FILLER PIC X(10) VALUE '3MONDAY'.
     02   FILLER PIC X(10) VALUE '4TUESDAY'.
     02   FILLER PIC X(10) VALUE '5WEDNESDAY'.
     02   FILLER PIC X(10) VALUE '6THURSDAY'.
     02   FILLER PIC X(10) VALUE '7FRIDAY'.
01   WEEKDAY-TABLE REDEFINES WEEKDAY-TABLE-SKELETON.
     02   TABLE-ELEMENT OCCURS 7 TIMES
          INDEXED BY TABLE-INDEX
          ASCENDING KEY IS T-WEEKDAY-NUMBER.
          03   T-WEEKDAY-NUMBER PIC 9.
          03   DAY-OF-WEEK-IN     PIC X(09).
```

[Procedure Division segment]

```
SEARCH ALL TABLE-ELEMENT AT END PERFORM ERROR-PARA-2
WHEN T-WEEKDAY-NUMBER (TABLE-INDEX) = WEEKDAY-NUMBER
MOVE DAY-OF-WEEK-IN (TABLE-INDEX) TO DAY-OF-WEEK-OUT.
```

Input Data for Program 34

```
01/01/2000
12/31/1978
12/31/1980
07/04/1976
07/04/1978
10/30/1927
05/15/1948
11/05/1700
04/KH/1980
03/00/1865
12/12/1623
13/25/1705
05/13/1677
06/28/1959
09/29/1800
02/06/1400
02/25/1853
08/16/2155
```

Program 34

```
1         IDENTIFICATION   DIVISION.
2         PROGRAM-ID.      JULIAN-TABLE.
3         AUTHOR.          IRVIN POREMBA.
4         INSTALLATION.    NYU.
5         DATE-WRITTEN.    APRIL 3, 1982.
6         DATE-COMPILED.   APRIL 28, 1982.
7         SECURITY.        HENRY MULLISH.
8      * * * * * * * * * * * * * * * * * * * * * * * * * * * * * * * * * * * * * * * * * * *
9      *     THIS PROGRAM READS IN DATA CARDS PUNCHED:                                    *
10     *                                                                                  *
11     *     COLUMNS  1-2: MONTH                                                           *
12     *     COLUMN     3: SLASH                                                           *
13     *     COLUMNS  4-5: DAY                                                             *
14     *     COLUMN     6: SLASH                                                           *
15     *     COLUMNS 7-13: YEAR                                                            *
16     *                                                                                  *
17     *     THE PROGRAM USES THE DATA TO FIND THE                                        *
18     *     JULIAN DATE FOR EACH GREGORIAN DATE GIVEN,                                   *
19     *     ALONG WITH THE DAY OF THE WEEK AND WHETHER                                   *
20     *     THE YEAR IS A LEAP YEAR OR NOT.                                              *
21     * * * * * * * * * * * * * * * * * * * * * * * * * * * * * * * * * * * * * * * * * * *
22
23     ENVIRONMENT DIVISION.
24     CONFIGURATION SECTION.
25     SOURCE-COMPUTER. CYBER-170-720.
26     OBJECT-COMPUTER. CYBER-170-720.
27     SPECIAL-NAMES.
28     INPUT-OUTPUT SECTION.
29     FILE-CONTROL.
30         SELECT IN-FILE ASSIGN TO INPUT.
31         SELECT OUT-FILE ASSIGN TO OUTPUT.
32
33     DATA DIVISION.
34     FILE SECTION.
35
36     FD    IN-FILE
37           LABEL RECORDS ARE OMITTED.
38
39     01    RECORD-IN.
40           02    MONTH-IN           PIC 9(02).
41           02    SLASH-1            PIC X(01).
42           02    DAY-IN             PIC 9(02).
43           02    SLASH-2            PIC X(01).
44           02    YEAR-IN            PIC 9(04).
45           02    FILLER             PIC X(70).
46
47     FD    OUT-FILE
48           LABEL RECORDS ARE OMITTED.
49
50     01    LINE-OUT                 PIC X(133).
51
52     WORKING-STORAGE SECTION.
53     77    PAGE-COUNT               PIC 9999 VALUE ZERO.
54     77    CARD-COUNT               PIC 99999 VALUE ZERO.
55     77    CARD-COUNT-2             PIC 99 VALUE ZERO.
56     77    TOTAL-DAYS               PIC 999 VALUE ZERO.
57     77    CENTURY                  PIC 99.
58     77    YEAR-X                   PIC 9999.
59     77    LEAP-YEAR                PIC 999.
60     77    WEEKDAY-NUMBER           PIC 9.
61     77    YEAR-MINUS-ONE           PIC 9999.
62     77    INT-YEAR-1-DIV-4         PIC 9999.
63     77    INT-YEAR-1-DIV-100       PIC 99.
64     77    INT-YEAR-1-DIV-400       PIC 99.
65     77    TOTAL-NUMERATOR          PIC 9999.
66     77    TOTAL-NUMERATOR-DIV-7    PIC 9(04).
67     77    MORE-CARDS               PIC X(03) VALUE 'YES'.
68
69     01    WEEKDAY-TABLE-SKELETON.
70           02    FILLER             PIC X(10) VALUE '1SATURDAY'.
71           02    FILLER             PIC X(10) VALUE '2SUNDAY'.
72           02    FILLER             PIC X(10) VALUE '3MONDAY'.
```

```
73              02    FILLER                  PIC X(10) VALUE '4TUESDAY'.
74              02    FILLER                  PIC X(10) VALUE '5WEDNESDAY'.
75              02    FILLER                  PIC X(10) VALUE '6THURSDAY'.
76              02    FILLER                  PIC X(10) VALUE '7FRIDAY'.
77
78       01    WEEKDAY-TABLE REDEFINES WEEKDAY-TABLE-SKELETON.
79              02 TABLE-ELEMENT OCCURS 7 TIMES INDEXED BY TABLE-INDEX
80                   ASCENDING KEY IS T-WEEKDAY-NUMBER.
81                   03 T-WEEKDAY-NUMBER      PIC 9.
82                   03 DAY-OF-WEEK-IN        PIC X(09).
83
84       01    HEADER-1.
85              02    FILLER                  PIC X(01) VALUE SPACES.
86              02    FILLER                  PIC X(05) VALUE 'PAGE'.
87              02    PAGE-COUNT-OUT          PIC Z,ZZ9.
88              02    FILLER                  PIC X(04) VALUE SPACES.
89              02    FILLER                  PIC X(16) VALUE 'JULIAN CALENDAR'.
90              02    FILLER                  PIX X(10) VALUE 'CONVERSION'.
91
92       01    HEADER-2.
93              02    FILLER                  PIC X(01) VALUE SPACES.
94              02    FILLER                  PIC X(10) VALUE ALL '*'.
95              02    FILLER                  PIC X(04) VALUE SPACES.
96              02    FILLER                  PIC X(26) VALUE ALL '*'.
97
98       01    HEADER-3.
99              02    FILLER                  PIC X(01) VALUE SPACES.
100             02    FILLER                  PIC X(04) VALUE 'CARD'.
101             02    FILLER                  PIC X(06) VALUE SPACES.
102             02    FILLER                  PIC X(09) VALUE 'GREGORIAN'.
103             02    FILLER                  PIC X(05) VALUE SPACES.
104             02    FILLER                  PIC X(06) VALUE 'JULIAN'.
105             02    FILLER                  PIC X(08) VALUE SPACES.
106             02    FILLER                  PIC X(03) VALUE 'DAY'.
107
108      01    HEADER-4.
109             02    FILLER                  PIC X(01) VALUE SPACES.
110             02    FILLER                  PIC X(05) VALUE 'COUNT'.
111             02    FILLER                  PIC X(08) VALUE SPACES.
112             02    FILLER                  PIC X(04) VALUE 'DATE'.
113             02    FILLER                  PIC X(08) VALUE SPACES.
114             02    FILLER                  PIC X(04) VALUE 'DATE'.
115             02    FILLER                  PIC X(07) VALUE SPACES.
116             02    FILLER                  PIC X(07) VALUE 'OF WEEK'.
117
118      01    HEADER-5.
119             02    FILLER                  PIC X(01) VALUE SPACES.
120             02    FILLER                  PIC X(06) VALUE ALL '*'.
121             02    FILLER                  PIC X(04) VALUE SPACES.
122             02    FILLER                  PIC X(10) VALUE ALL '*'.
123             02    FILLER                  PIC X(04) VALUE SPACES.
124             02    FILLER                  PIC X(07) VALUE ALL '*'.
125             02    FILLER                  PIC X(04) VALUE SPACES.
126             02    FILLER                  PIC X(09) VALUE ALL '*'.
127
128      01    DETAIL-LINE.
129             02    FILLER                  PIC X(01) VALUE SPACES.
130             02    CARD-COUNT-OUT          PIC ZZ,ZZ9.
131             02    FILLER                  PIC X(04) VALUE SPACES.
132             02    MONTH-OUT               PIC 99.
133             02    SLASH-1-OUT             PIC X(01).
134             02    DAY-OUT                 PIC 99.
135             02    SLASH-2-OUT             PIC X(01).
136             02    YEAR-OUT                PIC 9999.
137             02    FILLER                  PIC X(04) VALUE SPACES.
138             02    JULIAN-DAY-OUT          PIC 999.
139             02    YEAR-2-OUT              PIC 9999.
140             02    FILLER                  PIC X(04) VALUE SPACES.
141             02    DAY-OF-WEEK-OUT         PIC X(09).
142             02    FILLER                  PIC X(04) VALUE SPACES.
143             02    BLANK-OR-LEAP-YEAR      PIC X(09).
144
145      01    DETAIL-LINE-2.
146             02    FILLER                  PIC X(01) VALUE SPACES.
147             02    CARD-COUNT-OUT-2        PIC ZZ,ZZ9.
```

```
148      02   FILLER             PIC X(04) VALUE SPACES.
149      02   MONTH-OUT-2        PIC X(02).
150      02   SLASH-1-OUT-2      PIC X(01).
151      02   DAY-OUT-2          PIC X(02).
152      02   SLASH-2-OUT-2      PIC X(01).
153      02   YEAR-OUT-2         PIC X(04).
154      02   FILLER             PIC X(04) VALUE SPACES.
155      02   FILLER             PIC X(15) VALUE 'GREGORIAN DATE'.
156      02   FILLER             PIC X(07) VALUE 'INVALID'.
157
158   PROCEDURE DIVISION.
159
160   MAIN-LINE-ROUTINE.
161      PERFORM OPEN-FILES.
162      PERFORM NEW-PAGE.
163      PERFORM START-UP.
164      PERFORM PROCESS-DATA UNTIL MORE-CARDS EQUAL 'NO'.
165      PERFORM CLOSE-UP.
166      STOP RUN.
167
168   OPEN-FILES.
169      OPEN INPUT IN FILE.
170      OPEN OUTPUT OUT-FILE.
171
172   NEW-PAGE.
173      MOVE SPACES TO LINE-OUT.
174      WRITE LINE-OUT AFTER PAGE.
175
176      START-UP.
177      READ IN-FILE AT END MOVE 'NO' TO MORE-CARDS
178          MOVE ' **NO DATA IN DECK**' TO LINE-OUT
179          WRITE LINE-OUT AFTER 30.
180      IF MORE-CARDS EQUAL 'YES' PERFORM WRITE-HEADINGS.
101
182   PROCESS-DATA.
183      ADD 1 TO CARD-COUNT.
184      ADD 1 TO CARD-COUNT-2.
185      IF MONTH-IN NOT NUMERIC
186          OR DAY-IN NOT NUMERIC
187          OR YEAR-IN NOT NUMERIC
188          OR MONTH-IN > 12
189          OR MONTH-IN < 1
190          OR DAY-IN > 31
191          OR DAY-IN < 1
192          OR YEAR-IN < 1582
193          PERFORM ERROR-PARA
194          PERFORM CHECK-READ
195      ELSE
196          PERFORM GO-PARA THRU CHECK-READ.
197
198   CLOSE-UP.
199      CLOSE IN-FILE, OUT-FILE.
200
201   GO-PARA.
202      GO TO JAN, FEB, MAR, APR, MAY, JUNE, JULY, AUG, SEPT,
203          OCT, NOV, DEC DEPENDING ON MONTH-IN.
204
205   DEC.    ADD 30 TO TOTAL-DAYS.
206   NOV.    ADD 31 TO TOTAL-DAYS.
207   OCT.    ADD 30 TO TOTAL-DAYS.
208   SEPT.   ADD 31 TO TOTAL-DAYS.
209   AUG.    ADD 31 TO TOTAL-DAYS.
210   JULY.   ADD 30 TO TOTAL-DAYS.
211   JUNE.   ADD 31 TO TOTAL-DAYS.
212   MAY.    ADD 30 TO TOTAL-DAYS.
213   APR.    ADD 31 TO TOTAL-DAYS.
214   MAR.    ADD 28 TO TOTAL-DAYS.
215   FEB.    ADD 31 TO TOTAL-DAYS.
216   JAN.    ADD DAY-IN TO TOTAL-DAYS.
217      MOVE YEAR-IN TO CENTURY.
218      IF CENTURY EQUAL ZERO PERFORM LEAP-1
219      ELSE PERFORM LEAP-2.
220
221   WEEKDAY.
222      SUBTRACT 1 FROM YEAR-IN GIVING YEAR-MINUS-ONE.
```

```
223          DIVIDE 4 INTO YEAR-MINUS-ONE GIVING INT-YEAR-1-DIV-4.
224          DIVIDE 100 INTO YEAR-MINUS-ONE GIVING INT-YEAR-1-DIV-100.
225          DIVIDE 400 INTO YEAR-MINUS-ONE GIVING INT-YEAR-1-DIV-400.
226          ADD TOTAL-DAYS, YEAR-IN, INT-YEAR-1-DIV-4,
227              INT-YEAR-1-DIV-400 GIVING TOTAL-NUMERATOR.
228          SUBTRACT INT-YEAR-1-DIV-100 FROM TOTAL-NUMERATOR.
229          DIVIDE 7 INTO TOTAL-NUMERATOR GIVING TOTAL-NUMERATOR-DIV-7
230              REMAINDER WEEKDAY-NUMBER.
231          ADD 1 TO WEEKDAY-NUMBER.
232
233      SEARCH-WEEKDAY.
234          SEARCH ALL TABLE-ELEMENT AT END PERFORM ERROR-PARA-2
235              WHEN T-WEEKDAY-NUMBER (TABLE-INDEX) = WEEKDAY-NUMBER
236              MOVE DAY-OF-WEEK-IN (TABLE-INDEX) TO DAY-OF-WEEK-OUT.
237
238      WRITE-PARA.
239          MOVE CARD-COUNT TO CARD-COUNT-OUT.
240          MOVE MONTH-IN TO MONTH-OUT.
241          MOVE SLASH-1 TO SLASH-1-OUT.
242          MOVE DAY-IN TO DAY-OUT.
243          MOVE SLASH-2 TO SLASH-2-OUT.
244          MOVE YEAR-IN TO YEAR-OUT.
245          MOVE TOTAL-DAYS TO JULIAN-DAY-OUT.
246          MOVE YEAR-IN TO YEAR-2-OUT.
247          WRITE LINE-OUT FROM DETAIL-LINE AFTER 2.
248
249      CHECK-READ.
250          READ IN-FILE AT END MOVE ZEROS TO CARD-COUNT-2
251              MOVE 'NO' TO MORE-CARDS.
252          IF CARD-COUNT-2 = 10 MOVE ZEROS TO CARD-COUNT-2
253              PERFORM NEW-PAGE
254              PERFORM WRITE-HEADINGS.
255          MOVE ZEROS TO TOTAL-DAYS.
256
257      WRITE-HEADINGS.
258          ADD 1 TO PAGE-COUNT.
259          MOVE PAGE-COUNT TO PAGE-COUNT-OUT.
260          WRITE LINE-OUT FROM HEADER-1 AFTER 1.
261          WRITE LINE-OUT FROM HEADER-2 AFTER 1.
262          WRITE LINE-OUT FROM HEADER-3 AFTER 2.
263          WRITE LINE-OUT FROM HEADER-4 AFTER 1.
264          WRITE LINE-OUT FROM HEADER-5 AFTER 1.
265
266      LEAP-1.
267          DIVIDE 400 INTO YEAR-IN GIVING YEAR-X
268              REMAINDER LEAP-YEAR.
269          IF LEAP-YEAR EQUAL ZERO
270              MOVE 'LEAP YEAR' TO BLANK-OR-LEAP-YEAR
271          ELSE MOVE SPACES TO BLANK-OR-LEAP-YEAR.
272          IF LEAP-YEAR EQUAL ZERO AND MONTH-IN > 2
273              ADD 1 TO TOTAL-DAYS.
274
275      LEAP-2.
276          DIVIDE 4 INTO YEAR-IN GIVING YEAR-X
277              REMAINDER LEAP-YEAR.
278          IF LEAP-YEAR EQUAL ZERO
279              MOVE 'LEAP YEAR' TO BLANK-OR-LEAP-YEAR
280          ELSE MOVE SPACES TO BLANK-OR-LEAP-YEAR.
281          IF LEAP-YEAR EQUAL ZERO AND MONTH-IN > 2
282              ADD 1 TO TOTAL-DAYS.
283
284      ERROR-PARA.
285          MOVE CARD-COUNT TO CARD-COUNT-OUT-2.
286          MOVE MONTH-IN TO MONTH-OUT-2.
287          MOVE SLASH-1 TO SLASH-1-OUT-2.
288          MOVE DAY-IN TO DAY-OUT-2.
289          MOVE SLASH-2 TO SLASH-2-OUT-2.
290          MOVE YEAR-IN TO YEAR-OUT-2.
291          WRITE LINE-OUT FROM DETAIL-LINE-2 AFTER 2.
292
293      ERROR-PARA-2.
294          MOVE ' **ERROR IN PROGRAMMING**' TO LINE-OUT.
295          WRITE LINE-OUT AFTER 2.
296          PERFORM CLOSE-UP.
297          STOP RUN.
```

Output for Program 34

PAGE 1		JULIAN CALENDAR CONVERSION		
* * * * * * * * *		* *		
CARD COUNT	GREGORIAN DATE	JULIAN DATE	DAY OF WEEK	
* * * * *	* * * * * * * * * *	* * * * * * *	* * * * * * * * *	
1	01/01/2000	0012000	SATURDAY	LEAP YEAR
2	12/31/1978	3651978	SUNDAY	
3	12/31/1980	3661980	WEDNESDAY	LEAP YEAR
4	07/04/1976	1861976	SUNDAY	LEAP YEAR
5	07/04/1978	1851978	TUESDAY	
6	10/30/1927	3031927	SUNDAY	
7	05/15/1948	1361948	SATURDAY	LEAP YEAR
8	11/05/1700	3091700	FRIDAY	
9	04/KH/1980	GREGORIAN DATE INVALID		
10	03/00/1865	GREGORIAN DATE INVALID		

PAGE 2		JULIAN CALENDAR CONVERSION		
* * * * * * * * *		* *		
CARD COUNT	GREGORIAN DATE	JULIAN DATE	DAY OF WEEK	
* * * * *	* * * * * * * * * *	* * * * * * *	* * * * * * * * *	
11	12/12/1623	GREGORIAN DATE INVALID		
12	13/25/1705	GREGORIAN DATE INVALID		
13	05/13/1677	1331677	THURSDAY	
14	06/28/1959	1791959	SUNDAY	
15	09/29/1800	2721800	MONDAY	
16	02/06/1400	GREGORIAN DATE INVALID		
17	02/25/1853	0561853	FRIDAY	
18	08/16/2155	2282155	SATURDAY	

10.9   Double-Dimensioned Tables

So far we have confined our study of tables to single levels. A single-level table, or a one-dimensional table, has a single OCCURS clause and a single subscript or index. On occasions, however, within some repeated element there is another repeated element. In such a case we have a 2-dimensioned table. COBOL permits single-, double-, and even triple-level tables. For each level used, a separate OCCURS clause must be specified.

The scenario for Program 35 follows. Gary Truax, the leading COBOL programmer for COBOL Consultants Inc., is sent by his company to do some consultation work for 2 different customers, Acme Corp. and Compute Inc. Each company has 2 departments, each of which pays consultants according to its own pay scales. Acme, for example, pays consultants at the rate of $50 per hour in their department 1, and $75 per hour, in their technical department, 2. Gary regularly consults for both companies in each department.

COBOL Consultants keeps track of the hours Gary Truax spends in the client companies and every month prepares a detailed billing report itemizing the charges for each company by department.

For the purposes of the program Acme Inc. is referred to as number 1 whereas Compute Inc. is known as number 2. By preassigning such numbers to the 2 companies, computation is simplified. Moreover, each of the 2 departments of each company is also referred to by the numbers 1 and 2, again for ease of handling. This is represented schematically on the following page.

Once the company to which we are referring is established, we have to be able to specify the department within that company in order to access the appropriate rate per hour to charge. Thus we have 2 separate levels of categories. Such a

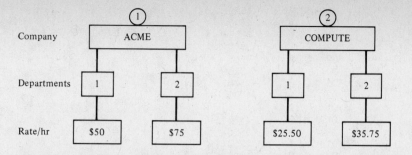

structure may be specified in COBOL by means of a 2-level table, sometimes referred to as a table with 2 dimensions. It may be written as:

```
01  COMPANY-BILLING-SKELETON.
    02  FILLER PIC X(12) VALUE '011500027500'.
    02  FILLER PIC X(12) VALUE '021255023575'.
01  COMPANY-BILLING REDEFINES COMPANY-BILLING-SKELETON.
    02  COMPANY-ELEMENT OCCURS 2 TIMES
                    INDEXED BY COMP-INDEX.
        05  DEPARTMENT-ELEMENT OCCURS 2 TIMES
                        INDEXED BY DEPART-INDEX.
            07  DEPART-NO PIC 9(01).
            07  HOURLY-RATE PIC 9(02)V9(02).
```

To understand how this table works, let us examine in detail the first element of the skeleton, which is:

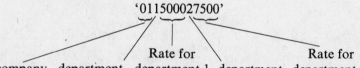

where the first 2 digits, 01, refer to company 1; the next 1, department 1; and the number 5000 (redefined with the PICTURE 99V99, to become 50.00), the rate per hour for department 1 of company 1. Next is 2, for department 2, followed by 7500, which is redefined to be 75.00.

Similarly, the second element of the skeleton,

'021255023575'

spells out in detail the rates of pay for company 2, departments 1 and 2.

The input to the program consists of the company number, the department number, and the number of hours to be billed.

In order to access the appropriate rate of pay, we make a search of the table to match the incoming company number with the company number in the table. Once the match has been made a second search is conducted to locate the correct department number within the company. Once this second search is successful the corresponding rate of pay is accessed, and then it is multiplied by the number of hours worked (from the input data) to compute the charge.

Humans, being so fallible, might possibly mistype the incoming data. If, say, the input refers to a company numbered 03, obviously this would be in error. Similarly, if a department were specified that was neither 1 or 2, it, too, would be in error. Should the company number be in error there would be little point in searching for the department number because it could not exist. Therefore a test is made before the second search to detect whether an error was found in the first one. If an error was found, a message is printed. Should the first search succeed but the second fail, the error message is printed for this case, too.

Input for Program 35

```
02      2       1000
01      1       2525
02      1       4000
```

01	2	1550
01	1	4200
01	1	1250
02	1	3500
02	2	7500
02	2	1325
03	5	1200
02	1	1230
01	1	1425
01	2	1755
02	1	3620
01	1	1250
02	01	1240
01	2	2575
02	2	3300
01	1	4500
01	2	1250
01	3	1200
02	1	1100
02	1	4000
01	1	2500
02	2	3000
02	1	3000

Program 35

```
1       IDENTIFICATION  DIVISION.
2       PROGRAM-ID.     BILLING.
3       AUTHOR.         IRVIN POREMBA.
4       INSTALLATION.   NYU.
5       DATE-WRITTEN.   JUNE 24, 1982.
6       DATE-COMPILED.  JUNE 24, 1982.
7       SECURITY.       HENRY MULLISH.
8       * * * * * * * * * * * * * * * * * * * * * * * * * * * * * * * * * * * * * * * * * * * * * * *
9       *       THIS PROGRAM READS IN DATA CARDS PUNCHED:                          *
10      *                                                                          *
11      *       COLUMNS    1-2: COMPANY NUMBER                                     *
12      *       COLUMN       5: DEPARTMENT NUMBER                                  *
13      *       COLUMNS 10-13: HOURS WORKED                                        *
14      *                                                                          *
15      *       THIS PROGRAM FINDS THE RATE OF PAY FOR                            *
16      *       THE COMPANY AND DEPARTMENT AND COMPUTES                           *
17      *       A BILL FOR THE SERVICES GIVEN TO THE DEPARTMENT                   *
18      *       AND AT THE END A GRAND TOTAL FOR ALL BILLING                      *
19      *       IS PRINTED OUT.                                                    *
20      * * * * * * * * * * * * * * * * * * * * * * * * * * * * * * * * * * * * * * * * * * * * * * *
21
22      ENVIRONMENT DIVISION.
23      CONFIGURATION SECTION.
24      SOURCE-COMPUTER. CYBER-170-720.
25      OBJECT-COMPUTER. CYBER-170-720.
26      SPECIAL-NAMES.
27      INPUT-OUTPUT SECTION.
28      FILE-CONTROL.
29          SELECT IN-FILE ASSIGN TO INPUT.
30          SELECT OUT-FILE ASSIGN TO OUTPUT.
31
32      DATE DIVISION.
33      FILE SECTION.
34
35      FD  IN-FILE
36          LABEL RECORDS ARE OMITTED.
37
38      01  RECORD-IN.
39          02   COMPANY        PIC 9(02).
40          02   FILLER         PIC X(02).
41          02   DEPARTMENT     PIC 9(01).
42          02   FILLER         PIX X(04).
43          02   HOURS-WORKED   PIC 9(02)V9(02).
44          02   FILLER         PIC X(66).
45
46      FD  OUT-FILE
```

```
47              LABEL RECORDS ARE OMITTED.
48
49     01    LINE-OUT                    PIC X(133).
50
51     WORKING-STORAGE SECTION.
52
53     01    INDEPENDENT-ITEMS-USED.
54           02    ANY-MORE-CARDS       PIC X(03) VALUE 'YES'.
55           02    BILL                 PIC 9(04)V9(02).
56           02    CARD-COUNT           PIC 9(04) VALUE ZEROS.
57           02    CARD-COUNT-2         PIC 99 VALUE ZEROS.
58           02    CARD-FLAG            PIC 99 VALUE 20.
59           02    ERROR-FLAG           PIC X(03).
60           02    GRAND-BILL           PIC 9(08)V9(02) VALUE ZERO.
61           02    PAGE-COUNT           PIC 999 VALUE ZEROS.
62
63
64     01    COMPANY-BILLING-SKELETON.
65           02    FILLER               PIC X(12) VALUE '011500027500'.
66           02    FILLER               PIC X(12) VALUE '021255023575'.
67
68     01    COMPANY-BILLING REDEFINES COMPANY-BILLING-SKELETON.
69           02    COMPANY-ELEMENT OCCURS 2 TIMES
70                                  INDEXED BY COMP-INDEX.
71                 05 COMPANY-NO        PIC 9(02).
72                 05 DEPARTMENT-ELEMENT OCCURS 2 TIMES
73                                  INDEXED BY DEPART-INDEX.
74                 07 DEPART-NO         PIC 9(01).
75                 07 HOURLY-RATE       PIC 9(02)V9(02).
76
77     01    HEADER-1.
78           02    FILLER               PIC X(06) VALUE 'PAGE'.
79           02    PAGE-COUNT-OUT       PIC ZZ9.
80           02    FILLER               PIC X(13) VALUE SPACES.
81           02    FILLER               PIC X(16) VALUE 'MONTHLY BILLING'.
82           02    FILLER               PIC X(10) VALUE 'FOR COBOL'.
83           02    FILLER               PIC X(11) VALUE 'CONSULTANTS'.
84
85     01    HEADER-2.
86           02    FILLER               PIC X(01) VALUE SPACES.
87           02    FILLER               PIC X(08) VALUE ALL '*'.
88           02    FILLER               PIC X(13) VALUE SPACES.
89           02    FILLER               PIC X(37) VALUE ALL '*'.
90
91     01    HEADER-3.
92           02    FILLER               PIC X(08) VALUE SPACES.
93           02    FILLER               PIC X(07) VALUE 'CARD'.
94           02    FILLER               PIC X(09) VALUE 'COMPANY'.
95           02    FILLER               PIC X(12) VALUE 'DEPARTMENT'.
96           02    FILLER               PIC X(09) VALUE 'HOURLY'.
97           02    FILLER               PIC X(10) VALUE 'HOURS'.
98           02    FILLER               PIC X(03) VALUE 'NET'.
99
100    01    HEADER-4.
101          02    FILLER               PIC X(08) VALUE SPACES.
102          02    FILLER               PIC X(09) VALUE 'COUNT'.
103          02    FILLER               PIC X(09) VALUE 'NAME'.
104          02    FILLER               PIC X(11) VALUE 'NUMBER'.
105          02    FILLER               PIC X(07) VALUE 'RATE'.
106          02    FILLER               PIC X(11) VALUE 'WORKED'.
107          02    FILLER               PIC X(04) VALUE 'BILL'.
108
109    01    HEADER-5.
110          02    FILLER               PIC X(08) VALUE SPACES.
111          02    FILLER               PIC X(05) VALUE ALL '*'.
112          02    FILLER               PIC X(02) VALUE SPACES.
113          02    FILLER               PIC X(07) VALUE ALL '*'.
114          02    FILLER               PIC X(02) VALUE SPACES.
115          02    FILLER               PIC X(02) VALUE SPACES.
116          02    FILLER               PIC X(06) VALUE ALL '*'.
117          02    FILLER               PIC X(02) VALUE SPACES.
118          02    FILLER               PIC X(06) VALUE ALL '*'.
119          02    FILLER               PIC X(02) VALUE SPACES.
120          02    FILLER               PIC X(09) VALUE ALL '*'.
121
122    01    DETAIL-LINE.
```

```
123        02    FILLER               PIC X(08) VALUE SPACES.
124        02    CARD-COUNT-OUT       PIC Z,ZZ9.
125        02    FILLER               PIC X(02) VALUE SPACES.
126        02    COMPANY-OUT          PIC X(07).
127        02    FILLER               PIC X(06) VALUE SPACES.
128        02    DEPART-NO-OUT        PIC 9(01).
129        02    FILLER               PIC X(07) VALUE SPACES.
130        02    HOURLY-RATE-OUT      PIC $$9.99.
131        02    FILLER               PIC X(02) VALUE SPACES.
132        02    HOUR-WORKED-OUT      PIC Z9.99.
133        02    FILLER               PIC X(03) VALUE SPACES.
134        02    BILL-OUT             PIC $$,$$9.99.
135
136   01   TOTAL-LINE.
137        02    FILLER               PIC X(05) VALUE SPACES.
138        02    FILLER               PIC X(17) VALUE 'TOTAL OF BILLS:'.
139        02    GRAND-BILL-OUT       PIC $$$,$$$,$$9.99.
140
141   PROCEDURE DIVISION.
142
143   MAIN-LINE-ROUTINE.
144        PERFORM OPEN-FILES.
145        PERFORM NEW-PAGE.
146        PERFORM START-UP.
147        PERFORM PROCESS-DATA UNTIL ANY-MORE-CARDS EQUAL 'NO'.
148        PERFORM CLOSE-UP.
149        STOP RUN.
150
151   OPEN-FILES.
152        OPEN INPUT IN-FILE.
153        OPEN OUTPUT OUT-FILE.
154
155   NEW-PAGE.
156        MOVE SPACES TO LINE-OUT.
157        WRITE LINE-OUT AFTER PAGE.
158
159   START-UP.
160        READ IN-FILE AT END MOVE 'NO' TO ANY-MORE-CARDS
161             MOVE ' **NO DATA IN DECK**' TO LINE-OUT
162             WRITE LINE-OUT AFTER 30.
163        IF ANY-MORE-CARDS EQUAL 'YES' PERFORM WRITE-HEADINGS.
164
165   PROCESS-DATA.
166        IF CARD-COUNT-2 EQUAL CARD-FLAG PERFORM NEW-PAGE
167             MOVE ZEROS TO CARD-COUNT-2
168             PERFORM WRITE-HEADINGS.
169        ADD 1 TO CARD-COUNT, CARD-COUNT-2.
170        PERFORM SEARCH-RATE.
171        READ IN-FILE AT END PERFORM TOTAL-PARA
172        READ IN-FILE AT END PERFORM TOTAL-PARA
173             MOVE 'NO' TO ANY-MORE-CARDS.
174
175   CLOSE-UP.
176        CLOSE IN-FILE, OUT-FILE.
177
178   SEARCH-RATE.
179        MOVE 'NO' TO ERROR-FLAG.
180        SET COMP-INDEX TO 1.
181        SET DEPART-INDEX TO 1.
182        SEARCH COMPANY-ELEMENT AT END PERFORM ERROR-PARA
183        WHEN COMPANY-NO (COMP-INDEX) = COMPANY
184             NEXT SENTENCE.
185        IF ERROR-FLAG EQUAL 'NO' SEARCH DEPARTMENT-ELEMENT
186             AT END PERFORM ERROR-PARA
187        WHEN DEPART-NO (COMP-INDEX, DEPART-INDEX) = DEPARTMENT
188             PERFORM COMPUTE-PAY.
189
190   COMPUTE-PAY.
191        MULTIPLY HOURS-WORKED BY
192             HOURLY-RATE (COMP-INDEX, DEPART-INDEX) GIVING
193             BILL ROUNDED.
194        ADD BILL TO GRAND-BILL.
195        MOVE CARD-COUNT TO CARD-COUNT-OUT.
196        PERFORM DECODE.
197        MOVE DEPARTMENT TO DEPART-NO-OUT.
198        MOVE HOURS-WORKED TO HOUR-WORKED-OUT.
```

```
199          MOVE BILL TO BILL-OUT.
200          MOVE HOURLY-RATE (COMP-INDEX, DEPART-INDEX)
201          TO HOURLY-RATE-OUT.
202          WRITE LINE-OUT FROM DETAIL-LINE AFTER 2.
203
204     DECODE.
205          IF COMPANY EQUAL 1 MOVE 'ACME' TO COMPANY-OUT
206          ELSE IF COMPANY EQUAL 2 MOVE 'COMPUTE' TO COMPANY-OUT.
207
208     TOTAL-PARA.
209          MOVE GRAND-BILL TO GRAND-BILL-OUT.
210          PERFORM NEW-PAGE.
211          WRITE LINE-OUT FROM TOTAL-LINE AFTER 30.
212
213     WRITE-HEADINGS.
214          ADD 1 TO PAGE-COUNT.
215          MOVE PAGE-COUNT TO PAGE-COUNT-OUT.
216          WRITE LINE-OUT FROM HEADER-1 AFTER 1.
217          WRITE LINE-OUT FROM HEADER-2 AFTER 1.
218          WRITE LINE-OUT FROM HEADER-2 AFTER 1.
219          WRITE LINE-OUT FROM HEADER-3 AFTER 2.
220          WRITE LINE-OUT FROM HEADER-4 AFTER 1.
221          WRITE LINE-OUT FROM HEADER-5 AFTER 1.
222
223     ERROR-PARA.
224          MOVE 'YES' TO ERROR-FLAG.
225          MOVE 'ERROR IN DATA' TO LINE-OUT.
226          WRITE LINE-OUT AFTER 2.
```

Output for Program 35

PAGE 1   MONTHLY BILLING FOR COBOL CONSULTANTS

* * * * * * * * * *

* * * * * * * * * *

CARD COUNT	COMPANY NAME	DEPARTMENT NUMBER	HOURLY RATE	HOURS WORKED	NET BILL
* * * * *	* * * * * * *	* * * * * * * * * *	* * * * * *	* * * * * *	* * * * * * * * *
1	COMPUTE	2	$35.75	10.00	$357.50
2	ACME	1	$50.00	25.25	$1,262.50
3	COMPUTE	1	$25.50	40.00	$1,020.00
4	ACME	2	$75.00	15.50	$1,162.50
5	ACME	1	$50.00	42.00	$2,100.00
6	ACME	1	$50.00	12.50	$625.00
7	COMPUTE	1	$25.50	35.00	$892.50
8	COMPUTE	2	$35.75	75.00	$2,681.25
9	COMPUTE	2	$35.75	13.25	$473.69
ERROR IN DATA					
11	COMPUTE	1	$25.50	12.30	$313.65
12	ACME	1	$50.00	14.25	$712.50
13	ACME	2	$75.00	17.55	$1,316.25
14	COMPUTE	1	$25.50	36.20	$923.10
15	ACME	1	$50.00	12.50	$625.00
ERROR IN DATA					
17	ACME	2	$75.00	25.75	$1,931.25
18	COMPUTE	2	$35.75	33.00	$1,179.75
19	ACME	1	$50.00	45.00	$2,250.00
20	ACME	2	$75.00	12.50	$937.50

PAGE 2   MONTHLY BILLING FOR COBOL CONSULTANTS

* * * * * * * * * *

* * * * * * * * * *

CARD COUNT	COMPANY NAME	DEPARTMENT NUMBER	HOURLY RATE	HOURS WORKED	NET BILL
* * * * *	* * * * * * *	* * * * * * * * * *	* * * * * *	* * * * * *	* * * * * * * * *
ERROR IN DATA					
22	COMPUTE	1	$25.50	11.00	$280.50
23	COMPUTE	1	$25.50	40.00	$1,020.00
24	ACME	1	$50.00	25.00	$1,250.00
25	COMPUTE	2	$35.75	30.00	$1,072.50
26	COMPUTE	1	$25.50	30.00	$765.00

TOTAL OF BILLS: $25,151.94

10.10 Triple-Dimensioned Tables

As mentioned earlier, COBOL permits a maximum of 3 levels in a single table. The purpose of the next program is to illustrate how such a table is handled.

Let us assume that all colleges have been categorized according to their level of difficulty. Let category 1 be the lowest level and category 5 the highest. Now within each category (level) we wish to refer to each of the 4 years of attendance: freshman, sophomore, junior, and senior. Within each year we have 2 semesters: fall and spring. Thus we have a table composed of 3 different levels.

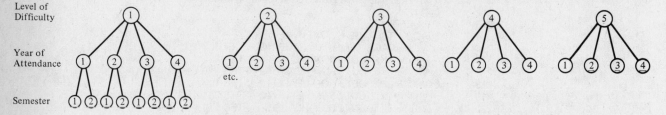

Suppose now that a foundation anxious to encourage higher education sets up a National Scholarship Payment Account to assist selected students (possibly those studying COBOL) in meeting their financial obligations according to the level of difficulty of the school in attendance, the year of attendance, and the particular semester currently being attended. The table of financial assistance may be expressed graphically as follows.

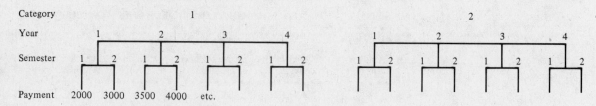

or in tabular form.

	COLLEGE CATEGORY				
	1	2	3	4	5
FRESHMAN					
Fall	$2,000	$2550	$3575	$4435	$4850
Spring	3,000	3100	3750	4500	5000
SOPHOMORE					
Fall	3,500	3770	3975	4700	5100
Spring	4,000	4150	4375	4955	5225
JUNIOR					
Fall	4,350	4400	4500	5000	5375
Spring	4,875	4965	5050	5229	5495
SENIOR					
Fall	5,000	5125	5200	5395	5600
Spring	5,200	5250	5300	5550	5856

The program has been set up to allow for up to 99 different categories of college. Here is how such a triple-level table is set up in COBOL.

```
01   SCHOLARSHIP-RATE-SKELETON.
     02    FILLER              PIC X(46) VALUE
     '01112000230002135002400031435024875415000025200'.
     02    FILLER              PIC X(46) VALUE
     '05114850250002151002522531537525495415600025856'.
     02    FILLER              PIC X(46) VALUE
     '04114435245002147002495531500025229415395525550'.
     02    FILLER              PIC X(46) VALUE
     '03113575237502139752437531450025050415200025300'.
     02    FILLER              PIC X(46) VALUE
     '02112550231002137702415031440024965415125525250'.
```

```
01   SCHOLARSHIP-RATE REDEFINES SCHOLARSHIP-RATE-SKELETON.
   02   COLLEGE-ELEMENT OCCURS 5 TIMES INDEXED BY COLLEGE-INDEX.
      03   T-COLLEGE        PIC 9(02).
      03   CLASS-ELEMENT OCCURS 4 TIMES INDEXED BY CLASS-INDEX.
         05   T-CLASS       PIC 9(01).
         05   SEMESTER-ELEMENT OCCURS 2 TIMES
                            INDEXED BY SEM-INDEX.
            07  T-SEMESTER PIC 9(01).
            07  T-RATE        PIC 9(04).
```

To understand the table skeleton, we would find it helpful to examine the first entry that identifies the college categories.

```
    Freshman        Sophomore        Junior          Senior
       |                |               |               |
       |                |               |               |
'0 1 1 1 2 0 0 0 2 3 0 0 0 2 1 3 5 0 0 2 4 0 0 0 3 1 4 3 5 0 2 4 8 7 5 4 1 5 0 0 0 2 5 2 0 0'
    /     | Pymt |  Pymt    |  Pymt  |  Pymt    |  Pymt  |  Pymt    |  Pymt  |  Pymt
   /      |      |          |        |          |        |          |        |
College  Fall    Spring     Fall    Spring     Fall    Spring     Fall    Spring
```

For each different level there must be a different table index. These are COLLEGE-INDEX, CLASS-INDEX, and SEM-INDEX in the program. If COLLEGE-INDEX has a value of 1, CLASS-INDEX has a value of 3, and SEM-INDEX has a value of 2, the appropriate payment of $4875 may be selected.

Input for Program 36

PAULINE LANDAU	0411
JULIO BARRNECHE	0121
JIM PORETTA	0322
VLADIMIR KRIMNUS	0511
CALVIN YEE	0522
LENNY FRENANDEZ	0311
JOSEPH KWOK	0131
SIMONE ZAPUN	0321
MERI COHEN	0111
SABRINA ELLIS	0312
JO HERRIOT	0222
MITCHELL NUSBAUM	0241
PETER SWIDERSKI	0432
GEORGE BARROW	0342
IRVIN POREMBA	0542
STANLEY YOUNG	0422
DEBBIE TURNER	0212
JOHN KESICH	0221
KORMAN SHEDLO	0142

Program 36

```
1       IDENTIFICATION   DIVISION.
2       PROGRAM-ID.      THREE-LEVEL-TABLE.
3       AUTHOR.          IRVIN POREMBA.
4       INSTALLATION.    NYU.
5       DATE-WRITTEN.    APRIL 25, 1982.
6       DATE-COMPILED.   MAY 6, 1982.
7       SECURITY.        HENRY MULLISH.
8       ***********************************************************************
9       *    THIS PROGRAM READS IN DATA CARDS PUNCHED:                       *
10      *                                                                    *
11      *    COLUMNS  1-25: STUDENT NAME                                     *
12      *    COLUMNS 31-32: TYPE OF COLLEGE                                  *
13      *    COLUMN     33: CLASS (1-FRESHMAN, 2-SOPHOMORE,                  *
14      *                          3-JUNIOR, 4-SENIOR)                       *
15      *    COLUMN     34: SEMESTER (1-FALL, 2-SPRING)                      *
16      *                                                                    *
17      *    THIS PROGRAM PRINTS OUT THE SCHOLARSHIP PAYMENT                 *
18      *    THAT A STUDENT RECEIVES ACCORDING TO THE                        *
19      *    STUDENT'S TYPE OF COLLEGE, CLASS, AND THE                       *
20      *    SEMESTER THAT THE STUDENT IS CURRENTLY IN.                      *
21      ***********************************************************************
```

```
22
23     ENVIRONMENT DIVISION.
24     CONFIGURATION SECTION.
25     SOURCE-COMPUTER. CYBER-170-720.
26     OBJECT-COMPUTER. CYBER-170-720.
27     SPECIAL-NAMES.
28     INPUT-OUTPUT SECTION.
29     FILE-CONTROL.
30         SELECT IN-FILE ASSIGN TO INPUT.
31         SELECT OUT-FILE ASSIGN TO OUTPUT.
32     DATA DIVISION.
33     FILE SECTION.
34
35     FD   IN-FILE
36         LABEL RECORDS ARE OMITTED.
37
38     01   RECORD-IN.
39         02   STUDENT-NAME          PIC X(25).
40         02   FILLER                PIC X(05).
41         02   COLLEGE               PIC 9(02).
42         02   CLASS                 PIC 9(01).
43         02   SEMESTER              PIC 9(01).
44         02   FILLER                PIC X(46).
45
46     FD   OUT-FILE
47         LABEL RECORDS ARE OMITTED.
48
49     01   LINE-OUT                  PIC X(133).
50
51     WORKING-STORAGE SECTION.
52
53     01   INDEPENDENT-ITEMS-USED.
54         02   ANY-MORE-CARDS        PIC X(03) VALUE 'YES'.
55         02   CARD-COUNT            PIC 9(04) VALUE ZERO.
56         02   CARD-COUNT-2          PIC 9(02) VALUE ZERO.
57         02   PAGE-COUNT            PIC 9(03) VALUE ZERO.
58         02   TOTAL-PAYMENT         PIC 9(07) VALUE ZERO.
59         02   1-SEARCH-ERROR        PIC X(03).
60         02   2-SEARCH-ERROR        PIC X(03).
61
62     01   SCHOLARSHIP-RATE-SKELETON.
63         02   FILLER                PIC X(46) VALUE
64     '0111200023000213500240003143502487541500025200'.
65         02   FILLER                PIC X(46) VALUE
66     '0511485025000215100252225315375254954156002856'.
67         02   FILLER                PIC X(46) VALUE
68     '0411443524500214700249553150002522941539525550'.
69         02   FILLER                PIC X(46) VALUE
70     '0311357523750213975243753145002505041520025300'.
71         02   FILLER                PIC X(46) VALUE
72     '0211255023100213770241503144002496541512525250'.
73
74     01   SCHOLARSHIP-RATE REDEFINES SCHOLARSHIP-RATE-SKELETON.
75         02   COLLEGE-ELEMENT OCCURS 5 TIMES INDEXED BY COLLEGE-INDEX.
76             03  T-COLLEGE         PIC 9(02).
77             03  CLASS-ELEMENT OCCURS 4 TIMES INDEXED BY CLASS-INDEX.
78                 05  T-CLASS       PIC 9(01).
79                 05  SEMESTER-ELEMENT OCCURS 2 TIMES
80                                   INDEXED BY SEM-INDEX.
81                     07  T-SEMESTER PIC 9(01).
82                     07  T-RATE    PIC 9(04).
83
84     01   HEADER-1.
85         02   FILLER                PIC X(01) VALUE SPACES.
86         02   FILLER                PIC X(05) VALUE 'PAGE'.
87         02   PAGE-COUNT-OUT        PIC ZZ9.
88         02   FILLER                PIC X(10) VALUE SPACES.
89         02   FILLER                PIC X(09) VALUE 'NATIONAL'.
90         02   FILLER                PIC X(12) VALUE 'SCHOLARSHIP'.
91         02   FILLER                PIC X(15) VALUE 'PAYMENT ACCOUNT'.
92
93     01   HEADER-2.
94         02   FILLER                PIC X(01) VALUE SPACES.
95         02   FILLER                PIC X(08) VALUE ALL '*'.
96         02   FILLER                PIC X(10) VALUE SPACES.
```

```
 97            02    FILLER              PIC X(36) VALUE ALL '*'.
 98
 99     01    HEADER-3.
100            02    FILLER              PIC X(01) VALUE SPACES.
101            02    FILLER              PIC X(17) VALUE 'CARD'.
102            02    FILLER              PIC X(19) VALUE 'STUDENT'.
103            02    FILLER              PIC X(11) VALUE 'COLLEGE'.
104            02    FILLER              PIC X(10) VALUE 'CLASS'.
105            02    FILLER              PIC X(11) VALUE 'SEMESTER'.
106            02    FILLER              PIC X(11) VALUE 'SCHOLARSHIP'.
107
108     01    HEADER-4.
109            02    FILLER              PIC X(01) VALUE SPACES.
110            02    FILLER              PIC X(18) VALUE 'COUNT'.
111            02    FILLER              PIC X(19) VALUE 'NAME'.
112            02    FILLER              PIC X(11) VALUE 'RANK'.
113            02    FILLER              PIC X(11) VALUE 'RANK'.
114            02    FILLER              PIC X(11) VALUE 'YEAR'.
115            02    FILLER              PIC X(07) VALUE 'PAYMENT'.
116
117     01    HEADER-5.
118            02    FILLER              PIC X(01) VALUE SPACES.
119            02    FILLER              PIC X(05) VALUE ALL '-'.
120            02    FILLER              PIC X(03) VALUE SPACES.
121            02    FILLER              PIC X(25) VALUE ALL '-'.
122            02    FILLER              PIC X(03) VALUE SPACES.
123            02    FILLER              PIC X(07) VALUE ALL '-'.
124            02    FILLER              PIC X(03) VALUE SPACES.
125            02    FILLER              PIC X(08) VALUE ALL '-'.
126            02    FILLER              PIC X(03) VALUE SPACES.
127            02    FILLER              PIC X(08) VALUE ALL '-'.
128            02    FILLER              PIC X(03) VALUE SPACES.
129            02    FILLER              PIC X(11) VALUE ALL '-'.
130
131     01    DETAIL-LINE.
132            02    FILLER              PIC X(01) VALUE SPACES.
133            02    CARD-COUNT-OUT      PIC Z,ZZ9.
134            02    FILLER              PIC X(03) VALUE SPACES.
135            02    STUDENT-NAME-OUT    PIC X(25).
136            02    FILLER              PIC X(06) VALUE SPACES.
137            02    COLLEGE-OUT         PIC 9(01).
138            02    FILLER              PIC X(06) VALUE SPACES.
139            02    CLASS-OUT           PIC X(08).
140            02    FILLER              PIC X(04) VALUE SPACES.
141            02    SEMESTER-OUT        PIC X(06).
142            02    FILLER              PIC X(05) VALUE SPACES.
143            02    PAYMENT-OUT         PIC $$,$$9.00.
144
145     01    TOTAL-LINE.
146            02    FILLER              PIC X(01) VALUE SPACES.
147            02    FILLER              PIC X(18) VALUE 'TOTAL SCHOLARSHIP'.
148            02    FILLER              PIC X(20) VALUE 'AMOUNT IN DOLLARS:'.
149            02    TOTAL-PAYMENT-OUT PIC $$,$$$,$$9.00.
150
151     01    ERROR-LINE.
152            02    FILLER              PIC X(01) VALUE SPACES.
153            02    CARD-COUNT-OUT-2    PIC Z,ZZ9.
154            02    FILLER              PIC X(03) VALUE SPACES.
155            02    MESSAGE-OUT         PIC X(50).
156            02    FILLER              PIC X(01) VALUE SPACES.
157            02    ERROR-OUT           PIC X(02).
158
159     PROCEDURE DIVISION.
160
161     MAIN-LINE-ROUTINE.
162            PERFORM OPEN-FILES.
163            PERFORM NEW-PAGE.
164            PERFORM START-UP.
165            PERFORM PROCESS-DATA UNTIL ANY-MORE-CARDS EQUAL 'NO'.
166            PERFORM CLOSE-UP.
167            STOP RUN.
168
169     OPEN-FILES.
170            OPEN INPUT IN-FILE.
171            OPEN OUTPUT OUT-FILE.
```

```
172
173    NEW-PAGE.
174        MOVE SPACES TO LINE-OUT.
175        WRITE LINE-OUT AFTER PAGE.
176
177    START-UP.
178        READ IN-FILE AT END MOVE 'NO' TO ANY-MORE-CARDS
179            MOVE ' * *NO DATA IN DECK* *' TO LINE-OUT
180            WRITE LINE-OUT AFTER 30.
181        IF ANY-MORE-CARDS EQUAL 'YES' PERFORM WRITE-HEADINGS.
182
183    PROCESS-DATA.
184        ADD 1 TO CARD-COUNT, CARD-COUNT-2.
185        MOVE 'NO' TO 1-SEARCH-ERROR, 2-SEARCH-ERROR.
186        PERFORM SEARCH-RATE.
187        READ IN-FILE AT END MOVE 'NO' TO ANY-MORE-CARDS
188            PERFORM GRAND-TOTAL
189            MOVE ZEROS TO CARD-COUNT-2.
190        IF CARD-COUNT-2 = 15 MOVE ZEROS TO CARD-COUNT-2
191            PERFORM NEW-PAGE
192            PERFORM WRITE-HEADINGS.
193
194    CLOSE-UP.
195        CLOSE IN-FILE, OUT-FILE.
196
197    GRAND-TOTAL.
198        PERFORM NEW-PAGE.
199        MOVE TOTAL-PAYMENT TO TOTAL-PAYMENT-OUT.
200        WRITE LINE-OUT FROM TOTAL-LINE AFTER 30.
201
202    SEARCH-RATE.
203        SET COLLEGE-INDEX TO 1.
204        SET CLASS-INDEX TO 1.
205        SET SEM-INDEX TO 1.
206        SEARCH COLLEGE-ELEMENT AT END PERFORM ERROR-1
207        WHEN COLLEGE = T-COLLEGE (COLLEGE-INDEX)
208            NEXT SENTENCE.
209        IF 1-SEARCH-ERROR = 'NO'
210            SEARCH CLASS-ELEMENT AT END PERFORM ERROR-2
211            WHEN CLASS = T-CLASS (COLLEGE-INDEX, CLASS-INDEX)
212                NEXT SENTENCE.
213        IF 1-SEARCH-ERROR = 'NO' AND 2-SEARCH-ERROR = 'NO'
214            SEARCH SEMESTER-ELEMENT AT END PERFORM ERROR-3
215            WHEN SEMESTER = T-SEMESTER
216                (COLLEGE-INDEX, CLASS-INDEX, SEM-INDEX)
217                PERFORM WRITE-IT.
218
219    WRITE-IT.
220        MOVE T-RATE (COLLEGE-INDEX, CLASS-INDEX, SEM-INDEX)
221            TO PAYMENT-OUT.
222        ADD T-RATE (COLLEGE-INDEX, CLASS-INDEX, SEM-INDEX)
223            TO TOTAL-PAYMENT.
224        MOVE CARD-COUNT TO CARD-COUNT-OUT.
225        MOVE STUDENT-NAME TO STUDENT-NAME-OUT.
226        MOVE COLLEGE TO COLLEGE-OUT.
227        PERFORM DECODE.
228        WRITE LINE-OUT FROM DETAIL-LINE AFTER 2.
229
230    DECODE.
231        IF CLASS = 1 MOVE 'FRESHMAN' TO CLASS-OUT
232        ELSE IF CLASS = 2 MOVE 'SOPHOMORE' TO CLASS-OUT
233            ELSE IF CLASS = 3 MOVE 'JUNIOR' TO CLASS-OUT
234                ELSE MOVE 'SENIOR' TO CLASS-OUT.
235        IF SEMESTER = 1 MOVE 'FALL' TO SEMESTER-OUT
236        ELSE MOVE 'SPRING' TO SEMESTER-OUT.
237
238    WRITE-HEADINGS.
239        ADD 1 TO PAGE-COUNT.
240        MOVE PAGE-COUNT TO PAGE-COUNT-OUT.
241        WRITE LINE-OUT FROM HEADER-1 AFTER 1.
242        WRITE LINE-OUT FROM HEADER-2 AFTER 1.
243        WRITE LINE-OUT FROM HEADER-2 AFTER 1.
244        WRITE LINE-OUT FROM HEADER-3 AFTER 2.
245        WRITE LINE-OUT FROM HEADER-4 AFTER 1.
246        WRITE LINE-OUT FROM HEADER-5 AFTER 0.
```

```
247
248     ERROR-1.
249          MOVE 'YES' TO 1-SEARCH-ERROR.
250          MOVE CARD-COUNT TO CARD-COUNT-OUT-2.
251          MOVE 'COLLEGE NUMBER FOUND IN ERROR SEARCH TERMINATED'
252               TO MESSAGE-OUT.
253          MOVE COLLEGE TO ERROR-OUT.
254          WRITE LINE-OUT FROM ERROR-LINE AFTER 2.
255
256     ERROR-2.
257          MOVE 'YES' TO 2-SEARCH-ERROR.
258          MOVE CARD-COUNT TO CARD-COUNT-OUT-2.
259          MOVE 'CLASS NUMBER FOUND IN ERROR SEARCH-TERMINATED'
260               TO MESSAGE-OUT.
261          MOVE CLASS TO ERROR-OUT.
262          WRITE LINE-OUT FROM ERROR-LINE AFTER 2.
263
264     ERROR-3.
265          MOVE CARD-COUNT TO CARD-COUNT-OUT-2.
266          MOVE 'SEMESTER NUMBER FOUND IN ERROR SEARCH TERMINATED'
267               TO MESSAGE-OUT.
268          MOVE SEMESTER TO ERROR-OUT.
269          WRITE LINE-OUT FROM ERROR-LINE AFTER 2.
```

Output for Program 36

PAGE 1 · NATIONAL SCHOLARSHIP PAYMENT ACCOUNT

* * * * * * *   *

* * * * * * *   *

CARD COUNT	STUDENT NAME	COLLEGE RANK	CLASS RANK	SEMESTER YEAR	SCHOLARSHIP PAYMENT
1	PAULINE LANDAU	4	FRESHMAN	FALL	$4,435.00
2	JULIO BARRNECHE	1	SOPHOMORE	FALL	$3,500.00
3	JIM PORETTA	3	SOPHOMORE	SPRING	$4,375.00
4	VLADIMIR KRIMNUS	5	FRESHMAN	FALL	$4,850.00
5	CALVIN YEE	5	SOPHOMORE	SPRING	$5,225.00
6	LENNY FRENANDEZ	3	FRESHMAN	FALL	$3,575.00
7	JOSEPH KWOK	1	JUNIOR	FALL	$4,350.00
8	SIMONE ZAPUN	3	SOPHOMORE	FALL	$3,975.00
9	MERI COHEN	1	FRESHMAN	FALL	$2,000.00
10	SABRINA ELLIS	3	FRESHMAN	SPRING	$3,750.00
11	JO HERRIOT	2	SOPHOMORE	SPRING	$4,150.00
12	MITCHELL NUSBAUM	2	SENIOR	FALL	$5,125.00
13	PETER SWIDERSKI	4	JUNIOR	SPRING	$5,229.00
14	GEORGE BARROW	3	SENIOR	SPRING	$5,300.00
15	IRVIN POREMBA	5	SENIOR	SPRING	$5,856.00

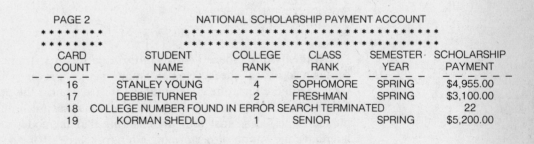

PAGE 2 · NATIONAL SCHOLARSHIP PAYMENT ACCOUNT

* * * * * * *   *

* * * * * * *   *

CARD COUNT	STUDENT NAME	COLLEGE RANK	CLASS RANK	SEMESTER YEAR	SCHOLARSHIP PAYMENT
16	STANLEY YOUNG	4	SOPHOMORE	SPRING	$4,955.00
17	DEBBIE TURNER	2	FRESHMAN	SPRING	$3,100.00
18	COLLEGE NUMBER FOUND IN ERROR SEARCH TERMINATED				22
19	KORMAN SHEDLO	1	SENIOR	SPRING	$5,200.00

TOTAL SCHOLARSHIP AMOUNT IN DOLLARS: $78,950.00

10.11 Reading in a Table from Data Cards

In the previous programs in which the concept of tables was illustrated, the table was explicitly defined in the Data Division with a fixed number of elements. The number of elements coincided exactly with the integer number that was specified in the OCCURS clause.

There are many situations, however, where the number of elements varies over the course of time. An inventory of the types of items sold by a supermarket is one such situation. In these cases the types of items being sold change every week, if not every day.

Instead of modifying the table itself each time a change is made, a table may be read in at execution time. Moreover, one need not know exactly how many elements there are in the table, just an upper bound—some maximum figure—is required.

To illustrate this concept, suppose we assign some 4-digit numeric code to various items of furniture that might be sold in a furniture store. We decide in advance that there will never be more than 999 different items so that 999 is our upper bound. We may now define the table in the Data Division by using a special form of the OCCURS clause designed especially for this purpose. It is:

```
01  FURNITURE-TABLE.
    02  TABLE-ELEMENT OCCURS 1 TO 999 TIMES
                    DEPENDING ON TABLE-COUNT
                    INDEXED BY TABLE-INDEX.
        03  FURN-CODE PIC 9999.
        03  FURN-NAME PIC X(25).
```

where a "trailer-card" bearing the number 9999 in the first 4 positions is placed at the end of the data. Now we proceed with the program.

Input for Program 37

```
0001SOFA
0005HIGH CHAIR
0015LOVE SEAT
0023RECLINER CHAIR
0031BRASS BED
0032BUNKBED
0033PLATFORM BED
0039GLASS COFFEE TABLE
0044OAK WOOD TABLE ENDS
0047FORMICA DINING TABLE
0056TEAK BOOKCASE
0059WALNUT CHEST
0072CHINESE RUG
0075INDOOR-OUTDOOR CARPET
0081OAK WOOD DESK
0082GLASS TOP DESK
0086 DESK CHAIR
0110THREE PIECE COUCH
0112SOFA BED
0234WOOD BURNING FIREPLACE
0357LAWN CHAIRS
9999
```

Initially, the index, TABLE-INDEX, is set to 1. Immediately after each data card is read in, it is checked to determine whether it is the trailer-card. If it is not the trailer-card, the furniture code number is tested against the previous code number to be sure that the cards are in sequence—in this case, ascending order. The first code number is tested against zero. By ensuring that the codes are in sequence, we can later have the option of performing a binary search. If the data card is in order, 1 is added to TABLE-COUNT, the data item in the DEPENDING ON clause. The current value of TABLE-COUNT is tested to make sure it does not exceed 999, the upper bound specified in the OCCURS clause. If this test is also passed, WORK-PARA is performed. This paragraph sets up the table internally, increasing the value of TABLE-INDEX by 1 each time by means of the instruction:

```
SET TABLE-INDEX UP BY 1
```

The READ instruction then reads in the subsequent card. This process is repeated until all the table elements have been read in from data cards; in other words, until the trailer-card is encountered. At this point the table is searched by means of the instruction:

```
PERFORM TABLE-WRITING VARYING TABLE-INDEX FROM 1 BY 1 UNTIL
TABLE-INDEX > TABLE-COUNT
```

which prints out the table.

Program 37

```
1        IDENTIFICATION   DIVISION.
2        PROGRAM-ID.      TABLE-12.
3        AUTHOR.          IRVIN POREMBA.
4        INSTALLATION.    NYU.
5        DATE-WRITTEN.    APRIL 28, 1982.
6        DATE-COMPILED.   APRIL 28, 1982.
7        SECURITY.        HENRY MULLISH.
8
9        * * * * * * * * * * * * * * * * * * * * * * * * * * * * * * * * * * * * * * * * * * * * * *
10       *      THIS PROGRAM READS IN A TABLE. THE DATA CARDS      *
11       *      ARE PUNCHED:                                       *
12       *                                                         *
13       *      COLUMNS  1-4: FURNITURE-CODE                       *
14       *      COLUMNS 5-29: TYPE OF FURNITURE                    *
15       *                                                         *
16       *      THE PROGRAM READS IN THE DATA CARDS AND            *
17       *      CREATES A TABLE. AFTERWARDS THE TABLE IS           *
18       *      PRINTED OUT UNDER A HEADING.                       *
19       * * * * * * * * * * * * * * * * * * * * * * * * * * * * * * * * * * * * * * * * * * * * * *
20
21       ENVIRONMENT DIVISION.
22       CONFIGURATION SECTION.
23       SOURCE-COMPUTER. CYBER-170-720.
24       OBJECT-COMPUTER. CYBER-170-720.
25       SPECIAL-NAMES.
26       INPUT-OUTPUT SECTION.
27       FILE-CONTROL.
28            SELECT IN-FILE ASSIGN TO INPUT.
29            SELECT OUT-FILE ASSIGN TO OUTPUT.
30
31       DATA DIVISION.
32       FILE SECTION.
33
34       FD   IN-FILE
35            LABEL RECORDS ARE OMITTED.
36
37       01   TABLE-IN.
38            02   FURNITURE-CODE        PIC 9999.
39            02   FURNITURE-NAME        PIC X(25).
40
41       FD   OUT-FILE
42            LABEL RECORDS ARE OMITTED.
43
44       01   LINE-OUT                    PIC X(133).
45
46       WORKING-STORAGE SECTION.
47
48       77   MORE-CARDS              PIX X(03) VALUE 'YES'
49       77   FURNITURE-CODE-SAVE     PIC 9999 VALUE ZERO.
50       77   TABLE-COUNT             PIC 9999 VALUE ZERO.
51       77   TABLE-COUNT-2           PIC 99 VALUE ZERO.
52
53       01   FURNITURE-TABLE.
54            02   TABLE-ELEMENT          OCCURS 1 TO 999 TIMES
55                                        DEPENDING ON TABLE-COUNT
56                                        INDEXED BY TABLE-INDEX.
57                 03  FURN-CODE          PIC 9999.
58                 03  FURN-NAME          PIC X(25).
59
60       01   HEADER-1.
61            02   FILLER                 PIC X(13) VALUE SPACES.
```

```
62             02    FILLER                      PIC X(15) VALUE 'FURNITURE TABLE'.
63
64     01    HEADER-2.
65             02    FILLER                      PIC X(13) VALUE SPACES.
66             02    FILLER                      PIC X(15) VALUE ALL ' * '.
67
68     01    HEADER-3.
69             02    FILLER                      PIC X(10) VALUE 'FURNITURE'.
70             02    FILLER                      PIC X(13) VALUE 'CODE'.
71             02    FILLER                      PIC X(14) VALUE 'FURNITURE NAME'.
72
73     01    HEADER-4.
74             02    FILLER                      PIC X(01) VALUE SPACES.
75             02    FILLER                      PIC X(14) VALUE ALL ' * '.
76             02    FILLER                      PIC X(04) VALUE SPACES.
77             02    FILLER                      PIC X(25) VALUE ALL ' * '.
78
79     01    DETAIL-LINE.
80             02    FILLER                      PIC X(06) VALUE SPACES.
81             02    FURNITURE-CODE-OUT   PIC 9999.
82             02    FILLER                      PIC X(09) VALUE SPACES.
83             02    FURNITURE-NAME-OUT   PIC X(25).
84
85     PROCEDURE DIVISION.
86
87     MAIN-LINE-ROUTINE.
88             PERFORM OPEN-FILES.
89             PERFORM NEW-PAGE.
90             PERFORM START-UP.
91             PERFORM PROCESS-DATA UNTIL MORE-CARDS EQUAL 'NO'.
92             PERFORM CLOSE-UP.
93             STOP RUN.
94
95     OPEN-FILES.
96             OPEN INPUT IN-FILE.
97             OPEN OUTPUT OUT-FILE.
98
99     NEW-PAGE.
100            MOVE SPACES TO LINE-OUT.
101            WRITE LINE-OUT AFTER PAGE.
102
103    START-UP.
104            READ IN-FILE AT END MOVE 'NO' TO MORE-CARDS
105                    MOVE '  * * *NO DATA IN DECK * * *' TO LINE-OUT
106                    WRITE LINE-OUT AFTER 30.
107            SET TABLE-INDEX TO 1.
108
109    PROCESS-DATA.
110            IF FURNITURE-CODE = 9999 PERFORM SEARCH-PARA
111            ELSE IF FURNITURE-CODE NOT > FURNITURE-CODE-SAVE
112                    PERFORM ERROR-PARA
113                    ELSE ADD 1 TO TABLE-COUNT
114                        IF TABLE-COUNT > 999 PERFORM TABLE-TOO-LARGE
115                        ELSE PERFORM WORK-PARA.
116
117    CLOSE-UP.
118            CLOSE IN-FILE, OUT-FILE.
119
120    WORK-PARA.
121            MOVE FURNITURE-CODE TO FURN-CODE (TABLE-INDEX).
122            MOVE FURNITURE-NAME TO FURN-NAME (TABLE-INDEX).
123            MOVE FURNITURE-CODE TO FURNITURE-CODE-SAVE.
124            SET TABLE-INDEX UP BY 1.
125            READ IN-FILE AT END PERFORM ERROR-NO-TRAILER.
126
127    SEARCH-PARA.
128            MOVE 'NO' TO MORE-CARDS.
129            PERFORM WRITE-HEADINGS.
130            PERFORM TABLE-WRITING
131                VARYING TABLE-INDEX FROM 1 BY 1
132                    UNTIL TABLE-INDEX > TABLE-COUNT.
133
134    TABLE-WRITING.
```

```
135         ADD 1 TO TABLE-COUNT-2.
136         MOVE FURN-CODE (TABLE-INDEX) TO FURNITURE-CODE-OUT.
137         MOVE FURN-NAME (TABLE-INDEX) TO FURNITURE-NAME-OUT.
138         WRITE LINE-OUT FROM DETAIL-LINE AFTER 2.
139         IF TABLE-COUNT-2 EQUAL 15 MOVE ZEROS TO TABLE-COUNT-2
140             PERFORM NEW-PAGE
141             PERFORM WRITE-HEADINGS.
142
143     WRITE-HEADINGS.
144         WRITE LINE-OUT FROM HEADER-1 AFTER 1.
145         WRITE LINE-OUT FROM HEADER-2 AFTER 1.
146         WRITE LINE-OUT FROM HEADER-2 AFTER 1.
147         WRITE LINE-OUT FROM HEADER-3 AFTER 2.
148         WRITE LINE-OUT FROM HEADER-4 AFTER 1.
149
150     ERROR-NO-TRAILER.
151         MOVE 'NO' TO MORE-CARDS.
152         MOVE ' **NO TRAILER CARD IN DECK, PROGRAM TERMINATED**'
153             TO LINE-OUT.
154         WRITE LINE-OUT AFTER 30.
155
156     ERROR-PARA.
157         MOVE 'NO' TO MORE-CARDS.
158         MOVE ' **DATA CARD NOT IN SEQUENCE, PROGRAM TERMINATED**'
159             TO LINE-OUT.
160         WRITE LINE-OUT AFTER 30.
161
162
163     TABLE-TOO-LARGE.
164         MOVE 'NO' TO MORE-CARDS.
165         MOVE ' **TABLE ITEMS EXCEEDS 999, PROGRAM TERMINATED**'
166             TO LINE-OUT.
167         WRITE LINE-OUT AFTER 30.
```

Output for Program 37

```
                        FURNITURE TABLE
                        * * * * * * * * * * *
                        * * * * * * * * * *

      FURNITURE CODE                    FURNITURE NAME
      * * * * * * * * * * *             * * * * * * * * * *
            0001                        SOFA
            0005                        HIGH CHAIR
            0015                        LOVE SEAT
            0023                        RECLINER CHAIR
            0031                        BRASS BED
            0032                        BUNKBED
            0033                        PLATFORM BED
            0039                        GLASS COFFEE TABLE
            0044                        OAK WOOD TABLE ENDS
            0047                        FORMICA DINING TABLE
            0056                        TEAK BOOKCASE
            0059                        WALNUT CHEST
            0072                        CHINESE RUG
            0075                        INDOOR-OUTDOOR CARPET
            0081                        OAK WOOD DESK
```

```
                        FURNITURE TABLE
                        * * * * * * * * * * *
                        * * * * * * * * * *

      FURNITURE CODE                    FURNITURE NAME
      * * * * * * * * * * *             * * * * * * * * * *
            0082                        GLASS TOP DESK
            0086                        DESK CHAIR
            0110                        THREE PIECE COUCH
            0112                        SOFA BED
            0234                        WOOD BURNING FIREPLACE
            0357                        LAWN CHAIRS
```

Review Questions

1. What is the maximum number of levels permitted in a table in COBOL?
2. What is the role played by the OCCURS clause?
3. What role does the REDEFINES clause play in tables?
4. Is it possible to add to an index-name?
5. What is necessary in order for the SEARCH verb to be used?
6. What is the difference between SEARCH and SEARCH ALL?
7. If a binary search is required, what must be present in the table elements?
8. What is the difference between subscripting and indexing?

Exercises

1. The Lobbus Manufacturing Co., Inc. records on 80-column cards each sale as follows.

Column 1–5	salesman number
6–8	product number
13–18	quantity sold
19–26	total sale price 9(6)V99

The product number, together with its associated manufacturer's cost per unit item, is stored in a table.

Write a program that prints a listing, one line per card, showing salesman number, product number, quantity sold, manufacturer's cost (quantity sold times cost per item), sales price, and net profit on loss per sale. For each salesman, a total line should be printed showing total quantity, total sales, and total profit or loss. Finally, a grand total line should be printed showing the total quantity sold, total of sales, and total profit or loss. Assume that the input deck is sorted in order of salesman number.

Table of Unit Costs

PRODUCT NUMBER	COST PER UNIT ITEM
001	00.019
005	00.912
011	01.622
019	04.915
077	00.125
078	00.115
084	08.652
100	10.115
125	02.225
350	05.350
412	05.500

2. A local philanthropist in a moment of extreme gratitude to his alma mater decided to contribute toward the tuition costs of each paying student in the current academic year according to the following scheme.

STUDENT	PERCENT
Freshmen	20
Sophomores	18
Juniors	12
Seniors	10
Graduates	15
Doctoral candidates	40

For each student a card is punched in the following way.

columns 1–25	student's name
30–38	Social Security number
40	academic category (1 = freshmen...
	6 = doctoral candidates)
46–55	student's address
70–73	regular annual fees 9(4)

Write a COBOL program that uses a table to print a listing made up of

a. edited card count (assume about 10,000 students are registered)
b. student's name
c. student's address
d. academic category (freshmen,... doctoral candidate)
e. Social Security number with 2 blanks as separators
f. percentage reduction
g. regular annual fees (edited)
h. amount of discount (edited)
i. balance to be paid by student (edited)
j. In the middle of the next new page the edited total amount to be paid by the benefactor should be printed, together with some pertinent comments about how much the efforts are appreciated, how long he or she will be remembered with esteem in the halls of academia...

3. Write a COBOL program to process a payroll file composed of data cards punched according to the format shown here.

col 1–25	name of employee
30–31	number of dependents
50–54	gross pay (999V99)

A table should be set up in memory (details follow the statement of this problem). It shows the tax rates for all employees, depending on the number of dependents. For each employee calculate the amount of withholding tax and the net pay after deducting the tax from the gross pay. The tax is computed by multiplying the gross pay by the tax rate. Keep a count of the cards and print out the following.

a. the card sequence number (edited)
b. the name of employee
c. the gross pay (edited)
d. the number of dependents (edited)
e. the applicable tax rate (edited)
f. the amount of tax (edited)
g. the net pay (edited)

If the number of dependents is less than 1 or greater than 10, display an error message but continue processing.

As an additional exercise on a separate page print the total gross pay, total tax withheld, and total net pay for the whole file of cards.

Tax Rate Based on Dependents

NUMBER OF DEPENDENTS	TAX RATE (PERCENT)
1	10.00
2	7.00
3	5.90
4	5.00
5	4.30
6	3.85
7	3.30
8	2.90
9	2.60
10 or more	2.35

4. An enterprising magazine distributor offers his customers a set rate for subscriptions to 10 leading magazines. If the subscription is for a period of 3 years or more the customer gets a 30% reduction. Here are the names of the magazines and the relevant details.

Business Week	BSW	$30.00
Fortune	FT	35.00
Forbes	FRB	35.00
Electronic News	EN	28.00
Barron's	BRN	40.00
Newsweek	NSWK	23.00
Time	TM	25.00
TV Guide	TVG	16.00
Creative Computing	CC	28.00
Playboy	PLBY	18.00

Each customer card is punched as follows.

col 1–30	customer name
35–38	magazine code
40–41	number of years of subscription

Set up a table to enable a report to be printed with all the available information.

5. A car rental firm sets up the following charges for renting automobiles.

MAKE OF CAR	CODE NUMBER FOR CAR	RATE PER DAY ($)
Oldsmobile	216	25.00
Pontiac	711	20.50
Porsche	482	50.00
Mercedes	009	50.00
Cadillac	332	30.00
Dodge	486	15.00
Plymouth	219	12.00
Chrysler	111	17.50
Chevrolet	443	11.95
Buick	592	13.45
Datsun	123	9.95
Toyota	456	10.50
Rolls-Royce	246	65.00

When a customer returns a car an input record is composed as shown.

col 1–25	customer name
30–32	code number for make of car rented
40–43	number of days rented

Write a program containing a table that is accessed by the code number on each data record. The input records should be counted and all the relevant information should be printed in a neat report, which should include:
a. the card count
b. the name of the customer
c. the make of the car
d. the code of the car
e. the rate per day
f. the number of days the car is rented
g. the charge for rental

On a separate page the total charges should be printed somewhere near the middle of the paper.

Sorting

COBOL sure takes a lot of time and effort—but it's fun!

(Debbie Hammer)

In this chapter you will learn how to use the extremely utilitarian sort facility of COBOL. In particular, you will be introduced to:

- the SORT statement
- the additional sort-work area that is usually required in the SELECT clause.
- the SD entry
- ascending and descending keys
- USING and GIVING as used with the SORT verb
- the INPUT PROCEDURE
- the RELEASE clause
- the concept of a Procedure Division Section
- the OUTPUT PROCEDURE
- the RETURN clause
- a legitimate use of the GO TO statement

11.1 The USING and GIVING Clause

Those readers who have had some computer programming experience in languages other than COBOL will recall that the task of sorting a series of scores or names is quite an intellectual feat. This is not so in COBOL. The language provides the programmer with a tailor-made package of routines, which does the job for him. As usual, however, certain careful attention to detail is imperative. Once such detail has been mastered, sorting becomes rather trivial.

The need for sorting in business applications is virtually limitless. Accounts may have to be printed and processed in order of ascending or possibly descending account number, transactions may have to be reported in ascending order of company name (as they would appear in a dictionary, for example), or according to some combination of an alphabetical and a numeric sort such as state name, branch number, and department number.

For all these different types of sorts the key word is SORT, a COBOL word that brings into play the routines required to accomplish the desired purpose. These routines are, on most COBOL systems, part of a complex SORT/MERGE module, normally supplied by the manufacturer. This module represents a very important part of the system's *software* as opposed to the printer, card reader, disk, and so on, which make up the system's *hardware*.

Sorting may be done on alphabetic, alphanumeric, and numeric data using the SORT verb. In order to take advantage of the SORT facility, one must include several minor additions in the program. The first of these changes occurs in the Environment Division where an additional SELECT clause is needed to assign a special area of memory for the sort to occur. It is the same SELECT clause with which we are already familiar, although certain computers or systems require the programmer to use a specific name in the ASSIGN clause. In WATBOL, for example, the area must be named UT-S-SORTWK01 or UR-S-SORTWK01. For simplicity we will illustrate 2 of our programs demonstrating the SORT feature by means of programs run on an IBM 370 system where the area of memory may be called by any name (we have used UT-S-SORTER), which (minus the initial UT-S) is specified in the control cards.

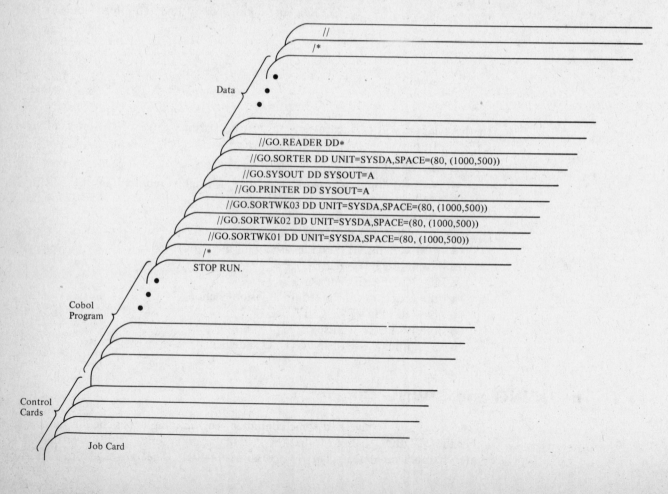

In the Data Division, provision must be made for a description of the file that is to be sorted. A sort-file must be described by an SD entry—Sort-file Description—in much the same way that the input and output files must always be described by an FD entry. Unlike the other files, however, the sort-file does not take a LABELS RECORDS clause because it is already predefined by the system. The SD entry must be the last entry in the File Section. That is to say, if there is no other section present (such as Working-Storage Section), it is followed immediately by the Procedure Division. Following the SD is the name of the sort-file—the same name as that specified in the SELECT clause. As in the case of an FD, an 01-level entry must follow the SD. Individual fields may be specified within this record.

Suppose we have to sort 3 records, each of which contains a last name, first name, and Social Security number.

```
KRUGER    DOV      123456789
LINCOLN   ABE      987654321
REAGAN    RONALD   777777777
```

By inspection it is clear that these 3 records are in ascending order of the last name. This is the order in which they would be found in a telephone directory, for example. However, they could be sorted in ascending order of the first name. In that case they would be written as:

```
LINCOLN   ABE      987654321
KRUGER    DOV      123456789
REAGAN    RONALD   777777777
```

Finally, it would also be possible to sort them in, say, ascending order of Social Security number, in which case the records would be:

```
KRUGER    DOV      123456789
REAGAN    RONALD   777777777
LINCOLN   ABE      987654321
```

In the first sequence the records are sorted in ascending order of the last name. The last name is spoken of as the *key* under which the records—the complete records—are sorted. In the second case the key is the first name and in the last instance the key is the Social Security number.

Suppose now we had several records in which the last name were the same, which is often the case as can easily be confirmed by looking inside any telephone directory. For example,

```
KRUGER    DOV      123456789
KRUGER    STANLEY  222444666
LINCOLN   ABE      987654321
LINCOLN   MARY     111333555
REAGAN    RONALD   777777777
REAGAN    NANCY    135135135
```

Sorting these records in ascending order of the last name leads to ambiguity. Some additional information must now be supplied. Let us say that for identical last names, we wish to sort according to ascending order of the first name. The sorted records would now be:

```
KRUGER    DOV      123456789
KRUGER    STANLEY  222444666
LINCOLN   ABE      987654321
LINCOLN   MARY     111333555
REAGAN    NANCY    135135135
REAGAN    RONALD   777777777
```

In this case we have 2 keys: last name and first name. In COBOL one is permitted up to 12 different keys.

The SORT verb takes the following form.

SORT sort-file-name

ON { ASCENDING / DESCENDING } KEY data-name

USING file-name-1 GIVING file-name-2.

For our first sort program we will read the following series of records.

Input for Program 38

LAST NAME	FIRST NAME	SOCIAL SECURITY NUMBER
SMALL	LINDA	142755533
POREMBA	IRVIN	342425393
FLINT	JAMES	145883214
POREMBA	MICHAEL	425352475
FLINT	JAMES	352667523
MULLISH	HENRY	456251478
HANLON	DEBBIE	454578965
POREMBA	EMMA	123425599
POREMBA	LEON	114237755
GREENBERG	SANDRA	443578692
MANN	ALAN	432115678
CAIN	SUSAN	556758341
MANN	SIDNEY	124331144
MANN	CHARLES	431256614
HANLON	DEBBIE	127755666
HANLON	DEBBIE	578612439

The program sorts these records in ascending order of the last name, descending order of the first name, and ascending order of the Social Security number.

Notice the similarity between the input record RECORD-IN and the sort record SORT-RECORD. They are virtually identical except for the fact that the sort record-names have been changed to reflect that they belong to the sort record. Each corresponding entry is of the same length. Notice also that the output record length is also 80 characters.

In the Procedure Division we have some surprises. Only the single SORT instruction is there (apart from the paragraph-name and the STOP RUN).

```
SORT SORT-FILE
    ASCENDING  KEY SORT-LAST-NAME
    DESCENDING KEY SORT-FIRST-NAME
    ASCENDING  KEY SORT-SOC-SEC-NO
        USING  IN-FILE
        GIVING OUT-FILE.
```

No file is opened and no file is closed. No READ instruction appears, no MOVE instruction is present, and no WRITE instruction is there, as we will see in the following program. Nevertheless, it produced the output *exactly* as desired. Interesting!

Program 38

```
00001      IDENTIFICATION  DIVISION.
00002      PROGRAM-ID.     SORT1.
00003      AUTHOR.         IRVIN POREMBA.
00004      INSTALLATION.   NYU.
00005      DATE-WRITTEN.   JUNE 18, 1982.
00006      DATE-COMPILED.  JUN 27, 1982.
00007      SECURITY.       HENRY MULLISH.
```

```
00008       * * * * * * * * * * * * * * * * * * * * * * * * * * * * * * * * * * * * * * *
00009       *      THIS PROGRAM READS IN DATA CARDS PUNCHED:                          *
00010       *                                                                         *
00011       *      COLUMNS  1-15: LAST NAME                                           *
00012       *      COLUMNS 21-30: FIRST NAME                                          *
00013       *      COLUMNS 36-44: SOCIAL SECURITY NUMBER                              *
00014       *                                                                         *
00015       *      THE PROGRAM SORTS THE DATA ACCORDING TO                            *
00016       *      ASCENDING ORDER OF THE LAST NAME. IF TWO                           *
00017       *      PERSONS HAVE THE SAME LAST NAME, THEY ARE                          *
00018       *      SORTED IN DECENDING ORDER OF THEIR FIRST NAME.                     *
00019       *      IF THEY ALSO HAVE THE SAME FIRST NAME, THEY                        *
00020       *      ARE SORTED IN ASCENDING ORDER OF SOCIAL                            *
00021       *      SECURITY NUMBER.                                                   *
00022       * * * * * * * * * * * * * * * * * * * * * * * * * * * * * * * * * * * * * * *
00023
00024       ENVIRONMENT    DIVISION.
00025       CONFIGURATION  SECTION.
00026       SOURCE-COMPUTER. IBM-370-158.
00027       OBJECT-COMPUTER. IBM-370-158.
00028       SPECIAL-NAMES. CO1 IS A-NEW-PAGE.
00029       INPUT-OUTPUT   SECTION.
00030       FILE-CONTROL.
00031           SELECT IN-FILE ASSIGN TO UT-S-READER.
00032           SELECT OUT-FILE ASSIGN TO UT-S-PRINTER.
00033           SELECT SORT-FILE ASSIGN TO UT-S-SORTER.
00034
00035       DATA DIVISION.
00036       FILE SECTION.
00037
00038       FD    IN-FILE
00039             LABEL RECORDS ARE OMITTED.
00040
00041       01    RECORD-IN.
00042             02    LAST-NAME          PIC X(15).
00043             02    FILLER             PIC X(05).
00044             02    FIRST-NAME         PIC X(10).
00045             02    FILLER             PIC X(05).
00046             02    SOC-SEC-NO         PIC 9(09).
00047             02    FILLER             PIC X(36).
00048
00049       FD    OUT-FILE
00050             LABEL RECORDS ARE OMITTED.
00051
00052       01    LINE-OUT               PIC X(80).
00053       SD    SORT-FILE.
00054
00055       01    SORT-RECORD.
00056             02    SORT-LAST-NAME     PIC X(15).
00057             02    FILLER             PIC X(05).
00058             02    SORT-FIRST-NAME    PIC X(10).
00059             02    FILLER             PIC X(05).
00060             02    SORT-SOC-SEC-NO    PIC 9(09).
00061             02    FILLER             PIC X(36).
00062
00063       PROCEDURE DIVISION.
00064
00065       MAIN-LINE-SORT.
00066           SORT SORT-FILE
00067               ASCENDING KEY SORT-LAST-NAME
00068               DESCENDING KEY SORT-FIRST-NAME
00069               ASCENDING KEY SORT-SOC-SEC-NO
00070                       USING IN-FILE
00071                       GIVING OUT-FILE.
00072
00073           STOP RUN.
```

Output for Program 38

```
CAIN          SUSAN        556758341
FLINT         JAMES        145883214
FLINT         JAMES        352667523
```

GREENBERG	SANDRA	443578692
HANLON	DEBBIE	127755666
HANLON	DEBBIE	454578965
HANLON	DEBBIE	578612439
MANN	SIDNEY	124331144
MANN	CHARLES	431256614
MANN	ALAN	432115678
MULLISH	HENRY	456251478
POREMBA	MICHAEL	425352475
POREMBA	LEON	114237755
POREMBA	IRVIN	342425393
POREMBA	EMMA	123425599
SMALL	LINDA	142755533

Program 38 takes advantage of 2 key COBOL words, USING and GIVING. When used in the context of the SORT verb they perform all the work that is necessary to sort the data in accordance with the instructions that are specified by the ASCENDING/DESCENDING key clauses. In this particular example there are 3 keys, namely, SORT-LAST-NAME, SORT-FIRST-NAME, and SORT-SOC-SEC-NO. Because SORT-LAST-NAME is specified first, it is the *primary* sorting key. Each key may be either ascending or descending, although more often than not it is the ascending order that is used, for this is usually the more natural order. In the SORT statement SORT-LAST-NAME is specified to be in ascending order. The *second* key that is listed is SORT-FIRST-NAME; this is called a *secondary* key. As you see, it has been specified that this key should be sorted in descending order. Finally, the last-named key is SORT-SOC-SEC-NO, which is to be sorted in ascending order. Because it is the last key mentioned, it is the least significant one. In other words, first the data is sorted on the primary key and in the event of similar data, according to the secondary key, and if again the data is similar, according to the tertiary key, in this case SORT-SOC-SEC-NO. So you see the *order* in which the keys are specified is of critical importance. The order implies hierarchy.

The USING clause of the SORT statement:

a. opens the input file, which must be in the closed condition
b. reads the input file
c. moves each record of data to the SD area so that sorting may be initiated
d. "releases" each record of the sort-file to a special area of memory where the sorting actually takes place
e. closes the input file.

The GIVING clause of the SORT statement, on the other hand,

a. opens the output file, which must be in the closed condition
b. "returns" each sorted record to the SD area
c. moves the sorted records to the output area
d. writes each sorted record (beginning at the top of a new page) to the output device
e. closes the output file

As you can see, the USING and GIVING clauses are veritable workhorses. They provide the programmer with the ability to produce a sorted listing of data with almost no effort at all. It is true that the USING and GIVING clauses do not allow for any selective handling of either the input or the output, but that is not their intent. The INPUT PROCEDURE and the OUTPUT PROCEDURE provide this capability. The USING and GIVING options are analogous to having an automobile equipped with automatic shift. It is extremely easy and convenient to use but for the driver who insists on fast starts and hairpin turns the automatic shift leaves something to be desired.

A summary of the critical points you should know follow.

1. A maximum of 12 keys is permitted.
2. A special SELECT is necessary in FILE-CONTROL.

3. The SD is not opened or closed or has a LABEL RECORDS clause associated with it. If it has such a clause, it is treated as a comment and ignored under the 1974 standard.
4. Each key used must be specified to be either ascending or descending.
5. SD is used instead of FD.
6. All SD names are really redefines of the input file records.
7. SD is another area of memory.
8. If the USING and GIVING clauses are used, neither the input nor the output files are either opened or closed by the programmer.
9. The USING clause opens the input file, reads the data, moves the data to the SD area, releases the data to the sort module for sorting, and closes the input file.
10. The GIVING clause opens the output file, returns the sorted records to the SD area, moves the records to the output area, writes the records on the output device—usually the printer—and closes the output file.

11.2 INPUT PROCEDURE

Suppose we have some data and want only *some* of it sorted and printed. For example, our data might consist of student names, state of residence, and year of birth, as shown.

Input for Program 39

PETERFREUND MICHAEL	NY	1960
LUM KIN	NY	1960
NUMEROFF KAREN	MA	1960
CHIN SUSAN	NY	1960
BREIDBART SHAUN	NY	1960
GROSSMAN SUSAN	NJ	1960
SHULMAN POLLY	NJ	1960
WECKER ALAN	NY	1960
ELET YVONNE	WA	1955
WILLIAMS ROY	NY	1960
LEVINE MICHAEL	VA	1960
JENKINS BUDDY	VA	1950
GARELICK RHONDA	NY	1960
COHEN MADDY	NY	1960
HERNANDEZ MARCO	NY	1960
ACKERMAN SUSAN	NJ	1960
POREMBA IRVIN	NY	1960
STRONG AMY	IL	1953

If we wanted to sort and print the sorted data according to last name, state of birth, and year of birth, but with the proviso that only those records in which the state of birth was New York and the year of birth was 1960, it is clear that we could not resort to the USING clause because its effect would be to sort *all* the data. What we need is to have some control over which records are to be sorted.

When selection of input data is required we must resort to an INPUT PROCEDURE in which we manage the data in whatever way we choose. An INPUT PROCEDURE is the alternative to the USING clause. If an INPUT PROCEDURE is elected, the Procedure Division must be divided into SECTIONs. In all the other divisions the section names were provided by the COBOL language. In the Procedure Division section names are user-defined. We have opted to use the names MAIN-SORTING SECTION for the section of the Procedure Division that includes the sort and CHECK-THE-RECORD SECTION for the remainder of the program. The rule in COBOL is that if one section is used in the Procedure Division, every statement must be included in a section. If we had divided previous programs into sections—which we were perfectly entitled to do—we could have performed those sections. However, because it really was not necessary to resort to sections in previous programs, we did not. When using either an INPUT PROCEDURE or an OUTPUT PROCEDURE we are forced to use sections.

The MAIN-SORTING SECTION of the next program reads:

```
MAIN-LINE-SORT.
    SORT SORT-FILE ASCENDING KEY SORT-NAME
    INPUT PROCEDURE CHECK-THE-RECORD
    GIVING OUT-FILE.
    STOP RUN.
```

where the ascending key SORT-NAME is specified and the name of the INPUT PROCEDURE is declared to be CHECK-THE-RECORD. What this means conceptually is that the input procedure CHECK-THE-RECORD is to be "performed." This implies that there is a portion of the Procedure Division that is called CHECK-THE-RECORD SECTION.

We now focus our attention within the CHECK-THE-RECORD SECTION. We, ourselves, have to open the input file and read the input file. Only if STATE-IN is equal to 'NY' and YEAR-BORN is equal to 1960 is that particular record "released" to the sort module. The instruction to "release" a record is, as you will already have guessed, the word, RELEASE. When all the data has been examined and the selected records released to the sort module, the input file is closed and control is yielded to the GIVING clause of the SORT verb. This has the desired effect of printing all the sorted records of the selected data.

Before leaving this program, we should make an important point. The rule about using sections in the Procedure Division is that once a section has been entered, it may be exited only via the last physical instruction of that section. Therefore a GO TO CLOSE-UP has been included. On the 1974 standard the GO TO may be abbreviated to GO.

Program 39

```
00001       IDENTIFICATION  DIVISION.
00002       PROGRAM-ID.     SORT2.
00003       AUTHOR.         IRVIN POREMBA.
00004       INSTALLATION.   NYU.
00005       DATE-WRITTEN.   JUNE 18, 1982.
00006       DATE-COMPILED.  JUN 18, 1982.
00007       SECURITY.       HENRY MULLISH.
00008       * * * * * * * * * * * * * * * * * * * * * * * * * * * * * * * * * * * * * * * * *
00009       *     THIS PROGRAM READS DATA CARDS PUNCHED:                          *
00010       *                                                                     *
00011       *       COLUMNS  1-35: NAME                                           *
00012       *       COLUMNS 41-42: STATE LIVING IN                                *
00013       *       COLUMNS 46-49: YEAR OF BIRTH                                  *
00014       *                                                                     *
00015       *       THIS PROGRAM SORTS ONLY THE DATA IN WHICH                     *
00016       *       THE PERSON WAS BORN IN 1960 AND LIVES IN                      *
00017       *       NEW YORK. THE DATA IS SORTED IN ALPHABETIC                    *
00018       *       ORDER OF THE PERSON'S NAME.                                   *
00019       * * * * * * * * * * * * * * * * * * * * * * * * * * * * * * * * * * * * * * * * *
00020
00021       ENVIRONMENT    DIVISION.
00022       CONFIGURATION  SECTION.
00023       SOURCE-COMPUTER. IBM-370-158.
00024       OBJECT-COMPUTER. IBM-370-158.
00025       SPECIAL-NAMES. C01 IS A-NEW-PAGE.
00026       INPUT-OUTPUT SECTION.
00027       FILE-CONTROL.
00028           SELECT IN-FILE ASSIGN TO UT-S-READER.
00029           SELECT OUT-FILE ASSIGN TO UT-S-PRINTER.
00030           SELECT SORT-FILE ASSIGN TO UT-S-SORTER.
00031
00032       DATA DIVISION.
00033       FILE SECTION.
00034
00035       FD  IN-FILE
00036           LABEL RECORDS ARE OMITTED.
00037
```

```
00038     01    RECORD-IN.
00039           02    NAME-IN          PIC X(35).
00040           02    FILLER           PIC X(05).
00041           02    STATE-IN         PIC X(02).
00042           02    FILLER           PIC X(03).
00043           02    YEAR-BORN        PIC 9(04).
00044           02    FILLER           PIC X(31).
00045
00046     FD    OUT-FILE
00047           LABEL RECORDS ARE OMITTED.
00048
00049     01    LINE-OUT               PIC X(80).
00050
00051     SD    SORT-FILE.
00052
00053     01    SORT-RECORD.
00054           02    SORT-NAME        PIC X(35).
00055           02    FILLER           PIC X(05).
00056           02    SORT-STATE       PIC X(02).
00057           02    FILLER           PIC X(03).
00058           02    SORT-YEAR        PIC 9(04).
00059           02    FILLER           PIC X(31).
00060
00061     WORKING-STORAGE SECTION.
00062     77    ANY-MORE-CARDS         PIC X(03) VALUE 'YES'.
00063
00064     PROCEDURE DIVISION.
00065
00066     MAIN-SORTING SECTION.
00067
00068     MAIN-LINE-SORT.
00069           SORT SORT-FILE
00070           ASCENDING KEY SORT-NAME
00071           INPUT PROCEDURE CHECK-THE-RECORD
00072           GIVING OUT-FILE.
00073           STOP RUN.
00074
00075     CHECK-THE-RECORD SECTION.
00076
00077     MAIN-LINE-ROUTINE.
00078           PERFORM OPEN-FILE.
00079           PERFORM START-UP.
00080           PERFORM PROCESS-DATA UNTIL ANY-MORE-CARDS EQUAL 'NO'.
00081           GO TO CLOSE-UP.
00082
00083     OPEN-FILE.
00084           OPEN INPUT IN-FILE.
00085
00086     START-UP.
00087           READ IN-FILE AT END MOVE 'NO' TO ANY-MORE-CARDS
00088                 DISPLAY '**NO DATA IN DECK**'.
00089
00090     PROCESS-DATA.
00091           IF STATE-IN EQUAL 'NY' AND YEAR-BORN EQUAL 1960
00092           MOVE NAME-IN TO SORT-NAME
00093           MOVE STATE-IN TO SORT-STATE
00094           MOVE YEAR-BORN TO SORT-YEAR
00095           RELEASE SORT-RECORD.
00096           READ IN-FILE AT END MOVE 'NO' TO ANY-MORE-CARDS.
00097
00098     CLOSE-UP.
00099           CLOSE IN-FILE.
```

Output for Program 39

```
BREIDBART SHAUN          NY      1960
CHIN SUSAN               NY      1960
COHEN MADDY              NY      1960
GARELICK RHONDA          NY      1960
HERNANDEZ MARCO          NY      1960
LUM KIN                  NY      1960
PETERFREUND MICHAEL      NY      1960
POREMBA IRVIN            NY      1960
WECKER ALAN              NY      1960
WILLIAMS ROY             NY      1960
```

11.3   OUTPUT PROCEDURE

Just as we need an INPUT PROCEDURE when exercising some control over the input data to a sort, so we must resort to an OUTPUT PROCEDURE when exerting some control over the printing of the sorted records.

To illustrate this concept we use the following data.

Input for Program 40

```
FREEDMAN       LINDA        02500
POREMBA        IRVIN        10005
FREEDMAN       LINDA        11525
POREMBA        IRVIN        02500
POREMBA        IRVIN        05775
HALL           RUBIN        03675
HALL           RUBIN        05000
HALL           RUBIN        03000
FREEDMAN       LINDA        01250
FREEDMAN       LINDA        04555
HALL           RUBIN        12500
HALL           RUBIN        11025
POREMBA        IRVIN        10000
```

This data represents the names of traffic violators and the amounts of their fines in 999V99 format. The purpose of the program is to first sort the data in ascending order of the fine. Because no prior selection is required, the USING clause is implemented. However, when printing out the output we would like to see instead of an ordinary sorted, sequential list of the input records, a report showing each violator and the related fines listed on a separate page, together with a total of the fines, using a control break to eject to a new page and to suppress the printing of duplicate names. Such control necessitates the use of an OUTPUT PROCEDURE. In the program that follows the OUTPUT PROCEDURE is called CONTROL-BREAK. Thus a CONTROL-BREAK SECTION must be in the program. Once again, a GO or a GO TO is used to exit from the last physical instruction of the section.

The OUTPUT PROCEDURE opens the output file prior to operating on the input records, which are already sorted as a result of the USING clause in the SORT statement. Now we want to "return" the sorted records to the sort area. This is done by the RETURN statement, which has the format:

RETURN sort-file AT END imperative statement(s)

which looks remarkably like the COBOL READ instruction. In fact it may be conceptualized as reading from the sorted file of records.

Program 40

```
1         IDENTIFICATION   DIVISION.
2         PROGRAM-ID.      SORTING-3.
3         AUTHOR.          IRVIN POREMBA.
4         INSTALLATION.    NYU.
5         DATE-WRITTEN.    JUNE 27, 1982.
6         DATE-COMPILED.   JUNE 27, 1982.
7         SECURITY.        HENRY MULLISH.
8     * * * * * * * * * * * * * * * * * * * * * * * * * * * * * * * * * * * * * * * * * * * * * * *
9     *       THIS PROGRAM READS DATA CARDS PUNCHED:                            *
10    *                                                                         *
11    *       COLUMNS  1-35: NAME                                               *
12    *       COLUMNS 41-45: AMOUNT OF FINE                                     *
13    *                                                                         *
14    *       THIS PROGRAM SORTS THE DATA IN ALPHABETIC ORDER                   *
15    *       OF THE PERSON'S NAME AND ASCENDING ORDER OF THE                   *
16    *       FINES. THEN IT PRINTS OUT THE SORTED                              *
17    *       INFORMATION USING A CONTROL BREAK ON THE                          *
18    *       PERSON'S NAME AND ALSO PRINTS THE TOTAL AMOUNT                     *
19    *       OF FINES FOR EACH PERSON.                                         *
20    * * * * * * * * * * * * * * * * * * * * * * * * * * * * * * * * * * * * * * * * * * * * * * *
```

```
21
22          ENVIRONMENT    DIVISION.
23          CONFIGURATION SECTION.
24          SOURCE-COMPUTER. CYBER-170-720.
25          OBJECT-COMPUTER. CYBER-170-720.
26          SPECIAL-NAMES.
27          INPUT-OUTPUT SECTION.
28          FILE-CONTROL.
29              SELECT IN-FILE ASSIGN TO INPUT.
30              SELECT OUT-FILE ASSIGN TO OUTPUT.
31              SELECT SORT-FILE ASSIGN TO SORTFILE.
32
33          DATA DIVISION.
34          FILE SECTION.
35
36          FD    IN-FILE
37              LABEL RECORDS ARE OMITTED.
38
39          01    RECORD-IN.
40              02    NAME-IN              PIC X(35).
41              02    FILLER               PIC X(05).
42              02    FINE-IN              PIC 9(03)V9(02).
43              02    FILLER               PIC X(35).
44
45          FD    OUT-FILE
46              LABEL RECORDS ARE OMITTED.
47
48          01    LINE-OUT                 PIC X(133).
49
50          SD    SORT-FILE.
51
52          01    SORT-RECORD.
53              02    SORT-NAME            PIC X(35).
54              02    FILLER               PIC X(05).
55              02    SORT-FINE            PIC 9(03)V9(02).
56              02    FILLER               PIC X(35).
57
58          WORKING-STORAGE SECTION.
59          77    ANY-MORE-CARDS           PIC X(03) VALUE 'YES'.
60          77    CARD-COUNT               PIC 9(04) VALUE ZERO.
61          77    NAME-SAVE                PIC X(35).
62          77    PAGE-COUNT               PIC 9(02) VALUE ZERO.
63          77    TOTAL-FINE               PIC 9(06)V9(02) VALUE ZERO.
64
65          01    HEADER-1.
66              02    FILLER               PIC X(01) VALUE SPACES.
67              02    FILLER               PIC X(05) VALUE 'PAGE'.
68              02    PAGE-COUNT-OUT       PIC Z9.
69              02    FILLER               PIC X(02) VALUE SPACES.
70              02    FILLER               PIC X(25) VALUE 'COUNT'.
71              02    FILLER               PIC X(25) VALUE 'NAME'.
72              02    FILLER               PIC X(05) VALUE 'FINE'.
73
74          01    HEADER-2.
75              02    FILLER               PIC X(01) VALUE SPACES.
76              02    FILLER               PIC X(07) VALUE ALL '-'.
77              02    FILLER               PIC X(02) VALUE SPACES.
78              02    FILLER               PIC X(05) VALUE ALL '-'.
79              02    FILLER               PIC X(05) VALUE SPACES.
80              02    FILLER               PIC X(35) VALUE ALL '-'.
81              02    FILLER               PIC X(05) VALUE SPACES.
82              02    FILLER               PIC X(07) VALUE ALL '-'.
83
84          01    DETAIL-LINE.
85              02    FILLER               PIC X(10) VALUE SPACES.
86              02    CARD-COUNT-OUT       PIC Z,ZZ9.
87              02    FILLER               PIC X(05) VALUE SPACES.
88              02    NAME-OUT             PIC X(35).
89              02    FILLER               PIC X(05) VALUE SPACES.
90              02    FINE-OUT             PIC $$$9.99.
91
92          01    DETAIL-LINE-2.
93              02    FILLER               PIC X(10) VALUE SPACES.
94              02    FILLER               PIC X(13) VALUE 'TOTAL AMOUNT'.
95              02    FILLER               PIC X(10) VALUE 'OF FINES:'.
96              02    TOTAL-FINES-OUT      PIC $$$$,$$9.99.
```

```
97
98        PROCEDURE DIVISION.
99
100       MAIN-SORTING SECTION.
101
102       MAIN-LINE-SORT.
103           SORT SORT-FILE
104           ASCENDING KEY SORT-NAME
105           ASCENDING KEY SORT-FINE
106               USING IN-FILE
107           OUTPUT PROCEDURE CONTROL-BREAK.
108           STOP RUN.
109
110       CONTROL-BREAK SECTION.
111
112       MAIN-LINE-ROUTINE.
113           PERFORM OPEN-FILE.
114           PERFORM NEW-PAGE.
115           PERFORM START-UP.
116           PERFORM PROCESS-DATA UNTIL ANY-MORE-CARDS EQUAL 'NO'.
117           GO TO CLOSE-UP.
118
119       OPEN-FILE.
120           OPEN OUTPUT OUT-FILE.
121
122       NEW-PAGE.
123           MOVE SPACES TO LINE-OUT.
124           WRITE LINE-OUT AFTER PAGE.
125
126       START-UP.
127           RETURN SORT-FILE AT END MOVE 'NO' TO ANY-MORE-CARDS
128               MOVE '  **NO DATA IN DECK**' TO LINE-OUT
129               WRITE LINE-OUT AFTER 30.
130           IF ANY-MORE-CARDS EQUAL 'YES' PERFORM WRITE-HEADINGS
131           ADD 1 TO CARD-COUNT
132           PERFORM NEW-NAME.
133
134       PROCESS-DATA.
135           ADD 1 TO CARD-COUNT.
136           IF SORT-NAME EQUAL NAME-SAVE PERFORM SAME-NAME
137           ELSE PERFORM VIOLATOR-TOTAL
138               PERFORM NEW-PAGE
139               PERFORM WRITE-HEADINGS
140               PERFORM NEW-NAME.
141
142       SAME-NAME.
143           MOVE CARD-COUNT TO CARD-COUNT-OUT.
144           MOVE SPACES TO NAME-OUT.
145           MOVE SORT-FINE TO FINE-OUT.
146           ADD SORT-FINE TO TOTAL-FINE.
147           WRITE LINE-OUT FROM DETAIL-LINE AFTER 2.
148           RETURN SORT-FILE AT END MOVE 'NO' TO ANY-MORE-CARDS.
149
150       NEW-NAME.
151           MOVE CARD-COUNT TO CARD-COUNT-OUT.
152           MOVE SORT-NAME TO NAME-SAVE.
153           MOVE SORT-NAME TO NAME-OUT.
154           MOVE SORT-FINE TO FINE-OUT.
155           ADD SORT-FINE TO TOTAL-FINE.
156           WRITE LINE-OUT FROM DETAIL-LINE AFTER 2.
157           MOVE ZEROS TO TOTAL-FINE.
158           RETURN SORT-FILE AT END MOVE 'NO' TO ANY-MORE-CARDS.
159
160       VIOLATOR-TOTAL.
161           MOVE TOTAL-FINE TO TOTAL-FINES-OUT.
162           WRITE LINE-OUT FROM DETAIL-LINE-2 AFTER 3.
163
164       WRITE-HEADINGS.
165           ADD 1 TO PAGE-COUNT.
166           MOVE PAGE-COUNT TO PAGE-COUNT-OUT.
167           WRITE LINE-OUT FROM HEADER-1 AFTER 1.
168           WRITE LINE-OUT FROM HEADER-2 AFTER 0.
169
170       CLOSE-UP.
171           PERFORM VIOLATOR-TOTAL.
172           CLOSE OUT-FILE.
```

Output for Program 40

PAGE 1	COUNT	NAME	FINE
	1	FREEDMAN LINDA	$12.50
	2		$25.00
	3		$45.55
	4		$115.25
	TOTAL AMOUNT OF FINES:		$185.80

PAGE 2	COUNT	NAME	FINE
	5	HALL RUBIN	$30.00
	6		$36.75
	7		$50.00
	8		$110.25
	9		$125.00
	TOTAL AMOUNT OF FINES:		$322.00

PAGE 3	COUNT	NAME	FINE
	10	POREMBA IRVIN	$25.00
	11		$57.75
	12		$100.00
	13		$100.05
	TOTAL AMOUNT OF FINES:		$257.80

11.4 Using Both an INPUT and OUTPUT PROCEDURE

The logical conclusion to the 3 previous programs is to illustrate a program with both an INPUT and an OUTPUT PROCEDURE. In our example we wish to sort the following data into ascending order of the last name, ascending order of the first name, and descending order of the commission.

Input for Program 41

```
MULLISH          HENRY          000001
MULLISH          HENRY          000115
ARPIN            ED             000043
ARPIN            ED             000016
LEE              SHIRLEY        000108
WHITELOCKE       SUSAN          000128
LEE              SHIRLEY        000089
LEE              SHIRLEY        000048
MULLISH          HENRY          000029
WHITELOCKE       SUSAN          000016
WHITELOCKE       SUSAN          000143
ARPIN            MABEL          000009
POREMBA          IRVIN          001234
POREMBA          IRVIN          000568
POREMBA          IRVIN          000079
```

We will use an INPUT PROCEDURE to print out a suitable heading before the data is read; next, print out the raw data before it is sorted, and then sort the data and print it again with a suitable heading on a fresh page. The SORT instruction now reads:

```
SORT SORT-FILE
ON ASCENDING KEY SORT-LAST-NAME
ON ASCENDING KEY SORT-FIRST-NAME
ON DESCENDING KEY SORT-COMMISSION
INPUT PROCEDURE WRITE-RAW-DATA
OUTPUT PROCEDURE WRITE-SORTED-DATA.
```

Because the first 2 keys are both ascending, the phrase ON ASCENDING KEY has to be written only once.

Program 41

```
1        IDENTIFICATION   DIVISION.
2        PROGRAM-ID.      SORTING-4.
3        AUTHOR.          IRVIN POREMBA.
4        INSTALLATION.    NYU.
5        DATE-WRITTEN.    JUNE 27, 1982.
6        DATE-COMPILED. JUNE 27, 1982.
7        SECURITY.        HENRY MULLISH.
8        * * * * * * * * * * * * * * * * * * * * * * * * * * * * * * * * * * * * * * * * * * * * * * * * * * *
9        *       THIS PROGRAM READS IN DATA CARDS PUNCHED AS              *
10       *       FOLLOWS:                                                 *
11       *                                                               *
12       *       COLUMNS  1-20: LAST NAME                                 *
13       *       COLUMNS 25-35: FIRST NAME                                *
14       *       COLUMNS 40-45: AMOUNT OF COMMISSION                      *
15       *                                                               *
16       *       THE PROGRAM THEN PRINTS OUT THE RAW DATA                 *
17       *       ON A NEW PAGE AND THEN ON ANOTHER NEW PAGE,              *
18       *       PRINTS OUT THE DATA FULLY EDITED AFTER IT HAS            *
19       *       BEEN SORTED IN ASCENDING ORDER OF LAST NAME,             *
20       *       ASCENDING ORDER OF FIRST NAME, AND DESCENDING            *
21       *       ORDER OF COMMISSION.                                     *
22       * * * * * * * * * * * * * * * * * * * * * * * * * * * * * * * * * * * * * * * * * * * * * * * * * * *
23
24       ENVIRONMENT   DIVISION,
25       CONFIGURATION SECTION.
26       SOURCE-COMPUTER. CYBER-170-720.
27       OBJECT-COMPUTER. CYBER-170-720.
28       SPECIAL-NAMES.
29       INPUT-OUTPUT SECTION.
30       FILE-CONTROL.
31           SELECT IN-FILE ASSIGN TO INPUT.
32           SELECT OUT-FILE ASSIGN TO OUTPUT.
33           SELECT SORT-FILE ASSIGN TO SORTFILE.
34
35       DATA DIVISION.
36       FILE SECTION.
37
38       *    DEFINE INPUT OF PROGRAM.
39
40       FD   IN-FILE
41            LABEL RECORDS ARE OMITTED.
42
43       01   RECORD-IN.
44            02    LAST-NAME          PIC X(20).
45            02    FILLER             PIC X(04).
46            02    FIRST-NAME         PIC X(11).
47            02    FILLER             PIC X(04).
48            02    COMMISSION         PIC 9(06).
49            02    FILLER             PIC X(35).
50
51       *    DEFINE OUTPUT OF RAW DATA.
52
53       FD   OUT-FILE
54            LABEL RECORDS ARE OMITTED.
55
56       01   LINE-OUT               PIC X(133).
57
58       *    DEFINE OUTPUT OF SORTED DATA.
59
60       SD   SORT-FILE.
61
62       01   SORT-DATA.
63            02    SORT-LAST-NAME     PIX X(20).
64            02    FILLER             PIC X(04).
65            02    SORT-FIRST-NAME    PIC X(11).
66            02    FILLER             PIC X(04).
```

```
67              02    SORT-COMMISSION    PIC 9(06).
68
69      WORKING-STORAGE SECTION.
70      77    MORE-CARDS              PIC X(03) VALUE 'YES'.
71      77    MORE-CARDS-2            PIC X(03) VALUE 'YES'.
72
73      01    HEADER-1.
74            02    FILLER            PIC X(26) VALUE SPACES.
75            02    FILLER            PIC X(13) VALUE 'UNSORTED DATA'.
76
77      01    HEADER-2.
78            02    FILLER            PIC X(26) VALUE SPACES.
79            02    FILLER            PIC X(13) VALUE ALL '*'.
80
81      01    HEADER-3.
82            02    FILLER            PIC X(28) VALUE SPACES.
83            02    FILLER            PIC X(11) VALUE 'SORTED DATA'.
84
85      01    HEADER-4.
86            02    FILLER            PIC X(28) VALUE SPACES.
87            02    FILLER            PIC X(11) VALUE ALL '*'.
88
89      01    HEADER-5.
90            02    FILLER            PIC X(05) VALUE SPACES.
91            02    FILLER            PIC X(10) VALUE 'LAST NAME'.
92            02    FILLER            PIC X(10) VALUE SPACES.
93            02    FILLER            PIC X(11) VALUE 'FIRST NAME'.
94            02    FILLER            PIC X(04) VALUE SPACES.
95            02    FILLER            PIC X(10) VALUE 'COMMISSION'.
96
97      01    HEADER-6.
98            02    FILLER            PIC X(01) VALUE SPACES.
99            02    FILLER            PIC X(20) VALUE ALL '*'.
100           02    FILLER            PIC X(04) VALUE SPACES.
101           02    FILLER            PIC X(11) VALUE ALL '*'.
102           02    FILLER            PIC X(04) VALUE SPACES.
103           02    FILLER            PIC X(10) VALUE ALL '*'.
104
105     01    DETAIL-LINE.
106           02    FILLER            PIC X(01) VALUE SPACES.
107           02    LAST-NAME-OUT     PIC X(20).
108           02    FILLER            PIC X(04) VALUE SPACES.
109           02    FIRST-NAME-OUT    PIC X(11).
110           02    FILLER            PIC X(05) VALUE SPACES.
111           02    COMMISSION-OUT    PIC $$$$,$$9.
112
113     PROCEDURE DIVISION.
114
115     SORT-CARD SECTION.
116
117     MAIN-LINE-SORT.
118         SORT SORT-FILE
119         ON ASCENDING KEY SORT-LAST-NAME
120         ON ASCENDING KEY SORT-FIRST-NAME
121         ON DESCENDING KEY SORT-COMMISSION
122         INPUT PROCEDURE WRITE-RAW-DATA
123         OUTPUT PROCEDURE WRITE-SORTED-DATA.
124         STOP RUN.
125
126     WRITE-RAW-DATA SECTION.
127
128     MAIN-LINE-ROUTINE-1.
129         PERFORM OPEN-FILES.
130         PERFORM NEW-PAGE-1.
131         PERFORM START-UP-1.
132         PERFORM PROCESS-DATA-1 UNTIL MORE-CARDS EQUAL 'NO'.
133         GO TO CLOSE-UP-1.
134
135     OPEN-FILES.
136         OPEN INPUT IN-FILE.
137         OPEN OUTPUT OUT-FILE.
138
139     NEW-PAGE-1.
140         MOVE SPACES TO LINE-OUT.
141         WRITE LINE-OUT AFTER PAGE.
```

```
142
143     START-UP-1.
144         READ IN-FILE AT END MOVE 'NO' TO MORE-CARDS
145             MOVE ' ***NO DATA IN DECK***' TO LINE-OUT
146             WRITE LINE-OUT AFTER 2.
147         IF MORE-CARDS EQUAL 'YES' PERFORM WRITE-HEADINGS.
148
149     PROCESS-DATA-1.
150         MOVE LAST-NAME TO LAST-NAME-OUT.
151         MOVE FIRST-NAME TO FIRST-NAME-OUT.
152         MOVE COMMISSION TO COMMISSION-OUT.
153         WRITE LINE-OUT FROM DETAIL-LINE AFTER 2.
154         MOVE LAST-NAME TO SORT-LAST-NAME.
155         MOVE FIRST-NAME TO SORT-FIRST-NAME.
156         MOVE COMMISSION TO SORT-COMMISSION.
157         RELEASE SORT-DATA.
158         READ IN-FILE AT END MOVE 'NO' TO MORE-CARDS.
159
160     WRITE-HEADINGS.
161         WRITE LINE-OUT FROM HEADER-1 AFTER 1.
162         WRITE LINE-OUT FROM HEADER-2 AFTER 1.
163         WRITE LINE-OUT FROM HEADER-2 AFTER 1.
164         WRITE LINE-OUT FROM HEADER-5 AFTER 2.
165         WRITE LINE-OUT FROM HEADER-6 AFTER 1.
166
167     CLOSE-UP-1.
168         CLOSE IN-FILE, OUT-FILE.
169
170     WRITE-SORTED-DATA SECTION.
171
172     MAIN-LINE-ROUTINE-2.
173         PERFORM OPEN-FILE.
174         PERFORM START-UP-2.
175         PERFORM PROCESS-DATA-2 UNTIL MORE-CARDS-2 EQUAL 'NO'.
176         GO TO CLOSE-UP-2.
177
178     OPEN-FILE.
179         OPEN OUTPUT OUT-FILE.
180
181     START-UP-2.
182         MOVE SPACES TO LINE-OUT.
183         WRITE LINE-OUT AFTER PAGE.
184         WRITE LINE-OUT FROM HEADER-3 AFTER 1.
185         WRITE LINE-OUT FROM HEADER-4 AFTER 1.
186         WRITE LINE-OUT FROM HEADER-4 AFTER 1.
187         WRITE LINE-OUT FROM HEADER-5 AFTER 2.
188         WRITE LINE-OUT FROM HEADER-6 AFTER 1.
189         RETURN SORT-FILE AT END MOVE 'NO' TO MORE-CARDS-2.
190
191     PROCESS-DATA-2.
192         MOVE SORT-LAST-NAME TO LAST-NAME-OUT.
193         MOVE SORT-FIRST-NAME TO FIRST-NAME-OUT.
194         MOVE SORT-COMMISSION TO COMMISSION-OUT.
195         WRITE LINE-OUT FROM DETAIL-LINE AFTER 2.
196         RETURN SORT-FILE AT END MOVE 'NO' TO MORE-CARDS-2.
197
198     CLOSE-UP-2.
199         CLOSE OUT-FILE.
```

Output for Program 41

```
                        UNSORTED DATA
                     * * * * * * * * * * * *
                     * * * * * * * * * * * *

            LAST NAME              FIRST NAME          COMMISSION
* * * * * * * * * * * * * * * * * * *   * * * * * * * * *   * * * * * * * * *
            MULLISH                HENRY                   $1
            MULLISH                HENRY                 $115
            ARPIN                  ED                     $43
            ARPIN                  ED                     $16
            LEE                    SHIRLEY               $108
            WHITELOCKE             SUSAN                 $128
            LEE                    SHIRLEY                $89
```

LEE	SHIRLEY	$48
MULLISH	HENRY	$29
WHITELOCKE	SUSAN	$16
WHITELOCKE	SUSAN	$143
ARPIN	MABEL	$9
POREMBA	IRVIN	$1,234
POREMBA	IRVIN	$568
POREMBA	IRVIN	$79

SORTED DATA
* * * * * * * * * * * * *
* * * * * * * * * * * *

LAST NAME	FIRST NAME	COMMISSION
* * * * * * * * * * * * * * * * * * *	* * * * * * * * * *	* * * * * * * * * *
ARPIN	ED	$43
ARPIN	ED	$16
ARPIN	MABEL	$9
LEE	SHIRLEY	$108
LEE	SHIRLEY	$89
LEE	SHIRLEY	$48
MULLISH	HENRY	$115
MULLISH	HENRY	$29
MULLISH	HENRY	$1
POREMBA	IRVIN	$1,234
POREMBA	IRVIN	$568
POREMBA	IRVIN	$79
WHITELOCKE	SUSAN	$143
WHITELOCKE	SUSAN	$128
WHITELOCKE	SUSAN	$16

Review Questions

1. May alphabetic as well as numeric data be sorted?
2. Where must the SD entry be placed in a SORT program?
3. What is the effect of the USING clause?
4. What is the effect of the GIVING clause?
5. In the SORT instruction

```
SORT SORTING-FILE
DESCENDING KEY SSN
ASCENDING KEY ABC
DESCENDING KEY XYZ
USING INPUT-FILE
GIVING OUTPUT-FILE.
```

   a. How many sorting keys are present?
   b. Which is the primary key?
   c. Which is the secondary key?
   d. Which is the tertiary key?
6. If some selection process has to be done on the input data, what special provision must be made?
7. If an INPUT or OUTPUT PROCEDURE is to be used, how must the Procedure Division be structured?
8. What is implied by the clause

```
OUTPUT PROCEDURE ABCDE?
```

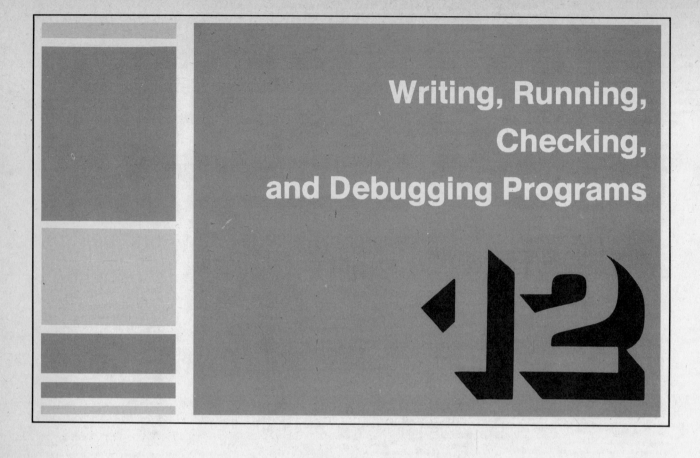

Writing, Running, Checking, and Debugging Programs

Are the error diagnostics at night better than those you get during the day?

(Carl Keck)

Writing a computer program to solve a particular problem represents only the middle segment of a 3-phase operation. Once the problem has been defined, a method of solving it has to be developed; this is the first phase. Next, the method has to be translated into the instructions, operations, and options that are available to the COBOL programmer. The program is then written on paper or, better yet, on coding forms, or the instructions are typed into a video terminal or keypunched onto cards. The time required to write a program may be measured in minutes, hours, days, or even weeks, depending on the complexity of the problem and the skill and ability of the programmer.

When looking at a COBOL textbook such as this one, the reader can easily get the mistaken impression that all the programs that are illustrated worked the first time they were run or were written originally how they appear in their published form. It should be clearly understood that this is far from the truth. Almost all the programs required extensive amendments before they were regarded as satisfactory for inclusion in the text. One can only imagine the frustration and anguish that accompanied the evolution of the programs from their original to their final states. In most cases, however, the sense of satisfaction and gratification achieved when a program behaves *exactly* as it is supposed to far outweighs the irritation, even the torment, experienced along the way. Students freely concede that you can't get satisfaction without a certain amount of frustration. In the words of the popular song, "you can't have one without the other." In fact the computer is an awfully

272

dumb machine. It does exactly what you tell it to do, not necessarily what you intended it to do, which can sometimes prove to be quite infuriating. Finding and eliminating errors—the so-called debugging stage—is the third phase.

Because the kinds of errors that can occur are so varied, one has to adopt some type of strategy when writing a program. The errors could be those of logic, syntax, or just typos; data-names can easily be misspelled and/or reserved words can be used in other than their legitimate places. Making mistakes is inevitable. One has to be reconciled to this unpleasant fact and, having accepted it, program accordingly. For example, intermediate results may be displayed by inserting into the program a liberal sprinkling of DISPLAY statements for the first run or two of the program. This might help to clear up the initial mistakes, or, as commonly called, the *bugs*. Once the bugs have been cleared up—in official jargon, once the program has been *debugged*—the DISPLAY statements can be eliminated. In what may be termed "defensive programming," one can prepare for many different types of errors to whatever extent is possible. Any effort expended in devising tricks or traps to catch bugs will pay off handsomely, for the time spent in finding a bug can far exceed the time required in anticipating it. In other words, preparation is far better than perspiration.

12.1　Types of Diagnostic Messages

The compiler is designed to help the programmer as much as possible, spending part of its time checking for errors of syntax. If such an error is found, a *diagnostic* message is printed out, matching the number of the line in violation with the description of the detected error. The different kinds of diagnostic messages run into the hundreds. In fact if you would like to see a complete list of the diagnostics that can be done on the IBM 370, try running the following simple, 5-line program. The PROGRAM-ID name ERRMSG is a special name that is reserved for this purpose.

Program 42

```
IDENTIFICATION DIVISION.
PROGRAM-ID. ERRMSG.
ENVIRONMENT DIVISION.
DATA DIVISION.
PROCEDURE DIVISION.
```

In essence, program errors fall into 2 categories: those that become manifest during compilation and those that become apparent during execution of the program. On most systems 4 types of errors are flagged, which is done by printing out the number of the line in violation, an error code, and finally, the error message itself. On IBM compilers the 4 types of errors are coded W, C, E, and D. Sometimes as the result of a single error more than one will appear.

W-Level Diagnostics

The least severe of the errors is the warning, coded with the letter W. It does not interfere with running the program and informs the programmer that the instruction, although not entirely in keeping with the rules, has been accepted. A typical W-level diagnostic would be a warning that a data-name is too long and therefore is truncated, or an item has been moved into a field that is too small to contain all of it (which could easily have been the programmer's intent). Often these W-type diagnostic messages are ignored, but it is recommended that the errors be corrected and the program rerun. If they are not corrected, anyone subsequently looking at the program listing will probably waste time checking over every diagnostic to ensure that it is not a potential source of error.

C-Level Diagnostics

In a C-level diagnostic the compiler has detected some sort of ambiguity and has guessed at the intended operation. If the guess is correct, all is well and the program is not in need of human intervention. Thus the results will be fine, but only on *condition* that the compiler has made the right guess. This is why it is called a C-level diagnostic. We strongly advise that all C-level diagnostics be corrected before the program is regarded as acceptable.

E-Level Diagnostics

The compiler detects the 2 previous levels of diagnostics (W and C) during compilation, the initial phase that the program undergoes. Sometimes, however, errors do not become apparent until the program is actually in execution, the second of the 2 phases of a program run. Errors detected during execution are regarded with such severity that processing the program is immediately halted. These fatal execution errors are flagged with the code letter E. The omission of a required program name is a primary candidate for an E-level diagnostic. The violation must be corrected before the program is resubmitted.

D-Level Diagnostics

The D-level diagnostic is the most severe kind that is possible in COBOL. It stands for "disaster." This is the diagnostic that is printed out in the event of a compiler error, a contingency over which the programmer has no control. It is extremely rare and ordinarily the programmer may never see a D-level error during an entire career. Running a FORTRAN program on a COBOL compiler might produce a D-level diagnostic!

In WATBOL, the student COBOL compiler that we will discuss later on, diagnostic messages are put into 5 categories rather than into 4. The first is the MESSAGE, which is nonfatal and may be caused by omitting a space after a period. Next is the WARNING, which is also nonfatal and may be triggered by having a PROGRAM-ID name with a length greater than 8. Next in severity is the EXTENSION diagnostic, which flags each nonstandard but acceptable instruction. This is intended merely to advise the programmer that although the instruction is acceptable on the current compiler, it might not work on another. Because transportability of programs is often a major concern, perhaps all nonstandard extensions to the language should be avoided. An ERROR is a severe violation caused by, say, the instruction:

DIVIDE A BY B.

As you will recall, this form of the divide instruction must use the GIVING clause. The equivalent of the "disaster" in WATBOL is the TERMINATION diagnostic that few students ever see.

On Cyber computers there are 5 levels, too. They are:

T: trivial, nonfatal
W: warning, nonfatal
F: an unresolved semantic error such that the statement cannot be compiled, for example, an 02-level item with no preceding 01 level.
C: catastrophic; compiler error
N: nonstandard

So you see these 3 totally different compilers produce almost identical error messages. If the diagnostics on your particular compiler are not exactly the same, they will surely be close enough for you to understand them. To understand this subject further, examine carefully the following program, which has been designed to print a simple heading on a new page. The method adopted to accomplish this is to move the constant '1' to the carriage-control position of the output line. Many programmers prefer this procedure to the PAGE option. It would be instructive for you to pretend that you are the compiler and determine if the program is in order. After all, the compiler has to examine minutely every instruction and entry in your program before it can convert the program to binary.

Program 43

```
1       IDENTIFICATION   DIVISION.
2       PROGRAM-ID.      HEADINGS.
3       AUTHOR.          IRVIN POREMBA.
4       INSTALLATION.    NYU.
5       DATE-WRITTEN.    JUNE 9, 1982.
6       DATE-COMPILED.   JUNE 13, 1982.
7       SECURITY.        HENRY MULLISH.
8       * * * * * * * * * * * * * * * * * * * * * * * * * * *
9       *       THIS PROGRAM WRITES            *
10      *       A SIMPLE HEADING               *
11      *       ON A NEW PAGE                  *
12      * * * * * * * * * * * * * * * * * * * * * * * * * * *
13
14      ENVIRONMENT DIVISION.
15      CONFIGURATION SECTION.
16      SOURCE-COMPUTER. CYBER-170-720.
17      OBJECT-COMPUTER. CYBER-170-720.
18      SPECIAL-NAMES.
19      INPUT-OUTPUT SECTION.
20      FILE-CONTROL.
21          SELECT OUT-FILE ASSIGN TO OUTPUT.
22
23      DATA DIVISION.
24      FILE SECTION.
25
26      FD   OUT-FILE
27          LABEL RECORDS ARE OMITTED.
28
29      01   LINE-OUT.
30          02  CARRIAGE-CONTROL   PIC X(01).
31          02  PRINT-LINE         PIC X(132).
32
33      WORKING STORAGE SECTION.
34
35      01   HEADER-1.
36          02  FILLER             PIC X(05) VALUE SPACES.
37          02  FILLER             PIC X(06) VALUE 'COBOL'.
38          02  FILLER             PIC X(12) VALUE 'PROGRAMMING'.
39          02  FILLER             PIC X(04) VALUE 'INC.'.
40
41      03   HEADER-2.
42          02  FILLER             PIC X(05) VALUE SPACES.
43          02  FILLER             PIC X(11) VALUE 'DEPARTMENT'.
44          02  FILLER             PIC X(12) VALUE 'OF COMPUTER.
45          02  FILLER             PIC X(07) VALUE 'SCIENCE'.
46
47      01   HEADER-3.
48          02  FILLER             PIC X(05) VALUE SPACES.
49          02  FILLER             PIC X(09) VALUE 'NEW YORK'.
50          02  FILLER             PIC X(16) VALUE 'UNIVERSITY 10003'.
51
52      PROCEDURE DIVISION.
53
54      MAIN-LINE-ROUTINE.
55          PERFORM OPEN-FILE.
56          PERFORM NEW-PAGE.
57          PERFORM WRITE-HEADINGS.
58          PERFORM CLOSE-UP.
59          STOP RUN.
```

```
60
61        OPEN-FILE.
62            OPEN OUTPUT OUT-FILE.
63
64        NEW-PAGE.
65            MOVE '1' TO CARRIAGE-CONTROL.
66            MOVE SPACES TO PRINT-LINE.
67            WRITE LINE-OUT.
68            MOVE SPACES TO CARRIAGE-CONTROL.
69
70        WRITE-HEADINGS.
71            MOVE HEADER-1 TO PRINT-LINE.
72            WRITE LINE-OUT AFTER 2.
73            MOVE HEADER-2 TO PRINT-LINE.
74            WRITE LINE-OUT AFTER 1.
75            MOVE HEADER-3 TO PRINT-LINE.
76            WRITE LINE-OUT AFTER 1.
77
78        CLOSE-UP.
79            CLOSE OUT-FILE.
```

The program "bombed," to use the jargon of computer programmers. It might be eye-opening for you to know that the compiler listed no fewer than 19 errors—in such a simple program, too! Here is the list of diagnostics as printed by the COBOL computer on the Cyber 170/720. The diagnostics are shown under the headings SEV for severity, LINE for line number, COL for column number, and ERROR for the nature of the error.

Output for Program 43 (I)

```
SEV  LINE  COL  ERROR
F    33    8    3001  THIS ELEMENT MAY NOT APPEAR IN THIS CONTEXT.
W    33    31   3212  A DUPLICATE PERIOD HAS BEEN ENCOUNTERED. THE PRECEDING ONE IS IGNORED.
W    36    NA   4020  IN THE FILE OR LINKAGE SECTION, THE VALUE CLAUSE IS ONLY ALLOWED WITH CONDITION NAME ENTRIES.
W    37    NA   4020  IN THE FILE OR LINKAGE SECTION, THE VALUE CLAUSE IS ONLY ALLOWED WITH CONDITION NAME ENTRIES.
W    38    NA   4020  IN THE FILE OR LINKAGE SECTION, THE VALUE CLAUSE IS ONLY ALLOWED WITH CONDITION NAME ENTRIES.
F    39    NA   4011  A PICTURE CLAUSE IS ONLY ALLOWED WITH AN ELEMENTARY ITEM.
W    39    NA   4020  IN THE FILE OR LINKAGE SECTION, THE VALUE CLAUSE IS ONLY ALLOWED WITH CONDITION NAME ENTRIES.
W    39    NA   8045  LITERAL EXCEEDS ITEM LENGTH. VALUE TRUNCATED.
F    41    NA   4010  A PICTURE CLAUSE IS REQUIRED FOR THIS ELEMENTARY ITEM.
W    42    NA   4020  IN THE FILE OR LINKAGE SECTION, THE VALUE CLAUSE IS ONLY ALLOWED WITH CONDITION NAME ENTRIES.
W    43    NA   4020  IN THE FILE OR LINKAGE SECTION, THE VALUE CLAUSE IS ONLY ALLOWED WITH CONDITION NAME ENTRIES.
W    44    NA   4020  IN THE FILE OR LINKAGE SECTION, THE VALUE CLAUSE IS ONLY ALLOWED WITH CONDITION NAME ENTRIES.
W    44    NA   8045  LITERAL EXCEEDS ITEM LENGTH. VALUE TRUNCATED.
F    44    51   1011  THIS NON-NUMERIC LITERAL HAS NO TERMINAL QUOTE. A QUOTE FOLLOWING COLUMN 72 IS ASSUMED.
W    45    NA   4020  IN THE FILE OR LINKAGE SECTION, THE VALUE CLAUSE IS ONLY ALLOWED WITH CONDITION NAME ENTRIES.
W    48    NA   4020  IN THE FILE OR LINKAGE SECTION, THE VALUE CLAUSE IS ONLY ALLOWED WITH CONDITION NAME ENTRIES.
W    49    NA   4020  IN THE FILE OR LINKAGE SECTION, THE VALUE CLAUSE IS ONLY ALLOWED WITH CONDITION NAME ENTRIES.
W    50    NA   4020  IN THE FILE OR LINKAGE SECTION, THE VALUE CLAUSE IS ONLY ALLOWED WITH CONDITION NAME ENTRIES.
F    73    17   7180  AN ERROR WAS DETECTED IN THE DESCRIPTION OF THIS ITEM. THAT ERROR MUST BE CORRECTED BEFORE
                      THIS STATEMENT CAN BE COMPILED CORRECTLY.
                 **       19 ERRORS LISTED        **
                 **       1 UNLISTED TRIVIAL ERROR  **
```

The first error is fatal and refers to line 33, column 8. An examination of line 33 reveals immediately that the hyphen has been omitted from WORKING-STORAGE. This is indeed a serious error. Because WORKING-STORAGE has not been recognized by the compiler, the period in the same line is flagged as a duplicate period. Because there is, in effect, no WORKING-STORAGE section present, every entry that contains a VALUE clause will automatically be in error. So lines 36, 37, 38, 39, 41, 42, 43, 44, 45, 48, 49, and 50 will be in error. The letters NA stand for "not applicable." Placing a hyphen in between WORKING and STORAGE eliminates all these diagnostics. The error messages are sometimes quite mystifying, but remember, the compiler is fixed and cannot know exactly what was intended. It does the best it can.

Placing the hyphen in WORKING-STORAGE in line 33 certainly improves the situation. Here is the list of diagnostics printed with this single correction made. The number of listed errors has now been reduced from 19 to 7, certainly a step in the right direction. Instead of 5 fatal errors we now have only 4.

Output for Program 43 (II)

```
SEV  LINE  COL  ERROR
F    39    NA   4011  A PICTURE CLAUSE IS ONLY ALLOWED WITH AN ELEMENTARY ITEM.
W    39    NA   8045  LITERAL EXCEEDS ITEM LENGTH. VALUE TRUNCATED.
F    41    NA   4010  A PICTURE CLAUSE IS REQUIRED FOR THIS ELEMENTARY ITEM.
W    44    NA   4051  A TERMINAL PERIOD IS REQUIRED FOR THIS DATA ENTRY.
W    44    NA   8045  LITERAL EXCEEDS ITEM LENGTH. VALUE TRUNCATED.
F    44    51   1011  THIS NON-NUMERIC LITERAL HAS NO TERMINAL QUOTE. A QUOTE FOLLOWING COLUMN 72 IS ASSUMED.
F    73    17   7180  AN ERROR WAS DETECTED IN THE DESCRIPTION OF THIS ITEM. THAT ERROR MUST BE CORRECTED
                      BEFORE THIS STATEMENT CAN BE COMPILED CORRECTLY.
                      * *      7 ERRORS LISTED         * *
                      * *      1 UNLISTED TRIVIAL ERROR    * *
```

Line 39 is flagged as a fatal error. The reason is that A PICTURE clause is only allowed with an elementary item. Really! A close scrutiny of line 39 reveals that there is absolutely nothing wrong with it. What the devil is the compiler complaining about? In such cases it usually pays to look in the neighborhood of the alleged error. A glance at line 41 indicates the source of the problem. Can you see the culprit? The record-name HEADER-2 is assigned an 03-level number instead of 01, which every record description must contain. Giving it an 03-level number implies that it is subordinate to its preceding 02-level item.

Changing line 41 to an 01 instead of an 03 clears up the problem dramatically. In the output for the next run of the program, we have now reduced the number of listed errors to 3. We are getting close.

Output for Program 43 (III)

```
SEV  LINE  COL  ERROR
W    44    NA   4051  A TERMINAL PERIOD IS REQUIRED FOR THIS DATA ENTRY.
W    44    NA   8045  LITERAL EXCEEDS ITEM LENGTH. VALUE TRUNCATED.
F    44    51   1011  THIS NON-NUMERIC LITERAL HAS NO TERMINAL QUOTE. A QUOTE FOLLOWING COLUMN 72 IS ASSUMED.
                      * *      3 ERRORS LISTED         * *
                      * *      1 UNLISTED TRIVIAL ERROR    * *
```

Line 44 is responsible for each of the 3 diagnostics, 2 of which are merely warnings and one is a fatal error. The first warning states that a terminal period is required. However, on careful inspection it is clear that a terminal period is, in fact, there. The next warning says that the literal exceeds the item length; an outright lie—OF COMPUTER is exactly 12 characters long (including the space) and a PICTURE OF X(12) is perfect. So let us look now at the third diagnostic message, the fatal one, which draws our attention specifically to column 51 of line 44. This points to the leading apostrophe. However, where is the closing apostrophe? Alas, it has been omitted!

The following program is the corrected version, which produces no diagnostics whatever, just the expected output.

Program 43 (corrected)

```
1        IDENTIFICATION   DIVISION.
2        PROGRAM-ID.      HEADINGS.
3        AUTHOR.          IRVIN POREMBA.
4        INSTALLATION.    NYU.
5        DATE-WRITTEN.    JUNE 9, 1982.
6        DATE-COMPILED.   JUNE 13, 1982.
7        SECURITY.        HENRY MULLISH.
8        * * * * * * * * * * * * * * * * * * * * * * * * * * * *
9        *      THIS PROGRAM WRITES              *
10       *      A SIMPLE HEADING                 *
11       *      ON A NEW PAGE                    *
12       * * * * * * * * * * * * * * * * * * * * * * * * * * * *
13
14       ENVIRONMENT    DIVISION.
15       CONFIGURATION  SECTION.
16       SOURCE-COMPUTER. CYBER-170-720.
```

```
17        OBJECT-COMPUTER. CYBER-170-720.
18        SPECIAL-NAMES.
19        INPUT-OUTPUT SECTION.
20        FILE-CONTROL.
21            SELECT OUT-FILE ASSIGN TO OUTPUT.
22
23        DATA DIVISION.
24        FILE SECTION.
25
26        FD   OUT-FILE
27            LABEL RECORDS ARE OMITTED.
28
29        01   LINE-OUT.
30            02   CARRIAGE-CONTROL  PIC X(01).
31            02   PRINT-LINE        PIC X(132).
32
33        WORKING-STORAGE SECTION.
34
35        01   HEADER-1.
36            02   FILLER            PIC X(05) VALUE SPACES.
37            02   FILLER            PIC X(06) VALUE 'COBOL'.
38            02   FILLER            PIC X(12) VALUE 'PROGRAMMING'.
39            02   FILLER            PIC X(04) VALUE 'INC.'.
40
41        01   HEADER-2.
42            02   FILLER            PIC X(05) VALUE SPACES.
43            02   FILLER            PIC X(11) VALUE 'DEPARTMENT'.
44            02   FILLER            PIC X(12) VALUE 'OF COMPUTER'.
45            02   FILLER            PIC X(07) VALUE 'SCIENCE'.
46
47        01   HEADER-3.
48            02   FILLER            PIC X(05) VALUE SPACES.
49            02   FILLER            PIC X(09) VALUE 'NEW YORK'.
50            02   FILLER            PIC X(16) VALUE 'UNIVERSITY 10003'.
51
52        PROCEDURE DIVISION.
53
54        MAIN-LINE-ROUTINE.
55            PERFORM OPEN-FILE.
56            PERFORM NEW-PAGE.
57            PERFORM WRITE-HEADINGS.
58            PERFORM CLOSE-UP.
59            STOP RUN.
60
61        OPEN-FILE.
62            OPEN OUTPUT OUT-FILE.
63
64        NEW-PAGE.
65            MOVE '1' TO CARRIAGE-CONTROL.
66            MOVE SPACES TO PRINT-LINE.
67            WRITE LINE-OUT.
68            MOVE SPACES TO CARRIAGE-CONTROL.
69
70        WRITE-HEADINGS.
71            MOVE HEADER-1 TO PRINT-LINE.
72            WRITE LINE-OUT AFTER 2.
73            MOVE HEADER-2 TO PRINT-LINE.
74            WRITE LINE-OUT AFTER 1.
75            MOVE HEADER-3 TO PRINT-LINE.
76            WRITE LINE-OUT AFTER 1.
77
78        CLOSE-UP.
79            CLOSE OUT-FILE.
```

Output for Program 43

```
COBOL PROGRAMMING INC.
DEPARTMENT OF COMPUTER SCIENCE
NEW YORK UNIVERSITY 10003
```

The fact that a program produces no diagnostics is, unfortunately, no guarantee that it is correct. After all, if DATA-NAME-1 and DATA-NAME-2 had to be added together and you inadvertently multiplied them, there is no way the computer can detect such an error of logic. One must never assume that just because the output "looks so grand and reliable" that it is necessarily correct. The program must first be checked out with carefully selected data that is designed to test as many contingencies as is humanly possible. Computed results should be checked against independently calculated ones. Here the pocket calculator can be very helpful. Handing in incorrect results to a teacher negatively affects your grade. (Teachers and their graders invariably use pocket calculators to check computed results; so why don't you, too?) By the same token, submitting an erroneous report to a superior in industry can be catastrophic. Remember, a computer calculates at phenomenal speeds and can produce incorrect results at those speeds.

12.2   COBOL Debugging Aids

Clearly, infinite care and great attention to detail is called for. To assist you in this all-important task, several alternatives are provided, some or even all of which may be incorporated into a COBOL program. As already mentioned, a liberal sprinkling of DISPLAY statements is always a good idea. As soon as the program checks out correctly these statements may be eliminated. However, COBOL provides the programmer with other specially designed debugging tools to help overcome those most embarrassing moments when neither compilation-time nor execution-time bugs have been detected, yet no output is produced. These techniques are used simultaneously with other elementary tricks, such as using dummy data designed to test for all possible contingencies and then real data to check out the program for the specific application under the normal prevailing conditions.

One of the most common debugging features on the IBM 370 family of computers is what is known as the *trace*. Suppose we have a program whose Procedure Division is composed of a series of paragraphs, each, of course, with its own unique paragraph-name. The instruction READY TRACE, when inserted in the Procedure Division (in the B margin), causes the system to print out during execution the names of each paragraph-name that is executed in the order of execution. On some systems these paragraph-names are printed along the width of the page and on others, underneath each other. To "switch off" the trace, as it were, the instruction RESET TRACE is used. This feature is particularly helpful in isolating errors of logic. As soon as the error has been isolated and corrected, the trace statements should be removed from the deck.

Under the 1968 standard another favorite device was to place EXHIBIT statements at key points, or "check points," along the program. In its most elementary form the EXHIBIT statement behaves simply as a DISPLAY statement. For example, inserting

EXHIBIT RETAIL-PRICE

at a point of the program in the B margin, where RETAIL-PRICE is a data-name in the program, will print out its value at that point. Similarly, inserting

EXHIBIT 'REACHED RETAIL-PRICE-PARA'

will print out the message in quotes.

The instruction

EXHIBIT GROSS-PAY, '   IS THE GROSS PAY'

will print out first the value of the data-name GROSS-PAY, which is followed in turn on the same line by the message in quotes. In order to ensure that there is a separation between the value printed out for GROSS-PAY and its accompanying message one deliberately includes a blank as the first character of the quoted message.

A more interesting version of the EXHIBIT statement is the form that prints out first the *name* of the data-name, then an equal sign, a space, and finally, the actual value of the data-name. For example, the instruction

EXHIBIT NAMED GROSS-PAY

will print out the data-name and its value in the following form:

GROSS-PAY = 123456

where the actual data-name is followed by an equals sign with a blank on each side. By the same token, the instruction

EXHIBIT NAMED GROSS-PAY 'WEEKLY WAGE ONLY'

would print out when executed

GROSS-PAY = 123456 WEEKLY WAGE ONLY

For those occasions when it is desired to print out the value of a data-name only if its value *has changed from the last time the instruction was executed*, yet another form of the EXHIBIT may be used. For example, if we want to check whether GROSS-PAY had changed its value, we can write

EXHIBIT CHANGED GROSS-PAY

If the value of GROSS-PAY had in fact changed, its present value would have been printed out, preceded by an equals sign and a blank.

Finally, there is a version of the EXHIBIT that combines both the NAMED and the CHANGED options. As you might have guessed, it is the CHANGED NAME option, as in

EXHIBIT CHANGED NAME GROSS-PAY

where the value of GROSS-PAY will be printed alongside the print out GROSS–PAY = , only if its value has changed.

Another option that is usually found associated with the EXHIBIT statement is the ON option. For example,

ON 650 EXHIBIT NAMED GROSS-PAY

will print out the word GROSS–PAY = , followed by the current value of GROSS–PAY after the instruction has been executed 650 times. The EXHIBIT statement is not included in the 1974 standard.

12.3 Job Control Language (JCL) for the IBM 370 OS System

In order to run any COBOL program, one needs to punch certain control cards that must accompany the program. The Job Control Language (JCL) cards, which we will describe here, apply to the IBM 360/370 system, probably the most popular commercial computer system in the world today.

The COBOL program itself together with its data and associated control cards constitutes a "job." In order to identify the user to the system, the very first control card (often referred to as the *job card*) contains the user's account number and the name of the user. This enables the system to ascertain that the account is valid and verifies the associated user's name. In addition to this information, the user must supply a job name composed of up to 8 characters. A job name must begin with an alphabetic character but may be followed by either alphabetic or numeric characters. No special symbols such as a period, comma, or a minus sign, and so on, may be used—and this includes the blank space. The job name serves to identify the particular job to the supervisory system.

Figure 12-1 shows a typical job card.

The job card must begin with a slash in columns 1 and 2 and is immediately followed by the job name. The word JOB, which starts in column 12, must be

```
1 2 3        12   16              26
//FIRST     JOB  (XXXX, XXXX),    'HENRY MCKAY'
```

Figure 12-1

preceded and followed by a space. Within the parentheses, beginning with column 16, there is the account number, which is supplied to authorized users by the installation. After the closing parenthesis there is a comma, followed immediately (that means no space!) by the name of the user, which is enclosed within apostrophes.

The second control card is generally the EXEC card, which specifies the particular compiler to be used. At New York University it is currently the version COBOLU (the ANSI compiler). Other compilers that may be available at various installations are COBOLE, COBOLF, COBUCS, and COBACG, which will all compile and execute a COBOL program.

Figure 12-2 shows a typical EXEC card.

The third control card is punched

```
//COB.SYSIN DD *
```

This card specifies that the COBOL program itself follows immediately. Therefore the 4 divisions of the program follow this //COB.SYSIN DD * card. After the program there is a card punched with /* in columns 1 and 2, which indicates the end of the program. What follows after the /* card depends on the nature of the program.

1. If the only input/output verb used in the program is DISPLAY (as in Program 1 in the text), the only cards necessary are:

```
//GO.SYSOUT DD SYSOUT = A
//
```

Figure 12-2

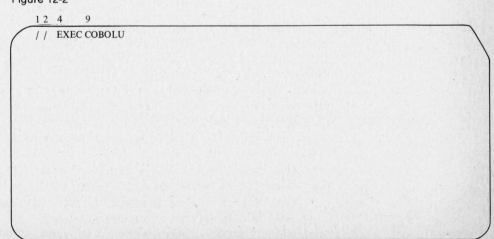

```
1 2  4    9
/ /  EXEC COBOLU
```

2. If the ACCEPT also is used in the program, the following setup is necessary.

```
//GO.SYSOUT DD SYSOUT = A
//GO.SYSIN DD *
```

data card(s) to be read by ACCEPT

```
/*
//
```

3. If just WRITE's are used, as was done in Program 5, the following JCL is required:

```
//GO.mnemonic-name DD SYSOUT = A
//
```

The mnemonic-name is the programmer-selected name that is associated with the file in question. For an output file a common choice is PRINTER, but PAYFILE, ACCTREC, and ACCTPAY are just as acceptable. Whatever name is chosen must appear in the SELECT clause in the Environment Division.

4. For a program using READ's, WRITE's, and DISPLAY's, the necessary JCL is

```
/*
//GO.SYSOUT DD SYSOUT = A
//GO.READER DD *
```

data

```
/*
//
```

where the output file is assigned to SYSOUT and the input file to READER in the SELECT clauses.

5. If the programmer wishes any output produced by a DISPLAY instruction to be printed on a *separate* page, the JCL is

```
/*
//GO.SYSOUT DD SYSOUT = A
//GO.PRINTER DD SYSOUT = A
GO.READER DD *
```

data

```
/*
//
```

The complete deck looks as shown in Figure 12-3.

12.4 Interpreting System Termination Codes

When writing a COBOL program, one, of course, takes the utmost care. It often transpires (much too frequently as a matter of fact), however, that despite our valiant attempts, errors of logic or of keypunching do creep in. The system has been designed so that if it detects an error and abnormally ends (ABENDS) the program, it categorizes the source of the error according to a system code. These codes are usually prefixed by 0C (zeroC), followed by a digit and are printed out before the listing of the program.

The termination code 0C1 is generally caused by an attempt to read or write a file that has not yet been opened, or one that has been closed.

Code 0C2 is caused by a missing or a misspelled DD statement in the JCL.

Code 0C4 is caused by subscripting beyond the length of the table. An uninitialized subscript or index will also cause an 0C4, as indeed will an attempt to

Figure 12-3

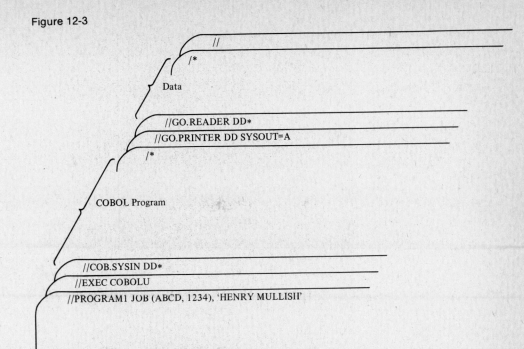

enter a so-called "protected" area. Once again, an attempt to read an unopened file may cause an 0C4 error message.

An uninitialized subscript or index can cause an 0C5 error. Other causes include subscripts that are too large, an OPEN statement that has failed due to JCL errors, or a misspelled or missing DD statement. Still other causes are attempting to close an already closed file, making an improper exit from a PERFORM, or attempting to access an input or output area before a READ or an OPEN instruction for the file in question is executed.

Code 0C6 may be caused by an improper exit from a PERFORM statement.

Code 0C7 is probably the most frequent execution time-error message encountered by students who are novices in COBOL language. The most common reason for an 0C7 error message is that the data is not of the correct form. Blank spaces within a numeric field will cause an 0C7 error, as indeed will the inclusion of a decimal point, comma, dollar sign, or any other nonnumeric character.

Finally, a program that for some reason exceeds the allotted execution time may be terminated and the completion code 322 printed. Two possible reasons for this error are: (1) the computation actually requires a greater time period than either the user has specified in the JCL or the "default" time allows or (2) the program is caught in an infinite loop.

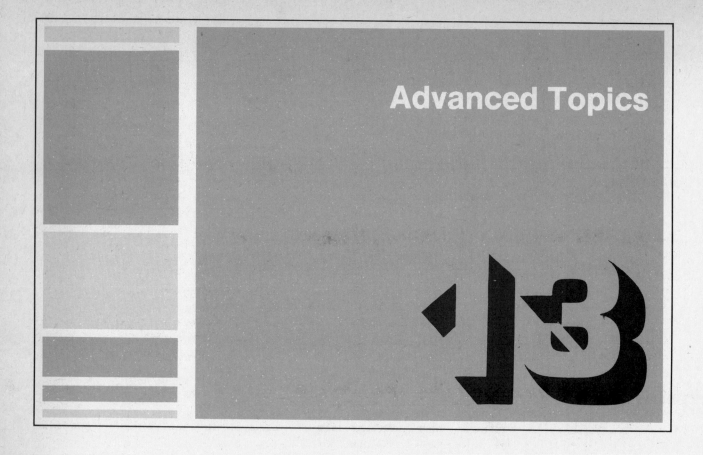

Advanced Topics

COBOL is the key to all kinds of opportunities.

(Pauline Landau)

13.1 The Telephone Problem

It is customary for the standard 7-digit telephone number to be composed of a 2-letter exchange code, followed by a digit, followed by a 4-digit number. For example, some typical telephone numbers are AC–2–1234, SU–5–9801, and MU–4–4444. The recent tendency is to replace the letter codes with numerics. The result is that almost all newly assigned telephone numbers are composed of 7 numerics. For some people, remembering a 7-digit telephone number is far more difficult than one composed of 2 letters followed by 5 numeric digits. The following program has been devised to assist such people.

It will be noticed that in the standard telephone dial (see the figure on page 286) there are 10 finger positions for the digits 0 through 9 (the program is equally applicable to push-button instruments). Associated with the digit 2, for example, there are the letters ABC. Digits 3 through 9 on the dial also have letters associated with them, as shown in the diagram. The digits 0 and 1 do *not* have corresponding alphabetics.

The purpose of this program is to read a given 7-digit telephone number and to print out every possible alphabetic combination corresponding to that telephone number. Within the 2187 combinations it is hoped at least one word or name will be included that somehow describes the individual who has the telephone number, thereby avoiding the difficulty of having to remember the 7 digits. One could then simply dial the 7-lettered word or name.

Because the digits 0 and 1 do not have corresponding letters, some kind of decision has to be made if the telephone number in question contains one or both of these 2 digits. Either the telephone number can be rejected outright or a substitution can be made. For example, the zero can be replaced by the letter Z, which incidentally does not appear on the telephone dial. As for the digit 1, this could be substituted with, say, a minus sign. This version of the program rejects any telephone number that contains a zero or a 1.

The telephone number is "inspected" for the presence of a 1 or a 0 by means of the INSPECT statement. This statement is new with the 1974 standard and replaces the EXAMINE statement of the 1968 standard. Although the INSPECT is a "souped-up" version of the EXAMINE statement, you might have to become familiar with both because you can never know in advance which standard you will be using.

The EXAMINE statement has 2 different formats. As with the INSPECT (which has 3 different formats), the EXAMINE is used to examine incoming data and to manipulate the characters in specific ways. Because both these statements are capable of character manipulation, they are often used for what is known as *data validation*. That is, they are used to inspect data and to verify that the data is valid. Other uses are character translation and text-editing.

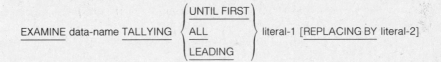

EXAMINE data-name TALLYING { UNTIL FIRST / ALL / LEADING } literal-1 [REPLACING BY literal-2]

For example,

EXAMINE ABC TALLYING ALL SPACES.

ABC is a data-name with a PICTURE of X(06) containing, say, 'ƀƀƀDOG'. The instruction tallies up all the spaces that are present in the data-name ABC. TALLY is a special register that is always automatically initialized to zero. The value of TALLY would be 3, because there is a total of 3 spaces in ABC.

For example,

EXAMINE DEF TALLYING ALL '*'

where DEF is a data-name with a PICTURE of X(05) containing '1*2*3'. This time TALLY would yield the number 2 because there are 2 asterisks in the field under examination.

Assume that GHI is a data-name with a PICTURE of 9(04) containing 'ƀƀ23'. For example,

EXAMINE GHI TALLYING LEADING SPACES REPLACING BY ZEROS.

This time TALLY would be equal to 2 (because there are 2 leading spaces) and GHI would change its contents to 0023.

In the second format for the EXAMINE statement there is no provision for tallying up any occurrences. Instead, it allows only for replacing characters with others.

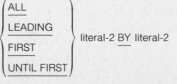

EXAMINE data-name REPLACING { ALL / LEADING / FIRST / UNTIL FIRST } literal-2 BY literal-2

For example, assume that JKL is a data-name with a PICTURE of X(08) containing 12/13/48.

EXAMINE JKL REPLACING ALL '/' BY SPACE.

This would change JKL to 12 13 48.

So you see, the EXAMINE statement is capable of performing character manipulation in addition to keeping track of the number of occurrences that a certain character appears.

The INSPECT statement is quite similar in function to the EXAMINE but has some features that are even more powerful. In its simplest form it is:

$$\underline{\text{INSPECT}} \text{ data-name-1 } \underline{\text{TALLYING}} \text{ data-name-2 FOR} \left\{ \begin{array}{l} \underline{\text{ALL}} \\ \underline{\text{LEADING}} \end{array} \right\} \left\{ \begin{array}{l} \text{data-name-3} \\ \text{literal} \end{array} \right\}$$

Whereas the EXAMINE provides a ready-made data-name TALLY, the INSPECT asks the programmer to supply his or her own, which, of course, must be initialized to zero.

In the program the instructions:

INSPECT TELEPHONE-NUMBER TALLYING COUNT-ZEROS FOR ALL ZEROS
INSPECT TELEPHONE-NUMBER TALLYING COUNT-ONES FOR ALL '1'

inspect the telephone number and count the number of occurrences of all zeros and ones. The tally of zeros is placed in COUNT-ZEROS and the count of all 1's is stored in COUNT-ONES. If either of these counts turns out to be greater than zero the telephone number is rejected.

Here is a typical telephone dial.

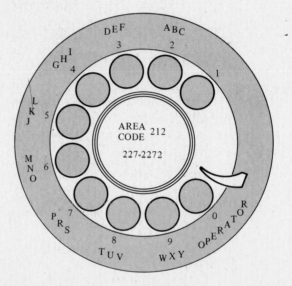

The input to the program is a 7-digit telephone number, punched in columns 1 through 7. The output consists of a printout of the telephone number to be converted, followed by the 2187, (3^7), possible alphabetic combinations corresponding to that telephone number, printed in 11 columns on each page.

In order to understand how the program works, we will first consider the simple case of a 3-digit telephone number, 247. The letters associated with these 3 digits are:

2	4	7
ABC	GHI	PRS

The idea is to select systematically each of the letters in turn until all combinations are exhausted. The first combination, taking the first letter from each group of 3, is AGP. Next is AGR followed by AGS; taking the succeeding 2 letters in turn from the third group. At this point the rightmost group, PRS, is exhausted. Then we take the first letter of the first group, A, followed by the second letter of the second group, H, followed in turn by each of the letters of the third group. We therefore arrive at the combinations AHP, AHR, and AHS. Next we combine A with the third letter of the second group, I, matching it up successively with PRS of the third group to obtain the combinations AIP, AIR, and AIS. This exhausts both the third and the second groups. At this point, we begin with the second letter of the first group, combining it in turn with each letter of the second and third group, exactly as before. This gives us the combinations:

```
BGP   BGR   BGS
BHP   BHR   BHS
BIP   BIR   BIS
```

Finally, the letter C of the first group is combined with each letter of the second and third groups, creating the combinations

```
CGP   CGR   CGS
CHP   CHR   CHS
CIP   CIR   CIS
```

Thus we have arrived at each of the possible combinations by using the digits 2, 4, and 7. In essence we have accessed each of the letters associated with these 3 digits as follows.

```
1  1  1
1  1  2
1  1  3
1  2  1
1  2  2
1  2  3
1  3  1
1  3  2
1  3  3
2  1  1
   :
3  2  3
3  3  3
```

In the program where we deal with 7 digits rather than with 3, this scheme is accomplished by exploiting the advanced version of the PERFORM statement, to be described shortly.

Each digit 2 through 7 is associated with one of 8 groups of 3 letters.

2	3	4	5	6	7	8	9
ABC	DEF	GHI	JKL	MNO	PRS	TUV	WXY

In order to refer to each letter within a group for a particular digit, we vary pointers called LETTER-POINTER-1 through LETTER-POINTER-7 "from 1 by 1 until" the letter-pointer is greater than 3.

Therefore to point to each letter in succession of each group associated with each of the 7 digits of the telephone number, we set up a "nest" of PERFORM loops. Each pointer is initialized to 1 and LETTER-POINTER-7 begins the cycle from 1 to 3. As soon as it becomes greater than 3, LETTER-POINTER-6 is increased to 2 and LETTER-POINTER-7 is reinitialized to 1. This process continues until *all* pointers are greater than 3, at which point all possible combinations are printed out.

The statement used to execute the nest of loops is the somewhat intimidating version of the PERFORM whose formal notation is:

$$\underline{\text{PERFORM}} \text{ procedure-name-1} \quad \begin{Bmatrix} \underline{\text{THROUGH}} \\ \underline{\text{THRU}} \end{Bmatrix} \text{procedure-name-2}$$

$$\underline{\text{VARYING}} \begin{Bmatrix} \text{data-name-1} \\ \text{index-1} \end{Bmatrix} \quad \underline{\text{FROM}} \begin{Bmatrix} \text{data-name-2} \\ \text{index-2} \\ \text{literal-1} \end{Bmatrix}$$

$$\underline{\text{BY}} \begin{Bmatrix} \text{data-name-3} \\ \text{literal-2} \end{Bmatrix} \quad \underline{\text{UNTIL}} \text{ condition-1}$$

$$\left[\underline{\text{AFTER}} \begin{Bmatrix} \text{data-name-4} \\ \text{index-3} \end{Bmatrix} \quad \underline{\text{FROM}} \begin{Bmatrix} \text{data-name-5} \\ \text{index-4} \\ \text{literal-3} \end{Bmatrix} \right.$$

$$\underline{\text{BY}} \begin{Bmatrix} \text{data-name-6} \\ \text{literal-4} \end{Bmatrix} \quad \underline{\text{UNTIL}} \text{ condition-2}$$

$$\left[\underline{\text{AFTER}} \begin{Bmatrix} \text{data-name-7} \\ \text{index-5} \end{Bmatrix} \quad \underline{\text{FROM}} \begin{Bmatrix} \text{data-name-8} \\ \text{index-6} \\ \text{literal-5} \end{Bmatrix} \right.$$

$$\left. \left. \underline{\text{BY}} \begin{Bmatrix} \text{data-name-9} \\ \text{literal-9} \end{Bmatrix} \quad \underline{\text{UNTIL}} \text{ condition-3} \right] \right]$$

As you will notice, a maximum of 3 data-names may be varied with a single such PERFORM instruction. However, because the required process calls for 7 data-names to vary, this obstacle is overcome by breaking it up into 3 different segments.

Again, remember that the only telephone number digits we can handle are 2 through 9, for both 0 and 1 have no alphabetic equivalents. The digits 2 through 9 are used as subscripts. However, these 8 digits must begin with a subscript of 1 through 8. Therefore 1 is subtracted from each of the valid 7 digits.

Using the letter-pointer and the decremented digits, we are now able to access the appropriate letters from the table. For example, if the decremented digit is equal to 3 and the letter-pointer has a value of 1, the corresponding letter would be G because the first letter of the third group, GHI, is G. Once a letter has been accessed for each of the 7 digits of the telephone number, we have the desired combination.

Instead of printing out the number per line (which would be most wasteful of paper), a method is used to print the somewhat voluminous output with 11 numbers per line. This is accomplished by the use of the OCCURS clause in the detail-line.

Program 44

```
1       IDENTIFICATION  DIVISION.
2       PROGRAM-ID.     TELEPHONE.
3       AUTHOR.         IRVIN POREMBA.
4       INSTALLATION    NYU.
5       DATE-WRITTEN.   APRIL 28, 1982.
6       DATE-COMPILED.  JUNE 20, 1982.
7       SECURITY.       HENRY MULLISH.
8
9       ************************************************************
10      *       THIS PROGRAM READS IN A TELEPHONE NUMBER          *
11      *       PUNCHED:                                          *
12      *                                                         *
13      *       COLUMN 1: FIRST DIGIT                             *
14      *       COLUMN 2: SECOND DIGIT                            *
15      *       COLUMN 3: THIRD DIGIT                             *
16      *       COLUMN 4: FOURTH DIGIT                            *
17      *       COLUMN 4: FIFTH DIGIT                             *
18      *       COLUMN 6: SIXTH DIGIT                             *
19      *       COLUMN 7: SEVENTH DIGIT                           *
20      *                                                         *
21      *       THE PROGRAM TESTS EACH TELEPHONE NUMBER TO        *
22      *       BE SURE THAT IT IS BOTH NUMERIC AND DOES NOT      *
23      *       CONTAIN ANY ZEROS OR ONES. IF IT IS A VALID       *
24      *       NUMBER THE PROGRAM PRINTS OUT THE 2,187           *
25      *       DIFFERENT ALPHABETIC COMBINATIONS CORRESPONDING   *
26      *       TO THAT TELEPHONE NUMBER.                         *
27      ************************************************************
```

```
28
29      ENVIRONMENT    DIVISION.
30      CONFIGURATION  SECTION.
31      SOURCE-COMPUTER. CYBER-170-720.
32      OBJECT-COMPUTER. CYBER-170-720.
33      SPECIAL-NAMES.
34      INPUT-OUTPUT SECTION.
35      FILE-CONTROL.
36          SELECT IN-FILE ASSIGN TO INPUT.
37          SELECT OUT-FILE ASSIGN TO OUTPUT.
38
39      DATA DIVISION.
40      FILE SECTION.
41
42      FD   IN-FILE
43           LABEL RECORDS ARE OMITTED.
44
45      01   RECORD-IN.
46           02    TELEPHONE-NUMBER.
47                 03    FIRST-DIGIT      PIC 9.
48                 03    SECOND-DIGIT     PIC 9.
49                 03    THIRD-DIGIT      PIC 9.
50                 03    FOURTH-DIGIT     PIC 9.
51                 03    FIFTH-DIGIT      PIC 9.
52                 03    SIXTH-DIGIT      PIC 9.
53                 03    SEVENTH-DIGIT    PIC 9.
54           02    FILLER                 PIC X(73).
55
56      FD   OUT-FILE
57           LABEL RECORDS ARE OMITTED.
58
59      01   LINE-OUT                      PIC X(133).
60
61      WORKING-STORAGE SECTION.
62
63      01   INDEPENDENT-ITEMS-USED.
64           02    ANY-MORE-CARDS    PIC X(03) VALUE 'YES'.
65           02    POSITIONER        PIC 99 VALUE ZEROS.
66           02    COUNT-ZEROS       PIC 9.
67           02    COUNT-ONES        PIC 9.
68
69      01   POINT-TO-LETTER.
70           02    LETTER-POINTER-1    PIC 9.
71           02    LETTER-POINTER-2    PIC 9.
72           02    LETTER-POINTER-3    PIC 9.
73           02    LETTER-POINTER-4    PIC 9.
74           02    LETTER-POINTER-5    PIC 9.
75           02    LETTER-POINTER-6    PIC 9.
76           02    LETTER-POINTER-7    PIC 9.
77
78      01   CONVERSION-TABLE-SKELETON.
79           02    FILLER    PIC X(12) VALUE 'ABCDEFGHIJKL'.
80           02    FILLER    PIC X(12) VALUE 'MNOPRSTUVWXY'.
81
82      01   CONVERSION-TABLE REDEFINES CONVERSION-TABLE-SKELETON.
83           02    TABLE-ELEMENT OCCURS 8 TIMES.
84                 03    LETTERS OCCURS 3 TIMES.
85                       05 FILLER    PIC X(01).
86
87      01   COMPLETED-WORD.
88           02    LETTER-1    PIC X(01).
89           02    LETTER-2    PIC X(01).
90           02    LETTER-3    PIC X(01).
91           02    LETTER-4    PIC X(01).
92           02    LETTER-5    PIC X(01).
93           02    LETTER-6    PIC X(01).
94           02    LETTER-7    PIC X(01).
95
96      01   HEADER-1.
97           02    FILLER       PIC X(01) VALUE SPACES.
98           02    FILLER       PIC X(13) VALUE 'THE TELEPHONE'.
99           02    FILLER       PIC X(01) VALUE SPACES.
100          02    FILLER       PIC X(12) VALUE 'NUMBER IS:'.
101          02    PHONE-OUT    PIC 9999999.
102
```

```
103     01   DETAIL-LINE.
104          02   FILLER              PIC X(01) VALUE SPACES.
105          02   WORD-OUT OCCURS 11 TIMES.
106               03   FILLER         PIC X(12).
107
108     PROCEDURE DIVISION.
109
110
111     MAIN-LINE-ROUTINE.
112          PERFORM OPEN-FILES.
113          PERFORM NEW-PAGE.
114          PERFORM START-UP.
115          PERFORM PROCESS-DATA UNTIL ANY-MORE-CARDS EQUAL 'NO'.
116          PERFORM CLOSE-UP.
117          STOP RUN.
118
119     OPEN-FILES.
120          OPEN INPUT IN-FILE.
121          OPEN OUTPUT OUT-FILE.
122
123     NEW-PAGE.
124          MOVE SPACES TO LINE-OUT.
125          WRITE LINE-OUT AFTER PAGE.
126
127     START-UP.
128          READ IN-FILE AT END MOVE 'NO' TO ANY-MORE-CARDS
129               MOVE ' **NO DATA IN DECK**' TO LINE-OUT
130               WRITE LINE-OUT AFTER 30.
131          IF ANY-MORE-CARDS EQUAL 'YES' MOVE SPACES TO DETAIL-LINE.
132
133     PROCESS-DATA.
134          MOVE TELEPHONE-NUMBER TO PHONE-OUT.
135          WRITE LINE-OUT FROM HEADER-1 AFTER 1.
136          IF TELEPHONE-NUMBER NUMERIC PERFORM INSPECTION-PARA
137          ELSE PERFORM ERROR-1.
138          READ IN-FILE AT END MOVE 'NO' TO ANY-MORE-CARDS.
139          IF ANY-MORE-CARDS EQUAL 'YES' PERFORM NEW-PAGE.
140
141     CLOSE-UP.
142          CLOSE IN-FILE, OUT-FILE.
143
144     INSPECTION-PARA.
145          MOVE ZEROS TO COUNT-ONES, COUNT-ZEROS.
146          INSPECT TELEPHONE-NUMBER TALLYING COUNT-ZEROS FOR ALL ZEROS.
147          INSPECT TELEPHONE-NUMBER TALLYING COUNT-ONES FOR ALL '1'.
148          IF COUNT-ZEROS > 0 OR COUNT-ONES > 0 PERFORM ERROR-2
149               ELSE PERFORM NEST-LOOPS-1.
150
151     NEST-LOOPS-1.
152          SUBTRACT 1 FROM FIRST-DIGIT, SECOND-DIGIT, THIRD-DIGIT,
153               FOURTH DIGIT, FIFTH-DIGIT, SIXTH-DIGIT, SEVENTH-DIGIT.
154          PERFORM NEST-LOOPS-2
155          VARYING LETTER-POINTER-1 FROM 1 BY 1 UNTIL
156               LETTER-POINTER-1 > 3
157          AFTER LETTER-POINTER-2 FROM 1 BY 1 UNTIL
158               LETTER-POINTER-2 > 3
159          AFTER LETTER-POINTER-3 FROM 1 BY 1 UNTIL
160               LETTER-POINTER-3 > 3.
161          WRITE LINE-OUT FROM DETAIL-LINE AFTER 1.
162
163     NEST-LOOPS-2.
164          PERFORM NEST-LOOPS-3
165          VARYING LETTER-POINTER-4 FROM 1 BY 1 UNTIL
166               LETTER-POINTER-4 > 3
167          AFTER LETTER-POINTER-5 FROM 1 BY 1 UNTIL
168               LETTER-POINTER-5 > 3
169          AFTER LETTER-POINTER-6 FROM 1 BY 1 UNTIL
170               LETTER-POINTER-6 > 3.
171
172     NEST-LOOPS-3.
173          PERFORM LINE-POSITION
174          VARYING LETTER-POINTER-7 FROM 1 BY 1 UNTIL
175               LETTER-POINTER-7 > 3.
176
```

```
177    ERROR-1.
178        MOVE 'NONNUMERIC CHARACTERS IN TELEPHONE NUMBER'
179            TO LINE-OUT.
180        WRITE LINE-OUT AFTER 10.
181
182    ERROR-2.
183        MOVE 'ZEROS OR ONES IN TELEPHONE NUMBER REJECT' TO
184            LINE-OUT.
185        WRITE LINE-OUT AFTER 10.
186
187    LINE-IN POSITION.
188        IF POSITIONER < 11 ADD 1 TO POSITIONER
189            PERFORM MOVE-LETTERS
190        ELSE WRITE LINE-OUT FROM DETAIL-LINE AFTER 1
191            MOVE ZEROS TO POSITIONER
192            MOVE SPACES TO DETAIL-LINE.
193
194    MOVE-LETTERS.
195        MOVE LETTERS (FIRST-DIGIT, LETTER-POINTER-1) TO LETTER-1.
196        MOVE LETTERS (SECOND-DIGIT, LETTER-POINTER-2) TO LETTER-2.
197        MOVE LETTERS (THIRD-DIGIT, LETTER-POINTER-3) TO LETTER-3.
198        MOVE LETTERS (FOURTH-DIGIT, LETTER-POINTER-4) TO LETTER-4.
199        MOVE LETTERS (FIFTH-DIGIT, LETTER-POINTER-5) TO LETTER-5.
200        MOVE LETTERS (SIXTH-DIGIT, LETTER-POINTER 6) TO LETTER-6.
201        MOVE LETTERS (SEVENTH-DIGIT, LETTER-POINTER-7) TO LETTER-7.
202        MOVE COMPLETED-WORD TO WORD-OUT (POSITIONER).
```

Output for Program 44

THE TELEPHONE NUMBER IS: 2606789
ZEROS OR ONES IN TELEPHONE NUMBER REJECT

THE TELEPHONE NUMBER IS: AR66679
NONNUMERIC CHARACTERS IN TELEPHONE NUMBER

```
THE TELEPHONE NUMBER IS: 2272272
AAPAAPA  AAPAAPB  AAPAAPC  AAPAARA  AAPAARB  AAPAARC  AAPAASA  AAPAASB  AAPAASC  AAPABPA  AAPABPB
AAPABRA  AAPABRB  AAPABRC  AAPABSA  AAPABSB  AAPABSC  AAPACPA  AAPACPB  AAPACPC  AAPACRA  AAPACRB
AAPACSA  AAPACSB  AAPACSC  AAPBAPA  AAPBAPB  AAPBAPC  AAPBARA  AAPBARB  AAPBARC  AAPBASA  AAPBASB
AAPBBPA  AAPBBPB  AAPBBPC  AAPBBRA  AAPBBRB  AAPBBRC  AAPBBSA  AAPBBSB  AAPBBSC  AAPBCPA  AAPBCPB
AAPBCRA  AAPBCRB  AAPBCRC  AAPBCSA  AAPBCSB  AAPBCSC  AAPCAPA  AAPCAPB  AAPCAPC  AAPCARA  AAPCARB
AAPCASA  AAPCASB  AAPCASC  AAPCBPA  AAPCBPB  AAPCBPC  AAPCBRA  AAPCBRB  AAPCBRC  AAPCBSA  AAPCBSB
AAPCCPA  AAPCCPB  AAPCCPC  AAPCCRA  AAPCCRB  AAPCCRC  AAPCCSA  AAPCCSB  AAPCCSC  AARAAPA  AARAAPB
AARAARA  AARAARB  AARAARC  AARAASA  AARAASB  AARAASC  AARABPA  AARABPB  AARABPC  AARABRA  AARABRB
AARABSA  AARABSB  AARABSC  AARACPA  AARACPB  AARACPC  AARACRA  AARACRC  AARACRC  AARACSA  AARACSB
AARBAPA  AARBAPB  AARBAPC  AARBARA  AARBARB  AARBARC  AARBASA  AARBASB  AARBASC  AARBBPA  AARBBPB
AARBBRA  AARBBRB  AARBBRC  AARBBSA  AARBBSB  AARBBSC  AARBCPA  AARBCPB  AARBCPC  AARBCRA  AARBCRB
AARBCSA  AARBCSB  AARBCSC  AARCAPA  AARCAPB  AARCAPC  AARCARA  AARCARB  AARCARC  AARCASA  AARCASB
AARCBPA  AARCBPB  AARCBPC  AARCBRA  AARCBRB  AARCBRC  AARCBSA  AARCBSB  AARCBSC  AARCCPA  AARCCPB
AARCCRA  AARCCRB  AARCCRC  AARCCSA  AARCCSB  AARCCSC  AASAAPA  AASAAPB  AASAAPC  AASAARA  AASAARB
AASAASA  AASAASB  AASAASC  AASABPA  AASABPB  AASABPC  AASABRA  AASABRB  AASABRC  AASABSA  AASABSB
AASACPA  AASACPB  AASACPC  AASACRA  AASACRB  AASACRC  AASACSA  AASACSB  AASACSC  AASBAPA  AASBAPB
AASBARA  AASBARB  AASBARC  AASBASA  AASBASB  AASBASC  AASBBPA  AASBBPB  AASBBPC  AASBBRA  AASBBRB
AASBBSA  AASBBSB  AASBBSC  AASBCPA  AASBCPB  AASBCPC  AASBCRA  AASBCRB  AASBCRC  AASBCSA  AASBCSB
AASCAPA  AASCAPB  AASCAPC  AASCARA  AASCARB  AASCARC  AASCASA  AASCASB  AASCASC  AASCBPA  AASCBPB
AASCBRA  AASCBRB  AASCBRC  AASCBSA  AASCBSB  AASCBSC  AASCCPA  AASCCPB  AASCCPC  AASCCRA  AASCCRB
AASCCSA  AASCCSB  AASCCSC  ABPAAPA  ABPAAPB  ABPAAPC  ABPAARA  ABPAARB  ABPAARC  ABPAASA  ABPAASB
ABPABPA  ABPABPB  ABPABPC  ABPABRA  ABPABRB  ABPABRC  ABPABSA  ABPABSB  ABPABSC  ABPACPA  ABPACPB
ABPACRA  ABPACRB  ABPACRC  ABPACSA  ABPACSB  ABPACSC  ABPBAPA  ABPBAPB  ABPBAPC  ABPBARA  ABPBARB
ABPBASA  ABPBASB  ABPBASC  ABPBBPA  ABPBBPB  ABPBBPC  ABPBBRA  ABPBBRB  ABPBBRC  ABPBBSA  ABPBBSB
ABPBCPA  ABPBCPB  ABPBCPC  ABPBCRA  ABPBCRB  ABPBCRC  ABPBCSA  ABPBCSB  ABPBCSC  ABPCAPA  ABPCAPB
ABPCARA  ABPCARB  ABPCARC  ABPCASA  ABPCASB  ABPCASC  ABPCBPA  ABPCBPB  ABPCBPC  ABPCBRA  ABPCBRB
ABPCBSA  ABPCBSB  ABPCBSC  ABPCCPA  ABPCCPB  ABPCCPC  ABPCCRA  ABPCCRB  ABPCCRC  ABPCCSA  ABPCCSB
ABRAAPA  ABRAAPB  ABRAAPC  ABRAARA  ABRAARB  ABRAARC  ABRAASA  ABRAASB  ABRAASC  ABRABPA  ABRABPB
ABRABRA  ABRABRB  ABRABRC  ABRABSA  ABRABSB  ABRABSC  ABRACPA  ABRACPB  ABRACPC  ABRACRA  ABRACRB
ABRACSA  ABRACSB  ABRACSC  ABRBAPA  ABRBAPB  ABRBAPC  ABRBARA  ABRBARB  ABRBARC  ABRBASA  ABRBASB
ABRBBPA  ABRBBPB  ABRBBPC  ABRBBRA  ABRBBRB  ABRBBRC  ABRBBSA  ABRBBSB  ABRBBSC  ABRBCPA  ABRBCPB
ABRBCRA  ABRBCRB  ABRBCRC  ABRBCSA  ABRBCSB  ABRBCSC  ABRCAPA  ABRCAPB  ABRCAPC  ABRCARA  ABRCARB
ABRCASA  ABRCASB  ABRCASC  ABRCBPA  ABRCBPB  ABRCBPC  ABRCBRA  ABRCBRB  ABRCBRC  ABRCBSA  ABRCBSB
ABRCCPA  ABRCCPB  ABRCCPC  ABRCCRA  ABRCCRB  ABRCCRC  ABRCCSA  ABRCCSB  ABRCCSC  ABSAAPA  ABSAAPB
ABSAARA  ABSAARB  ABSAARC  ABSAASA  ABSAASB  ABSAASC  ABSABPA  ABSABPB  ABSABPC  ABSABRA  ABSABRB
ABSABSA  ABSABSB  ABSABSC  ABSACPA  ABSACPB  ABSACPC  ABSACRA  ABSACRB  ABSACRC  ABSACSA  ABSACSB
ABSBAPA  ABSBAPB  ABSBAPC  ABSBARA  ABSBARB  ABSBARC  ABSBASA  ABSBASB  ABSBASC  ABSBBPA  ABSBBPB
ABSBBRA  ABSBBRB  ABSBBRC  ABSBBSA  ABSBBSB  ABSBBSC  ABSBCPA  ABSBCPB  ABSBCPC  ABSBCRA  ABSBCRB
ABSBCSA  ABSBCSB  ABSBCSC  ABSCAPA  ABSCAPB  ABSCAPC  ABSCARA  ABSCARB  ABSCARC  ABSCASA  ABSCASB
```

```
ABSCBPA  ABSCBPB  ABSCBPC  ABSCBRA  ABSCBRB  ABSCBRC  ABSCBSA  ABSCBSB  ABSCBSC  ABSCCPA  ABSCCPB  ABSCCPC
ABSCCRA  ABSCCRB  ABSCCRC  ABSCCSA  ABSCCSB  ABSCCSC  ACPAAPA  ACPAAPB  ACPAAPC  ACPAARA  ACPAARB  ACPAARC
ACPAASA  ACPAASB  ACPAASC  ACPABPA  ACPABPB  ACPABPC  ACPABRA  ACPABRB  ACPABRC  ACPABSA  ACPABSB  ACPABSC
ACPACPA  ACPACPB  ACPACPC  ACPACRA  ACPACRB  ACPACRC  ACPACSA  ACPACSB  ACPACSC  ACPBAPA  ACPBAPB  ACPBAPC
ACPBARA  ACPBARB  ACPBARC  ACPBASA  ACPBASB  ACPBASC  ACPBBPA  ACPBBPB  ACPBBPC  ACPBBRA  ACPBBRB  ACPBBRC
ACPBBSA  ACPBBSB  ACPBBSC  ACPBCPA  ACPBCPB  ACPBCPC  ACPBCRA  ACPBCRB  ACPBCRC  ACPBCSA  ACPBCSB  ACPBCSC
ACPCAPA  ACPCAPB  ACPCAPC  ACPCARA  ACPCARB  ACPCARC  ACPCASA  ACPCASB  ACPCASC  ACPCBPA  ACPCBPB  ACPCBPC
ACPCBRA  ACPCBRB  ACPCBRC  ACPCBSA  ACPCBSB  ACPCBSC  ACPCCPA  ACPCCPB  ACPCCPC  ACPCCRA  ACPCCRB  ACPCCRC
ACPCCSA  ACPCCSB  ACPCCSC  ACRAAPA  ACRAAPB  ACRAAPC  ACRAARA  ACRAARB  ACRAARC  ACRAASA  ACRAASB  ACRAASC
ACRABPA  ACRABPB  ACRABPC  ACRABRA  ACRABRB  ACRABRC  ACRABSA  ACRABSB  ACRABSC  ACRACPA  ACRACPB  ACRACPC
ACRACRA  ACRACRB  ACRACRC  ACRACSA  ACRACSB  ACRACSC  ACRBAPA  ACRBAPB  ACRBAPC  ACRBARA  ACRBARB  ACRBARC
ACRBASA  ACRBASB  ACRBASC  ACRBBPA  ACRBBPB  ACRBBPC  ACRBBRA  ACRBBRB  ACRBBRC  ACRBBSA  ACRBBSB  ACRBBSC
ACRBCPA  ACRBCPB  ACRBCPC  ACRBCRA  ACRBCRB  ACRBCRC  ACRBCSA  ACRBCSB  ACRBCSC  ACRCAPA  ACRCAPB  ACRCAPC
ACRCARA  ACRCARB  ACRCARC  ACRCASA  ACRCASB  ACRCASC  ACRCBPA  ACRCBPB  ACRCBPC  ACRCBRA  ACRCBRB  ACRCBRC
ACRCBSA  ACRCBSB  ACRCBSC  ACRCCPA  ACRCCPB  ACRCCPC  ACRCCRA  ACRCCRB  ACRCCRC  ACRCCSA  ACRCCSB  ACRCCSC
ACSAAPA  ACSAAPB  ACSAAPC  ACSAARA  ACSAARB  ACSAARC  ACSAASA  ACSAASB  ACSAASC  ACSABPA  ACSABPB  ACSABPC
ACSABRA  ACSABRB  ACSABRC  ACSABSA  ACSABSB  ACSABSC  ACSACPA  ACSACPB  ACSACPC  ACSACRA  ACSACRB  ACSACRC
ACSACSA  ACSACSB  ACSACSC  ACSBAPA  ACSBAPB  ACSBAPC  ACSBARA  ACSBARB  ACSBARC  ACSBASA  ACSBASB  ACSBASC
ACSBBPA  ACSBBPB  ACSBBPC  ACSBBRA  ACSBBRB  ACSBBRC  ACSBBSA  ACSBBSB  ACSBBSC  ACSBCPA  ACSBCPB  ACSBCPC
ACSBCRA  ACSBCRB  ACSBCRC  ACSBCSA  ACSBCSB  ACSBCSC  ACSCAPA  ACSCAPB  ACSCAPC  ACSCARA  ACSCARB  ACSCARC
ACSCASA  ACSCASB  ACSCASC  ACSCBPA  ACSCBPB  ACSCBPC  ACSCBRA  ACSCBRB  ACSCBRC  ACSCBSA  ACSCBSB  ACSCBSC
ACSCCPA  ACSCCPB  ACSCCPC  ACSCCRA  ACSCCRB  ACSCCRC  ACSCCSA  ACSCCSB  ACSCCSC  BAPAAPA  BAPAAPB  BAPAAPC
BAPAARA  BAPAARB  BAPAARC  BAPAASA  BAPAASB  BAPAASC  BAPABPA  BAPABPB  BAPABPC  BAPABRA  BAPABRB  BAPABRC
BAPABSA  BAPABSB  BAPABSC  BAPACPA  BAPACPB  BAPACPC  BAPACRA  BAPACRB  BAPACRC  BAPACSA  BAPACSB  BAPACSC
BAPBAPA  BAPBAPB  BAPBAPC  BAPBARA  BAPBARB  BAPBARC  BAPBASA  BAPBASB  BAPBASC  BAPBBPA  BAPBBPB  BAPBBPC
BAPBBRA  BAPBBRB  BAPBBRC  BAPBBSA  BAPBBSB  BAPBBSC  BAPBCPA  BAPBCPB  BAPBCPC  BAPBCRA  BAPBCRB  BAPBCRC
BAPBCSA  BAPBCSB  BAPBCSC  BAPCAPA  BAPCAPB  BAPCAPC  BAPCARA  BAPCARB  BAPCARC  BAPCASA  BAPCASB  BAPCASC
BAPCBPA  BAPCBPB  BAPCBPC  BAPCBRA  BAPCBRB  BAPCBRC  BAPCBSA  BAPCBSB  BAPCBSC  BAPCCPA  BAPCCPB  BAPCCPC
BAPCCRA  BAPCCRB  BAPCCRC  BAPCCSA  BAPCCSB  BAPCCSC  BARAAPA  BARAAPB  BARAAPC  BARAARA  BARAARB  BARAARC
BARAASA  BARAASB  BARAASC  BARABPA  BARABPB  BARABPC  BARABRA  BARABRB  BARABRC  BARABSA  BARABSB  BARABSC
BARACPA  BARACPB  BARACPC  BARACRA  BARACRB  BARACRC  BARACSA  BARACSB  BARACSC  BARBAPA  BARBAPB  BARBAPC
BARBARA  BARBARB  BARBARC  BARBASA  BARBASB  BARBASC  BARBBPA  BARBBPB  BARBBPC  BARBBRA  BARBBRB  BARBBRC
BARBBSA  BARBBSB  BARBBSC  BARBCPA  BARBCPB  BARBCPC  BARBCRA  BARBCRB  BARBCRC  BARBCSA  BARBCSB  BARBCSC
BARCAPA  BARCAPB  BARCAPC  BARCARA  BARCARB  BARCARC  BARCASA  BARCASB  BARCASC  BARCBPA  BARCBPB  BARCBPC
BARCBRA  BARCBRB  BARCBRC  BARCBSA  BARCBSB  BARCBSC  BARCCPA  BARCCPB  BARCCPC  BARCCRA  BARCCRB  BARCCRC
BARCCSA  BARCCSB  BARCCSC  BASAAPA  BASAAPB  BASAAPC  BASAARA  BASAARB  BASAARC  BASAASA  BASAASB  BASAASC
BASABPA  BASABPB  BASABPC  BASABRA  BASABRB  BASABRC  BASABSA  BASABSB  BASABSC  BASACPA  BASACPB  BASACPC
BASACRA  BASACRB  BASACRC  BASACSA  BASACSB  BASACSC  BASBAPA  BASBAPB  BASBAPC  BASBARA  BASBARB  BASBARC
BASBASA  BASBASB  BASBASC  BASBBPA  BASBBPB  BASBBPC  BASBBRA  BASBBRB  BASBBRC  BASBBSA  BASBBSB  BASBBSC
BASBCPA  BASBCPB  BASBCPC  BASBCRA  BASBCRB  BASBCRC  BASBCSA  BASBCSB  BASBCSC  BASCAPA  BASCAPB  BASCAPC
BASCARA  BASCARB  BASCARC  BASCASA  BASCASB  BASCASC  BASCBPA  BASCBPB  BASCBPC  BASCBRA  BASCBRB  BASCBRC
BASCBSA  BASCBSB  BASCBSC  BASCCPA  BASCCPB  BASCCPC  BASCCRA  BASCCRB  BASCCRC  BASCCSA  BASCCSB  BASCCSC
BBPAAPA  BBPAAPB  BBPAAPC  BBPAARA  BBPAARB  BBPAARC  BBPAASA  BBPAASB  BBPAASC  BBPABPA  BBPABPB  BBPABPC
BBPABRA  BBPABRB  BBPABRC  BBPABSA  BBPABSB  BBPABSC  BBPACPA  BBPACPB  BBPACPC  BBPACRA  BBPACRB  BBPACRC
BBPACSA  BBPACSB  BBPACSC  BBPBAPA  BBPBAPB  BBPBAPC  BBPBARA  BBPBARB  BBPBARC  BBPBASA  BBPBASB  BBPBASC
BBPBBPA  BBPBBPB  BBPBBPC  BBPBBRA  BBPBBRB  BBPBBRC  BBPBBSA  BBPBBSB  BBPBBSC  BBPBCPA  BBPBCPB  BBPBCPC
BBPBCRA  BBPBCRB  BBPBCRC  BBPBCSA  BBPBCSB  BBPBCSC  BBPCAPA  BBPCAPB  BBPCAPC  BBPCARA  BBPCARB  BBPCARC
BBPCASA  BBPCASB  BBPCASC  BBPCBPA  BBPCBPB  BBPCBPC  BBPCBRA  BBPCBRB  BBPCBRC  BBPCBSA  BBPCBSB  BBPCBSC
BBPCCPA  BBPCCPB  BBPCCPC  BBPCCRA  BBPCCRB  BBPCCRC  BBPCCSA  BBPCCSB  BBPCCSC  BBRAAPA  BBRAAPB  BBRAAPC
BBRAARA  BBRAARB  BBRAARC  BBRAASA  BBRAASB  BBRAASC  BBRABPA  BBRABPB  BBRABPC  BBRABRA  BBRABRB  BBRABRC
BBRABSA  BBRABSB  BBRABSC  BBRACPA  BBRACPB  BBRACPC  BBRACRA  BBRACRB  BBRACRC  BBRACSA  BBRACSB  BBRACSC
BBRBAPA  BBRBAPB  BBRBAPC  BBRBARA  BBRBARB  BBRBARC  BBRBASA  BBRBASB  BBRBASC  BBRBBPA  BBRBBPB  BBRBBPC
BBRBBRA  BBRBBRB  BBRBBRC  BBRBBSA  BBRBBSB  BBRBBSC  BBRBCPA  BBRBCPB  BBRBCPC  BBRBCRA  BBRBCRB  BBRBCRC
BBRBCSA  BBRBCSB  BBRBCSC  BBRCAPA  BBRCAPB  BBRCAPC  BBRCARA  BBRCARB  BBRCARC  BBRCASA  BBRCASB  BBRCASC
BBRCBPA  BBRCBPB  BBRCBPC  BBRCBRA  BBRCBRB  BBRCBRC  BBRCBSA  BBRCBSB  BBRCBSC  BBRCCPA  BBRCCPB  BBRCCPC
BBRCCRA  BBRCCRB  BBRCCRC  BBRCCSA  BBRCCSB  BBRCCSC  BBSAAPA  BBSAAPB  BBSAAPC  BBSAARA  BBSAARB  BBSAARC
BBSAASA  BBSAASB  BBSAASC  BBSABPA  BBSABPB  BBSABPC  BBSABRA  BBSABRB  BBSABRC  BBSABSA  BBSABSB  BBSABSC
BBSACPA  BBSACPB  BBSACPC  BBSACRA  BBSACRB  BBSACRC  BBSACSA  BBSACSB  BBSACSC  BBSBAPA  BBSBAPB  BBSBAPC
BBSBARA  BBSBARB  BBSBARC  BBSBASA  BBSBASB  BBSBASC  BBSBBPA  BBSBBPB  BBSBBPC  BBSBBRA  BBSBBRB  BBSBBRC
BBSBBSA  BBSBBSB  BBSBBSC  BBSBCPA  BBSBCPB  BBSBCPC  BBSBCRA  BBSBCRB  BBSBCRC  BBSBCSA  BBSBCSB  BBSBCSC
BBSCAPA  BBSCAPB  BBSCAPC  BBSCARA  BBSCARB  BBSCARC  BBSCASA  BBSCASB  BBSCASC  BBSCBPA  BBSCBPB  BBSCBPC
BBSCBRA  BBSCBRB  BBSCBRC  BBSCBSA  BBSCBSB  BBSCBSC  BBSCCPA  BBSCCPB  BBSCCPC  BBSCCRA  BBSCCRB  BBSCCRC
BBSCCSA  BBSCCSB  BBSCCSC  BCPAAPA  BCPAAPB  BCPAAPC  BCPAARA  BCPAARB  BCPAARC  BCPAASA  BCPAASB  BCPAASC
BCPABPA  BCPABPB  BCPABPC  BCPABRA  BCPABRB  BCPABRC  BCPABSA  BCPABSB  BCPABSC  BCPACPA  BCPACPB  BCPACPC
BCPACRA  BCPACRB  BCPACRC  BCPACSA  BCPACSB  BCPACSC  BCPBAPA  BCPBAPB  BCPBAPC  BCPBARA  BCPBARB  BCPBARC
BCPBASA  BCPBASB  BCPBASC  BCPBBPA  BCPBBPB  BCPBBPC  BCPBBRA  BCPBBRB  BCPBBRC  BCPBBSA  BCPBBSB  BCPBBSC
BCPBCPA  BCPBCPB  BCPBCPC  BCPBCRA  BCPBCRB  BCPBCRC  BCPBCSA  BCPBCSB  BCPBCSC  BCPCAPA  BCPCAPB  BCPCAPC
BCPCARA  BCPCARB  BCPCARC  BCPCASA  BCPCASB  BCPCASC  BCPCBPA  BCPCBPB  BCPCBPC  BCPCBRA  BCPCBRB  BCPCBRC
BCPCBSA  BCPCBSB  BCPCBSC  BCPCCPA  BCPCCPB  BCPCCPC  BCPCCRA  BCPCCRB  BCPCCRC  BCPCCSA  BCPCCSB  BCPCCSC
BCRAAPA  BCRAAPB  BCRAAPC  BCRAARA  BCRAARB  BCRAARC  BCRAASA  BCRAASB  BCRAASC  BCRABPA  BCRABPB  BCRABPC
BCRABRA  BCRABRB  BCRABRC  BCRABSA  BCRABSB  BCRABSC  BCRACPA  BCRACPB  BCRACPC  BCRACRA  BCRACRB  BCRACRC
BCRACSA  BCRACSB  BCRACSC  BCRBAPA  BCRBAPB  BCRBAPC  BCRBARA  BCRBARB  BCRBARC  BCRBASA  BCRBASB  BCRBASC
BCRBBPA  BCRBBPB  BCRBBPC  BCRBBRA  BCRBBRB  BCRBBRC  BCRBBSA  BCRBBSB  BCRBBSC  BCRBCPA  BCRBCPB  BCRBCPC
BCRBCRA  BCRBCRB  BCRBCRC  BCRBCSA  BCRBCSB  BCRBCSC  BCRCAPA  BCRCAPB  BCRCAPC  BCRCARA  BCRCARB  BCRCARC
BCRCASA  BCRCASB  BCRCASC  BCRCBPA  BCRCBPB  BCRCBPC  BCRCBRA  BCRCBRB  BCRCBRC  BCRCBSA  BCRCBSB  BCRCBSC
BCRCCPA  BCRCCPB  BCRCCPC  BCRCCRA  BCRCCRB  BCRCCRC  BCRCCSA  BCRCCSB  BCRCCSC  BCSAAPA  BCSAAPB  BCSAAPC
BCSAARA  BCSAARB  BCSAARC  BCSAASA  BCSAASB  BCSAASC  BCSABPA  BCSABPB  BCSABPC  BCSABRA  BCSABRB  BCSABRC
BCSABSA  BCSABSB  BCSABSC  BCSACPA  BCSACPB  BCSACPC  BCSACRA  BCSACRB  BCSACRC  BCSACSA  BCSACSB  BCSACSC
BCSBAPA  BCSBAPB  BCSBAPC  BCSBARA  BCSBARB  BCSBARC  BCSBASA  BCSBASB  BCSBASC  BCSBBPA  BCSBBPB  BCSBBPC
BCSBBRA  BCSBBRB  BCSBBRC  BCSBBSA  BCSBBSB  BCSBBSC  BCSBCPA  BCSBCPB  BCSBCPC  BCSBCRA  BCSBCRB  BCSBCRC
BCSBCSA  BCSBCSB  BCSBCSC  BCSCAPA  BCSCAPB  BCSCAPC  BCSCARA  BCSCARB  BCSCARC  BCSCASA  BCSCASB  BCSCASC
BCSCBPA  BCSCBPB  BCSCBPC  BCSCBRA  BCSCBRB  BCSCBRC  BCSCBSA  BCSCBSB  BCSCBSC  BCSCCPA  BCSCCPB  BCSCCPC
BCSCCRA  BCSCCRB  BCSCCRC  BCSCCSA  BCSCCSB  BCSCCSC  CAPAAPA  CAPAAPB  CAPAAPC  CAPAARA  CAPAARB  CAPAARC
CAPAASA  CAPAASB  CAPAASC  CAPABPA  CAPABPB  CAPABPC  CAPABRA  CAPABRB  CAPABRC  CAPABSA  CAPABSB
```

```
CAPACPA  CAPACPB  CAPACPC  CAPACRA  CAPACRB  CAPACRC  CAPACSA  CAPACSB  CAPACSC  CAPBAPA  CAPBAPB
CAPBARA  CAPBARB  CAPBARC  CAPBASA  CAPBASB  CAPBASC  CAPBBPA  CAPBBPB  CAPBBPC  CAPBBRA  CAPBBRB
CAPBBSA  CAPBBSB  CAPBBSC  CAPBCPA  CAPBCPB  CAPBCPC  CAPBCRA  CAPBCRB  CAPBCRC  CAPBCSA  CAPBCSB
CAPCAPA  CAPCAPB  CAPCAPC  CAPCARA  CAPCARB  CAPCARC  CAPCASA  CAPCASB  CAPCASC  CAPCBPA  CAPCBPB
CAPCBRA  CAPCBRB  CAPCBRC  CAPCBSA  CAPCBSB  CAPCBSC  CAPCCPA  CAPCCPB  CAPCCPC  CAPCCRA  CAPCCRB
CAPCCSA  CAPCCSB  CAPCCSC  CARAAPA  CARAAPB  CARAAPC  CARAARA  CARAARB  CARAARC  CARAASA  CARAASB
CARABPA  CARABPB  CARABPC  CARABRA  CARABRB  CARABRC  CARABSA  CARABSB  CARABSC  CARACPA  CARACPB
CARACRA  CARACRB  CARACRC  CARACSA  CARACSB  CARACSC  CARBAPA  CARBAPB  CARBAPC  CARBARA  CARBARB
CARBASA  CARBASB  CARBASC  CARBBPA  CARBBPB  CARBBPC  CARBBRA  CARBBRB  CARBBRC  CARBBSA  CARBBSB
CARBCPA  CARBCPB  CARBCPC  CARBCRA  CARBCRB  CARBCRC  CARBCSA  CARBCSB  CARBCSC  CARCAPA  CARCAPB
CARCARA  CARCARB  CARCARC  CARCASA  CARCASB  CARCASC  CARCBPA  CARCBPB  CARCBPC  CARCBRA  CARCBRB
CARCBSA  CARCBSB  CARCBSC  CARCCPA  CARCCPB  CARCCPC  CARCCRA  CARCCRB  CARCCRC  CARCCSA  CARCCSB
CASAAPA  CASAAPB  CASAAPC  CASAARA  CASAARB  CASAARC  CASAASA  CASAASB  CASAASC  CASABPA  CASABPB
CASABRA  CASABRB  CASABRC  CASABSA  CASABSB  CASABSC  CASACPA  CASACPB  CASACPC  CASACRA  CASACRB
CASACSA  CASACSB  CASACSC  CASBAPA  CASBAPB  CASBAPC  CASBARA  CASBARB  CASBARC  CASBASA  CASBASB
CASBBPA  CASBBPB  CASBBPC  CASBBRA  CASBBRB  CASBBRC  CASBBSA  CASBBSB  CASBBSC  CASBCPA  CASBCPB
CASBCRA  CASBCRB  CASBCRC  CASBCSA  CASBCSB  CASBCSC  CASCAPA  CASCAPB  CASCAPC  CASCARA  CASCARB
CASCASA  CASCASB  CASCASC  CASCBPA  CASCBPB  CASCBPC  CASCBRA  CASCBRB  CASCBRC  CASCBSA  CASCBSB
CASCCPA  CASCCPB  CASCCPC  CASCCRA  CASCCRB  CASCCRC  CASCCSA  CASCCSB  CASCCSC  CBPAAPA  CBPAAPB
CBPAARA  CBPAARB  CBPAARC  CBPAASA  CBPAASB  CBPAASC  CBPABPA  CBPABPB  CBPABPC  CBPABRA  CBPABRB
CBPABSA  CBPABSB  CBPABSC  CBPACPA  CBPACPB  CBPACPC  CBPACRA  CBPACRB  CBPACRC  CBPACSA  CBPACSB
CBPBAPA  CBPBAPB  CBPBAPC  CBPBARA  CBPBARB  CBPBARC  CBPBASA  CBPBASB  CBPBASC  CBPBBPA  CBPBBPB
CBPBBRA  CBPBBRB  CBPBBRC  CBPBBSA  CBPBBSB  CBPBBSC  CBPBCPA  CBPBCPB  CBPBCPC  CBPBCRA  CBPBCRB
CBPBCSA  CBPBCSB  CBPBCSC  CBPCAPA  CBPCAPB  CBPCAPC  CBPCARA  CBPCARB  CBPCARC  CBPCASA  CBPCASB
CBPCBPA  CBPCBPB  CBPCBPC  CBPCBRA  CBPCBRB  CBPCBRC  CBPCBSA  CBPCBSB  CBPCBSC  CBPCCPA  CBPCCPB
CBPCCRA  CBPCCRB  CBPCCRC  CBPCCSA  CBPCCSB  CBPCCSC  CBRAAPA  CBRAAPB  CBRAAPC  CBRAARA  CBRAARB
CBRAASA  CBRAASB  CBRAASC  CBRABPA  CBRABPB  CBRABPC  CBRABRA  CBRABRB  CBRABRC  CBRABSA  CBRABSB
CBRACPA  CBRACPB  CBRACPC  CBRACRA  CBRACRB  CBRACRC  CBRACSA  CBRACSB  CBRACSC  CBRBAPA  CBRBAPB
CBRBARA  CBRBARB  CBRBARC  CBRBASA  CBRBASB  CBRBASC  CBRBBPA  CBRBBPB  CBRBBPC  CBRBBRA  CBRBBRB
CBRBBSA  CBRBBSB  CBRBBSC  CBRBCPA  CBRBCPB  CBRBCPC  CBRBCRA  CBRBCRB  CBRBCRC  CBRBCSA  CBRBCSB
CBRCAPA  CBRCAPB  CBRCAPC  CBRCARA  CBRCARB  CBRCARC  CBRCASA  CBRCASB  CBRCASC  CBRCBPA  CBRCBPB
CBRCBRA  CBRCBRB  CBRCBRC  CBRCBSA  CBRCBSB  CBRCBSC  CBRCCPA  CBRCCPB  CBRCCPC  CBRCCRA  CBRCCRB
CBRCCSA  CBRCCSB  CBRCCSC  CBSAAPA  CBSAAPB  CBSAAPC  CBSAARA  CBSAARB  CBSAARC  CBSAASA  CBSAASB
CBSABPA  CBSABPB  CBSABPC  CBSABRA  CBSABRB  CBSABRC  CBSABSA  CBSABSB  CBSABSC  CBSACPA  CBSACPB
CBSACRA  CBSACRB  CBSACRC  CBSACSA  CBSACSB  CBSACSC  CBSBAPA  CBSBAPB  CBSBAPC  CBSBARA  CBSBARB
CBSBASA  CBSBASB  CBSBASC  CBSBBPA  CBSBBPB  CBSBBPC  CBSBBRA  CBSBBRB  CBSBBRC  CBSBBSA  CBSBBSB
CBSBCPA  CBSBCPB  CBSBCPC  CBSBCRA  CBSBCRB  CBSBCRC  CBSBCSA  CBSBCSB  CBSBCSC  CBSCAPA  CBSCAPB
CBSCARA  CBSCARB  CBSCARC  CBSCASA  CBSCASB  CBSCASC  CBSCBPA  CBSCBPB  CBSCBPC  CBSCBRA  CBSCBRB
CBSCBSA  CBSCBSB  CBSCBSC  CBSCCPA  CBSCCPB  CBSCCPC  CBSCCRA  CBSCCRB  CBSCCRC  CBSCCSA  CBSCCSB
CCPAAPA  CCPAAPB  CCPAAPC  CCPAARA  CCPAARB  CCPAARC  CCPAASA  CCPAASB  CCPAASC  CCPABPA  CCPABPB
CCPABRA  CCPABRB  CCPABRC  CCPABSA  CCPABSB  CCPABSC  CCPACPA  CCPACPB  CCPACPC  CCPACRA  CCPACRB
CCPACSA  CCPACSB  CCPACSC  CCPBAPA  CCPBAPB  CCPBAPC  CCPBARA  CCPBARB  CCPBARC  CCPBASA  CCPBASB
CCPBBPA  CCPBBPB  CCPBBPC  CCPBBRA  CCPBBRB  CCPBBRC  CCPBBSA  CCPBBSB  CCPBBSC  CCPBCPA  CCPBCPB
CCPBCRA  CCPBCRB  CCPBCRC  CCPBCSA  CCPBCSB  CCPBCSC  CCPCAPA  CCPCAPB  CCPCAPC  CCPCARA  CCPCARB
CCPCASA  CCPCASB  CCPCASC  CCPCBPA  CCPCBPB  CCPCBPC  CCPCBRA  CCPCBRB  CCPCBRC  CCPCBSA  CCPCBSB
CCPCCPA  CCPCCPB  CCPCCPC  CCPCCRA  CCPCCRB  CCPCCRC  CCPCCSA  CCPCCSB  CCPCCSC  CCRAAPA  CCRAAPB
CCRAARA  CCRAARB  CCRAARC  CCRAASA  CCRAASB  CCRAASC  CCRABPA  CCRABPB  CCRABPC  CCRABRA  CCRABRB
CCRABSA  CCRABSB  CCRABSC  CCRACPA  CCRACPB  CCRACPC  CCRACRA  CCRACRB  CCRACRC  CCRACSA  CCRACSB
CCRBAPA  CCRBAPB  CCRBAPC  CCRBARA  CCRBARB  CCRBARC  CCRBASA  CCRBASB  CCRBASC  CCRBBPA  CCRBBPB
CCRBBRA  CCRBBRB  CCRBBRC  CCRBBSA  CCRBBSB  CCRBBSC  CCRBCPA  CCRBCPB  CCRBCPC  CCRBCRA  CCRBCRB
CCRBCSA  CCRBCSB  CCRBCSC  CCRCAPA  CCRCAPB  CCRCAPC  CCRCARA  CCRCARB  CCRCARC  CCRCASA  CCRCASB
CCRCBPA  CCRCBPB  CCRCBPC  CCRCBRA  CCRCBRB  CCRCBRC  CCRCBSA  CCRCBSB  CCRCBSC  CCRCCPA  CCRCCPB
CCRCCRA  CCRCCRB  CCRCCRC  CCRCCSA  CCRCCSB  CCRCCSC  CCSAAPA  CCSAAPB  CCSAAPC  CCSAARA  CCSAARB
CCSAASA  CCSAASB  CCSAASC  CCSABPA  CCSABPB  CCSABPC  CCSABRA  CCSABRB  CCSABRC  CCSABSA  CCSABSB
CCSACPA  CCSACPB  CCSACPC  CCSACRA  CCSACRB  CCSACRC  CCSACSA  CCSACSB  CCSACSC  CCSBAPA  CCSBAPB
CCSBARA  CCSBARB  CCSBARC  CCSBASA  CCSBASB  CCSBASC  CCSBBPA  CCSBBPB  CCSBBPC  CCSBBRA  CCSBBRB
CCSBBSA  CCSBBSB  CCSBBSC  CCSBCPA  CCSBCPB  CCSBCPC  CCSBCRA  CCSBCRB  CCSBCRC  CCSBCSA  CCSBCSB
CCSCAPA  CCSCAPB  CCSCAPC  CCSCARA  CCSCARB  CCSCARC  CCSCASA  CCSCASB  CCSCASC  CCSCBPA  CCSCBPB
CCSCBRA  CCSCBRB  CCSCBRC  CCSCBSA  CCSCBSB  CCSCBSC  CCSCCPA  CCSCCPB  CCSCCPC  CCSCCRA  CCSCCRB
CCSCCSA  CCSCCSB  CCSCCSC
```

13.2   The Number of Elapsed Days Problem

We have already encountered the program in which a date is inputted and the computer calculates the equivalent Julian date and the day of the week on which that date falls. The formula that was used for that calculation can be amended to compute the number of days that have elapsed between any 2 given dates. This concept of elapsed days is important in business because customers are often offered discounts if payment is received within certain given time limits. Also, banks may compute the interest on a loan depending on the number of days that has elapsed between the making of the loan and the time period before it is fully paid.

Suppose we want to know the number of days that have elapsed between January 1, 1980 and January 1, 1981. The starting date would be January 1, 1980 and the ending date January 1, 1981. Both these dates have Julian days of 001 and the formula requires the use of the Julian day as shown.

$$\begin{aligned} \text{Number of elapsed days} = \ & \text{Julian-day-end} - \text{Julian-day-beg.} \\ & + (\text{End-year} - \text{Beg.-year}) \times 365 \\ & + \frac{\text{End-year} - \text{Beg.-year}}{4} - \frac{\text{End-year} - \text{Beg.-year}}{100} \\ & + \frac{\text{End-year} - \text{Beg.-year}}{400} \end{aligned}$$

Suppose we want to know the number of days that have elapsed between, say, January 1, 1981 and March 15, 1981. We know by inspection that because there are 31 days in January, 30 days will have elapsed during that month. To the number 30 is added 28 for the number of the days in February, and finally, 15 is added for the 15 days in March.

$$30 + 28 + 15 = 73$$

The Julian day for January 1, 1981 is 001 and that for March 15 is 074. According to the formula,

$$\text{Number of elapsed days} = 74 - 1 + 0 + 0 - 0 + 0 = \underline{\underline{73}}$$

The number of elapsed days as calculated by using the preceding formula works out correctly for each of the following cases.

1. from a nonleap year to a nonleap year
2. from a leap year to a leap year
3. from a nonleap year to a leap year

However, for the special case where the beginning date is a leap year in which the month is either January or February, and the ending date is a nonleap year, the total number of elapsed days will be short by 1, using the formula. Therefore this special case must be tested for in the program and if found, 1 must be added to give the correct result.

Input for Program 45

```
01011980   01011981
09201980   03221981
01011970   01011980
07041776   05051981
01011800   01012000
05051981   01012000
01011950   01012000
05231825   01021960
02011595   02011900
06281959   05051981
01011900   05051981
01011950   01011981
02271865   02271981
03231910   05021999
01011981   05011981
```

Program 45

```
1       IDENTIFICATION  DIVISION.
2       PROGRAM-ID.     ELAPSED-DAYS.
3       AUTHOR.         IRVIN POREMBA.
4       INSTALLATION.   NYU.
5       DATE-WRITTEN.   MAY 1, 1982.
6       DATE-COMPILED.  JUNE 18, 1982.
7       SECURITY.       HENRY MULLISH.
```

```
8      * * * * * * * * * * * * * * * * * * * * * * * * * * * * * * * * * * * * * * * * * * * * * * * * * * *
9      *       THIS PROGRAM READS IN DATA CARDS PUNCHED:                              *
10     *                                                                              *
11     *       COLUMNS  1-8:  BEGINNING DATE                                          *
12     *       COLUMNS 14-21: ENDING DATE                                            *
13     *                                                                              *
14     *       THIS PROGRAM USES THE TWO DATES AND A FORMULA                          *
15     *       TO FIND THE TOTAL ELAPSED DAYS BETWEEN THE DATES                       *
16     *       WHICH IS PRINTED OUT ALONG WITH DATES.                                 *
17     * * * * * * * * * * * * * * * * * * * * * * * * * * * * * * * * * * * * * * * * * * * * * * * * * * * *
18
19     ENVIRONMENT    DIVISION.
20     CONFIGURATION  SECTION.
21     INPUT-OUTPUT     SECTION.
22     FILE-CONTROL.
23         SELECT IN-FILE ASSIGN TO INPUT.
24         SELECT OUT-FILE ASSIGN TO OUTPUT.
25
26     DATA DIVISION.
27     FILE SECTION.
28
29     FD   IN-FILE
30         LABEL RECORDS ARE OMITTED.
31
32     01   RECORD-IN.
33         02   DATE-1.
34             03   BEG-MONTH        PIC 9(02).
35             03   BEG-DAY          PIC 9(02).
36             03   BEG-YEAR         PIC 9(04).
37         02   FILLER              PIC X(05).
38         02   DATE-2.
39             03   END-MONTH        PIC 9(02).
40             03   END-DAY          PIC 9(02).
41             03   END-YEAR         PIC 9(04).
42         02   FILLER              PIC X(59).
43
44     FD   OUT-FILE
45         LABEL RECORDS ARE OMITTED.
46
47     01   LINE-OUT                PIC X(133).
48
49     WORKING-STORAGE SECTION.
50
51     01     INDEPENDENT-ITEMS-USED.
52         02   ANY-MORE-CARDS       PIC X(03) VALUE 'YES'.
53         02   CENTURY-YEAR         PIC 9(02).
54         02   CHECK-LEAP-YEAR      PIC 9(04).
55         02   CK-LEAP-YEAR         PIC X(03).
56         02   CK-MONTH             PIC 9(02).
57         02   DIFF-BET-2-YEARS     PIC 9(04).
58         02   INT-4                PIC 9(07).
59         02   INT-100              PIC 9(07).
60         02   INT-400              PIC 9(07).
61         02   JULIAN-DAY-BEG       PIC 9(03).
62         02   JULIAN-DAY-END       PIC 9(03).
63         02   LEAP-YEAR            PIC 9(02).
64         02   LEAP-YEAR-BEG-FLAG   PIC X(03).
65         02   LEAP-YEAR-END-FLAG   PIC X(03).
66         02   ONE-OR-0-LEAP-DAYS   PIC 9(01).
67         02   TOTAL-ELAPSED-DAYS   PIC 9(07).
68         02   YEAR-DIVIDED         PIC 9(04).
69
70     01   DETAIL-LINE.
71         02   FILLER              PIC X(01) VALUE SPACES.
72         02   FILLER              PIC X(19) VALUE 'THE NUMBER OF DAYS'.
73         02   FILLER              PIC X(16) VALUE 'ELAPSED BETWEEN'.
74         02   DATE-1-OUT.
75             03   BEG-MONTH-OUT    PIC 99/.
76             03   BEG-DAY-OUT      PIC 99/.
77             03   BEG-YEAR-OUT     PIC 9999.
78         02   FILLER              PIC X(05) VALUE 'AND'.
79         02   DATE-2-OUT.
80             03   END-MONTH-OUT    PIC 99/.
81             03   END-DAY-OUT      PIC 99/.
```

```
82                     03    END-YEAR-OUT     PIC 9999.
83              02    FILLER              PIC X(04) VALUE 'IS'.
84              02    ELAPSED-DAYS-OUT    PIC Z,ZZZ,ZZ9.
85
86       01   PAST-DAYS-SKELETON.
87              02    FILLER              PIC X(05) VALUE '01000'.
88              02    FILLER              PIC X(05) VALUE '02031'.
89              02    FILLER              PIC X(05) VALUE '03059'.
90              02    FILLER              PIC X(05) VALUE '04090'.
91              02    FILLER              PIC X(05) VALUE '05120'.
92              02    FILLER              PIC X(05) VALUE '06151'.
93              02    FILLER              PIC X(05) VALUE '07181'.
94              02    FILLER              PIC X(05) VALUE '08212'.
95              02    FILLER              PIC X(05) VALUE '09243'.
96              02    FILLER              PIC X(05) VALUE '10273'.
97              02    FILLER              PIC X(05) VALUE '11304'.
98              02    FILLER              PIC X(05) VALUE '12334'.
99
100      01   PAST-DAYS REDEFINES PAST-DAYS-SKELETON.
101             02    TABLE-ELEMENT OCCURS 12 TIMES.
102                    03    MONTH        PIC 9(02).
103                    03    DAYS         PIC 9(03).
104
105      PROCEDURE DIVISION.
106      MAIN-LINE-ROUTINE.
107             PERFORM OPEN-FILES.
108             PERFORM NEW-PAGE.
109             PERFORM START-UP.
110             PERFORM PROCESS-DATA UNTIL ANY-MORE-CARDS EQUAL 'NO'.
111             PERFORM CLOSE-UP.
112             STOP RUN.
113
114      OPEN-FILES.
115             OPEN INPUT IN-FILE.
116             OPEN OUTPUT OUT-FILE.
117
118      NEW-PAGE.
119             MOVE SPACES TO LINE-OUT.
120             WRITE LINE-OUT AFTER PAGE.
121
122      START-UP.
123             READ IN-FILE AT END MOVE 'NO' TO ANY-MORE-CARDS
124                    MOVE ' **NO DATA IN DECK**' TO LINE-OUT
125                    WRITE LINE-OUT AFTER 30.
126
127      PROCESS-DATA.
128             PERFORM CAL-FOR-BEGINNING-DATE.
129             PERFORM CAL-FOR-ENDING-DATE.
130             IF LEAP-YEAR-BEG-FLAG = 'YES'
131                    AND LEAP-YEAR-END-FLAG = 'NO'
132                    AND BEG-MONTH < 3
133                    ADD 1 TO TOTAL-ELAPSED-DAYS.
134             MOVE BEG-MONTH TO BEG-MONTH-OUT.
135             MOVE BEG-DAY TO BEG-DAY-OUT.
136             MOVE BEG-YEAR TO BEG-YEAR-OUT.
137             MOVE END-MONTH TO END-MONTH-OUT.
138             MOVE END-DAY TO END-DAY-OUT.
139             MOVE END-YEAR TO END-YEAR-OUT.
140             MOVE TOTAL-ELAPSED-DAYS TO ELAPSED-DAYS-OUT.
141             WRITE LINE-OUT FROM DETAIL-LINE AFTER 2.
142             READ IN-FILE AT END MOVE 'NO' TO ANY-MORE-CARDS.
143
144      CLOSE-UP.
145             CLOSE IN-FILE, OUT-FILE.
146
147      CAL-FOR-BEGINNING-DATE.
148             MOVE DAYS (BEG-MONTH) TO JULIAN-DAY-BEG.
149             MOVE BEG-MONTH TO CK-MONTH.
150             MOVE BEG-YEAR TO CHECK-LEAP-YEAR.
151             PERFORM CENTURY-YEAR-CK.
152             ADD ONE-OR-0-LEAP-DAYS TO JULIAN-DAY-BEG.
153             ADD BEG-DAY TO JULIAN-DAY-BEG.
154             MOVE CK-LEAP-YEAR TO LEAP-YEAR-BEG-FLAG.
155
```

```
156        CAL-FOR-ENDING-DATE.
157            MOVE DAYS (END-MONTH) TO JULIAN-DAY-END.
158            MOVE END-YEAR TO CHECK-LEAP-YEAR.
159            MOVE END-MONTH TO CK-MONTH.
160            PERFORM CENTURY-YEAR-CK.
161            ADD ONE-OR-0-LEAP-DAYS TO JULIAN-DAY-END.
162            ADD END-DAY TO JULIAN-DAY-END.
163            MOVE CK-LEAP-YEAR TO LEAP-YEAR-END-FLAG.
164            PERFORM CAL-ELAPSED-DAYS.
165
166        CENTURY-YEAR-CK.
167            MOVE 'NO' TO CK-LEAP-YEAR.
168            MOVE 0 TO ONE-OR-0-LEAP-DAYS.
169            MOVE CHECK-LEAP-YEAR TO CENTURY-YEAR.
170            IF CENTURY-YEAR = 0 PERFORM CENTURY-LEAP-YEAR
171            ELSE PERFORM NOT-CENTURY-LEAP-YEAR.
172
173        CENTURY-LEAP-YEAR.
174            DIVIDE 400 INTO CHECK-LEAP-YEAR GIVING YEAR-DIVIDED
175                REMAINDER LEAP-YEAR.
176            PERFORM CHECK-IF-LEAP-YEAR.
177
178        NOT-CENTURY-LEAP-YEAR.
179            DIVIDE 4 INTO CHECK-LEAP-YEAR GIVING YEAR-DIVIDED
180                REMAINDER LEAP-YEAR.
181            PERFORM CHECK-IF-LEAP-YEAR.
182
183        CHECK-IF-LEAP-YEAR.
184            IF LEAP-YEAR EQUAL 0 MOVE 'YES' TO CK-LEAP-YEAR.
185            IF LEAP-YEAR = 0 AND CK-MONTH > 2
186                MOVE 1 TO ONE-OR-0-LEAP DAYS.
187
188        CAL-ELAPSED-DAYS.
189            SUBTRACT BEG-YEAR FROM END-YEAR GIVING DIFF-BET-2-YEARS.
190            COMPUTE TOTAL-ELAPSED-DAYS = 365 * DIFF-BET-2-YEARS +
191                JULIAN-DAY-END − JULIAN-DAY-BEG.
192            COMPUTE INT-4 = DIFF-BET-2-YEARS / 4.
193            COMPUTE INT-100 = DIFF-BET-2-YEARS / 100.
194            COMPUTE INT-400 = DIFF-BET-2-YEARS / 400.
195            COMPUTE TOTAL-ELAPSED-DAYS = TOTAL-ELAPSED-DAYS + INT-4
196                + INT-100 + INT-400.
```

Output for Program 45

THE NUMBER OF DAYS ELAPSED BETWEEN 01/01/1980 AND 01/01/1981 IS	366
THE NUMBER OF DAYS ELAPSED BETWEEN 09/20/1980 AND 03/22/1981 IS	182
THE NUMBER OF DAYS ELAPSED BETWEEN 01/01/1970 AND 01/01/1980 IS	3,652
THE NUMBER OF DAYS ELAPSED BETWEEN 07/04/1776 AND 05/05/1981 IS	74,817
THE NUMBER OF DAYS ELAPSED BETWEEN 01/01/1800 AND 01/01/2000 IS	73,052
THE NUMBER OF DAYS ELAPSED BETWEEN 05/05/1981 AND 01/01/2000 IS	6,815
THE NUMBER OF DAYS ELAPSED BETWEEN 01/01/1950 AND 01/01/2000 IS	18,262
THE NUMBER OF DAYS ELAPSED BETWEEN 05/23/1825 AND 01/02/1960 IS	49,168
THE NUMBER OF DAYS ELAPSED BETWEEN 02/01/1595 AND 02/01/1900 IS	111,404
THE NUMBER OF DAYS ELAPSED BETWEEN 06/28/1959 AND 05/05/1981 IS	7,981
THE NUMBER OF DAYS ELAPSED BETWEEN 01/01/1900 AND 05/05/1981 IS	29,710
THE NUMBER OF DAYS ELAPSED BETWEEN 01/01/1950 AND 01/01/1981 IS	11,322
THE NUMBER OF DAYS ELAPSED BETWEEN 02/27/1865 AND 02/27/1981 IS	42,370
THE NUMBER OF DAYS ELAPSED BETWEEN 03/23/1910 AND 05/02/1999 IS	32,547
THE NUMBER OF DAYS ELAPSED BETWEEN 01/01/1981 AND 05/01/1981 IS	120

13.3   Discussion of the Elapsed Days Program

The beginning date and the ending date are read in from the data card in the form mmddyyyy. The first requirement is to determine the Julian day for each date. The Julian day is calculated with the help of a table in which for each of the 12 months is stored the number of days that have elapsed to the beginning of that month. For example, zero days have elapsed before January 1st and 031 days before February 1st, and so on.

By using the month (read in as data under the names BEG-MONTH and END-MONTH), one can access in the table the number of elapsed days prior to that month. Then a check is made to determine whether the year in question is a leap year. Because this exact calculation must be done for both dates, the data-name CK-MONTH is used for both months and CK-LEAP-YEAR is used for both years. The paragraph CENTURY-YEAR-CK is then performed to determine if the years in question are century years. If they are, a test is made to see whether they are evenly divisible by 400. If they are divisible by 400, they are leap years and 1 is moved to the flag ONE-OR-0-LEAP-DAYS, which eventually is added to the number of Julian days. If they are not century years, they are divided by 4, again to test whether they are leap years. If a leap year is determined, the literal 'YES' is moved to CK-LEAP-YEAR; otherwise, it remains at 'NO' to which it is initially set in the paragraph CK-LEAP-YEAR. Whatever the value is, whether 'YES' or 'NO', this value is saved under the name LEAP-YEAR-BEG-FLAG or LEAP-YEAR-END-FLAG, whichever is appropriate.

At this point we have correctly calculated the correct Julian day for each of the 2 dates. We are now ready to perform CAL-ELAPSED-DAYS, which computes the elapsed days between the 2 given dates. A test is now made for the special case that we raised earlier in the discussion. If the starting year is a leap year and the ending year is a nonleap year and the month of the leap year is prior to March, 1 is added to the elapsed days.

13.4 Printing a Histogram in COBOL

It is often desirable to represent a given frequency distribution of, for instance, production, hours worked, salaries, or ethnic origin of employees so that it will be easily comprehended. As the old maxim goes, "One picture is worth a thousand words."

For the benefit of those COBOL programmers who do not have access to a graphics display facility, the printer may be used to advantage to present such frequency distributions in the form of histograms.

The data to the next program is punched 40 numbers to a card, each number having a PICTURE of 9(02) and a range of 0 through 99. Rather than give a unique name to each number, advantage may be taken of the OCCURS clause. By writing in the input area:

```
01  RECORD-IN.
    02  NUMBER-IN OCCURS 40 TIMES PIC 9(02).
```

we find that each number, NUMBER-IN, assumes the same name but differs from the other numbers in terms of its position, that is, its subscript.

A table is then set up to store 10 categories of numbers.

1. 0–9	6. 50–59
2. 10–19	7. 60–69
3. 20–29	8. 70–79
4. 30–39	9. 80–89
5. 40–49	10. 90–99

Each of these "pockets" or bins is initialized to zero in the table and after each number is examined a 1 is added to the appropriate "pocket." In order to determine which bin to increment, one uses the following formula:

$$\text{integer portion}\left[\frac{\text{incoming number} - \text{lowest possible number}}{\text{range of the numbers}} + 1\right]$$

When all the input numbers have been read and the appropriate bin numbers have been incremented, we are ready to print the histogram.

In order to keep the frequencies within the bins to manageable proportions, one scales down each frequency, based on the largest frequency, according to the formula:

$$\frac{\text{frequency in bin}}{\text{largest frequency}} \times 10$$

The largest frequency is determined by setting the first frequency to the temporary maximum and checking each succeeding frequency against the maximum, substituting any newly found maximum for the old maximum whenever a new one is found. This is all done through the use of the PERFORM VARYING statement.

The maximum value of the *scaled* frequencies is used to print out the histogram. This is again found by resorting to the preceding method by using the PERFORM VARYING statement.

After the scaled frequency maximum value is found another PERFORM VARYING statement is used that goes from that maximum to zero in steps of -1. Beginning with the maximum, one checks each bin to determine whether it is equal in value or greater than the scaled frequency value. If it is one of these, an X is printed in the appropriate position in the detail-line. If it is not, a space is printed at that location.

Once all the bins have been checked the line is printed, which becomes part of the histogram itself. The value of the maximum is then decreased by 1 and the process is repeated until the current value of the frequency is equal to zero. At that point the histogram is complete.

Input for Program 46

```
45011924799910178076339171087007112108730586743798900393010050673343458308728636
54648624105370757894527564436662665901223044529852599694009885742968095617144095
82973360258264095946566366397292689550309392045722214251553520254561285526497845
01294704939919995002005581636060564833087502219463218045103082281348054326220018
```

Program 46

```
1       IDENTIFICATION   DIVISION.
2       PROGRAM-ID.      HISTOGRAM.
3       AUTHOR.          IRVIN POREMBA.
4       INSTALLATION.    NYU.
5       DATE-WRITTEN.    JUNE 23, 1982.
6       DATE-COMPILED.   JUNE 23, 1982.
7       SECURITY.        HENRY MULLISH.
8       ***************************************************************
9       *      THIS PROGRAM READS IN NUMBERS PUNCHED:                *
10      *                                                            *
11      *      RANDOM NUMBERS 40 PER DATA CARD.                      *
12      *                                                            *
13      *      THE PROGRAM FINDS THE BIN THAT THE RANDOM             *
14      *      NUMBER BELONGS TO AND ADDS 1 TO THAT BIN.             *
15      *      AFTER THIS PROCESS IS COMPLETED A GRAPH OF            *
16      *      THE BINS AND THEIR AMOUNTS IS PRINTED OUT             *
17      ***************************************************************
18      ENVIRNOMENT      DIVISION.
19      CONFIGURATION  SECTION.
20      SOURCE-COMPUTER. CYBER-170-720.
21      OBJECT-COMPUTER. CYBER-170-720.
22      SPECIAL-NAMES.
23      INPUT-OUTPUT SECTION.
24      FILE-CONTROL.
25          SELECT IN-FILE ASSIGN TO INPUT.
26          SELECT OUT-FILE ASSIGN TO OUTPUT.
27
28      DATA DIVISION.
29      FILE SECTION.
30
```

```
31     FD    IN-FILE
32           LABEL RECORDS ARE OMITTED.
33
34     01    RECORD-IN.
35           02    NUMBER-IN OCCURS 40 TIMES PIC 9(02).
36
37     FD    OUT-FILE
38           LABEL RECORDS ARE OMITTED.
39
40     01    LINE-OUT                  PIC X(133).
41
42     WORKING-STORAGE SECTION.
43
44     01    INDEPENDENT-ITEMS-USED.
45           02    ANY-MORE-CARDS      PIC X(03) VALUE 'YES'.
46           02    LARGEST-VALUE       PIC 999.
47           02    N-BIN               PIC 99.
48           02    NUMBER-OF-BINS      PIC 9(02) VALUE 10.
49           02    SMALLEST-NUMBER     PIC 9(02) VALUE ZERO.
50           02    SUB                 PIC 9(02) VALUE ZERO.
51
52     01    HISTO-TABLE-SKELETON.
53           02    FILLER              PIC X(03) VALUE '000'.
54           02    FILLER              PIC X(03) VALUE '000'.
55           02    FILLER              PIC X(03) VALUE '000'.
56           02    FILLER              PIC X(03) VALUE '000'.
57           02    FILLER              PIC X(03) VALUE '000'.
58           02    FILLER              PIC X(03) VALUE '000'.
59           02    FILLER              PIC X(03) VALUE '000'.
60           02    FILLER              PIC X(03) VALUE '000'.
61           02    FILLER              PIC X(03) VALUE '000'.
62           02    FILLER              PIC X(03) VALUE '000'.
63
64     01    HISTO-TABLE REDEFINES HISTO-TABLE-SKELETON.
65           02    TABLE-ELEMENT OCCURS 10 TIMES.
66              03    BIN-VALUE        PIC 9(03).
67
68     01    HEADER-1.
69           02    FILLER              PIC X(27) VALUE SPACES.
70           02    FILLER              PIC X(10) VALUE 'HISTOGRAM'.
71           02    FILLER              PIC X(10) VALUE 'OF NUMBERS'.
72
73     01    HEADER-2.
74           02    FILLER              PIC X(27) VALUE SPACES.
75           02    FILLER              PIC X(20) VALUE ALL '*'.
76
77     01    HEADER-3.
78           02    FILLER              PIC X(06) VALUE SPACES.
79           02    FILLER              PIC X(45) VALUE ALL '*'.
80
81     01    HEADER-4.
82           02    FILLER              PIC X(12) VALUE '*'.
83           02    FILLER              PIC 9 VALUE 1.
84           02    FILLER              PIC X(03) VALUE '*'.
85           02    FILLER              PIC 9 VALUE 2.
86           02    FILLER              PIC X(03) VALUE '*'.
87           02    FILLER              PIC 9 VALUE 3.
88           02    FILLER              PIC X(03) VALUE '*'.
89           02    FILLER              PIC 9 VALUE 4.
90           02    FILLER              PIC X(03) VALUE '*'.
91           02    FILLER              PIC 9 VALUE 5.
92           02    FILLER              PIC X(03) VALUE '*'.
93           02    FILLER              PIC 9 VALUE 6.
94           02    FILLER              PIC X(03) VALUE '*'.
95           02    FILLER              PIC 9 VALUE 7.
96           02    FILLER              PIC X(03) VALUE '*'.
97           02    FILLER              PIC 9 VALUE 8.
98           02    FILLER              PIC X(03) VALUE '*'.
99           02    FILLER              PIC 9 VALUE 9.
100          02    FILLER              PIC X(03) VALUE '*'.
101          02    FILLER              PIC 99 VALUE 10.
102          02    FILLER              PIC X(02) VALUE '*'.
103
104    01    DETAIL-LINE.
105          02    FILLER              PIC X(06) VALUE SPACES.
106          02    LINE-COUNT-OUT      PIC ZZ9.
```

```
107              02    FILLER                  PIC X(01) VALUE ' * '.
108              02    CHARACTER-OUT OCCURS 10 TIMES.
109                 03    X-OUT                PIC X(04).
110
111      PROCEDURE DIVISION.
112
113      MAIN-LINE-ROUTINE.
114          PERFORM OPEN-FILES.
115          PERFORM NEW-PAGE.
116          PERFORM START-UP.
117          PERFORM PROCESS-DATA UNTIL ANY-MORE-CARDS EQUAL 'NO'.
118          PERFORM CLOSE-UP.
119          STOP RUN.
120
121      OPEN-FILES.
122          OPEN INPUT IN-FILE.
123          OPEN OUTPUT OUT-FILE.
124
125      NEW-PAGE.
126          MOVE SPACES TO LINE-OUT.
127          WRITE LINE-OUT AFTER PAGE.
128
129      START-UP.
130          READ IN-FILE AT END MOVE 'NO' TO ANY-MORE-CARDS
131              MOVE ' * * NO DATA IN DECK * * ' TO LINE-OUT
132              WRITE LINE-OUT AFTER 30.
133
134      PROCESS-DATA.
135          PERFORM HISTO-PARA VARYING SUB FROM 1 BY 1
136              UNTIL SUB > 40.
137          READ IN-FILE AT END PERFORM WRITE-HISTOGRAM
138              MOVE 'NO' TO ANY-MORE-CARDS.
139
140      CLOSE-UP.
141          CLOSE IN-FILE, OUT-FILE.
142
143      HISTO-PARA.
144          COMPUTE N-BIN = (NUMBER-IN (SUB) − SMALLEST-NUMBER) /
145              NUMBER-OF-BINS + 1.
146          ADD 1 TO BIN-VALUE (N-BIN).
147
148      WRITE-HISTOGRAM.
149          WRITE LINE-OUT FROM HEADER-1 AFTER 1.
150          WRITE LINE-OUT FROM HEADER-2 AFTER 1.
151          WRITE LINE-OUT FROM HEADER-2 AFTER 1.
152          MOVE BIN-VALUE (1) TO LARGEST-VALUE.
153          PERFORM GET-LARGEST-VALUE VARYING N-BIN FROM 2 BY 1
154              UNTIL N-BIN > NUMBER-OF-BINS.
155          PERFORM SCALING VARYING N-BIN FROM 1 BY 1 UNTIL
156              N-BIN > NUMBER-OF-BINS.
157          MOVE BIN-VALUE (1) TO LARGEST-VALUE.
158          PERFORM GET-LARGEST-VALUE VARYING N-BIN FROM 2 BY 1
159              UNTIL N-BIN > NUMBER-OF-BINS.
160          PERFORM WRITE-LINE VARYING LARGEST-VALUE FROM LARGEST-VALUE
161              BY −1 UNTIL LARGEST-VALUE = 0.
162          WRITE LINE-OUT FROM HEADER-3 AFTER 1.
163          WRITE LINE-OUT FROM HEADER-4 AFTER 1.
164
165      GET-LARGEST-VALUE.
166          IF BIN-VALUE (N-BIN) > LARGEST-VALUE MOVE
167              BIN-VALUE (N-BIN) TO LARGEST-VALUE.
168
169      SCALING.
170          COMPUTE BIN-VALUE (N-BIN) = BIN-VALUE (N-BIN) /
171              LARGEST-VALUE * 10.
172
173      WRITE-LINE.
174          MOVE LARGEST-VALUE TO LINE-COUNT-OUT.
175          PERFORM POSITION-XS VARYING N-BIN FROM 1 BY 1 UNTIL
176              N-BIN > 10.
177          WRITE LINE-OUT FROM DETAIL-LINE AFTER 1.
178
179      POSITION-XS.
180          IF BIN-VALUE (N-BIN) = LARGEST-VALUE OR BIN-VALUE (N-BIN)
181              > LARGEST-VALUE MOVE 'X' TO X-OUT (N-BIN)
182          ELSE MOVE SPACES TO X-OUT (N-BIN).
```

Output for Program 46

```
                        HISTOGRAM OF NUMBERS
                  * * * * * * * * * * * * * * * * * *
                  * * * * * * * * * * * * * * * * * *
        10*   X
         9*   X                                                    X
         8*   X           X               X                        X
         7*   X           X         X     X     X                  X
         6*   X           X         X     X     X     X            X
         5*   X     X     X     X   X     X     X     X     X     X
         4*   X     X     X     X   X     X     X     X     X     X
         3*   X     X     X     X   X     X     X     X     X     X
         2*   X     X     X     X   X     X     X     X     X     X
         1*   X     X     X     X   X     X     X     X     X     X
        * * * * * * * * * * * * * * * * * * * * * * * * * * * * * * * * * * * * * * * *
        *     1  *  2  *  3  *  4 * 5  *  6  *  7  *  8  *  9  *  10*
```

13.5 Introduction to Modular Programming

In the commercial world where programming is used so extensively, frequently the same kind of procedure may be necessary for different types of operations. Once a particular technique is written, debugged, and verified to be in perfect working order, it would be both costly and foolhardy to go to the trouble to rewrite that very same procedure when it is required in a new application. After all, why reinvent the wheel once it has already been invented.

COBOL has a special facility that enables the programmer to incorporate into an existing program any previously written procedure, provided it is written according to a prescribed format. These procedures are regarded as modules. This approach to writing complex programs is particularly efficient and is widely used in the industrial world of data processing.

In order to illustrate this concept of modular programming, let us take a rather simple case. The purpose of the main program is to read the data composed of 2 numbers. These numbers are processed by the module that simply adds the 2 numbers, returning the result back to the main program, which prints out the pair of inputted numbers and their sum.

The mechanism by which information is transferred from the main program to the module is initiated by the CALL statements. The CALL statement is of the form:

CALL 'the program module' USING data-names

where the program module must be enclosed by quotation marks. Once the information is transmitted to the CALLed module, it is processed there and the result is returned to the main program, either by executing an EXIT PROGRAM or, for IBM computers, GOBACK instruction. Control is then returned to the statement following the CALL statement.

The USING clause specifies the data that is to be transferred to and from the module. However, care must be taken to ensure that whatever items are being transmitted are on the 01 or the 77 level.

The module must also have the 4 standard divisions, its own PROGRAM-ID name, and what is called a LINKAGE SECTION, which is part of the Data Division. The purpose of the Linkage Section is to describe the data that is common to both the main program and the module.

RECORD-IN is identical in both the main program and the module. However, DETAIL-LINE, which also appears in both the main program and the module, is described differently, because we are only interested in the item TOTAL-OUT when the information is transmitted back to the main program. In order to skip over the first 58 positions of the common area, one uses a FILLER with a PICTURE of X(58).

Input for Program 47

```
0253  2500
1000  1000
0000  0000
1234  1234
2500  2500
1235  1425
5566  2534
0025  0357
1238  1478
1985  4567
9985  4325
7568  4265
1786  0357
1598  7586
4537  7532
0001  0001
```

Program 47

```
1       IDENTIFICATION   DIVISION.
2       PROGRAM-ID.   MAINPROGRAM.
3       AUTHOR.         IRVIN POREMBA.
4       INSTALLATION.   NYU.
5       DATE-WRITTEN.   JUNE 11, 1982.
6       DATE-COMPILED.  JUNE 16, 1982.
7       SECURITY.       HENRY MULLISH.
8       * * * * * * * * * * * * * * * * * * * * * * * * * * * * * * * * * * * * * * * * * * * *
9       *       THIS PROGRAM READS DATA CARDS PUNCHED:                              *
10      *                                                                           *
11      *       COLUMNS  1-4:  FIRST NUMBER                                         *
12      *       COLUMNS 11-14: SECOND NUMBER                                        *
13      *                                                                           *
14      *       THIS PROGRAM(MAINPROGRAM) CALLS A                                   *
15      *       SUBPROGRAM(MODULE) WHICH ADDS TWO NUMBERS                           *
16      *       AND RETURNS THE RESULT TO THE MAIN PROGRAM                          *
17      *       WHICH PRINTS IT OUT.                                                *
18      * * * * * * * * * * * * * * * * * * * * * * * * * * * * * * * * * * * * * * * * * * * *
19
20      ENVIRONMENT  DIVISION.
21      CONFIGURATION  SECTION.
22      SOURCE-COMPUTER. CYBER-170-720.
23      OBJECT-COMPUTER. CYBER-170-720.
24      SPECIAL-NAMES.
25      INPUT-OUTPUT    SECTION.
26      FILE-CONTROL.
27          SELECT IN-FILE ASSIGN TO INPUT.
28          SELECT OUT-FILE ASSIGN TO OUTPUT.
29
30      DATA DIVISION.
31      FILE SECTION.
32
33
34      FD   IN-FILE
35           LABEL RECORDS ARE OMITTED.
36
37      01   RECORD-IN.
38           02   NUMBER-1          PIC 9(04).
39           02   FILLER            PIC X(06).
40           02   NUMBER-2          PIC 9(04).
41           02   FILLER            PIC X(66).
42
43      FD   OUT-FILE
44           LABEL RECORDS ARE OMITTED.
45
46           01   LINE-OUT          PIC X(133).
47
48      WORKING-STORAGE SECTION.
49      77   ANY-MORE-CARDS         PIC X(03) VALUE 'YES'.
50
51      01   DETAIL-LINE
52           02   FILLER            PIC X(01) VALUE SPACES.
```

```
53          02    FILLER              PIC X(15) VALUE 'FIRST NUMBER = '.
54          02    NUMBER-1-OUT        PIC ZZZ9.
55          02    FILLER              PIC X(05) VALUE SPACES.
56          02    FILLER              PIC X(16) VALUE 'SECOND NUMBER = '.
57          02    NUMBER-2-OUT        PIC ZZZ9.
58          02    FILLER              PIC X(05) VALUE SPACES.
59          02    FILLER              PIC X(08) VALUE 'TOTAL = '.
60          02    TOTAL-OUT           PIC ZZZZZ9.
61
62      PROCEDURE DIVISION.
63
64      MAIN-LINE-ROUTINE.
65          PERFORM OPEN-FILES.
66          PERFORM NEW-PAGE.
67          PERFORM START-UP.
68          PERFORM PROCESS-DATA UNTIL ANY-MORE-CARDS EQUAL 'NO'.
69          PERFORM CLOSE-UP.
70          STOP RUN.
71
72      OPEN-FILES.
73          OPEN INPUT IN-FILE.
74          OPEN OUTPUT OUT-FILE.
75
76      NEW-PAGE.
77          MOVE SPACES TO LINE-OUT.
78          WRITE LINE-OUT AFTER PAGE.
79
80      START-UP.
81          READ IN-FILE AT END MOVE 'NO' TO ANY-MORE-CARDS
82              MOVE ' **NO DATA IN DECK**' TO LINE-OUT
83              WRITE LINE-OUT AFTER 30.
84
85      PROCESS-DATA.
86          CALL 'MODULE' USING RECORD-IN, DETAIL-LINE.
87          MOVE NUMBER-1 TO NUMBER-1-OUT.
88          MOVE NUMBER-2 TO NUMBER-2-OUT.
89          WRITE LINE-OUT FROM DETAIL-LINE AFTER 2.
90          READ IN-FILE AT END MOVE 'NO' TO ANY-MORE-CARDS.
91
92      CLOSE-UP.
93          CLOSE IN-FILE, OUT-FILE.
```

```
1       IDENTIFICATION   DIVISION.
2       PROGRAM-ID.      MODULE.
3       *      THIS SUBPROGRAM ADDS THE TWO NUMBERS TOGETHER.   *
4
5       ENVIRONMENT   DIVISION.
6
7       DATA DIVISION.
8
9       LINKAGE SECTION.
10
11      01    RECORD-IN.
12          02    NUMBER-1        PIC 9(04).
13          02    FILLER          PIC X(06).
14          02    NUMBER-2        PIC 9(04).
15          02    FILLER          PIC X(66).
16
17      01    DETAIL-LINE.
18          02    FILLER          PIC X(58).
19          02    TOTAL-OUT       PIC ZZZZZ9.
20
21      PROCEDURE DIVISION USING RECORD-IN, DETAIL-LINE.
22
23      ADD-NUMBERS.
24          ADD NUMBER-1, NUMBER-2 GIVING TOTAL-OUT.
25
26      RETURN-TO-MAIN-PROGRAM.
27          EXIT PROGRAM.
```

Output for Program 47

FIRST NUMBER = 253	SECOND NUMBER = 2500	TOTAL = 2753
FIRST NUMBER = 1000	SECOND NUMBER = 1000	TOTAL = 2000
FIRST NUMBER = 0	SECOND NUMBER = 0	TOTAL = 0
FIRST NUMBER = 1234	SECOND NUMBER = 1234	TOTAL = 2468
FIRST NUMBER = 2500	SECOND NUMBER = 2500	TOTAL = 5000
FIRST NUMBER = 1235	SECOND NUMBER = 1425	TOTAL = 2660
FIRST NUMBER = 5566	SECOND NUMBER = 2534	TOTAL = 8100
FIRST NUMBER = 25	SECOND NUMBER = 357	TOTAL = 382
FIRST NUMBER = 1238	SECOND NUMBER = 1478	TOTAL = 2716
FIRST NUMBER = 1985	SECOND NUMBER = 4567	TOTAL = 6552
FIRST NUMBER = 9985	SECOND NUMBER = 4325	TOTAL = 14310
FIRST NUMBER = 7568	SECOND NUMBER = 4265	TOTAL = 11833
FIRST NUMBER = 1786	SECOND NUMBER = 357	TOTAL = 2143
FIRST NUMBER = 1598	SECOND NUMBER = 7586	TOTAL = 9184
FIRST NUMBER = 4537	SECOND NUMBER = 7532	TOTAL = 12069
FIRST NUMBER = 1	SECOND NUMBER = 1	TOTAL = 2

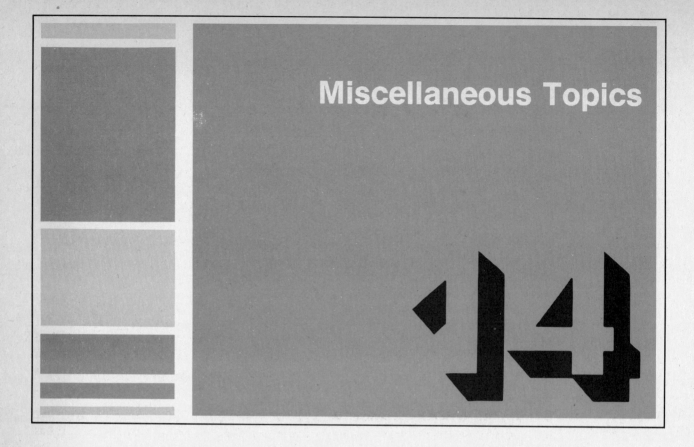

Miscellaneous Topics

Writing a complete COBOL program is like composing a symphony.

(Meri Cohen)

14.1 Signed Numbers

In almost all the programs we have encountered so far, all numeric fields have been assigned a picture of one or more 9's. For example, the data-names for Social Security numbers, identification numbers, hours worked, rate per hour, all have fields of 9's. When assigning a picture of all 9's, one implies that the number in question is positive. In fact if the result of a subtraction of 2 numbers were negative, and its result had a picture of all 9's only, the result would be printed as a positive number, which would be the absolute value of the correct result. In certain situations this could lead to disastrous consequences. Its associated picture must be preceded by the letter S, in order to ensure that the appropriate sign of a number is retained. Many professional programmers consider it good programming practice to use the letter S in the pictures of all numeric fields. For example, suppose in Working-Storage we have the 2 following 77-level items.

```
77   UNSIGNED-FIELD PICTURE 999.
77   SIGNED-FIELD PICTURE S999.
```

If in the Procedure Division, we then execute the following statements.

```
MOVE -50 TO UNSIGNED-FIELD, SIGNED-FIELD.
DISPLAY UNSIGNED-FIELD, SIGNED-FIELD.
```

The numbers

50   −50

will be stored internally and printed as shown. In the case of the unsigned field, UNSIGNED-FIELD, with the picture of 999 rather than S999, the printed result of 50 is obviously incorrect. It is important to note that the presence of an S in a numeric field does not alter the size of the field and should not be counted when totaling the characters in the record.

One way to read a negative number as a numeric data item is to precede the number with a negative sign. One must first make sure that the associated picture is preceded by an S and that the negative sign is *multipunched* over the rightmost digit. However strange this concept appears, the correct negative value will be read in. Once again, the minus sign is not counted in the width of the data field.

The SIGN Clause

The 1974 standard provides the programmer with a method of reading in data that has minus signs to either the left or the right. Normally a negative number punched on data cards is assumed to have the negative sign overpunched on the rightmost digit. Using the SIGN clause, one may specify whether the sign (usually negative) is punched to the left or to the right of the number. For example,

−12345   +12345   12345−   12345+

would be acceptable punched data items, provided the SIGN clause was used. It has the form

$$[\underline{\text{SIGN}} \text{ IS}] \left\{ \begin{array}{c} \underline{\text{LEADING}} \\ \underline{\text{TRAILING}} \end{array} \right\} [\underline{\text{SEPARATE}} \text{ CHARACTER}]$$

This instruction may be part of an input record description in the Data Division. Here are some examples of how the SIGN clause may be used, indicating the effective size of the corresponding field.

DATA ITEM AS PUNCHED ON CARD	ENTRY DESCRIPTION	SIZE OF PUNCHED FIELD
1̄23	PICTURE S999	3
12̄3	PICTURE S999 SIGN IS TRAILING	3
123+	PICTURE S999 SIGN TRAILING SEPARATE	4
−123	PICTURE S999 SIGN IS LEADING SEPARATE CHARACTER	4

If the SIGN clause is omitted, it is assumed to be SIGN IS TRAILING. Only if the SEPARATE option is used is the character S in the PICTURE clause included in the size of the field.

14.2 The STOP Statement

Throughout this text we have terminated each program by execution of the statement STOP RUN. Because this instruction permanently stops execution of the program, it cannot be restarted short of reading it in again. However, this is not the only form of the STOP; it is possible to instruct the computer both to pause and print a message by means of the following form of the instruction.

STOP LITERAL

This statement also causes the computer to stop executing. The literal in question may be either a numeric or a nonnumeric literal. For example, we might have

STOP 'OUT OF DATA'.

or

STOP 1234.

In both these cases the execution of the STOP instruction causes a pause in execution. This time, however, the program may be restarted by the intervention of the operator. The literal specified in the STOP instruction is printed on the printer before the computer comes to a halt.

In the case of a numeric literal a list of numeric error codes might be established and given to the operator; when one of these errors is encountered, the operator will be able to consult a list of error codes and determine what action to take to rectify the matter. The operator can then restart the job.

14.3 The USAGE Clause

As the reader already knows, all COBOL instructions are ultimately converted into the language that the computer really understands, namely, the binary language. If one were to pry open the cover of the computer memory, one would be confronted by a dazzling array of switches that are represented only by zeros and ones, and nothing else. Nevertheless for various purposes the formats of certain data are stored differently, depending on their intended usage. The informed programmer is at liberty to state the intended usage of the data. By doing so, he or she can optimize the efficiency of the program. The clause

USAGE IS

may be used for describing data that may be one of the following types.

```
DISPLAY
{ COMPUTATIONAL-3 }
{ COMP-3          }
{ COMPUTATIONAL }
{ COMP          }
```

where COMPUTATIONAL-3 may be abbreviated to COMP-3, and likewise, COMPUTATIONAL to COMP. However, the clause USAGE IS may always be omitted entirely.

DISPLAY is the term used to describe the manner in which both input and output information is stored internally. Assembly language programmers, those programmers who code programs in a language much closer to that of the computer, refer to this mode of representation as *zoned decimal* or *unpacked* format. If there is no usage clause specified in the record description, USAGE is assumed to be DISPLAY. DISPLAY is therefore said to be the default option. In the first of the next 2 examples the USAGE clause is explicitly stated, whereas in the second, it is implied. Nevertheless both examples are treated equally by the COBOL compiler:

```
05 WAGES PICTURE 999V99 USAGE IS DISPLAY.
05 WAGES PICTURE 999V99.
```

Computational data (data that will be used for arithmetic purposes) may be efficiently stored in its so-called packed form. COBOL programmers can specify this format by writing:

USAGE IS COMPUTATIONAL-3.

or

USAGE IS COMP-3.

or

COMPUTATION-3.

or simply

COMP-3.

If a number is stored in DISPLAY format, and used in a calculation, it first has to be converted from DISPLAY format (unpacked) to COMP-3 (packed), the calculation is done in COMP-3, and finally, the result is converted to DISPLAY (unpacked) for printing the result. Each conversion, of course, takes precious computer time. When COMP-3 is used, all these conversions to and from packed format are avoided and the execution of the program is made much more efficient. The COMP-3 format is specified for numeric fields only and is never used for either reading cards or printing.

The COMPUTATIONAL form (binary), or COMP as it is usually written, is invariably used for storing data in strict binary form. There are many purposes for which binary arithmetic is considered both more efficient and desirable. Counting operations are often specified to be COMPUTATIONAL. If one attempts to display data sorted in COMPUTATIONAL form, the output will be printed in binary, a form that we humans have much trouble in deciphering. If, however, such data is DISPLAYED or EXHIBITED, it will be printed in display form, leaving it in its original form internally. Many professional programmers use COMP for counters, subscripts, table values, and data-names strictly for computation.

14.4 Hardware

The computing environment is generally divided into *hardware* and *software*. The main frame of the computer, for example, is generally the most conspicuous part of the hardware. Other hardware elements are the disks, operating panel, card reader, line printer, and drum. The following picture shows an IBM 370/145 computer center with its various hardware members. The disk storage unit is in the far right corner, whereas the card punch is in the far left. The card reader is front left and the high-speed printer is front right. All the way to the left there are the tape drives and in the back left there is the operator's console.

The keypunch machine is often the standard hardware device for punching input cards. A trained keypunch operator is capable of keypunching cards rapidly

and accurately by means of the so-called "drumcard." It is beyond the scope of this book to describe in detail how the drum may be exploited, but it is nonetheless recommended that an introduction to its use be requested of the keypunch operator.

There is also another machine (not illustrated), which is called a *verifier*. Once a program deck has been punched, it may then be checked with a verifier machine, preferably by an operator other than the one who punched the deck initially. Each card is treated as if it were to be repunched. No holes are punched this time; instead, spring-loaded plungers take the place of the punch mechanism. If holes actually appear where they are supposed to, the plungers penetrate the holes and the column is considered to be correctly keypunched. If, however, there is a discrepancy between the punched card and what the verifier operator has keyed in, a red light is actuated to alert the operator to the discrepancy. Either the card has been initially punched incorrectly or an error has been made during the verification process. Either way, the appropriate action must be taken. In effect, therefore, verifying a deck is tantamount to repunching the whole deck again, a time-consuming luxury not everyone can afford.

Magnetic Tapes

Some commercial installations record all their business transactions on magnetic tape. Some have libraries consisting literally of hundreds of magnetic tape reels. In early computers, magnetic tape was actually made of a long strip of paper-thin steel. Modern computers, however, use continuous strips of plastic tape, coated on one side with a metallic oxide. Usually the tape is one-half inch wide and can be in any of the standard lengths of 250, 600, 1200, or 2400 feet securely wound around plastic reels. This is the same type of tape as that used in tape recorders, where audio signals are recorded on the tape. With a computer, however, data is recorded by a system of magnetized spots that conform to a specific pattern for each specific character. These "bits," as they are called, correspond to the form in which the information is actually stored in the internal memory of the computer. Notice the mounted tape on the right-hand side of the preceding picture, just above the video screen.

Disk Storage

Despite the considerable advantages that magnetic tapes offer for storing masses of information, a significant disadvantage is that in order to get from one item of information to another, one must scan the entire length of tape between the 2 items. In other words, to access the seven hundred and fiftieth record on the tape, 749 records must first be read before the desired record can be accessed. Obviously for many situations, this method of accessing information can be extremely inefficient and expensive.

With the invention of *disk* drives, a much faster method of accessing mass data was provided, and today they are one of the most common means of storing voluminous data. A disk pack rotates at a constant speed much like a phonograph record. Instead of only one platter, the disk pack usually contains 11 metal disks that are permanently attached to a central spindle as shown in Figure 14-1. No information may be written on either the top surface of the uppermost disk or the undersurface of the lowermost disk. On each of the surfaces there are a specific number of concentric circles called *tracks*. In the Model 2316 disk pack, for example, there are 200 concentric circles (tracks) on each of the 20 usable surfaces. There are therefore 20 × 200 tracks per disk pack, making a total of 4000 tracks on which data can be either written or accessed. Although these concentric circles get smaller

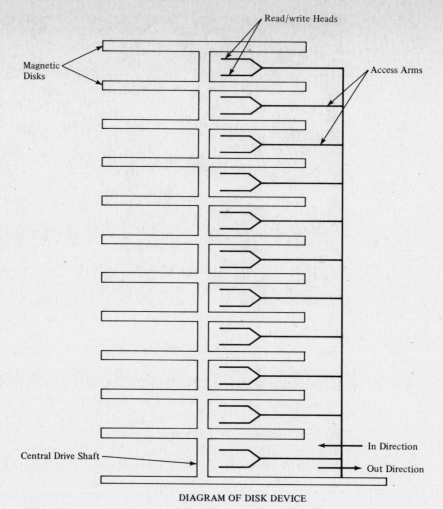

DIAGRAM OF DISK DEVICE

Figure 14-1

toward the center of the disk, each of the tracks, regardless of position, has the same data capacity.

As in the case of magnetic tape, data is recorded on disk as magnetic spots called bits, corresponding to the manner in which the data is stored internally.

When data is either written on the disk or read from the disk, movable read/write heads move in and out to the appropriate track. Although only one track may be accessed at any given moment, whenever the access mechanism moves, all 20 read/write heads move simultaneously. For any position therefore 20 tracks can be accessed without moving the head mechanism. Each set of these 20 tracks is regarded as a *cylinder*. Unlike magnetic tape, information on disk may be directly accessed. For this reason, disk is the kind of device referred to as a DASD (pronounced *das-dee*), which stands for Direct Access Storage Device.

14.5 Software

No computer is of any value if it does not come equipped with the system routines to control it. These system routines contain the supervisory routine, library routines, compilers, and utility routines. The software may be viewed in a manner analogous to the automobile, which requires fuel for it to function. Writing the programs for the software packages can range in complexity from a simple COBOL program to a highly sophisticated assembler (binary) program. The overall computer system therefore is a very intimate marriage of both hardware and software, each requiring the other for success.

14.6   File Structure

Although it has not as yet been specifically stated, the FILE SECTION defines all those data areas that are part of the input or the output files. These files will also have been defined in the ENVIRONMENT DIVISION, where by means of a SELECT clause the particular files are defined and assigned to input-output devices. For every SELECT clause contained in the ENVIRONMENT DIVISION, a file-name is declared.

When a READ instruction is executed in the PROCEDURE DIVISION, data is transmitted to the input area reserved for that input file. Similarly, whenever a WRITE statement is executed, all the information stored in an output area is transmitted to the specified output device.

As you will have noticed in every program, each file mentioned in the file section is described with an FD entry. FD in fact stands for File Description. Each file may be a card file, tape file, or disk file.

A file invariably consists of many individual records, each of which may be recorded in one of 3 different modes. One of the standard entries refers to the mode in which the data is recorded. It is the recording mode clause that has the generalized format:

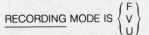

RECORDING MODE IS $\left\{ \begin{array}{c} F \\ V \\ U \end{array} \right\}$

where F stands for fixed; V, for variable; and U, for unspecified. If all the records within a file are of the same length, such as is the case with a card file (every card must contain 80 characters), the RECORDING MODE IS F.

For those situations in which record lengths are not fixed, they may be designated as variable or unspecified. In the following diagram (Figure 14-2), reading from left to right, the file is composed of 5 records made up of 20, 50, 100, 150, 20, and 200 characters, respectively.

In such a situation the RECORDING MODE IS V, for *variable*. It is only fair to say that for records of variable length additional programming burdens are encountered and therefore variable-length records are discouraged.

If the records are of neither variable nor fixed length, the clause RECORD-ING MODE IS U (for *unspecified*) is used, Again, files with unspecified recording modes are seldom encountered except in more sophisticated situations.

Because the RECORDING MODE clause is optional, it may, of course, be omitted. In such cases the computer itself determines whether the file is variable or fixed.

Figure 14-2

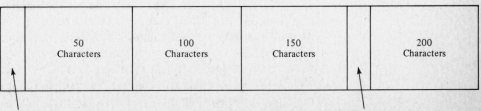

| | 50 Characters | 100 Characters | 150 Characters | | 200 Characters |

20 Characters   20 Characters

A required clause under the FD is LABEL RECORDS, which has the following generalized format.

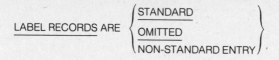

Label records are created as the first and last records of a magnetic tape or disk and supply important identifying information to the system. These are *created* on output files and are *checked* on input files. LABEL RECORDS ARE STANDARD has the effect of triggering the COBOL routines for writing the labels on output files or for checking the labels on input files.

The writing of header and trailer records does not apply to unit-record devices such as the card reader or line printer. For unit-record files therefore we write

LABEL RECORDS ARE OMITTED.

A third optional clause under the FD is the RECORD CONTAINS clause, which has the following format.

RECORD CONTAINS integer CHARACTERS.

As the clause suggests, the RECORD CONTAINS clause indicates the number of characters that it contains. For example, RECORD CONTAINS 133 CHARACTERS would describe a print file with 133-position records. The usual size of a printed line is 132 characters. We write 133, however, because the first position is reserved for carriage control purposes. It is positions 2 through 133 of the records that are actually printed. An input card file may have an entry that reads RECORD CONTAINS 80 CHARACTERS.

When tapes or disk are used, a BLOCK CONTAINS clause may be included. It has the general form:

$$
\text{BLOCK CONTAINS integer}
\begin{Bmatrix}
\text{RECORDS} \\
\text{CHARACTERS}
\end{Bmatrix}
$$

Tape or disk files are often blocked for reasons of expediency. If many logical records are contained within a block, more efficient use of the file is accomplished because less time is consumed in accessing the recorded information. Usually the COBOL programmer is not expected to know the most efficient block size (or the *blocking factor*, as it is called) but is informed of this by a systems expert. If an FD does in fact include a BLOCK CONTAINS clause, no further entry is required to perform the operations on that blocked data. This clause is never used when unit record devices are designated. In such cases the entire clause is omitted.

The last optional entry permitted in the file description is the DATA RECORD clause, which is of the form:

$$
\text{DATA}
\begin{Bmatrix}
\text{RECORD IS} \\
\text{RECORDS ARE}
\end{Bmatrix}
\text{record-name-1 [record-name-2]} \ldots
$$

The DATA RECORD(S) clause defines the names of the record or records within the file. Naturally if there is only one record in the file, DATA RECORD is used. These assigned record names, it is pointed out, must be unique to the program and must conform to the rules for constructing user-supplied names. It would be reasonable to suppose that if more than one data record is specified, additional core is required. This is in fact *not* the case for a single input or output area (as the case may be); it is merely redefined by subsequent record definitions.

Because the DATA RECORD(S) clause is the last optional entry for all file descriptions, it is always followed by a period to designate the end of the FD.

Here are some typical examples of file descriptions.

1. FD IN-FILE
LABEL RECORDS ARE OMITTED
RECORD CONTAINS 80 CHARACTERS
DATA RECORD IS SALES-RECORD.
2. FD MASTER-FILE
RECORDING MODE IS F
LABEL RECORDS ARE STANDARD
RECORD CONTAINS 65 CHARACTERS
BLOCK CONTAINS 10 RECORDS
DATA RECORDS ARE ACCTS-RECEIVABLE, ACCTS-PAYABLE.

14.7 The WATBOL Compiler

The tendency today is for COBOL programmers to get their training at educational institutions, either under the auspices of a particular computer manufacturer or in one of the various colleges. There are even high schools where COBOL is now taught as a regular part of the curriculum. One of the glaring realities in an educational environment is that novices make unlimited errors. This is perfectly natural and is to be expected. After all, part of the educational process is to purge oneself of the incorrect thinking that causes these errors.

In the University of Waterloo in Ontario, Canada, there is a Computer Systems Group that has succeeded in writing a special COBOL compiler that is geared for the student. It permits many if not most of the options available on the full COBOL compiler and is particularly useful in that detected errors are more explicitly documented. Usually a dollar sign, for example, is printed out on the program listing immediately beneath the area of the violation, thereby directing the programmer's attention to the part of the statement that has created the diagnostic. The compiler is "fast and dirty," as well as rich in its diagnostic capability.

A "fast and dirty" compiler is one that is fast during compilation, the phase during which most if not all a student's program errors will be found. Such a compiler is not suited for commercial purposes because the generated code is not optimized and would result in unduly long execution times. Because student problems are generally short, running them in inefficient machine code is not particularly disturbing. Furthermore, the operating system assigns a very high priority to jobs running under WATBOL. The result is that a student can obtain a fast turnaround, which is always a treasured asset.

In naming the compiler produced by this group at the University of Waterloo, the first 3 letters of Waterloo were attached to the last 3 letters of COBOL, giving us WATBOL.

At New York University, where WATBOL was routinely used as the student compiler, turnaround time was about 10 minutes, compared to at least an hour using the regular COBOL compiler. Furthermore, all the time used in running WATBOL (as distinct from COBOL) was gratis, whereas regular COBOL time is strictly budgeted. No greater inducement was necessary to encourage students to run their programs on the WATBOL compiler.

Instead of the 4 levels of diagnostics recognized by the standard COBOL compiler, namely, W, C, E, and D, the WATBOL compiler issues compile-time diagnostics at 5 levels of severity. They are MESSAGE, WARNING, EXTENSION, ERROR, and TERMINATION.

A nonfatal MESSAGE is issued for minor infractions of the rules, such as omitting a space after a period or a comma. Execution of the program, however, continues.

More severe violations of COBOL rules are flagged by a WARNING. Using a program name greater in length than 8 characters or including a minus sign in it (invariably referred to as a hyphen) would cause a WARNING. A WARNING is also not fatal.

Because WATBOL allows for various nonstandard instructions known as "extensions," WATBOL prints out the word EXTENSION for each statement that incorporates such an extension. The purpose of the diagnostic is to alert the user that if the program is to be run subsequently on another computer that does not allow for that particular extension, the program will have to be amended accordingly.

A more severe violation is flagged by the word ERROR. In this case execution of the program is usually halted because to continue might result in incorrect output.

An even more severe violation is flagged by the word TERMINATION. As its name suggests, it terminates execution of the program.

A typical example of a WATBOL diagnostic is shown here. An attempt is made to execute the instruction.

```
DIVIDE A1 BY A2.
```

As you may recall, when the preposition BY is used in the DIVIDE statement, the GIVING clause must also be used. The diagnostic is printed as follows.

```
61          DIVIDE A1 BY A2.
                            $
* * * * *ERROR 537 MISSING KEYWORD GIVING.
```

In this case, instruction 61 is in violation of the rules of syntax. A dollar sign is printed beneath the period, indicating the point where the violation has been detected. On the next line, after the 5 asterisks, there is printed the error number (in this case, ERROR 537) and a description of the nature of the error.

You may recall earlier in the text, when we discussed the MULTIPLY verb, the point was made that one cannot say

```
MULTIPLY A1 TIMES A2
```

however acceptable this may be in conversational English. One has to write, of course,

```
MULTIPLY A1 BY A2.
```

Here is what happens if this error is attempted in WATBOL. It gives two rather than one diagnostic. Error 532 points out that instead of the word TIMES the preposition BY has been assumed. Then immediately afterward, error 850 announces that it has detected a missing or invalid operand. Presumably the data-name A2 is lost or ignored because of the first diagnostic.

```
67          MULTIPLY A1 TIMES A2.
                               $
* * * * *ERROR 532 MISSING KEYWORD-BY ASSUMED.
* * * * *ERROR 850 MISSING OR INVALID OPERAND.
```

To obtain a list of all possible diagnostics that are available on the WATBOL compiler, one only has to run the following short program. The program name is a special 8-character WORD, namely, COBERMSG, for COBOL error messages.

Program 48

COBERMSG

```
IDENTIFICATION DIVISION.
PROGRAM-ID. COBERMSG.
ENVIRONMENT DIVISION.
DATA DIVISION.
PROCEDURE DIVISION.
    STOP RUN.
```

The output to this program is quite voluminous but will be of great interest to the novice programmer. Of even greater interest and usefulness is a list of the complete set of reserved, key words recognized by the WATBOL compiler. This may be obtained by running the identical program to the preceding one for producing the error messages. The only change that should be made is that the program name has to be COBKEYWD instead of COBERMSG. It is recommended that when writing programs in WATBOL the list of reserved words be kept close by for ready reference.

There are, however, some incompatibilities between WATBOL and IBM COBOL, which include the following.

1. Whereas in COBOL no spaces may appear before the separators comma, semicolon, and period, spaces are optional in WATBOL.

2. Nonnumeric literals may be enclosed within either single or double quotes but not a combination of them. In other words, the literals 'GROSS-PAY' and "WAGES" are both acceptable but 'NET-INCOME" is not. However, the inclusion of either of the quote signs is permitted, provided that it is enclosed by a pair of the other quote signs. For example, 'FICA"S-AMOUNT' and "FICA'S-AMOUNT" are both valid nonnumeric literals in WATBOL.

3. In COBOL a comment card is specified by punching an asterisk in column 7. Unlike COBOL, in WATBOL a comment card cannot immediately precede a continuation card.

4. Some program text is allowed on the same line as Division or Section headers in WATBOL, but this is not a recommended practice.

5. Multiple receiving fields are permitted in ADD, SUBTRACT, MULTIPLY, DIVIDE and COMPUTE statements. For example,

```
ADD A B GIVING C D.
```

In this case the sum of A and B will be stored in both C and D. By the same token,

```
COMPUTE W X = Y + Z
```

will store the sum of Y and Z in both W and X.

6. The debugging aids READY TRACE and RESET TRACE are permitted. Instead of the paragraph names of the executed program being printed out, their internally stored statement numbers are printed. What appears on the output is a succession of statement numbers.

7. The input file must be assigned to SYSIN and the output file, to SYSOUT.

8. The simple WRITE statement on SYSOUT is treated equivalently as the COBOL statement WRITE AFTER ADVANCING. In other words, they both cause the printer to space before printing. Because the WRITE AFTER ADVANCING option necessitates a blank in column 1 for carriage control, the simple WRITE in WATBOL should have 133 characters per line or, on some systems, 121 characters.

9. Output produced by the WATBOL compiler prints immediately after the program listing. Therefore it may be desirable to resort to SPECIAL-NAMES to go to the top of a new page before printing.

10. Uncleared areas of output are printed with double quotation marks.

A typical WATBOL program control card setup is now shown.

```
//JOB      JOB(XXXX,XXXX), 'YOUR NAME', CLASS = C
$JOB       WATBOL ANYNAME
           {COBOL PROGRAM}
$ENTRY     (WHETHER DATA IS USED OR NOT)
           {DATA CARDS (IF USED)}
$EOF
/*.
//
```

At different installations, minor changes may be necessary.

14.8 The Unwritten Murphy's Law

There is a most pervasive law that programmers the world over soon learn to respect even though no legislative body ever passed it nor does it appear in any nation's constitution. Universally spoken of simply as Murphy's Law, its origin is rather obscure, but it is an axiom that unfortunately proves its validity time and time again. It may be stated in various ways; some of the most common versions are:

1. In any field of detailed endeavor, anything that can go wrong *will* go wrong.
2. If left to themselves, things always go from bad to worse.
3. If there is a possibility of several things going wrong, the one that will in fact go wrong is the one that will do the most damage.
4. Nature invariably sides with the hidden flaw.
5. (This is really Chisholm's Law, a variant of Murphy's Law.) If everything seems to be going well, it is clear that something important has been overlooked.
6. (This is actually Gumperson's Law, another variant of Murphy's Law.) If anything can go wrong, it will, and what's more, it will go wrong at precisely the worst possible moment.

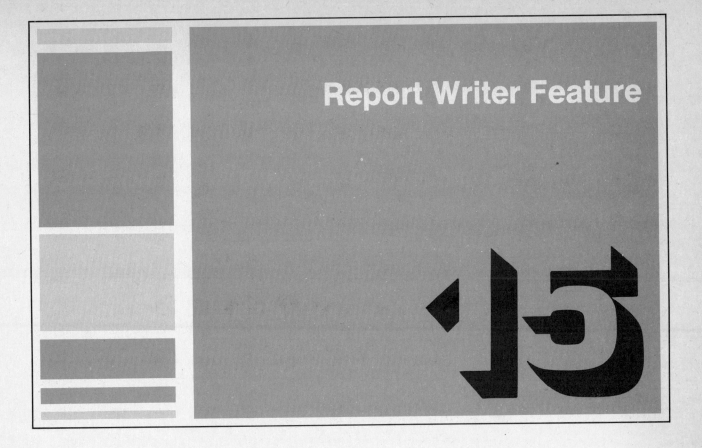

Report Writer Feature

You don't get to the meat of a COBOL program until you're already tired of writing.

(Leslie Jones)

In previous chapters we saw how writing a report can lead to a somewhat lengthy Procedure Division. Depending on the depth of detail required, the logic can become quite complicated. Because the writing of reports plays such a major role in business data processing, ANSI COBOL provides us with a special module, known as the Report Writer feature. This gives us the ability to print a heading to a report, a page heading at the top of each page, detail-lines of various kinds—the major substance of the report, page footings at the bottom of each page of the report, footings for subtotals and totals, and finally, a report footing for the conclusions of the report.

Many COBOL programmers have to program reports for a great variety of purposes. For these programmers the Report Writer feature will be of particular interest, because it will relieve them of much of the housekeeping chores. In Report Writer the programmer is given the opportunity to describe the physical appearance of a report rather than having to specify the precise, detailed procedures that otherwise would be necessary to produce that report. As a result, the amount of coding in the Procedure Division is radically reduced and the programming task is made that much easier.

As is usual in life, one doesn't get something for nothing. It is interesting to know that about 30% of all the reserved words are due to the Report Writer feature of COBOL. It is kind of a language within the COBOL language. If one is to take advantage of the Report Writer feature, a certain amount of effort must be expended in learning it. It is true that when seen for the first time, the amount of detail that has to be absorbed and correctly implemented looks complicated and possibly overwhelming. Often the Report Writer is presented so that it gives the impression that no matter how effective a tool it might be, it certainly isn't worth learning. This is simply not so. As does anything that is worthwhile, it does require a certain amount of strict attention to detail. Once the Report Writer has been mastered, it can then be applied in all kinds of reports, thereby easing the burden on the programmer considerably.

15.1 A One-Page Report

As our first illustration, let us take an atypical example—an uncomplicated program—one requiring no computation and no input data. Program 49 will only print in a predetermined manner a heading to a report. The design of the heading—the report heading—is first sketched out on a special format sheet called a print layout form, which is usually supplied by the manufacturer. A completed print layout form is presented in Figure 15-1 to show what we want to accomplish.

One could easily write suitable Data and Procedure Division instructions to produce this output without resorting to the Report Writer feature, but the point is how to do it by using the Report Writer feature.

When the Report Writer is used all reports are automatically started at the top of a new page. Our task at the moment is to print a single page with a particular format, which is nothing more than a title page that begins on the top line of the new page. Specifically, we note that the first line, which reads

THIS IS THE ONLY PAGE OF THE REPORT

begins in column 22 and is composed of 35 alphabet characters. The next line of output, which is

IT USUALLY CONTAINS

is a 19-alphabetic character literal that begins 2 lines after the previous printed line and commences in column 30. Then we come to the third line

COMPANY NAME

which is printed 4 lines after the previous one. The phrase begins in column 34 and

Figure 15-1

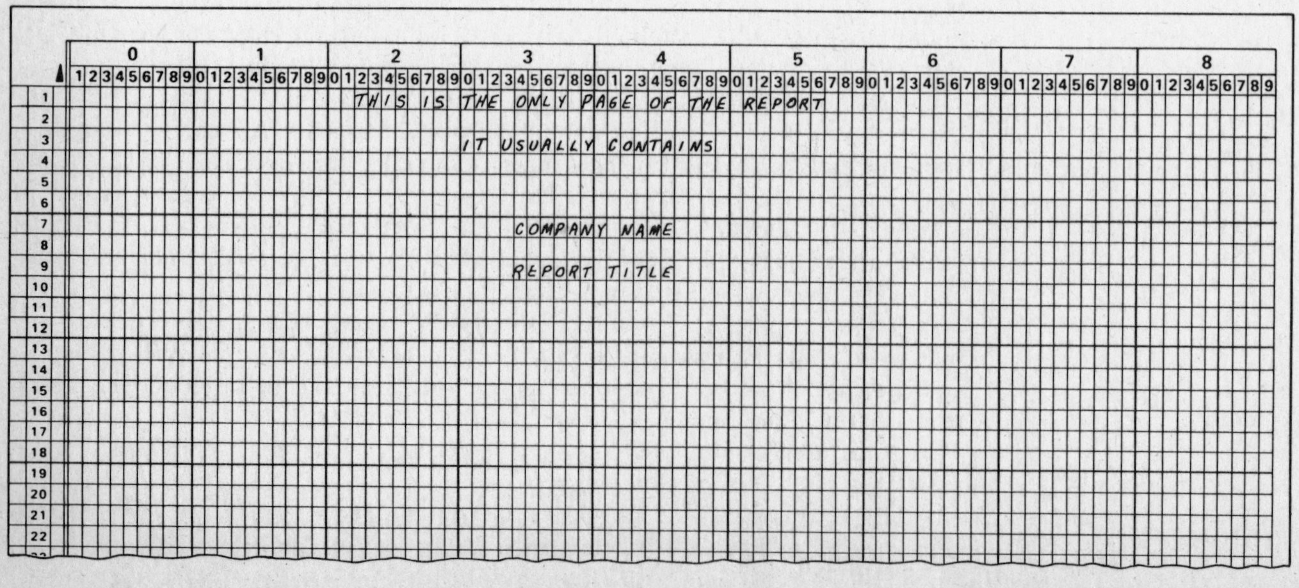

consists of 12 alphabetic characters. Finally, 2 lines below the last line (which was written on line 7 of the chart), we print the 12-character alphabetic literal

REPORT TITLE

beginning in column 34, thus lining up directly with the printed line above it. This represents the conclusion of the output.

What we have outlined is the crux of the so-called Report Section, which must be included in any COBOL program utilizing the Report Writer feature. We will now state some of the rules that apply to the Report Writer feature, showing how the detailed description fits into the general pattern.

1. A name must be selected for the report file. We have named it, expectedly, REPORT-FILE. Because this file is our output file, it is assigned to the printer in the SELECT clause and a file description—the usual FD—must be specified.

This file description differs from others we have encountered thus far in that previously a REPORT IS clause did not have to be included. When using the Report Writer feature, however, this clause is mandatory. It is encumbent upon us now to give a name to the report. What better name could we choose than ONLY-PAGE? So the FD must include the clause

REPORT IS ONLY-PAGE

2. A new section must now be introduced. It is called the Report Section, which is a detailed description of the report. The report file description is specified by an RD-level entry in the same way that a file description is specified by an FD-level entry. Under this RD-level entry we can stipulate the maximum number of lines to be printed per page. It has arbitrarily been decided to limit the number of lines per page to 30. Furthermore, we may specify under the RD-level entry the line number on which the heading is to appear. According to the print layout form, the heading is to begin on the top line of the page. All this information is stated in a most succinct form by:

```
REPORT SECTION.
RD      ONLY-PAGE
        PAGE LIMIT IS 30 LINES
        HEADING 1.
```

Analogous to the 01 level of an FD-level entry is an 01-level for an RD-level entry. This is followed by a so-called TYPE clause. There are a variety of TYPE clauses, but the one we are interested in now is the one called report heading, which may be specified by its abbreviation RH.

Subordinate to the 01 level we specify, in terms of line number, column number, and line content, is the precise information we wish to print in the report. Referring to the print layout form, we describe the successive lines of the report in language almost identical to that already indicated. The first line of the report, for example, is specified within the 01-level entry:

```
01   TYPE IS REPORT HEADING
     02 LINE NUMBER IS 1
     COLUMN NUMBER IS 22 PICTURE X(35)
     VALUE 'THIS IS THE ONLY PAGE OF THE REPORT'.
```

The second line is specified by the 02-level entry

```
02   LINE PLUS 2
     COLUMN 30 PICTURE X(19)
     VALUE 'IT USUALLY CONTAINS'.
```

This has the effect of printing the phrase "IT USUALLY CONTAINS" on line 3 (plus 2 lines from the previous printed line). This is a **relative** way of specifying a line position, as opposed to the **direct** method.

The only portion of the program still to be described is the Procedure Division.

3. The output file is opened in the ordinary way. (This particular program does not have an input file).

4. The report specified in the FD and the RD entries must be activated by the INITIATE verb. It has the effect of initializing certain important counters provided by the Report Writer feature.

5. The report is generated internally by the GENERATE verb.

6. At the end of the job the processing of the report is completed by the TERMINATE verb. Although the TERMINATE instruction completes the processing of the report, it does not close the file. This must be done in the ordinary way.

Here is the complete program producing a single-page report (although an elementary one) that has been generated by the Report Writer feature of COBOL.

Program 49

```
00001       IDENTIFICATION   DIVISION.
00002       PROGRAM-ID.      REPORT1.
00003       AUTHOR.          IRVIN POREMBA.
00004       INSTALLATION.    NYU.
00005       DATE-WRITTEN.    JUNE 29, 1982.
00006       DATE-COMPILED.   JUN 30, 1982.
00007       SECURITY.        HENRY MULLISH.
00008       * * * * * * * * * * * * * * * * * * * * * * * * * * * * * * * * * * * * * * * * * * * * *
00009       *       THIS PROGRAM USES THE REPORT WRITER FEATURE               *
00010       *       TO WRITE A SINGLE-PAGE REPORT.                            *
00011       * * * * * * * * * * * * * * * * * * * * * * * * * * * * * * * * * * * * * * * * * * * * *
00012
00013       ENVIRONMENT    DIVISION.
00014       CONFIGURATION  SECTION.
00015       SOURCE-COMPUTER. IBM-370-145.
00016       OBJECT-COMPUTER. IBM-370-145.
00017       SPECIAL-NAMES. C01 IS A-NEW-PAGE.
00018       INPUT-OUTPUT SECTION.
00019       FILE-CONTROL.
00020            SELECT REPORT-FILE ASSIGN TO UT-S-PRINTER.
00021
00022       DATA DIVISION.
00023       FILE SECTION.
00024
00025       FD   REPORT-FILE
00026            LABEL RECORDS ARE OMITTED.
00027            REPORT IS ONLY-PAGE.
00028
00029       REPORT SECTION.
00030
00031       RD   ONLY-PAGE
00032            PAGE LIMIT IS 30 LINES
00033            HEADING 1.
00034
00035       01   TYPE IS REPORT HEADING.
00036            02   LINE NUMBER IS 1
00037                 COLUMN NUMBER IS 22  PIC X(35)
00038                 VALUE 'THIS IS THE ONLY PAGE OF THE REPORT'.
00039            02   LINE PLUS 2
00040                 COLUMN 30              PIC X(19)
00041                 VALUE 'IT USUALLY CONTAINS'.
00042            02   LINE PLUS 4
00043                 COLUMN 34              PIC X(12)
00044                 VALUE 'COMPANY NAME'.
00045            02   LINE PLUS 2
00046                 COLUMN 34              PIC X(12)
00047                 VALUE 'REPORT TITLE'.
00048
00049       PROCEDURE DIVISION.
00050
00051       REPORT-ROUTINE.
00052            OPEN OUTPUT REPORT-FILE.
00053            INITIATE ONLY-PAGE.
00054            GENERATE ONLY-PAGE.
00055            TERMINATE ONLY-PAGE.
00056            CLOSE REPORT-FILE.
00057            STOP RUN.
```

Output for Program 49

THIS IS THE ONLY PAGE OF THE REPORT
IT USUALLY CONTAINS

COMPANY NAME
REPORT TITLE

15.2   Direct-Line Referencing

Another way to specify the position of the line being printed is to refer directly to
the line number. In other words, we may specify a line position "absolutely" rather
than by referring to a previous program line. A rule that must be observed, however,
is that once a relative reference has been used in any group, it cannot be followed by
a direct reference.

What follows is a program similar to the previous one except that all the line
references are direct or absolute. The output is identical to the preceding one.

Program 50

```
00001     IDENTIFICATION   DIVISION.
00002     PROGRAM-ID.      REPORT2.
00003     AUTHOR.          IRVIN POREMBA.
00004     INSTALLATION.    NYU.
00005     DATE-WRITTEN.    JUNE 29, 1982.
00006     DATE-COMPILED.   JUN 30, 1982.
00007     SECURITY.        HENRY MULLISH.
00008     * * * * * * * * * * * * * * * * * * * * * * * * * * * * * * * * * * * * * * * * * *
00009     *     THIS PROGRAM USES THE REPORT WRITER FEATURE                 *
00010     *     TO WRITE A SINGLE-PAGE REPORT. DIRECT LINE                  *
00011     *     REFERENCING IS USED.                                        *
00012     * * * * * * * * * * * * * * * * * * * * * * * * * * * * * * * * * * * * * * * * * *
00013
00014     ENVIRONMENT DIVISION.
00015     CONFIGURATION SECTION.
00016     SOURCE-COMPUTER. IBM-370-145.
00017     OBJECT-COMPUTER. IBM-370-145.
00018     SPECIAL-NAMES. C01 IS A-NEW-PAGE.
00019     INPUT-OUTPUT SECTION.
00020     FILE-CONTROL.
00021         SELECT REPORT-FILE ASSIGN TO UT-S-PRINTER.
00022
00023     DATA DIVISION.
00024     FILE   SECTION.
00025
00026     FD   REPORT-FILE
00027          LABEL RECORDS ARE OMITTED.
00028          REPORT IS ONLY-PAGE.
00029
00030     REPORT SECTION.
00031
00032     RD   ONLY-PAGE
00033          PAGE LIMIT IS 30 LINES
00034          HEADING 1.
00035
00036     01   TYPE IS REPORT HEADING.
00037          02 LINE NUMBER IS 1
00038             COLUMN NUMBER IS 22  PIC X(35)
00039             VALUE 'THIS IS THE ONLY PAGE OF THE REPORT'.
00040          02 LINE NUMBER IS 3
00041             COLUMN 30              PIC X(19)
00042             VALUE 'IT USUALLY CONTAINS'.
00043          02 LINE NUMBER IS 7
00044             COLUMN 34              PIC X(12)
00045             VALUE 'COMPANY NAME'.
00046          02 LINE NUMBER IS 9
```

```
00047          COLUMN 34              PIC (X)12
00048            VALUE 'REPORT TITLE'.
00049
00050     PROCEDURE DIVISION.
00051
00052     REPORT-ROUTINE.
00053          OPEN OUTPUT REPORT-FILE.
00054          INITIATE ONLY-PAGE.
00055          GENERATE ONLY-PAGE.
00056          TERMINATE ONLY-PAGE.
00057          CLOSE REPORT-FILE.
00058          STOP RUN.
```

Output for Program 50

THIS IS THE ONLY PAGE OF THE REPORT
        IT USUALLY CONTAINS

        COMPANY NAME
        REPORT TITLE

15.3   A Report Writer Program with a Control Break

Programs 49 and 50 were presented merely to familiarize the reader with some of the fundamentals in writing a report by using the Report Writer feature. It is most unlikely that any COBOL programmer would resort to Report Writer merely to prepare a one-page report. A more realistic situation is presented in the next program, where the input deck is composed of a series of cards, each of which is punched with a salesman's name, a product item number, and the quantity of items sold. The data is punched in the format shown in Figure 15-2.

The data cards are arranged such that all cards bearing the same salesman's name are grouped together. The purpose of the program is merely to produce a report by using the Report Writer feature that lists the salesman's name, item number, and quantity sold, all preceded by a suitable title page. However, each time there is a change of the salesman's name, we wish to total the quantity sold by that salesman and to print it out with an appropriate control footing. We have selected as a control footing the phrase SALESMAN TOTAL > > ---- > , followed by a line of asterisks. For each salesman the name is printed only once.

The most important point to understand in the program that follows is that it is the change of the salesman's name that triggers the printing of the control footing, the total quantity sold by that salesman, and so on. For this reason the salesman's name is considered to be a control break, one of the most frequently used features of the Report Writer.

Figure 15-2

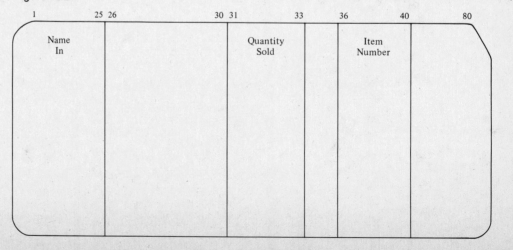

The outline of the title page described by the first 01-level entry of the Report Section is similar in most respects to what we have already encountered in the 2 previous programs, but we have introduced 2 new features, which will be described shortly.

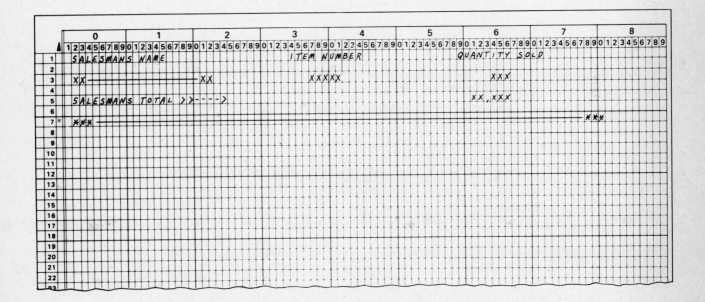

Program 51

```
00001          IDENTIFICATION  DIVISION.
00002          PROGRAM-ID.     REPORT3.
00003          AUTHOR.         IRVIN POREMBA.
00004          INSTALLATION.   NYU.
00005          DATE-WRITTEN.   JULY 1, 1982.
00006          DATE-COMPILED.  JUL 1, 1982.
00007          SECURITY.       HENRY MULLISH.
```

```
00008    * * * * * * * * * * * * * * * * * * * * * * * * * * * * * * * * * * * * * * * * *
00009    *      THIS PROGRAM READS IN DATA CARDS PUNCHED:                              *
00010    *                                                                             *
00011    *      COLUMNS  1-25: NAME                                                     *
00012    *      COLUMNS 31-33: QUANTITY SOLD                                            *
00013    *      COLUMNS 36-40: ITEM NUMBER                                              *
00014    *                                                                             *
00015    *      THIS PROGRAM USES THE CONTROL BREAK FEATURE OF                          *
00016    *      THE REPORT WRITER TO CREATE A REPORT.                                   *
00017    * * * * * * * * * * * * * * * * * * * * * * * * * * * * * * * * * * * * * * * * *
00018
00019    ENVIRONMENT    DIVISION.
00020    CONFIGURATION  SECTION.
00021    SOURCE-COMPUTER. IBM-370-145.
00022    OBJECT-COMPUTER. IBM-370-145.
00023    SPECIAL-NAMES. CO1 IS A-NEW-PAGE.
00024    INPUT-OUTPUT    SECTION.
00025    FILE-CONTROL.
00026         SELECT IN-FILE ASSIGN TO UT-S-READER.
00027         SELECT REPORT-FILE ASSIGN TO UT-S-PRINTER.
00028
00029    DATA DIVISION.
00030    FILE SECTION.
00031
00032    FD   IN-FILE
00033         LABEL RECORDS ARE  OMITTED.
00034
00035    01   RECORD-IN.
00036         02    NAME-IN        PIC X(25).
00037         02    FILLER         PIC X(05).
00038         02    QTY-SOLD       PIC 9(03).
00039         02    FILLER         PIC X(02).
00040         02    ITEM-NO        PIC 9(05).
00041         02    FILLER         PIC X(40).
00042
00043    FD   REPORT-FILE
00044         LABEL RECORDS ARE OMITTED
00045         REPORT IS SALES.
00046
00047    WORKING-STORAGE SECTION.
00048    77   ANY-MORE-CARDS        PIC X(03) VALUE 'YES'.
00049
00050    REPORT SECTION.
00051
00052    RD   SALES
00053         CONTROL IS NAME-IN
00054         PAGE LIMIT IS 30 LINES
00055         HEADING 1
00056         FIRST DETAIL 3
00057         LAST DETAIL 25.
00058
00059    01   TYPE IS REPORT HEADING NEXT GROUP IS NEXT PAGE.
00060         02    LINE NUMBER IS 1
00061               COLUMN 22 PIC X(36)
00062               VALUE 'THIS IS THE TITLE PAGE OF THE REPORT'.
00063         02    LINE PLUS 2
00064               COLUMN 30 PIC X(19)
00065               VALUE 'IT USUALLY CONTAINS'.
00066         02    LINE PLUS 4
00067               COLUMN 34 PIC X(12)
00068               VALUE 'COMPANY NAME'.
00069         02    LINE PLUS 2
00070               COLUMN 34 PIC X(12)
00071               VALUE 'REPORT TITLE'.
00072         02    LINE PLUS 2
00073               COLUMN 38 PIC X(04)
00074               VALUE 'DATE'.
00075         02    LINE PLUS 4
00076               COLUMN 20 PIC X(41)
00077               VALUE 'IF THE REPORT IS TO BE PRINTED ON A'.
00078         02    LINE PLUS 2
00079               COLUMN 25 PIC X(31)
00080               VALUE 'PAGE BY ITSELF YOU MUST SPECIFY'.
00081         02    LINE PLUS 2
00082               COLUMN 29 PIC X(23)
00083               VALUE 'NEXT GROUP IS NEXT PAGE'.
```

```
00084          02    LINE PLUS 0
00085                COLUMN 29 PIC X(23)
00086                VALUE '---- ----- -- ---- ----'.
00087          02    LINE PLUS 2
00088                COLUMN 25 PIC X(31)
00089                VALUE 'IN THE REPORT GROUP DESCRIPTION'.
00090
00091     01   TYPE IS PAGE HEADING
00092          LINE NUMBER IS 1.
00093          02    COLUMN IS 2 PIC X(14)
00094                VALUE 'SALESMANS NAME'.
00095          02    COLUMN IS 34 PIC X(11)
00096                VALUE 'ITEM NUMBER'.
00097          02    COLUMN IS 59 PIC X(13)
00098                VALUE 'QUANTITY SOLD'.
00099
00100   · 01   DETAIL-LINE
00101          TYPE IS DETAIL
00102          LINE NUMBER PLUS 1.
00103          02    COLUMN 2 GROUP INDICATE PIC X(25)
00104                SOURCE IS NAME-IN.
00105          02    COLUMN 37          PIC 9(05)
00106                SOURCE IS ITEM-NO.
00107          02    COLUMN IS 59       PIC ZZ9
00108                SOURCE IS QTY-SOLD.
00109
00110     01   TYPE IS CONTROL FOOTING NAME-IN.
00111          02    LINE NUMBER PLUS 1.
00112                03    COLUMN 2    PIC X(24)
00113                      VALUE 'SALESMANS TOTAL > > ----> '.
00114                03    COLUMN 61   PIC ZZ,ZZ9
00115                      SUM QTY-SOLD.
00116          02    LINE PLUS 1
00117                COLUMN 2 PIC X(78)
00118                VALUE ALL ' * '.
00119
00120   PROCEDURE DIVISION.
00121
00122   MAIN-LINE-ROUTINE.
00123        PERFORM OPEN-FILES.
00124        PERFORM START-UP.
00125        PERFORM PROCESS-DATA UNTIL ANY-MORE-CARDS EQUAL 'NO'.
00126        PERFORM CLOSE-UP.
00127        STOP RUN.
00128
00129   OPEN-FILES.
00130        OPEN INPUT IN-FILE.
00131        OPEN OUTPUT REPORT-FILE.
00132
00133   START-UP.
00134        READ IN-FILE AT END MOVE 'NO' TO ANY-MORE-CARDS
00135             DISPLAY ' * *NO DATA IN DECK * *'.
00136        IF ANY-MORE-CARDS EQUAL 'YES' INITIATE SALES.
00137
00138   PROCESS-DATA.
00139        GENERATE DETAIL-LINE.
00140        READ IN-FILE AT END MOVE 'NO' TO ANY-MORE-CARDS.
00141
00142   CLOSE-UP.
00143        TERMINATE SALES.
00144        CLOSE IN-FILE, REPORT-FILE.
```

Output for Program 51

```
                    THIS IS THE TITLE PAGE OF THE REPORT
                         IT USUALLY CONTAINS


                          COMPANY NAME
                          REPORT TITLE
                             DATE
                 IF THE REPORT IS TO BE PRINTED ON A
                  PAGE BY ITSELF YOU MUST SPECIFY
                     NEXT GROUP IS NEXT PAGE
               _ _ _ _ _ _ _ _ _ _ _ _ _ _ _ _ _
                 IN THE REPORT GROUP DESCRIPTION
```

SALESMANS NAME	ITEM NUMBER	QUANTITY SOLD
ROBERT SMITH	12534	300
	14888	250
	12000	147
	11111	500
	25322	750
	42599	253
	12345	100
SALESMANS TOTAL > > ---->		2,300

* *

IRVIN POREMBA	44444	400
	19999	125
	12555	435
	45366	125
	14555	120
	12356	450
SALESMANS TOTAL > > ---->		1,655

* *

ALAN ROBERTS	78564	350
	43215	250
	12389	560
	12378	145
	78965	130

SALESMANS TOTAL > > ---->		1,435

* *

15.4   Description of Report Section in Program 51

Once again, the Report Description is prefaced by the section header REPORT SECTION and is followed by the RD-level entry in which it is stated succinctly that the data-name NAME-IN is the control break. All we need to write is

CONTROL IS NAME-IN

The page limit is again set to 30 lines and this limit applies to every page that is generated by the report. All headings will begin on line 1, for wc have specified

HEADING 1

Because we wish to start the first detail-line on line 3 and the last on line 25, we include the clauses

FIRST DETAIL 3
LAST DETAIL 25.

The phrase NEXT GROUP IS NEXT PAGE causes the printing described in the next 01-level entry to be printed on a new page. It is an option that, if used, is incorporated into the TYPE clause. If it is omitted and the page limit is not exceeded, the next group described will be printed on the same page as the title page.
The underlining of the phrase

NEXT GROUP IS NEXT PAGE

is accomplished by printing a succession of underbar symbols on the same line as the phrase to be underlined. By writing

LINE PLUS 0

(in line 00084), we suppress the line feed of the printer. Consequently, the printer overprints the same line, thus underlining the line already printed.
Another TYPE clause is PAGE HEADING, containing all the information to be printed at the top of each successive page. The abbreviation PH may be used instead of PAGE HEADING.

Yet another clause is DETAIL, which may be abbreviated to DE. It appears in the 01-level entry DETAIL-LINE. As its name implies, it contains the information that is required for printing out each detail-line in the report. In the RD-level entry just described the FIRST DETAIL line of each page is specified to be printed on line 3. In the same group entry there is another clause we have not yet encountered, the GROUP INDICATE clause. This provides the means to suppress the printing of any elementary level item in the DETAIL group, except for its first appearance after a control break or when a new page is triggered, although a control break has not occurred. Because this is an output item, it must be accompanied by a suitable PICTURE clause. The specific data-name to be "group indicated" is included in the SOURCE IS clause. It is obvious then that the SOURCE IS clause is only the familiar MOVE verb where the item to be moved is specified in the input field called RECORD-IN. Although both ITEM-NO and QTY-SOLD are included in the DETAIL-LINE group, they are not affected by the GROUP INDICATE clause and therefore are not suppressed. If the intention had been to GROUP INDICATE each of these items, a separate GROUP INDICATE clause would have had to appear.

Finally, we come to the last of the 01-level entries, whose type is CONTROL FOOTING. CONTROL FOOTING applies to the data-name we called NAME-IN in the program. Whenever a control break on NAME-IN occurs, the relevant information from this group entry is printed out according to the manner specified within the group. This footing will be automatically printed before the detail-line for the new name that triggers the control break.

However, we still have another special reserved word to explain, namely, SUM. The role of SUM is to maintain an accumulative total for the designated data-name. Because we have the value QTY-SOLD qualified by the SUM clause, the Report Writer feature sets up a counter whose value is printed out at each control break. In addition, after it is printed out, the counter is reset to zero for the next accumulation.

In the Procedure Division the input file IN-FILE and the output file REPORT-FILE are opened. In START-UP the first data card is read. So long as there is at least one data card present, the RD item SALES is INITIATEd. The Report Writer word, INITIATE, sets all summed totals to zero, page-counter to 1, and the line-counter to zero.

When the paragraph PROCESS-DATA is performed the GENERATE verb is activated. It generates each detail-line of output and increments the sum counters, line-counters, and page-counters, whichever is necessary. Then subsequent data cards are read until the end of file is triggered. At that point the paragraph CLOSE-UP is executed. Here the program is terminated by means of the TERMINATE clause.

15.5 A Report Writer Program with Two Control Breaks

In REPORT 4, the next of our introductory Report Writer programs, the program is an amendment of Program 51 in that instead of a single control break there are now 2—FINAL and NAME-IN.

Program 52

```
00001     IDENTIFICATION   DIVISION.
00002     PROGRAM-ID.      REPORT4.
00003     AUTHOR.          IRVIN POREMBA.
00004     INSTALLATION.    NYU.
```

```
00005      DATE-WRITTEN.   JULY 1, 1982.
00006      DATE-COMPILED. JUL 2, 1982.
00007      SECURITY.       HENRY MULLISH.
00008      * * * * * * * * * * * * * * * * * * * * * * * * * * * * * * * * * * * * * * * * *
00009      *     THIS PROGRAM READS DATA CARDS PUNCHED:                      *
00010      *                                                                 *
00011      *     COLUMNS  1-25: NAME                                         *
00012      *     COLUMNS 31-33: QUANTITY SOLD                                *
00013      *     COLUMNS 36-40: ITEM NUMBER                                  *
00014      *                                                                 *
00015      *     THIS PROGRAM USES THE REPORT WRITER FEATURE                 *
00016      *     TO CREATE A REPORT WITH TWO CONTROL BREAKS: ONE             *
00017      *     FOR THE NAME AND ONE FOR THE END OF THE REPORT.             *
00018      * * * * * * * * * * * * * * * * * * * * * * * * * * * * * * * * * * * * * * * * *
00019
00020      ENVIRONMENT    DIVISION.
00021      CONFIGURATION  SECTION.
00022      SOURCE-COMPUTER. IBM-370-145.
00023      OBJECT-COMPUTER. IBM-370-145.
00024      SPECIAL-NAMES. CO1 IS A-NEW-PAGE.
00025      INPUT-OUTPUT     SECTION.
00026      FILE-CONTROL.
00027           SELECT IN-FILE ASSIGN TO UT-S-READER.
00028           SELECT REPORT-FILE ASSIGN TO UT-S-PRINTER.
00029
00030      DATA DIVISION.
00031      FILE SECTION.
00032
00033      FD   IN-FILE
00034           LABEL RECORDS ARE OMITTED.
00035
00036      01   RECORD-IN.
00037           02    NAME-IN          PIC X(25).
00038           02    FILLER           PIC X(05).
00039           02    QTY-SOLD         PIC 9(03).
00040           02    FILLER           PIC X(02).
00041           02    ITEM-NO          PIC 9(05).
00042           02    FILLER           PIC X(40).
00043
00044      FD   REPORT-FILE
00045           LABEL RECORDS ARE OMITTED
00046           REPORT IS SALES.
00047
00048      WORKING-STORAGE SECTION.
00049      77   ANY-MORE-CARDS         PIC X(03) VALUE 'YES'.
00050
00051      REPORT SECTION.
00052
00053      RD   SALES
00054           CONTROLS ARE FINAL, NAME-IN
00055           PAGE LIMIT IS 32 LINES
00056           HEADING 1
00057           FIRST DETAIL 8
00058           LAST DETAIL 23
00059           FOOTING 28.
00060
00061      01   TYPE IS REPORT HEADING.
00062           02    LINE NUMBER IS 1
00063                 COLUMN NUMBER IS 27 PIC X(27)
00064                 VALUE 'HENRY AND IRV SALES COMPANY'.
00065           02    LINE NUMBER IS 3
00066                 COLUMN IS 34      PIC X(12)
00067                 VALUE 'SALES REPORT'.
00068
00069      01   TYPE IS PAGE HEADING.
00070           02    LINE NUMBER IS 6.
00071                 03   COLUMN IS 2    PIC X(14)
00072                      VALUE 'SALESMAN NAME'.
00073                 03   COLUMN IS 34   PIC X(11)
00074                      VALUE 'ITEM NUMBER'.
00075                 03   COLUMN IS 59   PIC X(13)
00076                      VALUE 'QUANTITY SOLD'.
00077
00078      01   DETAIL-LINE
00079           TYPE IS DETAIL LINE NUMBER IS PLUS 1.
00080           02    COLUMN IS 2        PIC X(25)
```

```
00081                    GROUP INDICATE
00082                    SOURCE IS NAME-IN.
00083             02    COLUMN IS 37      PIC 9(05)
00084                    SOURCE IS ITEM-NO.
00085             02    COLUMN IS 64      PIC ZZ9
00086                    SOURCE IS QTY-SOLD.
00087
00088       01    TYPE IS CONTROL FOOTING NAME-IN.
00089             02    LINE NUMBER PLUS 2
00090                    03   COLUMN 2       PIC X(24).
00091                          VALUE 'SALESMAN TOTAL > > ----> '.
00092                    03   SUB
00093                          COLUMN IS 61    PIC ZZ,ZZ9
00094                          SUM QTY-SOLD.
00095             02    LINE PLUS 1.
00096                    03   COLUMN 2       PIC X(78)
00097                          VALUE ALL ' * '.
00098
00099       01    TYPE IS CONTROL FOOTING FINAL LINE NEXT PAGE.
00100             02    COLUMN IS 2      PIC X(27)
00101                    VALUE 'TOTAL QUANTITY SOLD > > ----> '.
00102             02    COLUMN IS 60      PIC ZZZ,ZZ9
00103                    SUM SUB.
00104
00105       01    TYPE IS PAGE FOOTING LINE 30.
00106             02    COLUMN IS 62      PIC X(11)
00107                    VALUE 'PAGE NUMBER'.
00108             02    COLUMN IS 76      PIC Z9
00109                    SOURCE PAGE-COUNTER.
00110
00111       01    TYPE IS REPORT FOOTING.
00112             02    LINE PLUS 2
00113                    COLUMN IS 33       PIC X(13)
00114                    VALUE 'END OF REPORT'.
00115
00116   PROCEDURE DIVISION.
00117
00118   MAIN-LINE-ROUTINE.
00119       PERFORM OPEN-FILES.
00120       PERFORM START-UP.
00121       PERFORM PROCESS-DATA UNTIL ANY-MORE-CARDS EQUAL 'NO'.
00122       PERFORM CLOSE-UP.
00123       STOP RUN.
00124
00125   OPEN-FILES.
00126       OPEN INPUT IN-FILE.
00127       OPEN OUTPUT REPORT-FILE.
00128
00129   START-UP.
00130       READ IN-FILE AT END MOVE 'NO' TO ANY-MORE-CARDS
00131            DISPLAY ' * *NO DATA IN DECK * *'.
00132       IF ANY-MORE-CARDS EQUAL 'YES' INITIATE SALES.
00133
00134   PROCESS-DATA.
00135       GENERATE DETAIL-LINE.
00136       READ IN-FILE AT END MOVE 'NO' TO ANY-MORE-CARDS.
00137
00138   CLOSE-UP.
00139       TERMINATE SALES.
00140       CLOSE IN-FILE, REPORT-FILE.
00141
```

Output for Program 52

```
                         HENRY AND IRV SALES COMPANY
                              SALES REPORT
SALESMAN NAME                               ITEM NUMBER        QUANTITY SOLD
ROBERT SMITH                                   12534               300
                                               14888               250
                                               12000               147
                                               11111               500
                                               25322               750
                                               42599               253
                                               12345               100
SALESMAN TOTAL > > ---->                                           2,300
* * * * * * * * * * * * * * * * * * * * * * * * * * * * * * * * * * * * * * * * * *
```

IRVIN POREMBA	44444	400
	19999	125
	12555	435
	45366	125
	14555	120
	12356	450
SALESMAN TOTAL > > ---->		1,655

* *

PAGE NUMBER 1

SALESMAN NAME	ITEM NUMBER	QUANTITY SOLD
ALAN ROBERTS	78564	350
	43215	250
	12389	560
	12378	145
	78965	130
SALESMAN TOTAL > > ---->		1,435

* *

PAGE NUMBER 2

SALESMAN NAME	ITEM NUMBER	QUANTITY SOLD
TOTAL QUANTITY SOLD > > ---->		5,390

PAGE NUMBER 3

END OF REPORT

15.6 Discussion of Program 52

The CONTROL IS or the CONTROLS ARE clause in the RD-level entry is the means by which the Report Writer feature is advised of the control breaks. This time there are 2 such control breaks: FINAL and NAME-IN.

FINAL is a COBOL reserved word. It is a control break condition that is activated by the end of the data. Following the word FINAL in the CONTROLS ARE clause there is NAME-IN, which also acts as a control break whenever a change in the NAME-IN field of the input data exists. Of course, one may have a long list of other control breaks; what appears last is the least inclusive. When controls are tested the most inclusive (highest) control is tested first, then the second, and so on.

These terms might seem somewhat strange at first. What is implied is a system of hierarchy of levels. For example, at New York University there is a renowned College of the Arts and Sciences; within the college there is a School of Mathematics, which includes the Computer Science Department, which in turn offers an excellent course in COBOL programming. In this system the most inclusive level is New York University and the least inclusive is the course in COBOL. New York University would therefore be the first to be mentioned and COBOL, the last. Another example might be country, region, state, and city.

In order to print certain information at the foot of each page of the report, a special TYPE clause is used. It is the PAGE FOOTING clause, which may be abbreviated to PF. The PAGE FOOTING in the program specifies that information is to be printed on line 30. In particular, the literal PAGE NUMBER is to appear starting in column 62. Following this phrase the actual page number is to be printed. This role, however, is taken care of automatically by the Report Writer feature. A page-counter called PAGE-COUNTER is incremented each time a new page is printed. Therefore by specifying SOURCE IS PAGE-COUNTER, one can access this information directly.

Finally, at the foot of the report, that is, at its conclusion, we want to print the phrase END OF REPORT. This is accomplished by resorting to the special TYPE called REPORT FOOTING, which may be abbreviated to RF.

15.7   A Simple Computation with Report Writer

Provision is made within Report Writer to enable the programmer to carry out any calculation of his or her choosing. These calculations are performed by means of the same arithmetic verbs that are available in regular COBOL. That is to say, the verbs ADD, SUBTRACT, MULTIPLY, DIVIDE, and COMPUTE are used.

In the next and final program to be illustrated by using Report Writer, each data card contains 2 numbers that are added together and divided by 2 to compute its average.

Once again, the Report Section must be the last section of the Data Division. Because several 77-level items are present, the Report Section follows them. It will be noticed that the computation of the average is performed prior to the execution of the GENERATE statement.

Program 53

```
1        IDENTIFICATION   DIVISION.
2        PROGRAM-ID.      REPORT5.
3        AUTHOR.          IRVIN POREMBA.
4        INSTALLATION.    NYU.
5        DATE-WRITTEN.    JULY 7, 1982.
6        DATE-COMPILED.   JULY 8, 1982.
7        SECURITY.        HENRY MULLISH.
8        ****************************************************************
9        *     THIS PROGRAM READS IN DATA CARDS PUNCHED:              *
10       *                                                            *
11       *     COLUMNS 1-4: FIRST-NUMBER                              *
12       *     COLUMNS 6-9: SECOND NUMBER                             *
13       *                                                            *
14       *     THIS PROGRAM USES THE REPORT WRITER FEATURE            *
15       *     TO CREATE A REPORT PRINTING OUT THE NUMBERS            *
16       *     AND THEIR AVERAGE.                                     *
17       ****************************************************************
18
19       ENVIRONMENT    DIVISION.
20       CONFIGURATION  SECTION.
21       SOURCE-COMPUTER. CYBER-170-720.
22       OBJECT-COMPUTER. CYBER-170-720.
23       SPECIAL-NAMES.
24       INPUT-OUTPUT    SECTION.
25           SELECT IN-FILE ASSIGN TO INPUT.
26           SELECT REPORT-FILE ASSIGN TO OUTPUT.
27
28       DATA DIVISION.
29           FILE SECTION.
30
31       FD   IN-FILE
32            LABEL RECORDS ARE OMITTED.
33
34       01   RECORD-IN.
35            02    NUMBER-1         PIC 9(04)
36            02    FILLER           PIC X(01).
37            02    NUMBER-2         PIC 9(04).
38            02    FILLER           PIC X(71).
39
40       FD   REPORT-FILE
41            LABEL RECORDS ARE OMITTED
42            REPORT IS AVERAGE.
43
44       WORKING-STORAGE SECTION.
45       77    ANY-MORE-CARDS        PIC X(03) VALUE 'YES'.
46       77    AVG-NUMBERS           PIC 9(04)V99.
47       77    TOTAL-NUMBER          PIC 9(05).
48
49       REPORT SECTION.
50
51       RD    AVERAGE
```

```
52          PAGE LIMIT IS 30 LINES
53          HEADING 1
54          FIRST DETAIL 5
55          LAST DETAIL 25.
56
57    01    TYPE IS PAGE HEADING.
58          02 LINE IS 1
59          COLUMN 15                PIC X(22)
60          VALUE 'AVERAGE OF TWO NUMBERS'.
61          02 LINE PLUS 1
62          COLUMN 15                PIC X(22)
63          VALUE ALL ' * '.
64
65    01    DETAIL-LINE
66          TYPE IS DETAIL
67          LINE PLUS 2.
68          02 COLUMN 2               PIC X(15)
69          VALUE 'FIRST NUMBER = '.
70          02 COLUMN 27              PIC ZZZ9
71          SOURCE IS NUMBER-1.
72          02 COLUMN 23              PIC X(16)
73          VALUE 'SECOND NUMBER = '.
74          02 COLUMN 39              PIC ZZZ9
75          SOURCE IS NUMBER-2.
76          02 COLUMN 45              PIC X(10)
77          VALUE 'AVERAGE = '.
78          02 COLUMN 55              PIC ZZZ9.99
79          SOURCE IS AVG-NUMBERS
80
81    PROCEDURE DIVISION.
82
83    MAIN-LINE-ROUTINE.
84          PERFORM OPEN-FILES.
85          PERFORM START-UP.
86          PERFORM PROCESS-DATA UNTIL ANY-MORE-CARDS EQUAL 'NO'.
87          PERFORM CLOSE-UP.
88          STOP RUN.
89
90    OPEN-FILES.
91          OPEN INPUT IN-FILE.
92          OPEN OUTPUT REPORT-FILE.
93
94    START-UP.
95          READ IN-FILE AT END MOVE 'NO' TO ANY-MORE-CARDS
96              DISPLAY ' * * NO DATA IN DECK * * '.
97          IF ANY-MORE-CARDS EQUAL 'YES' INITIATE AVERAGE.
98
99    PROCESS-DATA.
100         ADD NUMBER-1, NUMBER-2 GIVING TOTAL-NUMBER.
101         DIVIDE 2 INTO TOTAL-NUMBER GIVING AVG-NUMBERS.
102         GENERATE DETAIL-LINE.
103         READ IN-FILE AT END MOVE 'NO' TO ANY-MORE-CARDS.
104
105   CLOSE-UP.
106         TERMINATE AVERAGE.
107         CLOSE IN-FILE, REPORT FILE.
```

Output for Program 53

```
                          AVERAGE OF TWO NUMBERS
                    * * * * * * * * * * * * * * * * * * *
     FIRST NUMBER =   123     SECOND NUMBER = 4567     AVERAGE = 2345.00
     FIRST NUMBER = 1222      SECOND NUMBER = 4566     AVERAGE = 2894.00
     FIRST NUMBER = 1234      SECOND NUMBER = 5678     AVERAGE = 3456.00
     FIRST NUMBER = 1000      SECOND NUMBER = 1000     AVERAGE = 1000.00
     FIRST NUMBER =     0     SECOND NUMBER =    0     AVERAGE =    0.00
     FIRST NUMBER = 1257      SECOND NUMBER = 4567     AVERAGE = 2912.00
     FIRST NUMBER =   500     SECOND NUMBER =  100     AVERAGE =  300.00
     FIRST NUMBER =   385     SECOND NUMBER = 4520     AVERAGE = 2452.50
     FIRST NUMBER = 1234      SECOND NUMBER = 9876     AVERAGE = 5555.00
     FIRST NUMBER =    30     SECOND NUMBER =   25     AVERAGE =   27.50
```

Review Questions

1. Select any program you have written and rewrite it by using the Report Writer feature.
2. Write a program by using Report Writer that will read in as input a set of accounts receivable cards sorted by month and punched in the following format.

> col 1–15 name of month
>   21–46 customer name
>   61–65 amount due (999V99)
>   76–80 invoice number

Generate a report that lists and totals all the accounts receivable for each of the months. Each month's transactions should appear on a separate page with a suitable heading, including a page number.

At the end of the report the total accounts receivable for the year should be printed.

3. Write a report by using Report Writer to process a salesman's commissions. The commission a salesman is paid is based on his or her number of years of service with the company, in accordance with the following table.

YEARS OF SERVICE	RATE OF COMMISSION (%)
1	5.0
2	6.8
3	7.5
4	8.0
5	10.0
6	11.0
7	13.0
8	15.0
9	17.5
10 or more	20.0

The input cards are punched as follows.

> col 1–20 salesman's name
>   30–35 number of items sold
>   40–45 price per item (9999V99)
>   50–51 number of years of service

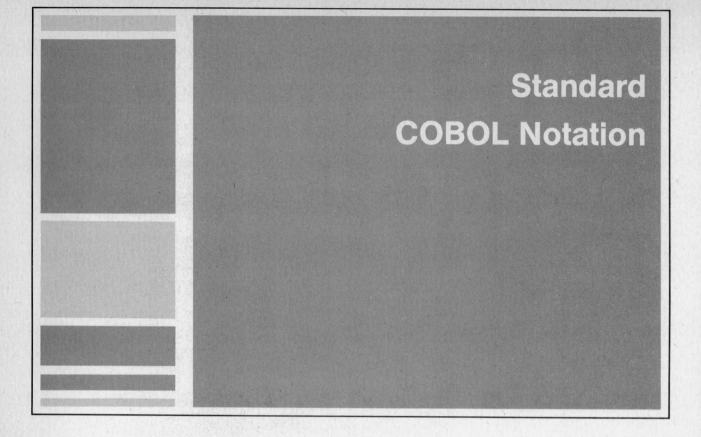

Standard COBOL Notation

Throughout this text the reader will have been exposed to a rather extensive repertoire of the COBOL language. These elements of the language may be used only where they are appropriate, and only when they are in strict conformity with the syntactical rules of the COBOL language. Often certain optional features are permitted, or may be omitted at the discretion of the programmer. In order that the reader may know at a glance precisely what is mandatory and what is optional with any specific instruction, each one in this appendix is written in a universally accepted notation that conforms to the following conventions.

1. All words written in uppercase are COBOL keywords. If they are under-lined, they are a keyword that *must* be used for a particular feature. If the word is not underlined, the keyword is optional but is generally included for ease of comprehension, greater clarity, and improved readability.
2. All words written in lowercase represent entries that must be supplied by the programmer.
3. Any part of an instruction that is enclosed in brackets [ ] is optional.
4. If there are alternatives for a given instruction, these will be included in braces { }. One of the stated alternatives must be selected by the programmer.
5. If a clause is to be repeated as many times as a programmer desires, this is indicated by an ellipsis (...), which, as you can see, is a succession of 3 dots.

Some elementary formal COBOL notations together with applied examples follow.

COBOL INSTRUCTION FORMATS

a. GO TO procedure-name-1

GO TO DISCOUNT-PARA

b. ADD data-name-1 TO data-name-2

ADD BONUS TO WAGES

c. DIVIDE data-name-1 INTO data-name-2 [ROUNDED] [ON SIZE ERROR imperative-statement]

DIVIDE MONTHS INTO YEAR.
DIVIDE   5 INTO WORK-WEEK ROUNDED.
DIVIDE TOTAL-DEPENDENTS INTO NET-INCOME
    ON SIZE ERROR DISPLAY 'ERROR ON DIVIDE'.
DIVIDE AMT INTO CREDITS ROUNDED
    SIZE ERROR STOP RUN.

IDENTIFICATION DIVISION FORMATS

IDENTIFICATION DIVISION.

(ID DIVISION.*)

PROGRAM-ID. program-name.

AUTHOR. [comment-entry]...

INSTALLATION. [comment-entry]...

DATE-WRITTEN. [comment-entry]...

DATE-COMPILED. [comment-entry]...

SECURITY. [comment-entry]...

ENVIRONMENT DIVISION FORMATS

ENVIRONMENT DIVISION.

CONFIGURATION SECTION.

SOURCE-COMPUTER. computer-name.

OBJECT-COMPUTER. computer-name.

SPECIAL-NAMES. [channel-name IS mnemonic-name]

INPUT-OUTPUT SECTION.

FILE-CONTROL. SELECT file-name ASSIGN TO system-name

DATA DIVISION.
FILE SECTION.
FD file-name.

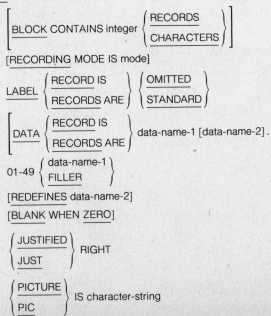

$$\left[\text{BLOCK CONTAINS integer} \left\{ \begin{array}{l} \text{RECORDS} \\ \text{CHARACTERS} \end{array} \right\} \right]$$

[RECORDING MODE IS mode]

$$\underline{\text{LABEL}} \left\{ \begin{array}{l} \text{RECORD IS} \\ \text{RECORDS ARE} \end{array} \right\} \left\{ \begin{array}{l} \text{OMITTED} \\ \text{STANDARD} \end{array} \right\}$$

$$\left[\text{DATA} \left\{ \begin{array}{l} \text{RECORD IS} \\ \text{RECORDS ARE} \end{array} \right\} \text{data-name-1 [data-name-2]} \ldots \right]$$

$$\text{01-49} \left\{ \begin{array}{l} \text{data-name-1} \\ \text{FILLER} \end{array} \right\}$$

[REDEFINES data-name-2]

[BLANK WHEN ZERO]

$$\left\{ \begin{array}{l} \text{JUSTIFIED} \\ \text{JUST} \end{array} \right\} \text{RIGHT}$$

$$\left\{ \begin{array}{l} \text{PICTURE} \\ \text{PIC} \end{array} \right\} \text{IS character-string}$$

$$\left[\text{[SIGN IS]} \left\{ \begin{array}{l} \underline{\text{LEADING}} \\ \underline{\text{TRAILING}} \end{array} \right\} \left[\underline{\text{SEPARATE}} \text{ CHARACTER} \right] \right]$$

[OCCURS integer TIMES [DEPENDING ON data-name INDEXED BY index-name-1
[index-name-2]...]

[USAGE IS usage-type]

[VALUE IS literal]

$$\left[\text{88-condition-name} \left\{ \begin{array}{l} \underline{\text{VALUE}} \text{ IS} \\ \underline{\text{VALUES}} \text{ ARE} \end{array} \right\} \text{literal-1 } [\underline{\text{THRU}} \text{ literal-2}] \text{ [literal-3 } [\underline{\text{THRU}} \text{ literal-4}]] \dots \right]$$

[WORKING-STORAGE SECTION.]

[77 level-description]...

[01 record-description]...

BASIC FORMATS FOR TABLE HANDLING

Format 1

$$\underline{\text{OCCURS}} \text{ integer TIMES} \left[\left\{ \begin{array}{l} \underline{\text{ASCENDING}} \\ \underline{\text{DESCENDING}} \end{array} \right\} \text{KEY IS data-name-1 [data-name-2} \dots \text{]} \dots \right] \dots$$

[INDEXED BY index-name-1 [index-name-2]...]

Format 2

OCCURS integer-2 TO integer-2 TIMES [DEPENDING ON data-name-1]

$$\left[\left\{ \begin{array}{l} \underline{\text{ASCENDING}} \\ \underline{\text{DESCENDING}} \end{array} \right\} \text{KEY IS data-name-2 [data-name-3]} \dots \right] \dots$$

[INDEXED BY index-name-1 [index-name-2]...]

Format 3 [IBM version]

OCCURS integer-2 TIMES [DEPENDING ON data-name-1]

$$\left[\left\{ \begin{array}{l} \underline{\text{ASCENDING}} \\ \underline{\text{DESCENDING}} \end{array} \right\} \text{KEY IS data-name-2 [data-name-3]} \dots \right] \dots$$

[INDEXED BY index-name-1 [index-name-2]...]

THE REDEFINES CLAUSE

Level-number data-name-1 REDEFINES [data-name-2]...

PROCEDURE DIVISION INSTRUCTIONS

The ACCEPT Instruction

Format 1

$$\underline{\text{ACCEPT}} \text{ data-name} \left[\underline{\text{FROM}} \left\{ \begin{array}{l} \underline{\text{SYSIN}} \\ \underline{\text{CONSOLE}} \\ \text{mnemonic-name} \end{array} \right\} \right]$$

Format 2

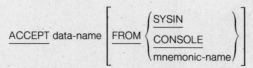

$$\underline{\text{ACCEPT}} \text{ data-name } \underline{\text{FROM}} \left\{ \begin{array}{l} \underline{\text{DATE}} \\ \underline{\text{DAY}} \\ \underline{\text{TIME}} \end{array} \right\}$$

The ADD Instruction

Format 1

ADD $\begin{Bmatrix} \text{data-name-1} \\ \text{constant-1} \end{Bmatrix}$ $\begin{bmatrix} \text{data-name-2} \\ \text{constant-2} \end{bmatrix}$ ... TO data-name-m [ROUNDED]

[data-name-n [ROUNDED]] ... [ON SIZE ERROR imperative-statement(s)]

Format 2

ADD $\begin{Bmatrix} \text{data-name-1} \\ \text{constant-1} \end{Bmatrix}$ $\begin{Bmatrix} \text{data-name-2} \\ \text{constant-2} \end{Bmatrix}$ $\begin{bmatrix} \text{data-name-3} \\ \text{constant-3} \end{bmatrix}$ ... GIVING identifier-m

[ROUNDED] [identifier-n [ROUNDED]] ... [ON SIZE ERROR imperative statement(s)]

Format 3

ADD $\begin{Bmatrix} \text{CORRESPONDING} \\ \text{CORR} \end{Bmatrix}$ data-name-1 TO data-name-2 [ROUNDED] [ON SIZE ERROR imperative
statement(s)]

CLOSE file-name-1 [file-name-2] ...

COMPUTE data-name-1 [ROUNDED] = $\begin{Bmatrix} \text{data-name-2} \\ \text{constant} \\ \text{arithmetic-expression} \end{Bmatrix}$

[ON SIZE ERROR imperative statement(s)]

The DISPLAY Instruction

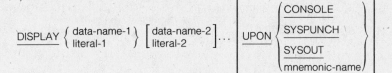

DISPLAY $\begin{Bmatrix} \text{data-name-1} \\ \text{literal-1} \end{Bmatrix}$ $\begin{bmatrix} \text{data-name-2} \\ \text{literal-2} \end{bmatrix}$ ... $\begin{bmatrix} \text{UPON} \begin{Bmatrix} \text{CONSOLE} \\ \text{SYSPUNCH} \\ \text{SYSOUT} \\ \text{mnemonic-name} \end{Bmatrix} \end{bmatrix}$

Format 1

DIVIDE $\begin{Bmatrix} \text{data-name-1} \\ \text{constant} \end{Bmatrix}$ INTO data-name-2 [ROUNDED][ON SIZE ERROR imperative-statement(s)]

Format 2

DIVIDE $\begin{Bmatrix} \text{data-name-1} \\ \text{constant-1} \end{Bmatrix}$ $\begin{Bmatrix} \text{INTO} \\ \text{BY} \end{Bmatrix}$ $\begin{Bmatrix} \text{data-name-2} \\ \text{constant-2} \end{Bmatrix}$
GIVING data-name-3 [ROUNDED] [REMAINDER data-name-4]
[ON SIZE ERROR imperative-statement(s)]

The EXIT Statement

paragraph-name, EXIT

The GO TO Statement

Format 1

GO TO procedure-name

Format 2

GO TO procedure-name-1 [procedure-name-2] ... DEPENDING ON data-name

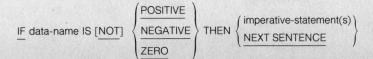

IF data-name IS [NOT] $\begin{Bmatrix} \text{POSITIVE} \\ \text{NEGATIVE} \\ \text{ZERO} \end{Bmatrix}$ THEN $\begin{Bmatrix} \text{imperative-statement(s)} \\ \text{NEXT SENTENCE} \end{Bmatrix}$

$$\left[\begin{Bmatrix} \text{ELSE} \\ \text{OTHERWISE} \end{Bmatrix} \begin{Bmatrix} \text{imperative statement(s)} \\ \text{NEXT SENTENCE} \end{Bmatrix} \right]$$

The IF Statement

$$\text{IF data-name IS [NOT]} \begin{Bmatrix} \text{NUMERIC} \\ \text{ALPHABETIC} \end{Bmatrix} \text{THEN} \begin{Bmatrix} \text{imperative statement(s)} \\ \text{NEXT SENTENCE} \end{Bmatrix}$$

$$\left[\begin{Bmatrix} \text{ELSE} \\ \text{OTHERWISE} \end{Bmatrix} \begin{Bmatrix} \text{imperative statement(s)} \\ \text{NEXT SENTENCE} \end{Bmatrix} \right]$$

$$\text{IF [NOT] condition-name THEN} \begin{Bmatrix} \text{imperative statement(s)} \\ \text{NEXT SENTENCE} \end{Bmatrix} \left[\begin{Bmatrix} \text{ELSE} \\ \text{OTHERWISE} \end{Bmatrix} \right.$$

$$\left. \begin{Bmatrix} \text{imperative statement(s)} \\ \text{NEXT SENTENCE} \end{Bmatrix} \right]$$

The MOVE Instruction

Format 1

$$\text{MOVE} \begin{Bmatrix} \text{data-name-1} \\ \text{literal-1} \end{Bmatrix} \text{TO data-name 2 [data-name-3]}\ldots$$

Format 2

$$\text{MOVE} \begin{Bmatrix} \text{CORRESPONDING} \\ \text{CORR} \end{Bmatrix} \text{record-name-1 TO record-name-2}$$

The OPEN Statement

$$\text{OPEN} \begin{Bmatrix} \text{INPUT file-name(s)} \\ \text{OUTPUT file-name(s)} \end{Bmatrix}$$

The PERFORM Instruction

Format 1

$$\text{PERFORM para-name-1} \begin{Bmatrix} \text{THRU} \\ \text{THROUGH} \end{Bmatrix} \text{para-name-2} \left[\begin{Bmatrix} \text{data-name} \\ \text{integer} \end{Bmatrix} \text{TIMES} \right]$$

Format 2

$$\text{PERFORM para-name-1} \begin{Bmatrix} \text{THRU} \\ \text{THROUGH} \end{Bmatrix} \text{para-name-2 UNTIL condition}$$

Format 3

$$\text{PERFORM para-name-1} \begin{Bmatrix} \text{THRU} \\ \text{THROUGH} \end{Bmatrix} \text{para-name-2}$$

$$\text{VARYING data-name-1 FROM} \begin{Bmatrix} \text{data-name-2} \\ \text{constant-2} \end{Bmatrix}$$

$$\text{BY} \begin{Bmatrix} \text{data-name-3} \\ \text{constant-3} \end{Bmatrix} \text{UNTIL condition-1}$$

$$\left[\text{AFTER data-name-4 FROM} \begin{Bmatrix} \text{data-name-5} \\ \text{constant-5} \end{Bmatrix} \right.$$

$$\left. \text{BY} \begin{Bmatrix} \text{data-name-6} \\ \text{constant-6} \end{Bmatrix} \text{UNTIL condition-2} \right]$$

$$\left[\underline{\text{AFTER}} \text{ data-name-7 } \underline{\text{FROM}} \left\{ \begin{array}{l} \text{data-name-8} \\ \text{constant-8} \end{array} \right\}\right.$$

$$\left.\underline{\text{BY}} \left\{ \begin{array}{l} \text{data-name-9} \\ \text{constant-6} \end{array} \right\} \underline{\text{UNTIL}} \text{ condition-3}\right]$$

The programmer is free to define a series of paragraphs by a SECTION name in the Procedure Division. This alternative avoids having to use the THRU option. One can therefore select a suitable SECTION name, say, PARA-1-TO-PARA-10 SECTION and write the instruction:

PERFORM PARA-1-TO-PARA-10.

rather than the instruction:

PERFORM PARA-1 THRU PARA-10.

Many professional programmers prefer to PERFORM sections.

The READ Statement

READ file-name RECORD [<u>INTO</u> record-name]

$$\left\{ \begin{array}{l} \underline{\text{AT END}} \\ \underline{\text{INVALID}} \text{ KEY} \end{array} \right\} \text{ imperative-statement(s)}$$

The SEARCH Statement

Format 1

$$\underline{\text{SEARCH}} \text{ data-name-1 } \left[\underline{\text{VARYING}} \left\{ \begin{array}{l} \text{index-name-1} \\ \text{data-name-2} \end{array} \right\}\right]$$

[AT <u>END</u> imperative-statement(s)]

$$\underline{\text{WHEN}} \text{ condition-1} \left\{ \begin{array}{l} \text{imperative-statement(s)} \\ \underline{\text{NEXT SENTENCE}} \end{array} \right\}$$

$$\left[\underline{\text{WHEN}} \text{ condition-2} \left\{ \begin{array}{l} \text{imperative-statement(s)} \\ \underline{\text{NEXT SENTENCE}} \end{array} \right\}\right]\dots$$

Format 2

<u>SEARCH ALL</u> data-name [AT <u>END</u> imperative-statement(s)]

$$\underline{\text{WHEN}} \text{ condition} \left\{ \begin{array}{l} \text{imperative-statement(s)} \\ \underline{\text{NEXT SENTENCE}} \end{array} \right\}$$

The SET Instruction

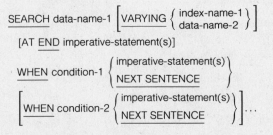

$$\underline{\text{SET}} \text{ index-name} \left\{ \begin{array}{l} \underline{\text{TO}} \left\{ \begin{array}{l} \text{integer-1} \\ \text{data-name-1} \end{array} \right\} \\ \left\{ \begin{array}{l} \underline{\text{UP BY}} \\ \underline{\text{DOWN BY}} \end{array} \right\} \left\{ \begin{array}{l} \text{integer-1} \\ \text{data-name-1} \end{array} \right\} \end{array} \right\}$$

The STOP Instruction

$$\underline{\text{STOP}} \left\{ \begin{array}{l} \underline{\text{RUN}} \\ \text{literal} \end{array} \right\}$$

The SUBTRACT Statement

Format 1

$$\underline{\text{SUBTRACT}} \left\{ \begin{array}{l} \text{data-name-1} \\ \text{constant-1} \end{array} \right\} \left\{ \begin{array}{l} \text{data-name-2} \\ \text{constant-2} \end{array} \right\}$$

[<u>FROM</u> data-name-3 [<u>ROUNDED</u>]]

[data-name-4 [<u>ROUNDED</u>]]...

[ON <u>SIZE ERROR</u> imperative-statement(s)]

Format 2

SUBTRACT $\begin{Bmatrix} \text{data-name-1} \\ \text{constant-1} \end{Bmatrix} \begin{matrix} \text{data-name-2} \\ \text{constant-2} \end{matrix} \dots$

[FROM $\begin{Bmatrix} \text{data-name-3} \\ \text{constant-3} \end{Bmatrix}$

GIVING data-name-4 [ROUNDED]

[ON SIZE ERROR imperative-statement(s)]

Format 3

SUBTRACT $\begin{Bmatrix} \text{CORRESPONDING} \\ \text{CORR} \end{Bmatrix}$ record-name-1

FROM record-name-2 [ROUNDED]

[ON SIZE ERROR imperative-statement(s)]

The WRITE Instruction

WRITE record-name-1 [FROM record-name-2]

$\left[\begin{Bmatrix} \text{BEFORE} \\ \text{AFTER} \end{Bmatrix} \text{ADVANCING} \begin{Bmatrix} \text{integer LINE} \\ \text{data-name LINE} \\ \text{mnemonic-name} \end{Bmatrix} \right]$

THE SORT MODULE INSTRUCTIONS

Data Division

SD sort-file-name
   RECORDING MODE IS mode

DATA $\begin{Bmatrix} \text{RECORD IS} \\ \text{RECORDS ARE} \end{Bmatrix}$ record-name-1 [record-name-2]...

RECORD CONTAINS integer CHARACTERS

$\left[\text{LABEL} \begin{Bmatrix} \text{RECORD IS} \\ \text{RECORDS ARE} \end{Bmatrix} \begin{Bmatrix} \text{STANDARD} \\ \text{OMITTED} \end{Bmatrix} \right]$

Procedure Division

RELEASE sort-record-name [FROM record-name]
RETURN sort-file-name RECORD
[INTO record-name] AT END imperative-statement(s)

SORT file-name-1 ON $\begin{Bmatrix} \text{ASCENDING} \\ \text{DESCENDING} \end{Bmatrix}$ KEY

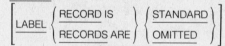

data-name-1 [data-name-2]... ON $\begin{Bmatrix} \text{ASCENDING} \\ \text{DESCENDING} \end{Bmatrix}$ KEY

data-name-3 [data-name-4...]...

$\begin{Bmatrix} \text{INPUT PROCEDURE IS} \quad \text{procedure-name-1} \quad \text{[THRU procedure-name-2]} \\ \text{USING} \quad\quad\quad\quad\quad\quad \text{file-name-2} \end{Bmatrix}$

$\begin{Bmatrix} \text{OUTPUT PROCEDURE} \quad \text{procedure-name-3} \quad \text{[THRU procedure-name-4]} \\ \text{GIVING} \quad\quad\quad\quad\quad\quad \text{file-name-3} \end{Bmatrix}$

REPORT WRITER—BASIC FORMATS

FILE-SECTION—REPORT Clause

$\begin{Bmatrix} \text{REPORT IS} \\ \text{REPORTS ARE} \end{Bmatrix}$ report-name-1 [report-name-2]...

Report Section

REPORT SECTION.

RD report-name.

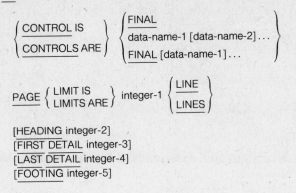

$$\left\{ \begin{matrix} \underline{\text{CONTROL}} \text{ IS} \\ \underline{\text{CONTROLS}} \text{ ARE} \end{matrix} \right\} \left\{ \begin{matrix} \underline{\text{FINAL}} \\ \text{data-name-1 [data-name-2]} \ldots \\ \underline{\text{FINAL}} \text{ [data-name-1]} \ldots \end{matrix} \right\}$$

$$\underline{\text{PAGE}} \left\{ \begin{matrix} \underline{\text{LIMIT}} \text{ IS} \\ \underline{\text{LIMITS}} \text{ ARE} \end{matrix} \right\} \text{ integer-1} \left\{ \begin{matrix} \underline{\text{LINE}} \\ \underline{\text{LINES}} \end{matrix} \right\}$$

[HEADING integer-2]
[FIRST DETAIL integer-3]
[LAST DETAIL integer-4]
[FOOTING integer-5]

REPORT WRITER DESCRIPTION ENTRIES

Format 1

01 [DATA-NAME-1]

$$\underline{\text{LINE NUMBER}} \text{ IS} \left\{ \begin{matrix} \text{integer-1} \\ \underline{\text{PLUS}} \text{ integer-2} \\ \underline{\text{NEXT PAGE}} \end{matrix} \right\}$$

$$\underline{\text{NEXT GROUP}} \text{ IS} \left\{ \begin{matrix} \text{integer-1} \\ \underline{\text{PLUS}} \text{ integer-2} \\ \underline{\text{NEXT PAGE}} \end{matrix} \right\}$$

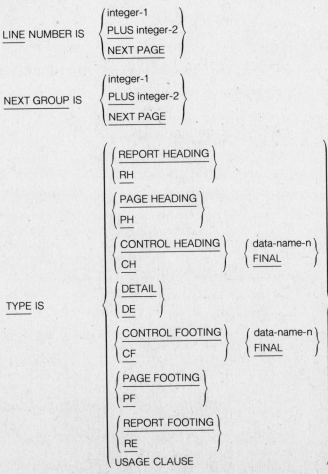

TYPE IS
$$\left\{ \begin{matrix} \left\{ \begin{matrix} \underline{\text{REPORT HEADING}} \\ \underline{\text{RH}} \end{matrix} \right\} \\ \left\{ \begin{matrix} \underline{\text{PAGE HEADING}} \\ \underline{\text{PH}} \end{matrix} \right\} \\ \left\{ \begin{matrix} \underline{\text{CONTROL HEADING}} \\ \underline{\text{CH}} \end{matrix} \right\} \left\{ \begin{matrix} \text{data-name-n} \\ \underline{\text{FINAL}} \end{matrix} \right\} \\ \left\{ \begin{matrix} \underline{\text{DETAIL}} \\ \underline{\text{DE}} \end{matrix} \right\} \\ \left\{ \begin{matrix} \underline{\text{CONTROL FOOTING}} \\ \underline{\text{CF}} \end{matrix} \right\} \left\{ \begin{matrix} \text{data-name-n} \\ \underline{\text{FINAL}} \end{matrix} \right\} \\ \left\{ \begin{matrix} \underline{\text{PAGE FOOTING}} \\ \underline{\text{PF}} \end{matrix} \right\} \\ \left\{ \begin{matrix} \underline{\text{REPORT FOOTING}} \\ \underline{\text{RE}} \end{matrix} \right\} \\ \text{USAGE CLAUSE} \end{matrix} \right\}$$

Format 2

level-number [data-name-1]

        LINE clause-see format 2
        USAGE clause

Format 3

level-number [data-name-1]

        COLUMN NUMBER IS integer-1

        GROUP INDICATE

        JUSTIFIED clause

        LINE clause-see format 1

        PICTURE clause

        RESET ON $\begin{Bmatrix} \text{data-name-1} \\ \text{FINAL} \end{Bmatrix}$

        BLANK WHEN ZERO clause

        SOURCE is data-name-3 data-name-4...

        SUM data-name-3 [data-name-4]... [UPON data-name-5]

        VALUE IS literal-1

        USAGE clause

Format 4

01   DATA-NAME-1

       BLANK WHEN ZERO clause

       COLUMN clause-see format 3

       GROUP clause-see format 3

       JUSTIFIED clause

       LINE clause see format 1

       PICTURE clause

       RESET clause-see format 3

       $\begin{Bmatrix} \text{SOURCE clause} \\ \text{SUM clause} \\ \text{VALUE clause} \end{Bmatrix}$ -see format 3

       TYPE clause-see format 1

       USAGE clause

REPORT WRITER FORMATS FOR THE PROCEDURE DIVISION

GENERATE data-name

INITIATE report-name-1 [report-name-2]...

TERMINATE report-name-1 [report-name-2]...

USE BEFORE REPORTING data-name

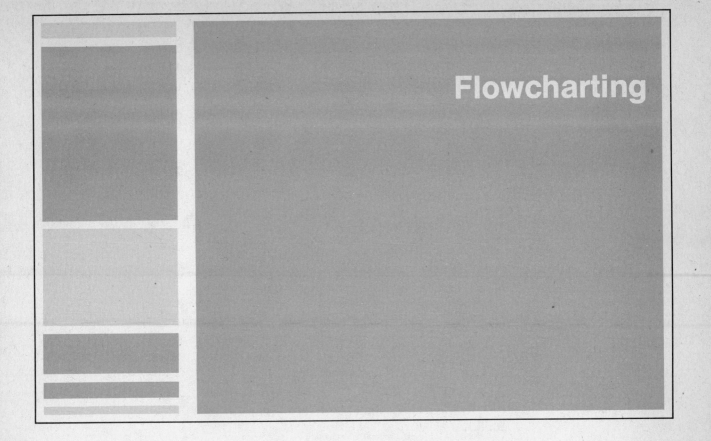

Flowcharting

Flowcharts are the blueprints from which the logic employed in a program can be represented diagrammatically. As such, they perform an extremely useful role for both the writer of the program and anyone who has to assume responsibility for the maintenance of the program. Flowcharts provide additional documentation for programs and are usually drawn before the actual programs are written. To paraphrase a well-known proverb, a flowchart is worth a thousand words.

Since the early days of computer programming, a convention has developed regarding the symbols that are customarily used in flowcharts. The following symbols have been standardized by the American National Standards Institute (ANSI). Each symbol represents a particular function such as reading, writing, processing, and decision making.

The basic concepts within a program are usually written within the appropriate flowchart symbols. On looking at the flowchart, one can usually get a sense of the overall logic that is used within the program at a single glance. Once a flowchart has been written and carefully checked, the programmer can be confident that all the logical paths are consistent and that there are no undetermined paths—"loose ends" so to speak.

Programs in which the logic is straightforward may not in fact require flowcharts because the programs can be written directly from the statement of the problem. However, for those programs in which the logic is fairly complicated, and the decisions that have to be made are quite numerous, a prewritten flowchart is invariably worth the time and effort spent in writing it.

Flowcharting Symbols	Meaning
	Input or output by means of punched cards
	Input or output in which a printed document is used
	An unspecified input-output medium
	Input-output in which magnetic disk is used for storage
	Any computational process within the computer
	The beginning or end of a program segment
	A decision box which shows the paths to be taken upon the presence or absence of a given condition

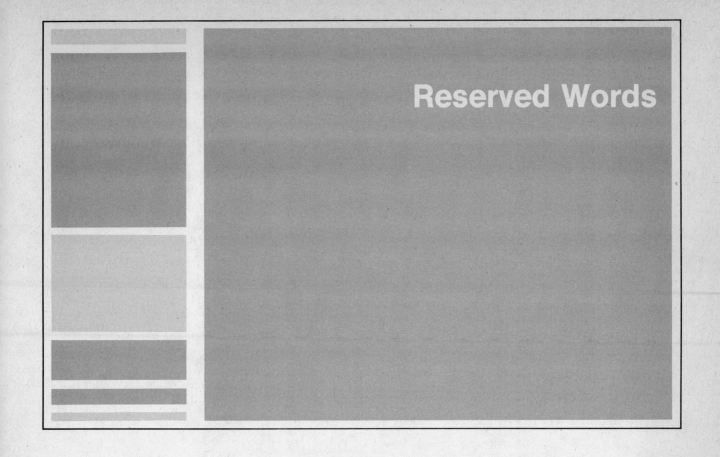

Reserved Words

WATBOL KEYWORD LIST

ACCEPT	CHANGED	CYL-OVERFLOW
ACCESS	CHARACTER	C01
ACTUAL	CHARACTERS	C02
ADD	CLOCK-UNITS	C03
ADDRESS	CLOSE	C04
ADVANCING	COBOL	C05
AFTER	CODE	C06
ALL	COLUMN	C07
ALPHABETIC	COM-REG	C08
ALPHANUMERIC	COMMA	C09
ALPHANUMERIC-EDITED	COMMUNICATION	C10
ALTER	COMP	C11
ALTERNATE	COMP-1	C12
AND	COMP-2	
APPLY	COMP-3	DATA
ARE	COMP-4	DATE
AREA	COMPUTATIONAL	DATE-COMPILED
AREAS	COMPUTATIONAL-1	DATE-WRITTEN
ASCENDING	COMPUTATIONAL-2	DAY
ASSIGN	COMPUTATIONAL-3	DAY-OF-WEEK
AT	COMPUTATIONAL-4	DE
AUTHOR	COMPUTE	DEBUG
	CONFIGURATION	DEBUG-CONTENTS
BASIS	CONSOLE	DEBUG-ITEM
BEFORE	CONSTANT	DEBUG-LINE
BEGINNING	CONTAINS	DEBUG-NAME
BLANK	CONTROL	DEBUG-SUB-1
BLOCK	CONTROLS	DEBUG-SUB-2
BOTTOM	COPY	DEBUG-SUB-3
BY	CORE-INDEX	DEBUGGING
	CORR	DECIMAL-POINT
CALL	CORRESPONDING	DECLARATIVES
CANCEL	COUNT	DELETE
CBL	CSP	DELIMITED
CD	CURRENCY	DELIMITER
CF	CURRENT-DATE	DEPENDING
CH	CYL-INDEX	DEPTH

347

DESCENDING	INITIATE	OTHERWISE
DESTINATION	INPUT	OUTPUT
DETAIL	INPUT-OUTPUT	OV
DISABLE	INSERT	OVERFLOW
DISP	INSPECT	
DISPLAY	INSTALLATION	PAGE
DISPLAY-ST	INTO	PAGE-COUNTER
DIVIDE	INVALID	PERFORM
DIVISION	IS	PF
DOWN		PH
DUPLICATES	JUST	PIC
DYNAMIC	JUSTIFIED	PICTURE
		PLUS
EGI	KEY	POINTER
EJECT	KEYS	POSITION
ELSE		POSITIONING
EMI	LABEL	POSITIVE
ENABLE	LABEL-RETURN	PREPARED
AND	LAST	PRINT-SWITCH
END-OF-PAGE	LEADING	PRINTING
ENDING	LEAVE	PRIORITY
ENTER	LEFT	PROCEDURE
ENTRY	LENGTH	PROCEDURES
ENVIRONMENT	LESS	PROCEED
EOP	LIBRARY	PROCESS
EQUAL	LIMIT	PROCESSING
EQUALS	LIMITS	PROGRAM
ERROR	LINAGE	PROGRAM-ID
ESI	LINAGE-COUNTER	
ETI	LINE	QUEUE
EVERY	LINE-COUNTER	QUOTE
EXAMINE	LINES	QUOTES
EXCEEDS	LINKAGE	
EXCEPTION	LOCK	RANDOM
EXHIBIT	LOW-VALUE	RANGE
EXIT	LOW-VALUES	RD
EXTEND	LOWER-BOUND	READ
EXTENDED-SEARCH	LOWER-BOUNDS	READY
		RECEIVE
FD		RECORD
FILE	MASTER-INDEX	RECORD-OVERFLOW
FILE-CONTROL	MEMORY	RECORDING
FILE-LIMIT	MERGE	RECORDS
FILE-LIMITS	MESSAGE	REDEFINES
FILLER	MODE	REEL
FINAL	MODULES	REFERENCES
FIRST	MORE-LABELS	RELATIVE
FOOTING	MOVE	RELEASE
FOR	MULTIPLE	RELOAD
FROM	MULTIPLY	REMAINDER
		REMARKS
	NAMED	REMOVAL
GENERATE	NEGATIVE	RENAMES
GIVING	NEXT	REORG-CRITERIA
GO	NO	REPLACING
GOBACK	NOMINAL	REPORT
GREATER	NOT	REPORTING
GROUP	NOTE	REPORTS
	NSTD-REELS	REREAD
HEADING	NUMBER	RERUN
HIGH-VALUE	NUMERIC	RESERVE
HIGH-VALUES	NUMERIC-EDITED	RESET
HOLD		RETURN
	OBJECT-COMPUTER	RETURN-CODE
I-O	OBJECT-PROGRAM	REVERSED
I-O-CONTROL	OCCURS	REWIND
ID	OF	REWRITE
IDENTIFICATION	OFF	RF
IF	OH	RH
IN	OMITTED	RIGHT
INDEX	ON	ROUNDED
INDEXED	OPEN	RUN
INDICATE	OPTIONAL	
INITIAL	OR	SA
INITIALIZE	ORGANIZATION	SAME

SD	SUBTRACT	TRAILING
SEARCH	SUM	TRANSFORM
SECTION	SUPERVISOR	TYPE
SECURITY	SUPPRESS	
SEEK	SUSPEND	UNEQUAL
SEGMENT	SYMBOLIC	UNIT
SEGMENT-LIMIT	SYNC	UNSTRING
SELECT	SYNCHRONIZED	UNTIL
SELECTED	SYSIN	UP
SEND	SYSIPT	UPON
SENTENCE	SYSLST	UPPER-BOUND
SEPARATE	SYSOUT	UPPER-BOUNDS
SEQUENTIAL	SYSPCH	UPSI-0
SERVICE	SYSPUNCH	UPSI-1
SET	S01	UPSI-2
SIGN	S02	UPSI-3
SIZE		UPSI-4
SKIP1	TABLE	UPSI-5
SKIP2	TALLY	UPSI-6
SKIP3	TALLYING	UPSI-7
SORT	TAPE	USAGE
SORT-CORE-SIZE	TERMINAL	USE
SORT-FILE-SIZE	TERMINATE	USING
SORT-MERGE	TEXT	
SORT-MESSAGE	THAN	VALUE
SORT-MODE-SIZE	THEN	VALUES
SORT-RETURN	THROUGH	VARYING
SOURCE	THRU	
SOURCE-COMPUTER	TIME	
SPACE	TIME-OF-DAY	WHEN
SPACES	TIMES	WITH
SPECIAL-NAMES	TO	WORDS
STANDARD	TOP	WORKING-STORAGE
START	TOTALED	WRITE
STATUS	TOTALING	WRITE-ONLY
STOP	TRACE	WRITE-VERIFY
STRING	TRACK	
SUB-QUEUE-1	TRACK-AREA	ZERO
SUB-QUEUE-2	TRACK-LIMIT	ZEROES
SUB-QUEUE-3	TRACKS	ZEROS

The following is a list of the 1974 ANSI reserved words.

ACCEPT	CLOCK-UNITS	DEBUG-SUB-1	ESI
ACCESS	CLOSE	DEBUG-SUB-2	EVERY
ADD	COBOL	DEBUG-SUB-3	EXCEPTION
ADVANCING	CODE	DEBUGGING	EXIT
AFTER	CODE-SET	DECIMAL-POINT	EXTEND
ALL	COLLATING	DECLARATIVES	
ALPHABETIC	COLUMN	DELETE	FD
ALSO	COMMA	DELIMITED	FILE
ALTER	COMMUNICATION	DELIMITER	FILE-CONTROL
ALTERNATE	COMP	DEPENDING	FILLER
AND	COMPUTATIONAL	DESCENDING	FINAL
ARE	COMPUTE	DESTINATION	FIRST
AREA	CONFIGURATION	DETAIL	FOOTING
AREAS	CONTAINS	DISABLE	FOR
ASCENDING	CONTROL	DISPLAY	FROM
ASSIGN	CONTROLS	DIVIDE	
AT	COPY	DIVISION	GENERATE
AUTHOR	CORR	DOWN	GIVING
	CORRESPONDING	DUPLICATES	GO
BEFORE	COUNT	DYNAMIC	GREATER
BLANK	CURRENCY		GROUP
BLOCK		EGI	
BOTTOM	DATA	ELSE	HEADING
BY	DATE	EMI	HIGH-VALUE
	DATE-COMPILED	ENABLE	HIGH-VALUES
CALL	DATE-WRITTEN	END	
CANCEL	DAY	END-OF-PAGE	I-O
CD	DE	ENTER	I-O-CONTROL
CF	DEBUG-CONTENTS	ENVIRONMENT	IDENTIFICATION
CH	DEBUG-ITEM	EOP	IF
CHARACTER	DEBUG-LINE	EQUAL	IN
CHARACTERS	DEBUG-NAME	ERROR	INDEX

INDEXED	OBJECT-COMPUTER	REPORT	SYMBOLIC
INDICATE	OCCURS	REPORTING	SYNC
INITIAL	OF	REPORTS	SYNCHRONIZED
INITIATE	OFF	RERUN	
INPUT	OMITTED	RESERVE	TABLE
INPUT-OUTPUT	ON	RESET	TALLYING
INSPECT	OPEN	RETURN	TAPE
INSTALLATION	OPTIONAL	REVERSED	TERMINAL
INTO	OR	REWIND	TERMINATE
INVALID	ORGANIZATION	REWRITE	TEXT
IS	OUTPUT	RF	THAN
	OVERFLOW	RH	THROUGH
JUST		RIGHT	THRU
JUSTIFIED	PAGE	ROUNDED	TIME
	PAGE-COUNTER	RUN	TIMES
KEY	PERFORM		TO
	PF		TOP
LABEL	PH	SAME	TRAILING
LAST	PIC	SD	TYPE
LEADING	PICTURE	SEARCH	
LEFT	PLUS	SECTION	
LENGTH	POINTER	SECURITY	UNIT
LESS	POSITION	SEGMENT	UNSTRING
LIMIT	POSITIVE	SEGMENT-LIMIT	UNTIL
LIMITS	PRINTING	SELECT	UP
LINAGE	PROCEDURE	SEND	UPON
LINAGE-COUNTER	PROCEDURES	SENTENCE	USAGE
LINE	PROCEED	SEPARATE	USE
LINE-COUNTER	PROGRAM	SEQUENCE	USING
LINES	PROGRAM-ID	SEQUENTIAL	
LINKAGE		SET	VALUE
LOCK		SIGN	VALUES
LOW-VALUE	QUEUE	SIZE	VARYING
LOW-VALUES	QUOTE	SORT	
	QUOTES	SORT-MERGE	WHEN
		SOURCE	WITH
MEMORY		SOURCE-COMPUTER	WORDS
MERGE	RANDOM	SPACE	WORKING-STORAGE
MESSAGE	RD	SPACES	WRITE
MODE	READ	SPECIAL-NAMES	
MODULES	RECEIVE	STANDARD	ZERO
MOVE	RECORD	STANDARD-1	ZEROES
MULTIPLE	RECORDS	START	ZEROS
MULTIPLY	REDEFINES	STATUS	
	REEL	STOP	+
NATIVE	REFERENCES	STRING	−
NEGATIVE	RELATIVE	SUB-QUEUE-1	*
NEXT	RELEASE	SUB-QUEUE-2	/
NO	REMAINDER	SUB-QUEUE-3	**
NOT	REMOVAL	SUBTRACT	>
NUMBER	RENAMES	SUM	<
NUMERIC	REPLACING	SUPPRESS	=

Printed Sheets
to Aid the Programmer

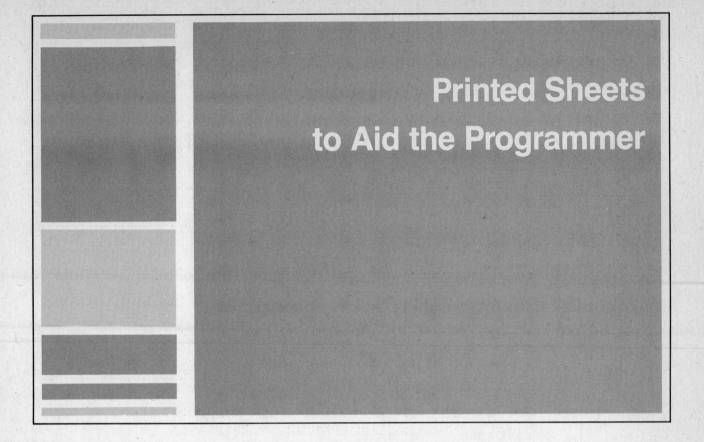

COBOL CODING SHEET

| PAGE NO. | PROGRAM NAME | | | PAGE | | OF | |
| 1   3 | PROGRAMMER'S NAME | | DATE | IDENT | 73 | | 80 |

| LINE NO. | | | | | | |
| 4   6 | 7 | 8 | 12 | 16 | 40 | 72 |

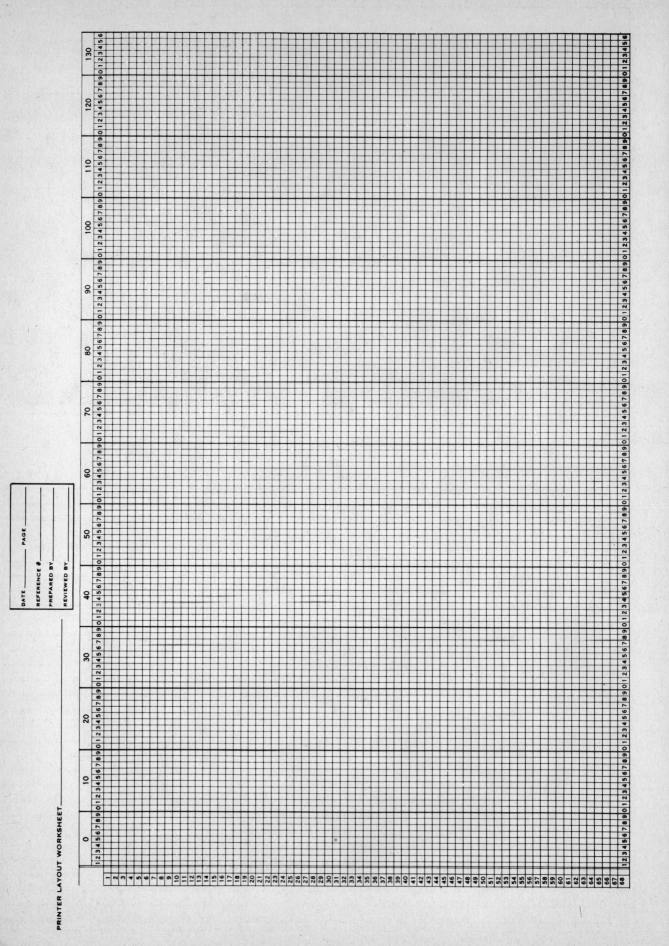

PRINTER LAYOUT WORKSHEET

DATE _____ PAGE _____
REFERENCE ● _____
PREPARED BY _____
REVIEWED BY _____

352

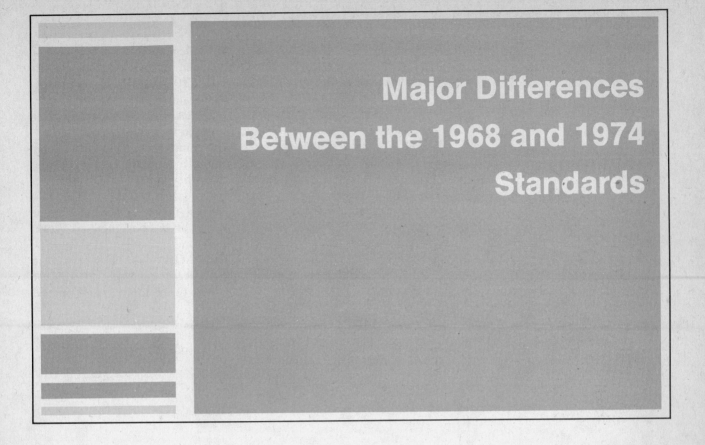

Major Differences Between the 1968 and 1974 Standards

Most of the programs illustrated in this book were run on a computer that used the 1974 standard compiler. However, it should be emphasized that not all COBOL installations have upgraded their compilers to the 1974 standard. At the time of publication an estimated 50% of all American installations provided access to the 1974 standard compiler, a proportion that is bound to increase in the near future.

In truth, the number of changes from the 1968 to the 1974 standard is not substantial, particularly from the point of view of the beginning programmer. At most, some minor change to a program might be necessary before it can run without trouble. A list of the major differences follows.

1968 STANDARD	1974 STANDARD
1. The REMARKS paragraph is the last option in the Identification Division.	The REMARKS paragraph has been eliminated totally. Comments (an asterisk in position 7) replace the REMARKS paragraph and may be inserted anywhere in the program.
2. A comma, semicolon, or period may not be preceded by a space.	The punctuation rules regarding spaces have been relaxed. A comma, semicolon, period, and a left parenthesis may be followed by a space.
3. In the WRITE statement the word LINES is used; LINE is not permitted.	The word LINE is equivalent to LINES and both may be used.
4. The editing symbol slash (/), is not available.	The editing symbol slash may be used in both numeric and alphanumeric edited fields.
5. The SIGN clause is not available.	The SIGN clause is available.

353

6. Multiple answer fields may not be specified for any arithmetic statement.

   Multiple answer fields may be specified for ADD, SUBTRACT, MULTIPLY, DIVIDE, and COMPUTE statements.

7. The INSPECT statement is not available.

   The EXAMINE statement has been replaced with the INSPECT.

8. Multiple subscripts and indexes must be separated by commas when they appear within parentheses.

   The commas may be omitted from multiple subscripts and indexes when they appear within parentheses.

9. 77-level items, if used, must appear at the beginning of Working-Storage.

   77-level items do not have to be placed at the beginning of Working-Storage.

10. The PAGE option of the WRITE statement is not available.

    The PAGE option may be used in the WRITE statement to eject the printer to the top of a new page.

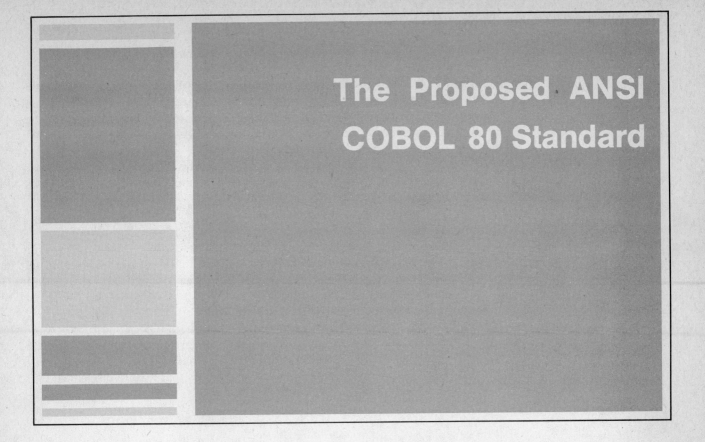

The Proposed ANSI COBOL 80 Standard

If you were to look at a COBOL program written in the 1960s you would not have any difficulty following it because the language has not changed very much from those early days of COBOL processing. In fact, you would probably be surprised at how familiar-looking it would be. The changes that COBOL has undergone have been evolutionary rather than revolutionary.

Well, the COBOL language may be headed for another step forward in its continuing evolution. It is possible that the 1974 standard you have so assiduously studied throughout this textbook may be replaced by an enhanced version called COBOL 80. But the changes that are contemplated will hardly be of consequence to you if you are not already dealing with concepts far in advance of the material presented in this book.

COBOL 80 is so called because its specifications were laid down in 1980. It is only fair to say, however, that at the time this book goes to press there is an enormous swell of resistance to the proposed standard on the part of the data processing community. The American National Standards Institute X3J4 subcommittee, charged with monitoring the reaction of COBOL users, is well aware of the fact that, as currently proposed, it will not receive overwhelming support. As a matter of fact, in a survey conducted to test user reaction to the proposed standard, the majority were strongly opposed to it, mainly because of its incompatibility with the 1974 version which, incidentally, is still used by only about half the data processing community. Since it is such an improvement over the 1968 standard, the popularity of the 1974 standard is almost certain to increase as the years go by. The way matters stand now there is a high likelihood that the X3J4 technical subcommittee will have to go back and review the important subject of upward compatibility—that is to say, what changes would have to be made to existing programs in order to run them on the new standard. Many industry managers have estimated that the conversion costs would be staggering; some have threatened to take the American National Standards Institute to court if the new standard is released in its present form.

Part of the opposition to the new proposed standard stems from the fact that, as is usual when converting to a new standard, the number of reserved words is increased. This means that if programs written under the earlier standard contain user-defined data-names that under the new standard are reserved words, those programs will have to be modified. Extensive analyses of the costs that would be involved in converting to the new standard have been undertaken and many feel that they are so large as not to warrant the conversion.

Before giving you details of some of the proposed changes, here are some of the arguments as detailed in an open letter dated December 1981 from the DPMA's principal representative to the ANS Committee, X3:

1. There is a lack of consensus on the new specifications.
2. ANS COBOL capabilities must continually move forward and keep up with the "state of the art" in data processing but this must not be done at the cost of changing millions of lines of source code, code which is in place and running throughout the world.
3. Reprogramming of existing programs should be, if not eliminated entirely, then certainly minimized.
4. Features and elements in the previous standard should almost never be deleted, as the benefit of deletion almost never outweighs the reprogramming costs involved to an installation that uses that feature or element.
5. Do not help a few to be "portable" by causing everybody to be incompatible.

In the new standard the following list contains the proposed new reserved words. Some of them are already reserved on some manufacturer-enhanced compilers:

ADDING	END-MULTIPLY
ALPHABET	END-PERFORM
ALPHABETIC-LOWER	END-READ
ALPHABETIC-UPPER	END-RECEIVE
ALPHANUMERIC	END-RETURN
ALPHANUMERIC-EDITED	END-REWRITE
ANY	END-SEARCH
COMMON	END-START
CONTENT	END-STRING
CONTINUE	END-SUBTRACT
CONVERSION	END-UNSTRING
CONVERTING	END-WRITE
DAY-OF-WEEK	EVALUATE
DEBUG-LENGTH	EXTERNAL
DEBUG-NUMERIC-CONTENTS	FALSE
DEBUG-SIZE	GLOBAL
DEBUG-START	INITIALIZE
DEBUG-SUB	NUMERIC-EDITED
DEBUG-SUB-N	ORDER
DEBUG-SUB-ITEM	OTHER
DEBUG-SUB-NUM	PURGE
END-ADD	REFERENCE
END-CALL	REFERENCE-MODIFIER
END-COMPUTE	REPLACE
END-DELETE	STANDARD-2
END-DIVIDE	TEST
END-EVALUATE	THEN
END-IF	TRUE

Probably the most important addition to COBOL in the proposed version is the distinct trend towards ease of structured programming. It permits the user for the first time to explicitly delimit a statement in the Procedure Division. A clue to this is seen in the list of proposed additional reserved words. No fewer than 19 of them begin with END-.

How often beginning COBOL programmers forget to close the files before terminating the run. It is now proposed that execution of STOP RUN closes all files.

It is proposed that the number of subscripts allowed be raised from 3 to 48. This number 48 is felt by many to be excessive. What is now proposed is that either it remain at 3 or it be raised to 7, as was done in the latest version of Fortran (Fortran 77).

Probably the most frequently occurring error in COBOL is to write ADD A TO B GIVING C. In the new proposed standard this is acceptable.

From the point of view of the individual COBOL programmer, the enhancements proposed for COBOL 80 can only make his or her task of writing programs even more rewarding and enjoyable.

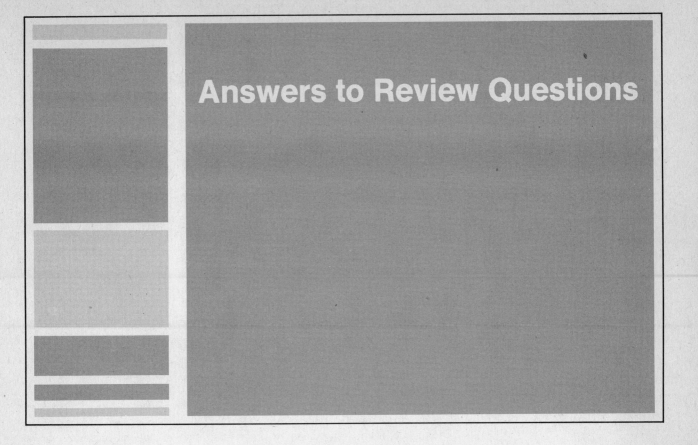

Answers to Review Questions

Chapter 1

1. The source program is written in the high-level language — in this case, COBOL. During compilation it is converted to the binary language. Once in binary it is an object program.
2. The compiler
3. COmmon Business Oriented Language
4. **c**
5. **d**
6. **a**
7. **c**
8. **a**
9. **d**
10. **d**
11. **c**
12. **a.** is invalid because both entries should be in the A margin
    b. is invalid because there must not be a hyphen between IDENTIFICATION and DIVISION
    c. is invalid because a program name cannot contain a question mark
    d. is invalid because the period is missing and COBOL is a reserved word
    e. is invalid because the period is missing after PROGRAM-ID
    f. is invalid because the dollar sign symbol is not permitted in a program name
    g. is invalid because DATA is a reserved word
    h. is valid
13. **c**
14. **d**
15. **a**
16. **a**
17. **d**

Chapter 2

1. A program is a sequence of instructions that is designed to solve a particular problem.
2. 80. Some computers, however, take a 96-column card.
3. If the card is used for data, columns 1 – 80 are available. However, if it is being used for a COBOL instruction, columns 73 – 80 are ignored. Therefore those columns may be used for identification and sequencing purposes.
4. The Identification Division
5. The Environment Division
6. The Data Division
7. The Procedure Division
8. The DISPLAY statement
9. The ACCEPT statement
10. Yes, the word DIVISION is misspelled.
11. Under the 1974 standard there is no limit.
12. STOP RUN
13. That is it was written for a pre-1974 standard compiler.
14. By placing the asterisk symbol *, in position 7
15. It performs (executes) the specified paragraph and returns to the statement following the PERFORM.
16. No, it would not work because the performed paragraph, POEM, performs itself. In mathematics this process is called "recursion" and is permitted in certain advanced scientifically oriented languages; certainly not in COBOL.
17. Absolutely not!
18. When using the 1974 COBOL compiler, every statement in the Procedure Division must have a paragraph name. For this reason the Procedure Division is always followed by a paragraph name. Paragraph names, or procedure names as they are also called, are always area A entries.
19. PROGRAM-ID names and paragraph names (both regarded as procedure names) may contain all numerics. Data-names, on the other hand, must contain at least one alphabetic.

Chapter 3

1. The Environment Division
2. The File Section
3. The file-name
4. It makes the line a comment.
5. No, FD is the required reserved word.
6. It is used to name a field that is not referenced.
7. **a**, **b**, **c**, **d**, **f**, **g**, and **j**.
8. They must be OPENed.
9. They must be CLOSEd.
10. The OPEN statement must specify whether the file being OPENed is an INPUT or OUTPUT file. The CLOSE statement does not require these specifications and if they were included an error would be created.
11. One READs a file and WRITEs a record. This may be remembered easily by recalling that during the WAR the RAF (Britain's Royal Air Force) played a major role in leading the Allied Forces to victory. The key words here are capitalized.

   WAR = Write A Record, and RAF = Read A File.

12. By using the instruction:

   WRITE record AFTER ADVANCING PAGE

13. Because if any "junk" is there it will be printed out.
14. By writing C01 IS NEW-PAGE (or some such name) in the SPECIAL-NAMES paragraph and, in the Procedure Division, by using this form of the WRITE statement

   WRITE record AFTER ADVANCING NEW-PAGE.

15. The READ has an AT END clause and the ACCEPT doesn't. Also, the word READ is followed by a *file*-name, whereas the ACCEPT is followed by a *record*-name.
16. The first period encountered.
17. It is the fundamental construct for repeating a segment of coding.
18. It refers to the first position of a line that is printed with the WRITE statement. This does not apply to the DISPLAY.
19. A numeric literal is any item that is represented by a number such as +5.6, −17, 1981, and so on. It may be signed, contain a decimal point, and have up to 18 numeric digits. A numeric literal may be operated on arithmetically. On the other hand, a nonnumeric literal such as 'CAT', 'DOG', 'SALARY', and so on cannot be used in an arithmetic operation.
20. **b**
21. **b**
22. **c**
23. **d**
24. **d**
25. **b** and **d**
26. **c**
27. **a** and **d**
28. None
29. All
30. A figurative constant

Chapter 4

1. **a.** FINANCE, **b.** FIN, **c.** F, **d.** FINANCE ¢¢¢
2. **a.** 746   **b.** 46   **c.** 6   **d.** 00746
3. It is a 77-level item, which is not capable of being broken down into further subdivisions and is always placed in the Working-Storage Section.
4. Both verbs are reserved for "low volume" use because they are slow in execution. The DISPLAY is limited to 120 characters and does not have the AFTER ADVANCING clause of its counterpart, the WRITE statement.
5. **a.** NL, **b.** NNL, **c.** NL, **d.** DN, **e.** NNL, **f.** NL, **g.** NL, **h.** DN, **i.** DN

Chapter 5

1. It moves the literal ' = = = = = ' to the FILLER field.
2. An implied MOVE
3. Because the period determines the scope (the range) of the IF statement.
4. **a.** LABEL RECORDS clause is omitted.
   b. The OPEN must state whether the file is INPUT or OUTPUT.
   c. Unless BLANKS is previously defined, the entry should be MOVE SPACES TO OUT-FIELD.
   d. Unless YES is otherwise defined, it should be enclosed within quote signs.
5. No, only the record name in the output section can be written by using the WRITE statement. The record could be printed, however, with the DISPLAY.
6. **a** and **b** are valid; the others are invalid.
7. **a, b, e, h, i, l, m**
8. **a, b,** and **d** are correct.
9. Only **a** is valid; all the rest contain reserved words.
10. None of them is valid.
11. The READ instruction should read AT END, not ON END. This clause has GO AWAY rather than GO TO AWAY, but the word TO may be omitted on the 1974 standard.
12. SUBTRACT 1 FROM C.
    MULTIPLY C BY D.
    ADD 1 TO C.
    SUBTRACT C FROM D GIVING C.

13. Because the period does not immediately follow the STOP RUN statement, the AT END clause terminates with ADD 1 TO DAYS. This means that before the AT END condition is raised, execution of the program commences with the MOVE instruction, not the ADD. Furthermore, the ADD instruction will never be executed because even on the AT END condition the STOP RUN instruction is encountered first, before the ADD is acted on.

14. **a.** IF X EQUAL 5 GO TO EOJ-PARA.

   b. IF A > B AND C < D PERFORM TOTALS-PARA.

   c. IF E > F OR E = F MOVE 'CAT' TO FLAG.
   or
   IF E > F OR = F MOVE 'CAT' TO FLAG.

   d. IF G < H MOVE 15 TO I.
   or
   IF G < H COMPUTE I = 15.
   but not
   IF G < H 15 = I.

   e. IF A < 10 OR B < 10 OR C < 10 STOP RUN
   Note here that it is only the subject of the comparison that may be implied, not the object.

   f. IF X > Y COMPUTE P = 2 * P
   COMPUTE R = 3 * R.

Chapter 6

1. Without the decimal point; the value is right-justified into the specified field, filled out with leading zeros (if there is room), and the implied decimal point is provided for by the V symbol in the corresponding PICTURE of the input item.

2. Never

3. The rightmost digit is overpunched with the minus sign. The corresponding PICTURE must be prefixed with the sign symbol S.

4. **a.** 3904, **b.** 472, **c.** ¢¢¢56, **d.** ¢¢074, **e.** ¢0048, **f.** 5000, **g.** ¢¢¢¢1, **h.** ¢10203, **i.** ¢¢¢¢¢

5. **a.** 123.400, **b.** 001.23, **c.** 0123.45, **d.** 1.68, **e.** 6.80, **f.** .21, **g.** .28, **h.** 012.340, **i.** 234

6. **a.** $123, **b.** $123, **c.** $234, **d.** $123, **e.** $123, **f.** $3,456.00, **g.** $1,234.00, **h.** ¢¢¢$12.00, **i.** ¢¢¢$12,345.00

7. **a.** $*123, **b.** **123, **c.** 123, **d.** ***, **e.** $12,345.00, **f.** $123.45, **g.** $***123.45

8. **a.** 12,345, **b.** 123,456, **c.** 000,003, **d.** 1,234,567, **e.** $¢¢¢123.00, **f.** $¢1,234.00, **g.** $¢¢¢123.00, **h.** ¢¢¢$.01
   Note: In example (h) the dollar sign replaces the most significant digit, 1. As soon as this happens, the zeros become *leading* zeros and therefore are suppressed.

9. **a.** 12¢345, **b.** 1¢2¢3¢4, **c.** 1¢¢48¢¢9, **d.** 12¢¢¢34, **e.** 109¢28¢2011, **f.** 123000
   g. 1¢234000, **h.** ¢234000

10. **a.** +123, **b.** 123 +, **c.** +123, **d.** +123, **e.** +56, **f.** +23, **g.** −123, **h.** +123, **i.** 123 +
    Note: In examples (e) and (f) the plus sign suppresses the most significant digit in an analogous manner to that of the dollar sign. Also, note that numbers without a sign are treated as positive numbers.

11. **a.** ¢123, **b.** −123, **c.** 123 −, **d.** −1234, **e.** −123, **f.** −123, **g.** −123, **h.** −23,
    i. 123¢¢, **j.** 123¢¢, **k.** 123DB, **l.** 123CR
    Note: In example **h** the leading minus sign suppresses the most significant digit.

12. **a.** PIX is invalid but PIC is perfectly acceptable.

    b. A PICTURE cannot have both a V and a decimal point.

    c. A PICTURE cannot have 2 floating symbols; here both the dollar sign and the Z are floating, which is not permitted.

    d. This PICTURE will not create a diagnostic but it doesn't make very much sense. If the number is to be edited as a dollar and cents amount it would be desirable to see a decimal point in the position occupied by the V, which would not print out at all.

    e. The Z suppresses *leading* zeros, not intervening zeros. The symbol B is appropriate here.

    f. An arithmetic comparison cannot be made with a numeric edited item in the same way that no arithmetic operation may be performed on an edited item.

Chapter 7

2. 01   MILITARY.
      02 ID   PIC 9(08).
      02 FILLER PIC X(06).
      02 WAGE   PIC 999V99.
      02 FILLER PIC X(15).
      02 YEARS   PIC 99.
      02 FILLER PIC X(44).

3. **a.** STUDENT-HISTORY
   b. YEAR-OF-BIRTH, YEAR-GRADUATED-HIGH-SCHOOL, COLLEGE-CREDITS-EARNED
   c. COLLEGE-CREDITS-EARNED
   d. 80 columns
   e. 3; 1
   f. 999
   g. 9999
   h. FILLER
   i. 1

4. qualified; Procedure; CORRESPONDING; IN; OF

5. **a.** false, **b.** true, **c.** true, **d.** true

Chapter 8

1. It enables the programmer to assign more than a single name and/or PICTURE clause to a given storage area.
2. Yes, the REDEFINES area may be equal to or smaller than the redefined area but not greater.
3. Yes
4. Yes, but it is not recommended.
5. 831225
6. The data name QQQQQQ could be broken down into 3 levels, each with a PICTURE of 99.
7. 12/25/83
8. The ROUNDED option is used.
9. The ROUNDED option is simply not specified.
10. The field becomes ' * = * = * = * = * '
11. It is a change of value in a field for which some special action is to be taken.
12. By using the ACCEPT/FROM/DAY and ACCEPT/FROM/TIME options

Chapter 9

1. Never
2. Always
3. No, it may be placed anywhere in the Data Division.
4. No, it may be used only in a conditional statement.
5. A figurative constant is a keyword that provides a way of introducing a value into a program. Some examples are: SPACE, SPACES, ZERO, ZEROS, ZEROES, ALL, QUOTE.
6. SIGN IS LEADING SEPARATE CHARACTER
7. SIGN IS TRAILING SEPARATE CHARACTER
8. Only one

Chapter 10

1. Three
2. It specifies the number of repeated items on a given level.

3. It helps to provide the means to convert the skeleton into a table, if necessary, with different PICTUREs.
4. No, you can SET UP BY ... or SET DOWN BY ... .
5. An index
6. When the SEARCH verb is used a sequential search is made and the index must be set in the program. The SEARCH ALL is a binary search and does not need the index to be set at all.
7. The table elements must contain either an ascending or descending key, which must be specified in the OCCURS clause.
8. Subscripting is sequential and does not use the SEARCH verb. Every subscript has a PICTURE and a VALUE. Indexes do not have either a PICTURE or a VALUE; they use the SEARCH verb and are specified by means of the INDEXED BY clause.

Chapter 11

1. Yes
2. It must be the last entry in the File Section.
3. It opens the input file, reads the data, sends the data to be sorted, and closes the input file.
4. It opens the output file, sends the sorted data to be printed, and closes the output file.
5. **a.** 3
   b. SSN
   c. ABC
   d. XYZ
6. Instead of the USING clause, an INPUT PROCEDURE must be used.
7. In sections
8. That a section named ABCDE is to be performed

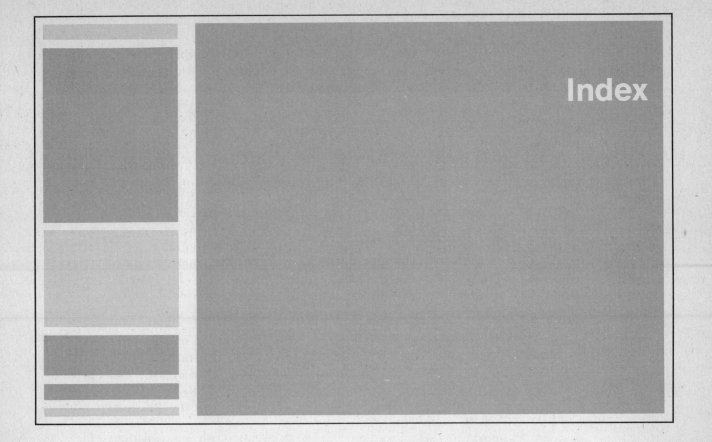

Index

82 83 84 85 9 8 7 6 5 4 3 2 1